Conte...

4   Map of princ

7   Map of touri...

11   Introductio...

12   Regions and landscapes

16   Historical table and notes

22   Languages, politics and government

23   Art and architecture

35   Literature

37   Music

37   Folklore and traditions

40   Townscapes

41   Food and drink

45   Belgium

257 Grand Duchy of Luxembourg

281 Practical information

289 Books and films

290 Phrasebook

291 Bilingual list of place names

292 Calendar of events

296 Admission times and charges

329 Index

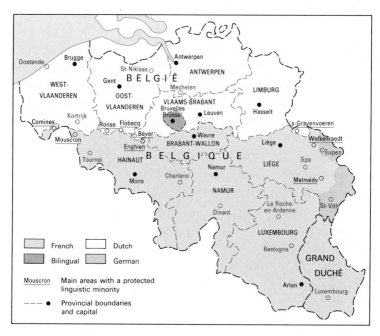

French   Dutch

Bilingual   German

Mouscron   Main areas with a protected
            linguistic minority

--- ●   Provincial boundaries
            and capital

Principal sights

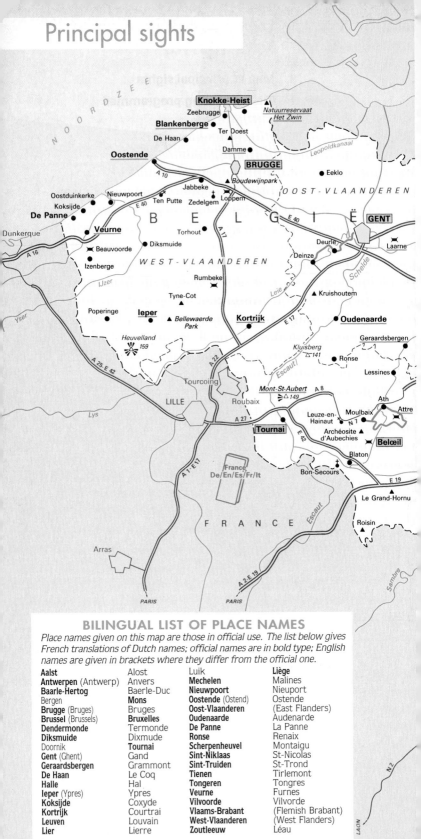

BILINGUAL LIST OF PLACE NAMES

Place names given on this map are those in official use. The list below gives French translations of Dutch names; official names are in bold type; English names are given in brackets where they differ from the official one.

Aalst	Alost	Luik	**Liège**
Antwerpen (Antwerp)	Anvers	**Mechelen**	Malines
Baarle-Hertog	Baerle-Duc	**Nieuwpoort**	Nieuport
Bergen	**Mons**	**Oostende** (Ostend)	Ostende
Brugge (Bruges)	Bruges	**Oost-Vlaanderen**	(East Flanders)
Brussel (Brussels)	**Bruxelles**	**Oudenaarde**	Audenarde
Dendermonde	Termonde	**De Panne**	La Panne
Diksmuide	Dixmude	**Ronse**	Renaix
Doornik	**Tournai**	**Scherpenheuvel**	Montaigu
Gent (Ghent)	Gand	**Sint-Niklaas**	St-Nicolas
Geraardsbergen	Grammont	**Sint-Truiden**	St-Trond
De Haan	Le Coq	**Tienen**	Tirlemont
Halle	Hal	**Tongeren**	Tongres
Ieper (Ypres)	Ypres	**Veurne**	Furnes
Koksijde	Coxyde	**Vilvoorde**	Vilvorde
Kortrijk	Courtrai	**Vlaams-Brabant**	(Flemish Brabant)
Leuven	Louvain	**West-Vlaanderen**	(West Flanders)
Lier	Lierre	**Zoutleeuw**	Léau

Michelin map 409 also has a bilingual list of place names

4

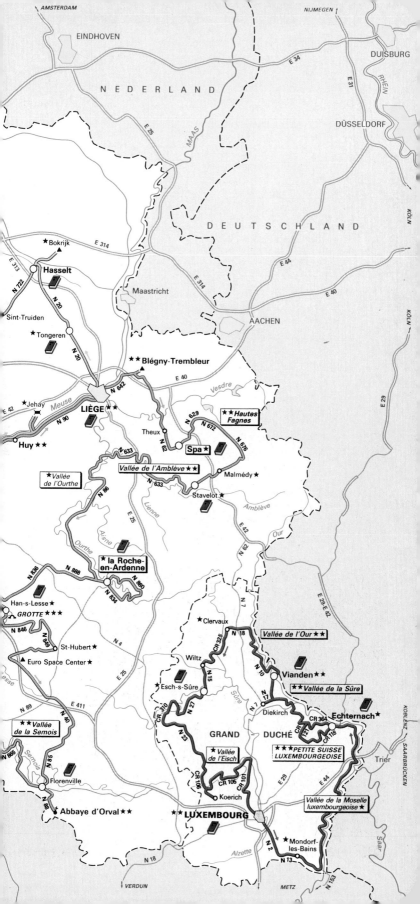

Ardennes Landscape

Introduction

Regions and landscapes

Although Belgium covers a rather small geographical area 30 513km² (11 781sq miles) it has a population of 9 180 063 (January 1994). This is one of the highest population densities in Europe: 300 inhabitants per km² (Great Britain: 228). The Grand Duchy of Luxembourg has a population of 378 400 in a geographical area of 2 586km² (998sq miles), and a population density of 146 inhabitants per km². People and merchandise in the two States circulate freely, thanks to a remarkable communications infrastructure (numerous waterways both rivers and canals and a very comprehensive road network). In Belgium this infrastructure is such that it enables the population to move around on a daily basis, on a scale unparalleled anywhere else in the world. Almost half of the Belgian and Luxembourg workforce is employed in industry alone, with the most important sectors being metallurgy, textiles and the chemical industry in Belgium, and iron and steel works in Luxembourg.

BELGIUM

At its widest point, southeast to northwest, Belgium measures 329km-204 miles across. It has relatively diverse scenery, and the Belgian territory itself is divided into three distinct areas *(see map below)*.

Lower Belgium (up to 100m – 328ft in altitude)

Antwerpen
Principal cities: **Antwerp**, Mechelen
Area: 2 867km-1 782sq miles
Population: 1 522 125

West-Vlaanderen
Principal cities: **Bruges**, Ostend, Kortrijk
Area: 3 134km-10 947 sq miles
Population: 1 101 236

Oost-Vlaanderen
Principal city: **Ghent**
Area: 2 982km²-1 853sq miles
Population: 1 306 377

Limburg
Principal city: **Hasselt**
Area: 2 422km²-1 505sq miles
Population: 698 349

The coast – The 70km-43.5 miles of straight coastline is the only part of Belgium which borders the sea. The beautiful beaches of fine white sand have made this coast into a much-frequented holiday venue. The other side of the coin is that they have not made it easy to build ports, for which costly special arrangements (access canals, outer harbours) have been necessary to compensate for their distance from the coast. The seafront has only one sheltered place, the mouth of the River IJzer (Yser) where Nieuwpoort has been built. Zeebrugge is a man-made fishing port. Antwerp *(qv)*, Belgian's largest commercial port, is at the end of a very long estuary which crosses the Dutch province of Zeeland.

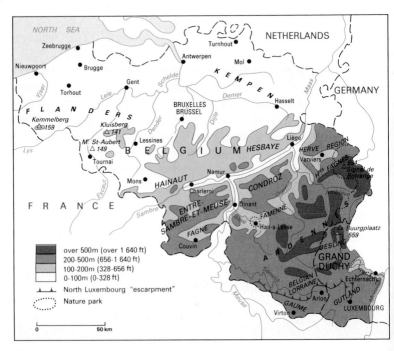

The coast has developed out of all recognition since the Middle Ages and is now edged with promenades for pedestrians and cyclists alternating with wide strips of **dunes** covered with seagrass. In the past, it was marshy land crisscrossed by an infinite number of waterways. As time passed these gradually became choked with mud, as in the case of the silting up of the Zwin tributary, which ruined Bruges as a centre of trade. Man himself completed the work of Nature by creating a polder area beyond the dunes.

The polders – Although they are not the size of the Dutch ones, the polders have been created in the same way. They were once swamps, which have been drained and dried out, and which are now protected against the tides by locks. In 1914 it only took the opening of Nieuwpoort's sluice gates to flood the entire hinterland *(see Nieuwpoort)*. The soil of the polders is very fertile.

Kempen – What was once known as Taxandria extends over several provinces and into the Netherlands. The sands and pebbles carried along by the rivers Scheldt, Meuse and Demer have accumulated in the vast plain between the rivers. Lakes and marshland are scattered over the Kempen region, with only heather and Norwegian pines growing on its poor soil.

Although there are now few inhabitants in Kempen, it was once a favourite place for the monks to build their monasteries (Postel, Westmalle and Tongerlo). Some of the land was reclaimed and cultivated in the 19C, while other areas were used for military manoeuvres (Leopoldsburg, founded in 1850). More recently the region has become home to a Centre of Nuclear Studies at Mol (1952) as well as to some industrial concerns, attracted by the presence of the Albert Canal built in 1939. The only valuable natural resource is coal. This was discovered at the end of the 19C near Genk, but the coal seams have been gradually abandoned because it is no longer cost-effective to mine them.

Another sandy region – This region, with its occasional valleys, extends throughout Flanders between the coast and the polders and the rivers Leie and Scheldt. Several peaks are all that remain of the more resistant strata: **Kemmelberg, Kluisberg** and **Mont St Aubert**.

The land is cultivated much more intensively here than in Kempen, and the area is much more densely populated. The cultivated fields are edged with poplars. Low farmhouses are dotted around the countryside. The textile industry has established itself near the Scheldt and in the regions surrounding Kortrijk, Tournai and Ghent in particular.

Some regions are thickly wooded, such as **Houtland**, near Torhout.

It is easy to reach the ancient strata, making it possible to create many quarries (porphyry in Lessines and Tournai). This has been a highly urbanised area since the heyday of the drapers during the Middle Ages. The great cities of Ghent, Antwerp and Brussels developed in these regions where transport was so easy.

Central Belgium (100-200m-328-656ft in altitude)

Brabant
Principal city: **Brussels**
Area: 3 358km^2-1 296sq miles
Population: 1 908 828

Hainaut
Principal cities: Tournai, **Mons**, Charleroi
Area: 3 785km^2-1 461sq miles
Population: 1 116 079

A cretaceous plain extends over the centre of the countryside, surrounding the Sambre and Meuse Valleys, rising gradually from a moderate altitude towards the Ardennes massif to the south, finally reaching an altitude of about 200m-656ft. The soil is a mixture of clay and silt in the plain and loess on the slopes. This relatively fertile land is used for both agriculture and pastureland. The old forest that was the haunt of the charcoal burners and which covered a good part of the country during the Roman period, has virtually disappeared; **Soignes Forest** *(qv)* is all that now remains.

The **Hesbaye** plateau to the east and the **Hainaut** to the west are covered with a layer of very fertile loess. This is agricultural country, where villages tuck themselves away in valleys, and farms are large and isolated. The limestone, sandstone or brick buildings (the latter often whitewashed) usually surround a vast central courtyard, which is reached through a single, sometimes monumental, gateway. The **coal-mining basin** is to the south of Central Belgium, at the point where it meets the Ardennes mountains, where a fault brought the carboniferous layers to the surface; it lies in a long dip in the land which is crossed by the rivers Sambre and Meuse from Charleroi to Liège and extended by the coal-mining area around Mons, the Borinage. The highest concentration of metal-working industries is found on this "Sambre-Meuse furrow" (the Liège, Charleroi and Louvière regions).

Ardennes

Namur
Principal cities: **Namur**, Dinant
Area: 3 666km-1 415sq miles
Population: 411 178

Liège
Principal cities: **Liège**, Spa
Area: 3 862km-1 490sq miles
Population: 888 129

Luxembourg
Principal cities: La Roche-en-Ardenne, **Arlon**
Area: 4 439km-1 713sq miles
Population: 227 462

Hautes Fagnes

The **Signal de Botrange** (beacon), at an altitude of 694m-2 276ft, is the highest point in Belgium. It is actually the remains of a worn mountain massif from the Primary era which extends the German Eifel range. The parallel mountain folds roll from east to west, making it difficult to establish communication routes outside the valleys running from south to north. This region, which is famous for the forests dating from the Roman period (the name "Ardennes" comes from the name of a goddess, Arduinna), can be divided into the Lower and Upper Ardennes.

Lower Ardennes – This series of plateaux, at an average altitude of 200-500m-656-1 640ft, is located south of the Meuse. The **Condroz** (named after the Germanic tribe, the Condrusi) is quite a fertile region, composed of limestone and schist. The main town is Ciney. **Entre-Sambre-et-Meuse** lies south of Charleroi. The great hollows of **Famenne** (main town: Marche-en-Famenne) and **Fagne** are typically swampy, wooded regions of sandstone and schist. Deep, narrow valleys gouged out by the rivers Lesse, Ourthe and Meuse run between these plateaux. Caves can be seen all along the valleys. The humid **Herve region,** used mostly for pastureland, and the Verviers region are part of Lower Ardennes. The French border region south of Couvin *(qv)*, known as the **Pays des Rièzes et des Sarts,** is over 300m-984ft in altitude. This is one point where the Ardennes shelf emerges.

Upper Ardennes – These plateaux, over 500m-1 640ft in altitude, are essentially convex. The most rugged crests make up the inhospitable area of Hautes Fagnes, which includes the highest point in Belgium. Peat bogs have developed on the very water-logged, poorly drained ground here.

Part of this region has been planted with coniferous trees, spruces for the most part. The winding river valleys, such as that of the Amblève, are more welcoming.

The typical Ardennes farmhouse is a great forbidding barracks of a place. It is a sort of cube of rough-rendered walls, with the living areas and the barn under the same ridged roof. One of the sides is sometimes half-timbered.

The region of the Upper Ardennes, lacking in natural resources and ill-favoured by the harsh climate and difficulty of access, did not develop at the same pace as the rest of the country for many years. It has now opened up to tourism.

The **Belgian Lorraine** (Arlon) and the **Gaume** (Virton) regions belong geologically to the southern part of Luxembourg. As in France, the Lorraine village consists of rows of closely built farms on either side of very wide streets. In southern Gaume the houses have pantiles, which is not at all usual in Belgium.

THE GRAND DUCHY OF LUXEMBOURG

Capital: **Luxembourg**
Area: 2 586km-1 606sq miles
Population: 384 062

Luxembourg consists of two very different geographical regions.

Oesling, in the north, is a plateau which joins the Ardennes and Eifel ranges. At its highest point it reaches 559m-1833ft (Buurgplaatz). The harsh climate is comparable to that of the Ardennes. Oesling is a region of forests, which occupy about one-third of the territory of the Grand Duchy of Luxembourg.

Gutland to the south has a milder climate as it is at a lower altitude, sloping gently down towards the French Lorraine. It is formed of superposed strata of sandstone and limestone, alternating with clay and marl. The Luxembourg vineyards *(see Vallée de la Moselle Luxembourgeoise)* are southeast of the Gutland, on the hills overlooking the Moselle region.

Erosion has created **"escarpments"** where the hard rock of the ancient mountain massif meets softer rock. These long, sheer rock faces are covered with beech forests. The northern one, of Luxembourg sandstone, crosses the Arlon region at Echternach and runs along the north of Luxembourg's "Petite Suisse". The southern one extends along the border and carries on into Belgium to just south of Virton.

One-third of Luxembourg's population lives in the capital. Although the density is fairly low in Oesling where the main sector of the economy is tourism, Gutland, which is suitable for farming, is also the industrial area (coalfields in Esch-sur-Alzette).

CAVES

A complete circle of rivers, the Meuse, the Ourthe and the Lesse, encloses the region of Condroz, on the central Ardennes plateau. The rivers flow on the perimeter of the plateau, cutting through schist and limestone to form deep river beds.

Water infiltration – The effect of water is particularly noticeable in the calcareous areas, where it erodes the surface of the plateau to form chasms such as the **Fondry des Chiens** in Nismes, or the various types of abysses which can be found here and there throughout the region.

Cave formation – Water flowing into these chasms dissolves the limestone forming subterranean rivers, which are often no more than the underground stretch of a river at ground level. The Lesse is an example of this, disappearing near Han to reappear 10km-6.25miles further on. It runs through the **Grotte de Han,** the most famous cavern in Belgium, renowned for its great chamber. The great chamber at the **Grotte de Rochefort,** Sabbath Hall, is equally impressive.

In most cases the subterranean river has a tendency to cut deeper and deeper. Because of this, the old river bed higher up fills up only during floods, and otherwise dries up completely. It is sometimes possible to take a boat through the lower gallery. At **Remouchamps,** the boat trip lasts for about 1km-0.5mile.

Some of the caves formed in this way were inhabited during the prehistoric period (Goyet, Furfooz, Han, etc.).

Concretions – Underground, the water deposits the limestone it has accumulated from filtering through the soil, thus forming the fantastic shapes of concretions. **Stalactites,** projections downwards from the roof, are the best known, along with **stalagmites,** columns rising up from the floor.

Gravity-defying eccentrics are the delicate concretions produced by crystallisation, which often "grow" diagonally. Although they are generally white and formed of calcite, they are sometimes tinted with minerals: for example, iron oxide produces a reddish colour, and manganese gives a brownish one.

Resurgences – Water running through subterranean galleries eventually re-emerges at ground level once more. At Han-sur-Lesse the resurgent river is visible near the point where visitors end the tour.

FLORA AND FAUNA

Nature reserves and country parks are particularly carefully managed, as much in the most densely populated areas as in the Ardennes, to protect flora and fauna.

Parc Naturel Germano-Luxembourgeois

Nature reserves – These areas are strictly protected by the various regions or by private associations. Some of them are open to the public, at least in part; others may only be visited with a guide. Particularly good reserves in Flanders include **De Kalmthoutse Heide, De Mechelse Heide,** where heather is the predominant vegetation, and **Het Zwin,** which is more ornithologically orientated. In the Ardennes there is the **Hautes Fagnes,** famous for its peat bogs, in the province of Namur the **Lesse and Lomme nature reserve** and the **Furfooz** nature reserve (these two reserves are known locally as "parcs naturels"), and in the province of Hainaut the **Virelles** lake at Chimay.

Nature parks – These parks include valleys, forests, villages, etc. covered by conservancy orders. A distinction is made between national nature parks, designated by the State, and regional nature parks, designated by some other public authority. Belgium has a large national nature park, the **Hautes Fagnes-Eifel** *(qv),* which extends into Germany.

Like Belgium, Luxembourg shares a large nature park with Germany, the **Germano-Luxembourg nature park.** Indicated by signs marked with a sprig of holly, it extends across particularly wild or picturesque areas. The major tourist centres of Echternach, Vianden and Clervaux lie within its boundaries.

Leisure parks – In these parks the natural setting is maintained for the maximum benefit of visitors, sports enthusiasts and ramblers alike. Some parks contain an ornithological nature reserve or a game park, others a stretch of water making it possible to engage in various water sports. The leisure parks are quite numerous in the Kempen region, where they can usually be found in the midst of extensive pine forests.

Historical table and notes

Celts and Romans

BC	The Belgians, of Celtic origin, fight vainly against Julius Caesar, who finally defeats them in 57. Three years later the Eburoni revolt, led by Ambiorix, is crushed.
AD 1C-3C	**Pax Romana.** Modern Belgium is divided into three Roman provinces: Belgica Prima (capital: Trier), Belgica Secunda (capital: Rheims) and Germania Secunda (capital: Cologne). Tongeren and Tournai are major towns.
4C-5C	Barbarian invasions. The Franks settle in Taxandria (Kempen) and Luxembourg. The first conversions to Christianity take place.

Merovingians to feudal system

5C	Tournai comes under the rule of the Salian Franks. Childeric, father of Clovis, founds the Merovingian dynasty. Clovis makes Tournai an episcopal seat following his conversion.
7C	Second wave of conversions to Christianity. Blossoming of the great abbeys.
843	**Treaty of Verdun:** the Carolingian Empire is divided between France (to the west of the Scheldt) and Germania, leaving a narrow band of territory between the two, running from the North Sea to the Mediterranean, which is given to Lothair I. Upon his death this territory is divided into three parts: Italy, Burgundy and **Lotharingia**. The frontiers of the latter correspond approximately to modern Belgium, minus Flanders (which depends on the French crown).
862	Baldwin of the Iron Arm becomes first Count of **Flanders** *(see Kortrijk, Rumbeke).*
962	Lotharingia is annexed to the Germanic Holy Roman Empire.
963	Count Sigefroi of the Moselle founds the county of Luxembourg *(qv).*
980	**Notger**, prince-bishop of **Liège** *(qv)*, gains temporal power over his territory.

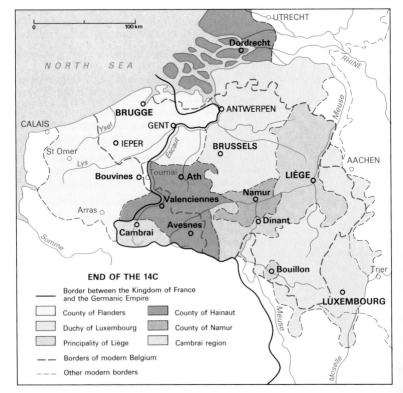

END OF THE 14C

— Border between the Kingdom of France and the Germanic Empire

☐ County of Flanders   ☐ County of Hainaut
☐ Duchy of Luxembourg   ☐ County of Namur
☐ Principality of Liège   ☐ Cambrai region

- - - Borders of modern Belgium
- - - Other modern borders

Early 11C	Flanders expands at the expense of Imperial territories. This is the rise of Imperial Flanders. The Count of Flanders is vassal to both the King of France and the Holy Roman Emperor.
12C-13C	**Emancipation of the Flemish cities:** The period from the 12C to the 14C is marked by growth in trade, particularly in the weaving of wool. The new wealth of the towns gives them communal autonomy. This is the golden age for Bruges *(qv)*. Although a vassal of the King of France, Flanders' economic activities link it loosely to England and the Holy Roman Empire. This causes a rift between the people with an eye to their economic interests and the nobility supported by the French. The king of France, **Philip Augustus**, makes heavy claims on the northern States and a coalition forms against him. The Flemish are supported by King John (Lackland) of England and Emperor Otto IV of Germany. Nevertheless, in 1214 Philip Augustus is victorious at the **Battle of Bouvines**, at the expense of the Count of Flanders, Ferrand.
1300	Philip the Fair annexes Flanders *(qv)*, but the population revolts, and on 11 July 1302 the **Battle of the Golden Spurs** ends in victory for the Flemish people over Philip the Fair's French knights.
1308	Henri VII of Luxembourg becomes Holy Roman Emperor under the name of Henry IV *(qv)*.
1337	Beginning of the **Hundred Years War** between the English and the French, in dispute over the French crown. Revolt against the Count of Flanders in Ghent *(qv)*.
1354	The county of Luxembourg is raised to the status of duchy.
1369	The Duke of Burgundy, **Philip the Bold**, marries Margaret of Male, daughter of the Count of Flanders, Louis of Male.

FOREIGN RULE

The Dukes of Burgundy

1384	On the death of Louis of Male, Philip the Bold inherits his territories. Thus Flanders becomes part of the Duchy of Burgundy.
1429-1477	Reigns of the Dukes of Burgundy **Philip the Good** and **Charles the Bold**. A great period of prosperity. Philip the Good founds the **Order of the Golden Fleece** at the time of his marriage with Isabella of Portugal. With the acquisition of Luxembourg in 1441, he completes the unification of the countries this side of the border (as opposed to those on the other side, in Burgundy). The Dukes of Burgundy are surrounded by a sumptuous court, and become major patrons of the arts. In 1468, Charles the Bold sacks the town of Liège, which is in revolt, and annexes the principality. On his death in 1477 his daughter **Mary of Burgundy** inherits his territories and marries Maximilian of Austria. The two-headed eagle replaces the Burgundian coat of arms.

The Habsburgs

1482-1519	On the death of Mary of Burgundy, Maximilian becomes regent of the Low Countries (thus named to differentiate them from the High Countries, or Upper Germany, his country). In 1494 Maximilian gives the Low Countries to his son **Philip the Handsome**. In 1496 Philip marries Joanna, daughter of the Catholic King of Spain. Their son Charles is born in 1500 in Ghent; he is the future **Emperor Charles V**. He is brought up in Flanders, partly by his aunt, Margaret of Austria, daughter of Maximilian *(qv)*, who becomes governor after the death of Philip the Handsome in 1506.
1519-1555	**Reign of Emperor Charles V:** Charles I, King of Spain, becomes Emperor Charles V on the death of Maximilian. His empire, "where the sun never sets", includes the Burgundian lands, the Austrian Empire and Spain, together with all the American and Asian colonies. He extends the territory of the Low Countries both to the north and to the south. In 1548 Emperor Charles V establishes Franche-Comté and the seventeen provinces of the Low Countries in the "Burgundy circle", with Brussels as capital.

The Spanish Netherlands

| 1555-1598 | **Reign of Philip II of Spain:** in 1555 Emperor Charles V hands over the rule of the Low Countries to his son, Philip II. While Emperor Charles V had been strongly attached to the country of his birth and had protected it fiercely, his son is first and foremost a Spaniard. As a fervent Catholic, he fights against the Protestants ("iconoclasts"), who ransack the churches of his religion. During his reign, the nationalistic spirit of the |

Low Countries boils over, and the struggle for political liberties keeps pace with the battle of the Calvinists for religious tolerance. In 1567 Philip II appoints the **Duke of Alva** governor of the Low Countries and charges him with quashing the Calvinistic "heresy" and with combatting the Dutch revolt, led by guerilla-style groups of **"Geuzen"** (rebel-nobility). The Counts of Egmont and Hornes are executed in Brussels *(qv)*. In 1576 the "Spanish Fury" is unleashed in Antwerp, then in Ghent. In the wake of this Philip II is forced to concede the **Pacification of Ghent** which liberates the seventeen provinces of the Low Countries from Spanish troops. In 1579, after the **Confederation of Arras** brings together the Catholic provinces which have chosen to stay under Spanish rule, the Protestant provinces form the **Union of Utrecht** (the provinces of the present Netherlands), followed by the republic of the United Provinces.

1598-1621	Reign of Archdukes Albert and Isabella, daughter of Philip II.
1648	With the **Treaty of Münster** Philip IV of Spain recognises the independence of the United Provinces and grants them the north of Brabant, northern Limburg and Flemish Zeeland. Belgium's future territory begins to take shape.
1659-1678	The **Treaty of the Pyrenees** between France and Spain places Artois under French rule and leads to the marriage of Louis XIV with Maria Theresa of Spain. According to a Brabant custom favouring children of a first marriage, she stands to inherit the entire region through her mother. In 1663 Louis XIV declares the **War of Devolution** against the Spanish Netherlands to take possession of his wife's inheritance. He then annexes southern Flanders (Lille). The Triple Alliance ends this war with the **Treaty of Aachen.** However, Louis XIV declares the **War of the Netherlands** in 1678, which concludes with the **Treaty of Nijmegen** in 1678; Flanders and Hainaut are excised.

The Austrian Netherlands

1701-1713	**War of the Spanish Succession:** Charles II of Spain dies with no direct descendants, leaving as heir Philip of Anjou, the grandson of his sister Maria Theresa and Louis XIV. However, England, Holland, Denmark and the German princes back the Archduke of Austria against France in the claim to succession.
1740-1748	War of the Austrian Succession. Louis XV invades Belgium, which is returned to Austria under the terms of the Treaty of Aachen.
1780-1789	**Emperor Joseph II**, an enlightened despot, nonetheless fails to take local idiosyncracies into account, thus sparking the peoples' revolt: Belgian nationalism becomes a reality. In 1789 the Brabant Revolution drives out the Austrians and assembles the States General in Brussels. The Austrians are temporarily expelled.

French Rule

1795	After the victories at Jemappes (1792) and Fleurus (1794), Republican France annexes the Austrian Netherlands and the principality of Liège. It establishes nine *départements* which are eventually to become the nine present provinces.

The Kingdom of the Netherlands

1814	**Napoleon's Defeat:** Belgium and Holland form the Kingdom of the Netherlands, with William I of Orange as sovereign. He also becomes Grand Duke of Luxembourg.
1815	The **Battle of Waterloo**, followed by the **Congress of Vienna.** Eupen and Malmédy are then annexed to Prussia.
1830	Belgium finally wins independence from Holland, which has held dominion over the Belgians since the Congress of Vienna following the Brussels Revolution *(see Brussels)*. Belgium renounces its claims on Flemish Zeeland, northern Brabant and part of Limburg. The German-speaking part of Luxembourg remains under the rule of William I.

From independence to the present day

1831	The London Conference acknowledges Belgian independence. The Constitution is drawn up and the crown given to Leopold of Saxe-Coburg-Gotha, who becomes first King of the Belgians under the name of **Leopold I** (1831-1865). War breaks out between the Belgians and the Dutch.
1839	William I acknowledges Belgian independence. Belgium overcomes severe economic difficulties (famine in Flanders, 1845-1848) and sets the Industrial Revolution in motion. Luxembourg, tied economically to Germany from 1842, experiences substantial industrial growth.

1865-1909	Reign of **Leopold II**.
1890	**Independence of Luxembourg: Adolf of Nassau** is Grand Duke from 1890 to 1905. **William IV** succeeds him (1905-1912).
1894	Universal suffrage is established in Belgium.
1908	The Congo, which has been Leopold II's personal property since 1855, becomes a Belgian colony.
1909	**Albert I** becomes King of the Belgians.
1912	**Marie-Adelaide** becomes Grand Duchess of Luxembourg.
1914-1918	**First World War:** Germany occupies Luxembourg and virtually all of Belgium, where Albert I, the "Soldier King", heads the resistance. Liège *(qv)* is captured, then Namur *(qv)*, Brussels and Antwerp *(qv)*. The Belgian army falls back to the coast. The Battle of the IJzer (Yser) *(qv)* takes place, brought to a close by the flooding of the polders. The front settles on the Ypres salient *(qv)*, then the hills of Flanders *(see Ypres)*.
1919	Treaty of Versailles: Belgium regains Eupen, Malmédy, Moresnet and St-Vith. **Grand Duchess Charlotte of Luxembourg** succeeds her sister Marie-Adelaide, who is forced to abdicate.
1922	Economic union concluded between Belgium and Luxembourg.
1934	Accidental death of Albert I *(see Meuse namuroise)*. **Leopold III** succeeds him (1934-1944). His wife, Queen Astrid, meets an accidental death the following year (1935).
1940-1944	**Second World War:** Germany occupies Belgium and Luxembourg. Battle of the Bulge *(see Bastogne)*.
1944-1951	Charles of Belgium is Regent.
1948	The Customs & Excise union of Benelux is concluded: **Be**lgium-**Ne**therlands-**Lux**embourg.
1951	Leopold III abdicates in favour of his son, who becomes King of the Belgians under the name of **Baudouin I**.
1957	Belgium and Luxembourg become members of the EEC (European Economic Community). Brussels is the capital of the EEC.
1960	The economic union of Benelux, instituted in 1958, comes into effect. The Eyskens government grants independence to the Belgian Congo, which becomes the Congo-Kinshasa, then Zaïre. Marriage of King Baudouin with Doña Fabiola de Mora y Aragón.
1964	**Jean of Nassau**, Grand Duke of Luxembourg, succeeds Grand Duchess Charlotte.
1977	Agreement drawn up establishing three federal regions: Brussels, Flanders, Wallonia.
1980	Referendum on regionalisation; new institutions in Flanders and Wallonia.
1989	The Brussels conurbation is officially recognised as an autonomous region called Bruxelles-Capitale.
1991-1993	Adoption (1991), ratification (1992) and enforcement (1993) of the Treaty of Maastricht setting up the European Union.
1993	Baudouin I dies and is succeeded by **Albert II**.
1994	Belgium becomes a federal state.

King Baudouin I

Reigns of successive Royal Families

Carolingians

977-991	Charles of France, Duke of Lower Lotharingia
991-1005	Otto I, Duke of Lower Lotharingia

House of Louvain

1005-1015	Lambert I, Count of Louvain, known as the Elder
1015-1038	Henry I, Count of Louvain
1038-1041	Otto of Louvain
1041-1063	Lambert II, Count of Louvain, called Balderic
1063-1079	Henry II, Count of Louvain
1079-1095	Henry III, Count of Louvain
1095-1140	Godefroid I the Bearded
1140-1142	Godefroid II the Younger
1142-1190	Godefroid III the Valiant
1190-1235	Henry I the Warrior
1235-1248	Henry II the Magnanimous
1248-1261	Henry III the Merciful
1261-1294	John I the Victorious
1294-1312	John II the Peace-Loving
1312-1355	John III the Triumphant
1355-1406	Jeanne
1406-1415	Anthony (Valois of Burgundy)
1415-1427	John IV
1427-1430	Philip I of Saint-Pol

House of Burgundy

1430-1467	Philip the Good
1467-1477	Charles the Bold
1477-1482	Mary of Burgundy
1482-1493	Maximilian of Austria
1493-1506	Philip I the Handsome (Habsburg of the Low Countries)
1506-1515	Margaret of Austria

Spanish rule

1515-1555	Emperor Charles the Fifth
1555-1598	Philip II (Habsburg of Spain)
1598-1621	Isabel of Austria and Albert
1621-1633	Isabel of Austria
1633-1665	Philip IV
1665-1700	Charles II
1700-1706	Philip V of Anjou (Bourbon)

Austrian rule

1713-1740	Charles VI (Habsburg of Austria)
1740-1780	Maria Theresa
1780-1790	Joseph II (Lorraine)
1790-1792	Leopold II
1792-1795	Francis II

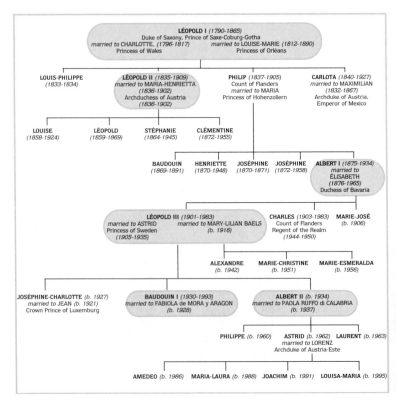

King Albert II and Queen Paola

French rule

1795-1799 Directoire: Commissaire Bou-
teville
1799-1804 Consulate: Napoleon Bonaparte
1804-1815 Empire: Napoleon I

Dutch government

1815-1830 William I of Orange-Nassau

Independence

1830-1831 Regency of Baron Surlet de
Chokier
1831-1865 Leopold I of Saxe-Coburg-
Gotha
1865-1909 Leopold II
1909-1934 Albert I
1934-1951 Leopold III
1944-1950 Regency of Prince Charles
1951-1993 Baudouin I
1993- Albert II

Belgium and Luxembourg
Independence and dynastic change

The battle of Waterloo (18 June 1815) put an end to Napoleon's dreams of empire-building and the Congress of Vienna (1814-15) reorganized Europe after the turmoil of the Napoleonic Wars and the Hundred Days. This comprehensive settlement created an autonomous grand duchy with William I of **Orange-Nassau** of the kingdom of the Netherlands (Belgium and Holland) as Grand Duke. However William promptly integrated the Grand Duchy into his kingdom as another province.

After the 1830 Revolution, marked by the "September Days" in Brussels, the Belgian provinces were separated from Holland and achieved independence as the kingdom of Belgium with Brussels as capital and Leopold of the **Saxe-Coburg** branch of the **Ernestine Wettins** as the first King of the Belgians.

Until the 19C the Ernestine Wettins were only another of the many small European dynasties but following several well-connected marriages they rose to unprecedented heights; Leopold became king of the Belgians as Leopold I in 1831, Albert married Queen Victoria in 1840, Ferdinand married Maria II of Portugal in 1836, while a fourth became prince of Bulgaria in 1887 and king in 1908. Leopold I's successors of the house of Saxe-Coburg have ruled Belgium ever since.

When Belgium revolted in 1830 the people of Luxembourg suppported the movement and the 1831 London Conference decided to divide Luxembourg. The western French-speaking part was given to Belgium and the eastern portion was to form the heart of a new independent grand duchy of Luxembourg retaining links with the Netherlands. The Dutch King William I was obstructive and it was 1839 before the separation took place. Independence came in 1890 on the death of the Dutch King William III whose male heirs had predeceased him. Adolf of the **Weilbourg** branch of the house of **Nassau** became Grand Duke in 1890 and was followed by his son William IV (1905-12). William in turn was succeeded by his daughter Marie-Adelaide who abdicated in 1919 in favour of her sister the Grand Duchess Charlotte. The Belgian and Luxembourg dynasties were linked in 1953 when the present Grand Duke Jean married Josephine-Charlotte of Belgium.

Use the Map of Principal Sights to plan an itinerary

Languages, politics and government

BELGIUM

Belgium's multilingualism has important consequences for the political and administrative structure of the country.

A trilingual country – Three languages are spoken in Belgium: Dutch in Flanders (60% of the Belgian population), French in Wallonia (39%) and German or a Germanic dialect in the Eupen region (slightly less than 1%). The linguistic borders correspond roughly to those of the provinces, except in Brabant *(see map p 3)*. Brussels is a sort of enclave within the Flemish region, being bilingual with a French-speaking majority. Dutch is one of the western branches of the Germanic language and resembles both German and English.

The linguistic quarrel – The linguistic border dates back as far as the 5C, when Rome abandoned the north of the country to the Germanic tribes. The Gallo-Roman language in the south resisted Germanic influence despite Salian Frank occupation. "Walha" (the origin of the word "Walloon") meant "foreigner" to the Franks.
Dutch literature developed in Flanders from the 12C, but disappeared almost entirely after the break from the Netherlands at the end of the 16C. It was not until the reign of William I from 1814 to 1830 that a certain rebirth of Dutch took place; in reaction to this the members of the 1831 Constituent Assembly imposed French as the only official language. Since then the sometimes violent antagonism between Flemish and French speakers has dominated Belgium's domestic history. There have been successive measures to "reinstate" the Dutch language:
1898: the equality law decrees that all laws should be passed in Dutch and French. The king has to take his oath in both languages.
1930: the University of Ghent adopts Flemish.
1932: regional monolingualism replaces bilingualism, except in Brussels.

Political and administrative organisation – Belgium is a parliamentary, representative, constitutional monarchy. Its constitution dates from 1831 and has undergone several amendments, the last one in 1993.
The king chooses the prime minister, who then forms his own government. The parliament has two Chambers: the Senate (71 senators) and the Chamber of Representatives (150). Every royal decree must be counter-signed by a minister. The legislative elections are held by direct, universal suffrage.

Political and administrative organisations linked to the linguistic communities
– On one hand, there is a division into three **Communities:** Flemish, French and German-speaking responsible for cultural affairs, health, social affairs and education (which is conducted in each language). On the other, the country is also divided into three **Regions:** Brussels, Flanders and Wallonia responsible for everything on a regional level – housing, employment, the environment, and economic development. Since 1980 Flanders and Wallonia have had actual legislative assemblies elected by universal suffrage, and their own executive bodies chosen from within each region.
Under the terms of the law of 12 January 1989 Bruxelles-Capitale became a political region in its own right, with a Council, an executive and extensive powers. On 18 June 1989 there was a major new institutional change when Council elections were held for the region of Bruxelles-Capitale. For the first time in Belgium the inhabitants themselves elected those who would be their representatives in the regional Council.

Administrative divisions – Belgium is currently divided into ten Provinces *(see map p 3 and the text on the regions and landscapes)*. Each province has a capital where the provincial government is located.

LUXEMBOURG

Languages – Three languages are spoken in the Grand Duchy of Luxembourg. The Luxembourg dialect, a Moselle patois, is used everyday. German is used for culture in general. French is the official language, and that used for literature. It is taught in all schools and at all educational levels; at secondary school most classes are held in French.

Political organisation – The constitution dates from 17 October 1868 and has been revised several times. The Grand Duke holds executive power and chooses his own government. Legislative power belongs to the Chamber of Deputies. The members are elected every five years by direct universal suffrage.

Art and architecture

Over the centuries various peoples have flocked into Belgium and Luxembourg, bringing with them major artistic movements: the Romans, the French, the Germans, the Burgundians, the Austrians, the Spanish, the Dutch. Each left its trace.

Nevertheless two very distinct and original styles, both of which gave rise to real masterpieces, were born and developed in Belgian cities: the Mosan school in the principality of Liège and Flemish art, which flourished especially during the reign of the Dukes of Burgundy.

From Prehistory to the Carolingian Empire

A few megaliths (Wéris) have survived from the prehistoric era. Archeological digs carried out in the towns once occupied by the Romans have brought to light a multitude of objects bearing witness to the skill of the craftsmen including pottery, glass, bronze and terracotta statuettes, and jewellery. The **Treviri Region** (Arlon and Luxembourg) has produced innumerable statues, votive stelae, including the famous stones with four divinities, and funerary monuments on which the bas-reliefs, now in museums, show scenes of everyday life *(illustration p 64)*.

Funerary artefacts from the 5C to the 9C, in the regions ruled by the Salian Franks (Tournai) and the Ripuarian Franks (Arlon and Luxembourg), included damascene (inlaid) iron weapons, jewellery and brooches in bronze or gold, set with glass beads. Charlemagne set up court at Aachen and introduced Christianity throughout his empire. He was at the root of a cultural renewal which manifested itself above all in the art of illumination. The churches of Lobbes and Theux are characteristic of the Carolingian style with their forepart, their wooden ceilings, their square pillars and the gallery located west of the nave.

Romanesque art (11C, 12C)

Towns and abbeys developed during this period. Belgium was divided into two parts. West of the Scheldt, Flanders belonged to France; regions to the east, through which the River Meuse flowed, belonged to the Holy Roman Empire. Romanesque art spread in particular along the trade routes lying in these two valleys. Two distinct movements formed – Scaldian art (from Scaldis, or the Scheldt) and Mosan art (named after the Meuse). Both were full of originality, even though churches in both regions share many common characteristics, such as basilical design, transept, chancel with radiating chapels and flat wooden ceiling.

Scaldian Romanesque art

In the Scaldian regions, devastated by the passage of hordes of marauding Vikings, Romanesque architecture is now evident only in isolated buildings such as the collegiate church in **Soignies.** The building of **Tournai Cathedral** led to the construction in the 12C of several churches based on the same architectural style. The main features visible from the outside of these buildings are the tower at the transept crossing and turrets on the west front; inside, the Norman influence in the tribunes and galleries is also typical.

Cathédrale Notre-Dame, Tournai

23

A number of civic buildings are also examples of Scaldian art (Tournai, Ghent, Aalst). Above the ground floor with round-arched openings, the windows, divided into two by a colonnette, are aligned between two stone string courses. In Gravensteen castle in Ghent, the Romanesque arches of the windows divided by colonnettes bear a strong resemblance to the design used in private houses.

Sculpture in the region from the 12C onwards, favoured by the availability of local Tournai stone *(qv)*, is quite remarkable. Outstanding examples can be seen on doorways and capitals (Tournai Cathedral) and fonts (Zedelgem, Dendermonde).

Mosan Romanesque art

The art which developed in the diocese of Liège (that is to say, the Meuse valley and the surrounding countryside), in particular during the 11C and 12C, is known as Mosan Romanesque art. The **principality of Liège**, which included Aachen, was already a leading area for arts and crafts during the Gallo-Roman period and it came very much under Carolingian influence. Later, owing to particularly close relations with the archbishopric of Cologne (on which the diocese of Liège depended) and the Rhine, the Rhenish Romanesque style began to exercise an influence as well.

In the 13C, French style predominated. This put an end to Mosan influence on architecture.

Architecture – Mosan regional Romanesque architecture retained a number of elements from Carolingian art, of which it is in some ways the continuation. First of all Ottonian architecture, which spread in Germany in the 10C and at the beginning of the 11C under Otto I, left its mark on part of the **collegiate church in Nivelles,** which was consecrated in 1046. Nivelles belonged at that time to the bishopric of Liège which was dependent on the Holy Roman Empire.

The forepart of the churches became more imposing in the 12C, being flanked with staircase turrets (Église St-Denis and Église St-Jean in Liège) or, more rarely, two square towers (Église St-Barthélemy in Liège). The outside of the church was decorated with Lombard arches. The apse occasionally included a second gallery on the outside (St-Pieterskerk in Sint-Truiden). There was often a crypt in the church, and sometimes beautiful cloisters (Nivelles, Tongeren).

Several of these characteristics can be seen in the later section of the collegiate church in Nivelles, as well as in many rural churches (Hastières-par-delà, Celles, Xhignesse).

Copper-, Gold- and Silversmithing – The art of melting and beating copper or brass was commonplace in the Meuse Valley first in Huy, then in Dinant. It is probably the reason for the great liturgical goldsmithing tradition which was to spread throughout the Mosan region, resulting in the production of immensely ornate shrines, reliquaries, crucifixes and book bindings. From 1107 to 1118 **Renier de Huy** made the famous brass font for the Église St-Barthélemy in Liège. Its classic perfection is quite exceptional for the period.

Thereafter the work became more complex, more elaborate in subject matter and more varied in materials used.

Godefroy de Huy used champlevé enamel for most of his work, in particular for the reliquary of the head of Pope St Alexander made for the Abbey of Stavelot and now exhibited in the Musée du Cinquantenaire in Brussels.

Nicolas de Verdun, who marked the transition from Romanesque to Gothic, created the reliquary of Our Lady for Tournai cathedral in 1205.

The monk **Hugo d'Oignies** produced his delicate, sophisticated works at the beginning of the 13C. They are now on display in

Font by Renier de Huy,
Église St-Barthélemy, Liège

Namur, in Oignies Convent. There are also many anonymous works, such as the 12C Visé reliquary, or the 13C Stavelot reliquary *(illustration p 188)*. Both of them fall within the limits of Mosan art.

Sculpture – Mosan art produced superb woodcarvings such as the Tongeren Christ, and the famous Virgins in Majesty known as the **Sedes Sapientiae**, or Seat of Wisdom. Further examples include the Walcourt carvings in the Museum of Religious and Mosan Art as well as in Église St-Jean in Liège.

The sculptures in stone are equally interesting, especially the capitals (Tongeren) and the bas-reliefs (*Dom Rupert Madonna,* in the Musée Curtius in Liège). Many Mosan church fonts have basins carved with heads on each of the four corners (Waha) and the lip decorated with ornamental foliage and animals (St-Séverin).

Gothic Art (13C to 15C)

Religious architecture – Rhenish art gradually gave way in ecclesiastical buildings to the French Gothic style, which imported by the monastic communities from France, or which spread throughout the area from Tournai.

Nevertheless, Gothic art appears later in Belgium than in France. The first example was the **chancel in Tournai cathedral** (1243), which was inspired by the cathedral in Soissons (Aisne, France). The style spread slowly. There are a number of clear variations that are specific to Belgium or to particular regions. The Gothic church is wider in Belgium than in France and is often not as high. On the other hand, the bell tower reaches a very impressive height (123m-403ft in Antwerp), even when it has been left unfinished, as in Mechelen.

Scaldian Gothic – This style retains some Romanesque features, but its main feature is the development of triple lancet windows, or **triplets** (O.L.-Vrouwekerk van Pamele in Oudenaarde, St.-Nikolaas in Ghent).

Brabant Gothic – It was not until the 14C that Gothic art appeared in Brabant. The architects took their inspiration from the great French cathedrals (Cathédrale des Sts-Michel-et-Gudule in Brussels). However, their modifications created a distinctive style which spread outside the province (Antwerp cathedral). Otherwise, this art remained rather sobre and never developed the excesses of Flamboyant Gothic.

The Brabant church is a large building with three aisles and an ambulatory with radiating chapels. Its main feature is the massive tower forming the west porch (the most beautiful example is in Mechelen), and side aisle chapels surmounted by triangular gables lined up like a row of houses. There is often no transept (Halle basilica), and the rose windows have commonly been replaced with larger windows.

The interior has a very distinctive style. The nave is supported by solid cylindrical pillars, whose capitals were originally decorated with a double row of curly cabbage leaves; large statues of the Apostles were later added to the other side of these pillars. The vaulting is of a fairly early Gothic style.

The side aisle chapels open into each other, creating new aisles. Finally, the triforium is sometimes replaced by a very intricately traceried balustrade, without a gallery.

The most representative church of this type is the basilica in Halle.

Civic architecture – From the end of the 13C, architectural originality manifested itself predominantly in **civic buildings**, especially in Flanders. Among these buildings were belfries, covered markets or town halls.

The cloth trade encouraged the creation and growth of the towns. The inhabitants defended their prosperity by obtaining certain privileges, town charters providing guarantees for their industry. For their meetings and their commercial activities they constructed impressive buildings which bore witness to jealously defended local autonomy and busy community life. The buildings were arranged around the central market square (Grand-Place/Grote Markt).

Belfries – The belfry towers over the market square, symbolising civic power. It stands alone (Tournai, Ghent) or is integrated into a public building, such as a covered market (Bruges, Ieper) or the town hall (Brussels).

It is designed as a keep with watch turrets and battlements. The prison is below ground level, with two rooms, one on top of the other, above it, with a cantilevered oriel window or balcony from which proclamations were made. The bell chamber *(qv)* is at the top, along with the lodge for the watchmen and heralds. Crowning everything is a weathervane symbolising the city, and shaped like a dragon, the Flemish lion, a warrior, a saint (Brussels), or a local character (Oudenaarde).

Covered Markets – The community developed hand in hand with the cloth trade. In the 15C there were 4 000 weavers in Ghent out of a total population of 50 000. Certain covered markets even had the privilege of offering official sanctuary normally provided only by churches and cemeteries.

The covered market consisted of a rectangular building divided into spaces for stalls inside. The area used for meetings and storage was upstairs. The most beautiful covered markets are to be seen in Bruges, dating from the end of the 13C, and in Ieper, dating from the same period and rebuilt after the First World War.

In both Bruges and Ieper the covered market contains the belfry because up to the end of the 14C it generally served as the Town Hall.

Town Halls – The most beautiful town halls (Bruges, Leuven, Brussels, Oudenaarde) were built from the late 14C onwards, when the cloth trade was declining.

Bruges Town Hall constructed in 1376 set a good precedent. The architecture still resembles that of a chapel. Brussels Town Hall followed. Those in Leuven and Ghent were built during the Renaissance. The one in Oudenaarde is a synthesis of its predecessors.

Outside, the façade is decorated with recesses containing statues of Flemish counts and countesses and the town's patron saints.

On the first floor is the great aldermen's hall, notable for its luxurious decoration (frescoes, tapestries or paintings, and always with a massive fireplace). It was used for meetings presided over by the burgomaster, as well as a hall for local festivities.

The ground floor of the Town Hall in Damme is used as a covered market.

The Gothic style is also evident in Flemish private houses. This is especially true of Bruges where the 16C saw the development of a very distinctive style tending toward Flamboyant architecture. Windows were surmounted by a moderately ornate tympanum. Later, the windows and tympanum were set adjacent to each other beneath an ogee arch.

Sculpture – A school of sculpture developed in Brabant (Brussels, Leuven) and in Antwerp and Mechelen during the second half of the 15C and the beginning of the 16C. It produced innumerable wooden altarpieces showing remarkably fine craftsmanship. They are also outstanding for the picturesque realism with traces of Gothic techniques.

An outstanding example of these **Brabant altarpieces,** apart from the one in Hakendover produced in 1430 (the oldest altarpiece in Belgium and also one of the most elegantly made) is the magnificent St George altarpiece (1493) exhibited in the Musée du Cinquantenaire in Brussels.

Hôtel de Ville, Brussels

The same picturesque quality marks the sculpture on **church stalls.** The armrests and misericords (seat supports) in Brabant churches are decorated with satirical figures full of imagination, unforgiving illustrations of the human vices. Those in Diest are among the most remarkable examples.

Decorative arts – The Belgian Gothic style exhibits great originality particularly in the decoration of the interiors of ecclesiastical or civic buildings. Woodworking (altarpieces, statues, stalls, beams) is as remarkable as stonecarving, as illustrated by the Flamboyant **rood-screens** in Lier, Walcourt and Tessenderlo. Mosan gold- and silversmithing did not survive beyond the 13C. Coppersmithing, however, spread throughout the country, giving rise to magnificent chandeliers, fonts, or lecterns in the shape of eagles, pelicans or gryphons.

Exceptional works were also produced in painting *(qv)* and tapestry *(qv)*.

The Renaissance (16C)

The Italian Renaissance had little impact on Belgium, and then not until 1530.

Architecture – While ecclesiastical buildings retained the Gothic style, civic architecture gradually adopted the style of the Italian Renaissance.

Oudenaarde Stadhuis (1526-1530) has upheld the Gothic tradition, partially at least, whereas the Stadhuis in Antwerp (1564) designed by **Cornelis Floris II de Vriendt** (1514-1575) reflects a change in tastes, as do the courtyard of the Prince-Bishops' palace in Liège (1526) and the guild halls on Grand-Place in Antwerp (late 16C).

This is particularly evident on the façades where there are engaged columns, pilasters and statues (Antwerp Stadhuis), friezes (the Oude Griffie in Bruges), and gables trimmed with volutes and crowned with statues (Stadhuis in Veurne). The windows often have moulded tympana above them, a regional characteristic inherited from the Gothic style.

Indeed, the extent and exuberance of this decoration has earned Flemish Renaissance style the name **"pre-baroque"**.

During the second half of the 16C, during the period of Spanish rule, a style known as **hispano-flemish** developed in castle architecture. It is typified by onion domes such as the ones at Ooidonk, turrets as at Rumbeke, or crowstepped gables like those in Beersel *(illustration p 92)*. These decorative elements give the buildings a picturesque and characteristic appearance, as do the onion domes which feature on top of church bell towers.

Sculpture – Renaissance sculpture in Belgium is best manifested in the somewhat intellectual works by the Mons artist **Jacques DuBroeucq** (c1500-1584), most of which are kept in Mons' collegiate church of Ste-Waudru ((qv statues of the Virtues). He also designed the castles in Binche and Mariemont, which no longer exist.

Cornelis Floris II de Vriendt, the architect of the Stadhuis in Antwerp, also created the magnificent tabernacle in Zoutleeuw.

The works of **Jerome Duquesnoy the Elder** (c1570-1641), renowned for his *Manneken Pis (illustration p 95)*, bear a resemblance to those of Cornelis Floris, especially the Aalst tabernacle.

Jean Mone (died1548), sculptor to Emperor Charles V, was born in Metz, France. He specialised in funerary monuments (Enghien, Hoogstraten) and altarpieces (Halle) in the purest Italian tradition.

Baroque art (17C)

The early 17C was a period of relative peace after the wars of religion and independence. Spain was represented by Archdukes Albert and Isabella, whose sumptuous court was in Brussels. These Catholic sovereigns had many ecclesiastical buildings constructed.

Until the middle of the century, however, the great artistic centre was still Antwerp *(qv)*, where Rubens died in 1640.

Religious architecture – **Cobergher** *(qv)* completed the dome-topped Scherpenheuvel basilica at the beginning of the century, at the request of the archdukes. It is this building which marks the birth of the Baroque style in Belgium.

Numerous ecclesiastical buildings were constructed for the Society of Jesus (Jesuits), such as St.-Carolus Borromeuskerk in Antwerp, Église St-Loup in Namur, St-Michielskerk in Leuven. They drew their inspiration from the Gesù church built in Rome in the previous century.

By the end of the century several Premonstratensian abbey churches had adopted the Baroque style, among them Grimbergen, Averbode, and Ninove. They are grandiose buildings with a layout in the form of a trefoil cross and a particularly long chancel reserved for the monks. Sometimes the churches are topped with a cupola, as is the case in Grimbergen.

Civic architecture – Noteworthy buildings from this period include the Mons belfry.

The most beautiful set of urban buildings in the Baroque style is to be found on the **Grand-Place, Brussels.** Rebuilt after the 1695 bombardment, it reveals decorative liveliness taken to excess but it nevertheless retained something of the Renaissance spirit in the Doric, Ionic and Corinthian orders which lend rhythm to the façades, as well as in the balustrades on some of the pediments.

In the Mosan region, 17C private houses are characteristically bereft of any flights of fancy. The brick walls are divided up by rows of stone, between which there are tall mullion windows. The Musée Curtius in Liège is an excellent example.

Sculpture – Many churches of this period were decorated inside with sculptures by the Antwerp artist **Artus Quellin the Elder** (1609-1668) who was very much influenced by Rubens, or with works by his cousin **Artus Quellin the Younger** (1625-1697).

Lucas Fayd'herbe (1617-1697), the artist from Mechelen who was also a student of Rubens, created enormous statues resting against columns in the nave and on altarpieces.

François Duquesnoy (1597-1643), son of Jerome *(see above)*, worked mainly in Rome. He was famous for his cherubs, or "putti", which were graceful figurines made of marble, terracotta or ivory. He is also credited, together with his brother **Jerome Duquesnoy the Younger** (1602-1654), with producing numerous ivory crucifixes which resemble each other in the delicacy and elegance of the craftsmanship (Château de Spontin).

Jean Delcour (1627-1707) in Liège worked with Bernini in Rome and sculpted elegant effigies of Madonnas and saints *(qv)*.

Antwerp artist **Hendrik Frans Verbruggen** (1655-1724) won renown for his woodcarvings. Examples include the Grimbergen confessionals decorated with life-sized figures. They are outstanding for the remarkable vigour and sense of movement. They were frequently imitated.

Belfry, Mons

For the Cathédrale des Sts-Michel-et-Gudule in Brussels, Verbruggen produced a proto-type of the pulpits known in Belgium as **truth pulpits**, on which sculptures and immense figures depict the truths of the Gospels.

The church stalls in Averbode, Floreffe and Vilvoorde, decorated with figures, are also remarkable examples of Belgian Baroque sculpture.

The 18C

The Baroque style persisted in ecclesiastical buildings, but at the end of the century, under the rule of Charles of Lorraine (1744-1780), the neo-Classical style began to spread. The **Place Royale in Brussels** was constructed in this style by the Frenchmen Guimard and Barré.

Laurent Dewez (1731-1812), architect to the governor, built the minster in Orval in 1760 in the same style (it has since been destroyed). He followed this with the church at Gembloux (1762-1779) and finally the église de Bonne-Espérance (1770-1776).

Baroque sculpture was still very much in evidence in churches. Pulpits tended more towards the Rococo, for example the elegant construction in oak and marble in St.-Baafskathedraal in Ghent. It was made by **Laurent Delvaux** (1696-1778), who thereafter adopted the neo-Classical style. **Theodoor Verhaegen** (1700-1759) made several pulpits, and a splendid confessional with majestic figures carved in wood in Ninove.

Michiel Vervoort the Elder (1667-1737) produced pulpits and confessionals decorated with statues, such as the ones in St.-Carolus Borromeuskerk in Antwerp.

The decorative arts came into their own in the 18C with tapestry and lace *(see below)*, ceramics in Tournai *(see Tournai)*, and cabinet-making in Liège *(see Liège)* where the pieces of furniture, drawing inspiration from the French style, adorned sumptuous interiors hung with painted leather or tapestries (Musée d'Ansembourg in Liège). In Liège, the richness of the interior decoration in the castles contrasts with the austerity of the local architecture (Aigremont).

The 19C and 20C

Architecture – At the beginning of the 19C, neo-Classicism triumphed in Brussels (Galeries St-Hubert, Colonne du Congrès, Théâtre de la Monnaie) and in Ghent (Grote Schouwburg and Law Courts). The end of the century saw a taste for architecture that harked back to Classical Antiquity. The most beautiful example is the Graeco-Roman Law Courts in Brussels, designed by **Poelaert** (1817-1879).

However, from 1890 onwards certain architects revolted against these copies of the past and sought new forms and materials. Belgium was one of the first countries to subscribe to the Art Nouveau movement, with architects such as **Paul Hankar** (1859-1901), **Henry van de Velde** (1863-1957) and above all **Victor Horta** (1861-1947). Traditional materials (stone, glass, wood) or new ones (steel, concrete) were used for rationally designed buildings in which the structure was linked harmoniously to the interior decoration until it became in itself a decorative element. The interior of the house by Horta (Musée Horta in St-Gilles, Brussels), the Waucquez shops containing Brussels's Comic Strip Centre and the Musée des Beaux-Arts in Tournai all demonstrate the attention to detail, form and originality which characterise this highly productive innovator.

After Horta, several architects plunged into modernism and attempted to resolve the problem of collective residences. This gave birth to the garden-cities of the 1920s, created by architects **Eggerickx** and **Van der Zwaelmen** ("Floréal" and "Le Logis" garden cities in Boitsfort, *qv*), Victor Bourgeois, **Huib Hoste, Adolphe Puissant** *(see Bruxelles)*.

More modern works include those of **André Jacqmain** in Louvain-la-Neuve, **Claude Strebelle** in Sart Tilman, **Lucien Kroll** in Woluwe-St-Pierre and **Roger Bastin** in Brussels (Musée d'Art moderne).

Sculpture – **Willem Geefs** (1805-1883), representing neo-Classicism, created the statue of Leopold I at the top of Colonne du Congrès in Brussels.

From 1830, the influence of Romanticism and the taste for quattrocento are evident in the sculptures of **Charles Fraikin** (1817-1893) and **Julien Dillens** (1849-1904) who participated with the exiled Rodin in decorating the Bourse in Brussels.

Thomas Vinçotte (1850-1925) created the group of charging horses on the Arc de triomphe du Cinquantenaire.

Jef Lambeaux (1852-1908) is popular for the surging passion emanating from his works, reminiscent of Jordaens (Brabo Fountain in Antwerp). **Constantin Meunier** (1831-1905) was a painter before turning to sculpture in 1885. He felt at one with the new industrial era and committed himself to representing the working man, the miner at his job.

The Impressionist period is represented, above all, by **Rik Wouters** (1882-1916), whose spontaneity bursts out of boldly executed works such as the *Crazy Virgin.*

Georges Minne (1866-1941) pioneered Expressionism, whose principal representatives were to be **Oscar Jespers** (1887-1970) and **Joseph Cantré**. A return to fundamental themes can be seen in the works of **Georges Grard** (1901-1984) which celebrates the fertile image of the female form. By the 1920s, non-figurative art had already appeared in the works of **Servranckx**, who was also a painter.

Notable post-war pioneers include **Maurice Carlier** and **Félix Roulin** (born in 1931) who hammered out a highly personal world in copper, adding elements of the human body (hands, mouths, arms, etc.) to various reliefs. The works of **Jacques Moeschal** (born in 1913), architect and sculptor, can be seen alongside motorways and decorating the urban landscape. They are made of steel and concrete. **Pol Bury** (born in 1922) inherited the Surrealist tradition in addition to being close to the CoBrA group *(see below)*. Since the 1950s he has devoted himself to designing "Kinetic" sculptures (continuously moving sculptures with motors or balls, hydraulic sculptures, etc.).

PAINTING

It is in painting that the people of Belgium, who are fond of colour and receptive to the world around them, have found their most characteristic mode of expression.

The Primitives – The 15C is the golden age of Flemish painting. A naturalist movement had already appeared by the end of the 14C, with Hennequin (or Jan) de Bruges, who drew the tapestry cartoons for *The Apocalypse* in Angers, and Melchior Broederlam, painter of the altarpieces for the Champmol charterhouse in Burgundy.

Their art remained nonetheless closely related to the art of **illumination** in which the Flemings excelled under the patronage of the Dukes of Burgundy. In the early 15C the Pol friars, Jan and Herman van Limburg, **miniaturists** of the *Très Riches Heures du duc de Berry* (Château de Chantilly, France) displayed an astonishingly detailed and vivid realism in their art of illumination.

The greatest painter was **Jan van Eyck** (*d*1441). The *Mystic Lamb* altarpiece *(qv)* remains one of the great wonders of painting of all time, by his use of perspective, realistic detail and bright colours softened by light. Van Eyck is also credited by many with the invention of oil painting.

Robert Campin, thought by some scholars to be the Master of Flémalle, worked in Tournai during the same period. One of his students was **Rogier van der Weyden** (Rogier de la Pasture) *(qv)*, who influenced among others **Dirk Bouts** *(qv)*.

Van Eyck was succeeded by the Bruges School *(qv)*, which included **Petrus Christus**, the great portraitist, and **Hans Memling**, who offers a charming synthesis of the pictorial themes of his period in his work, as much in his calm sophisticated religious compositions as in his exceptional, masterfully executed portraits. **Gérard David** continued in similar vein. In Ghent, **Hugo van der Goes** *(see Bruges)* painted panels demonstrating an original sense of composition.

Virgin with Child by Hugo van der Goes,
Musée d'Art ancien, Brussels

Musée d'Art ancien, Bruxelles/ARTEPHOT-COLORTHEQUE, Paris

The Renaissance – 16C. **Quentin Massys** (1466-1530) was the first painter to reveal Renaissance inspiration in his tasteful, sophisticated works. **Joachim Patinir** *(qv)* and **Herri met de Bles** *(qv)* devoted themselves to landscapes. **Pieter Bruegel the Elder** (*c*1525-1569), a follower of Hieronymous Bosch, produced lively, picturesque works revealing his gift for observation. His son Pieter Brueghel, known as **Hell Brueghel**, imitated him with not inconsiderable talent.

17C – Like the 15C this was a golden age for painting.

Pieter Paul Rubens *(qv)* was a universal artist who was sensitive to all the promptings of flesh and spirit. It was he who struck a balance between Flemish realism and Italian harmony.

Anthony van Dyck (1599-1641), who lived in England from 1632 onwards, was a student of Rubens. He was an extraordinary draughtsman who painted often dark and melancholy works. He also painted religious scenes and elegant society portraits.

Jacob Jordaens (1593-1678) was one of Rubens' assistants. He painted colourful works with vigourous brush strokes, often depicting earthy, realistic scenes. The animal painter **Frans Snyders** (1579-1657) taught **Paul De Vos** among his students, whose brother **Cornelis De Vos** specialised in portraits. Jan Brueghel, known as **Velvet Brueghel,** is famous for his paintings of flowers and landscapes. His son-in-law **David Teniers the Younger** (1610-1690) created a fashion in Belgium for scenes of peasant life, or genre painting. Developments slowed down somewhat in the 17C with the religious paintings of **Pieter Jozef Verhaghen** (1728-1811) *(qv),* who continued in Rubens' style.

19C-20C – The style of the excellent portraitist François Joseph **Navez** (1787-1869), a student of David, was essentially neo-Classical. Antoine **Wiertz** (1806-1865) was more Romantic.

In 1868 the Société Libre des Beaux-Arts in Brussels brought together the Realist painters **Félicien Rops** (1833-1898) *(qv),* **Charles De Groux** (1867-1930), **Alfred-Émile Stevens** (1823-1906) and **Constantin Meunier.**

Portrait of Marguerite by Fernand Khnopff

Musées Royaux des Beaux-Arts de Belgique

Except for **Théo van Rysselberghe** (1862-1926), who adopted Seurat's pointillist style, the painters of the late 19C paid no attention to new movements, in particular Impressionism. **Émile Claus** (1848-1924) depicted tranquil country life. **Henri Evenepoel** (1872-1899) studied daily life, whereas **Henri De Braekeleer** (1840-1888) lent a luminous poetry to scenes of bourgeois life. Jakob Smits *(qv)* painted the Kempen region. The **Symbolist movement** attracted William Degouves de Nuncques (1867-1935), Xavier Mellery (1845-1921) and Fernand Khnopff (1858-1921), who painted strange, sphinx-like women.

James Ensor *(qv)* set himself apart from artistic movements, demonstrating an unrivalled originality and talent.

Belgian painting made good progress with the work of the **Sint Martens-Latem group** *(qv).* **Valerius de Saedeleer** painted landscapes in the style of Brueghel, while **Gustave van de Woestijne** painted everyday people. The second wave of the Latem group's work was Expressionist, with **Albert Servaes,** who tended towards mysticism in his work, **Gust** (Gustave) **De Smet** and **Frits van den Berghe,** who was more Surrealist. **Constant Permeke** *(qv)* led this group. His landscapes and figures have a calm vigour about them and, like his sculptures, are endowed with a fairly primitive lyricism.

Musées Royaux des Beaux-Arts de Belgique

Flute Player by Rik Wouters

Fauvism was as important a movement in Brabant as Expressionism was in Flanders. The leading exponent was **Rik Wouters** (1882-1916), whose paintings showed a tendency towards constructivism (influenced by Cézanne). In the same school, **Jean Brusselmans** (1884-1953) drew his inspiration from his surroundings, depicting working class women, labourers, landscapes, and backstreet interiors.

Surrealism made its mark with **René Magritte** (1898-1967) and his fantastic worlds in which his precise technique was put to the service of his imagination. **Paul Delvaux** (1897-1994) painted characters roaming around against theatrical backdrops.

Joseph Peeters (1895-1960) and **Victor Servranckx** (1897-1965) were both precursors and theoreticians of abstract art in Belgium; Servranckx's geometric abstract works are reminiscent of Fernard Léger.

La Jeune Peinture Belge was founded just after the Second World War, in July 1945, bringing together Gaston Bertrand, Louis Van Lint, **Anne Bonnet**, Antoine Mortier and **Marc Mendelson.** This was the second wave of abstract art.

In 1948 the **CoBrA** group (**Co**penhagen, **Br**ussels, **A**msterdam) was founded by the Belgian writer Christian Dotremont and the Experimental Group of painters from Amsterdam. Principal exponents were the Dane Asger Jorn, the Dutchman Karel Appel and the Belgian **Pierre Alechinsky.** Cobra aimed to be a way of life, art freed from the intellect to express all types of experience.

Since 1960 Belgian painters have followed the great international movements.

TAPESTRY

Tapestry, designed to ornament the walls of castles and churches, is thought to have been introduced into Europe at the end of the 8C. The art of tapestry-making developed in particular from the 14C onwards and assumed considerable importance in Belgium.

Brussels had over 1 500 tapestry-makers at the beginning of the 16C. Tapestries woven in Belgium were ordered by the greatest princes in Europe, by the kings of Spain and by the Pope.

The first tapestries were usually religious compositions. Historic scenes appeared later, as did hunting scenes and allegorical or mythological scenes. Several tapestries illustrating the same theme are known as a set, or up to the 19C as a "room". Compositions were set against a background of flower-filled meadows.

Tournai – The main centre of production was initially Arras, under the rule of the Dukes of Burgundy. Its decline began in 1477, when the town was captured by Louis XI. Tournai, which was already the main rival of Arras, ended up by eclipsing it altogether. Tournai tapestries have no border. The story is depicted in several episodes set close together. There are no empty spaces. The areas between the sumptuously robed figures are filled in with plant decoration. The compositions are highly stylised, even when the subject is taken from a painting such as **The Judgement of Trajan and Herkenbald** (Bernisches Historiches Museum, Berne, Switzerland), which was inspired by works by Van der Weyden which have since been destroyed.

The most famous Tournai tapestries include *Sheep-shearing*, *The Story of Gideon* (disappeared) (1449-1453) and *The Story of Alexander* (1459), which were woven for Philip the Good and *The Battle of Roncevaux* (second half of the 15C).

Brussels – Tapestry had a place of honour in Brussels from the 14C onwards; nevertheless, the oldest known works from Brussels only date back to the second half of the 15C. In 1466, the Dukes of Burgundy commissioned their first tapestries.

Highly sophisticated in technique, the compositions were still essentially Gothic in style, as illustrated by the early 16C **David and Bathsheba.**

Brussels tapestry making reached its peak not long after this. A new style evolved under the impetus of **Van Orley** (*c*1488-1541). The composition became monumental, and the scenes very elaborate, dealing with a single, strongly emphasised subject. The figures are dressed in sumptuous costumes, the landscapes enriched with Renaissance buildings, plants are painstakingly reproduced, and the borders are filled with flowers, fruit and grotesques involving either animal or arabesque motifs.

From 1525 it is possible to discern the initials BB (Brussels Brabant) in the border framing the composition. Van Orley designed the series entitled **Honours**, commissioned by Emperor Charles V (*c*1520), **The Legend of Notre-Dame-du-Sablon** (1515-1518) and the **Hunts of Maximilian,**

The Legend of Notre-Dame-du-Sablon
Musées Royaux d'Art et d'Histoire, Brussels

which was made by Willem de Pannemaker, a member of a highly talented family of tapestry-makers. Nature is depicted in a remarkable way in the latter series.

Raphael painted the cartoons for the **Acts of the Apostles** (1515-1519) commissioned by Pope Leo X.

The painter **Pieter Coecke** produced the cartoons for *Mortal Sins* and *The Story of St Paul*.

The Legend of Herkenbald (1513) and the series **Virtues and Vices** are equally admirable works.

At the beginning of the 17C Brussels lost its supremacy in this field, although commissions continued to pour in. Many tapestries, such as *The Triumphs of the Holy Sacrament*, were made to cartoons by **Rubens**. They are outstanding for their sense of drama, their perspective effects and the importance of the border as a feature. Jordaens himself created several cartoons, including *Proverbs* and *Country Life*.

Antwerp, Bruges, Enghien and Geraardsbergen also produced tapestries during this period. At the end of the 17C and 18C Rubens' cartoons were still being used, but rustic subjects were more the vogue, and so paintings by **David Teniers the Younger** *(qv)* were frequently reproduced.

Oudenaarde – In Oudenaarde, where tapestry had been a great art since the 16C, the subjects have always been of a more modest type than in Brussels. The 18C witnessed the triumph of the landscapes called **verdures** *(qv)*, which other centres of tapestry production such as Enghien and Geraardsbergen had been making since the 16C. Oudenaarde, like Brussels, imitated the rustic paintings of David Teniers the Younger.

Contemporary Tapestry – The art of tapestry fell into decline at the end of the 18C. It was then revived in Mechelen, with the Gaspard de Wit Royal Tapestry Works *(qv)*, in Oudenaarde *(qv)* and in Tournai *(qv)*, where the group Force Murale, led by Roger Somville and Edmond Dubrunfaut, was created in 1945.

OTHER ART FORMS

Furniture – Oak Gothic furniture was limited to tables, benches and chests with linenfold decoration. During the Renaissance, tables and very high-backed chairs were embellished with heavy turned feet. The massive sideboards made in **Antwerp** had two main parts and featured entablatures supported by caryatids, uprights decorated with lions' heads (the Flemish lion) holding rings in their mouths, friezes and panels which were either moulded or sculpted to depict religious, historical or mythological scenes. Seats and walls were covered in the Spanish fashion, with embossed and painted leather which was produced in **Mechelen** from the beginning of the 16C, taking over from Cordoba. During this period the flanges and brackets of the beams in most of the civic buildings were sculpted. The fireplaces were embellished with Renaissance motifs.

Craftsmen began to use tropical woods from the end of the 16C. Cupboards, which soon took on gigantic proportions, were often veneered in ebony. **Antwerp** produced its famous ebony or rosewood cabinets, richly encrusted with ivory, mother-of-pearl or tortoiseshell. Some of them are decorated with painted panels from Rubens's studio.

The French taste for flowing lines came into fashion in the 18C. Elegant oak presses were produced in **Liège** and **Namur.**

Art Nouveau became very popular thanks to Henry van de Velde and Victor Horta, especially in the work of Serrurier-Bovy.

Furniture-making is still a flourishing industry in Mechelen and Liège.

Ceramics – The decoration of houses in the Middle Ages gave rise to a high level of production of **ceramic tiles** for walls and floors. Crockery in **glazed stoneware** came from the Rhine region, but also from **Raeren** and, from the 16C, from **Bouffioulx** (near Charleroi) as well. Nowadays the blue sandstone ware from **La Roche-en-Ardenne** is widely appreciated. **Faïence** (tin-glazed earthenware) was first produced in Antwerp in the 16C, using Italian techniques. Apart from traditional tiles, dishes and apothecaries' jars were also produced. Ceramics factories were established in the 18C and 19C in Nimy (near Mons), Liège, Namur, Brussels, Tournai and Andenne (the largest centre for fine earthenware).

At the present time, tableware is an important manufacturing activity in Belgium (La Louvière) and in the Grand Duchy of Luxembourg.

For **porcelain,** the main centre of production besides Andenne was **Tournai**, where a works was founded in the middle of the 18C. **Brussels** porcelain still has a good reputation.

Glassware – This craft was established in Hainaut in the 2C and perfected in the late 15C, under the influence of Venice. It made further strides in the 17C, owing this time to Bohemian and English influences. At the same time the use of coal as a fuel from the end of the 17C was instrumental in concentrating the production of window glass in the Charleroi basin.

The **Vonêche** crystal works, founded near Beauraing (Namur province) in 1802, was the largest in the French Empire until 1815. **Val St-Lambert** (west of Liège) took over from it after 1826. The Manage glassworks (near Charleroi) is reputed nowadays for the manufacture of perfume bottles.

Lace – While this craft is probably of Venetian origin, Flanders lays claim to the invention of bobbin (or pillow) lace. This is made on a cushion or pillow. Threads are held taut by bobbins and interwoven to form a web or a pattern, the work being continually fixed in place with pins.

Lace first appeared during the Renaissance and was designed to ornament clothing. Flemish paintings depict both adults and children in suits decorated with lace at the collar and on the sleeves. This craft was taught to young girls at school and soon became popular. It then regained its popularity once Belgium's period of political and religious strife had passed, and Flemish lace gained an unequalled reputation in the 17C. The principal centres of production during this period included **Brussels** (mainly needlepoint lace), **Bruges, Mechelen** and **Antwerp**.

In the 18C lacemaking reached its heyday, with patterns largely incorporating Rococo designs and embellishment in particular with floral motifs. Sadly the invention first of machine-made tulle, then the Jacquard loom, had an adverse effect on the popularity of needlepoint lacemaking.

There have, however, been successful efforts to preserve the craft of lacemaking. It is still practised in Bruges and Sint-Truiden. Bobbin lacemaking is once more being taught, and several new centres have sprung up, in particular at Lier, Mechelen and Poperinge. Zele is continuing the tradition of needlepoint lace. There is a centre of contemporary lacemaking in Brussels.

GLOSSARY OF ART AND ARCHITECTURAL TERMS USED IN THE GUIDE

Ambulatory: *illustration I.*

Apse: semicircular or semi-polygonal east end of a church, behind the altar.

Arcade: a line of small counterthrusting arches, usually raised on columns.

Avant-corps: the part of a building which projects obviously from the main body or façade.

Axial (or Lady) chapel: chapel in the main axis of the church (often dedicated to Our Lady, if the church itself is not); *illustration I.*

Bartizan: a battlemented parapet (watch tower); *illustration II.*

Bas-relief: carved or sculpted figures which are slightly proud of their background; low relief.

Bracket: piece of projecting stone or timber supporting a beam or cornice.

Brattice: temporary projecting wooden gallery or parapet used during sieges.

Cantilever: see bracket.

Capital: enlarged uppermost part of a column shaft.

Champlevé enamel: enamel poured into engraved patterns on metal surfaces and then smoothed down to the same level as the metal.

Chancel: the part of the church reserved for the clergy (sanctuary) and cantors (choir), which contains the high altar; *illustration I.*

Chapter-house: room in a monastery where the chapter of canons or nuns meets.

Chevet: French term for the exterior of the apse (the east end); *illustration I.*

Corbel: see bracket.

Crowstepped gable: triangular upper part of a wall which supports the two slopes of the roof and which has stepped edges.

Curtain wall: length of wall or rampart between two towers or bastions; *illustration III.*

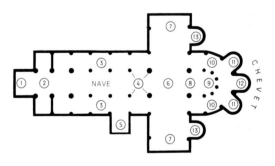

Ground plan – The more usual Catholic form is based on the outline of a cross with the two arms of the cross forming the transept:
① Porch – ② Narthex – ③ Side aisles (sometimes double) – ④ Bay (transverse section of the nave between 2 pillars) – ⑤ Side chapel (often pre-dates the church) – ⑥ Transept crossing – ⑦ Arms of the transept, sometimes with a side doorway – ⑧ Chancel, nearly always facing east towards Jerusalem; the chancel often vast in size was reserved for the monks in abbatial churches– ⑨ High altar – ⑩ Ambulatory: in pilgrimage churches the aisles were extended round the chancel, forming the ambulatory, to allow the faithful to file past the relics – ⑪ Radiating or apsidal chapel – ⑫ Axial chapel. In churches which are not dedicated to the Virgin this chapel in the main axis of the building is often consecrated to the Virgin (Lady Chapel) – ⑬ Transept chapel.

Foliated scroll: sculpted spiral ornamentation, decorated predominantly with stylised foliage motifs.

High relief: sculpted relief figures which are proud of their background by more than half their thickness (in between bas-relief and fully detached sculpture).

Lancet arch: a narrow, sharply pointed arch (resembling the head of a lance).

Lantern: a windowed structure at the top of a dome or turret permitting light to enter a building.

Machicolation: a projecting defensive parapet, supported by brackets, with holes in the floor through which missiles etc. can be dropped on the attackers; *illustrations II and III.*

Merlon: solid part of a battlemented parapet between two embrasures.

Moat: a trench, generally filled with water, surrounding and protecting a fortress.

Mullion: a stone upright separating panels in windows, doors or other openings.

Oriel: a bay window cantilevered out from a wall.

Palladian style: door or window openings in sets of three, divided by pilasters or columns and with triangular pediments above the outer two openings and a round-arched lintel above the central one.

Pilaster: an engaged rectangular column.

Pinnacle: apex of a building.

Polyptych: painting or sculpture composed of several hinged panels.

Radiating or apsidal chapel: *illustration I.*

Rood-screen: carved screen separating chancel and nave, generally bearing a large crucifix (rood) and sometimes representations of other figures present at the Crucifixion.

Round (arch etc.): semicircular.

Side aisle: aisle running along each side of the nave at the same height as it.

Stalls: *illustration IV.*

Stucco: mixture of marble dust and plaster bound with strong glue.

Transept: *illustration I.*

Transept arm: *illustration I.*

Tribune: raised platform at one end of a church, reserved for the seat of the bishop or other high-ranking church dignitary.

Triforium: shallow gallery running along the nave and chancel of a church, above the side aisles and below the clerestory.

Triptych: painting or sculpture composed of three hinged panels, which can be closed up.

Watch turret: *illustration II.*

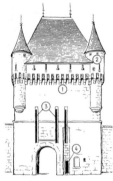

illustration II

Fortified gatehouse: ① Machicolations – ② Watch turrets or bartizan – ③ Slots for the arms of the drawbridge – ④ Postern.

illustration III

Fortified enclosure: ① Hoarding (projecting timber gallery – ② Machicolations (corbelled crenellations) – ③ Barbican – ④ Keep or donjon – ⑤ Covered watchpath – ⑥ Curtain wall – ⑦ Outer curtain wall – ⑧ Postern.

illustration IV

Stalls:
① High back – ② Elbow rest – ③ Cheek-piece – ④ Misericord.

MICHELIN GREEN GUIDES

Art and Architecture
Ancient monuments
Picturesque routes
Landscape
Geography
History
Touring programmes
Plans of towns and buildings

A selection of guides for holidays in France and abroad

Literature

The enormous extent and variety of Belgian literature is virtually unknown outside the country itself. Literary works, in particular those by Flemish speakers, have a pronounced local flavour and are characterised also by an unquestionable originality.

French-speaking Belgium – In earlier centuries the country produced some famous chroniclers. In the 14C, there was Froissart; in the 15C, Philippe de Commines. The 16C produced Jean Lemaire de Belges, born in Bavay.
In the 18C the hallmark of the Maréchal de Ligne *(qv)*, a memorialist, was his cosmopolitan approach.
A highly original and active literary movement has developed in Belgium during the last century.
Following the great precursor **Charles de Coster**, author of the celebrated work *The Glorious adventures of Tyl Ulenspiegel* (1867), came the group "La Jeune Belgique" (1881) and a period of upsurge in literary activity from novelists, such as the Antwerp writer **Georges Eekhoud** (1854-1927) and Camille Lemonnier (1844-1913) *(Un Mâle, 1881)*, from poets, such as the Ghent author Van Lerberghe (1861-1907) who wrote the exquisite *Chanson d'Ève* in 1904, Max Elskamp (1862-1931), or **Georges Rodenbach** (1855-1898), made famous by his short stories entitled *Vies encloses* and his novel *Bruges la Morte* (1892). Some writers earned worldwide renown. Among them were the great poet **Émile Verhaeren** *(qv)* and the Ghent author **Maurice Maeterlinck** (1862-1949), mysterious and melancholy writer of the play *Palleas and Melisande*, and also an essayist *(La Vie des abeilles)* and Nobel Prize winner in 1911.
From subsequent generations, outstanding writers include Maurice Carême (1899-1978), Robert Goffin (*b.* 1898), Jean de Boschère (1878-1953), **Marcel Thiry** (1897-1977), author of *Toi qui pâlis au nom de Vancouver*, Marie Gevers (1883-1975), who has been compared to the French author Colette, the Brussels writer Franz Hellens (1881-1972) who wrote novels set mainly in fantasy worlds, and Pierre Nothomb (1887-1967) *(La Vie d'Adam)* who also wrote a few novels.
The Mons author **Charles Plisnier** (1896-1952) was a famous novelist and winner of the Prix Goncourt (for *Mariages* and *Faux Passeports*). **Fernand Crommelynck** (1886-1970) was best-known for an earthy play *The Magnificent Cuckold*, and **Michel De Ghelderode** (1898-1962) was a prolific, audacious playwright.

Maurice Grevisse (1895-1980) wrote *Bon Usage* (1936), and M Joseph Hanse (1902-1992) wrote *Nouveau Dictionnaire des difficultés du français moderne*, both significant reference works in the field of grammar and linguistics.
Writers who have achieved international fame include the Namur author **Henri Michaux** (1899-1984), who took French nationality, the Liège writer of detective stories **Georges Simenon** (1903-1989), creator of the famous Inspector Maigret in 1930 and author of many analytical novels, the essayist **Suzanne Lilar** (1901-1992) who wrote works such as *le Journal de l'Analogiste* or *Le Couple*, the historian **Carlo Bronne** (1901-1987); and the novelist **Françoise Mallet-Joris** (*b*1930) who lives in Paris. In the world of the comic-strip **Hergé** (1907-1983), creator of Tintin in 1929 (*Tintin au pays des Soviets*), lived to see his

Tintin by Hergé

albums translated into languages from all over the world. **Folon's** little character in a hat has achieved fame on billboards the world over.
The songwriter-composer **Jacques Brel** (*Le Plat Pays*) (1929-1978) can be ranked among Belgium's poets. Also deserving of a mention is an author from Brussels, **Pierre Mertens** (Prix Médicis, 1987), author of *Éblouissements*.
There are a number of institutions which defend French literature such as the Académie royale de langue et de littérature françaises (1921), l'Association des Ecrivains belges and the Journal des Poètes whose editor is Arthur Haulot.

Flemish-speaking Belgium – Flemish literature was born in the 12C, and gained momentum first in the 13C with the poetess Hadewijch and the poet and moralist **Jacob van Maerlant** *(qv)*, then in the 14C, with the mystic **Jan van Ruusbroec** *(qv)*, considered to be the father of Dutch prose.
Writers who distinguished themselves in the 19C include the Antwerp citizen **Hendrik Conscience** *(qv)*, Romantic author of novels and short stories, and the great Catholic poet **Guido Gezelle** *(qv)*.

The 20C has had a number of outstanding poets such as the sensual, mystic **Karel van de Woestijne** (1878-1929), and the modernist Expressionist Paul van Ostaijen (1896-1928). Cyriel Buysse (1859-1932) figures among the novelists, along with **Stijn Streuvels** (1871-1969), who drew his inspiration from the flat landscapes in the southwest of the country (*De Vlaschaard* – The Flax Field), Herman Teirlinck (1879-1967), prolific novelist and dramatist, Willem Elsschot (1882-1960), **Ernest Claes** *(qv)* with his mischievous tales, **Felix Timmermans** *(qv)*; and Gerard Walschap (1896-1989).

After 1930 poetry was dominated by **Jan van Nijlen** (1884-1965), **Richard Minne** (1891-1965), **Karel Jonckheere** (1906-1933), **Anton van Wilderode** (*b*1918), and **Christine D'Haen** (*b*1923).

A second wave of modernist writers appeared in about 1948, including the talented Bruges author **Hugo Claus** (*b*1929), who is a dramatist (*Andréa ou la Fiancée du matin*, 1955; *Vendredi*, 1970), novelist (*Het verdriet van Belgiè* – The Sorrows of Belgium, 1983) and poet. Other highly-acclaimed writers are Paul Snoek (1933-1983); and Hugues Pernath (1931-1976).

Contemporary Flemish novelists include **Marnix Gijsen** (1899-1984), who first rose to fame with his philosophical tale *Joachim van Babylon*, Louis Paul Boon (1912-1979), a writer of realistic, passionate prose (*Route de la Chapelle*, 1953; *Menuet*, 1955) and a painter besides, **Johan Daisne** (1912-1978), some of whose works (*L'Homme au crâne rasé*, 1947; *Un soir un train* (1950) inspired filmmaker **André Delvaux** (1965 and 1968), **André Demedts** (1906-1992), **Hubert Lampo** (*b*1920), Ward Ruysslinck (*b*1929), Jef Geeraerts (*b*1930), interested by the Belgian Congo issue (*Je ne suis qu'un nègre*, 1961; *Gangrène I-IV*, 1968-1977), and **Ivo Michiels** (*b*1923), whose formal research could be seen as part of the European avant-garde movement (*Le Livre Alpha*, 1963). **Jean Ray** (1887-1964), born in Ghent, took the pen-name John Flanders. He wrote detective stories in Dutch and tales of the fantastic in French, including *Malpertuis* (1943) which was adapted for the cinema in 1972.

Luxembourg – Luxembourg has a few writers in the French language, such as Marcel Noppeney (1877-1966).

A poet expressing himself in the local language of Letzebuergisch, **Michel Rodange** (1827-1876) wrote a version of the animal epic by Van den Vos Reinaerde.

The Glorious Adventures of Tyl Ulenspiegl, by Charles De Coster:

"In Damme in Flanders, when May opened the blossom on the hawthorn bushes, was born Ulenspiegl, son of Claes.

An old midwife called Katheline wrapped the infant in warm swaddling clothes and, having looked at his head, pointed to a piece of skin.

"He's born under a lucky star!" she said, happily.

Soon, though, she pointed to a small black spot on the infant's shoulder and lamented:

"Alas! That is the black mark left by the Devil's finger."

"Mr. Satan," said Claes, "was up early, then, if he's had time to leave his mark on my son."

"Oh but he hadn't gone to bed," said Katheline," for the cock is only just beginning to crow."

And she left, placing the baby in Claes' arms.

Dawn broke through the night clouds, the swallows skimmed over the meadows, mewing as they went, and the dazzling purple face of the sun peeped over the horizon.

Claes opened the window and, speaking to Ulenspiegl, said,

"My lucky son, may I introduce Lord Sun who has come to greet the land of Flanders. Look at him as often as you can and later on, when you are in a scrape and don't know what to do to get out of it, seek advice from him. The sun is clear and hot. Be as sincere as it is clear and as good as it is hot."

"Claes, my husband," said Soetkin, "You're preaching to the deaf. Come and drink, my son."

And the mother gave the newborn babe her beautiful, natural bottles."

Music

Whether in Wallonia or Flanders, Belgium has always been a fertile ground for music. In the 15C and 16C Belgian composers, such as the Mons musician Roland de Lassus *(qv)*, were among the foremost in Europe.

In the 17C and 18C, however, first-class musicians were less common. The Liège composer **Grétry** *(qv)* wrote many comic operas, and his *Mémoires* ou *Essais sur la Musique* are full of original ideas.

The creation of the Conservatoires royaux (academy of music) in 1830 brought about a change for the better. **Fétis**, first director of the Brussels Conservatoire, acquired an international reputation with his theoretical and musicological works, as also did Gevaert, who succeeded him in 1871. Among Fétis' students, Edgar Tinel can perhaps be considered the greatest master of religious music in Belgium at the turn of this century.

After a nomadic life as a young virtuoso, **Henri Vieuxtemps**, born in Verviers *(qv)*, became a violin teacher at the Brussels Conservatoire in 1871. He founded the Franco-Belgian school for violin with his teacher, Bériot.

The great symphony composer **Paul Gilson** (1865-1942), a student of Gevaert, is one of the figures of contemporary Belgian music who has had the greatest impact on his period. A prolific composer in every genre, he had many disciples, including Jean Absil (1893-1974). Following the example of the Group of Six, founded in Paris in 1918 and headed by Erik Satie, several of Gilson's students formed the Group of Synthesists, with the aim of integrating the contributions of modern music into classical forms.

In 1867 in Antwerp a movement in favour of music with a distinctly Flemish character was born led by **Peter Benoit** (1834-1901). He created the first Flemish School of Music, which became a Conservatoire in 1898. As a composer of oratorios in Flemish illustrating themes particular to Flanders, he was often emulated.

Wallonia was no less prolific. **César Franck** (1822-1890), born in Liège and a naturalised French citizen, was a great innovator, for whom fame, however, only came posthumously. His student Guillaume Lekeu died in 1894 without fully realising his potential. Eugène Isaye (1858-1931), the great Liège violinist, and Joseph Jongen are also noteworthy.

Henry Pousseur (born in 1929) and Karel Goeyvaerts are the leaders of the serial music movement.

The Chapelle musicale Reine Élisabeth, founded in 1939, offers Belgian artists and a few foreign musicians an opportunity to continue their studies after completing the Conservatoire.

Folklore and traditions

See Calendar of events at the end of the guide.

Folklore in Belgium is extremely important and very much alive. It reflects a happy gregarious people, faithful to the past and its customs. Each major city has its own museum displaying traditions which have been preserved over the years, customs inherent to rural areas and to towns, especially Flemish towns where guilds played a major role, traditions of Flanders in the north and Wallonia in the south, influenced to some extent by Picardy.

A history which has mixed peoples of diverse origins only served to enrich this heritage, which is especially evident during festivals. All year long there is a succession of events, of religious or secular origin, which date back many years and serve as reminders of legends or ancient mysteries. From the most devout of processions (Veurne Penitents) to the bawdiest of festivities, these special events are constantly increasing in number or being revived. The slightest pretext is an opportunity for a public gathering or a pageant.

Everything is organised a long time in advance by the members of different "societies" or brotherhoods, who for several months pour their energies into preparing for the festival. When the big day comes, their members dress up in costume, meet old friends, have a meal and let the beer flow. Very often the festival or parish fête *(kermesse* or *ducasse: see below)* is combined with religious ceremonies.

These events, which are representative of the Belgian soul, have been immortalised by Brueghel and, more recently, by James Ensor.

Carnivals – Carnival-time is celebrated almost all over Belgium. This celebration, probably of pagan origins, takes place around Mardi Gras, or Shrove Tuesday. It was presented by Christianity as a symbol of rejoicing before the period of Lenten fasting and penitence. Twenty days later, Refreshment Sunday represents a break in the austerity of Lent.

The three most famous carnivals in Belgium take place in Binche, Eupen and Malmédy. Binche is renowned mainly for its **Gilles** *(qv)*, who only appear on Shrove Tuesday. However the festivities last four days, and before the Gilles appear there have already been processions of "Trouilles de nouilles" and "mam'zelles". Eupen is well-known for the Rhenish carnival which takes place on Shrove Monday.

As for Malmédy, the **"Cwarmê"** *(qv)* is original in incorporating satirical revues and the famous "haguètes" among the costumed figures. Other noteworthy festivals include the one in Aalst, with its parade of giants and Bayard the horse, and in Blankenberge.

During Lent – Certain customs have come to be associated with this period, such as the beheading of a goose or rooster by horsemen of the Antwerp region. Refreshment Sunday (Mid-Lent) is celebrated particularly enthusiastically at Stavelot with the **Blancs-Moussis**, amusing figures in huge white hooded garments and with long red noses, who hark back to the period when the Stavelot Abbey monks participated in the carnival. The Chinels, irresistable Punch and Judy characters, parade in Fosses-la-Ville *(qv)*. This festival is also very lively in Maaseik.

A Passion Play (Jeu de la Passion) takes place in Ligny. It is a series of tableaux drawn from the Gospels which also make allusions to the modern world. The Spanish left a heritage of penitence during Holy Week, a tradition which is upheld on Good Friday in particular in Veurne, where the famous Stations of the Cross procession takes place, involving hooded penitents, each bearing a cross. The same tradition is also upheld in Lessines *(qv)*.

Giants – Many of the parades in Belgium include giants. Although the number of giants has increased since the beginning of this century, the custom of including giants seems to date back to the 15C. The tradition began in Belgium and spread to Spain, owing to the Spanish occupation. The first giant character probably appeared in a religious procession or an "Ommegang", in which he symbolised Goliath or St Christopher. Goliath is in fact still present at the festival *(ducasse)* in Ath, where he is nicknamed Mr Gouyasse. He joins combat with David in a symbolic re-enactment of the Bible story.

Secular characters gradually appeared at these events. Even Bayard the horse came to be included, ridden by the four Aymon sons (in Aalst and Dendermonde). Giants appear also in Nivelles (Argayon, Argayonne, their son Lolo and the horse Godet), in Geraardsbergen, in Lier and in Arlon. The more famous giants include Polydor, Polydra and little Polysorke in Aalst, Cagène and his companion Florentine in Beloeil, Pie and Wanne and their son Jommeke in Tervuren, Count Baldwin IV the Builder and Alix of Namur in Briane. A parade in Heist brings together 120 giants from all over Flanders.

Bonfires – These are the Lenten bonfires, at which a guy is sometimes burned. The most famous bonfire is the **tonnekensbrand** in Geraardsbergen. A cask is set on fire after the throwing of *Krakelingen* biscuits.

Processions – Religious holidays, combining deep piety with secular traditions, are celebrated with processions which often incorporate historical pageants and even bright and colourful carnival parades. In the Middle Ages few people knew how to read, and over the course of the centuries the procession became a way of teaching Biblical themes. In addition to the usual characters representing apostles, prophets or angels, there were also floats on which tableaux illustrated scenes from religious history.

Some of them are extremely impressive, such as the **Holy Blood Procession** in Bruges *(qv)*. The faithful would follow the statue or reliquary of the saint across the fields for quite long distances over 30km-19miles in Ronse *(qv)* praying and singing hymns as they went.

Plays and pageants – Derived from religious and medieval origins, and bearing a resemblance to the mystery plays, these re-enact old legends during processions. One of the best-known is the one in Rutten, which commemorates the death of St Evermeire in the 8C. In Mons, the **Chariot of Gold** (Car d'Or) procession involves the various guilds with their patron saints and statues of the Virgin Mary, with the Chariot of Gold itself bringing up the rear. The "Lumeçon" Combat recalls a pageant dating from the Middle Ages.

Witches and their sabbaths are remembered in Ellezelles, to commemorate the execution of five witches in 1610. In Vielsalm it is the "macrâlles", spell-casting witches, who are the stars of a comic celebration.

In Wingene, the Brueghel festival illustrates paintings by the great master.

The Ducasse and the Kermesse – The words *ducasse* (from *dédicace*, meaning a Catholic holiday, one of the most famous *ducasses* is in Ath) and *kermesse* ("church fair" in Flemish) now both designate a fête held in honour of the patron saint of a town or village. This holiday has retained certain aspects of its religious origins (Mass and procession) but now includes traditional pageants, stalls, competitions and sometimes a car boot sale.

Holy Blood Procession, Bruges

Military parades – The first military parades begin at the end of May in the Entre Sambre-et-Meuse region *(qv)*, and offer an opportunity to admire the resplendent uniforms of the parading troops, in a rigorous military ceremony. One of the most surprising aspects of these parades is the use of Napoleonic uniforms. Zouaves, grenadier guards, dragoons, mamelukes and sappers are accompanied by a canteen-keeper.

The May tree – On 30 April, 1 May or during the month of May certain towns, such as Hasselt, Genk and Tongeren in the province of Limburg, solemnly plant a May tree as a symbol of renewal. In Brussels this tree is called the Meyboom or Tree of Joy (planted in August).

Historical pageants – These vividly re-enacted, sumptuous pageants of days gone by breathe new life into past grandeur. In Brussels, the **Ommegang** was once presided over by Emperor Charles V and his court; in Bruges, the Golden Tree pageant *(qv)* recalls the days of the Dukes of Burgundy.

Puppets – Puppet theatre appeared in Liège in the 19C and was a great success owing to the famous Tchantchès character *(qv)*. The Liège puppet is moved by means of a rod fixed to the top of its head. It is carved out of wood, painted and covered with cloth. The repertoire draws as much on history as on legend and on modern life and is aimed mainly at adult audiences. The theatre founded by Toone in Brussels *(qv)* dates from the same period.

The hero of puppet theatre nowadays is Woltje, who speaks a colourful Brussels dialect. The repertoire has kept its classics (the four Aymon sons, Till Eulenspiegel) while continuing to add new plays.

Other theatres in Antwerp, Ghent and Mechelen perform works in Flemish.

Folklore Museums and Open-Air Museums – Belgium is rich in folklore museums, which are always located in old buildings (hospitals, hospices, convents, etc.) and evoke traditions which vary from one region to another. For example:

Antwerp: **Volkskundemuseum** (Folklore Museum);

Binche: **Musée international du Carnaval et du Masque**★ (International Museum of Carnivals and Masks);

Bruges: **Museum voor Volkskunde**★ (Folklore Museum);

Ghent: **Museum voor Volkskunde**★ (Folklore Museum);

Liège: **Musée de la Vie wallonne**★★ (Museum of Walloon Life);

Mons: **Musée du Folklore et de la Vie montoise**★ (Museum of Mons Life);

Tournai: **Musée du Folklore** (Folklore Museum).

Two large open-air museums exhibit traditional regional architecture in the Ardennes, at **Le Fourneau St-Michel**★★ *(qv)* museum of rural life in Wallonia; in Flanders, the **Bokrijk**★★ *(qv)* open-air museum.

Townscapes

Belgian towns, especially Flemish ones, have a characteristic layout based on the autonomy they have enjoyed since the 13C *(see Historical Table and Notes)*. This is reflected by the impressive civic buildings *(see Architecture)* the belfry, the Town Hall and the covered market. Towns are imbued with remarkable charm by the canals, the cheerful music of the bells, the peacefulness of the Beguine convents, the welcoming atmosphere of the cafés and pubs.

Market Squares – These squares (Grote Markt or Grand-Place) are surrounded by the town's main buildings, including the Town Hall, the covered market and the belfry. The guild halls with richly sculpted façades decorated with the statue of a patron saint or symbolic animal are to be seen here too. The town stocks used to be set up on these squares. They were also used for executions, as well as for markets and major celebrations, theatre performances, parades and cavalcades with all the attendant pomp and ceremony. The best known market squares are in Brussels, Bruges, Antwerp and Mechelen.

Bells – The carillon chimes regularly ring out their melodies, lending a rhythm to town life. Carillons were not always installed in the belfry, but sometimes in the cathedral, as is the case in Mechelen and Antwerp.
The word "carillon" comes from "carignon", meaning a group of four bells. Carillons were connected to a clock (the first town clock appeared in 1370), and their various chimes were set to play just before the sounding of the hour. They were tapped by hand with a hammer for many years. The first mechanical chimes, made to play by the clock mechanism, were created in the 15C. The discovery of the manual keyboard, used for the first time in 1510 in Oudenaarde, made it possible to increase the number of bells. In 1583 the invention of the pedal board in Mechelen enabled bass stops to be used, thus enriching the variety of sound possible. The art of founding the bells has been refined to a quite remarkable degree, so that most of the major carillons now consist of at least 47 bells. The most famous examples in Belgium are in Mechelen, Bruges, Nieuwpoort, Antwerp, Ghent, Leuven, Florenville. There is a bell-ringers' school in Mechelen.

Jack o' the clocks – From the 14C, belfries were adorned with a clock and jack o' the clocks, metal figures which strike the hours by tapping a little bell with a hammer. Jack o' the clocks are a delightful sight to be found in Kortrijk, Nivelles, Brussels (Mont des Arts), Virton, Lier and Sint-Truiden.

Beguine convents – Beguine convents, often a little off the beaten track and enclosed inside walls, constitute a picturesque little town-within-a-town. Small cottages clustered together around a church and garden house the Beguine nuns. The members of these lay sisterhoods observe certain rules governing, for example, mode of dress and attendance of religious services (Mass), but they are not bound by any vows and are entitled to possess money of their own. They are free during the day to pursue their various occupations, but the doors of the Beguine convent close at nightfall. The little community is under the direction of a Superior known as the "Grande Demoiselle".
The origin of Beguine convents is unknown. The first establishment of this type is supposed by some to have been founded by Lambert le Bègue in Liège at the end of the 12C. On the other hand, tradition attributes their creation to Saint Begga, who was the Mother Superior of a convent in Andenne, where she died in 694. By the 13C Beguine convents had developed their definitive structure as independent enclosed communities with their own church. In 1566 the Protestant "iconoclasts" destroyed many of the Beguine convents, which were then rebuilt at the end of the 16C and the 17C.
These quiet, peaceful convents are perhaps the clearest embodiment of the mystic side of Belgium. There are now about twenty of them in the north of the country, and some are still occupied by a small number of Beguine nuns (St.-Amandsberg in Ghent) or by religious orders (the Benedictines in Bruges). For the most part, however, the towns rent the empty houses to the elderly, or sometimes to students, as in Leuven.

Almshouses – Financed by the guilds, these were a sort of sanctuary for the old or the poverty-stricken. They were rows of low, whitewashed brick maisonettes.

Estaminets – *Estaminet* is the Walloon word for a café. They are friendly places where people can meet and have a glass of beer, play cards and gossip. They are also a favourite gathering point for "coulonneux" (pigeon fanciers). What better place to sit and watch the world go by over a cup of coffee with a cinnamon biscuit (speculaas) or a Belgian chocolate!

Every year the **Michelin Red Guide Benelux**
presents a wealth of up-to-date information in a compact
form. It is the ideal companion for a holiday, a long weekend or business trip.

It is worth buying the current edition

Food and drink

Belgium

The Belgians are fond of the good life and appreciate the merits of a well-laden table. While a number of dishes reflect French influence, local preparations have successfully withstood being swamped, and the Walloon and Flemish provinces are justifiably proud of their culinary specialities.

Vegetable broth or clear beef or chicken soups *(bouillons)* are common starters to a meal.

Ardennes ham or sausage, cold fish, seafood with mayonnaise, shrimp rissoles or eels in a herb sauce may also feature as an hors d'oeuvre.

The main course offers a choice of many regional specialities including rabbit with prunes, Flemish *karbonaden* (braised beef, beer and onions), *oie à l'instar de Visé* (goose boiled then fried in the style of Visé, near Liège) or, in hunting season, a sample of the game with which the Ardennes abounds (hare, venison, young wild boar, mallard duck, pheasant).

Local vegetables include hops shoots (in March) in a mousseline sauce, Brussels chicory baked with cheese and ham, Brussel sprouts and Mechelen asparagus. There are some delicious varieties of cheese those from Herve, in particular the pungent, strongly-flavoured Remoudou, Maredsous, similar to the French St-Paulin cheese (mild); cheese from Brussels, and the Flemish Présent cheese.

The mixed fruit, rhubarb or sugar tarts of the Ardennes are mouthwatering. Overijse and the surrounding region are renowned for hothouse grapes, while Limburg produces plums preserved in vinegar syrup.

Belgian ice cream is delicious, and of course the excellent reputation of Belgian chocolates, especially the "pralines" (chocolates with creamy or nutty fillings), speaks for itself.

Drinks – Beer is the most common drink in Belgium. Quality French wines can be found in good restaurants. Belgium also produces spirits and liqueurs, for example mandarin orange liqueur, Spa Elixir (a type of Chartreuse), as well as the strong juniper berry flavoured geneva *(jenever)* from Hasselt, Deinze and Liège, where it is known as *péquet*.

Luxembourg

Particular specialities include suckling pig in aspic, smoked or cured Ardennes ham, other smoked meats such as smoked neck of pork with broad beans *(judd mat gaardebounen)*. Game is available in season. Kachkéis is a salted handmade cheese. September is the time to taste the local plum tarts.

All this is washed down with Moselle wine *(see Luxembourg Vallée de la MOSELLE LUXEMBOURGEOISE)* or beer, which is drunk by most people here. The liqueurs (various types of plum, blackcurrant) are well-known.

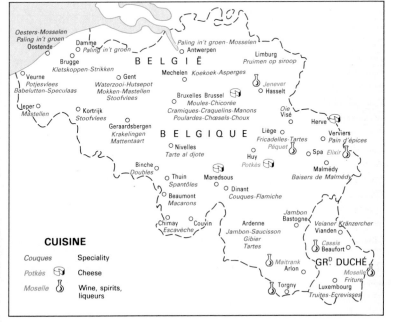

Brief gastronomic glossary

Babelutten (babelutes): hard butter toffees.

Baisers de Malmédy: meringues filled with whipped cream.

Cassis: blackcurrant liqueur.

Chicorée or chicon (Witloof): chicory.

Choesels: offal cooked in a Madeira sauce with mushrooms.

Couques (Koeken): in Brussels, sweet, lightly spiced bread; in Dinant, hard gingerbread sweetened with honey.

Cramiques (Kramieken): currant buns.

Craquelins (Krakelingen): buns with a sugary filling.

Doubles: two pancakes filled with Herve or Maredsous cheese.

Escavèche: fried fish preserved in a spicy marinade.

Filet américain: type of steak tartare.

Filet d'Anvers: portion of smoked beef or horse.

Flamiche: cheese tart made from Romedenne, a local cheese, served hot.

Fricadelles: meat balls.

Friture de la Moselle: fried whitebait.

Herve: soft cheese.

Hutsepot (Hochepot): mixed stew of pork, beef and mutton.

Jenever (genièvre): gin.

Karbonaden (Stoofvlees): beef braised in beer or water with onions, spices, vinegar and sugar.

Kletskoppen: thin butter biscuits made with almonds and hazelnuts.

Koekoek (Coucou):

Lierse Vlaaikens: plum tarts.

Macarons: macaroons.

Maitrank: aperitif from Arlon *(qv)*.

Manons: chocolates with a fresh cream filling.

Maredsous: soft cheese.

Mastellen: aniseed biscuits.

Mokken: type of macaroon flavoured with cinnamon or aniseed.

Mosselen (Moules): mussels.

Oesters (Huîtres): oysters.

Oie: goose.

Pain d'épices: gingerbread.

Paling in 't groen (Anguilles au vert): eels sautéed in butter and stewed in a sauce of finely chopped parsley, chervil, sorrel, sage, citronella and onions.

Péquet: strongly flavoured gin from Liège.

Pistolet: small round roll.

Potjesvlees: type of potted meat made from veal, rabbit and chicken.

Potkès (Boulette de Huy): savoury fromage blanc.

Poulardes: pullets.

Pruimen op siroop: prunes in syrup.

Remoudou: strong, pungent cheese of the Herve region.

Saucisson: dried sausage.

Spantôles: sweet biscuits named after a well-known canon.

Speculaas (spéculos): small biscuit flavoured with brown sugar and cinnamon.

Stoofvlees (carbonades): braised beef cooked in beer?

Strikken (Noeuds): biscuits made with butter and brown sugar.

Tartes: tarts.

Tarte al djote: cheese tart made from eggs, cardoons (akin to artichokes) and cream, served hot.

Tarte au stofé: tart made from fromage blanc, eggs, almonds and apple purée.

Truite: trout.

Veianer Kränzercher: small rings of choux pastry.

Waterzooi: type of clear fish or chicken soup.

BEER

Beer is Belgium's national drink. On average, every Belgian drinks 118 litres (about 200 pints) a year. There are nearly 100 breweries in the country and an endless variety of beers. Pale or dark, bitter or sweet, light or strong, there is a Belgian beer for every taste.

Beer was already known in Antiquity, then later the Gauls started to make barley beer which they called **"cervoise"**. During the Middle Ages brewing beer was a privilege of the monasteries. It spread widely throughout Flanders; indeed the word "beer" might itself be derived from the Flemish "bier".

Aalst and Poperinge are Belgium's main hops-growing regions, and the harvest is brought home in September. There are two signposted tourist routes to enable visitors to explore these regions. One is around Kobbegem ("Hopperoute": "Hops route") and the other is around Poperinge ("Hoppelandroute": "Hops country route").

The brewing process –
Barley grains are soaked in water until they germinate. The sprouting grains are then dried, roasted in a kiln and ground to a powder (malt): this is the **malting process.** The **brewing process** turns the starch in the finely ground malt into a sugary juice – the **wort** – by mixing the malt with pure water and hops and cooking it. It is this process which is the most important and characteristic part of beer-making. Brewing actually does two things: as well as turning the barley malt starch into sugar, it draws out the soluble malt substances. The quantity of hops added to the boiling wort affect the degree of bitterness and aromatic quality in the finished beer.

Cheese made with beer, and Chimay special "Grande Réserve"

Fermentation, the final stage, turns the wort into beer. The wort is left in large vats for several days, and yeast added to it to change the maltose sugar into ethyl alcohol and carbon monoxide

Varieties – Three types of beer are produced in this way, depending on variations in the fermentation process:

– **Low fermentation** beers, such as "pilsen"-type (lager) beer. Fermentation and more particularly the aging process take place at a low temperature. The best-known breweries are at Leuven (Interbrew breweries) and Waarloos, south of Antwerp (Alken-Maes breweries).

– **High fermentation** beers. Fermentation takes place at a "high" temperature of 15° to 20°C-59° to 68°F. Most "special" beers are in this category, and so are the famous **Trappist beers** which are still brewed in the great Cistercian abbeys. These are the beers of Orval, Chimay *(qv),* Rochefort *(qv),* Westmalle and St-Sixtus (in Westvleteren) and they are not to be confused with the abbey beers.

– **Spontaneous fermentation** beers, which include typically Belgian beers such as gueuze, kriek and lambic. These are made by letting the fermentation take place at its own pace, without the addition of yeast, in huge vats or casks. After being kept for about one to two years the beer is designated a **"lambic".**

One or a blend of several lambics is drawn off into bottles in which a second fermentation takes place, after which it becomes what is known as a **"gueuze". "Kriek"** is characterised by a red colour and fruity taste, from cherries having been steeped in it at the lambic stage.

Breweries and brewing museums open to the public
Musée de la Gueuze – Anderlecht in Brussels
Brasserie nationale – in Bascharage 6km from Rodange, Grand Duchy
Musée de la Brasserie – in the Brewers Guild Hall, Brussels
A choice of several Breweries – in Leuven
Brewery – Hoegaarden 13km from Tienen

Polyptych of the Adoration of the Mystic Lamb (detail), Jan van Eyck, St-Baafskathedraal, Ghent

Belgium

AALST

Oost-Vlaanderen – Population 74 857
Michelin maps 409 fold 3 or 213 fold 5
Town plan in the current Michelin Red Guide Benelux

Aalst, on the banks of the River Dender, was once a commercial town and now has an industrial estate grouping together a number of active industrial concerns. Large breweries have grown up as a result of regional hop-growing. Aalst is also a centre for the cut-flower business.

Carnival – The festivities *(see the Calendar of Events at the end of this guide)* begin on the Sunday before Shrove Tuesday, with a great parade of giants, including Bayard the Horse *(qv)*, and floats, immense papier mâché constructions often political and satirical in theme.

On Shrove Monday there is a second parade and the throwing of onions *(ajuinworp)* from the top of the buildings on Grand-Place.

Carnival - Bayard the Horse

Excitement reaches its peak on Shrove Tuesday, with the Vuil Jeannetten men comically dressed as women.

SIGHTS

Grote Markt – The statue of **Dirk Martens**, a native of Aalst, stands in the middle of this irregularly-shaped square; it was he who introduced the technique of printing to Flanders (1473).

Schepenhuis – This gracious 15C building, formerly the Town Hall, was extensively restored in the 19C. The 13C features which remain are the façades on the right-hand side and at the rear where there is a crowstepped gable and windows surmounted with trefoil arcades.
A charming 16C flamboyant oriel to the right brightens up the main façade.
The tall slender belfry dates from the 15C; it bears the town motto "Nec spe nec metu" ("neither by hope nor by fear") under two recesses containing two warriors. The statues represent the Count of Flanders and the Count of Aalst; the carillon consists of 52 bells.

Beurs van Amsterdam – The Amsterdam Stock Exchange is an arcaded building which dates from the 17C and 18C. It has a beautiful brick-and-stone façade, with four scrolled pediments and an onion-domed campanile.
It once belonged to the Barbarions, members of the **Chamber of Rhetoric**, a literary society which composed and performed songs and theatrical works.

Stadhuis – The 19C colonnaded Town Hall has a gracious 18C Rococo façade on the far side of the courtyard.

St-Martinuskerk – Herman de Waghemakere and a member of the Keldermans family built this Flamboyant Gothic sandstone collegiate church in the Brabant style. The nave is unfinished, but the **architecture★** in the transept and apse with ambulatory and radiating chapels is quite beautiful.

Interior – The inside of the church has a certain elegant simplicity. Note the round pillars and leaf-decorated capitals typical of the Brabant style, as well as the side aisle in the transept and the openwork triforium balustrade. A large work by Rubens, *St Roch Patron Saint of the Plague-Stricken*, forms the altarpiece which can be seen in the south transept; the frame is said to have been made to a plan drawn by the great artist.
Gaspar de Crayer's painting on the left has Rubens-like characteristics.
On the north side of the chancel there is a splendid black and white marble **tabernacle★** carved in 1604 by Jerome Duquesnoy the Elder. The three juxtaposed turrets are decorated with charming statuettes (the Virtues, the Evangelists, the Fathers of the Church, angels bearing the instruments of Christ's Passion).
The first ambulatory chapel on the south side has an *Adoration of the Shepherds* attributed to Ambrosius Francken in which the Italian influence is obvious (the Virgin Mary's very pure gentle face, the stylised positions of the figures).

Dirk Martens's gravestone is in the fourth chapel, and the remains of delicate freely drawn late-15C frescoes can be seen in the axial chapel.

Oud-Hospitaal ⊘ – *The old hospital lies in the street leading from the east end of St-Martinuskerk.*
Provisions and supplies used to be delivered here by boat, as the River Dender once flowed just behind the hospital. The restored buildings flanking cloisters and a chapel have been turned into a **museum** of archeology and regional decorative arts.

AARSCHOT

Vlaams-Brabant – Population 26 622
Michelin maps 409 H 3 or 213 fold 8

The collegiate church bell tower overlooks the little industrial town of Aarschot (pronounced "arskot"), in the **Hageland** region on the banks of the River Demer. The Austrians and Burgundians pillaged the town in the 15C, followed by the Spaniards in the 16C. Joseph II of Austria had the fortifications razed to the ground in 1782. Aarschot also suffered during the two World Wars, but has since risen from its ruins.

Pieter Jozef Verhaghen (1728-1811), who continued the work of the great 17C masters, was born here. His canvases embellish several churches, in particular in Leuven, where he spent the last years of his life. Aarschot inhabitants are jokingly referred to as "cobblestone beaters", from the time when watchmen doing their rounds reassured town citizens of their presence by tapping their feet on the cobblestones. An amusing "Kasseistamper" statue illustrates this nickname above a fountain near the Market Square.

SIGHTS

O.-L.-Vrouwkerk ⊘ – The chancel of this beautiful collegiate church built of local ferruginous sandstone dates from the 14C, and the nave from the beginning of the 15C. The tower comprising the façade rises to a height of 85m – 279ft (by comparison, the tower in Mechelen has a height of 98m – 321ft), its lower part brightened by alternate use of limestone and sandstone.
On entering there is a strikingly beautiful view of the nave; the upward sweep of its slender lines is heightened by the ribbing on the transverse arches. The same colouring as the tower is found in the chancel, which is concealed by a Late Gothic rood-screen. This is surmounted with a 15C triumphal cross and decorated with scenes of the Passion and Resurrection.
The pulpit and the confessionals are in the 17C Flemish Baroque style.
The choirstalls (1515) in the chancel are decorated with satirical carvings (hurdy-gurdyist, Lay of Aristotle, wolf and stork, trades). Note also the wrought-iron chandelier (1500) attributed to Quentin Massys. A painting by P J Verhaghen *(Disciples of Emmaus)* can be seen in a chapel on the south side of the ambulatory. In a chapel on the north side there is a remarkable painting on wood by an unknown 16C master of the Flemish school, the **Mystic Wine-press.** The Seven Sacraments are on the predella. The miraculous statue of Our Lady of Aarschot (1596) is in the north arm of the transept.

Begijnhof – Just past the Renaissance house by the church tower stands a row of 17C dwellings, all that remains of the former Beguine convent founded in 1259. The 16C **ducal mills** can be seen to the right on the banks of the Demer; there is an enclosure that forms a charming reconstruction of a Beguine convent on the left, now part of a hospice.

St.-Rochustoren – *On Grand-Place.*
The 14C brown sandstone tower was used in the Middle Ages as the law courts. It now houses the tourist office.

Viewpoint – There is a good view of the town and its surroundings from the **Aurelianustoren** (Aurelian Tower), sometimes called the Orleans Tower, the remains of the old fortifications.
Follow the Leuven signs from Grand-Place.

EXCURSION

St.-Pieters-Rode – *8km – 5 miles south. Leave by the Leuven road. A short distance on, turn left towards St.-Joris-Winge, then turn right.*
Château d'Horst is a beautiful polygonal mansion surrounded by water and flanked by a 14C keep. This, together with the entrance porch, is the only remaining trace of the building which Emperor Maximilian's troops destroyed in 1489. The rest of the castle is built of brick with stone string courses and dates from the 16C. The grounds around the castle have been turned into a recreational centre, like the nearby lake *(fishing and boating in season).*

Vallée de l'AISNE

Luxembourg

Michelin maps 409 J4-5 or 214 fold 7 – Local map see Vallée de l'OURTHE

The narrow Aisne River wends its way through the valley of the same name between wooded slopes until it flows into the River Ourthe.

PONT D'EREZÉE TO BOMAL *16km – 10 miles allow 2 hours*

The charming scenic tramway, **Tramway Touristique de l'Aisne** ⊙, follows the Aisne valley from the Pont d'Erezée (bridge) up through the rugged valley to the village of Forge.

Wéris – *6km – 3.75 miles north of Pont d'Erezée*. The charming 11C **church** dedicated to Ste-Walburge in Wéris is built on slate columns. There is a 16C sculpted tabernacle known as the "théothèque" to the right of the high altar. There are still several megaliths in Wéris, in particular a **dolmen** formed of blocks of local pudding-stone *(northwest heading towards Barvaux, to the left not far from the road).*

The road follows the Aisne Valley.

The enormous sandstone wall of **La Roche à Frêne** can be seen on the right. The road then goes through **Aisne**, the village after which the river is named, in which there are hot springs. Bomal is at the confluence of the Rivers Aisne and Ourthe.

Vallée de l'AMBLÈVE ★★

Liège

Michelin maps 409 J4-K4 or 213 folds 22, 23 and 214 folds 7, 8

The river which runs through the Amblève Valley rises in the Hautes Fagnes-Eifel nature park *(qv)*. Winding along an erratic, rustic course at first, it gouges out a wide V-shaped valley further downstream, forming large meanders between sloping banks clad in a thick carpet of green.

STAVELOT TO COMBLAIN-AU-PONT

46km – 28.5 miles allow 2 hours – Local maps below and under Vallée de l'OURTHE

★**Stavelot** – *See STAVELOT.*

Leave Stavelot and head towards Trois-Ponts.

Level with the confluence of the Salm the road passes quite near **Trois-Ponts** *(qv)* before reaching **Coo** *(qv).*

The **Congo viewpoint** is on the left shortly after **Stoumont**, a village perched high above the Amblève. There is a marvellous **view**★ of the valley, so sparsely inhabited and thickly wooded here that in summer it resembles a tropical forest.

From Targnon the road follows the river until it flows into the Ourthe.

Just after Targnon, the N 645 on the left leads up the delightful **Lienne Valley**.

★**Fonds de Quareux** – A little bridge under the railway line leads *(on foot)* to the banks of the Amblève. The river rushes down here, foaming over enormous boulders of hard quartz which have broken away from the surrounding rocky massif.

Nonceveux – This community is on the south bank, tucked inside a meander. The north bank has become a summer holiday resort.

Follow the **Ninglinspo** torrent on foot *(15min; leave from the large car-park on the right, just outside the town)* to reach the Chaudière, a natural basin of reddish stone at the foot of two small waterfalls.

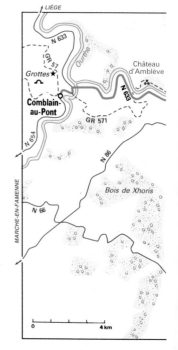

Just before going under the Remouchamps viaduct, there is a glimpse of the Château de Montjardin on the left, perched amidst the greenery overlooking the river.

Sougné-Remouchamps – *See SOUGNÉ-REMOUCHAMPS.*

The Château d'Amblève once stood on an outcrop downstream from **Aywaille**. Legend has it that the four Aymon sons *(qv)* stayed here.
The road soon comes to Comblain-au-Pont and the confluence of the Amblève with the Ourthe.

Comblain-au-Pont – *See Vallée de l'OURTHE.*

Domaine d'ANNEVOIE-ROUILLON ★

Namur

Michelin maps 409 H4 or 214 fold 5 Local map see La MEUSE NAMUROISE

The château and gardens in the Annevoie Estate are a beautiful example of 18C architecture and landscaping.
There is a wonderful floral display including tulips and hyacinths in spring, and roses and begonias in summer.

★★**Gardens** ⊙ – The estate has belonged to the Montpelliers since 1675. It was at the end of the 18C that one of the members of the family conceived the idea of these gardens flowing with water, compromising between formal French and romantic Italian gardens, which would charm visitors with the sparkling diversity and imaginative design of their groves and fountains. It is pleasant to stroll beneath century-old foliage and admire the Buffet d'Eau (display of fountains opposite the house), the Petit Canal and, after a short climb, the Grand Canal, with limetrees edging its banks. Besides these highlights there are also one or two strikingly original Baroque garden seats.

Château ⊙ – The old part (1627) on the right can be recognized by the pattern of pink bricks running just under the edge of the roof. The château was enlarged in 1775, the same time that the gardens, its perfect complement, were created.
The rooms **inside**★ are decorated with 18C woodwork and furniture, as well as family portraits and bouquets, all of which provide an elegant atmosphere.
The music room in the corner is particularly impressive with its delicate stucco decor by the Italian Moretti brothers; there are also beautiful views of the gardens.

*Consult the **Index** to find an individual town or sight.*

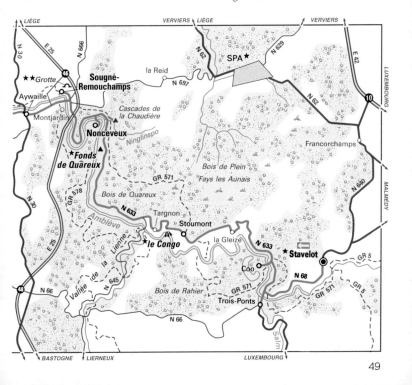

Antwerp, Belgium's second city, is one of the world's largest ports. It lies on the east bank of the Scheldt, which flows into the North Sea 88km – 54.5 miles to the northwest (the town is linked to the west bank by three tunnels for motorists and one for cyclists and pedestrians).

In sharp contrast to its role as an economic centre, which is perhaps most plainly in evidence in the bustling diamond merchants' district around the central railway station, Antwerp has nonetheless preserved all the charm of Flemish towns in its Old Town, overlooked by the graceful cathedral tower. It is a great pleasure to wander along the narrow streets or through the spacious squares, bordered by houses decorated with crowstepped gables and scrollwork or with tall many-windowed façades. There is the opportunity not only of visiting museums, richly stocked with works of art, or historical houses, in which the interiors served as models for the Flemish masters, but also of discovering theatres, stores (on the Meir and Keyserlei), elegant boutiques (in the pedestrian zone around Schoenmarkt, Komedieplaats, Leopoldstraat), restaurants, markets, antique dealers and art galleries.

Antwerp is the birthplace of a number of celebrities, including the writer **Hendrik Conscience** (1812-1883), author of the historical novel *De Leeuw van Vlaanderen* (1838) and the painter **Constant Permeke** *(qv)*. The most noteworthy, however, remain the printer **Plantin** *(qv)* and the painter **Rubens** *(qv)*, whose personalities are most strongly evoked by a visit to where they used to live.

HISTORICAL NOTES

Antwerp "owes the Scheldt to God, and everything else to the Scheldt" (Edmond de Bruyn, 1914).

Mysterious origins – The first settlement on the present site dates back to the third century. The name of the town seems to be derived from the word "aanwerpen", which means "alluvial deposits". According to a 16C legend, however, the name comes from the exploit of a Roman soldier, Silvius Brabo. The story goes that Brabo challenged the giant Druon Antigon, who regularly pillaged shipping on the Scheldt, ultimately cutting off the giant's hand and flinging it into the river. This explains why the city's coat-of-arms represents two cut-off hands next to a castle (the Steen); the word "handwerpen" means "to throw a hand".

The golden age (15C-16C) – Antwerp built its first ramparts in the 11C, and began to grow as an economic power in the 13C, specialising in the trade of fish, salt and grain and in the importing of English wool. The Hanseatic League established a branch here in the 15C. Antwerp was already in competition with Bruges, where the port was beginning to silt up.

The 16C decided the town's destiny. At the beginning of the century the Portuguese, who had discovered the Indian trade route, set up a European distribution centre for the spices and precious objects brought back from far-off lands. The first commodities exchange was built in 1515; the town was then under the protection of Emperor Charles V and had a population of more than 100 000. A new stock exchange established in 1531, as well as the use of modern banking techniques (bills of exchange and letters of credit), made Antwerp a world centre of trade, with more than 1 000 representatives of foreign commercial companies opening premises in the city. Printing evolved there in the middle of the century, largely through the efforts of Christopher Plantin. By 1560 Antwerp was Europe's second largest city after Paris. This was a golden age too for architecture, with the construction of the cathedral, the butchers' and brewers' guild halls and the Town Hall, and for art, with the Antwerp school represented by Quentin Massys, Joachim Patinir, Gossaert and Brueghel.

The decline – Under Philip II, who was an uncompromising Catholic, the Inquisition led to the Wars of Religion, which put an end to this prosperity. In 1566 the cathedral was ransacked and desecrated by Calvinist iconoclasts. Harsh repression followed, led by the Duke of Alva, and then in 1576 the Spanish garrison launched a terrifying attack on the town known as the "Spanish fury".

Antwerp's Calvinists had joined the revolt against the Spaniards; Alexander Farnese, great-grandson of the pope of the same name and governor of the Low Countries, had to lay siege for a year before he could recapture the town in 1585. In 1648 the Treaty of Münster closed the Scheldt to traffic; it was not reopened until 1795.

A desirable position – In 1794 the town was in the hands of the French. When Napoleon came in 1803 he immediately realised how strategically well-placed it was, a "cocked pistol aimed at England". He developed the port and had the first dock excavated, known today as the Bonaparte dock or Bonapartedosk (**DT**). In 1914 Antwerp resisted the German army from 28 September to 9 October, enabling Belgian troops to fall back to the River Ijzer (Yser) at Nieuwpoort. Antwerp's port was fully functional shortly after liberation in September 1944, in spite of the V1 and V2 bombings.

Traditional industry and trade: diamonds – In 1476 Louis de Berken, from Bruges, perfected diamond-cutting; this was to become a major industry in Antwerp. The arrival in the 16C of several Jewish families from Portugal gave it a new impetus. The trade in diamonds, mainly imported from the East Indies at that time, became virtually a Portuguese monopoly with Vasco de Gama's discovery of the Indian sea route. Antwerp's craftsmen rapidly won renown. The South African diamond rush began in 1869, while at the same time the town underwent a major increase in its population with a large influx of Jews from Eastern Europe. Today the diamond trade is handled by a number of Jewish families who have been established for centuries, as well as by traders from India, Zaïre, and Lebanon, while the cutting of diamonds remains the province of people from Antwerp.

A new growth linked to the port – Antwerp is now Belgium's largest port, its main trading city and a major industrial centre. The port is being expanded *(see the enlarged inset map on 409 folds 8 and 9)* northwards to the border with the Netherlands. It covers over 13 780ha – 31 579 acres, comprising 127km – 79 miles of waterfront, 949km – 590 miles of railway, 1 400ha – 3 459 acres of docks, a large amount of stock handling equipment and enormous storage depots. The building of a large dock to the north of Kanaaldok has greatly increased mooring capacity. Seven locks *(sluis)* connect the Scheldt with the docks. The Berendrecht lock, opened in 1988, is the biggest in the world: 763 000cu m – 791 994cu yds in volume, 500m – 0.4 miles long by 68m – 74yds wide. The Zandvliet lock has a volume of 613 000cu m – 801 804cu yds.

The volume of traffic through Antwerp's port depends in large part on Belgium's economy, but also on its being a transit point to Germany, France, the Netherlands, Switzerland and Italy. Imports consist of petroleum products, minerals, coal, wood products, grain and raw chemicals; exports are usually fertilisers, cements and metallurgical and chemical products. As for storage, Antwerp has excellent warehouse installations making it a crucial link in the distribution chain. Sizeable industries have developed near the port, dependent on its existence: oil refineries, car assembly plants, food industries, ship construction and repair.

TIPS FOR ANTWERP

Tourist Office – The Antwerp Tourist Board, Dienst voor Toerisme, Grote Markt 15, Antwerp, ☎ (03) 232 01 03 is open Mondays to Fridays 9am to 6pm, weekends and holidays 9am to 5pm. A monthly calendar of activities, a brochure of city walks and city maps are all available at the tourist office.

Guided tours – In summer there are bus tours of the city; they leave from Grote Markt and have a recorded commentary in four languages.

Public transport – A tram or bus ticket costs 40F and a ten-trip card only costs 250F. One ticket is valid on all trams and buses for one hour.

★★★GROTE-MARKT AND CATHEDRAL *tour: half a day*

This district is a maze of squares, narrow streets and passages, in which a remarkable number of niches containing statues of the Madonna are to be found; there are more than 300 of them. They were often the masterpieces of sculptors seeking to obtain membership of the Guild of St Luke.

★**Grote Markt** (**FY**) – The cathedral's slender, graceful spire rises above the irregularly-shaped Grote-Markt, which is surrounded by 16C and 17C **guild halls** with very tall façades consisting almost entirely of windows. They are crowned with crowstepped or scrolled gables, often bristling with delicate pinnacles.

Look towards the Stadhuis and note the five beautiful guild halls to the right, built mostly in the Renaissance style, dating from the late 16C. They are l'Ange Blanc, appropriately topped with an angel, the Maison des Tonneliers built for the Coopers' guild with its statue of St Matthew, the very tall **Vieille Arbalète** (literally *Old Crossbow*) surmounted with an equestrian statue of St George, the Maison des jeunes Arbalétriers used by the guild of Young Crossbowmen and dating from 1500 and the Maison des Merciers, the drapers' hall, decorated with an eagle.

Stadhuis (**FY H**) ⊙ – The Town Hall was built in 1564 by Cornelis Floris. The façade is 76m – 282ft long, and displays a successful combination of Flemish elements (dormers, gables) with those of the Italian Renaissance (a loggia just under the roof, pilasters between the windows, niches). The richly decorated central part lightens the austere orderly appearance of the tall mullion windows. The interior was completely remodelled in the 19C.

Brabo Fountain – This spirited work by Jef Lambeaux (1887) depicts Silvius Brabo brandishing the giant Druon's hand in a legendary gesture *(qv)*. The water falls directly onto the square's cobblestones.

Brabo Fountain and the Guild Halls in Grote-Markt

★Vlaaikensgang (FYZ) – The porch at no 16 of the **Oude Koornmarkt** leads into this pretty little old Antwerp street, which has retained its village atmosphere.
Return to the Oude Koornmarkt.

Handschoenmarkt (FY 82) – This triangular square surrounded by old houses just in front of the cathedral used to be a glove market. The well is crowned with an elegant wrought-iron canopy, with Brabo on the top preparing to throw the giant's hand. It stood in front of the Town Hall until 1565, and is attributed to Quentin Massys, a wrought-ironworker who is said to have become a painter because of love.

★★★Kathedraal (FY) ⊘ – The cathedral is the most admirable of all of Antwerp's buildings; it is also the largest in Belgium, standing on almost 1ha – 2.5 acres. Although construction began with the east end in 1352 and was finished as late as 1521, the whole is nevertheless quite harmonious. Several builders succeeded one another: Jacob Van Thienen, Jan Appelmans and his son Pieter, Jan Tac, Everaert Spoorwater, Herman and Domien de Waghemakere and Rombout Keldermans.

The cathedral was originally the home of *Our Lady of the Tree*, a statue found on a branch after a Viking invasion. This statue was destroyed in 1580, but a copy still exists in the church of Notre-Dame-du-Sablon in Brussels *(qv)*.

★★★Tower – As is also the case in Mechelen and Ghent, the wonder of the cathedral is the tower. It is 123m – 403ft tall, a miracle of ornamentation and delicacy. The magnificent bell tower crowning it is "straight as a summons, beautiful as a mast, bright as a candle", as wrote Verhaeren. It was built in a century by Pieter Appelmans and Herman and Domien de Waghemakere. It houses a carillon of 47 bells.

The second tower was left unfinished in the 16C. Four people seem to be busily at work at its foot. They were chiselled by Jef Lambeaux (1906) in honour of the architect Pieter Appelmans.

A curious onion dome has topped the transept crossing since the 16C.

Interior – *A brochure indicating where works of art can be found is available at the entrance.*

The inside of the cathedral is exceptionally large, comprising seven aisles, 125 pillars without capitals and a transept 117m – 384ft long by 65m – 213ft wide. There are many remarkable **works of art** contrasting with the cool majesty of the place.

In the central nave, the **pulpit** sculpted by Michel van der Voort in 1713 is a surprising sight, its effect heightened by flights of stairs crowned with birds and a ring of tumbling cherubs floating beneath a Fame falling from heaven. The pulpit section itself is supported by four female figures representing the four continents (Europe, Africa, Asia and America).

There are many works by **Rubens**. Above the high altar there is an **Assumption** (1626), one of his better representations on this theme, which captivates the viewer with its colourfulness broken up by touches of light. The **Raising of the Cross** (1610) in the north transept, originally intended for St Walburga's Church, is a violent, diagonal composition depicting a wonderfully noble head of Christ; the wildly tortuous postures of the vigorous soldiers throw their muscles into relief. The **Descent from the Cross** (1612) in the south transept is more classical in style: the body of the dead

Christ and his white shroud stand out against the dark background and the red of St John's clothing; the blond hair of Mary Magdalene is resplendent while the martyred man seems to be slipping, barely supported, into the arms of a lividly pale Mary. Commissioned by the Harquebusiers' guild, of which St Christopher was patron saint, all the themes in this altarpiece represent the "bearers of Christ": St Christopher, Mary with Christ in her womb during the Visitation, Jesus being held by Simeon during the Presentation in the Temple, and the body of Christ being carried during the Descent from the Cross. Rubens' **Resurrection** (1612) is to the south in the second chapel in the ambulatory. De Backer's **Last Judgement** with panels depicting the Plantin family is in the fourth chapel in the ambulatory. Other notable works of art include Quellin the Younger's Baroque sarcophagus for Bishop Capello (1676), Frans Francken the Elder's triptych *Jesus among the Doctors of the Church* (1586), Murillo's *St Francis*, the *Last Supper* by Otto Venius and the *Marriage at Cana* by Martin de Vos.

Return to Grote-Markt and take Rue Wisselstraat.

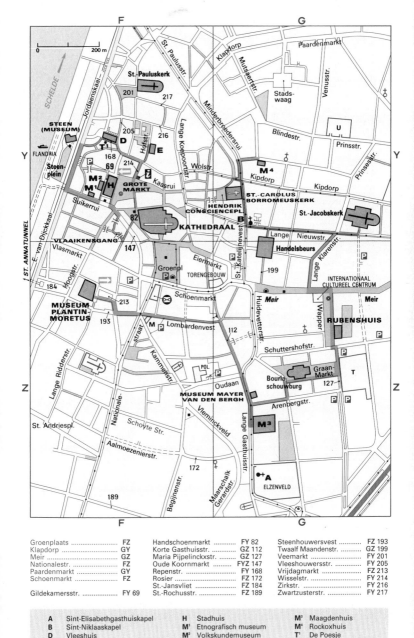

Groenplaats	FZ	Handschoenmarkt	FY 82	Steenhouwersvest	FZ 193
Klapdorp	GY	Korte Gasthuisstr.	GZ 112	Twaalf Maandenstr.	GZ 199
Meir	GZ	Maria Pijpelinckxstr.	GZ 127	Veemarkt	FY 201
Nationalestr.	FZ	Oude Koornmarkt	FYZ 147	Vleeshouwerstr.	FY 205
Paardenmarkt	GY	Repenstr.	FY 168	Vrijdagmarkt	FZ 213
Schoenmarkt	FZ	Rosier	FZ 172	Wisselstr.	FY 214
		St.-Jansvliet	FZ 184	Zirkstr.	FY 216
Gildekamersstr.	FY 69	St.-Rochusstr.	FZ 189	Zwartzusterstr.	FY 217

A	Sint-Elisabethgasthuiskapel	H	Stadhuis	M³	Maagdenhuis
B	Sint-Niklaaskapel	M¹	Etnografisch museum	M⁴	Rockoxhuis
D	Vleeshuis	M²	Volkskundemuseum	T¹	De Poesje
E	Oude Beurs				

ANTWERPEN

Carnotstr. ....EU 3
Dambruggestr. ....ETU 39
Gemeentestr. ....DU 63
de Keyserlei ....DU 103
Leysstraat ....DU 123
Offerandestr. ....EU 136
Pelikaanstr. ....DU 151
Quellinstr. ....DU 165
Turnhoutsebaan
  (Borgerhout) ....EU

van Aedtstraat ....DT 3
Amsterdamstr. ....DT 4
Ankerrui ....DT 6
Ballaerstr. ....DV 12
Bolivarplaats ....CV 15
Borsbeekbrug ....EX 16
van Breestr. ....DV 19
Brialmontlei ....DV 21
Britselei ....DV 22
Broederminstr. ....CV 24
Brouwersvliet ....DT 25
Brusselstr. ....CV 27
Cassierstr. ....DT 31
Charlottalei ....DV 33
Cockerillkaai ....CV 36
Cuperusstr. ....EV 37
Diksmuidelaan ....EX 43
Emiel Banningstr. ....CV 51
Emiel Vloorsstr. ....CX 52
Emile Verhaerenlaan ....CT 54
Erwtenstraat ....ET 55
Van Eycklei ....DV 57
Falconplein ....DT 58
Franklin Rooseveltpl. ....DU 60
Gen. Armstrongweg ....CX 64
Gerard Le Grellelaan ....DX 66
de Gerlachekaai ....CV 67
Gitschotellei ....EX 70
Graaf van Egmontstr. ....CV 72
Haantjeslei ....CDV 79
Halenstr. ....ET 81
Hessenplein ....DT 84
Jan de Voslei ....CX 90
Jan van Gentstr. ....CV 91
Jezusstraat ....DU 96
Justitiestraat ....DV 97
Kasteelpleinstr. ....DV 102
Kloosterstraat ....CU 105
Kol. Silvertopstr. ....CX 106
Koningin Astridplein ....DEU 109
Koningin Elisabethlei ....DX 110
Korte Winkelstr. ....DTU 114
Lange Lobroekstr. ....ET 117
Lange Winkelstr. ....DT 118
Leopold de Waelplein ......CV 120
Leopold de Waelstr. ....CV 121
Londenstr. ....DT 124
Maria-Henriettalei ....DV 129
Mercatorstr. ....DEV 130
Namenstr. ....CV 133
Van den Nestlei ....EV 135
Ommeganckstr. ....EU 138
Orteliuskaai ....DT 141
Osystraat ....DU 142
Oude Leeuwenrui ....DT 148
Platinkaai ....CU 153
Ploegstr. ....EU 154
Pluvierstraat ....CU 156
Posthofbrug ....EX 157
Prins Albertlei ....DX 159
Provinciestr. ....EUV 162
Pyckestraat ....CX 163
Quinten Matsijslei ....DUV 166
Rolwagenstr. ....EV 171
Schijnpoortweg ....ET 174
Van Schoonhovestr. ....DEU 175
Simonsstr. ....DEU 178
St.-Bernardsesteenweg ....CX 180
St.-Gummarusstr. ....DT 181
St.-Jansplein ....DT 183
St.-Jozefsstr. ....DV 186
St.-Michielskaai ....CU 187
Stuivenbergplein ....ET 196
Viaduct Dam ....ET 202
Viséstraat ....ET 204
Volkstraat ....CV 207
Vondelstr. ....DT 208

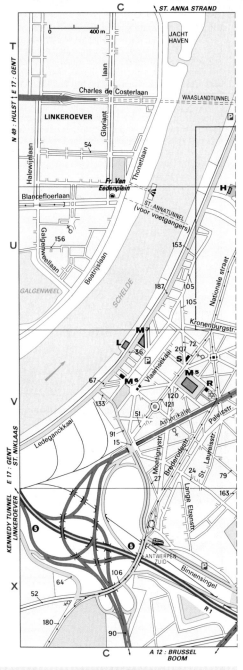

H	Stadhuis	
K	Brouwershuis	
L	Mini-Antwerpen	
M⁵	Koninklijk Museum voor Schone Kunsten	
M⁸	Museum voor Fotografie	

Oude Beurs (**FY E**) ⊙ – The former commodities exchange dates from 1515. Public administration offices occupy the building today. Behind the classical façade there is a charming paved courtyard surrounded by porticos and overlooked by a watchtower.

★**Vleeshuis** (**FY D**) ⊙ – The butchers' guild hall, an imposing Gothic building with a tall roof pierced by dormer windows, is to be found in the old harbour district. Stripes of white sandstone decorate the brick walls, which are framed by delicate turrets. The hall was built for the butchers' guild by one of the cathedral's architects between 1501 and 1504. It now houses a museum of archeology, numismatology and decorative arts from Antwerp.

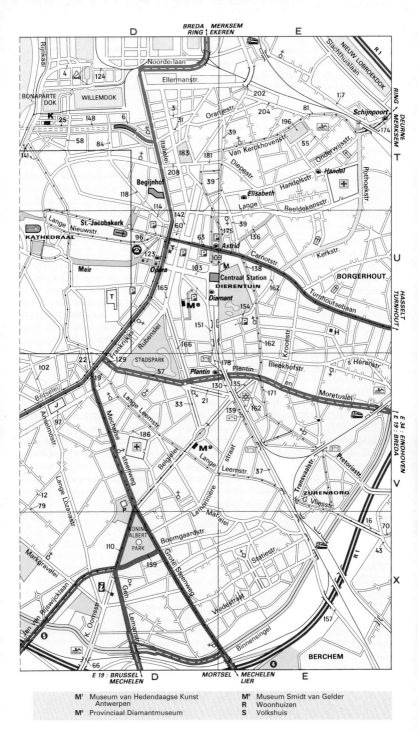

M¹	Museum van Hedendaagse Kunst Antwerpen	M⁹	Museum Smidt van Gelder
		R	Woonhuizen
M⁸	Provinciaal Diamantmuseum	S	Volkshuis

Various works are exhibited on the ground floor, beneath the beautiful Gothic vaulting of the great hall, and on the first floor. They include collections of silverware, glazed earthenware, wrought-ironwork, 15C statues, the 1514 Averbode altarpiece, panels of 16C Antwerp glazed earthenware tiles representing the conversion of St Paul, and antique furniture.

The **musical instrument collection★**, especially the harpsichords for which Antwerp was renowned in the 17C (the Ruckers family was the leading manufacturer), is particularly varied.

Take Repenstraat.

The **"Poesje"** (**FY T¹**) a famous Antwerp puppet theatre, is in a basement in the adjacent building.

★**Nationaal Scheepvaartmuseum** (FY) ☉ – The maritime museum is in the Steen fortress built after 843 on the Scheldt to defend the new frontier established by the Treaty of Verdun *(qv)*. Having been a prison since the early 14C, the castle was enlarged by Emperor Charles V around 1520, and then restored in the 19C and 20C. An interesting exhibition traces maritime and river life, with particular reference to Belgium, from its beginnings to the present time, aided by numerous pictures, models, instruments, sculptures and documents. There is also a department of industrial archeology (maritime park) open to visitors where a collection of boats is on display (including the river boat *Lauranda* used for temporary exhibitions). In front of the Steen is a statue of the legendary mischievous imp of Antwerp, **Lange Wapper.**

Traffic on the estuary is visible from the terraces on the **Steenplein** promenade. Boat trips leave from here for the tour of the port *(see below)*. All along this quay modern houses (Van Roosmalenhuis, on the corner of Goede Hoopstraat and St.-Michielskaai) alternate with superb older buildings.

★**Etnografisch museum** (FY M¹) ☉ – On the Suikerrui terraced houses dating from the 16C to the 19C now house Antwerp's ethnographic collections. Visitors are greeted by the famous statue of the Luba-Hembas' ancestor (Zaïre), to which André Malraux alluded in his "imaginary museum". This statue introduces the African section, organised by theme: precious objects, everyday objects, those used for magic (masks, voodoo dolls). The South Sea Islands section highlights Melanesian tribes, in which ancestor worship and social ranking are important elements: note the drum from the New Hebrides with a vertical slit to symbolise high rank; see also the Asmat (New Guinea) sculptures carved from tree-ferns for funerary rites, such as the magnificent ancestor's post called "bis". In the Americas section on the first floor, there is again this idea of an ancestor's post with the Haida Indians' (Canada) totem pole. A child's kayak nearby evokes Eskimo society, while a number of pre-Colombian earthenware pieces represent South and Central American civilisations; see also the brilliantly coloured Amazonian feather masks. On the second floor the collections are connected with Buddhism and Hinduism. Japan is represented by the 16C statue of Kannon Bosatsu in gilded laquered wood, as well as by paintings depicting "the nine meditations on the impurity of the body". The lamaistic objects include a remarkable 19C map of Lhassa and a unique series of 54 miniatures representing a mandala. On the third floor there are arts and crafts from China (Celadon ware), Japan, Afghanistan and Turkey.

Gildekamersstraat (FY 69) – This narrow thoroughfare skirts the rear of the Town Hall and is bordered by beautiful old houses, one of which is a folklore museum.

Volkskundemuseum (FY M²) ☉ – The extensive varied collections in the Folk Museum are devoted to Flemish popular art. The ground floor concerns life outside the home: street scenes, façades, games, signs, the *kermesse* represented by a marvellous Mortier street organ. The festive atmosphere continues into the stairway with the heads of the giants Druon and Pallas. The first floor handles certain aspects of Flemish daily life: toy collection, reconstruction of an apothecary's shop, display cases devoted to magic and superstitions. The second floor illustrates home life and the community lifestyle that is so important in Belgium (De Poesje puppet theatre).

★★FROM THE MUSEUM PLANTIN-MORETUS TO THE ROCKOXHUIS *time: one day*

★★★**Museum Plantin-Moretus** (FZ) ☉ – This museum occupies 34 rooms in the house and printing works built by the famous printer Plantin and enlarged in the 17C and 18C by his descendants, the Moretus family. It provides a fascinating history of humanism and old books in 16C and 17C Netherlands, through its beautiful old furniture, tapestries, gilded leatherwork, paintings, well-stocked libraries, collections of typography and drawings, engravings, old manuscripts and valuable editions.

The "Prince of Printers"

Christopher Plantin, a native of the Tours area in France, arrived in Antwerp in 1549 and became a printer in 1555 under the sign of the Golden Compasses; this emblem illustrated his motto "Labore et Constantia", the moving point representing work and the fixed point constancy.

The perfection of the publications produced on his sixteen presses (the Estienne family in France had only four) and his reputation for culture and erudition earned him the admiration of the greatest men of his time, including Philip II who made him his official royal printer and granted him the monopoly of sales of liturgical works in Spain and the Spanish colonies. Plantin created the famous Antwerp school of engraving, in collaboration with his friend, the governor and merchant Jerome Cook; Rubens himself would later head this institution. Plantin's greatest typographical success was his **Biblia Regia**, printed in five languages (Hebrew, Syrian, Greek, Latin and Aramaic). He died in 1589.

Museum visit – *The rooms are numbered and should be visited in order.* Visitors are greeted by the welcoming tranquillity of the courtyard, surrounded by leaded stained glass windows framed by Virginia creeper. Go through the main drawing room decorated with portraits by Rubens, then the shop, the proofreading room, Plantin's office and that of Justus Lipsius, Plantin's erudite friend. The presses in the printing shop date from the 16C, 17C and 18C; they still print *The Happiness of This World,* a sonnet by Plantin.

The famous *Biblia Regia* is exhibited on the first floor, along with the Gutenberg Bible, of which there are only thirteen copies left in the world. The wonderful libraries contain more than 25 000 old works, and the Max Horn Room has almost all the works of French literature from the 16C, 17C and 18C in magnificently bound first editions. The foundry is on the second floor.

Mad Meg (detail), by Bruegel the Elder

★★**Museum Mayer van den Bergh** (**GZ**) ⊘ – This museum is located in a neo-Gothic house dating from the early 20C and extended in 1974. The museum houses a remarkable collection of works of art, brought together in under ten years by the collector Fritz Mayer van den Bergh (1858-1901), who showed real genius in his purchases of medieval sculpture, illuminated manuscripts, ivories, tapestries and paintings.

Ground floor – Room 3 contains two 12C statue-columns from the cloisters of Notre-Dame-en-Vaux in Châlons-sur-Marne, France, as well as the 13C altarpiece painted on wood by Simeon and Machilos de Spoleto. A 15C triptych of Christ on the Cross by Quentin Massys is exhibited in Room 4 and is a testament to the painter's talent. The beauty and serenity of the landscape forms a strong contrast to the apparent suffering of the figures.

First floor – Beautiful Byzantine and Gothic ivories are exhibited in Room 6. Particularly arresting, however, is the carved group of *Jesus and St John* by the master Heinrich von Konstanz (*c*1300), as is the small Dutch diptych (1400) representing the Nativity and St Christopher (the Resurrection of Christ is depicted on the reverse side).

Room 9 contains the museum's finest exhibit. The painting entitled **Mad Meg**★★ *(De Dulle Griet)* by Bruegel the Elder is an apocalyptic vision of war in remarkable fiery colours. Next to it, the *Twelve Flemish Proverbs (see illustration, p 297)* shows another facet of Bruegel's astounding talent. The *Census at Bethlehem* and *Winter Landscape* are by his sons.

Maagdenhuis (**GZ M³**) ⊘ – One part of this former orphanage has been turned into a museum. There are many paintings (by Rubens), *St Jerome* by Van Dyck, sculptures and a collection of 16C Antwerp ceramic bowls.

The area between the Maagdenhuis and Rubenshuis is pleasant, with peaceful squares and a number of theatres and restaurants.

Bourlaschouwburg (**GZ**) – The Bourla Theatre lies on Komedieplaats and is housed in a remarkably-shaped neo-Classical building designed by the architect Pierre Bruno Bourla. The engaged columns on the façade frame the busts of famous authors and composers, while from above the attic the Muses accompanied by Apollo hail the crowds below. The ceiling in the first entrance hall was decorated by the Antwerp artist Jan Vanriet. The foyer with its impressive dome seems to encourage visitors to stop for a moment and admire the surroundings. Recent restoration work has been undertaken to adapt the theatre to current technical requirements.

★★**Rubenshuis** (**GZ**) ⊘ – Rubens' presence is everywhere in the museums and churches of Antwerp, but can be sensed most strongly in this grand house bought in 1610, one year after he married Isabella Brant.

Rubens turned it into a sumptuous palace, after carrying out major extension work and the construction of an immense studio. Having borne him three children his first wife died; four years after her death he married the very young Hélène Fourment. They had five more children who were brought up here.

Rubens: a painter from Antwerp

Rubens was born in exile near Cologne on 28 June 1577, where his father, an alderman of Antwerp, had been forced to take refuge when suspected of heresy. Rubens first saw Antwerp, in ruins, at the age of 12, after his father's death.

He studied with Verhaecht and Van Noort; from 1594 to 1598 he worked in the painter Otto Venius's studio and then he became a master in the Guild of St Luke.

He spent some time in Italy and returned to Antwerp in 1608, when the town was enjoying a period of peace under the Infanta Isabella. This was the apotheosis for Rubens and his school. Flemish and cosmopolitan, Catholic and an unbeliever, masterful and productive, he embodied the town's spirit of genius. Acting as the sovereigns' official ambassador, he succeeded in combining features of Italianism with the Flemish tradition in painting.

His students and assistants include the most prestigious names: Jan Brueghel, known as "Velvet" Brueghel; and the three Antwerp painters Jordaens, Van Dyck and Snyders. His influence extended both to sculpture (the Quellins and Verbruggen) and Baroque architecture.

He died in Antwerp in 1640 and was buried in St.-Jacobskerk.

Tour – The entire house was refurbished in 1946. In the north wing, the Flemish-style living quarters are embellished with old tiles, gilded leatherwork, 17C furniture and numerous paintings (note Rubens' self-portrait in the dining-room). In the south wing, the studio has a gallery from which admirers could contemplate his paintings.

The studio's Baroque façade with its philosophers' busts and mythological statuary can be admired from the courtyard. A portico links the two lodges and opens onto a garden through three arches which Rubens reproduced in some of his canvases.

The 17C garden has been redesigned in accordance with period paintings and engravings.

The Meir (**GZ**) – This is the town's prestigious main thoroughfare. The former royal palace, a beautiful 18C rococo building in which a number of sovereigns resided, is on the corner of the Meir (no 50) and the Wapper. The palace is now the International Cultural Centre (exhibitions, films).

St.-Jacobskerk (**GY**) ⊘ – The **interior**★ of this Late Gothic church is richly decorated in Baroque style. Among the paintings note Otto Venius's *Virgin Mary* in the south aisle and *The Calling of St Peter* by Jordaens in the ambulatory on the south side.

Rubens' funerary chapel behind the chancel contains one of his last works, *The Virgin and the Saints* (1634); it is said that he depicted himself in St George's armour, the Virgin being Isabella Brant, and Mary Magdalene Hélène Fourment. Jordaens' *St Charles healing the Plague-stricken in Milan* hangs in the neighbouring chapel.

The restored Gothic clock, believed to date from the second half of the 15C, is on display in a room at the back of the church.

Handelsbeurs (**GZ**) ⊘ – The Stock Exchange stands at a crossroads, its glass-paned dome dominating the houses tightly packed around it.

Domien de Waghemakere built the first exchange, which soon became too crowded *(qv)*. He created a new one, which was inaugurated in 1531. It was very active throughout the 16C but was destroyed by fire in 1858. The architect Schadde rebuilt it in 1872 in the same style, and the present building consists of a hall with tiers of galleries beneath a superb glass roof.

St.-Niklaaskapel (GY B) – This 15C chapel is home to a puppet theatre (Poppenschouwburg). There is a charming little courtyard, surrounded by old buildings, tucked away behind it.

★**Hendrik Conscienceplein** – This quiet cobbled square blends harmoniously with the surrounding 17C and 19C buildings and the façade of the church dedicated to St Charles Borromeo.

★**St.-Carolus Borromeuskerk** (GY) ⊘ – The beautiful **Baroque façade** of the church dedicated to St Charles Borromeo breaks up horizontally into three classical registers, with a central medallion based on a drawing by Rubens and two offset lantern turrets. Adjacent to the apse is an elegant Baroque bell tower, on which Renaissance themes are superposed. It was the work of Pieter Huyssens.

The Jesuits built the church between 1615 and 1621, and it was initially dedicated to St Ignatius, before taking the name of St Charles Borromeo.

The interior is still striking, despite the 1718 fire which destroyed the ceilings painted by Peter Paul Rubens and Anthony Van Dyck in the side aisles. The building is barrel-vaulted and has tribunes communicating with the nave through tall, brightly-lit galleries. The chancel and Lady Chapel still have their marble ornamentation.

Rubens' painting of the *Assumption* and other altarpieces commissioned from the artist in 1620 for the decoration of this church are now in the Museum of Fine Art in Vienna.

There is 18C carved wood panelling running under the arcades; between each confessional guarded by four angels there are medallions tracing the lives of St Ignatius *(south side)* and St Francis Xavier *(north side)*.

Museum ⊘ – The gallery, funerary crypt and vestry are open to visitors, as well as five rooms in the museum exhibiting collections of antique lace.

★**Rockoxhuis** (GY M⁴) ⊘ – Nikolas Rockox (1560-1640), a friend of Rubens, burgomaster of Antwerp and a humanist, was an enthusiastic collector of objets d'art. His 17C patrician home has been restored and is now a museum. *(An audiovisual presentation in English, French and Dutch traces Antwerp's cultural history from 1560 to 1640.)* Note the magnificent furniture (particularly the cupboards called "ribbanken", and the finely decorated ebony cabinets), the beautiful pieces of ceramic ware, an extensive collection of paintings which includes in particular works by Patinir (Room 1), Van Dyck (two studies of a man's head), Jordaens, Teniers the Younger, Rubens (Room 2), Momper (Room 3), Snyders (*Antwerp Fish Market*, Room 5) and Pieter Brueghel the Younger (copy of Bruegel the Elder's *Proverbs*, Room 6).

OTHER SIGHTS

Central Antwerp

St.-Pauluskerk (FY) ⊘ – *Entrance on St.-Paulusstraat.*
This Late Gothic church was begun in 1517 and completed in 1639, and is surmounted by a Baroque bell tower (1680).

Baroque furnishings and beautiful 17C wooden panels on the confessionals, which are framed by huge expressive figures, richly embellish the majestic **interior**★. Statues surround the chancel, which is narrower than the nave, giving an impression of depth further accentuated by the elevated position of the monumental marble altarpiece. In the north aisle paintings from the Rubens' school depict the Mysteries of the Rosary. This series of works includes one by Rubens himself depicting the *Flagellation*, a powerful painting in muted colours. There are two other works by Rubens in the transept, dating from about 1609: *Adoration of the Shepherds* (north transept) and *Dispute on the Nature of the Holy Sacrament* (south transept).

Sint-Elisabethgasthuiskapel (GZ A) ⊘ – This chapel is part of the old 13C St Elizabeth's hospital which was closed down in 1986 and restored as an arts centre (Elzenveld). The Brabant Gothic nave has capitals decorated with curly kale motifs; it dates from the early 15C. The chancel is the same length and was added between 1442 and 1460. The black-and-white marble high altar by Artus Quellin the Younger dominates the Baroque decoration; above the altar is a statue of the Virgin Mary. Among the works of art note paintings by Godfried Maes and Frans Francken the Younger.

Outside Central Antwerp

★★★**Koninklijk Museum voor Schone Kunsten** (CV M⁵) ⊘ – The Royal Museum of Fine Art is housed in a 19C building with an imposing façade consisting of Corinthian columns surmounted by bronze chariots by Vinçotte. It contains an exceptional collection of paintings, in particular works by Rubens and Flemish Primitive painters. The Guild of St Luke collected most of the early art from 1442 onwards. A large collection of modern art is on the ground floor.

First floor (ancient art) – It is interesting to begin in Room **N** which houses works by non-Belgian painters, before following the evolution of Flemish painting. In this room there are several real treasures to be admired: four small panels by **Simone Martini** (14C), including one representing the *Annunciation* executed with a delicacy reminiscent of miniature painting; the famous *Virgin Surrounded by Red and Blue Angels* which **Fouquet** endowed with Agnès Sorel's lovely features; the elegant, serene *Calvary* by **Antello de Messina**; **Jean Clouet's** splendid portraits, particularly that of the *Dauphin of France*, the son of Francis I; and finally a few works by **Lucas Cranach**, including *Charity* and *Eve* which he marked with his insignia (a tiny serpent holding a ring in its mouth).

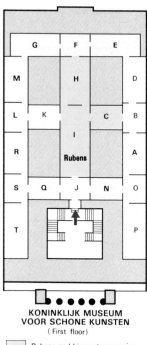

**KONINKLIJK MUSEUM
VOOR SCHONE KUNSTEN**
(First floor)

░ Rubens and his contemporaries

░ Flemish Primitives and Renaissance

Room **Q** is devoted to 15C Flemish Primitives. True masterpieces by the period's greatest painters are here: **Van Eyck's** *St Barbara*, a meticulously drawn work depicting the saint in front of a Gothic tower still under construction, and the delicately-coloured *Madonna at the Fountain*; **Van der Weyden's** *Seven Sacraments Triptych*, set inside a vast Gothic church with each sacrament personified as an angel bearing a banner, as well as his *Portrait of Philippe de Cro*; and the **Master of Frankfurt's** self-portrait with his wife, the Antwerp school's oldest known work (1496). Admire also **Memling's** *Portrait of a Man* and in the neighbouring room (**S**) three paintings representing *Christ Surrounded by Angel Musicians*.

Rooms **R** and **L** are devoted to 16C painting. Works from that period still have the main characteristics of Flemish Primitives but are nevertheless subject to Italian influence, as can be seen by **Quentin Massys'** *Mary Magdalene* or his famous *Triptych of the Entombment of Christ*. **Joachim Patinir's** painting of the *Flight into Egypt* in Room **L** represents an important step in the evolution of landscape painting. **Jan Massys'** *Portrait of Judith* is in the same room, along with an entire series of portraits by **Pourbus**, Jan Gossaert (known as **Mabuse**), and the Master of Antwerp. Room **M** is devoted to the **Brueghels**, especially the more or less faithful copies and imitations of works by Velvet Brueghel executed by his descendants, including *Bridal Dance*. Rooms **G**, **F** and **E** contain paintings by Jan Fyt and Martin de Vos.

Room **I**, devoted to Rubens, is reached by going through Room **C**, in which his preparatory sketches are exhibited. The many compositions showing the master's evolution, such as the *Baptism of Christ* painted in Italy, and the *Venus Frigida* (inspired by the marble statue of Venus crouching down, in the Vatican), are still classical paintings along with the *Triptych of the Incredulity of St Thomas*. Realism comes to the fore in the bloody *Christ in the Hay*, while pathos is conveyed through works such as *Last Communion of St Francis*, *Blow of the Spear* and *The Trinity* with its striking foreshortenings. Finally, *The Adoration of the Magi* (1624), with its brilliant colours and expressive figures, marks one of the finest periods of 17C Flemish painting. Room **H** recalls Rubens' collaborators through **Van Dyck's** distinguished portraits, his Piètas or the large *Crucifixion* in subtle tones or **Jordaens'** astonishing scenes of everyday life, such as *Family Concert*.

Room **A** exhibits still life paintings and works by animal painters, including Snyders whose paintings overflow with food or brim over with fish.

Room **T** displays 17C Dutch paintings, including **Rembrandt's** *Portrait of a Preacher*.

Ground floor (modern art) – This gives a very full view of the Belgian school after 1830. Note **Henri De Braekeleer's** *L'Homme à la chaire*, painted in the brewers' guild hall, a large collection of **James Ensor** paintings illustrating the artist's development from his first quasi-Impressionist works representing his friends' and acquaintances' homes to paintings filled with strange masks and skeletons, such as *Intrigue* (1890) and *Skeletons Fighting for the Body of a Hanged Man* (1891). **Rik Wouters'** light-filled paintings, such as *Woman Ironing*, are examples of Fauvism. The **Sint-Martens-Latem** group is well represented by the Expressionist **Permeke's** brutal style *(Fisherman's Woman, Snow, Seascape, Pale Clouds)*, the **De Smet** brothers, **Van den Berghe**, **Servaes** (the series of paintings entited *Peasant Life*) and **Van de Woestijne**. Surrealism is particularly well represented by **Magritte** *(16 September)* and **Delvaux**. Among contemporary works, note Pierre Alechinsky's large canvas painted in 1964, *Last Day*, which shows the evolution of his experiences during his period with the Cobra group, reacting against the desolation of the post-war world.

Some of the old warehouses between the Fine Art Museum and the quays have been converted into art galleries or museums (Museum of Photography, Museum of Contemporary Art).

Woonhuizen "De Vijf Werelddelen" (CV R) – Not far from the Museum of Fine Art on the corner of Plaatsnijderstraat and Schilderstraat is the remarkable "Five Continents" house dating from 1901. This Art Nouveau building designed by the architect Frans Smet-Verhas was built for a shipowner, hence the wooden ship's bow. A fine loggia above has stained-glass windows bearing the names of the world's five continents.

Volkshuis "Help U zelve" (CV S) – The architect Emiel van Averbeke, who was acclaimed as "Antwerp's Horta", built the Liberal People's House "Help U zelve" in conjunction with Jan van Asperen in 1898. The splendid recently restored façade is partially decorated with mosaics and has two gables topped with sculptures.

★**Museum voor Fotografie (CV M⁶)** ⊘ – The first floor of the Photography Museum traces each step in the history of photography since the "camera obscura" by means of a remarkable collection of equipment including daguerreotypes, dark rooms, detective cameras, spy cameras hidden in walking sticks or in a tie, folding equipment and more modern equipment. An exhibition of work by some of the world's greatest photographers illustrates the history of the art form. The shots were taken by Atget, Man Ray, Kertesz, Sanders, Cartier-Bresson, Brassaï, Capa, Avedon, Irving Penn, Ansel Adams, etc.

The second floor is devoted to stereoscopic photography, illustrated by the "Panorama Kaiser", and to cinema.

Two ground floor galleries, one named after Lieven Gevaert (born in Antwerp in 1868), house temporary exhibitions.

Museum van Hedendaagse Kunst Antwerpen-MUHKA (CUV M⁷) ⊘ – The Contemporary Art Gallery situated near the quaysides of the Scheldt is housed in a recently extended former grain elevator dating from 1926. It displays an interesting collection of modern art from the 1970s onwards. Widely acclaimed artists from Belgium (J Fabre, Van Snick, Lohaus, etc) and abroad (T Cragg, B Nauman, A Charlton, Boltanski, D Flavin) exhibit their works here. Take the lift up to the top of the building to admire H Duchateau's *Growing Ladder*.

The museum has helped to give the district a new lease of life, attracting numerous contemporary art galleries, restaurants and cafés.

Mini-Antwerpen (CV L) ⊘ – This miniature reconstruction of Antwerp *(still being completed)* has been laid out in an old shed on the wharf beside the Scheldt. A son-et-lumière brings the display to life. Note the workshops where new parts of the miniature town are built.

★★**Dierentuin (DEU)** ⊘ – The zoological gardens are situated in a park covering an area of 10ha – 25 acres between the central railway station and the Natural History Museum which was built in 1885. A statue of the museum's founder riding a camel can be seen over the entrance. The zoo has some rare species among its 5 000 animals, such as white rhinoceros and okapis (Moorish building). The brightly coloured Egyptian temple (1856) houses elephants, giraffes, ostriches and Arabian oryx. Sculptor Rembrandt Bugatti often came here for inspiration. Nothing in the bird house separates the tropical birds in the bright light from the public in the shadows. Visitors can see nocturnal animals in their burrows from behind the large windows in the Nocturama. The planetarium, aquarium, Natural History Museum and Delphinarium offer additional attractions.

Centraal Station (DEU) – The main railway station (1900-1905) next to the zoological gardens was built by L De La Censerie. The two monumental neo-Baroque façades are topped by a huge 60m – 197ft high dome.

★**Openluchtmuseum voor Beeldhouwkunst Middelheim** ⊘ – *Leave by Karel Oomsstraat* **(DX)**

The Open-Air Sculpture Museum is set against a backdrop of vast well shaded lawns beneath the huge trees in Middelheim Park (12 hectares – 30 acres). It contains over 400 works from Rodin to present day artists. The "Middelheim-Hoog" section contains modern sculpture by both Belgian and foreign artists (Maillol, Bourdelle, Moore, Giacometti, Richier, Calder, Nevelson, Jespers, Gentils etc.). Note the fine sweeping lines of Henry Moore's *King and Queen* and the extremely dynamic *Mad Virgin* by Rik Wouters. Nature provided the inspiration for

Openluchtmuseum Middelheim

René Braem's white pavilion, which houses small or fragile sculptures in wood, terracotta, metal and plaster. "Middelheim-Laag" displays contemporary sculptures. Notable works include the 2 emotionally moving figures by Juan Muñoz, Richard Deacon's enigmatic sculpture and Panamarenko's *Poulet préhistorique*.

Provinciaal Diamantmuseum (DU M⁸) ⊘ – The Provincial Diamond Museum lies in the heart of the diamond district near the station. The properties and origin of this crystal are described on the third floor. The weight of diamonds, the hardest known matter, formed at a depth of 150-200km – 93-124 miles at a temperature of 2000°C – 3632°F, is calculated in carats. Up to the 18C the stones came from India, but now the principal mines are in South Africa, West Africa and Australia.
The second floor is devoted to industrial use of diamonds and the transformation of the raw stone into a jewel. A 19C diamond workshop has been reconstructed. The history of diamonds in Antwerp is retraced on the first floor.
Precious jewels are kept in the treasure room.

Begijnhof (DT) ⊘ – The houses of the Beguine convent cluster together in their brick enclosure. A street of uneven cobblestones frames an orchard surrounded by hedges. The church, rebuilt in the 19C, is embellished with Jordaens and Van Noort paintings. Note the *Christ Bound* in the oratory.

Brouwershuis (DT K) ⊘ – Gilbert van Schoonbeke had the Brewers' Guild Hall built around 1553 to supply water to the many breweries he had opened in the surrounding district. In 1581 the waterworks building became the seat of the brewers' guild. Visitors can see the refurbished stable, the horse treadmill and the water-raising system, as well as the reservoirs once connected to the canals. The workshop and more particularly the beautiful Council Room are upstairs; this room often figures in Henri De Braekeleer paintings *(qv)*. It is furnished with antiques, the walls are clad with 17C gilded Mechelen leather and there is a beautiful fireplace with twisted columns.

Museum Smidt van Gelder (DV M⁹) ⊘ – This museum is housed in a refined 18C interior, featuring beautiful furniture and valuable collections (Dutch painting, Chinese porcelain).

Provinciaal Museum Sterckshof (Zilvercentrum) ⊘ – *Leave by Turnhoutsebaan* **(EU)**.
The Sterckshof Provincial Museum lies in Rivierenhof Park in Duerne. It is housed in a pretty Flemish Renaissance château which was rebuilt in 1938 and is surrounded by a moat. The museum contains a fine collection of silverware.

★Wijk Zurenborg (EV) – This splendid district consisting of several streets around Cogels-Osylei has been remarkably well-preserved. It takes its name from a 16C pleasure-garden. The district dates from the 19C and presents a most impressive display of town houses built in revival, eclectic and Art Nouveau styles. A number of famous architects were employed in its construction including Jos Bascourt, Emiel Dieltiens, Frans Smet-Verhas and Jules Hofman. Certain groups of buildings look like veritable palaces, such as those at nos 32-36 Cogels-Osylei (1897-1899) designed by the architect Dieltiens and the three Flemish neo-Renaissance mansions at nos 25-29 on the same avenue, built to plans by J Bascourt. Also on the same avenue is the Huize "Zonnebloem" (Sunflower House) by Jules Hofman, which is striking on account of its sinuous lines. The house at no 80 is almost an exact copy of the St-Cyr painter's house in Brussels *(see Bruxelles/Brussel)*. The four houses at the corner of Generaal Van Merlenstraat and Waterloostraat are built in a more sober style and illustrate the four seasons. At no 11 Waterloostraat is the "Battle of Waterloo" residence designed by F Smet-Verhas. Note the portraits of Napoleon and Wellington, the large bow-window and the small corner turret.

THE PORT *See p 51*

Scheldetocht: boat trip on the Scheldt ⊘ – This boat trip takes passengers down the Scheldt to Kallo and provides an interesting glimpse of Antwerp's industrial development, but it does not go into the dock area.

The boat turns around at the Kallo lock *(sluis)* which can handle boats of up to 125 000 tonnes and will soon provide access to a canal (Baalhoekkanaal) linking the western part of the Scheldt to the Netherlands. This canal will be the backbone of a new complex of docks on the west bank, four of which are completed. There is already a variety of industries in this initial area of port extension (6 000 hectares – 14 826 acres), including a thermal power station.

The boat sails against the current along the west bank, with its large chemical plants, then comes to the little St Anne's beach, the mill and the marina.

Havenrondvaart: boat trip around the harbour ⊘ – This boat tour of the harbour shows the docks where cargo vessels and tankers berth. The industrial complexes, oil refineries, grain elevators, transporter bridges, dry docks, shipyards and the many reservoirs are most impressive. During the week, the amount of harbour traffic never ceases to amaze visitors.

Lillo-Fort – *15km – 9.4 miles along the east bank of the Scheldt.*

The old stronghold of Lillo, which is surrounded by water on all sides, hides a peaceful village behind a screen of woodland. The church presides over a charming central square and a little harbour. This is one of the last three villages in the old polders area which is remembered in the **Polder en zeemuseum** (Polders Museum). Doel *(see below)* can be seen from the dyke along the Scheldt.

EXCURSIONS

East of Antwerp: 30km – 18.75 mile round trip – *Leave Antwerp on Schijnpoortweg (ET 174 on the town plan).*

Braschaat – This town has a large recreational centre in an extensive park with swimming pools and a zoo.

The **road** from Braschaat to Schilde is most attractive. It is lined with banks of rhododendron bushes in several places, making a marvellous show in May and June when they are in bloom, especially on the stretch of road flanking the Botermelk estate on the other side of the swing bridge which crosses the Antwerp canal at Turnhout. There are several well-to-do homes tucked amidst the woods and flowers of 's Gravenwezel.

Vrieselhof Provinciaal Domein – This estate between Schilde and **Oelegem** offers pleasant walks in a beautiful flower-filled park *(signposted paths)*. The castle in its centre was rebuilt after its destruction in 1914 and now contains a textile museum, **Textielmuseum** ⊘. Techniques of spinning, weaving and fabric-printing are explained here; there are also exhibitions of lace, costume and contemporary textile art.

West Bank of the Scheldt to Doel – *25km – 15.5 miles. In Amerikalei, take the Kennedy tunnel towards Hulst, then head towards Antwerp-Linkeroever (west bank).*

A little garden strewn with ships propellers, anchors and lifebelts near the pedestrian and cyclist tunnel provides an interesting **view** of central Antwerp with its towering cathedral and skyscraper. The marina tucks itself out of sight further north, along with a little mill and St Anne's beach. A boating lake lies to the south (Galgenweel).

Take the road towards Hulst, then head for Doel.

The road crosses a strange region where the polders, traditionally used for stock raising, lie next to Kallo's great industrial complexes *(see above)*, for which the ground had to be drained.

Doel – This little village, protected from the Scheldt by an enormous dike, has a tiny fishing port. A windmill stands on top of the dike. Lillo can be seen directly opposite, its white mill standing out behind the trees. Equally visible are the chimney-stacks of the industrial estate. A nuclear power plant has been built near Doel.

De Kalmthoutse Heide and **Kalmthout Arboretum** – *25km – 15.5 miles to the north. Michelin map 212 fold15. Leave on Schijnpoortweg* (**ET 174**).

De Kalmthoutse Heide nature reserve (natuurreservaat) lies north of the Antwerp de Kempen region, about 2km – 1.25 miles from the town of Kalmthout near the border. It covers 732 hectares – 1 809 acres of sand dunes, heathland *(heide)*, pine forests and marshes, inhabited by numerous birds and crisscrossed by waymarked footpaths.

The **Kalmthout Arboretum** ⊘ *(located on the N111)*, dating from 1857, is as much a quiet place for a stroll as interesting terrain for botanists. A walk in the grounds *(there are no paths: be sure to wear sensible, sturdy shoes)* provides an opportunity to admire a large variety of trees and shrubs, including rare species grouped within an area of 10 hectares – 25 acres. In addition to the many coniferous trees, there are magnolias, rhododendrons and shrubs of the rose family (sloes, etc.). The presence of wild plants lends a particular charm to this very beautifully laid out park.

ANTWERP
See ANTWERPEN

ARLON
Luxembourg Ⓟ – Population 22 216
Michelin maps 409 K6 or 214 fold 18
Town plan in the current Michelin Red Guide Benelux

The old town of Arlon, built on a hill, is the provincial capital of Belgian Luxembourg. During the Roman occupation it was one of the major towns (Orolaunum) on the road from Reims to Trier. Fortified in the late 3C, it still has many Roman remains.
Arlon has suffered from fires and wars over the centuries.

Maitrank – This Arlon aperitif, known locally as May wine, consists of dry white wine flavoured with sprigs of woodruff (asperula) picked before flowering, full-bodied cognac and sugar; it is then served chilled with a slice of orange. Since 1954 the Maitrank Brotherhood has organised large popular festivals at the end of May *(see the Calendar of Events at the end of this guide)*.

Viewpoint – The **observation platform** ⊘ at the top of St Donat's Church, itself on the hill, provides a view of the town's slate roofs, St Martin's Church, and a panoramic view across four countries: Belgium, the Grand Duchy of Luxembourg, France and Germany *(viewing tables)*.

★**Musée luxembourgeois** ⊘ – The refurbished Luxembourg Museum contains interesting regional archeological and ethnographic collections.
The most outstanding exhibits in the remarkable **Gallo-Roman Lapidary section**★★ on the ground floor are a unique collection of funerary monuments and fragments of civic architecture from the town itself or the region. The fragments are carved with bas-reliefs either representing mythological (Bacchus, Hercules) or allegorical figures (dancers), or representing domestic scenes providing precise information about daily life in the first three centuries of our era: farmers, schoolmaster, draper's shop. Note in particular the magnificent, beautifully expressive **relief of "The Travellers"**, and also the very fine

Relief of "The Travellers"

Vervicii monument discovered in 1980 (combat between Achilles and Hector). There is a Merovingian collection upstairs (tombs, jewels), medieval and Renaissance furniture and a 16C altarpiece.

Tour romaine: thermes – The **Roman tower** ⊘ *(Grand-Place)* was part of a rampart, the structure of which can still be seen by visitors. The rampart was built on a large foundation consisting of fragments of demolished buildings, including the magnificent bas-reliefs which now have pride of place in the Musée luxembourgeois. One of these sculptures, representing Neptune, is still in its place in the wall under the tower *(access by metal ladder)*.
One can also see part of the *Relief of "The Travellers"* which is in the museum.
There are a few remains of the 4C **Roman baths** ⊘, as well as the 5C foundations of Belgium's oldest Christian **basilica** ⊘, near the **old cemetery** *(Rue des Thermes Romains)* with its beautiful stone crosses.

EXCURSION

★**Victory Memorial Museum** ⊙– *6km – 3.75 miles southeast, exit direct from the E 411 motorway.*
Twelve years of research were necessary to create this remarkable collection of **Second World War transport and combat vehicles**★★. Tanks, trucks, cars, ambulances, motorcycles and sidecars manufactured in Britain, Germany, Canada, the United States, France, Italy, Poland and Czechoslovakia are exhibited in a vast modern building. They have been completely restored and are in perfect working order. They are equipped with their weapons and surrounded by figures of soldiers in uniform. Several scenes have been reconstructed: Rommel in his command-car in North Africa, the Normandy landings, a dance recalling the Liberation, and the Battle of the Bulge in the snowy Ardennes.
A documentary entitled *From Africa to Berlin* is comprised of archive newsreel clips recalling the great moments from 1942 to May 1945.

ATH

Hainaut – Population 23 922
Michelin maps 409 E4 or 213 folds 16, 17

Ath lies at the confluence of the two River Denders which extend southward by a canal. Owing to its strategic location on a main road, the town was besieged by Louis XIV in 1667. After it fell, Ath became the first town to be fortified by Vauban. He had a relief-map made of Ath, the first of its type (1669). Ath underwent a second French siege in 1745 during the War of Austrian Succession and most of the fortifications were destroyed.
The humanist Justus Lipsius *(qv)* was a student at the old school during the 16C.
Blue granite quarries have been worked in the surrounding region (in Maffle).

The parade of giants – At the end of August *(see the Calendar of Events)* the harvest festival or **ducasse**★★ (from the word meaning "dedication" or "consecration") is held with its parades of giants. The festivities take place over two days. On Saturday at around 3pm, the marriage of Mr and Mrs Gouyasse (local dialect for "Goliath") is solemnised in St Julian's church during the Gouyasse evensong, then David and Goliath do battle in front of the Town Hall.
On Sunday at 10am and 3pm, the giants measuring over 4m – 13ft in height and weighing more than 100kg-220lbs, wend their way through the town, in a merry atmosphere of gaiety and fun. They include Monsieur and Madame Gouyasse, the four Aymon sons *(see La Meuse namuroise)* riding Bayard their horse, Samson symbolising the might of the armed forces, Ambiorix *(see Tongeren)* and Mam'zelle Victoire, who symbolises Ath itself.

SIGHTS

Grand-Place – On the main square is the **Town Hall**, completed in 1624. It was built to plans by **Coebergher** (c1561-1634). This astonishing individual was a painter, engineer, architect to the Archdukes Albert and Isabella. He also opened the first pawnshops in Flanders. The foyer has a beautiful fireplace, a carved doorway and a stone balustraded staircase.

Église St-Julien – The church dedicated to St Julian can be glimpsed from here with its tall 15C tower, half-destroyed by fire in 1817, and its corner turrets. Also visible is the 16C **église St-Martin** which has an oak *Crucifixion* outside consisting of a huge figure of Christ surrounded by the two thieves, the Virgin Mary and St John. Inside the building is a splendid *Entombment*, a monumental group probably dating from the late 16C.

Tour de Burbant – *Access via the narrow street, rue du Gouvernement, near the Police Station (Commissariat de Police).*
The Burbant Tower is a massive square flat-buttressed keep discreetly located near Grand-Place. The Count of Hainaut, Baldwin IV the Builder, had it constructed in 1166 to serve as a base, defend Hainaut's northern border with Flanders and monitor the movements of the local nobility. The tower is a vestige of the old feudal lordship of Ath and it takes its name from the former Carolingian country of Brabant to which the region once belonged. It is a veritable military complex consisting of 4m – 13ft thick walls and an interior laid out on four storeys. Note the lack of windows in the lower section and the impressive fireplace. During the 14C, the keep was mainly used as a prison. The surrounding enclosure, added during the 15C and 16C, has been restored and turned into a cultural centre.

Musée d'Histoire et de Folklore ⊙ – *Rue du Bouchain, access via the Esplanade.* The first room of the History and Folk Museum is crammed with miscellaneous objects unearthed during local digs and dating from the Paleolithic era to the

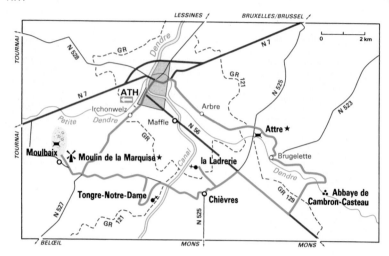

Bronze and Iron Ages. The next room takes the visitor back in time to the Middle Ages. Particularly noteworthy are an interesting late 14C *Entombment* from Mainvault and a splendid collection of chasubles. On the second floor, one of the rooms is devoted to the folklore of Ath and its famous Ducasse festival. The next room contains relief-maps of the town retracing the main stages in Ath's history, including its fortification by Vauban.

ADDITIONAL SIGHTS

Musée de la Pierre and Carrières de Maffle – *Chaussée de Mons. Take the Mons road to the south.*
The Maffle Quarries, which now include a Stone Museum, cover approximately ten hectares – twenty-five acres in the eastern part of the Dendre Valley. After industries moved out of the area from 1960 onwards, it was overrun by vegetation and the quarries have filled with water. Although it has become a nature reserve, it has nevertheless retained many traces of the former quarries and their industrial activity. A walk through the site reveals lime kilns, a powder magazine, a crane, a winch, etc.
A **museum** stands opposite the quarry in the former 19C quarry-master's house and the old workshops. It gives a full insight into the history of stone working in Belgium, especially in the region, through an exhibition of tools, machines and illustrated documents explaining how stone is worked from the extraction process to dressing, in addition to the development of transport techniques and the labourers' working conditions.

EXCURSIONS

Ath region – *Round tour of 38km – 23.75 miles local map see above leave Ath on the Mons road to the south, head for Irchonwelz, then turn right towards Villers-Notre-Dame.*
The region around Ath is devoted to arable and animal farming. The view runs for miles, broken only by ranges of poplars, large farms and hamlets.
Moulbaix – The pretty wooden **mill** called "**Moulin de la Marquise**"★ ⊙ (1614) is Hainaut's last working windmill. An unusual 19C house built in the Tudor style is concealed in the extensive park near the church.
Tongre-Notre-Dame – The 18C Renaissance style basilica contains a Romanesque enthroned Virgin in polychrome wood. Since the 17C, the statue has often been draped in rich robes and ornaments concealing all but the Infant Jesus's face. The statue, which stands on an altar built on the spot where the Virgin was said to have appeared in February 1081, is highly venerated and is the object of a pilgrimage.
The most notable features in the church's harmonious interior are the chancel, the six low-relief sculptures in white stone recounting the church's history and the splendid pulpit.
Chièvres – This little town belonged to the Egmonts in the 17C; one of the family members was beheaded in Brussels in 1568.
The 15-16C Gothic **Église St-Martin** ⊙ has a bell tower decorated with corner turrets. The church contains beautiful funerary monuments and a 15C lectern. The 15C **tour de Gavre** is a remnant of the old ramparts. The tower's brick gable can be seen from the church.
La Ladrerie is a pretty Romanesque chapel just outside the town in a farmyard in the Hunelle Valley. It was once part of a leper-hospital *(ladrerie)*.

Cambron-Casteau – The Cistercian **abbey** in Cambron-Casteau, founded in the 12C under the aegis of St Bernard, was one of the most prosperous in the land. It was rebuilt in the 18C, then destroyed by decree during the French Revolution. Only the ruins now remain.

The Classical style entrance of the **Parc Paradisio** ⊙ lies at the end of an avenue lined with lime trees. The abbey farm lies on the right of the entrance to the park. The buildings include a strange barn ("charril") that was once used to garage the farm carts. Above the barn is a dovecot. The park is dominated by the tall **tower** (54m – 177ft) of the abbey church. The four tombs with recesses containing recumbant figures, also in the church, recall that this was once a cemetery for Hainaut's nobility during the Middle Ages.

The surrounding gardens planted with trees several centuries old contain an ornithological park which harbours over 2,500 birds of a very wide range of different species, including parrots, cranes, storks, ibis, penguins, ducks and owls. The birds are kept in **large aviaries** (1 500 and 3 000m^2 – 16 140 and 32 280sq ft) in the dip of reconstituted marshland or quite simply live on the three lakes that can be seen from an impressive winding **flight of steps** (18C) edged with balustrades.

★**Attre** – *See below.*

ATTRE ★

Hainaut
Michelin maps 409 E4 or 213 fold 17 Local map opposite

Attre has a delightful château, which was built in 1752 by the Count of Gomegnies and finished by his son, Chamberlain to Emperor Joseph II. Its remarkably harmonious interior decoration is still intact.

★**Château** ⊙ – Four columns from Cambron-Casteau Abbey's rood-screen stand in front of the entrance. Two sphinxes with female busts frame the doorway.

The vestibule also served as a chapel; an altar has been set up in one of the corners. The very ornate handrail of the stairs is said to have been designed by 17C Parisian architect Blondel.

Many works of art and valuable collections adorn the rooms, including paintings by Snyders. The architect Dewez designed the remarkable parquet floors. Lovely 18C paintings attributed to Hubert Robert decorate the panelling of the main drawing room, in which there is also some very fine moulded plasterwork by the Italian Ferrari family. The Archducal Room is hung with the first painted wallpaper ever imported to Belgium (1760). The armchairs are covered in matching chintz. Chinese silk hangings decorate the Chinese Room's walls and seats.

Park – The Dender cuts across this very beautiful park. There is a 17C dovecot near the castle. The park's principal point of interest is the artificial rock, 24m – 79ft high, pierced by underground passageways. It was built for the Arch-Duchess Mary Christine of Saxony, who governed the Low Countries with her spouse Albert of Saxony. She used the little pavilion at the top as a hunting lodge.

AUDENARDE ★

See OUDENAARDE

Abbaye d'AULNE ★

Hainaut
Michelin maps 409 G4 or 214 fold 3 12km – 7.5 miles southwest of Charleroi

The imposing ruins of **Aulne Abbey** ⊙ stand at the end of the verdant Sambre Valley. This monastery, founded in the 7C by St Landelin in a spot surrounded by alders, was a daughter-house of Lobbes Abbey. A community of Cistercians from Clairvaux settled here in 1147. The abbey was burned down in 1794 and later restored to become the Herset Hospice in 1896; it was named after the founder, who was also the last abbot of Aulne.

Main courtyard – The stables are on the left and frame the 18C arcaded coachhouse. Next comes the 18C reception hall used by the Prince-Bishops of Liège. The guest quarters were at the back, where the abbot's palace was before 1767; only a tower remains.

Note on the right the late-18C arcades of the abbot's palace, as well as the west front of the church.

Église abbatiale – The imposing 16C Gothic abbey church is hidden behind a classical façade (1728). It still has its very beautiful chancel and transept; notice the tracery in the window in the south transept. The north transept leads first to the vestry, then the 18C chapter-house looking out on what little remains of the cloisters; both the vestry and chapter-house had the monks' dorters over them.

Take the path on the right to reach the part of the abbey where the old monks lived (on the left) and the infirmary (at the end, on the right). There is a remarkable view of the soaring majestic lines of the church formed by the **east end** and **transept★★** with immense lancet windows.

Go back the same way towards the cloisters. On the right is one of the refectories dating from the 18C, with very pretty vaulting made of spherical bricks supported in the centre by flared columns. This was the everyday refectory, called the "lean" one because no meat was eaten here.

AVERBODE ★
Vlaams-Brabant
Michelin maps 409 H2 or 213 fold 8 9km – 5.5 miles northwest of Diest

The Premonstratensians occupy Averbode Abbey which was founded by the Order in 1134-1135 in an area of pine forest where the three provinces of Antwerp, Limburg and Brabant meet. Besides traditional activities, the Fathers now run a retirement home as well as a publishing house producing books and weekly publications. Chamber music concerts are held here every year in the spring.

★ABBEY

Enter the courtyard through the 14C porch, surmounted by a ferruginous sandstone building, decorated with statues in Gothic niches. The abbot's house at the far end of the courtyard was rebuilt in the 18C style.

★**Church** – This beautiful abbey church, built from 1664 to 1672 by Van den Eynde, resembles those in Grimbergen and Ninove.

The Premonstratensians

This religious Order was founded by **St Norbert**. In 1120 he established the first community of the Order which he based on the Rule of St Augustine, at Prémontré near Laon in France. The Order spread rapidly to the old Low Countries where it was a great success. This is still one of Belgium's largest orders, the principal abbeys being Averbode, Parc and Tongerlo. The Premonstratensians, or Norbertines, are regular canons. While living in their community, they devote themselves to apostleship, which they conduct mostly in the parishes. They dress in white habits.

The façade with undulating lines displays the statues of St Norbert on the right and St John the Baptist, patron of the abbey, on the left. The interior has majestic proportions. The chancel is longer than the nave and is separated from it by two altarpieces which once formed the rood-screen. Visitors can see the richly carved 17C stalls beyond them.

Conventual buildings ⊙ – These buildings were burned down in 1942, except for the 18C cloisters, the chapter-house and the vestry decorated with beautiful 18C woodwork. Interesting paintings can be seen here: in the cloisters the portraits of abbots from the 17C are on view; in the chapter-house, there is a work by De Crayer.

Conventual cemetery – *Between the church and the road.*
The tomb of **Ernest Claes** and his wife lies here. This Flemish author (1885-1968) was born in Zichem *(qv)* and was especially fond of Averbode Abbey.

BASTOGNE
Luxembourg – Population 12 074
Michelin maps 409 K5 or 214 folds 17, 18

Bastogne is on the Ardennes plateau at an altitude of 515m – 1689ft. It is a former stronghold of which a 14C tower and the Trier Gate, **Porte de Trèves**, near the church dedicated to St Peter, still remain. Louis XIV's troops razed the fortifications in 1688. Bastogne has earned a reputation over the centuries for its excellent Ardennes ham as well as for its walnuts. Ever since General McAuliffe's famous sally in 1944 *(qv)*, the traditional walnut festival in December includes commemorative ceremonies.

The Battle of the Bulge (Battle of the Ardennes: Dec 1944-Jan 1945) and the siege of Bastogne – The Germans launched a counter-offensive against the Allied front on 16 December 1944, led by General von Rundstedt, whose objective was to take

Antwerp. The element of surprise combined with the persistant bad weather (fog and snow) brought the Germans immediate success. General von Manteuffel headed for the Meuse, leaving the Allied front line in a "bulge" (from which the battle took its name) around Bastogne which was held by the Americans. Now surrounded, the town became a strategic point.

The commanding officer, General **McAuliffe**, was rudely awakened on 22 December and asked to surrender. His terse answer to this ultimatum was "Nuts!", and so began the siege of Bastogne.

The sky cleared on 23 December, allowing supplies to be air-dropped into Bastogne. By Christmas Day, however, the Germans had advanced as far as Celles *(qv)*; this was as far as they were to get. The Allies threw everything they had into getting the upper hand. The US 3rd Army led by General Patton counterattacked on the southeast flank and entered Bastogne on 26 December. Allied planes were able to prevent fuel supplies getting to the Germans for their tanks. The US 1st Army reached the North at the beginning of January.

By 25 January, the German army's front line had been completely defeated.

SIGHTS

The tank gun turrets just outside the town on the main roads mark how closely the Germans surrounded the town in 1944.

Grand-Place (or Place McAuliffe) – There is an American assault tank on display here next to a bust of General McAuliffe. A milestone from the Road to Liberty, which runs from Ste-Mère-Église in Normandy to the outskirts of Bastogne, indicates the route taken by the American troops.

★**Église St-Pierre** – This 15C hall-church was built in the Flamboyant Gothic style. It has a square tower in front of it (11C-12C) surmounted by a projecting timber gallery.

The **interior**★ is remarkable. The vaulting was painted in 1536 and depicts scenes from the Old and New Testaments, as well as patron saints of guilds and religious brotherhoods. Note also a Baroque pulpit by the sculptor Scholtus; a 16C wooden Entombment, still somewhat Gothic in style; a Romanesque font with four sculpted heads on the corners; and a beautiful 16C chandelier in beaten iron, also called a "crown of light".

★**Le Mardasson** – *3km – 1.75 miles east.* A gigantic monument honouring the American soldiers who died in the Battle of the Bulge stands on a hill, where it was erected in 1950. The final milestone of the Road to Liberty is nearby.

"Le Mardasson" Memorial – The memorial is in the form of a five-pointed star, engraved with the story of the battle and the names of the various battalions that took part in it.

From the terrace at the top of the memorial, there is a **panoramic view** of Bastogne and the surrounding area; at each point of the star a viewing table indicates the main phases of the battle. The crypt, which was decorated by Fernand Léger, contains three altars.

★**Bastogne Historical Center** ◷ – This impressive building constructed in the shape of a star is devoted to the Battle of the Bulge. It contains collections of uniforms and vehicles, and two battle scenes have been reconstructed, one from the German side, the other from the American side.

The course of the battle is traced on an illuminated model and small screens *(commentary in several languages)* in the central amphitheatre. Finally, a film composed of sequences actually filmed during the battle is shown in the cinema.

BEAUMONT

Hainaut – Population 6 132
Michelin maps 409 F 5 or 214 fold 3

Beaumont lies at the junction of several major roads commanding the entrance to the "Hainaut boot". It is a small, old town perched on a hill. Delicious macaroons are made here using a recipe left by one of Napoleon's chefs when the French Emperor stayed in Beaumont on 14 June 1815, on his way to Waterloo.

The Three Auvergnats "Beaumont town, woe begone,
Come at noon, hung at one."
Such was the fate of three vagabonds from Auvergne, who forced a horserider on the road to Beaumont to carry their heavy bags. Once in the town the stranger revealed his identity: he was Emperor Charles V, come to visit the Low Countries (1549). The Emperor immediately had the three vagabonds hung in the public square.

Tour Salamandre ⊙ – This tower on a hillside was once part of the 12C fortifications. It has been restored and now houses a museum of local and regional history.

The crest of the Cro family, the local aristocracy, can be seen above one of the doors, along with their motto and the neck chain of the Order of the Golden Fleece. From the terrace at the top of the tower, there is a view of Beaumont, Hantes Valley and its old mill set against a backdrop of rolling countryside. The park laid out on the site of the fortress destroyed in 1655 belongs to a school.

EXCURSIONS

From Beaumont to Solre-sur-Sambre – *10km – 6.25 miles. Leave the town and head for Mons. Turn left shortly after Montignies.*

A part-Roman **bridge** with 13 arches stands not far from the ancient Roman road from Bavay to Trier. It spans the River Hantes in a pretty setting, forming a dam.

Solre-sur-Sambre – There is a 13C-14C **fortress** ⊙ at the foot of the town, partly hidden beyond the shaded moat. The austere façade consists of a square keep flanked by two great round towers with machicolations and pepperpot roofs.

Rance – *13km – 8 miles south.* Rance was famous for its marble industry and now disused quarry, which once produced red marble of coralline origin. The **Musée national du Marbre** ⊙, or national marble museum, is housed in the former Town Hall. Visitors can familiarise themselves here with the origins of the stone, see the types of marble most commonly found in Belgium, and the techniques used to extract and polish it *(marble polishing demonstration).*

Rance's **church** is adorned with many works carved in local marble.

BEAURAING ★

Namur – Population 7 781
Michelin maps 409 H 5 or 214 south of fold 5

Beauraing has been a famous place of pilgrimage ever since the appearance of the Virgin Mary to five local children between 29 November 1932 and 3 January 1933.

The sanctuaries – These have increased in number since 1943. There is a statue of the Virgin Mary in the garden, under the hawthorn where the apparitions took place; some of the stones the children knelt on are set in a pavement nearby. The **crypte St-Jean** is a little further down the street. Max van der Linden's Stations of the Cross, executed in colourful naïve-style ceramics, add life to the bare stone walls of the crypt. The thick-walled **monumental chapel** is lit by stained-glass windows erected in 1963-1964. The glass façade of the concrete complex built in 1968 to plans by the architect Roger Bastin overlooks the esplanade and its tiers of seats. Bastin's work comprises the **great crypt** and the **upper church** which can hold 7 000 worshippers. It is accessible to the ill or handicapped thanks to a special entrance ramp.

BELŒIL ★★

Hainaut – Population 12 489
Michelin maps 409 E 4 or 213 fold 16

Belœil château has belonged to the princes of Ligne since the 14C. The most illustrious member of the family was **Maréchal Charles-Joseph de Ligne** (1735-1814). This man of war, "the Prince Charming of Europe" renowned for his famous remark "Chaque homme a deux patries: la sienne et puis la France" (Every man has two countries, his own and France), was also a man of letters, as well as being the author of famous *Memoirs* and of a work entitled *Coup d'œil sur Belœil* in which he wittily described château and its gardens.

★★**Château** ⊙ – There was a fortress here as early as the 12C, but the château which can be seen today was built in the early 16C and extensively modified in the 17C and 18C to create an elegant stately home. The main building, which was burnt down in 1900, was rebuilt on the same foundations in 1902. The wings and the entrance lodges with mansard roofs remained intact. They date from the end of the 17C. The château is a veritable museum containing **splendid collections** ★★★ although its interior has still retained a residential character. Valuable furniture, remarkable tapestries, paintings, sculptures and porcelain collections adorn the various rooms. The many family mementoes also evoke 17C, 18C and 19C European history. Certain rooms contain Maréchal de Ligne's personal effects, particularly the mementoes given to him by Marie-Antoinette and Catherine the Great of Russia of whom he was a friend. The **library** ★ contains more than 20 000 books dealing mainly with the sciences. The three large paintings in the Ambassadors' Drawing Room recalling the diplomatic missions with which

Ph. Gajic/MICHELIN

Château de Belœil

the de Ligne family was entrusted illustrate the high points in the life of Prince Claude-Lamoral I de Ligne, who was Ambassador to King Philip IV of Spain and Viceroy of Sicily in 1669. The **chapel** which occupies the former stables contains religious objets d'art and a collection of coral sculptures brought back from Sicily by Prince Claude-Lamoral I.

★**Park** ⊘ – Work began to lay out the grounds in the 16C but the gardens were then modified on numerous occasions before Prince Claude-Lamoral II drew up the final plans in the 18C, on the advice of several landscape gardeners specialising in formal designs. Prince Charles-Joseph added a landscape garden. The grounds are laid out around a superb vista several miles in length, the **Grande Vue★★**, which leads to the **Great Neptune** basin, **Grande pièce d'eau de Neptune**, an ornamental lake covering an area of 16 hectares – 40 acres adorned with a group of statues dedicated to the Roman god of the sea (1761). Around the ornamental lake are alternating arbours and ponds providing an enticing setting for a stroll.

EXCURSION

Archéosite d'Aubechies ⊘ – *6km – 3.75 miles west on the 526, then turn right at Ellignies.* After years of productive excavation on the archeological site in Aubechies and the surrounding area, archeologists have reconstructed the various types of dwellings which succeeded one another from the early Neolithic period until the days of the Gauls. The six wattle and daub houses with their furnishings and utensils give the visitor a good idea of life at the time. The first, very large buildings were in fact communal dwellings; single-family homes did not come into existence until the Bronze Age.

The **Roman house** in the centre of the village of Aubechies, beyond the Scaldian Romanesque **church** (late 11C-early 12C) was built according to the plan of a 2C villa and now contains the finds unearthed during excavations of Gallo-Roman sites.

BINCHE★

Hainaut – Population 28 020
Michelin maps 409 F 4 or 214 fold 3
Town plan in the current Michelin Red Guide Benelux

Binche lies in the heart of Hainaut province, on an escarpment which was once encircled by a meander of the River Samme. It is a quiet picturesque village, still ringed by its 12C-14C walls bristling with 27 towers. The town suffered in 1554 under the troops of King Henri II of France, adversary of Emperor Charles V. Binche's economy is based on local trade, crafts linked to the production of the carnival costumes, and the off-the-peg clothes industry.

★★**Carnival** – Events are organised from January onwards: rehearsals for the drum-corps, followed by four Sundays when the future "Gilles" can be seen wearing their *"apertintailles"* (belts hung with bells).

BINCHE

The *"trouilles de nouilles"* ball takes place during the night of the Monday before Quinquagesima Sunday.

From 1000 onwards on **Quinquagesima Sunday** hundreds of people in fancy dress dance to the music of violas, barrel organs, accordions and drums. The high point of the afternoon is the parade of 1 500 local dancers. Monday is the day for groups of young people.

The Gilles – **Shrove Tuesday** is the only day when people "play the Gille" in Binche. A "Gille" never leaves his home town. The legendary Gilles appear any time from dawn onwards. Large or small, they all wear a linen costume decorated with heraldic lions, trimmed with ribbons and brilliantly white lace, and including two humps, one on the chest and one on the back. Wearing a belt of bells and clogs on their feet, they brandish a bundle of sticks *("ramon")* to ward off the evil spirits. Like the Pierrots,

Sailors and young beribboned Country-Folk, they can be seen in the streets of the town dancing slowly to the beat of the drum as they go to join their brotherhood. At about 10am they dance on Grand-Place, wearing wax masks with green spectacles. They parade through the town in the afternoon, sporting their magnificent ostrich-feather hats, delving into a basket for oranges to throw at and to the people they know (the windows along the route have been protected with grilles). This is followed by the **round dance** on Grand-Place, which is by this time packed with people.

The event is repeated at 7pm by the light of flares and ends in a glorious fireworks displays. The Gilles dance all night, escorted by the town's inhabitants. Tradition has it that the Gilles may drink nothing but champagne.

In 1872 these customs were said to be connected with the celebrations given in August 1549 by Mary of Hungary, Governor of the Low Countries, in honour of her

Gilles

brother Emperor Charles V, who had come to present his son, the future Philip II, to the country's nobility. The present Gilles are said to be descendants of the Indians crowned with feathers, who were said to have been brought before the emperor in honour of his recent conquest of Peru.

In fact Binche's carnival dates back at least as far as the 14C. The Gille is a serious figure cloaked in ritual. The customs (the dance of masked men, women are excluded; the giving of oranges – bread used to be given; the carrying of the *"ramon"*, the belt of bells) are all of very ancient origin, dating back to the days when dance had a religious and magical meaning.

★**OLD TOWN** *time: allow 1 hour 30min*

Grand-Place – The main square is the site of the **Town Hall** which was altered in the 16C by Mons sculptor and architect Jacques Du Broeucq. The belfry with its onion dome was a later addition.

Walk along the narrow street to the right of the Town Hall.

Follow the ramparts to the right around St George's Tower. It is the southern section of the town walls that are the most impressive.

Return via the postern gate known as the Posty.

The **Chapelle St-André** ⊘ (1537), which stands in the old cemetery on the left, contains sculpted modillions vividly illustrating the Dance of Death.

Collégiale St-Ursmer ⊘ – This collegiate church has a beautiful Renaissance rood-screen behind the porch. There is a 15C Entombment inside the church.

Parc communal – The gilded bronze statue at the entrance to the municipal park represents a Gille. The park was laid out in the ruins of the palace built by Du Broeucq in 1548 for Mary of Hungary. This impressive building, which was destroyed in 1554, overlooked the ramparts at the southernmost end of the town. There are some superb views from the top of the town walls.

★**Musée international du Carnaval et du Masque** ⊘ – The International Carnival and Mask Museum is housed in an old 18C Augustine school near the collegiate church. The museum collections take the visitor from carnival to carnival, from festival to festival, through many countries. The **mask collection★★**, with examples from all over the world, demonstrates the extent to which human imagination and creativity has been inspired by this art form in every age and every place: from the festival costumes of the South Sea Islands and the Amazon, to the astonishing masks from North America (Red Indians) and Africa, to the theatre masks of Asia and the often macabre masks of Latin America. Another part of the museum takes us to Europe's winter festivals and carnivals in Austria, Poland, Romania, Switzerland, Italy, Spain, France, not to mention the masquerades of Austria, the Czech and Slovak Republics, and Bulgaria. A large part of the museum is set aside for Wallonia's traditional carnivals, especially the one in Binche, completed by an audiovisual presentation in several languages and explanations of the origins and details of the Gilles' strange costume.

Each year there is an exhibition on a more particular theme concerning masks or carnivals.

EXCURSIONS

★★**Domaine de Mariemont** – *10km – 6 miles northeast. Leave Binche on the N 55 in the direction of Brussels, then turn left at Morlanwelz.*

Mariemont Estate is named after the governor Mary of Hungary who commissioned Du Broeucq to build the castle on a wooded hillside in 1546. Henri II destroyed the castle in 1554, as he did the one in Binche, and it was rebuilt and enlarged by Archdukes Albert and Isabella. In the 18C, Charles of Lorraine built a second castle of which the ruins can still be seen in the park. It was burnt down during conflict in 1794. The Warocqué family, a dynasty of industrialists, transformed the estate in the 19C and bequeathed it to the State in 1917, along with a large collection. This is exhibited today in a building constructed *c*1970 at the highest point of the park, on the site of the Warocqué mansion which was destroyed by fire in 1960.

★**Park** ⊘ – The ruins of the old castle can still be seen in this beautiful 45-hectare – 111-acre park which also contains a large number of sculptures by Belgian artists such as Victor Rousseau, Constantin Meunier and Jef Lambeaux. Rodin's *Burghers of Calais* is another of the works displayed here.

★★**Museum** ⊘ – The museum's rich archeological and art collections are pleasantly displayed. Works of art from great civilisations are on the first floor. The most outstanding exhibits come from Ancient Egypt (note the colossal head of a Ptolemaic queen), Greece (a Mariemont ephebe) and Rome (Boscoreale fresco) and from the **Far East** (enamelwork, lacquerwork, jade and Chinese porcelain). Gallo-Roman and Merovingian archeology is displayed in the basement, where there is also an exhibition illustrating the history of the Mariemont Estate and another displaying a large collection of **Tournai porcelain**. The second floor is used for contemporary exhibitions. The museum has a valuable **library** of manuscripts, bound works, etc.

Abbaye de Bonne-Espérance ⊘ – *6km – 4 miles south on the N55, in the direction of Merbes-le-Château, then Vellereille-les-Brayeux.*

A school now occupies this old Premonstratensian *(qv)* abbey, which Odo, a disciple of St Norbert, founded in 1126. A majestic 18C façade overlooks the main courtyard. On the right is the 15C Gothic tower of the abbey church.

Enter by the central doorway.

Pause to admire the beautiful oak double staircase in the hall. A door concealed beneath it leads to the cloisters.

The **cloisters**, which were altered in the 18C, still have their Gothic vaulting. The refectory has some particularly notable 18C decoration. A beautiful chapter-house completes the abbey buildings.

The **church** was built on the site of a 13C construction. It was designed by Laurent Dewez in the 18C in the neo-Classical style. The interior is characteristic of this type of architecture, with Corinthian columns and barrel vaulting decorated with stuccowork. The north transept chapel contains a Virgin and Child, a miraculous 14C statue carved in white Avesnes stone with a warm smile and finely executed dress.

The 1768 organ loft at the back of the nave comes from Affligem Abbey.

BLANKENBERGE ★

West-Vlaanderen – Population 16 813
Michelin maps 409 C 2 or 213 fold 2
Town plan in the current Michelin Red Guide Benelux

This small fishing port has become a large, well-organised seaside resort with a wide variety of activities. Blankenberge's main attractions include a casino, a long pier and a marina. The resort boasts several festivals *(see the Calendar of Events at the end of the guide)*; its carnival is particularly lively. The most popular events of the **Harbour Festival** in May are the folklore procession and the folk dancing. The blessing of the sea takes place in July. There is a famous procession of floral floats in August.

St.-Antoniuskerk – The church dedicated to St Anthony was consecrated in 1358. It has been modified on several occasions. The interior is adorned with beautiful 17C and 18C works of art including altarpieces, communion pew, a confessional, a pulpit, and an organ.

Blankenberge Pier

EXCURSIONS

Wenduine; De Haan; Klemskerke – *13km – 8 miles southwest.*

Wenduine – At the top of the highest of the dunes, Spioenkop, is a **viewpoint** from which there is an interesting vista of the beaches, the dunes and the resort with its old Town Hall rebuilt in the Flemish style. Note the small post windmill.

De Haan – This is a charming, flower-decked resort (De Haan-Centrum). The villas nestle amid the woodland and sand dunes crisscrossed by footpaths.

Klemskerke – This is a pretty village in the region of the polders. **St Clement's**, a hall church (the nave and side aisles are all the same height), contains 17C woodwork including pews and confessionals.
A post windmill stands nearby.

Use the Map of Principal Sights to plan an itinerary

BLATON

Hainaut
Michelin maps 409 D 4 or 213 fold 16

Blaton lies in a valley flanked by heather-covered hillsides (the Grande and the Petite Bruyère). Three canals supply the town with water.

Église de Tous-les-Saints – A tall 13C tower crowned by a 17C spire with onion dome rises high above the remainder of the Church of All the Saints which is one of the oldest religious sanctuaries in Hainaut province. It has retained its solid Romanesque pillars supporting the quadripartite vaulting constructed on an oblong plan. The austere nave is supported by thick columns with capitals decorated with crockets and stylised foliage in Tournai stone.
Note the Gothic statues in the niches to the right of the entrance.

EXCURSIONS

Stambruges – *5km – 3 miles east on the Mons road. Take the motorway and turn right.* The **Mer de Sable** (literally "Sea of Sand") is a sandy clearing among the pines and birches in the middle of the forest.

Bon-Secours – *7.5km – 4.5 miles west.* Bon-Secours is both a holiday resort and a place of pilgrimage. The basilica, at the top of a hill on the Franco-Belgian border, is neo-Gothic (1885) in style. It contains a statue of the Virgin that has been venerated since 1606.
A beautiful forest extends to the east and south, crossing partly into French territory. Deep in the forest lies the Château de l'Hermitage *(see Michelin Green Guide Flanders, Picardy and the Paris region).*

BLÉGNY-TREMBLEUR★★

Liège
Michelin maps 409 K 3 or 213 fold 23

The Blégny-Trembleur visitors' complex (complexe touristique) includes a tour of the mine and the Puits Marie museum, a train ride and various amenities including cafeteria, self-service restaurant and playground, etc.

Blégny-Trembleur colliery, the last in the Liège coal basin, has been kept in working order since its closure in 1980 as a reminder of the miners' way of life. The monks of Val-Dieu Abbey were already mining the surface coal in the 16C. The present shafts were excavated during the 19C. Women and children worked there and horses were lowered into the galleries to pull trucks, sometimes staying there until the end of their lives.

The mine and the mining process – The colliery consists of two shafts to ventilate the galleries, which descend through eight levels to a depth of 530m – 1 739ft below the surface. In these galleries, the coal was mined using the "advancing face" technique which consists of cutting parallel to the steepest angle of the coal seam. The seams could be mined until they were only 30cm – 12 inches thick. The miners worked in three eight-hour shifts. The morning shift was responsible for cutting, which consisted of working the coal loose with a jackhammer. The afternoon shift carried out the propping work, putting in pit props with wooden billets or metal shores. The night shift was responsible for backing (filling in holes with rubble) or caving (making the rocky roof cave in).

TOUR ⊙ *time: 2 hours 30min*

The tour is made even more interesting and poignant by the fact that the guides are ex-miners, describing their working conditions. There is also a film giving an insight into the colliery and the life of the miners.

Puits Marie – The pit's surface installations are open to the public. They have remained unchanged since the pit closure in 1980. They consist of the lamp works, the baths, showers and changing rooms, the compressor station where air was compressed for the ventilation and the jackhammers, and the sawmill where the pit props were made.

Puits no 1 – The 45m – 148ft high concrete tower of shaft no 1 was rebuilt during the last World War. The trucks were pulled halfway up the tower to the sorting station, and the stones were put on the slagheap.
The **underground installations** are reached by descending this shaft. The lift cage stops in a gallery 30m-98ft underground, and metal stairs lead along a passage, following a seam, to reach the next gallery 60m-196ft underground. The deafening sound of the ventilation system and the jackhammer worked by the guide, added to the narrowness of the coal face streaming with water, forcing the miners to lie down to work, combines to give a vivid picture of the miserable conditions in which the "black faces" laboured without a break for 8 hours at a stretch.
They were liable to suffer from silicosis, rheumatism and deafness from a very early age. Added to this were the dangers of pit-gas explosions, rock falls and pockets of water that could suddenly flood an entire gallery.

ADDITIONAL SIGHT AT THE VISITORS' COMPLEX

Tortillard: tourist train ⊙ – This little train travels through the valleys and orchards of the Herve region to reach **Mortroux** and its **Musée de la vie régionale** ⊙ . The folk museum displays the techniques used for small-scale production of Herve specialities, such as pear or apple syrup, cheese and butter.

Provinciaal Domein Van BOKRIJK★

Limburg
Michelin maps 409 J 3 or 213 fold 10

The Bokrijk provincial estate once belonged to Herkenrode Abbey. It has been laid out around a late-19C mansion and covers an area of 550 hectares – 1 359 acres, including 150 hectares – 371 acres of woodland and 40 hectares – 99 acres of lakes.

TOUR

★**Domaine récréatif** – This recreation centre includes the main amusement park, **Speeltuin**, comprising an adventure playground, a sports field and a rose garden, as well as a **nature reserve**, **Natuurreservaat "Het Wiek"**, laid out around a string of lakes, a deer enclosure, **Hertenkamp**, a remarkably well-maintained 10 hectare – 25 acre **arboretum★**, and several restaurants.
A narrow-gauge railway (autotrein) runs right round the estate.

★★**Openluchtmuseum** ⊙ – *Illustration p 300*. The open-air museum consists of reconstructions of a hundred or so buildings on a 90 hectare – 222 acre site. They illustrate Flemish provincial life of days gone by. There are four sectors, three of which are rural and one of which is urban. Each rural section corresponds to a cultural region. The infertile heathland of the **Kempen** region *(qv)* is represented by

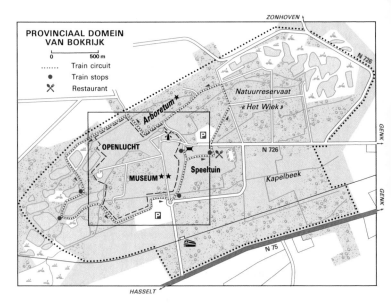

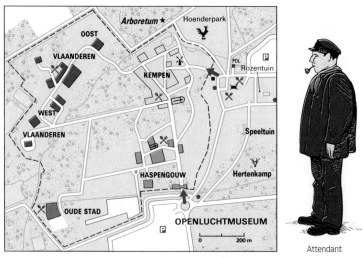

Attendant

a reconstructed village with civic buildings (church, inn) flanking a triangular square. A southern Limburg village inspired the section devoted to the undulating, fertile countryside of the **Hesbaye** and **Meuse** regions **(Haspengouw en het Maasland)**; it has a more "introverted" look to it than the Kempen village. The farmhouses of fertile **Lower Belgium (Oost-Vlaanderen, West-Vlaanderen)** are not grouped in a village. They come from various regions in East and West Flanders, which explains why they are so different. The historical houses from Antwerp (15C-18C) in the urban section **(Oude Stad)** were either copied or rebuilt here.

BOUILLON ★

Luxembourg – Population 5 396
Michelin maps 409 I 6 or 214 fold 16 Local map see Vallée de la SEMOIS
Town plan in the current Michelin Red Guide Benelux

The austere outlines of a fortress on a spur of a rock look down on the main town in the **Semois valley** *(qv)*. The old slate roofs crowd along the banks of the river where it forms a wide meander.

The Duchy of Bouillon – Bouillon grew up around the fortress standing in a key position on one of the main roads into Belgium.

The name is a reminder of **Godefroy de Bouillon,** who successfully ended the First Crusade (1096-1099) by taking Jerusalem. He had sold his duchy to the Prince-Bishop of Liège before leaving in 1096. Evrard de La Marck, Prince of Sedan, was one of the governors of the Duchy of Bouillon in the 15C. His descendents laid claim to the ducal title until it was inherited in 1594 by the Viscount Henri de La Tour d'Auvergne, the father of the famous French Marshal General Henri de Turenne. Louis XIV confiscated the castle, then later returned it to the family; Vauban was commissioned to provide it with fortifications. The town lay on the border between France and the principality of Liège but showed such an independent spirit that Vauban commented on its strong awareness of its sovereign freedom. Bouillon became a centre of liberal tendencies in the 18C, claiming links with the ideas put forward by the Encyclopaedists. The printer Pierre Rousseau introduced many of Voltaire's and Diderot's works here.

SIGHTS

★★**Château** ⊘ – The castle is Belgium's largest remaining example of medieval military architecture. Its existence is recorded as early as the 10C. Three 17C stone drawbridges, separated by small forts, defended the castle entrances. *Follow the numbered arrows.* Vauban's staircase, designed with great attention to purity of line, lies beyond the third bridge. It was built without either cement or mortar.

Visitors then see the "salle primitive", a chamber with stout 12C walls, and the 13C Godefroy de Bouillon Chamber hollowed out of the rock. It includes a large cross sunk into the floor and carved with images depicting the castle's history.

Château de Bouillon

77

Go out into the main courtyard. The **tour d'Autriche** (Austria Tower) was restored in 1551 by the Prince-Bishop of Liège, George of Austria; from it there are magnificent **views★★** of the fortress, the meander of the River Semois, the town and the old bridge to the north.

Visitors return to the entrance via the torture chamber where various instruments of torture have been re-created, the dungeons and the great underground passage which was both a means of reaching other parts of the castle and a warehouse. The water tank and the 54m – 177ft deep well are indications that water was not in short supply here.

★Musée Ducal ⊙ – The **History and Folklore section** of the Ducal Museum is in a delightful 18C house steeped in old-fashioned charm. It contains memorabilia of the Dukes of Bouillon and reminders of the region's folklore and crafts. There is a reconstruction of a typical Ardennes home (early 19C bedroom and kitchen) and of Pierre Rousseau's study. A weaver's workshop and a clog-maker's workshop can be seen in the attic.

The **Godefroy de Bouillon section** is in a restored court advisor's residence; it depicts life in the Middle Ages and the days of the Crusades. In addition to the mementoes brought back from the Levant by Crusaders, a model illustrates an attack on the castle, and a miniature model of the Bouillon fortress gives an excellent idea of its might in the 12C.

Abbaye de Cordemoy – *3km – 1.75 miles west along a narrow road.*
To reach the abbey, follow the deep narrow Semois Valley beyond the old **Gothic bridge** called Pont de la Poulie.

Notre-Dame-de-Clairefontaine Abbey stands in a peaceful setting. It was built in 1935 in the neo-Gothic style. It perpetuates the memory of a Cistercian abbey founded near Arlon by Ermesinde, the daughter of the Count of Luxembourg. The abbey was burnt down in 1794.

Henry van de Velde, a European artist of his time

Henry van de Velde (1863-1957) was born in Antwerp the son of a pharmacist. Painting was his first love and he moved from the Academy of Art in Antwerp to Carolus Duran's studio in Paris where he mixed with the avant-garde artists of the time. Through his friendship with the potter William Finch – who was of English parentage but had been born and educated in Belgium – he was to meet the members of the English Arts and Crafts Movement and 1893 was to mark the turning point of his career. Henry was only thirty when he abandoned painting for the decorative arts. He became a self-taught architect and his first project was to design his own home, Bloemenwerf, in the Brussels suburb of Uccle in a style reminiscent of the English cottage.

He then turned to designing furniture, textiles and other ornaments but they received a mixed reception at the Art Nouveau Salon in Paris. In 1904 Van de Velde became the director of the Arts School and School of Arts and Crafts in Weimar and set out to produce a new line of furniture and household appliances.

Van de Velde had moved almost imperceptibly from arts and crafts to the field of designing where he was keen to introduce a simplicity of design and purity of line – characteristics which were foreign to the Art Nouveau style of the period. He had however some difficulty imposing his ideas in the context of German art at the time, but his decorative arts school in Weimar with its advanced teaching methods, became the famous Bauhaus in 1919 when he appointed Walter Gropius to succeed himself as director. In 1925 the Bauhaus moved to the well-known Gropius-designed building in Dessau. In 1921 Henry van de Velde founded the National School of Architecture and decorative Arts known as La Cambre in Brussels.

His cultural roots were dual, French and German, and his desire to give concrete expression to his vision of art were to compromise him after the Liberation, when he was commissioned to oversee the reconstruction of Belgium's areas devastated by war. The last years of his life were spent in exile in Switzerland. Today he is best remembered as an artist of the Art Nouveau period but he was also a pioneer of modernism in its purist tradition.

BRUGGE★★★

BRUGES – West-Vlaanderen – Population 114 530
Michelin maps 409 C 2 or 213 fold 3

In winter or by moonlight, this is the *Bruges la Morte* described by Georges Roden-bach in his novel. The town seems to have come straight out of the Middle Ages. The houses are built of brick, worn smooth by the passing years. There are also majestic buildings and churches with clear, melodious chimes. All these buildings huddle on the banks of the canals, where swans glide gracefully across the dark waters. The town undergoes a metamorphosis during the summer and festivals, but it returns to its mystical silence near the Beguine convent and the Minnewater.

The great Flemish poet **Guido Gezelle** (1830-1899) was born and died in Bruges. He was a priest and teacher who spent his free time writing poetry. He sings of the Flanders that he discovered in the course of his travels, the region which inspired him to write so much beautiful verse.

★ **The Holy Blood Procession (La Procession du Saint-Sang)** – *Illustration p 37.* The Holy Blood Procession takes place on Ascension Day at 3pm when the Holy Blood reliquary is carried through the streets, preceded by the clergy, the innumerable religious brotherhoods and groups of people in costume. Some of them represent biblical scenes ranging from the original sin of Adam and Ève to the Passion of Christ; others represent the return from the Second Crusade, with Thierry of Alsace.

The **Golden Tree Pageant (Cortège de l'Arbre d'Or)** takes place in Bruges every five years. The pageant recalls the pomp and ceremony of the Burgundian period *(next procession in August 2001).*

The **Reiefeest** ⊙ is a canal festival, held every three years in August, when certain events in the town's history are relived.

HISTORICAL NOTES

Like most of the towns in northern Flanders, little is known of Bruges's relatively late origins (the earliest recorded mention of the town of Bruges dates back to 892). Count Baldwin Iron-Arm built the castle in the late 9C to protect the coast which was under continuous attack from the Vikings.

The sea, source of wealth – Bruges was already a flourishing city when Robert the Frisian made it the capital of his duchy in 1093. The River Reie linked the port to the Zwin estuary. Like many other towns in Flanders, this was a cloth-making community. Indeed, by the 12C it was a major importer of the English wool required for this industry. It headed the Hanseatic League of London, an association of several towns that traded with England. It was during this period that Damme was built, as an outer harbour on the Zwin estuary.

Bruges soon became a great exchange market, selling Flemish cloth and buying fish and timber from the Scandinavians, amber and fur from the Russians, wines from the Spaniards, cloth of gold from the Lombards, and silks and other Eastern products from the Venetians and Genoese.

By the 13C Bruges was one of the most active members of the powerful **Hanseatic League**, an association of northern European towns centring on Lübeck. The League held a monopoly on trade with Scandinavia and Russia. The Minnewater received 150 vessels every day.

Commercial wealth was accompanied by artistic activity in the town: St John's hospital was enlarged, as was St Saviour's church. The belfry, covered market and Church dedicated to Our Lady were built. Bruges also constructed town walls, of which four gates still remain.

The Town Hall was built at the end of the 14C, then in the 15C a characteristic **architectural style** developed with tympana above rectangular windows and many of the doors and windows framed by elegant ogee moulding.

Europe's first stock exchange was held in Bruges, in the open air.

Princely receptions – Conflict began in Flanders in 1280 between the patricians who supported the King of France ("leliaerts", or partisans of the fleur-de-lis), and the **Clauwaerts** ("people with claws", referring to those of the lion of Flanders).

Philip the Fair took the opportunity of annexing Flanders. During the royal procession known as the Joyeuse Entrée (1301) his wife, Queen Joan of Navarre, cried out when she saw the richly dressed citizens of Bruges who had come to greet her, "I thought I alone was queen, but I can see hundreds of others around me!" The people were angered by the luxury of this reception, which they were expected to pay for. At dawn on 13 May 1302 the Clauwaerts, led by Pieter de Coninck, massacred the French garrison. The uprising was known as the **"Bruges Matins"**. It led to a general rebellion in Flanders and the Battle of the Golden Spurs *(see Kortrijk).*

The Dukes of Burgundy began to spend more and more time in Flanders in the 15C. Philip the Good received his fiancée Isabella of Portugal in Bruges, in January 1429. The reception was unforgettably sumptuous: "Even in the smallest house in the town they were drinking from silver vessels." Philip founded the Order of the **Golden Fleece** during the marriage celebrations.

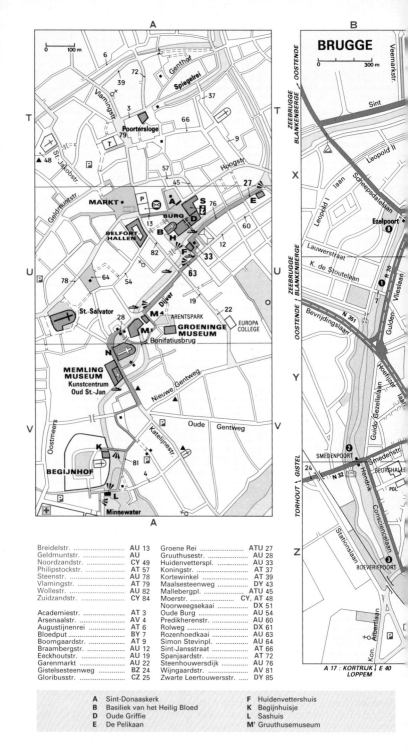

Breidelstr.	AU 13	Groene Rei	ATU 27
Geldmuntstr.	AU	Gruuthusestr.	AU 28
Noordzandstr.	CY 49	Huidenvetterspl.	AU 33
Philipstockstr.	AT 57	Koningstr.	AT 37
Steenstr.	AU 78	Kortewinkel	AT 39
Vlamingstr.	AT 79	Maalsesteenweg	DY 43
Wollestr.	AU 82	Mallebergpl.	ATU 45
Zuidzandstr.	CY 84	Moerstr.	CY, AT 48
		Noorweegsekaai	DX 51
Academiestr.	AT 3	Oude Burg	AU 54
Arsenaalstr.	AV 4	Predikherenstr.	AU 60
Augustijnenrei	AT 6	Rolweg	DX 61
Bloedput	BY 7	Rozenhoedkaai	AU 63
Boomgaardstr.	AT 9	Simon Stevinpl.	AU 64
Braambergstr.	AU 12	Sint-Jansstraat	AT 66
Eeckhoutstr.	AU 19	Spanjaardstr.	AT 72
Garenmarkt	AU 22	Steenhouwersdijk	AU 76
Gistelsesteenweg	BZ 24	Wijngaardstr.	AV 81
Gloribusstr.	CZ 25	Zwarte Leertouwersstr.	DY 85

A	Sint-Donaaskerk	**F**	Huidenvettershuis
B	Basiliek van het Heilig Bloed	**K**	Begijnhuisje
D	Oude Griffie	**L**	Sashuis
E	De Pelikaan	**M'**	Gruuthusemuseum

Flemish primitives in Bruges (15C)

Flemish primitives in Bruges (15C) – Bruges is the cradle of Flemish painting. It was here that **Jan van Eyck** (born in Maaseik) painted the *Adoration of the Lamb* which adorned Sint-Baafskathedraal in Ghent in 1432. Van Eyck used marvellous colours in the famous polyptych, abandoning golden backgrounds and conventional buildings and creating a realistic landscape with a startling sense of depth. He was also a distinguished portraitist. His genius is apparent in other works displayed in Bruges, including the *Virgin Mary with Canon van der Paele*, one painting as remarkable for the richness of the décor as for the treatment of the portrait of the donor. His follower, **Petrus Christus** (died c1473), produced the famous *Portrait de jeune fille* in Berlin's Dahlem Museum.

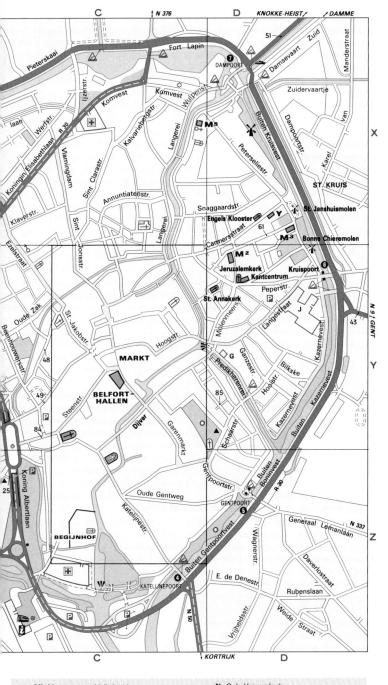

M² Museum voor Volkskunde	**N** O.-L.-Vrouwekerk
M³ Guido Gezellemuseum	**S** Paleis van het Brugse Vrije
M⁴ Brangwynmuseum	**Y** Schuttersgilde St.-Sebastiaan
M⁵ Museum O.L. Vrouw ter Potterie	**▲** Godshuizen

Van der Goes (c1440-1482) worked in Ghent and ended his days near Brussels *(qv)*, but his last and greatest work, *Death of the Virgin*, can be seen in Bruges. The sophisticated composition and emotional intensity are admirable for their rarity.

Memling (c1435-1494) is to Bruges what Rubens is to Antwerp. Hans Memling was of German origin, born near Mainz, but he settled in Bruges in 1465 after a stay in Cologne and perhaps also in Brussels. He completed a large number of commissioned works, including some for St John's Hospital, for the town magistrates, as well as for wealthy foreigners. The most outstanding works are still in Bruges. The serenity of his paintings sets him apart from his contemporaries. This, combined with his warm palette and perfection of the detail, renders his works both charming and intense. He is the painter of gentle Madonnas, feminine figures that are calm, even ethereal. His portraits are often considered more idealistic than those of Van Eyck.

Gerard David (c1460-1523) was born in Oudewater. He came to Bruges in 1483. David was a student of Memling, whose style he faithfully perpetuated, never abandoning the gravity and characteristic precision of his master's works *(Baptism of Christ)*.

During the Renaissance, a number of artists followed in his footsteps including **Adriaen Isenbrandt** from Haarlem, the Lombard **Ambrosius Benson, Jan Provost**, originally from Mons, and **Pieter Pourbus** from Gouda (Netherlands). These were the last great talents of the Bruges school, although a few anonymous painters should be also be mentioned, for example the Master of the Legend of St Ursula and the Master of the Legend of St Lucy.

"Sleeping Beauty" – Bruges's decline began in the late 15C, due largely to the silting up of the Zwin and the decline in the clothmaking industry.

Antwerp soon took over from Bruges. In 1488, the town revolted against Maximilian of Austria and took him prisoner. In 1520 it welcomed Emperor Charles V amid much pomp, a ceremonial organised by the painter Lancelot Blondeel.

The fury of the 16C Protestant "iconoclasts", the bands of "Geuzen" revolting against Spanish rule, and later, the French invasion in 1794, hastened the town's collapse and led to the destruction of many great buildings.

Renewal – Major construction projects were undertaken in the late 19C. The building of a breakwater at Zeebrugge *(qv)* linked by an 11km – 7 mile canal (finished in 1907) to Bruges's new port brought a certain degree of activity back to the town.

The installations were destroyed during the two World Wars and rebuilt in 1950. Since then, new industries have sprung up along the inner basin and the Baudouin Canal including glass works, mechanical engineering plants, chemical products and television assembly plants.

Bruges is very well-known for its bobbin lace.

The city is also a major educational centre thanks to the presence of the **Collège d'Europe** (**AU**), which was founded in 1949 and offers post graduates courses on European law, politics and economics.

TIPS FOR BRUGES

Try visiting this delightful medieval city out of season (October to March) when the crowds of tourists have gone. The softly falling snow and even a slight drizzle can add to the quiet and melancholy charm of the town.

The **Tourist Office** is located at Burg 11 and is open weekdays April to September 9.30am to 6.30pm, weekends and holidays 10am to 12 noon and 2pm to 6.30pm; the rest of the year weekdays 9.30am to 5pm, Saturdays and certain Sundays and holidays 9.30am to 1.15pm and 2pm to 5.30pm.

Transport

The historic centre should be visited on foot, so leave the car in the car park near the railway station or in one of the underground parks (see the town plan). The alternative is a **bicycle** and these can be hired from the railway station (special prices on offer for those who come by train), other hire shops in town and even from some hotels. The tourist office has a special brochure "5 times Bruges by bike" for sightseeing on two wheels. **Horse-drawn carriages** and **boat trips** are a more leisurely way of visiting the city but there are often long queues in summer. The carriages leave from Burg between March and October (10am to 6pm), except on Wednesday mornings, and cost around 800F for a 35min-ride (max of 5 people per carriage). The boats all follow the same 32 min circuit on the canals and can be boarded at any one of the landing stages (see the town plan). These operate from March to October 10am to 6pm and cost 150F for adults and 75F for children between 4 and 11.

Accommodation

The city has a wide variety of hotels to choose from, but it is necessary to book ahead when planning a visit for a festival or during the high season. The Tourist Office can also provide information on people offering bed and breakfast accommodation. There are two camp sites in the outskirts at Memling and Sint Michiels and the town has three youth hostels: Bauhaus, Langestraat 135-137, ☎ 34 10 93; Europa, Baron Ruzettelaan 143, Assebroek, ☎ 35 26 79k; and Herdersbrug, Louis Corseaukaai 46, Dudzele, ☎ 59 93 21.

Souvenirs

Chocolates, chocolates and more chocolates or take back a sample of one of the famous local brews. For the purist looking for genuine hand-made Bruges lace try the lace centre, Kantcentrum, in Peperstraat 3, or admire the collections in the Gruuthusemuseum or the Brangwynmuseum, Dijver 16.

★★★HISTORIC CENTRE AND CANALS *time: 2 days*

Visiting Bruges by night (from early May to the end of September) is an exceptional experience. The city, canals and old town walls are shown in all their beauty under the floodlights.

★★**Markt** (AU) – Life in Bruges centres on Grand-Place, flanked by houses with crowstepped gables, old guild halls and the covered market in the shadow of the magnificent town belfry. The statue of Pieter de Coninck and Jan Breydel serves as a reminder of the heros of the 1302 revolt *(qv).*
The canal led to the Markt until the 18C; it was here that boats used to berth.

★★★**Belfort-Hallen** (AU) – The belfry and covered market form a magnificent group of weathered, brick buildings.
The **belfry** ⊙ is a great symbol of civic pride and it is the most impressive of its kind in Belgium. The massive tower dates from the 13C, but the corner turrets were added in the 14C, and the top octagonal storey at the end of the 15C. Above the entrance porch, a few statues frame the balcony, from where new laws used to be proclaimed. The climb up to the top of the belfry *(366 steps)* includes a visit to the second-floor **treasury**. The town seal and charters used to be kept behind beautiful wrought-iron grilles. The **carillon** is higher up. It consists of 47 bells which chime every quarter hour. Finally, the remarkable **view**★★ from the top takes in all of Bruges and the surrounding countryside.
The **covered market** was constructed at the same time as the belfry and enlarged in the 14C and 16C. The four sections of the market surround a pretty courtyard. The arches in the south wing are home to a flower market. Note the old wooden façades just opposite.

★★**Burg** (AU) – This square is named after the castle (Burg) built by Baldwin Iron-Arm.
Four of Bruges's main buildings surround this square: from right to left, the basilica church dedicated to the Precious Blood, the Gothic Town Hall, the Renaissance court record office, and opposite, the old law courts.
One side of **St.-Donaaskerk** (**AU A**) is still standing. The church was built *c*900 in the Carolingian style and destroyed in 1799.
Horse-drawn carriages ⊙ wait for customers here.

★**Basiliek van het Heilig Bloed** (**AU B**) ⊙ – The basilica church houses a reliquary said to contain the Precious Blood of Christ, brought back from the Holy Land by Thierry of Alsace, Count of Flanders, on his return from the second Crusade.
The Romanesque 12C **lower chapel**★, dedicated to St Basil, was built by Thierry of Alsace. It has retained its original character, as can be seen by the massive cylindrical pillars. Note the Romanesque bas-relief of the Baptism of Christ on the reverse side of the tympanum over the door leading to a chapel on the right. There is a wooden statue of the Virgin Mary dating from 1300 in the south aisle.
A beautiful projecting doorway in a transitional Late Gothic-Renaissance style and a graceful 16C spiral staircase with surbased vaulting leads to the **chapel** dedicated to the Precious Blood. It was originally built in the Romanesque style but was altered in the 15C. It was decorated with murals in the 19C.
There is a little **museum** ⊙ beside the chapel. It contains the reliquary of the Precious Blood (1617), a prodigious example of goldsmithing. The reliquary is carried through the streets during the famous procession. There are also two magnificent triptych panels by Pieter Pourbus representing members of the Brotherhood of the Precious Blood.

Stadhuis (**AU H**) – The Town Hall was built at the end of the 14C in the Late Gothic style and was restored in the 19C. The façade is unusual not only for its rich decoration, but also for its sense of verticality, which is further accentuated by three turrets.
The **Gothic Room** ⊙ on the upper floor has panelled ogive vaulting, decorated at the intersection of the arches with beautiful hanging keystones.

Oude Griffie (**AU D**) – The old court record office now houses the Justice of the Peace. The Renaissance façade has harmonious lines, with three graceful scrolled gables.

Paleis van het Brugse Vrije (**AU S**) – The Freeman of Bruges Mansion was built in the neo-Classical style in the 18C, on the site of the old Freeman of Bruges building (1520) which was part of the Burg. A section of the older building has survived; it overlooks the canal. In the 14C the Freeman of Bruges was a councillor responsible for the management of the town's outlying areas.
The **musée provincial du Franc de Bruges** ⊙ contains the 16C **Freeman of Bruges fireplace**★, displayed in the Aldermen's Chamber. It was made to plans by Lancelot Blondeel who was also responsible for its building. The fireplace is Renaissance in style, built of black marble and oak, and decorated with an alabaster frieze telling the story of Susanna and the Elders. The upper part depicts several Flemish sovereigns. Emperor Charles V is shown in the centre, his sword upraised.
The copper handholds above the hearth were included for the aldermen to hold on to while drying their boots.
Take the narrow passageway leading off Blinde Ezelstraat.

Turn round to see the beautiful window over the arch, and the gables and turrets of the mansion once occupied by the Freeman of Bruges.

Take Steenhouwersdijk.

Groene Rei (**ATU 27**) – To the right of this tree-lined quay ("Green Quay") stands **De Pelikaan** (1714) (**AU E**), a low house with tall dormers. It is decorated with the emblem of a pelican. This used to be a hospital for the poor *(qv)*. From the end of the wharf there is a beautiful **view** of the canal, the belfry and the spire of the church of O.-L.-Vrouwekerke.

Huidenvettersplaats (**AU 33**) – This charming square, named after the town's tanners, contains a small column topped by two lions.

Rozenhoedkaai (**AU 63**) – This quay, literally "Rosary Quay", offers some of the most characteristic **views**★★ of Bruges. The pretty **Huidenvettershuis** (1631) (**AU F**) stands near the basin; it was the tanners' guild hall. Next to it is a turreted house. The tall roof of the chapel dedicated to the Precious Blood can be seen beyond, with the magnificent belfry to the left.

Dijver (**AU**) St-J. **Nepomucenusbrug** is topped with a statue of the patron saint of bridges, St John of Nepomuk. From the end of the wharf lined with lime trees, there is a splendid **view**★★ of an old bridge, the porch of the Gruuthusemuseum and the tower and spire of O.-L.-Vrouwekerk.

The flea market is held here on Saturday and Sunday afternoons *(March to the end of October)*.

★★★**Stedelijk Museum voor Schone Kunsten** (**Musée Groenige**) (**AU**) ⊘ – The Fine Arts Museum is noted for its collections of admirable masterpieces by Flemish Primitives. The first five

Rozenhoedkaai and the Belfry

rooms, set in a line, are exceptionally interesting. They deal with works by the Bruges school.

In Room 1 there are two fine works by **Van Eyck.** His *Madonna with Canon van der Paele* is striking for the brilliance of its colours, its luminous atmosphere and its fine details. The canon's portrait is remarkable. Van Eyck includes every wrinkle and wart. As for the *Portrait of Margaret van Eyck*, it illustrates the slightly surly middle-class dignity, the sense of duty and the piety of his wife. The work representing *St Luke painting the Virgin* is an old copy of a panel by Rogier Van der Weyden.

Van der Goes is represented in Room 2. His portraits and religious paintings depict fleeting expressions and a sense of movement. His *Death of the Virgin*, an exceptionally intense and dramatic painting, is among the works displayed. **Memling's** *Moreel Triptych*, depicting St Maur, St Christopher and St Giles is perhaps the painter's greatest masterpiece because of the mysticism, inner peace and contemplation that it illustrates. The works of two anonymous painters from Bruges hang in Room 3. The artists are known simply as the Master of the Legend of St Lucy and the Master of the Legend of St Ursula.

Works by **Gerard David** are hung in Room 4. They include the two panels of the *Judgement of Cambyses* (or the Story of the Unjust Judge) and the splendidly coloured triptych entitled the *Baptism of Christ*. Room 5 contains Hieronymus Bosch's strange and stunning *Last Judgement*, while Rooms 6 and 7 are given over to Jan Provost and Pieter Pourbus, who is represented by some remarkable portraits and a *Last Judgement*.

The exhibition of Flemish Expressionist works and contemporary Belgian painting (Delvaux, Magritte, Broodthaers) completes the museum collection.

Cross the narrow street to Arentspark.

Sleighs and carriages from the Gruuthusemuseum can be seen in display cases opposite the Brangwyn Museum *(qv)*.

Cross the humpbacked Bonifatiusbrug (**AUV**), a bridge in a wonderfully poetic setting★★. A bust serves as a reminder of the 16C Spanish humanist, Luis Vives, who spent the last years of his life in Bruges.

Take the street running between the Gruuthusemuseum and the north side of O.-L.-Vrouwekerk.

★★★**Memlingmuseum** (**AV**) ⊙ – This museum is in the old 12C St John's Hospital. Small **cloisters** housing a 17C **apothecary's** can be seen to the right of the entrance. The old wards contain works of art and objects illustrating the hospital's history. Memling's works are exhibited in the **church**.

The **St Ursula Shrine** is undoubtedly the most famous of Memling's works. The highly detailed images describe the life and martyrdom of St Ursula and the 11 000 virgins who were her companions. It illustrates their arrival in Cologne, then Basle and Rome, their return to Basle with the Pope, and their journey to Cologne where the saint was killed by the Huns. On the end panels are the Virgin Mary and St Ursula. The saint is shown sheltering the virgins under her mantle. Three other works surround the shrine, including two of the artist's most famous paintings.

The **Mystic Marriage of St Catherine of Alexandria** depicts the Infant Jesus slipping a ring onto the saint's finger while St Barbara is deeply engrossed in reading a book. To each side of the painting are scenes representing are the beheading of St John the Baptist, and St John the Evangelist on the island of Patmos. Memling reaches the height of grandeur with this highly symbolic triptych, completed in 1479. Some people believe that St Catherine and St Barbara are actually portraits of Mary of Burgundy and Margaret of York.

The **Adoration of the Magi** painted in 1479 is an important work if only for the perfect beauty of the Virgin Mary shown with her eyes lowered, and the youthful handsomeness of the black king Balthazar.

The **Descent from the Cross** triptych was executed in 1480 at the request of the priest Adrien Reyns, who appears on his knees on the inside of the leaf to the right. St Barbara, a very popular saint at that time, is depicted on the inside of the leaf to the left. The perturbing, diaphonous and enigmatic **Sambeth Sibyl** is to be seen in the chapel. The diptych of **Martin van Nieuwenhove**, with the portrait of the donor and the **Virgin with Apple**, was painted in 1487 and has wonderfully sophisticated lines and tones.

The recently restored 19C buildings house the **Kunstcentrum Oud St-Jan** (**AV**) which organises some excellent temporary exhibitions.

★★**Begijnhof** (**AV**) – The "Beguine convent of the vine" was founded in 1245 by Margaret of Constantinople, Countess of Flanders. The peaceful close lies beyond a beautiful Classical entrance near the canal. The 17C church and the white houses that were the Beguines' lodgings are set out around a vast green rectangle of lawn, brightened by a scattering of daffodils in the spring and planted with large trees. The Benedictines who took the place of the Beguine nuns retained the same style and colour of habit.

Begijnhof, Bruges

Begijnhuisje (AV K) ⊙ – At the Beguine House, go through the kitchen and rustically-furnished rooms to reach tiny cloisters with a brick well. The nearby bridge provides a beautiful **view** of the charming lock-keeper's house, **sashuis (AV L)**, in front of the **Minnewater,** one of the basins in the old harbour. This is the famous Lake of Love. A tower that was once part of the old town walls can be seen to the right. There is a story behind the swans gliding across these calm waters. In 1448 the citizens of Bruges imprisoned Maximilian of Austria and beheaded his councillor, Pierre Lanchais, whose crest featured a swan. Once Maximilian had been set free, he ordered the citizens of Bruges to keep swans on the town's canals from that day forward, to expiate their crime.

★★★**Boottocht** ⊙ – *The landing stages (aanlegplaatsen) for the boat trip are indicated on the town plan.*
This is one of the best ways for tourists in a hurry to enjoy Bruges. For others, this is a vital (and relaxing) complement to the visit on foot. The boats generally sail as far as the Beguine convent to the south and the Spiegelrei to the north.
At the far end of the **Spiegelrei,** literally "Mirror Quay", stand the statue of Van Eyck and the 15C Poortersloge (**AT**), flanked by a turret. The lodge contains the State archives. A stone bear, the town's symbol, is tucked in a niche *(not visible from the boat)*. The old toll house, Tonlieu, dating from 1477, is on the other side of the little square.

ADDITIONAL SIGHTS

★**Gruuthusemuseum (AU M¹)** ⊙ – The Gruuthuse mansion was originally used as a store and processing centre for *"grut"*, a mixture of flowers and dried plants combined with barley for brewing beer. The vast 15C residence built of warm red-toned brick houses a Museum of Decorative Arts at the end of the main courtyard.

The beautiful interior is very well-kept and has splendid fireplaces. The past lives on through the thousand or so old Flemish objects, many from Bruges, among them very beautiful furniture, sculptures, tapestries, musical instruments, weapons. Note the **bust of Emperor Charles V★** as a young man (1520) in the first room.
Louis van Gruuthuse's wooden oratory used to lead directly to the chancel of O.L.-Vrouwekerk.

Bust of Emperor Charles V, attributed to Konradt Meit, Gruuthusemuseum Bruges

★**O.-L.-Vrouwekerk (AV N)** ⊙ – The church dedicated to Our Lady dates mainly from the 13C. The most remarkable feature is the slender brick **tower** ⊙, 122m – 400ft tall.
Michelangelo's splendid white marble **Madonna and Child★★** is on the altar at the far end of the south aisle.
Chancel – The chancel contains the mausoleums of Charles the Bold and his daughter Mary of Burgundy. The Gothic **tomb★★** of Mary of Burgundy, who died at the age of 25 *(see Torhout)*, was designed by Jan Borman in 1498. The recumbant effigy is remarkable for its youthful face, graceful neck and long delicate hands with tapering fingers. The base is decorated with the crests of her ancestors.
The Renaissance monument to Charles the Bold dates from the 16C. Van Orley's *Crucifixion* decorates the high altar. Several funerary vaults decorated with frescoes were discovered beneath the chancel, among them Mary of Burgundy's original tomb. The funerary chapel of Pierre Lanchais is in the ambulatory. It contains the beautiful *Seven Sorrows of the Virgin*, a 16C Isenbrandt masterpiece. There is also a Crucifixion scene painted by Van Dyck. A 15C carved wooden gallery leads to the Gruuthusemuseum.

★**Brangwynmuseum (AU M⁴)** ⊙ – This late 18C town house is home to a beautiful collection of old Bruges landscapes (17C-19C) as well as large collection of lace. Works by the English decorative painter and engraver **Frank Brangwyn** (1867-1956) are displayed on the first floor.

Mary of Burgundy's Tomb

Jeruzalemkerk (DY) ⊙ – The curious lantern tower of this church can be seen from the corner of Balstraat. The church was built in the 15C by the Adornes family, merchants from Genoa. Pieter Adornes obtained a plan of the Church of the Holy Sepulchre during a pilgrimage to the Holy Land, and he used it as a model. The instruments of Christ's Passion can be seen on the altarpiece in the nave. The stained-glass windows date from the 16C and represent members of the Adornes family. The 15C recumbent effigies of Anselme Adornes and his wife are in the centre of the nave. The tomb of Christ has been reconstructed in the crypt.

The **Kantcentrum** (DY) ⊙, next to the Jeruzalemkerk, is a Lace Centre, where the delicate art of bobbin lacemaking is demonstrated.

★**Museum voor Volkskunde** (DY M²) ⊙ – The Folk Museum entrance is at 40 Rolweg, at the sign of the "Zwarte Kat", the "Black Cat Cafe". The folklore and traditions of Western Flanders are remembered in these charming old almshouses built by the cobblers' guild in the 17C. They contain collections of everyday objects and tools, as well as the reconstruction of a domestic interior and a shop.

Kruispoort (DY) – There are several sights to be seen in the vicinity of this gate which was once part of the town walls.

Three post **windmills** stand on the old walls to the north. The first one, **Bonne Chieremolen** (DXY), was brought here in 1911 from Olsene. The second one, **St.-Janshuismolen** (DX) ⊙, dates from 1770.

The **Guido Gezellemuseum** (DX M³) ⊙ is nearby, in the house where the poet was born.

The beautiful 16C and 17C archers' guild hall in Camersstraat, the **Schuttersgilde St.-Sebastiaan** (DX Y) ⊙, has portraits of the guild's "kings" and a collection of gold and silver plate.

The **Engels Klooster** (DX) ⊙ is in the same street. The domed chapel overlooking the so-called English cloisters dates from the 18C.

St.-Salvatorskathedraal (AU) ⊙ – The impressive Gothic brick cathedral, flanked by a 99m – 325ft high tower, overlooks a shady square.

The base of the tower was built in the 10C. The cathedral later burnt down several times and it was not completed until the 16C, the last sections to be built were the chapels in the chancel. The pinnacle of the tower was finished in the Romanesque style in the 19C.

Inside, the nave is supported by tall, slender clustered columns. The triforium and 13C clerestory windows in the chancel rise above walls which were rebuilt in the 15C. The cathedral is richly decorated. At the far end of the nave is the late 17C Baroque rood-screen, crowned by a beautiful statue of *God the Father* by Artus Quellin the Younger. The organ case above it dates from 1719. The pulpit was sculpted in 1785 by H Pulinx. Above the 15C choirstalls are the coats of arms of knights of the Golden Fleece. The thirteenth chapter of the Order was held here in 1478. Brussels tapestries from 1725 hang above them.

Schatkamer ⊙ – *Access via the south transept arm.* In addition to a few liturgical objects, the Treasury contains some interesting paintings. Note Dirck Bouts's *Martyrdom of St Hippolytus*. The left panel of this triptych is attributed to Van der Goes.

St.-Annakerk (DY) – The interior of this church was built in the Gothic style in the 17C. It was embellished with beautiful Baroque furnishings including a rood-screen, panelling and confessionals, a pulpit, etc.

Ezelpoort (BX) – The Ostend or "Donkey" Gate stands in a pretty, shady setting at the end of a canal. Swans glide on the peaceful surface of the waterway.

Godshuizen *(see key on town plan)* – The almshouses, of which there were many in Bruges from the 15C-18C, were financed by the guilds. They provided shelter for the elderly and the poverty-stricken. Most of them consist of rows of low, whitewashed and rather modest-looking brick houses. Each façade includes a door and a window with a tall dormer over it.

In addition to De Pelikaan *(qv)* and the little houses in the Folk Museum *(see above)*, do not miss the houses in Gloribusstraat (**CZ 25**), Moerstraat (**AT 48**), Zwarte-Leertouwersstraat (**DY 85**), Nieuwe Gentweg (**AV**) and Sinte-Katelijnestraat (**AV**).

Museum Onze-Lieve-Vrouw ter Potterie (**CDX M⁵**) ⊙ – The old 13C hospice of Our Lady of Pottery is at 79 Potterierei. It has a similar purpose to St John's Hospital. Although it still serves as an old people's home, part of it is now a museum. This section includes the ward, the 14C-15C cloisters, and the passageway to the richly decorated little Baroque church. Exhibits include 15C, 16C and 17C furniture, paintings, Flemish books of hours and objects relating to religious life and the veneration of the miraculous Virgin known as Our Lady of Pottery.

EXCURSIONS

Plan of the conurbation in the Michelin Guide Benelux.

★**Damme** – *7km – 4.3 miles northeast. See Damme for description of the town.*

Access by boat ⊙ – Damme can be reached by boat in season. *Departure from Noorweegse kaai landing-stage* (**DX 51**) *northeast of Bruges.*

The road runs along the Napoleon canal (built in 1812), a beautiful stretch of water reflecting the trees, bowed slightly by the wind.

St.-Michiels – *3km – 1.8 miles south.*

Boudewijnpark ⊙ – This park, named after King Baudouin, is attractive for many reasons. Two magnificent **barrel-organs**, one called De Senior (1880) and the other called De Condor, are exhibited in the large restaurant.

An enormous **astronomical clock**, the **Heirmanklok** ⊙, is housed in a vast building. The clock was built by Edgar Heirman. It is finely decorated and is brought to life through its many automata, much to the delight of visitors.

The **Dolfinarium** ⊙, facing the park entrance, puts on shows featuring dolphins and seals.

Tillegembos – These woods cover 44 hectares – 108 acres, and include signposted footpaths and a pond. Nearby is a typical inn and an old animal-powered oil-crusher (rosmolen).

Loppem – *7km – 4.3 miles south.*

Kasteel ⊙ – Loppem's neo-Gothic stately home, commissioned by the Baron and Baroness Charles van Caloen, was designed by London architect Edward Welby Pugin (1834-1875) and Baron Jean Béthune, who was also the architect of Maredsous Abbey *(see Vallée de la Molignée).* King Albert and his family stayed here in October and November 1918. It was here that the sovereign promised to establish universal suffrage and the "conversion to Flemish" of Ghent University. The neo-Gothic décor in the house provides the setting for an interesting collection of works of art including paintings, especially from the 16C and 17C, glazed earthenware (faïences), porcelain, etc. Among the paintings by the Dutch and Flemish schools, note *De Burg te Brugge* (Bruges Burg Square), executed in the early 17C. Jan van Caloen's collection is exhibited upstairs. It includes about sixty religious sculptures (13C-16C) of various origins (Netherlands, France, Italy, Spain, Germany).

There is a **maze** (doolhof) ⊙ in the park.

Zedelgem – *10.5km – 6.5 miles south. Leave Bruges on the N32* (**BZ**).

After crossing the A10, **Zeven-Kerken** comes into view on the right. The abbey, dedicated to St Andrew, is a major missionary centre. Its buildings surround a basilica with seven shrines which was built at the beginning of this century.

Turn right at the next crossroads.

St.-Laurentiuskerk in Zedelgem has a remarkable 11C-12C **font** ⊙. Four columns on a richly carved base support the basin which is decorated on all sides with scenes in relief. St Nicholas is represented on the four corners.

Male – *5km – 3.1 miles east on the N9* (**DY**).

Kasteel ⊙ – Male's huge castle surrounded by a moat has been occupied by the canonesses of St Trudo since 1954; it was once the residence of the Counts of Flanders. The Knights' Hall and the church, which was rebuilt in 1965, are open to visitors.

BRUGES★★★
See BRUGGE

BRUSSELS★★★
See BRUXELLES/BRUSSEL

Grand-Place, Brussels

Ch. Bastin/J. Evrard

BRUXELLES/BRUSSEL★★★

BRUSSELS – Brabant – Population 964 385 (conurbation)

Michelin maps 409 G 3, enlarged inset map on folds 21 and 22, or 213 fold 18

Brussels is the capital of Belgium, a royal residence and the seat of the European communities (EU, Euratom, ECSC) and of NATO. This very busy city incorporates a world of contrasts: the linguistic contrast between the Walloon and Flemish communities, not to mention the civil servants employed by the EU who often speak in English. The contrast between urban Brussels with its grand avenues offering uncluttered views and leading to buildings of historic interest, and its mazes of little streets lined with gabled houses. The contrast between its immense parks and the modern districts with their tall tower blocks such as the **World Trade Center**; last but not least, the contrast between the city's commercial function and its role as a cultural centre. Brussels has a highly active cultural life and is home to highly-acclaimed museums, a large number of theatres and other places of entertainment. Music has a special place here, due in part to the famous **Queen Elizabeth Competition** (piano, violin, composition, singing) in the spring. The **Europalia Festival** *(odd-numbered years)* draws on art forms and culture from other European countries.

Finally, Brussels is also a city of good living and wonderful food.

Brussels Conurbation – This was the name given in 1971 to a group of nineteen towns with Brussels, the largest of them all, in the centre. In 1989 the federal constitution divided Belgium into the autonomous regions of Flanders, Wallonia and Bruxelles-Capitale.

The **City of Brussels** consists mainly of the "pentagon" formed by the inner ringroad and the Laeken district.

The area inside the "pentagon" is divided into two parts. First there is: the commercial **Lower City**, which stretches into the Senne Valley (the river has been roofed over) and is concentrated around the Ilot Sacré

Ph. Maille/EXPLORER

Les Galeries Saint-Hubert

and Grand-Place. The other area of the town, the **Upper City**, lies on the Coudenberg and the other hills near Brussels Park. It includes the Palais Royal, the Parliament, the main ministries and the Law Courts (Palais de Justice).

The suburbs to the north and west, near the harbour and the canals, are highly industrialised. Those to the east and south, on the other hand, are attractive residential areas with large parks.

HISTORICAL NOTES

Uneventful Middle Ages – Brussels emerged at the end of the 10C when Charles, Duke of Lower Lotharingia, settled there. He had a castle built on Ile St-Géry, an island formed by two branches of the little River Senne. It was a marshy site, and the settlement was named Bruocsella, a Frankish word meaning "the house in the marshes".

During the prosperous period of clothmaking Brussels developed as a merchant city on the trading route between Flanders and Cologne.

Église Saint-Michel, a sign of the town's prosperity, was built on a hill; it became a collegiate church in 1047. It was then dedicated to St Gudula, the virgin whose piety triumphed over the devil when he extinguished her lantern while she was on her way to pray.

The first town walls were built in the 12C.

A new wall was built from 1357 to 1379. It was destroyed on the orders of Napoleon, and its location is now marked by the inner ringroad, known as the Petite Ceinture. Only one of the original seven fortified gateways has survived, the Porte de Hal to the south.

Throughout the Middle Ages, conflicts divided craftsmen and merchants, but the community as a whole remained loyal to its prince.

In the 15C Brussels turned to the arts, influenced by the merchant class and the Dukes of Burgundy. A magnificent Town Hall (Hôtel de Ville) was built, and decorated with paintings by Rogier van der Weyden. They were destroyed in 1695. The streets were adorned with fountains.

Brussels tapestry-makers produced marvellous works of art at the end of the 15C *(qv)*.

The woes of the capital of the Low Countries – In the 16C the town celebrated the arrival of Emperor Charles V, who was crowned in St Gudula's in 1516. The governor, Mary of Hungary, settled in Brussels in 1531, and the town gradually replaced Mechelen as the central seat of government of the Low Countries. Emperor Charles V abdicated at the Palais du Coudenberg in October 1555, handing over sovereignty of the Low Countries to his son Philip II.

Philip II drew Brussels into the religious strife of the 16C. The merchant class staged an armed uprising against Spanish rule symbolised by the Duke of Alva. The **Count of Egmont** and his companion, the Count of Hornes, died on the scaffold on Grand-Place in 1568. Egmont was the military gov-

> ### The Brussels coat of arms
> The coat of arms consists of a golden figure of St Michael slaying a black dragon on a red background. The shield is supported by two yellow lions, one of which is holding a banner bearing the coat of arms of Brabant and the other the city's coat of arms. Brussels dates back some one thousand years but its coat of arms was not designed until 25 March 1844 in accordance with a decree from King Leopold I. A statue of St Michael the archangel has however been on the top of the tower of the Hôtel de ville since 1455 (it was removed a short time ago for restoration purposes). The saint has also featured on the town's seal since 1229.
>
> Legend has it that Lambert II, Count of Louvain and Governor of Brussels (1041-1063), was sentenced to death by his father, Henry I, for having kidnapped the paternal fiancée. In order to escape his fate, Lambert II prayed to St Michael who enabled him to escape, altogether miraculously. The Count is then said to have proclaimed the archangel patron saint of the town.

ernor of Flanders and was condemned for having supported the Count of Hornes and William of Nassau in the Low Countries' revolt against Philip II. Goethe made him the hero of a tragedy (1787) which bears his name. The work was performed in 1810, to music by Beethoven.

In 1575 the town, which had shaken off Spanish rule, was recaptured by Farnese. The War of the Augsburg League was waged in 1695, and the French Maréchal de Villeroi laid siege to Brussels on the orders of Louis XIV, who hoped that this action would end the siege of Namur. The town centre lay in ruins and extensive reconstruction was required.

Governor Charles of Lorraine did a great deal to embellish Brussels. In 1795, when Brussels was under French rule, it became the "county town" in the *département* of Dyle. In 1815 the city once more became the capital of the Low Countries, an honour it was to share alternately with The Hague for 15 years.

An ever-open door – Brussels has lost count of the many famous French names to whom it played host in the 19C. The artist Jacques-Louis David spent the last ten years of his life here after being exiled in 1816. The French politicians Barbès, Proudhon and Blanqui, who were opposed to Napoleon, all came to live in Brussels. Victor Hugo stayed in a house on Grand-Place in 1852 and Baudelaire gave an unsuccessful series of lectures in 1864. It was also within the vicinity of the Grand-Place in 1873 that Verlaine shot his lover Rimbaud who had threatened to leave him, a crime for which he was imprisoned in Amigo Gaol and later in Mons.

The capital of Belgium – After the 1830 Revolution, marked by the " **September Days**" uprising in Brussels, the Belgian provinces separated from Holland and became independent. The kingdom of Belgium was established with Brussels as its capital. **King Leopold I** made his ceremonial entry into the city on 21 July 1831 (21 July has been a national holiday ever since).

The city has grown considerably since 1830, particularly at the turn of the century. The Université Libre was founded in 1834. Europe's first railway began operating in 1835, running from the Gare de l'Allée Verte (Brussels-Mechelen). The Congress Column was erected in 1859 to commemorate the National Congress which established Belgium's first constitution.

King Leopold II (1865-1909) launched several major projects which gave the town a new look. Anspach, who was to Brussels what Haussmann was to Paris, oversaw the building of the great central avenues. Several parks were created, including Laeken. A number of impressive buildings were erected, including: the Palais du Cinquantenaire with its arcade and the Tervuren Museum, both of them linked by Avenue de Tervuren; the basilica church on Koekelberg, which was completed in 1970. It stands on the grandiose Avenue Léopold-II.

Among the countless other notable buildings are the Musée d'Art Ancien, the Bourse de Commerce, the Théâtre de la Monnaie, and the Law Courts. The façade of the Palais Royal dates from this period.

Expansion after the First World War – The building of the **Jonction,** an underground tramway linking the Gare du Midi to the Gare du Nord which was inaugurated in 1952, transformed the district in between the Upper and Lower Cities. New architectural projects were launched such as the Banque Nationale and the Cité administrative (1958-1984), and the Mont des Arts district was created in an architecturally modernistic setting.

TIPS FOR BRUSSELS
Tourist information

The **TIB** (Office de Tourisme et d'Information de Bruxelles), Hôtel de Ville, Grand-Place, 1000 Brussels, ☎ (02) 513 89 40 is open daily 9am to 6pm, closed Sundays during winter and over the Christmas and New Year period. The tourist office provides a wide range of tourist products including a practical guide to Brussels called *Bruxelles Guide and Map.*

The **Belgian Tourist Office** at 61 Rue du Marché-aux-Herbes, 1000 Brussels, ☎ (02) 504 03 90 also provides visitors with literature about Brussels.

For a stay of several days the **Tourist Pass** is a must. The pass offers discount vouchers for numerous museums and attractions and free travel for a day on the public transport system. Buy the passport at your hotel or the TIB.

Public transport

Brussels has a well integrated transport network, where the two underground lines (indicated by a blue sign bearing a white "M"), are linked up with the 15 tram lines, some of which use tunnels to avoid the heavy traffic, and the numerous bus routes. A single ticket costs 50F, a 5-trip card costs 230F and a 10-trip card 305F. Your ticket or card must be stamped when you get onto a bus or go into a station.

Guided tours

The following organisations provide guided tours:

– **ARAU,** 55 Boulevard A Max, 1000 Brussels, ☎ (02) 219 33 45. This association offers tours-on-a-theme including Brussels 1900 (Art Nouveau), Brussels 1930 (Art Deco), a different view of Brussels, etc.

– **Arcadia,** 58 Rue Henri-Wafelaerts, 1060 Brussels, ☎ (02) 534 38 19. Theme tours.

– **De Boeck Sightseeingtours,** 8 Rue de la Colline, 1000 Brussels, ☎ (02) 513 77 44. Coach tours of the city.

– **La Fonderie,** 27 Rue Ransfort, 1080 Brussels, ☎ (02) 539 04 34). Industrial sightseeing tours on foot, by coach or by boat. Tours of Brussels' harbour and companies at work.

– **Itinéraires,** 157 Rue Hôtel des Monnaies, 1060 Brussels, ☎ (02) 539 04 34. Guided tours on a theme.

– **Pro vélo,** 32A Rue Ernest-Solvay, 1050 Brussels, ☎ (02) 502 73 55. Sightseeing tours by bike (high season only).

– **TIB,** Hôtel de Ville, Grand-Place, 1000 Brussels, ☎ (02) 513 89 40. Guided tours for individual sightseers in the summer months.

Markets

The Grand-Place is the magnificent setting for a daily flower market but on Sunday flowers give way to birds. An antiques market takes place every Saturday and Sunday morning on Grand Sablon and a flea market is held on Jeu de Balle not far from Grand-Place.

Useful phone numbers:

– Ambulance and fire brigade: 100
– Police and Gendarmerie: 101
– Doctors and Chemists on call: 479 18 18
– Dentists on call: 426 10 26
– Weather Forecast: 0900 27 003.

Brussels in detail

The new Michelin Green Guide to Brussels provides all you want to know about the Belgian capital in the usual handy format.

The various buildings constituting the Palais du Centenaire had already been built in the exhibition grounds on the Heysel plateau for the 1935 World Fair. The Atomium and the inner ring of the underground following the **inner ringroad** (petite ceinture) were built for the second **World Fair** in 1958.

A plethora of civic and private buildings has contributed to the city's modernisation since then. They include: the Royal Library (1969), the Centre européen du Berlaymont (1967), the building housing the Central Post Office and the city's administrative services (1971) and the Musée d'Art moderne (1978-1984).

The recently refurbished Forest-National sports and entertainments complex (1970) in Forest hosts concerts, shows and sporting events. The ultra-modern, well-equipped medical faculty of the Université Catholique de Louvain-la-Neuve *(qv)*, with its teaching hospital, was built in Woluwe-St-Lambert.

Brussels develops a new look – Nowadays, outside the "Ilot sacré" around the Grand-Place and its old buildings, Brussels is implementing extensive reconstruction projects.

Huge tower blocks have been erected west of the Gare du Nord, including the **World Trade Center** (**FQ**) and the Manhattan Center. The National Theatre is housed in the skyscraper known as the Centre International Rogier on **Place Rogier** (**FQ 213**). In nearby Rue Neuve is the City 2 shopping centre (**FQ**) which has been built partly underground.

Brussels is currently concentrating on the preservation of its architectural heritage and has undertaken the renovation of existing old buildings.

A project to improve the public transport system is also underway to complete urban development.

The "Ommegang" Procession

Hudder/EUREKA SLIDE

Together, the current underground system and the underground tramway network cover 40km – 25 miles and they are continuing to expand. Belgium's great artists have been commissioned to decorate the underground stations.

Traditions – The people of Brussels are faithful to their traditional folklore festivals, such as **Ommegang** *(see below)* or the planting of the Meyboom *(qv)*, and to their open-air markets, especially the bird market on Grand-Place, the antiques and book market on Place du Grand-Sablon, and the flea market on Place du Jeu-de-Balle.

The Ommegang Procession

In days gone by, every major town in Flanders or Wallonia celebrated the anniversary of its founding by a procession symbolising its splendour, morals and enthusiasm. The civilian, religious and military authorities all did their utmost to outdo their rivals at the *Ommegang*, literally "doing the rounds". Although its origins were religious (a statue of the Virign Mary was carried in triumph), the austere procession which began in the 13C quickly gained a more secular character. Over the years, it became the main event in the capital of Brabant, as famous for its extravagance and strangeness as it was for the magnificence encouraged by the sovereigns. The custom enjoyed its heyday in the 16C and it was attended by Emperor Charles V in 1549. It was revived in 1930 and the procession of guilds and local magistrates is now held on an annual basis *(see Calendar of Events)*. The Albert and Isabel bedcover *(see Cinquantenaire, Musées royaux d'Art et d'Histoire, room 106)* is decorated with a series of scenes illustrating the celebrations.

★★★ GRAND-PLACE ⏱ *time: 1 hour 30min*

The "gigantic square" admired by Victor Hugo and "rich theatre" celebrated by Jean Cocteau is unparalleled anywhere else in the world. It is seen at its best during the early morning flower market in the summer, at night when the floodlights throw the stunning gilded ornamentation of the buildings into sharp relief, or during the bird market on Sunday mornings. Every two years a Carpet of Flowers covers the cobblestones of Grand-Place for a few days in August *(see the Calendar of Events)*.

The Guild Halls – The guild halls were built after the French destroyed the town in 1695 and then restored in the 19C. Their beautiful Baroque façades surround Grand-Place. In general, they have several storeys decorated in the three architectural orders – Ionic, Doric and Corinthian. The buildings are then surmounted with scrolled gables and decorated with sculptures, gilded motifs and flame ornaments.

Every year in July, during the aristocratic **Ommegang** procession *(see the Calendar of Events)*, the Guilds have pride of place, along with the Serments (armed troops) and the Chambers of Rhetoric. The majestic parade, with hundreds of flags fluttering in the wind, is a re-enactment of the 1549 ceremony in the presence of Emperor Charles V and his sister Eleanor of Habsburg, widow of Francis I.

Walk round the Grand-Place anti-clockwise to see:

1-2 Le Roi d'Espagne – The King of Spain's Hall or the Bakers' Hall, topped with a dome and a gilded weather vane representing Fame.

3 La Brouette – The Wheelbarrow Hall for the Tallow Merchants' Guild.

4 Le Sac – The Sack Hall for the Coopers' and Cabinetmakers' Guild.

5 La Louve – The Wolf Hall for the Archers' Guild. This has a sculpture representing Romulus and Remus being suckled. On the second storey there are four statues depicting Truth, Falsehood, Peace and Discord.

6 Le Cornet – The Horn Hall for the Boatmen's Guild. Its gable is in the form of a frigate's poop.

7 Le Renard – The Fox Hall for the Drapers' Guild. A sculpted frieze runs above the first storey. On top is a statue of St Nicholas.

Hôtel de Ville – Town Hall (**H**) *(see below)*.

8 L'Étoile – Star Hall. The 't Serclaes memorial by Dillens beneath the arcade is said to ensure happiness for those who place their hands on the statue.

9 Le Cygne – The Swan Hall for the Butchers' Guild.

10 L'Arbre d'Or – The Golden Tree Hall for the Brewers' Guild. It is surmounted by a statue of Charles of Lorraine. The **Musée de la Brasserie** ⏱ is housed in the cellars. The museum includes a reconstruction of a 17C brewery and all the equipment for preparing beer. A brand new display explains the latest brewing techniques.

13-19 Maison des ducs de Brabant – The Dukes of Brabant Hall with its an impressive façade (1698), surmounted by a beautiful carved pediment and an attic storey in the manner of Palladio style, houses six guild halls. A row of busts representing the Dukes of Brabant decorates the pilasters.

24-25 La Chaloupe d'Or – The Golden Boat Hall for the Tailors' Guild.

26-27 Le Pigeon – The Pigeon Hall for the Painters' Guild. This is where Victor Hugo stayed in 1852.

28 La chambrette de l'Amman – The Amman's Garret. The "amman" was a magistrate representing the Duke of Brabant.

GUILD HALLS	
1-2	Le Roi d'Espagne
3	La Brouette
4	Le Sac
5	La Louve
6	Le Cornet
7	Le Renard
8	L'Étoile
9	Le Cygne
10	L'Arbre d'Or
24-25	La Chaloupe d'Or
26-27	Le Pigeon
28	La chambrette de l'Amman

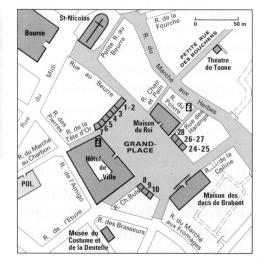

Carpet of Flowers on Grand-Place

Hôtel de ville (**H**) ⊙ – *Illustration p 26*. This pure Gothic Town Hall dates from the 13C and 15C. At the beginning of the 15C it consisted of no more than the south wing and the belfry. The present Lions' Staircase was then the main entrance. The slightly shorter north wing was added at a later date. On top of the building is a tower designed by Van Ruysbroeck, a marvel of daring elegance (96m – 315ft), crowned with a gilded copper statue of St Michael.

Note the beautiful Brussels tapestries inside, especially the ones in the Maximilian Room.

Maison du Roi – The King's Hall was rebuilt in the 19C, based on plans dating from 1515. This was the old Bakers' guild hall, before becoming the Duke's residence. No king has ever stayed here.

The **Musée de la ville de Bruxelles** ⊙ is housed here. It contains works of art tracing the city's history and its many local craft industries.

Among the 15C and 16C paintings and altarpieces located on the ground floor are the peaceful *Wedding Procession* attributed to Pieter Bruegel the Elder, and the *Saluzzo Altarpiece*, a masterpiece dating from the early 16C. The Brussels tapestries include the outstanding representation of the legend of Notre-Dame-du-Sablon (1516-1518) based on cartoons attributed to Bernard van Orley. The porcelain and silver collections contain beautiful examples of Brussels decorative art. Note the eight prophets from the Town Hall porch, in the room devoted to Gothic sculpture.

The city's growth and various transformations over the centuries are illustrated on the first floor by means of paintings, engravings, photographs and other objects, including a model of 13C Brussels.

The second floor covers the history of Brussels from its origins to the present day. The second room contains the various outfits which have been given to the Manneken Pis.

★★LES SABLON AND LE MONT DES ARTS *time: half a day*

Leave from Grand-Place and follow the route on the town plan p 98.

Rue de l'Étuve is lined with gabled houses, as are all the nearby quaintly-named streets.

★★**Manneken Pis** (**JZ**) – The Manneken Pis fountain, also known as "Little Julian", was sculpted by Jerome Duquesnoy the Elder in 1619. It provided the water supply for the district. The chubby little boy (*manneken*: little man), whose unselfconscious gesture has a certain cheeky charm, is said to symbolise the Brabant people's lively sense of humour and their vitality. The custom of giving him an outfit may have been established for reasons of decency, or more probably to honour Brussels' most famous and "oldest citizen". The donors range from Louis XV, who presented him a beautiful French outfit, to the Military Police, who presented him with a uniform. Almost every country has made a contribution to his wardrobe, which takes up an entire room in the Musée de la ville de Bruxelles *(see above)*.

Manneken Pis

The walk takes visitors past the **Tour Anneessens** (**JZ C¹**), one of the towers built as part of the 12C fortifications. Anneessens, who represented the tradesmen rebelling against the Austrian government, is said to have been imprisoned here before his execution in 1719.

★**Église Notre-Dame-de-la-Chapelle** (**JZ**) ☉ – *Restoration in progress*. This church is on the edge of the colourful Marolles district. While the 13C transept is in the Romanesque style, most of the building is characteristic of Brabant Gothic architecture. In particular, note the alignement of side gables and the tower-porch.
The painter Pieter Bruegel the Elder was buried in this church in 1569; his black marble memorial, surmounted by a copy of a work by Rubens entitled *Christ Giving the Keys to St Peter*, is in the fourth chapel in the south aisle. There is an interesting triptych by Henri de Clerck in 1619 in the fifth chapel in the south aisle. In the fourth chapel in the north aisle, note the beautiful **wooden statue**★ of St Margaret of Antioch (*c*1520). The Spinola marble tomb, dating from 1716, is in the chapel on the south side of the chancel.

★**Place du Grand-Sablon** (**KZ 112**) ☉ – This is the most elegant square in Brussels, surrounded by old houses, antique shops, numerous cafés and chic restaurants.

★**Église Notre-Dame-du-Sablon** (**KZ**) ☉ – This beautiful Flamboyant Gothic church was originally the chapel of the Crossbowmen's guild. The story goes that in 1348 the pious Baet Soetkens, saw a statue of the Virgin Mary in a dream. She brought it from Antwerp to Brussels in a small boat and presented it to the crossbowmen. The church became a place of pilgrimage and had to be enlarged in about 1400. The work was concluded in about 1550 with the main doorway. The "sacrarium", a small richly-decorated structure built to house the Holy Sacrament, was added to the side of the apse in 1549.
Inside, the chancel is marvellously high and airy; delicate colonnettes rise between the tall stained-glass windows. The pulpit dates from 1697. The south transept is embellished with a beautiful rose window. The chapels in the side aisles are connected to each another in true Brabant fashion. Their lower arches, like the ones of the chancel, are decorated with squinches bearing narrative carvings. Above the entrance is the statue of *Our Lady of the Tree (see Antwerpen)*.
The **Tours and Taxis (or Tassis) sepulchral chapel** is near the chancel. This is the family of Austrian origin that founded the international postal system in 1516. The black and white marble décor was the work of Lucas Faydherbe. The white marble statue of St Ursula is by Jerome Duquesnoy the Younger.
Magnificent tapestries attributed to Bernard Van Orley illustrate the legend of Notre-Dame-du-Sablon. They were made to decorate the side aisles. One is on show in the Musée de la Ville de Bruxelles. Another one is displayed in the Musées Royaux d'Art et d'Histoire.

★**Square du Petit-Sablon** (**KZ 195**) – This square is surrounded by columns bearing 48 charming bronze statuettes representing the trades of Brussels. Fraikin's statues of the Counts of Egmont and Hornes stand in the square itself, with statues of great 16C humanists. The **Palais d'Egmont** (**KZ**), also known as the Palais d'Arenberg, is on the southeast side. It is used for international receptions. Attractive old houses have been restored in Rue des Six-Jeunes-Hommes to the north. The **Musée instrumental** (**KZ M²**) *(see below)* is on the edge of the square, on the corner of Rue de la Régence.

★★★**Musées royaux des Beaux-Arts de Belgique** (**KZ**) – The Royal Belgian Museums of Fine Art consist of the Museum of Ancient Art and the Museum of Modern Art (**M¹**) *(see below)*.

★**Place Royale** (**KZ**) – This elegantly proportioned, Louis XVI style square lies at the top of the Coudenberg and is part of the district redevelopped at the end of the 18C by Charles of Lorraine. The square was designed by the French architects Guimard and Barré and is overlooked by a church (Église St-Jacques-sur-Coudenberg). There is a statue of Godefroy de Bouillon in the centre of the square, from which there is also a beautiful view of the Mont des Arts gardens, the tower of the Town Hall and the Law Courts (Palais de Justice). For some time now, excavations have been underway to uncover the Aula Magna, the great state room built during the reign of Philip the Good.

Place des Palais (**KZ**) – This is a vast esplanade, dominated by the **Palais Royal** ☉. The curved, colonnaded façade of the palace was built during the reign of Leopold II. If there is a flag flying, the sovereign is on Belgian soil. The sumptuous **Throne Room**★ dating from 1872, is decorated with huge chandeliers.
The **Palais des Académies** dating from 1823 stands at the eastern end of the square. This was once the residence of the Prince of Orange.
The **Palais des Beaux-Arts** (**KZ D**) built by Victor Horta between 1922 and 1928 stands discreetly to the west of the square, on the other side of Rue Royale. It hosts many major cultural events (exhibitions, concerts, cinema, theatre) and also houses the **Musée du Cinéma**.

★**Hôtel Bellevue** (**KZ M³**) – The neo-Classical Bellevue mansion was built between 1776 and 1777. Until 1902 it was a luxury hotel before being incorporated into the Palais Royal and used as a residence for Princess Clémentine, the daughter of Leopold II.

The first and second floors contain the **Musée de la Dynastie** ⊘ which contains a comprehensive collection of documents on the Belgian royal family from 1831 to the present day. A memorial to King Baudouin is due to be opened soon.

★**Parc de Bruxelles** (**KYZ**) – This is the former hunting ground of the Dukes of Brabant. It was laid out as formal gardens in the 18C by the Frenchman Barnabé Guimard and the Austrian Joachim Zinner, and peopled with statues including the delightful *Young Girl with a Shell* by A de Tombay.

Charles of Lorraine's palace (Detail)

Ch. Bastin et J. Evrard

★**Old England** (**KY B**) – The architect Paul Saintenoy (1862-1952) was commissioned to design this splendid Art Nouveau building (1899) by the Old England company, a British firm which opened premises in Brussels in 1886. The recent renovation work has restored these old shops to their former glory. The building is soon to house the Musical Instrument Museum.

Hôtel Ravenstein (**KZ E**) – This mansion dating from the 15C and 16C is on Rue Ravenstein, beyond Place Royale. Note the façade with its turret and the pretty inner courtyard.

Appartements de Charles de Lorraine (**KZ F**) ⊘ – The palace of Charles of Lorraine, with its neo-Classical façade, stands on the northwest side of Rue du Musée. This is actually the only surviving wing of the building constructed under this governor of the Low Countries. Work was carried out from 1756 to 1780, on the site of the old Nassau Mansion. The Print-room and chalcography section of the Bibliothèque Royale is on the ground floor. A monumental staircase leads to the first floor. Note the statue at its foot, representing Hercules (1770) with the features of the governor; it is by Laurent Delvaux. Do not miss the marvellous round drawing room decorated with a marble floor; the rose is made from 28 different types of Belgian marble. Equally interesting are the five refurbished rooms looking out onto Rue du Musée. The musée d'Art moderne can be seen from the windows, with its rooms below ground level forming a well of light.

Charles of Lorraine

Duke Charles Alexander of Lorraine and Bar (b Lunéville 1712, d Tervuren 1780), brother-in-law of Empress Maria Theresa of Habsburg, arrived in Brussels in March 1744 but left again in May of the same year to take command of the Imperial Army of the Rhine. On his return in April 1749 he immediately won the support of the people because, unlike many Spanish, Italian and German governors of earlier times, he was viewed as a fellow countryman who spoke the same language.

His court was famous for its splendour and brilliance. He encouraged patronage, was attentive to prestige but, at the same time, was also something of a rake. He was fascinated by alchemy. His rule brought the area a period of peace that enabled the arts and industry to flourish. Charles of Lorraine was also Grand Master of the Teutonic Order.

BRUXELLES
BRUSSEL

Adolphe-Max (Bd.) .... **JY 3**
Anspach (Bd.) .... **JY**
Beurre (Rue au) .... **JY 19**
Etuve (R. de l') .... **JZ 88**
Fripiers (R. des) .... **JY 105**
Grand-Sablon (Pl. du) .... **KZ 112**
Ixelles (Chée d') .... **KZ 129**
Marché-aux-Herbes
(R. du) .... **JY 168**
Marché-aux-Poulets (R. du) **JY 169**
Midi (R. du) .... **JYZ**
Neuve (Rue) .... **JY**
Reine (Galerie de la) ...... **JY 210**
Roi (Galerie du) .... **KY 214**
Toison d'Or (Av. de la) .... **KZ 238**

Albertine (Pl. de l') .... **JZ 4**
Assaut (R. d') .... **JY 10**
Baudet (R.) .... **KZ 15**
Bortier (Galerie) .... **JZ 23**
Bouchers
(Petite rue des) .... **JY 24**
Bouchers (R. des) .... **JY 25**
Bourse (Pl. de la) .... **JY 27**
Briques (Quai aux) .... **JY 29**
Chêne (R. du) .... **JZ 39**
Colonies (R. des) .... **KY 43**
Comédiens (R. des) .... **KY 45**
Commerce (R. du) .... **KZ 46**
Croix-de-Fer (R. de la) .... **KY 52**
Duquesnoy (Rue) .... **JYZ 66**
Ernest Allard (R.) .... **JZ 87**
Europe (Carr. de l') .... **KZ 90**
Fossé-aux-Loups (R.) ...... **JKY 99**
Impératrice (Bd. de l') ..... **JKY 124**

Joseph Lebeau (R.) .... **JZ 142**
Laeken (R. de) .... **JY 151**
Louvain (R. de) .... **KY 163**
Mercier (R. du Card.) ...... **KY 172**
Montagne (Rue de la) ...... **KY 172**
Musée (Pl. du) .... **KY 179**
Nord (Passage du) .... **JY 182**
Petit Sablon (Sq. du) ...... **KZ 195**
Presse (R. de la) .... **KY 201**
Princes (Galeries des) ..... **JY 205**
Ravenstein (R.) .... **KZ 207**
Rollebeek (R. de) .... **JZ 217**
Ruysbroeck (R. de) .... **KZ 219**
Ste-Catherine (Pl.) .... **JY 221**
Sainte-Gudule (Pl.) .... **KY 222**
Trône (R. du) .... **KZ 241**
Ursulines (R. des) .... **JZ 243**
Waterloo (Bd. de) .... **KZ 255**
6 Jeunes Hommes (R. des).. **JZ 268**

A Tour de Villers	**M²** Musée instrumental
B Old England	**M³** Hôtel Bellevue
C Hôtel Métropole	**M⁴** Bibliothèque Royale Albert Iᵉʳ
C¹ Tour Anneessens	**M⁵** Centre belge de la Bande Dessinée
D Palais des Beaux-Arts	**M⁶** Musée du Costume et de la Dentelle
E Hôtel Ravenstein	**M¹⁷** Musée du Cinéma
F Appartements de Ch. de Lorraine	**M¹⁸** Musée Bruxella 1238
F¹ Vitrine de P. Hankar	**M²⁰** Historium (Musée de Cire)
G Palais de la Dynastie	**M²²** Musée des Postes
G¹ Palais des Congrès	et des Télécommunications
H Hôtel de Ville	**N** Église St-Jean-Baptiste-au-Béguinage
K Colonne du Congrès	**N¹** Église Sts-Jean-et-Étienne-aux-Minimes
L Église Notre-Dame-du-Finistère	**Q** Tour Noire
M¹ Musée d'Art moderne	**T²** Théâtre de Toone

Michelin maps and town plans are oriented with north at the top of the page

Bibliothèque Royale Albert-Ier (**KZ M⁴**) ⊙ – The Albert I Royal Library was founded in the 15C during the reign of the Dukes of Burgundy. It has been open to the public since 1839 and was transferred to Mont des Arts in 1969. The magnificent collection consists of four million volumes available for consultation: manuscripts and printed material, prints and drawings, maps and plans, coins and medallions.

The building includes the **Nassau Chapel (chapelle de Nassau),** also known as St George's Chapel, which is a remnant of the old Nassau Mansion. This Flamboyant Gothic structure dates from 1520, and is now used for temporary exhibitions.

Musée du Livre and cabinets de donation ⊙ – The donation rooms in the Book Museum include reconstructions of Emile Verhaeren's study in St-Cloud near Paris, Michel de Ghelderode's study in Schaerbeek, as well as a room in memory of Henry van de Velde and his friend Max Elskamp.

The end room contains valuable manuscripts and printed material.

Musée de l'Imprimerie ⊙ – The Printing Museum exhibits a series of machines and printing-presses dating from the late 18C to the early 20C. They illustrate the history of printing (typography, copperplate engraving, lithography, offset) and the art of bookbinding and gilding.

Palais de la Dynastie (**KZ G**) – This building stands on the other side of the Mont des Arts gardens. The **Palais des Congrès** (Conference Centre) is in one wing. There is a jack o'the clock above the arcade portraying famous historic and folk figures.

From the top of the gardens, there is a beautiful view of the town hall spire and also the rows of houses rebuilt in the Flemish style.

Go down rue de la Madeleine.

Galerie Bortier (**JKZ 23**) – *Entrance at no 55 rue de la Madeleine or no 17 rue St-Jean.*

The Bortier Arcade with its Renaissance style décor was built in 1848 to plans by the architect Jean-Pierre Cluysenaar and is now mainly occupied by book shops.

Return to Grand-Place.

★★BOURSE, MONNAIE AND CATHEDRAL *time: half a day*

Leave from Grand-Place.

★★**Galeries St-Hubert** (**JKY**) – *Illustration p 90.* The St-Hubert Arcades stand at the start of Rue de la Montagne. The elegant Classical façade decorated with pilasters was built in 1846 to plans by the architect Cluysenaar. The central section is embellished with statues and bears the motto *"Omnibus omnia"* ("Everything for everybody").

The **Galerie du Roi** and **Galerie de la Reine,** with their Classical elevations, are roofed by round-arched glazed vaulting supported on a slender metal framework.

Galeries St-Hubert house luxury boutiques including a splendid book shop (Tropismes), elegant tea shops and restaurants, etc.

The **Galerie de la Reine** crosses the Rue des Bouchers with its many restaurants and leads into the **Galerie des Princes** on the left, which opens onto Rue de l'Écuyer through a large façade echoing the architectural motifs of the square.

Return to Rue des Bouchers.

★**Petite Rue des Bouchers** (**JY 24**) – The famous **Toone puppet theatre** ⊙ *(qv)* is in this tiny street lined with tourist restaurants.

Bourse (**JY**) – The Stock Exchange (1868-1873) is an impressive building reminiscent of the Paris Opera House designed by Charles Garnier. It was designed by Léon Suys in the Classical style although its simplicity is somewhat overshadowed by an abundance of decorative features. A number of artists including Auguste Rodin were involved in the sculpture work.

Bruxella 1238 (**JY M¹⁸**) ⊙ – *To the left of the Bourse, rue de la Bourse.*

This small archeology museum is situated on the site of a former Franciscan friary founded in 1238. Archeological digs carried out in 1988 uncovered the remains of the old church and monastery, numerous burial vaults, bones and fragments of pottery. Behind the Stock Exchange, surrounded by old houses, stands the tiny **Église St-Nicolas** ⊙ in Rue au Beurre. Inside the church, the chancel is out of line with the nave. Note the canvas attributed to Rubens, the *Virgin with Sleeping Child.*

Théâtre de la Monnaie (**JY**) – This was rebuilt by Poelaert in 1855 and was the scene of a historic event on 25 August 1830. During a production of Auber's *The Mute Girl of Portici,* while the famous aria on love of one's homeland *"Amour sacré de la patrie"* was being sung, the audience broke into a rebellion that was the prelude to the " September Days" *(qv).* The extensive renovation project carried out in 1985-1986 to plans drawn up by URBAT, A.2R.C. and the architect C Vandenhove has managed successfully to incorporate a post-modern section into the neo-Classical building. In the entrance hall the brightly coloured, flowing forms on the ceiling by Sam Francis constrast sharply with the spartan lines of the floor by Sol LeWitt. The royal room, which is now used for official receptions, was decorated by Charles Vandenhove in association with two other internationally renowned artists, Daniel Buren and Giulio Paolini. The renovation work has given the theatre state-of-the-art facilities.

Historium (JY M²⁰) ☉ – *In the Anspach Center*. A series of waxwork tableaux depicts the great events of Belgium's history since Caesar and the Conquest of Gaul.

Rue Neuve (JY) – This is the main pedestrian shopping precinct.

★**Place des Martyrs** (KY) – This urban complex designed in 1774-1775 has unfortunately been left to decline. However, restoration work is currently under way. At the centre of the square is Willem Geefs's monument (1838) dedicated to those who died in the 1830 Revolution.

★★**Centre belge de la Bande dessinée** (KY M⁵) ☉ – The Belgian Centre for Comic Strip Art is housed in the magnificent Art Nouveau building designed by Victor Horta in 1903 for Waucquez the textile wholesalers.
The vast entrance hall is lit by a street lamp, making the interior look like a public square. A bookshop, library and restaurant have been opened around the hall, and a monumental stone staircase with an ironwork balustrade leads up to the museum collections.
An exhibition on the mezzanine explains the various stages involved in the production of a comic strip (scenario, drawing, colouring, printing) The " treasury" is a collection of more than 3 000 original plates by the greatest comic strip writers of all times, displayed in groups of 300 in rotating exhibitions. An area is devoted to the actual production process.
On the first floor, beneath the immense glass roof, the **Musée de l'Imaginaire** beckons the visitor into the world of the great heroes of Belgian comic strips and their creators: Tintin (Hergé), Gaston Lagaffe (André Franquin), Spirou (Rob Vel), Bob and Bobette (Willy Vandersteen), Blake and Mortimer (Edgar Pierre Jacobs), Lucky Luke (Morris), Boule and Bill (Roba), the Smurfs (Peyo), etc.
The top floor of the Centre houses the Musée de la BD moderne which looks at the development of this art form in Belgium between 1960 and 1990.
The Centre is also a major location for temporary exhibitions.

Comic strips

People with a love of comic books will be delighted to find a trail referring specifically to the Ninth Art.
For the past while, a number of characters from comic strips have decorated several gable ends in the city:
– Boule and Bill by Roba, Rue du Chevreuil;
– Brousaille by Frank Pé, Plattesteen;
– Le Chat by Philippe Geluck, Boulevard du Midi;
– Néron by Marc Sleen, Place St-Géry;
– Ric Hochet by Tibet and Duchâteau, Rue des Bons Secours;
– Bob and Bobette by Willy Vandersteen, Rue de Laeken.
A brochure indicating the exact location of these murals can be obtained from the Tourist Office, Grand-Place, ☎ (02) 513 89 40.

★★**Cathédrale des Sts-Michel-et-Gudule** (KY) ☉ – The old collegiate church of St Michael and St Gudula has shared the title of cathedral of the Mechelen-Brussels archdiocese with the cathedral in Mechelen since 1962.
This beautiful Gothic building, the "ship anchored in the heart of Brussels", was built over several periods: the chancel dates from the 13C, the nave and side aisles from the 14C and 15C, and the towers from the 15C. The radiating chapels were added in the 16C and 17C. The façade's two lofty, powerful towers were designed by Van Ruysbroeck.
Starting at the east end, where the Brabant Gothic style made its first appearance, visitors arrive at the porch leading into the south transept. This is surmounted by a statue of St Gudula dating from the 15C.

Interior – *The chancel is currently undergoing restoration and is not therefore open to the public.* The Brabant style nave is impressively austere in appearance. There are 17C statues of the twelve apostles against the columns. On the Baroque pulpit, by H F Verbruggen, are carvings of Adam and Eve being driven out of the Garden of Eden.
Note the difference between the 14C south aisle, supported by columns, and the 15C north aisle, which is striking for the seeming weightlessness of its ribbed vaulting.

The chancel has great purity of line and a well-proportioned triforium with alternating strong and light supports. The Dukes of Brabant's mausoleum (1610) is topped by a lion.

The **stained-glass windows**★ are marvellous. The gallery at the end of the nave is decorated with a brilliantly coloured *Last Judgement*, dating from 1528. The rich blues and greens are particularly striking. The transept is lit by two sumptuous and beautifully designed 16C stained-glass windows (architecture, perspective, relief), executed using cartoons by Bernard van Orley. The window in the north transept represents Emperor Charles V and Isabella of Portugal, while the other in the south transept depicts King Louis II of Hungary, with his wife Mary, the sister of Emperor Charles V. Wonderful 16C stained-glass windows decorate the Chapel of the Holy Sacrament on the north side of the chancel. Others from the 17C, designed in true Rubens style, decorate the Lady Chapel to the south of the chancel. They depict episodes from the life of the Virgin Mary and, below, portraits of the donors.

The axial chapel, or Maes Chapel, contains a splendid alabaster altarpiece (1533) and a statue of the Virgin and Child (c1500), also in alabaster.

Excavations revealed the remains of the forepart of a Rhenish Mosan building in the nave, as well as the walls of an 11C Romanesque church. White flagstones in the nave trace the outline of the Romanesque church, and glass tiles allow visitors to see the remains for themselves.

Return to Grand-Place.

★★★MUSÉES ROYAUX DES BEAUX-ARTS DE BELGIQUE

The museums consist of the Musée d'Art ancien and the Musée d'Art moderne. The central buildings of these two museums are connected inside.

★★★**Musée d'Art Ancien (KZ)** ⏱ – The Museum of Ancient Art is housed in a classical building designed by Alphonse Balat between 1874 and 1880, extending into a modern wing. The museum is world-renowned for its collection of marvellous works by Flemish Primitives and famous masterpieces by Bruegel the Elder and Rubens.

15C-16C – This section exhibits some real treasures by the Flemish school as well as by the French, German, Dutch, Italian and Spanish schools. One of the oldest paintings is the *Life of the Virgin*, by an anonymous master from the Southern Low Countries (late 14C).

The work of the Tournai painter Rogier de la Pasture, otherwise known as **Rogier van der Weyden** is represented by: portraits of *Antoine, Great Bastard of Burgundy* and of *Laurent Froimont*, both marvels of simplicity; and a magnificent *Pietà* (Room 11), its drama heightened by a reddish light. Also in this room is a work by Van der Weyden's teacher, **Robert Campin**, who is thought by some scholars to be the **Master of Flémalle:** his *Annunciation,* which was a variation on the central panel from the

The Annunciation by the Master of Flémalle

BRUXELLES
BRUSSEL

Louise (Galerie) .... FS 161
Midi (Bd. du) .... ES

Baudoin (Bd.) .... EQ 16
Bienfaiteurs (Pl. des) .... GQ 21
Brabançonne (Av. de la) . GR 28
Edouard de Thibault (Av.) .. HS 72
Europe (Bd. de l') .... ES 89
Frans Courtens (Av.) .... HQ 102
Frère-Orban (Sq.) .... FR 104

Froissart (R.) .... GS 106
Gén. Eisenhower (Av.) .... GQ 108
Hal (Porte de) .... ES 114
Henri Jaspar (Av.) .... ES 117
Herbert Hoover (Av.) .... HR 118
Industrie (Quai de l') .... ER 126
Jan Stobbaerts (Av.) .... GQ 133

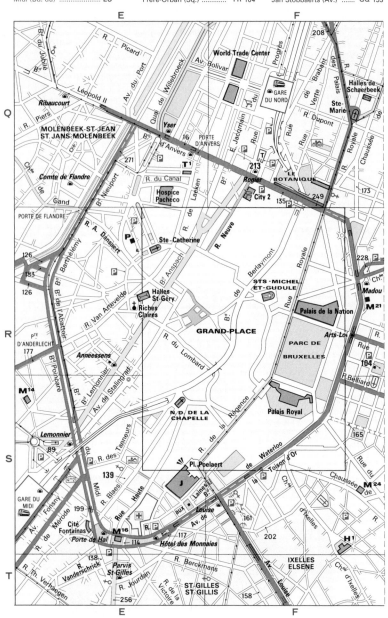

H¹   Maison communale
        d'Ixelles
J   Palais de Justice
M⁷   Musées royaux d'Art
        et d'Histoire

M⁸   Musée royal de l'Armée
        et d'Histoire militaire
M⁹   Muséum des Sciences naturelles
M¹¹ Musée communal d'Ixelles
M¹⁴ Musée de la Gueuze

*For information on the exhibitions,
shows and fairs in Brussels,
consult the weekly « MAD »
supplement in the daily paper called « Le Soir »
(the supplement is published on Wednesdays)
or buy the monthly magazine called « Kiosque »*

Jardin Botanique (Bd. du) ..	FQ 135	Mons (Chée de)	ER 177	Rogier (Pl.)	FQ 213
Jean Volders (Av.)	ET 138	Nerviens (Av. des)	GS 181	Roi Vainqueur (Pl. du)	HS 216
Jeu de Balle (Pl. du)	ES 139	Ninove (Chée de)	ER 183	Saint-Antoine (Pl.)	GT 220
Livourne (R. de)	FT 158	Palmerston (Av.)	GR 187	Scailquin (R.)	FR 228
Luxembourg (R. de)	FS 165	Porte de Hal (Av. de la)	ES 199	Victoria Regina (Av.)	FQ 249
Marie-Louise (Sq.)	GR 171	Prince Royal (R. du)	FS 202	Waterloo (Chée de)	ET 256
Méridien (R. du)	FQ 172	Reine (Av. de la)	FQ 208	9e de Ligne (Bd. du)	EQ 271

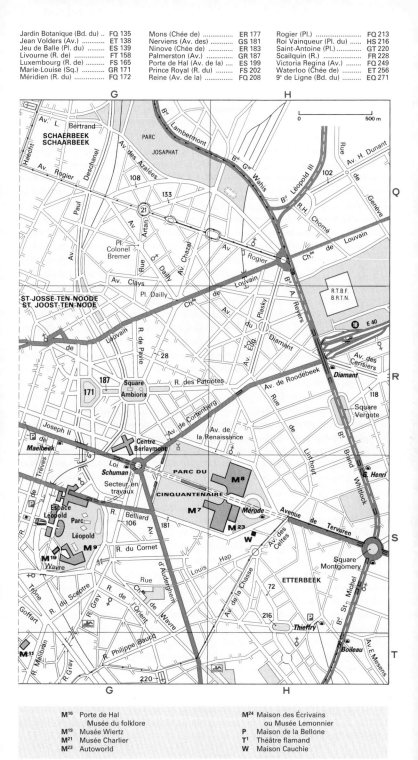

M16	Porte de Hal	M24	Maison des Écrivains
	Musée du folklore		ou Musée Lemonnier
M19	Musée Wiertz	P	Maison de la Bellone
M21	Musée Charlier	T1	Théâtre flamand
M23	Autoworld	W	Maison Cauchie

Sightseeing by train.
The TIB (Grand-Place) or Office du Tourisme belge
(63 Rue du marché-aux-Herbes) offers a sightseeing trip from
Jette to Boisfort with sound commentary provided by ARAU (Atelier de Recherche et d'Action Urbaines).
For information, contact the TIB ☎ 513 89 40 or the OPT ☎ 504 03 90

Merode Triptych exhibited in The Cloisters, New York is remarkable for the colours, the gentleness of the Virgin Mary's face and the precise detail with which the various objects have been portrayed. Van Eyck makes his influence felt in *Pietà*, one of the rare works by his student, **Petrus Christus.** The two panels of the *Justice of the Emperor Otto III,* one of the major masterpieces by **Dirck Bouts,** were commissioned in 1468 for Leuven Town Hall as "paintings of justice"; in fact they depict a miscarriage of justice. Works on display by the Bruges artist **Hans Memling** include the tender *Virgin and Child* and the *Martyrdom of St Sebastian,* with a beautiful background depicting a Flemish town. **Hieronymus Bosch** is represented by a *Calvary with Donor,* in which the landscape consists of chromatic nuances, and by a studio copy of his famous triptych, the *Temptation of St Anthony.* The *Virgin and Child* by **Hugo van der Goes** *(see Brugge)* is on display, a magnificent work with a slightly cold feel to it because of the colours chosen by the artist. The *Virgin with Milk Soup* by **Gerard David,** the last of the great Primitive painters, has a striking intimacy. **Quentin Massys** still shows the main characteristics of the Flemish Primitives, but his works are tinged with the Italian influence, foreshadowing the Mannerism favoured by the Antwerp school; examples of his work include the triptych of the *Holy Kinship* or *St Anne Altarpiece* and several paintings of the *Virgin and Child.* **Jan Gossaert,** also known as Mabuse, was a portraitist and court painter, who reveals a different facet of his art here with *Venus and Cupid,* one of the first Flemish works to feature a mythological subject. There is also a panel from the *Altarpiece of the Holy Cross Brotherhood* by **Bernard Van Orley,** painter to Margaret of Austria.

Room 31 is a veritable shrine to the work of **Bruegel the Elder.** Several of his masterpieces are exhibited here and they bear witness to the range of his talent and style. The *Fall of the Rebel Angels* shows the influence exerted by Hieronymus Bosch on Bruegel at the beginning of his career. Use of irony, realistic detail, and the tranquillity of the landscape, all of which are characteristic of Bruegel's work, are particularly evident in the famous *Census at Bethlehem* and *Fall of Icarus,* an unusual painting in which some people claim to see symbols from alchemy.

The rooms reserved for the **Delporte Legacy** include a Dutch Primitive panel, *Calvary and Resurrection,* the pretty round panels by Grimmer representing the *Seasons* and a lovely work by Bruegel the Elder, *Winter landscape with Skaters.*

17C-18C – The works of this period hang in the rooms around the great hall in the renovated galleries. **Rubens** is represented by very high quality paintings. His talent for large religious works is obvious in his beautifully coloured *Adoration of the Magi,* his *Ascent to Calvary* and his *Martyrdom of St Liévin.* His skill in producing more personal works is manifest in the famous *Negro Heads* and the *Portrait of Hélène Fourment,* which radiates mischievousness and charm; they can be seen in Room 52. A good deal of space is also devoted to **Jordaens** and several of his works are on display in Room 57, including the *Allegory of Fertility,* a lively painting with heightened sensuality. Among his other works are *The King Drinks* and *Susanna and the Elders.* There are also good works by Cornelis De Vos, Van Dyck, Teniers, Frans Hals, and this exceptional collection is completed by works by Dutch landscape and genre painters.

19C – *Ground floor.* This section displays works (paintings, sculptures and drawings) from neo-classicism, Romanticism, Realism and Luminism (*Linen Harvest* by Emiel Claus), as well as from Symbolism, represented in particular by **Fernand Khnopff** *(Memories,* and the enigmatic *Caresses).* Interesting works from the French school (Gauguin, Seurat, Signac, Vuillard and Monet) and the famous *Death of Marat,* painted in 1793 by Jacques-Louis David, are also exhibited here.

An entire room is devoted to **James Ensor,** who was a linchpin between the 19C and the 20C (*Le Lampiste,* 1880; *Scandalised Masks,* 1883; *Skeletons arguing over a Red Herring,* 1891).

★★Musée d'Art Moderne (KZ M¹) ⊙ – The Museum of Modern Art was inaugurated in 1984 and consists of two parts. The building with the main entrance on Place Royale is also used for temporary exhibitions (3 floors).

The Museum of Modern Art itself is an underground building, designed by the architects R Bastin and L Beek, who sank it down eight floors around a well of light. It houses permanent collections of 20C sculptures, paintings and drawings (from Fauvism to contemporary art).

The tour begins on level -2 in the agora, containing a large sculpture by Richard Long (*Utah Circle,* 1989) and paintings by Alan Charlton and Alan Green.

Level -3 is also devoted to contemporary art. There are striking sculptures by **Georges Segal** (figures in plaster moulded onto the models themselves) as well as works by Anselme Kiefer (*Bérénice,* 1989), Henry Moore, Pol Bury, Nam June Paik and paintings by Francis Bacon and Gaston Bertrand.

Going down through the various levels makes it possible to follow the evolution of artistic movements such as Fauvism, Expressionism, La Jeune Peinture Belge, CoBrA, Phases, Surrealism, Groupe Zéro, etc. Other particularly interesting works include those by **Rik Wouters** (*Lady with Yellow Neckband*, 1912; *Flute Player*, 1914), a very beautiful group by **Leon Spilliaert** (*Lady in Hat*, 1907; *Woman on a Dyke*, 1908; *Bather*, 1910), the representatives of the second Sint Martens-Latem school **(Permeke, Gustave De Smet** and **Frits van den Berghe)**, Abstract art with **Servranckx**, Baugniet and Peeters. The Belgian Futurists (P de Troyer and J Schmalzigaug), and the members of CoBrA **(Pierre Alechinsky, Karel Appel)**. The works by **Delvaux** *(Night Trains; Pygmalion; Public Voice)* and **Magritte** bear witness to the importance of Surrealism and Symbolism in Belgium in the 19C. A room is devoted to each of these artists. The Georgette and René Magritte Room contains works which were part of collections *(The Man of the Sea, Midnight Marriage, Empire of Lights, 1954),* as well as those bequeathed to the museum by the artist's widow *(Black Magic Pebble, Arnhem Domain).* Note also works by Wilfredo Lam, Hans Hartung, Joan Miró, Max Ernst, Paul Klee, Giorgio de Chirico, **Marcel Broodthaers**, Arman, etc.

Level -8 is more particularly concerned with contemporary art, with works by Belgian artists (Michel Mouffe, Mark Luyten, Dan van Severen, Bernd Lohaus, Marthe Wéry, Jan Vercruysse, Walter Swennen, Jef Geys and Jan Fabre) as well as foreign painters (Dan Flavin, Don Judd, Ulrich Ruckriem, Tony Cragg).

ADDITIONAL SIGHTS *town plans pages 98 and 102-103*

★★**Musée Instrumental** (**KZ M²**) ⊘ – Only part of the Musical Instrument Museum's collection, which consists of 6 000 instruments dating from the Bronze Age to the present, is exhibited. Wind instruments are on the ground floor, including saxophones, the invention of Adolphe Sax, a native of Dinant. The first floor is given over to keyboard instruments: virginals and spinets, which were very much in vogue from the 17C onwards, and harpsichords signed by famous names (Ruckers in Antwerp) and sometimes magnificently decorated. They were replaced in the 18C by the piano. String instruments on the second floor include harps, lutes and violins. There is also Joachim Tielke's beautiful viola da gamba (1701), which is marvellously decorated. The museum also has non-European instruments (from India, or the gamelan from Indonesia) and some from European folk art.

Colonne du Congrès (**KY K**) – The Congress Column was designed and inaugurated by Poelaert in 1859 to commemorate the National Congress which proclaimed the Belgian constitution after the 1830 Revolution. Willem Geefs' statue of Leopold II stands at its top. Two lions guard the tomb of the Unknown Soldier at the foot of the monument. There is an interesting overall view of the city from the "Esplanade" between the buildings of the Cité administrative.

★**Musée Charlier** (**FR M²¹**) ⊘ – *16 avenue des Arts.*
This museum is housed in two semi-detached houses in St-Josse, which were purchased in 1890 by the wealthy art collector, Henri van Cutsem. After having the two façades combined, van Cutsem commissioned his friend Victor Horta to design glass roofs which would provide the lighting effect for his collections. He then asked the artist Guillaume Charlier (1854-1925) to move in. The artist, who was the sole heir to his patron's estate on the latter's death in 1904, inherited the mansion and had a museum built by Victor Horta in Tournai to house H van Cutsem's collection of Impressionist oil paintings *(see Tournai).* The Charlier Museum contains a large number of paintings and sculptures by different artists, in addition to interesting collections of furniture, tapestries and decorative objects.

Palais de la Nation (**KY**) ⊘ – This palace was built during the days of Charles of Lorraine. It stands north of Brussels Park and was restored after a fire in 1883.
It is the seat of the Chamber of Representatives and the Senate. The **Salle des Séances du Sénat★** is particularly finely decorated.

Église du Finistère (**JKY L**) – This church is home to the statue of Our Lady of Finistère.

Église St-Jean-Baptiste-au-Béguinage (**JY N**) ⊘ – This church dedicated to St John the Baptist stands in a quiet district. It has a façade in three main parts in the Flemish Baroque style (1676).
The interior is beautifully proportioned, with Baroque decoration applied to the Gothic architecture. The entablature above the arches is very regular; it rests on the heads of winged angels at the intersections of the arches.
There is a figure of St Dominic slaying Heresy beneath the pulpit dating from 1757.
Note the marvellous paintings by the Brussels artist **Van Loon** and various Flemish artists.
The Beguine convent, which once had as many as 1 200 nuns, disappeared in the 19C.
Église Ste-Catherine (**JY**) stands nearby. It still has the **tower** (**JY**) from the old church, and the **Tour Noire** (**JY Q**), which was once part of the town's first walls.

Lace making

This art form probably came originally from Venice, although Flanders claims to have discovered bobbin-lace. It is made on a cushion or pillow. The threads are stretched on bobbins and crossed over to form either a net or a pattern. The piece of lace is pinned onto the pillow. The original form of lace was purely geometric (mid 15C) and used to decorate clothing. Flemish painters show people wearing lace collars and cuffs. The craft was taught to young girls in schools and soon became popular. Once the period of wars and conflicts was over, the craft became a source of prosperity again and, in the 17C, Flanders lace enjoyed an unrivalled reputation. Brussels was one of the main centres of lace making at the time, along with Bruges, Mechelen and Antwerp. The schools each had their own characteristics but, until the end of the 17C, the term "Flanders lace" was used to describe output from the southern part of the Spanish Netherlands, ie Antwerp, Ghent, Liège, Mechelen, Valenciennes and Brussels where most of the lace was needle-point.

During the early years of the 18C, Brussels lace became a net based on round stitches. The finer "drochel" net consisting of small, hexagonal stitches took pride of place as of 1760 in order to fit in with the ornate requirements of the Louis XV style. In those days, Brussels lace was the most highly sought-after and it was also the most expensive because it took a long time to make and required a great deal of care and attention. This explains why it was reserved almost exclusively for royal families.

Maison de la Bellone (ER P) ⊘ – This splendid patrician residence dating from the late 17C is not visible from the street. It is now the Maison du Spectacle which is an exhibition and information centre about the world of theatre and entertainment.
Musée du Costume et de la Dentelle (JY M[6]) ⊘ – The Costume and Lace Museum covers the various crafts related to costume-making from the 17C to the 20C, including Brussels lace, embroidery, and trimmings.

Place Poelaert (ES) – This square lies at the top of Galgenberg (literally "Gallows Hill") where the gibbet once hung. Overlooking the square is the immense **Palais de Justice** (ES J) ⊘, the Law Courts designed by Poelaert and built between 1866 and 1883. The main entrance consists of a huge peristyle leading into a majestic lobby. There is an extensive view from the terrace, of the Lower Town and the Marolles district with Notre-Dame-de-la-Chapelle.

★**Porte de Hal** (ES M[16]) – This gateway is the only trace of the 14C fortifications. It has been restored recently and now houses the **Musée du folklore** ⊘. The room on the first floor is quite magnificent with its six massive columns supporting pointed vaulting. The exhibits on the second floor are concerned with folk arts and crafts (old toys, dolls' houses). Temporary exhibitions are also organised here.

Place du Jeu-de-Balle (ES 139) – A **flea market** ⊘ is held on this large square in the heart of the popular **Marolles district.**

★**Le Botanique** (FQ) ⊘ – The immense greenhouses of the old Botanical Gardens now house a cultural centre for the French-speaking community of Belgium. Amenities include a library, a restaurant, cinemas, theatres, exhibition halls etc.

THE CINQUANTENAIRE *town plan pp 102-103*

Parc du Cinquantenaire (GHS) – The park was created in 1880, during the exhibition to celebrate the fiftieth anniversary of Belgium's independence. A large palace known as the Palais du Cinquantenaire stands in the grounds, its two wings joined by a monumental arcade designed by the architect Girault (1905). At the rear of the palace are two halls with metal rafters, dating from 1888. The north wing and hall contain the Army Museum; the south hall the Autoworld exhibition. The south wing contains the Royal Museums of Art and History.

★★★**Musées Royaux d'Art et d'Histoire** (HS M[7]) ⊘ – The Cinquantenaire Museum incorporating the Royal Museums of Art and History has been given a facelift. Over 50 new rooms have recently been opened, designed to blend in with the neo-classical architecture of the original building.
The collections in the Cinquantenaire are extremely diverse, especially as regards works from Antiquity, the decorative arts and non-European civilisations.

Antiquities (Western Asia, Greece, Rome, Egypt)
Western Asian civilisations are evoked on the ground floor (Palestine, Cyprus and Mesopotamia). A **model of Rome** can be seen from the mezzanine, showing the capital of the Roman Empire in the 4C, executed on a scale of 1:400 *(recorded commentary available with lighting)*. The first floor is devoted to Ancient Rome. The second floor

focuses on **Rome** (portrait gallery), **Etruria** and **Greece** (red and black figure vases). The great colonnade of Apamea has been reconstructed as a reminder of the Belgian missions in Syria. There is an overhead view of the famous Apamea mosaic in the centre of the great inner courtyard, a fabulous scene of hunters fighting wild beasts. This floor, created in 539, originally decorated a banqueting hall in Apamea, a Syrian town destroyed by the Persians in 612. The third floor is devoted to Egypt. Note a fragment from the **Book of the Dead**, the reconstruction of the **mastaba of Neferirtenef**, the **Dame de Bruxelles** (an archaic statue dating back to 2600 BC) and the very beautiful low relief representing **Queen Tiy**, wife of Amenhotep III. The fourth floor contains a plaster model of the burial complex of Djoser in Saqqarah.

Non-European Civilisations

The **America** rooms *(1st floor)* contain some splendid collections of pre-Columbian and ethnographic art. Note the magnificent feather cloak dating from the 16C, the monumental seated divinity from Mexico and a double scroll-shaped ornament (Columbia 600-1550).

Collections from Micronesia and Polynesia *(1st floor)* include archeological and ethnological objects which are exhibited according to theme. The museum has one of the world-famous statues from Easter Island.

The **India, China and Southeast Asia** section *(2nd floor)* illustrates the arts, religions and traditions of India (13C bronze statue of Civa), China (2 bodhisattvas *c*1200), Vietnam (pottery), Indonesia, Thailand and Tibet (extensive collection of thang-kas, religious and symbolic paintings by lamas).

Crafts

The Romanesque and Mosan room *(1st floor)* houses a treasure trove of ecclesiastical objets d'art, including the **Stavelot portable altar** (*c*1150-1160) made of brass and champlevé enamel, and some beautiful ivories.

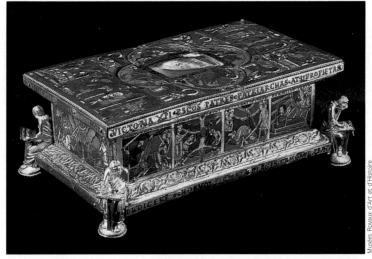

Stavelot portable altar

Musées Royaux d'Art et d'Histoire

The room devoted to decorative arts from the medieval to the Baroque periods *(1st floor)* contains **tapestries** that vie with each other in the delicacy of their execution and the splendour of their colours. They include the early 16C *Legend of Notre-Dame-du-Sablon* and the *Histoire de Jacob*. Jan Borman the Elder's **St George Altarpiece** (1493) stands out among the wooden **altarpieces** because of the intensely life-like figures.

There is some extremely valuable furniture on display including fine Antwerp cabinets and a reconstruction of the shop window designed by Victor Horta in 1912 for the Wolfers jewellery store.

Rooms on the second floor display examples of glassware (101 pieces by M Marinot), textiles, pottery and lace (**Albert and Isabella's bedspread**, 1599).

The **horsedrawn carriages** section *(ground floor)* houses a collection of coaches, sleighs, saddles, etc.

National Archeology

The room devoted to Belgian prehistory *(ground floor)* displays objects uncovered during digs (tools, jewellery and pottery). The Merovingian room *(ground floor)* includes a number of **tombs** discovered in Harmignies near Mons in addition to tools, weapons and jewellery.

Musée Royal de l'Armée et d'Histoire Militaire (HS M[8]) ⓥ – The Royal Army and Military History Museum illustrates the country's military history from 1789 to the present, through an extensive collection of uniforms, decorations, weapons and pictures. The armoured tank section includes Belgian vehicles (from 1935 onwards) as well as models from other countries (the ex-USSR, Great Britain, the United States and France). The **Air and Space section★**, in a large hall, has about a hundred planes. The Nieuport, a small French plane, served during the First World War, while the Spitfire and the Hurricane, both of them British, date from the Second World War.

The **Armoury★** contains some splendid arms (11C-18C) and armour (late 15C-17C) from old arsenals.

★★**Autoworld** (HS M[23]) ⓥ – Since 1986 some 450 vehicles, mostly cars, have been on display beneath the high glass roof of the south hall of the Palais du Cinquantenaire. While the exhibitions include some of the most beautiful models from the De Pauw collection, which used to be in the Manhattan Center Museum, as well as cars belonging to members of the Royal Veteran Car Club, most of the vehicles are from the prestigious **Ghislain Mahy collection.**

Born in Ghent in 1901, Mahy managed to collect more than 800 vehicles (powered by steam, electricity or petrol) over a period of forty years. They were often in pitiful condition when he purchased them, but they were always brought back to life in the collector's repair shop. There are now about 300 cars in perfect working order. Mahy bought the first car in 1944, a 1921 Ford. The collection came to include many American cars, such as the little 1917 Cadillac worth comparing with the one dating from 1928, and with the ones in the De Pauw collection *(ground floor, left)* dating from the 1930s and 50s. There are also many other famous makes (Buick, Chevrolet, Chrysler, Oldsmobile, Packard) and some that are less well known (Black, Detroit Electric, Willys-Overland). French vehicles include the 1896 Léon Bollée minicar, a 1908 Renault 14 continental hp with its characteristically-shaped bonnet, a 1911 Delaunay-Belleville, a 1920s Delage and a 1935 Hispano-Suiza. Particularly fine examples of British car manufacture include the makes of Bentley, Daimler, Humber, Jaguar and Rolls-Royce. Note the magnificent 1921 Silver Ghost. German car manufacture is represented by Adler, Mercedes, Horch and Opel, while Alfa-Romeo, Fiat and Lancia provide examples of Italian sophistication.

Musée Autoworld, Bruxelles - Ph. Cajic/MICHELIN, Paris

Minerva mascot

The Belgian makes deserve particular attention. They include examples from Belga Rise, FN, Fondu, Hermes, Imperia, Miesse, Nagant and Vivinus, not forgetting of course the famous **Minerva.**

Antwerp citizen Sylvain de Jong first built cycles, then motorcycles. This museum contains his 1902 prototype for the Minerva. Although the range initially consisted of only three models (2, 3 and 4 cylinders), it continued to expand until the 1930s. By 1911 the factory had 1 600 workers. In 1912 the company offered electric lights as an option on their automobiles, and by 1914 electric ignition had become available. In 1922 all four wheels had brakes. The firm acquired a solid reputation for enormously comfortable, superb quality automobiles, with very quiet engines. By 1930 Minerva had a range of cars from 12 to 40 continental hp. The golden age of the luxury car was drawing to a close, however, and customers were turning to less expensive makes. In 1934 the Minerva company went bankrupt.

The museum has about fifteen Minervas. The oldest one, dating from 1910, belonged to the Belgian Court during the reign of King Albert. The most luxurious is a 1930 model (40 continental hp), which could travel at speeds of up to 140km – 87 miles per hour.

★★**Maison Cauchie** (HS W) ⓥ – The home of architect and decorative artist Paul Cauchie stands at no 5 rue des Francs. The house dates from 1905 and has a remarkable façade almost entirely decorated in sgraffito, a technique similar to fresco painting.

Sgraffiti

At the end of last century, the authorities encouraged the development of art by organising competitions for the decoration of house fronts. The most commonly-used technique, because of its visibility from some distance away, was sgraffito which bears a resemblance to fresco painting. The surface is covered with a light-coloured base, then parts of the base are scratched away while still wet, leaving the support medium to show through and form a pattern or drawing. Some of the most fashionable sgraffiti from the Art Nouveau period are still visible today in Brussels:

– The house that belonged to Paul Hankar the architect, 71 Rue Defacqz, St-Gilles. The sgraffiti were created by A Crespin.

– The private mansion that belonged to Albert Clamberlani the artist, 48 Rue Defacqz, St-Gilles. The sgraffiti were the artist's own work.

– The house belonging to Edouard Ramaekers the architect, 35 Rue Le Corrège, Bruxelles-Extension. The work was created by an anonymous artist.

– A private house at 83 Rue Faider, Ixelles. The sgraffiti have been attributed to Privat Livemont.

– Houses in Rue Vanderschrick in St-Gilles. The work was created by an anonymous artist.

– The House belonging to the sgraffiti specialist Paul Cauchie, 5 rue des Francs, Etterbeek.

Maison Cauchie, Sgraffiti under the cornice

★★★**Muséum des Sciences Naturelles (Institut Royal)** (GS M⁹) ⊘ – The highlight of the dynamic Natural History Museum is its collection of **iguanodon skeletons★**. In 1878 the well-preserved bones of 29 of these reptilian dinosaurs were discovered in a mine in Bernissart, in the west of the country. The animals were herbivores from the Cretaceous period, and the species has long since been extinct.

Ten skeletons about 10m – 33ft long have been rebuilt, while others are exhibited as they were found, lying in the sand. In addition to these authentic specimens there are also animated robots of the tyrannosaurus, triceratops and allosaurus, etc. Other rooms give an insight into the life of invertebrates, the seas of the Jurassic and Cretaceous periods and polar animals. A vivarium gives the visitor a chance to observe a number of live species of giant spiders. The museum also has a fine collection of minerals. The whale room has an impressive display of 18 skeletons of Cetecea, including in particular that of the largest mammal of all times, the blue whale. There is also a splendid shell collection.

Musée Wiertz (GS M¹⁹) – *62 rue Vautier.*
This museum lies near Natural History Museum and is housed in the former studio and home of the artist. Wiertz was a visionary painter, a precursor of Symbolism and Surrealism in Belgium. The compositions in the main room are striking for their monumental size. Note also the unusual *Belle Rosine* and the macabre *Premature Burial.*

The squares – Near the Berlaymont is a district laid out from 1875 onwards by the architect Gédéon Bordiau. This example of modern town planning with eclectic and Art Nouveau style houses is worth taking time out to visit. Note the **Hôtel Van**

Eetvelde★ (1895-1898) at no 4 avenue Palmerston (**GR 187**), a brilliant work by Victor Horta and the **Maison du peintre de St-Cyr** (1900) at no 11 square Ambiorix (**GR**), a remarkably narrow building designed by Gustave Strauven.

Centre Berlaymont (**GR**) - *Restoration work in progress.*
This X-shaped complex of buildings (1967) at the Schuman roundabout was built on the site of a convent founded in the 17C by the Comtesse de Berlaymont. The Berlaymont was vacated by EU officials in late 1991 for safety reasons.

THE OTHER TOWNS IN THE BRUSSELS CONURBATION

To the east: Woluwe-St-Lambert and Woluwe-St-Pierre

Chapelle de Marie-la-Misérable (**DM**) – This charming chapel was built in 1360 in honour of a pious young girl who refused a young man's advances and was subsequently accused by him of theft. In punishment, she was buried alive. Miracles occurred on the spot where she had been put to death.
An old post **windmill** (**DL**) stands in a small wood not far to the north *(access via Avenue de la Chapelle-aux-Champs).*
The 18C **Château Malou** (**DM**) stands overlooking a lake in a vast park to the south. It has a gallery of works of art available on loan and hosts temporary exhibitions.
The delightful area of lakes known as the **Etangs Mellaerts** (**DN**) in **Woluwe-St-Pierre** is very popular in summer.

★**Palais Stoclet** (**CM P¹**) – *Closed to the public.*

Brussels, Capital of Art Nouveau (1893-1910)

Belgium was one of the first countries to become involved in the Art Nouveau Movement and the first buildings to be designed in this style were the Hôtel Tassel (**Victor Horta**, 1861-1947) and the house belonging to **Paul Hankar** (1859-1901). Art Nouveau is undoubtedly connected with a small progressive group of lay people, all of them young intellectuals who expressed enthusiastic support for this radically new style of architecture. Thanks to them, Art Nouveau was able to develop. Traditional building materials (stone, glass and timber) were still used but new materials (steel and concrete) were also included in designs that were created rationally. Horta was resolutely innovatory in the layout of private housing, creating a well of light on which all the rooms are centred. The interiors of his own home (now the **Musée Horta**) and of private mansions such as the Hôtel Van Eetvelde or the Hôtel Solvay are a remarkable example of a total work of art in which curves are the predominant feature.

Palais Stoclet

Ch. Bastin-J. Evrard

Paul Hankar, whose most outstanding designs were the Hôtel Clamberlani and the window of the De Backer flower shop, belonged to the more geometric tendency of Art Nouveau.
Henri Van de Velde (1863-1957) built his own villa, "Bloemenwerf", in 1895 on Avenue Vanderaey in Uccle, in a style reminiscent of an English cottage.
Among the major buildings of this period, there is also Saintenoy's **Old England** which is soon to house the **Musée instrumental**, the **Maison du St-Cyr** designed by Stauven (this building is remarkable for its narrow frontage), the houses in Rue Vanderschrick designed by Ernest Blérot, the poster-façade of the **Maison Cauchie** and the Hôtel Hannon designed by Jules Brunfaut.
The very famous **Palais Stoclet** designed by Joseph Hoffmann, an Austrian architect, was, like Dr. Van Neck's orthopaedic clinic designed by Antoine Pompe, a precursor of the modern style.

This magnificent residence with its pure architectural lines was built by the renowned Austrian architect, **Josef Hoffmann.** The construction work, which involved the sculptors Powolny, Luksch and Metzner in addition to the famous painter **Gustav Klimt,** lasted 6 years (1905-1911). The exterior has become a classic example of turn-of-the-century architecture. The perfect execution and modern-style forms have resisted the test of time quite remarkably. Note the magnificent staircase tower decorated with four figures and a bronze semi-circle by the sculptor Metzner.

★**Bibliotheca Wittockiana** (DM **B**[1]) ⏱ – *21 rue du Bémel. Guided tour by the librarian by appointment only, except for temporary exhibitions.*
This museum contains an extensive collection of bound works belonging to the industrialist Wittock. The valuable collection includes approximately one thousand one hundred volumes including some rare 16C to 20C bound editions. The collection of rattles covers forty centuries of history dating back to the Hittite period.

Musée du Transport urbain bruxellois (DM **M**[26]) ⏱ – *364b avenue de Tervuren.*
The Brussels Urban Transport Museum is housed in a former depot of the Société des Transports Intercommunaux de Bruxelles (STIB), the city's bus company. It provides an insight into the development of public transport through old trams and buses, information panels and documents.
The admission ticket includes a return journey on a 1930s tram to Soignes Forest (Tervuren Museum) or the Cinquantenaire (the journey takes approximately 1 hour).

To the south: St-Gilles and Ixelles

These two suburbs south of the town, beyond the Porte Louise, constitute a residential area. **Avenue Louise** was created in the middle of the 19C to link the Cambre Woods with the centre of the town; it is now home to elegant fashion boutiques and antique shops. Galerie Louise is a modern version of the Galeries St-Hubert. This district has a number of Art Nouveau buildings. The most outstanding example is Victor Horta's house.

★★**Musée Horta** (BN **M**[10]) ⏱ – The Horta Museum was set up in the two narrow houses that architect Victor Horta built between 1898 and 1901 as his home and studio. He wrote in his Memoirs: "People should please realise that I drew and created the design for each piece of furniture, each hinge and door-latch, the rugs and the wall decoration in each of the houses..." This enormous amount of work resulted in a marvel of harmony and elegance, a remarkable tribute to Art Nouveau as a style in which glass and iron play the leading role and in which curves and countercurves are combined so gracefully. The **staircase** is one of Horta's most beautiful creations. The lightness of the metal structure is accentuated by the golden light diffused by the glazed ceiling and the reflections from the multitude of mirrors *(see photograph pp 280-281).*

Hôtel Hannon ⏱ – *1 avenue de la Jonction.*
This Art Nouveau residence was built in 1903 by the architect Jules Brunfaut (1852-1942) and decorated by the French artists Louis Majorelle and Émile Gallé, the founder of the Nancy School. It was neglected for many years and most of the furniture has been lost. It was restored in 1988 and is now occupied by a photo gallery that pays homage to the industrialist Édouard Hannon, who was also a talented photographer. Note the window of the winter garden and its stained glass in a style reminiscent of Tiffany. The fresco on the staircase is also interesting; it was painted by the Rouen artist Paul-Albert Baudouin, a pupil of Puvis de Chavannes.
Nearby at no 55 avenue Brugmann is the house known as "**Les Hiboux**" (The Owls) which was built by Édouard Pelseneer in 1895.

★★**Musée communal d'Ixelles** (GT **M**[11]) ⏱ – *71 rue J-van-Volsem.*
Ixelles Museum was opened in 1892 in the buildings of a former slaughterhouse. It was extended in 1973 and partially restructured in 1994. The museum contains an excellent collection of 19C and 20C paintings and sculptures, by famous Belgian and French artists. The display includes a sketch by Dürer, *The Stork,* and original posters by Toulouse-Lautrec (the museum has 29 of them). Some rooms are devoted to high-class temporary exhibitions.

★★**Abbaye de Notre-Dame-de-la-Cambre** (CN **S**) – This old Cistercian abbey stands on the south shores of the Ixelles lakes. It now houses the École nationale supérieure d'architecture et des arts décoratifs, the college otherwise known as "La Cambre" and the Institut géographique national.
The beautiful **main courtyard,** with the abbey building flanked by pavilions at the corners and outbuildings in a semi-circular layout, forms a very harmonious 18C ensemble.
The **church** ⏱ dates from the 14C and there is a marvellous statue of **The Mocking of Christ ★** by Albert Bouts in the nave. The Stations of the Cross are by Anto Carte (1886-1954). The north transept contains the 17C reliquary of St Boniface, the Brussels citizen who became bishop of Lausanne and died in the monastery in the 13C.
The vaulting in the Lady chapel (south transept) rests on brackets carved with human figures and symbolic animals.

BRUXELLES
BRUSSEL

Broqueville (Av. de) .... CM 30
Charleroi (Chée de).......... BM 34
Croix-du-Feu (Av. des)...... BK 54
Démosthène Poplimont
(Av.)........................... BL 58
Edmond Parmentier (Av.) DM 69

Emile Bosckstael
(Bd.)........................... BL 75
Emile Bossaert (Av.) ...... AL 76
Emile Vandervelde
(Av.)........................... DM 82
France (R. de) .... BM 100
Houba de Strooper
(Av.)........................... BK 121
Jacques Sermon (Av.) .... BL 130
Jean Sobieski (Av.) .... BK 136

Jules van Praet (Av.)....... BKL 144
Madrid (Av. de) .... BK 166
Meysse (Av. de).............. BK 175
Port (Av. du) .... BL 198
Prince-de-Liège
(Bd.)........................... AM 204
Robiniers (Av. des).......... BL 211
Stockel (Chée de) .... DM 232
Veeweyde (R. de) .... AM 244
Vétérinaires (R. des)........ BM 247

B¹   Bibliotheca Wittockiana
M¹⁵ Demeure abbatiale de Dieleghem

M²⁶ Musée du Transport urbain bruxellois
P¹   Palais Stoclet

*The Michelin Green Guide Brussels (French and English editions)
reveals Belgium's capital city in all its guises, covering:*

- *the best-known sights in the city centre*
- *the secret treasures of lesser known districts*
- *the charms of the outlying districts*
- *the art treasures in the museums and galleries*
- *the best options for a shopping spree*
- *tips on the most typical cafés and restaurants*

ENVIRONS

KRAAINEM

Wezembeek (Av. de) .... DM 259

STROMBEEK-BEVER

Antwerpselaan .... BK 9

VILVOORDE

Parkstraat .... CK 192
Stationlei .... CK 231
Vuurkruisenlaan .... CK 252

ZAVENTEM

Henneaulaan................... DL 115

ZELLIK

Pontbeeklaan .... AK 197
Zuiderlaan........................ AL 264

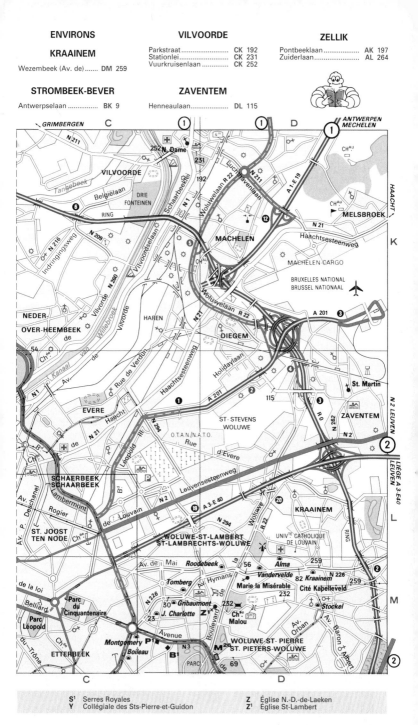

S¹ — Serres Royales
Y — Collégiale des Sts-Pierre-et-Guidon

Z — Église N.-D.-de-Laeken
Z¹ — Église St-Lambert

If you are a fan of Art Nouveau, don't miss:
- *Musée Horta (museum)*
- *Centre belge de la Bande Dessinée (Belgian comic strip centre)*
- *Maison Cauchie (town house)*
- *Hôtel Hannon (town house)*
- *Old England*
- *The squares*
- *Promenade des Etangs in Ixelles*

★**Bois de la Cambre** (**BCN**) – The woods form an oasis of greenery, with undulating countryside encircling a lake suitable for boating.

★**Musée Constantin-Meunier** (**BN M**[12]) ⊘ – *59 rue de l'Abbaye.*
The Constantin Meunier Museum is housed in the home and former studio of the artist (1831-1905). Alternately sculptor and painter, he devoted himself to depicting the world of work.

Maison communale d'Ixelles (**FST H**[1]) – The Town Hall was formerly the residence of La Malibran, the famous singer who married the Belgian violinist Bériot in 1836 and died the same year after falling from a horse.

Université Libre de Bruxelles (**CN U**) – Part of this university, which was founded in 1834, lies to the east of the La Cambre Woods. Another campus is near Ixelles cemetery.

Cimetière d'Ixelles (**CN**) – This is the burial place of, among others, French General Boulanger, who sought refuge in Brussels after his attempted coup d'état, and committed suicide in 1891 on the tomb of his mistress (avenue 3). There is a statue of Till Eulenspiegel on the tomb of Charles de Coster (avenue 1).

Watermael-Boitsfort

Église St-Clément (**CN**) – St Clement's church has preserved a certain rustic air, with its nave and 12C Romanesque tower.

Garden cities of "Le Logis" and "Floréal" (**CN**) – *Near Square des Archiducs.*
Built between 1921 and 1929, these garden cities were a model for Belgian low-income housing policies. At the end of April or the beginning of May there is a magnificent show of pink Japanese cherry blossom.

Uccle

★**Musée David-et-Alice-Van-Buuren** (**BN M**[13]) ⊘ – *41 Avenue Léo-Errera.*
David van Buuren's house, built in 1928, is a worthy setting for this museum. It contains part of the collection which belonged to this art lover. There is a version of Bruegel the Elder's **Fall of Icarus**, as well as landscapes by Hercules Seghers and Patinir, still-life paintings by Fantin-Latour, several works by Permeke, a series of paintings by Van de Woestyne, sculptures by Georges Minne and Delft ceramic ware.
The Art Deco style interior has retained the gentle atmosphere chosen by the art collector in which to display ancient and modern works.
The gardens are charming. They include a Scenic Garden, Garden of the Heart and a maze in which the various stages echo verses from the *Song of Solomon.*

Parc de Wolvendael (**BN**) – This vast park (10 hectares – 25 acres) harbours a small Louis XVI style pavilion.
At the edge of the park is the **Cornet** (**BN V**), a charming inn built in 1570, in which Eulenspiegel *(see Damme)* is said to have stayed. The **Russian Orthodox church** (**BN X**) nearby is a copy of a church in Novgorod.

Musée Van Buuren - The Garden of the Heart

Forest/Vorst

Église St-Denis (ABN) ⊙ – This charming Gothic church at the foot of the hill not far from Forest-National, contains the tomb of St Alène (12C). The former **abbaye de Forest** (ABN) houses a cultural centre. On the side bordering place St-Denis is a fine Louis XVI doorway.

Auderghem

Le Rouge Cloître (DN) – The monastery lies to the east of Auderghem in the Soignes Forest. It is now a restaurant. The painter Hugo van der Goes stayed here until his death in 1482. The outbuildings house an **Art Centre** and a **Soignes Forest Information Centre**.
Not far from here in the woods south of the Wavre road stands the **Château des Trois Fontaines** (DN) of which only a small red-brick building remains.
A vast park to the north surrounds **Château de Val Duchesse** (DN), where the Treaty of Rome was drawn up, and the delightful 12C **chapelle Ste-Anne**.

To the west: Anderlecht

★★Maison d'Érasme (AM) ⊙ – Erasmus's House, known as the "Swan" was built in 1468 and enlarged in 1515. It was one of the houses of the Anderlecht chapter where members of the community and their illustrious guests were lodged. In 1521 the most famous of these guests gave his name to the house. He was Erasmus (1469-1536).
Behind the brick walls of the shady close, there are five rooms furnished with Gothic and Renaissance furniture. The natural lighting is subdued, apparently serving as a reminder of the "prince of humanists".
On the ground floor are the rhetoric chamber, then the chapter-house containing paintings by old masters such as Hieronymus Bosch's superb *Adoration of the Magi*, **Erasmus's study** with its simple writing desk and the portraits of the philospher by Quentin Massys, Dürer and Holbein (copy).
The 16C statue at the foot of the staircase is said to represent Erasmus as a pilgrim.
The **white room** upstairs, once a dormitory, contains valuable first editions, including the first edition of *The Praise of Folly*, and engraved portraits of Erasmus and his contemporaries.

★Collégiale des Sts-Pierre-et-Guidon (AM Y) ⊙ – *Restoration work in progress.*
This beautiful Late Gothic collegiate church, dedicated to St Peter and St Guy of Anderlecht, dates from the 14C and the 15C. Its spire dates from the 19C.
Once inside, there are traces of frescoes (c1400) in the chapelle Notre-Dame-de-Grâce. They illustrate the life of St Guy who died in 1012 and is greatly venerated as the patron saint of peasants and the protector of horses. The late-11C crypt contains the tombstone of St Guy.

Béguinage (AM) – This Beguine convent was founded in 1252, partially rebuilt in 1756, and has since been restored.

★Musée de la Gueuze (ES M^{14}) ⊙ – *56 Rue Gheude.*
The museum in the capital's last remaining family brewery gives visitors an insight into the different stages in the production of traditional beers such as lambic, kriek, gueuze and faro.

Koekelberg

★Basilique nationale du Sacré-Cœur (ABL) ⊙ – *Photograph see over.* Building began on the basilica church dedicated to the Sacred Heart in 1905. The church was consecrated in 1951 and finally completed in 1970. The dome of this immense brick, concrete and stone building rises to 90m – 295ft above the Koekelberg hill. Against the apse stands a huge *Crucifixion* by Georg Minne.
Inside, the walls are faced with golden-yellow terracotta. They enclose a vast space. The transept is 108m – 354ft long. Notice especially the **ciborium** above the high altar. It is surmounted by a calvary and four bronze angels, kneeling, executed by Harry Elström. The many **stained-glass windows** diffuse a multi-coloured light. The windows in the nave were based on cartoons by Anto Carte.
It is possible to climb up to the **gallery-walkway** ⊙ and to the top of the **dome** ⊙, from where there is a panoramic **view** of Brussels.

To the north: Jette

Demeure abbatiale de Dieleghem (ABL M^{15}) – This residence is all that remains of an 11C abbey; it now houses the **musée national de la Figurine historique** ⊙ in beautiful Louis XVI rooms. This is a rich collection of figurines illustrating historic, mostly military, scenes from Antiquity to the present. The second floor houses the musée communal du Comté de Jette which retraces the history of the town from prehistoric times.

Basilique du Sacré-Cœur

Laeken

Église Notre-Dame-de-Laeken (BL Z) ⊘ – Poelaert built this church in the neo-Gothic style. The crypt contains the royal family's tombs.
The church also has a much venerated 13C statue of the Virgin Mary. The Gothic chancel of the old church can be seen in the cemetery in addition to the graves of several famous people. Rodin's statue of *The Thinker* marks the tomb of Jef Dillen.

Château Royal de Laeken (BL) ⊘ – The royal palace is located in the eastern section *(not open to the public)* of Laeken Park; this is the everyday residence of the Belgian sovereigns. The façade, rebuilt in 1902 by the architect Girault, can be seen beyond the entrance gates. There is a monument opposite, in the public park, in memory of Leopold I.
The Belvédère Pavilion, the residence of King Albert and Queen Paola, is discreetly placed not far from this royal monument.

★**Serres Royales de Laeken** (BK S¹) ⊘ – The royal greenhouses lie further to the north of the royal estate. Their architectural décor is splendid, and from a botanical point of view they are magnificent, but they are only rarely open to the public. The greenhouses were built towards the end of the last century by the architect, Balat. A number of galleries and pavilions containing tropical plants link the two main areas, the iron church *(not open to the public)* and the marvellous Winter Garden which is impressive for its sheer size. This veritable palace of glass, iron, cast iron and steel, is a bold synthesis of technical and aesthetic prowess.

Pavillon chinois (BK) ⊘ – The elegant Chinese pavilion (1901-1909) opposite the Japanese Tower was built by the architect Alexandre Marcel. The kiosk and exterior woodwork were made in Shanghai. On the ground floor, note the Delft room decorated with drawings illustrating La Fontaine's fables. There is a fine collection of Sino-Japanese ware manufactured for export with pieces exhibited in rotation.

An underground passageway running under the avenue J-van-Praet links the two buildings.

Tour japonaise (BK) ⊘ – The entrance pavilion of this Buddhist pagoda known as the Japanese Tower (1901-1904) is the reconstructed porch of the *Tour du monde* from the 1900 World Fair in Paris. The porch was designed by Alexandre Marcel and bought by Leopold II at the close of the exhibition. The tower and wing housing the main staircase were built in Brussels by the same architect. The architectural decoration was made in Japan. The tower is used for temporary exhibitions.

The nearby **fountain** is a reproduction of the famous *Neptune Fountain* in Bologna by Giambologna.

Heysel

★**Atomium** (BK) ⊘ – A reminder of the 1958 World Fair, the 102m – 335ft high Atomium dominates the Heysel plateau. It is a symbol of the atomic age, representing a molecule of iron crystal enlarged 165 billion times. The structure, made of steel sheathed in aluminum, consists of 9 spheres 18m – 59ft in diameter, linked by tubes 29m – 95ft long and 3m – 10ft in diameter, through which visitors move from one exhibition area to the next. Four of these spheres contain the Biogenium exhibition, "medicine on the move". The major break-throughs of medicine, microscopy, genetics, cellular biology, virology and immuno-logy are the main subjects handled through models, information panels and pho-tographs.

A lift leads to the uppermost sphere, from which there is a panoramic view of Brussels.

The **Bruparck** lies at the foot of the Atomium. This vast area contains Mini-Europe *(see below)*, the Kinepolis with nearly 30 cinemas, an Imax auditorium with a 600m²-6458ft² screen, the Océade (a water sports complex) and The Village, a group of cafés and restaurants.

The **Palais du Centenaire** can be seen further away to the north in the Parc des Expositions, which was created for the 1935 World Fair.

Mini-Europe (BK) ⊘ – All the EU countries are represented here by models (at a scale of 1:25) of buildings with a socio-cultural, historic or symbolic value. The exhibition in this 2.5 hectare – 6 acre park includes exhibits such as the Acropolis of Athens, Danish long-houses from the Viking period, the 15C Leuven Town Hall, a copy of the austere 16C Escurial monastery which Philip II had built to the northwest of Madrid, the 17C houses lining the canals of Amsterdam, and the English town of Bath designed by the 18C architects John Wood Senior and Junior etc.

There are also a few contemporary creations in the park, such as the Ariane rocket, the TGV high-speed train and a Jumbo-ferry.

EXCURSIONS

★★Forêt de Soignes

59km – 37 miles southeast. Leave by ③ on the plan.

★**Tervuren** – Tervuren **Park**★, lying to the northeast of Soignes Forest *(qv)*, was once a highly prized area for hunting; its attraction now lies in its carefully tended lawns and beautiful lakes. From the 13C to the 19C a glorious succession of castles, manor-houses and gardens made it an impressive sight. *Main entrance to the park for visitors in cars via Place de l'Église.*

★★**Koninklijk Museum voor Midden-Afrika** ⊘ – *Car park on Leuvensesteenweg.*
The Royal Museum of Central Africa originated in 1897 when King Leopold II of Belgium organised an exhibition in the Palais Colonial on the Congo, featuring the flora, fauna, art and ethnology of those faraway lands. It was such a success that it became a permanent museum, for which the architect Girault constructed the current building with its Louis XVI façade from 1904 to 1910.

The museum collections display a vast overview of Africa. The sculptures and other ethnographic exhibits represent various ethnic groups and, in particular, the two main centres of production of this form of artistic expression: Central Africa, especially the Belgian Congo or later Zaïre, and West Africa. The museum is also a centre for basic scientific research into the African continent.

Tour – Enter through the **rotunda**, from which there is a beautiful view of the park. The **great gallery** and a few other rooms leading off from it to the right contain a remarkable selection of African objects and works of art. In the gallery to the left of the rotunda the collections are exhibited by ethnographic theme (hunting, agriculture, craftmanship or social events, such as marriage or death); in the gallery to the right the objects are arranged by geographic area (Zaïre, North Angola, Rwanda and Burundi). There is a variety of amazing sculptures in wood, ivory, stone and metal (especially in Room 4). There is also a marvellously rich collection of jewels and accessories (Room 6). The rest of the tour provides interesting glimpses of Africa's colonial history (Livingstone and Stanley have a place of honour

BRUXELLES
BRUSSEL

Alfred Madoux (Av.) .... DN 6
Altitude 100 (Pl. de l') .... BN 7
Broqueville (Av. de) .... CM 30
Charleroi (Chée de) .... BM 34
Charroi (R. du) .... ABN 36
Delleur (Av.) .... CN 57
Edith Cavell (R.) .... BN 67

Edmond Parmentier
  (Av.) .... DM 69
Emile Vandervelde (Av.). DM 82
Flagey (Pl.) .... BN 93
Fonsny (Av.) .... BN 94
Foresterie (Av. de la) ...... CN 96
France (R. de) .... BM 100
Frans van Kalken (Av.).... AN 103
Gén. Jacques (Bd) .... CN 109
Houzeau (Av.) .... CN 123
Louis Schmidt (Bd) .... CN 162

Mérode (R. de)................ BN 174
Paepsem (Bd) .... AN 186
Parc (Av. du) .... BN 190
Plaine (Bd de la) .... CN 196
Prince-de-Liège (Bd) .... AM 204
Stockel (Chée de) .... DM 232
Tervuren (Chée de) .... DN 235
Th. Verhaegen (R.) .... BN 237
Triomphe (Bd. de) .... CN 240
Veeweyde (R. de) .... AM 244
Vétérinaires (R. des)........ BM 247

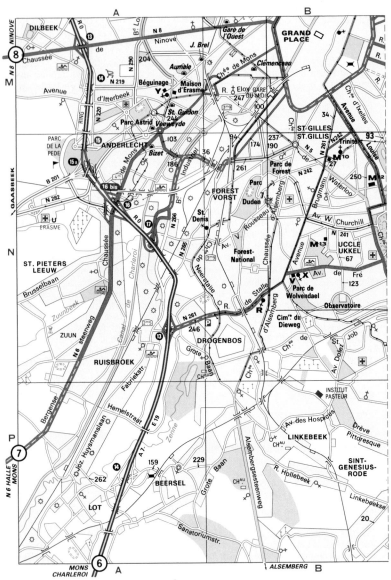

B¹   Bibliotheca Wittockiana
M¹⁰ Musée Horta
M¹² Musée Constantin Meunier
M¹³ Musée van Buuren

M²⁵ Musée des Enfants
M²⁶ Musée
      du Transport urbain bruxellois
P¹   Palais Stoclet

The Société des Transports intercommunaux de Bruxelles (STIB)
publishes an interesting brochure entitled
"L'Art Nouveau en transports en commun".
There is a list of corresponding routes
and three suggested itineraries
through city streets lined with outstanding Art Nouveau buildings.

Vieurgat (Chée de)	BN	250
W. Ceuppens (Av.)	BN	261
2e Rég. de Lanciers (Av. du)	CN	265

ENVIRONS

BEERSEL

Lotstraat	AP	159
Schoolstraat	AP	229

DROGENBOS

Verlengde Stallestraat	AN	246

KRAAINEM

Wezembeek (Av. de)	DM	259

LOT

Zennestraat	AP	262

ST-GENESIUS-RODE

Bevrijdingslaan	BP	20
Zonienwoudlaan	CP	263

R	Église Notre-Dame-des-Affligés	
S	Abbaye Notre-Dame-de-la-Cambre	
U	Université Libre de Bruxelles	
V	Le Cornet	
X	Église orthodoxe russe	
Y	Collégiale des Sts-Pierre-et-Guidon	

The school of Flemish primitives was originated by the innovatory style of Van Eyck: precise arrangement of space and mastery of perspective; detailed draughtsmanship; and luminosity of colour, due partly to the new use of oil-painting. Other Flemish primitives numbered Robert Campin (thought by some to be the Master of Flémalle), Rogier Van der Weyden, Petrus Christus, Dirk Bouts, Hugo Van der Goes and Hans Memling.

119

among the great explorers), the African mountain landscape of Ruwenzori at various altitudes, and the region's zoology (enormous dioramas), geology and mineralogy.

Return to the centre of Tervuren and follow the signs to the Arboretum.

★**Arboretum** ⊙ – Tervuren's geographical arboretum, created in 1902, takes up part of the woodland known as Bois des Capucins. It is divided into two sections focusing on the New and Old World. Tree species include those from temperate climates, classified by region: oaks, elms, ashes, birches and coniferous trees, and some tropical varieties.
Note the huge resinous trees from the Pacific (sequoias and Douglas firs).

Jezus-Eik (DN) – Walkers often stop at this spot, known to French-speakers as Notre-Dame-au-Bois ("Our Lady in the Wood"), to rest a little and enjoy a Brussels speciality: bread spread with soft white cheese *(fromage blanc)*, flavoured with onions and radishes.

★★**Forêt de Soignes (Zoniënwoud)** (DN) – This superb forest extends over an area of 4 380 hectares – 10 823 acres. It was once part of the ancient **charcoal-burners' forest** in the area west of the Ardennes forests, in which wood charcoal was produced in Roman times. Magnificent beech trees grow thickly in this undulating countryside which once rang with the cries of hunters. Deep in the valleys, there are many traces of abbeys and their estates. One such valley is **Groenendael** (Groenendaal), in a beautifully romantic **setting**★ dotted with lakes which was widely reputed from the 14C to the 18C for its abbey. The great mystic **Jan van Ruusbroec**, also called "the Admirable", lived here during the 14C. Besides major roads, there are many footpaths and bridle paths, and a few cycle paths, which offer the opportunity of a pleasant excursion.

La Hulpe – Stately houses and castles are widely scattered across the hills in this area. The 220 hectares – 544 acres of the **Domaine Solvay**, an estate which once belonged to the family of the industrialist Solvay, were bequeathed to the State.
The magnificent **park**★★ ⊙ dotted with lakes is overlooked by a **château** dating from 1840, which has been converted into a cultural centre.

Lac de Genval – Brussel's inhabitants often come to this lake at the weekend. The stretch of water is large enough to accommodate a variety of water sports. The wooded areas on the shores of the lake are a lovely setting for walks.

Château de Rixensart ⊙ – This is an impressive 17C square brick building in the Renaissance style, with turrets at the corners.
The estate has belonged to the Merode family for over a century; one of the family, Félix de Merode, was a member of the 1830 provisional government. One of his daughters married Montalembert, the famous French Catholic writer. Inside, there are beautiful tapestries (Beauvais, Gobelins), French paintings (Valentin, Nattier) and a collection of weapons brought back from the Egyptian campaign by the French mathematician Monge.

Waterloo

19km – 11.75 miles south

Leave by ⑥ on the plan.
See Waterloo for a description of the town.

Beersel and Huizingen

16km – 10 miles south

Beersel (AP) – This market town has a beautiful brick **fortress** ⊙ built between 1300 and 1310. It has been restored to its former glory using engravings depicting the castle in the late 17C.
It is a very romantic-looking place, surrounded by a moat. The machicolated watchpaths are reflected in its waters, along with the three watch turrets and crowstepped gables.

Huizingen – *Leave by ⑥ on the plan.*
The **domaine récréatif provincial** ⊙ is a recreation area covering 90 hectares – 22 acres. It is carefully maintained, and it constitutes a real oasis of greenery in the heart of an industrial region.

Gaasbeek

12km – 7.5 miles southwest.

★★**Château et parc de Gaasbeek** ⊙ – The castle in Gaasbeek, which stands on the edge of undulating grounds, was extensively restored in the late 19C and now houses a well-stocked museum. The whole estate was bequeathed by its owner in 1921, and has belonged to the Flemish community since 1981. The famous Count of Egmont spent the last three years of his life here.

The inner courtyard, Château de Gaasbeek

The **museum** has beautiful furniture, paintings, a large number of antique exhibits and magnificent **tapestries** (15C Tournai, 16C and 17C Brussels) depicting the five episodes in the story of Tobias (main staircase). The archives room contains Rubens's will. The view over the surrounding countryside from the terrace is reminiscent of the works of Bruegel the Elder who was a frequent visitor to the Payottenland, and who was particularly fond of painting at St.-Anna-Pede. The church from this region can be seen in one of his paintings.

Meise

14km – 8.75 miles north.

★★**Plantentuin** (**BK**) ⊙ – *Photograph below.* The Botanical Gardens lie within the grounds of the Bouchout estate for which this town north of Brussels is perhaps best known. The grounds are laid out with scientific precision, dense woodland

Plantentuin, Meise

121

areas alternating with lawns, lakes and remarkable lone-standing trees. Depending on the season, visitors taking a stroll through the park can see collections of hydrangeas, magnolias, rhododendrons, oak trees and maples. In the **Plantenpaleis** there is a signposted route leading through the world of tropical and subtropical plants. Do not miss the "Victoria" greenhouse with its "artists' palettes". Empress Charlotte, sister of Leopold II and widow of Maximilian, Emperor of Mexico, died in the castle which now houses temporary exhibitions. It forms a picturesque sight with its crenellated towers reflected in the calm waters of the old moat.

Grimbergen

16km – 10 miles north. Follow the A12 until Meise, then turn right.

Église abbatiale des Prémontrés – The Premonstretensian minster is one of the most interesting examples of Baroque architecture and ornamentation in Belgium (1660-1725). It was never actually completed. The chancel is very long and extends into a square tower. The interior owes its majestic proportions to the height of the vaulting and of the cupola. It still has its sumptuous furnishings, most notably four **confessionals★** carved with alternating allegories and characters from the Old and New Testament by the Antwerp sculptor Hendrik Frans Verbruggen. The 17C **stalls** are interesting. The church also contains 15 paintings by Flemish old masters (17C-18C).

The **main sacristy** (1763) north of the chancel is decorated with remarkable panelling. The fresco and grisailles on the ceiling are dedicated to St Norbert, founder of the Order.

There are beautiful 17C paintings in the small vestry.

Vilvoorde

12km – 7.5 miles north. Leave by the N1.

O.-L.-Vrouwkerk (**CK**) ⊙ – *Closed for restoration.*
This Gothic church has magnificent carved Baroque **choirstalls★** (1663). They were brought here from Groenendael Abbey *(qv)*.
The 17C pulpit is by Artus Quellin the Younger.

Zaventem

10km – 6.25 miles east. Leave by the Chaussée de Louvain; then turn left.

St.-Martinus (**DL**) – The church houses an interesting Van Dyck painting of *St Martin Dividing His Cloak.*

Canal du CENTRE
Hainaut
Michelin maps 409 F4 or 214 folds 2-3

The Canal du Centre was constructed between 1882 and 1917 to link the Meuse basin with that of the Scheldt and create a direct line of communication between Germany and France. The greatest problem was reducing the 90m – 295ft difference in height between the two basins. This was finally resolved by the building of 4 canal lifts and 6 locks which are still operational.

After the passing of the law of 9 March 1957 requiring major Belgian canals to meet European standards (a capacity for 1 350-tonne vessels), this canal was given a new course and the hydraulic lifts and locks were replaced with the Strépy-Thieu boat lift.

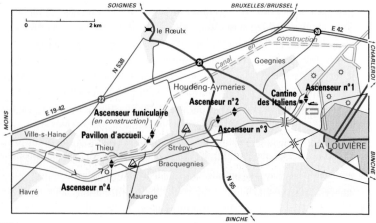

Hydraulic lift on the Canal du Centre

★**The hydraulic lifts** – These beautiful metal structures were designed by a London firm and built in the Cockerill works. They were actually put in place between 1888 and 1917. The principle is very simple: the barges enter two basins filled with water, one in the upper part of the canal and the other in the lower part. The two basins, which are fixed to enormous pistons, constitute a sort of hydraulic balance. The basins slide along two cylinders filled with water, linked by a pipe. The addition of extra water into the upper basin makes it sink, while the principle of communicating vessels makes the other one rise.

Ascenseur à bateaux de Strépy-Thieu – It was decided to construct a canal bridge leading to an enormous funicular lift, to complement the new course of the Canal du Centre.

A model, map with lights and an audiovisual presentation in the **visitor centre** ⊙ gives an idea of the size, technical details of the project that has been underway since 1982. The project chosen to resolve the problem of the 73.25m – 240ft difference in height in the canal's new course will result in impressive dimensions: a height of 110m – 361ft, length of 130m – 426ft, and width of 75m – 246ft wide. The weight being transferred to the ground is 300 000 tonnes. Two steel tanks measuring 112m – 367ft by 12m – 39ft, suspended by cables and balanced by counterweights, can move up or down independently in 6-7 minutes. It will take a barge only 40 minutes to pass the change in level. This means that the current waterway, which can only move 300-tonne boats in 5 hours, will be replaced so that it can handle 1 350-tonne boats in 2 hours.

An observation platform with viewing table enables visitors to see the progress made on the project.

Boat trip to the lifts ⊙ – *2 hour trip; departure from the Cantine des Italiens or Strépy-Bracquenies.*

This pleasant trip on the canal lined with trees and houses gives an insight into the life of bargees with the passage through the hydraulic lifts, and the turning or lift bridges worked by the bridgemen or lock-keepers. One of the landing-stages is near the **Cantine des Italiens**, living quarters built in 1945 for Italian coal miners. The trip on lifts 2 and 3 shows exactly how they work. In the machine room on the right bank near lift 3, visitors can see how very highly-compressed water is made and stored in the two towers to work the entrance gates to the lift, provide a watertight junction between the canal and the basin and operate the pistons. The return journey is made on a narrow-gauge tourist train running along the towpath and the lifts are again visible, but from the outside this time. To round off the visit, take a look at the various boats that have been restored and moored along the canal banks or take lift 1 to the **exhibition** ⊙ devoted to canal lifts throughout the world.

CHARLEROI

Hainaut – Population 356 858 (conurbation)
Michelin maps 409 G4 or 214 fold 3
Town plan in the current Michelin Red Guide Benelux

Charleroi is a major intersection of a number of main roads and railway lines; it is also near the coal-mining basin and is one of the main centres of the Belgian economy. Its busy streets, shops and liveliness all make the main city in the "Pays Noir" (Black Country) particularly attractive.

Two main districts lie at the heart of this sprawling city: the **upper city** around the modern belfry in the south and the **lower city**, the commercial district, which lies what was once an island in the Sambre, but where part of the river's course has been filled in.

Military past – In 1666 the government of the Spanish Low Countries, worried by Louis XIV's ambitions, had the village of Charnoy turned into a fortress; in homage to the Spanish king Charles II, it was renamed Charleroy. Louis XIV captured the fortified town in June 1667. Vauban strengthened the ramparts of the upper town, then built the lower town to maintain economic activity. Industry (glass works) was attracted to the region by its coal supply. Charleroi became the prize at stake in many a hard fought battle until 1868, when the ramparts were turned into boulevards. The town was captured by Jourdan in 1794 and served as a base first for the army of the French Republic, then for Napoleon's troops.

The Battle of Charleroi took place in 1914 (21-23 August). The French failed in their brave attempt to prevent the enemy from crossing the Sambre on 21 August; Charleroi fell. Nevertheless the German advance was stalled momentarily, until the French troops, almost surrounded, were forced to retreat on the evening of the 23 August, the day before German reinforcements arrived.

Industry – Industry has been attracted here mainly because of the coal. The first industrialists to settle here, from 1577 onwards, were the glass-makers. They were followed by metal-workers (foundries, nail-producing plants, wire and rolled sheet-metal). This sector underwent rapid expansion from the early 19C. Nowadays, the iron, steel and glass industries are still very much present, but manufacturing has diversified into electrical, electro-mechanical, chemical, pharmaceutical, printing and other industries. Two institutes of higher education train specialised technicians and engineers.

The Charleroi-Brussels canal links the Sambre to the Scheldt via Brussels and the maritime canal. The Sambre then flows into the Meuse at Namur.

The Entre-Sambre-et-Meuse processions – The towns and villages in the region to the south of Charleroi between the rivers Sambre and Meuse have an unusually high number of memories of war. They also feature prominently in the Belgian calendar of traditional events, because of the military marches that have been held here since the 17C.

The marches probably hark back to the troubled days of religious reformation, when religious processions were flanked by armed rural militias. Despite their military appearance, the events are organised in honour of a local patron saint.

On the saint's feast day a veritable army in miniature parades through the streets, sometimes escorting the statue of the saint. The "sappers" come first, then the drum corps, the fifes and the brass band. Then come the soldiers armed with guns, firing volleys into the air, accompanied by soldiers on horseback and even canteen-keepers. Since Napoleon's troops passed through this area, the uniform worn by the soldiers of the First Empire has been extremely popular.

About forty towns organise military processions *(qv)*. The St Roch procession at **Ham-sur-Heure** includes more than 700 people, among them the "Mons volunteers of the 1789 Brabant Revolution" *(see Turnhout)*.

The longest procession, covering a distance of 35km – 28 miles long and involving 5 000 people, is in **Gerpinnes**. The small **Musée des Marches folkloriques de l'Entre-Sambre-et-Meuse** ⊙ in the village displays the marchers' military costumes. The **Fosses-la-Ville** procession is as rare as it is splendid, taking place only once every 7 years *(qv)*.

Apart from the marches in the area between the Sambre and the Meuse, the Mary Magdalene procession in **Jumet** *(4km – 2.5 miles north of Charleroi)* is interesting too. This is the oldest procession in all of Wallonia, dating back to the year 1380. It is outstanding for the wide variety of costumes.

THE UPPER CITY *tour: 1 hour*

Beffroi – Like the Town Hall of which it is part, the belfry was built between 1930 and 1936. With a height of 70m – 230ft it rises above Place Charles-II and the surrounding streets set out in the form of a star. The Town Hall contains the **Musée des Beaux Arts** ⊙; exhibits include works by François-Joseph Navez (1787-1869) who studied with David, Pierre Paulus, Magritte and Delvaux.

Place du Manège – Part of the Sunday market is held on this huge square. Round it are the Palais des Expositions (1954) which is used for exhibitions, and the Palais des Beaux-Arts, a concert and entertainment hall that is the home of Belgium's Centre chorégraphique de la communauté française.

★**Musée du Verre** ⊘ – *10 boulevard Defontaine, near the Palais de Justice.*
The Institut national du Verre is easily recognisable for the reddish tinted glass in the windows. The exhibition is remarkable. The museum presents the art of glass-making and various techniques from their origins to the present, in a particularly interesting way *(recorded 40-minute commentary in several languages)*. The basement houses a permanent exhibition of Belgian glassware and is also used for temporary exhibitions.

Musée archéologique de Charleroi – A room in the basement of the musée du Verre recalls the region's Roman and Merovingian past, through the craftsmanship of the pottery and earthenware found in the Sambre basin.

EXCURSIONS

Mont-sur-Marchienne - *3km – 1.75 miles south. Access via the Porte de la Villette exit on the ring road, or the Mont-sur-Marchienne exit on the R 3 ring road.* The **Musée de la Photographie★** ⊘ is housed in a former neo-Gothic Carmelite convent. The history of photography is presented in the rooms surrounding the old cloisters. The visitor can follow the development of this art from its beginnings through the changes in equipment (from the camera obscura and daguerreotype to holography) and photographic style. Work by the world's greatest photographers illustrates this development. The museum aims to be a "living" institution, and has a library of more than 2 000 volumes on photography. It also organises temporary exhibitions throughout the year. The exhibitions feature very fine work which is later published.

Sambre Valley – *26km – 16 miles. Leave Charleroi by the N 53 in the Beaumont direction. 5km – 3 miles from the city centre, turn towards Montignies-le-Tilleul and head for Landelies by crossing the N 579, then the Sambre.*

Upstream from Landelies the Sambre River flows through a green, steep-sided valley, a setting which is greatly appreciated by anglers and sailing enthusiasts.

★**Abbaye d'Aulne** – *See Abbaye d'AULNE.*

Follow the road to Gozée.

There is a beautiful view of the ruins from above the abbey.

Gozée – It is worth taking a look at the **Zeupire Stone** *(on the left near a large café on the Beaumont road)*. It is a pink sandstone megalith weighing 20 tons which is thought to be the only surviving trace of an ancient cromlech.

Turn back and take the N 59.

Thuin – *See THUIN.*

Lobbes – The famous abbey was founded, like Aulne Abbey, in the 7C by St Landelin. It stood near the Sambre, but was destroyed in 1794.
The **collégiale St-Ursmer** is at the top of the hill, where it replaced a funerary church built by St Ursmer in about 713. The present collegiate church dates back to the Carolingian period and was enlarged in the 11C. The chancel and crypt are Romanesque, as are the porch and the west tower which are reminiscent of the Mosan school. A tower was added above the transept crossing in the 19C.
Note the tombs of St Ursmer and St Erme in the crypt. The pillars here were reworked in the 16C.

CHIMAY ★

Hainaut – Population 9 379
Michelin maps 409 F-G5 or 214 fold 13

The little town of Chimay lies at the foot of the "Hainaut boot", on the southern edge of the vast Rance forest. One of its best-known features is the castle, of which there is a lovely view from the bridge over the river known as the Eau Blanche. The castle is steeped in memories of the 14C author **Froissart**, who wrote some famous *Chroniques*. Another famous name connected with it is Mme Tallien.

The Princess of Chimay

Mme Tallien, born Theresa Cabarrus, was one of the most beautiful women of her time. In 1805 she married for the third time, taking as her husband François-Joseph de Caraman, Prince of Chimay. She spent the remainder of her otherwise turbulent life (1773-1835) in the calm surroundings of the château.
Having been saved from the scaffold in Bordeaux by the proconsul Tallien, she was then reimprisoned in Paris. From her cell she gave Tallien the courage to overthrow Robespierre, earning herself the name of Notre-Dame-de-Thermidor. Tallien married her shortly afterwards.

Château ⓥ – It initially belonged to the de Cro family. Then, in 1804, it passed to Riquet de Caraman, a descendant of the Riquet who built the Midi Canal in the 17C and a relative of the famous French politician and orator, Count Mirabeau. It was partially destroyed by a fire in 1935 and rebuilt according to old plans in the late Renaissance style. Its bluish grey limestone façade lies at the end of a vast esplanade.

Inside, there is a drawing room with a terrace standing 16m – 53ft above the Eau Blanche Valley. There are two portraits in this room recalling Mme Tallien, one by Gerard, the other painted when she was older. In 1863 her first son Joseph had the charming rococo theatre built and richly decorated with gilded stuccowork. It is a copy of the theatre in Fontainebleau (southeast of Paris). La Malibran was among the many artists invited to perform in Chimay.

The chapel, which has delightful surbased vaulting, contains the banners of Louis XI. They came from Carrouges in Normandy (Louis XI himself captured Chimay in 1447).

The King of Rome's christening robe and a range of Napoleonic memorabilia are on display in a small living room.

Collégiale des Sts-Pierre-et-Paul ⓥ – This 16C church was built of freestone and still has its beautiful 13C chancel. In it is a remarkable recumbent effigy of Charles de Cro, chamberlain and godfather to Emperor Charles V (died in 1552), as well as four plaques in memory of illustrious members of the de Chimay family. Note also the interesting 17C choirstalls and a triumphal cross (c1550). The first chapel on the south side upon entering the church contains the Latin epitaph of the chronicler Froissart who was also a canon in Chimay and died there in 1410. A monument can be seen on the square representing members of the de Chimay family. They include Mme Tallien and her husband wearing a cape.

EXCURSIONS

★**Étang de Virelles** ⓥ – *3km – 1.75 miles northeast.*
This nature reserve covers an area of 100 hectares – 247 acres. The popular lake is surrounded by woods and is one of the largest natural stretches of water in Belgium. The leisure area provides meals, pedalo hire, and a children's adventure playground.

Abbaye Notre-Dame-de-Scourmont – *10km – 6.25 miles south via Bourlers.*
Founded in 1850, the abbey is now a Trappist monastery. The austere buildings flank a central courtyard overlooked by the stark façade (1949) of the church. The monks make a beer known as "Trappiste de Chimay".

Michelin Green Guides are regularly revised
Use the most recent edition to ensure a successful holiday

COO

Liège
Michelin maps 409 K4 or 214 fold 8 – 8.5km – 5 miles west of Stavelot
Local map see Vallée de l'AMBLÈVE

This lively holiday resort (ski slopes at Wanne and Brume) lies in a mountain setting. It is well known for its magnificent **waterfall**★, where the seething, foaming waters of the Amblève pour down with a thunderous roar. *Floodlighting every evening.* In the 18C the Amblève formed a long meander at this point, which erosion had worn into an almost full circle. Could the monks of Stavelot have had the idea of boring through the rock to complete the work that Nature had already begun? In any case, a waterfall eventually formed as a result of the drop in level.

Montagne de Lancre – There is a broad **panoramic view**★ of the Amblève Valley from the tower built at the top of this mountain *(access by chairlift)*. The Coo-Trois-Ponts electric-powered pumping stations can also be seen. The meander is known as the Tour de Coo. It is contained by two dikes, forming the lower basin. Like Vianden *(qv)*, the pumps draw the water back up to the upper reservoirs in Brume at night so that extra power supplies can be produced for periods of peak consumption.

COURTRAI★

See KORTRIJK

COUVIN

Namur – Population 12 452
Michelin maps 409 G5 or 214 folds 13, 14

Couvin's rows of slate roofs can be seen along the tree-lined quays on the banks of the Eau Noire river. Overlooking the town is a limestone crag called Falize, on which a castle once stood. It was destroyed by Louis XIV in 1672. This is an attractive holiday town at the heart of a region dotted with waymarked footpaths and well-stocked rivers. Couvin is also famous for its cuisine: *poulet à la Couvinoise* (Couvin chicken), *escavèche* (fried fish dish) etc.

Ironsmelting is a very old industry in this region. There is an exhibition of firebacks at the Fonderies de l'Eau Noire.

In 872 Benedictines from the abbey of St-Germain-des-Prés in Paris brought Christianity to the region; this is why the main street is named Faubourg St-Germain.

Cavernes de l'Abîme ⊘ – These caves were once inhabited by prehistoric man and were also used as a refuge during the Roman period and the Middle Ages. An audiovisual presentation on Belgian prehistory is shown in one of the most impressive of the caves. A small museum complements the presentation. There is a delightful view of Couvin from the top of the steps outside.

Round tour of 17km – 10.5 miles to the west of Couvin – *Take the N 99 and turn left at Pétigny.*

★**Grottes de Neptune** ⊘ – *5km – 3.25 miles from Couvin.* The Eau Noire river, so called because of the black rocks on its bed, disappears underground in the Adugeoir chasm before reappearing near Nismes. Three tiers of galleries are open to the public with beautiful, well displayed rock formations. While the Eau Noire has not flowed through the upper gallery for centuries, it still fills the middle gallery when in spate. A pleasant boat trip takes visitors along the subterranean river in the lower gallery and gives them an opportunity to admire a spectacular **waterfall**. The end of the trip is enhanced by an exceptional sound and light show.

Return to Pétigny, take the N 99 again and turn left towards Nismes.

Nismes – After flowing through the Neptune Caves, the Eau Noire reappears above ground here and flows into the Eau Blanche to form the Viroin. Nismes is a popular summer holiday resort. There are many geological curiosities in the surrounding limestone area, including the **Fondry des Chiens** *(access by Rue Orgeveau)*, the most impressive of the twisting abysses bristling with monoliths which are dotted across the plateau east of the town. There is also a beautiful view of the surrounding countryside from here.

Mariembourg – This little town is named after Mary of Hungary, the governor of the Low Countries who had it built in 1542. The geometrically laid-out town was fortified (the town walls have now totally disappeared) and faced the Maubert-Fontaine fortress on French territory opposite. Mariembourg was reputed to be impregnable, but was captured in 1554 by King Henri II of France *(qv)*, forcing Emperor Charles V to create a new citadel, Philippeville *(qv)*. Mariembourg was recaptured by the Spanish in 1559 and was then handed over to the French a century later. It remained French until 25 July 1815, the date on which the town's defenders were forced to capitulate to the Prussians, although they were granted the "honours of war" for their courage.

Mariembourg is the departure point of the **Chemin de fer des Trois Vallées** ⊘, a tourist train that runs as far as Treignes via the picturesque **Viroin Valley**. It also goes through the Eau Blanche Valley on its way to Chimay.

Excursion in the border area – *20km – 12.5 miles south.*

The wild area of boggy moorland and forest near the French border is known as the **Pays des Rièzes et des Sarts.** The relatively infertile land is used partly for raising livestock. The region's butter and cheese are well known and widely appreciated.

Take the Rocroi road, then the N 964. Turn off towards Brûly-de-Pesche.

Brûly-de-Pesche – In a wood near a spring, on the site of a traditional pilgrimage in honour of St Méen, is **Hitler's bunker** ⊘. Hitler used it as his general headquarters from 6 June to 4 July 1940, directing the French campaign from here together with his staff. The small concrete bunker was built very quickly.

Cul-des-Sarts – The **Musée des Rièzes et des Sarts** ⊘, a folk museum depicting the traditional lifestyle in this locality, is in a little half-timbered house with a thatched roof behind the church.

DAMME ★

West-Vlaanderen – Population 10 749
Michelin maps 409 C2 or 213 fold 3 – 7km – 4.3 miles north of Bruges

The pretty little town of Damme has entered a decline that has given it a slightly melancholy air. It lies on the old Zwin estuary. It served as Bruges's outer harbour, and owed its expansion to the city whose history is so closely linked to its own. All sorts of merchandise passed through here, although Damme specialised particularly in the wine trade.

The marriage of Charles the Bold and Margaret of York was celebrated here with great pomp and ceremony in 1468; but by the end of the 15C, Damme was already suffering as a result of the decline in Bruges.

One of the earliest Flemish writers, **Jacob van Maerlant** (*c*1225-late 13C) came from here, as did **Till Eulenspiegel**. Eulenspiegel was the hero of the picaresque novel (1867) by Charles de Coster *(qv)* and waged continual conflict against the tyranny of Emperor Charles V and Philip II.

SIGHTS

★**Stadhuis** ⊘ – The Town Hall dates from the 15C and was restored in the 19C. The town market used to be held on the ground floor.

The fine façade, with its watch turrets and flight of steps, is decorated with pretty statues supporting narrative corbels carved with a combination of mischievous verve and charm. In a niche is a statue of Charles the Bold holding out a wedding ring to his fiancée, Margaret of York.

The interior has retained its magnificent carved beams. One of the figures is said to represent the writer Jacob van Maerlant.

O.-L.-Vrouwekerk ⊘ – The church dates from the 13C and 14C. The apse, between the flat chevets of the two side chapels, has beautiful lancet windows. When the town's population declined in the early 17C, after Damme had ceased to be a harbour and was, instead, becoming a citadel, it was decided that the church was too big, and the nave was demolished. The ruins still have a gallery with Tournai-style triplet windows.

A series of late-13C wooden statues of the Apostles can be seen inside. Note also the Baroque altarpiece against the north wall, and a statue of *Christ of Miracles* which is carried in religious processions such as the one dedicated to the Precious Blood in Bruges.

The tall square **tower**★ ⊘, which has lost its spire, is remarkable. It overlooks a charming little square shaded by lime trees and flanked by the great roofs of the hospice. There is a **view** of the town from the top of the tower. Hillocks mark the location of the 17C fortifications. The coast can be seen in clear weather.

St.-Janshospitaal ⊘ – The Hospital of St John was founded in the 13C, then later extended and turned into a hospice. The chapel and **museum** are open to the public.

The museum contains collections of furniture, paintings, faïences, liturgical objects and sculptures (statuette of St Margaret of Antioch) serving as reminders of the rich past of the hospital and the town.

Tijl Uilenspiegelmuseum ⊘ – The museum in honour of Till Eulenspiegel stands near the Stadhuis in a picturesque, double-gabled 15C house called De Grote Sterre (The Great Star). Books, drawings, paintings and stained-glass windows depict the famous Till and his entourage.

De Schellemolen ⊘ – This mill on the banks of the canal has been restored and now grinds cereals again.

*The Michelin Green Guide Brussels (French and English editions)
reveals Belgium's capital city in all its guises, covering:*
- *the best-known sights in the city centre*
- *the secret treasures of lesser known districts*
- *the charms of the outlying districts*
- *the art treasures in the museums and galleries*
- *the best options for a shopping spree*
- *tips on the most typical cafés and restaurants*

DENDERMONDE ★

Oost-Vlaanderen – Population 42 062
Michelin maps 409 F2 or 213 fold 5

Dendermonde is in a strategic position on the confluence of the Dender and the Scheldt (Dendermonde: mouth of the Dender). Louis XIV was forced to abandon his siege of the town in 1667 because of a flood brought about by the town's inhabitants. "Accursed town!" he cried, "I would need an army of ducks to capture you!"
Dendermonde suffered badly in September 1914 shortly after Antwerp's surrender. Every year *(see the Calendar of Events)* the town organises a parade of giants. The pageant led by Bayard the horse, ridden by the four Aymon sons *(qv)*, is held every ten years *(qv)*.
Legend has it that the famous horse was drowned in the Scheldt at Dendermonde, on Charlemagne's orders.

SIGHTS

Grote Markt – The square still has its old charm even though part of it has been rebuilt. There are two major buildings worth taking a look at here.

Stadhuis – This former cloth market, now the town hall, was rebuilt in the Flemish Renaissance style after the First World War. All that remained of the original was the square 14C belfry with its corner turrets.
There is a pretty view of the Dender (Oude Dender) from behind the Stadhuis.

Stedelijk Oudheidkundig Museum ⊘ – The municipal museum is located in the former meat market (vleeshuis) dating from 1460. It is flanked by an octagonal turret. Collections concerning the town's archeology and history are exhibited in a pretty medieval setting.

★★**O.-L.-Vrouwekerk** ⊘ – The church dedicated to Our Lady stands on a square surrounded by chestnut trees that can be seen from the rear of the museum. It was built in the 13C and 14C, and is surmounted by an octagonal tower above the transept crossing which is a blend of Gothic, Brabant and Scaldian styles.
There is a beautiful collection of **works of art**★ inside. Note the Romanesque font in the south aisle, in blue Tournai stone. The sides are decorated with symbolic pictures on the subject of baptism. The main events in the life of St Paul the Apostle are on the two friezes. He is depicted among the other Apostles on one side of the basin. Two paintings by Van Dyck can be seen nearby, one a Calvary scene and the other depicting the adoration of the Shepherds.
Another *Adoration of the Shepherds* is attributed to the 16C painter Herri met de Bles. The north transept and chancel still have 15C and 17C frescoes.

Begijnhof – *Access via the Brussels road (Brusselsestraat) then turn right.* Tall 17C houses encircle the inner courtyard. There are small **museums** ⊘ at nos 11, 24 and 25.

DEURLE

Oost-Vlaanderen
Michelin maps 409 D2 or 213 fold 4-11km – 6.75 miles southwest of Ghent

Deurle, on the edge of the Leie in the region dear to the hearts of the Flemish Expressionist painters of St.-Martens-Latem *(qv)*, stands half-hidden by the trees in the gardens of flower-bedecked villas.

Museum Gust De Smet ⊘ – The house to which Ghent artist Gustave (Gust) De Smet (1877-1943) retired to paint from 1935 until his death has become a museum. The studio and interior have remained unchanged and contain many works by this artist from the second group of St.-Martens-Latem artists.

Museum Léon De Smet ⊘ – This house was built in 1969 by the last companion of Gust De Smet's brother, Léon (1881-1966). It contains the painter's furniture and the everyday objects that he depicted in his paintings. About twenty of his paintings and drawings are exhibited.

Museum Mevrouw Jules Dhondt-Dhaenens ⊘ – This long white brick building next to the Léon De Smet Museum was built in 1969. It offers a good general view of Flemish Expressionism, which was based on the Latem school.
The museum houses works by great masters such as Permeke *(Lady in the Green Hat, Golden Landscape)*, Van den Berghe, Gust De Smet *(Twilight, Farm, Shooting Gallery)* and their precursor Albert Servaes whose works are steeped in tragic mysticism *(Executioner, The Passion, The Tomb, Resurrection)*.
This collection is completed by a few sculptures and an exhibition room.

DIEST ★

Vlaams-Brabant – Population 20 574
Michelin maps 409 I3 or 213 folds 8, 9

Diest lies in a bend of the Demer river and is a peaceful community surrounded by fortified walls, some of which are still standing.

Like Breda in the Netherlands, Dillenburg in Germany, and Orange in France, Diest was the fief of the **House of Orange,** of which the most famous member was William of Nassau or **William the Silent** (1533-1584), who led the revolt of the Low Countries against Spain. Heir to his cousin René de Chalon, Prince of Orange who was born in Diest, he founded the Orange-Nassau dynasty to which the present Queen Beatrix of the Netherlands belongs. Philip-William, William the Silent's eldest son, was buried in the church dedicated to St Sulpitius.

Diest was the birthplace of **St Jan Berchmans** who died here in 1621 at the age of 22. He became the patron saint of young people (his birthplace is at no 24 in the street named after him).

SIGHTS

Grote Markt (AZ 7) – The square is surrounded by interesting 16C to 18C houses and is also overlooked by the 18C Town Hall. The church stands in the middle of the square.

St.-Sulpitiuskerk (AZ) ◷ – This church was built from the 14C to the 16C in the Brabant style. The various stages of construction can be seen in the different types of stonework, from local ferruginous sandstone in the chancel and nave to white stone in the unfinished 16C tower. The church has a large carillon. There is an openwork triforium inside, as well as some interesting **works of art ★**. The beautiful 18C woodwork (pulpit, organ) is equally outstanding. The 15C **choir stalls** have amusing misericords representing the seven deadly sins and proverbs. Note also the

Guild chain of office

17C tabernacle with niches decorated in the Italian style, the 16C triptych entitled *Adoration of the Magi* and the 13C *Virgin and Child Enthroned* (Sedes Sapientiae).

The church plate is kept in a room behind the chancel.

★ **Stedelijk Museum (AZ H)** ◷ – The municipal museum is housed in the Town Hall crypts *(right-hand door under the flight of steps)*. The medieval setting shows the museum off to its best advantage. A 15C painting on wood depicting the **Last Judgement** is exhibited beneath the 14C red sandstone Gothic vaulting. There is also a marble statue of the *Madonna and Child* (1345) which was brought here from the Beguine convent and 15C and 16C armour.

The next room, which is clearly of Romanesque influence with brick cupolas set on short pillars, is an old seigneurial brewery. The well still exists. Notice the 15C chandelier made of deer horn, gold and silver.

The final sections in the museum comprise the guild room and aldermen's chamber, with their carved furniture and statues, and the gold- and silverwork cases containing beautiful 17C and 18C **guild chains of office.**

Lakenhalle (AZ B) – The linen market dates from the 14C. The façade was rebuilt in the 19C. A 15C cannon called the Holle Griet was placed nearby.

Go round the building to see the old façade.

There are two picturesque 15C **corbelled houses (AZ D)** at the crossroads of the nearby pedestrian precincts.

Almshouses – A few yards along Demerstraat are the 16C **Tongerlo abbey almshouses** known as Het Spijker **(AY)**. They are on the right, near a canal.

The 15C **Averbode almshouses (AY F)** are a little further along, half-hidden amidst foliage. The outbuildings date from the 20C.

Take your car to the Beguine convent, via Michel Theyssstraat.

★**Begijnhof (BY)** – The Beguine convent was founded in the 13C and is one of the largest in Belgium. It has a beautiful Baroque entrance (1671), with a niche containing a statue of the *Madonna and Child.*

The houses, with gables and niches, date from the 16C to the 18C. The house at no 5 Engelen Conventstraat (main street) is open to the public.

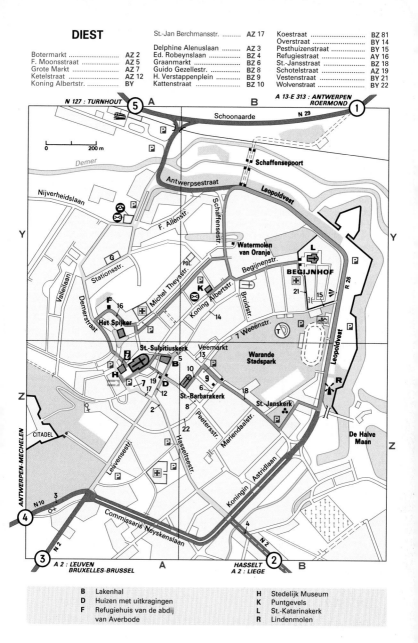

DIEST

Botermarkt	AZ 2	
F. Moonsstraat	AZ 5	
Grote Markt	AZ 7	
Ketelstraat	AZ 12	
Koning Albertstr.	BY	

St.-Jan Berchmansstr.	AZ 17	
Delphine Alenuslaan	AZ 3	
Ed. Robeynslaan	BZ 4	
Graanmarkt	BZ 6	
Guido Gezellestr.	BZ 8	
H. Verstappenplein	BZ 9	
Kattenstraat	BZ 10	

Koestraat	BZ 81	
Overstraat	BY 14	
Pesthuizenstraat	BY 15	
Refugiestraat	AY 16	
St.-Jansstraat	BZ 18	
Schotelstraat	AZ 19	
Vestenstraat	BY 21	
Wolvenstraat	BY 22	

B	Lakenhal
D	Huizen met uitkragingen
F	Refugiehuis van de abdij van Averbode
H	Stedelijk Museum
K	Puntgevels
L	St.-Katarinakerk
R	Lindenmolen

The Brabant Gothic style **St-Katarinakerk** (**BY L**) ⊘ has beautiful woodwork; note the pulpit dating from 1671 with its remarkably graceful sculptures, and the finely worked chancel parclose screen, from the same period. There are interesting statues.

Stop to admire the gables of the two old breweries at nos 72 and 74 Koning Albertstraat (**BY K**). They are decorated with carvings of brewer's tools.

Watermolen van Oranje (**BY**) – This 16C mill stands in the shade of a weeping willow. With its crowstepped gable reflecting in the nearby canal, it makes a very pretty picture.

Schaffensepoort (**BY**) – This gateway was built in two successive 19C fortified enclosures.

Leopoldvest (**BYZ**) – This boulevard runs along the town walls ("vest" means "rampart"), providing a pretty **view** of the Beguine convent. The convent gardens can be seen behind the brick enclosure, with the tall roofs of the houses huddling beyond.

The **Lindenmolen** (**BZ R**) is the next point of interest. It is a standard sort of 18C wooden mill which came from the nearby village of Assent. The surrounding area has been turned into a recreation area *(huge bathing area surrounded by sand)* called **De Halve Maan**.

Ruïnes van de St.-Janskerk (BZ) – The ivy-clad red sandstone ruins of the Gothic chancel of this church stand in the middle of a square.

H. Verstappenplein (BZ 9) – The main entrance to **Warande Park** can be seen from this square. Located on the hill where the castle once stood, this was once the hunting ground of the Princes of Orange. It is overlooked by their palace, dating from 1516 and flanked with a turret.

St.-Barbarakerk (BZ) ⊙ – This Baroque church has six sumptuous 17C carved wooden confessionals. One of these forms the base of the pulpit.

EXCURSION

Round tour of 37km – 23 miles – *Allow 2 hours. Leave on* ① *on the town plan and turn left.*

Tessenderlo-St.-Maartenskerk has a beautiful early 16C **rood-screen★**. Its three finely carved arcades rest on six pillars. Eight large statues of the Evangelists and the Fathers of the Church stand in the arches. Small figures in medieval costume enliven the four medallions above the arches, depicting scenes from the Life of the Virgin. Higher still, but beneath the openwork canopies, are scenes from the Life of Christ. The font was sculpted in the 12C.

★**Averbode** – *See AVERBODE.*

Zichem – Ernest Claes *(qv)* was born in this small market town. The church has a beautiful 16C triptych illustrating the Life of St Eustace, the patron saint. The stained-glass window over the high altar, dating from 1397, is the oldest in the country.

Scherpenheuvel – At the summit of a mountain which reaches 77m – 253ft in altitude is Belgium's national site of pilgrimage in veneration of the Virgin. A candlelight procession takes place in the afternoon of the Sunday following All Saints' Day.
Coebergher *(qv)* built the basilica between 1609 and 1627. It has seven sides and is topped by a Baroque dome, which marks the advent of this style in Belgium. It stands in the centre of a geometric urban layout, with seven avenues converging on it. A tall square tower rises behind it.
Six brightly coloured paintings by Van Loon, depicting the *Lives of St Anne and the Virgin*, are in the radiating chapels.

DIKSMUIDE

West-Vlaanderen – Population 15 270
Michelin maps 409 B2 or 213 folds 1, 2

In the Middle Ages Diksmuide was a port on the Yser River and a clothmaking town. It was destroyed in 1914, then bombed again in 1940. It was rebuilt, like Ypres, in the Flemish style. Diksmuide was one of the strategic points in the **Battle of the Yser** *(see Nieuwpoort)*. The name of the town is tied to the memory of Belgian soldiers and French marines under Admiral Ronarc'h who put up heroic resistance against all the odds from 16 October to 10 November 1914.

SIGHTS

Begijnhof – *Go past the entrance to the church and turn left at the Vismarkt.*
The Beguine convent has been rebuilt to resemble its predecessor. The white houses are set out around a well, on either side of a charming chapel with tall gables.

IJzertoren ⊙ – The Yser Tower is 84m – 275ft tall. It stands on the opposite bank of the Yser as a memorial to the heroes of the Battle of the Yser. It bears the letters A.V.V.-V.V.K., for the motto: Alles voor Vlaanderen, Vlaanderen voor Kristus (All for Flanders, Flanders for Christ).
There is a beautiful **panoramic view★** from the top *(lift)* over the Flanders Plain, the winding course of the Yser and the town of Diksmuide. On a clear day it is possible to see *(right to left)* the belfries of Bruges, Ostend, and Nieuwpoort, as well as the Flemish peaks De Rode and De Zwarte Berg *(viewing table)*.
The **museum** of the Battle of the Yser is on the first floor.

Dodengang ⊙ – *3km – 2 miles northwest on the west bank of the Yser.*
For four years (1914-1918) Belgian soldiers resisted the German advance in these trenches, known as the Trench of Death. They were only a few yards away from the lines of the German troops who had managed to cross the Yser here *(qv)* in October 1914 *(see Nieuwpoort)*.
A viewing table on the first floor of the building locates the strategic points. Visitors can then go through the two long corridors of the trenches, in which the sandbagged parapets have been faithfully reproduced in concrete.

DINANT★★

Namur – Population 12 085
Michelin maps 409 H5 or 214 fold 5 – Local maps see overleaf
and La MEUSE NAMURUROISE – Town plan in the current Michelin Red Guide Benelux

Dinant lies in a remarkable **setting★★** in the Meuse Valley. The massive solidity of the citadel and the onion-domed bell tower of the collegiate church dominate the town. Dinant, with its blue-roofed houses, covers the 4km – 2.5 miles between the river and the rock face.

This is a well-known tourist centre. Dinant's name is the origin of the French word **dinanderie**, the art of brass smelting and beating which has been practised here since the 12C. Dinant's other speciality is *couques*, honey cakes baked in decoratively carved wooden moulds.

The artist **Joachim Patinir** (or Patenier) was born here in the late 15C. He set biblical scenes in vast landscapes recalling the scenery of the Meuse valley. It was also the birthplace of Antoine Wiertz (1806-1865), a visionary painter who was a precursor of Symbolism and Surrealism in Belgium. As for **Adolphe Sax** (1814-1894), he was the inventor of... the saxophone.

A turbulent past – Dinant was constantly in conflict with Bouvines, Namur, Liège and the Dukes of Burgundy, all of them rivals in the brass-smithing business. The town was destroyed for this reason in 1466 by Charles the Bold. Owing to Dinant's strategic position in the Meuse Valley, it also witnessed a succession of conquering armies – King Henri II of France's troops In 1554, and Louis XIV of France's army in 1675 and 1692.

This is also one of the Belgian towns that suffered the most during the World Wars. In 1914 Dinant was sacked by the Germans; 1,100 homes were set alight and 674 civilians were shot. In 1940 and 1944, it was bombed and partly burned.

Boat trips ⊙ – *Landing stage opposite the Town Hall.*

SIGHTS

Collégiale Notre-Dame – Nothing is left of the sanctuary that became a collegiate church as far back as the 10C. The building underwent alteration in the 12C in the Romanesque style; all that remains of this church is the north door. The Gothic church was erected in a style imported from Burgundy and Champagne between the 13C and the end of the 14C. The onion dome and the elegant campanile, both of which were originally designed to be topped by a belfry, date from the period when the town was pillaged by Henri II's troops.

Interior – *Enter by the north door.* Although the church is small (the geographical location left little space for building), it produces the impression of grandeur and austerity that were characteristic of the Mosan School. The layout in the form of a Latin cross is given uniformity by the identical tiers throughout the building. The monostyle columns have octagonal capitals decorated with austere foliage in the regional style. The columns bear the weight of huge, moulded arches, a triforium with trefoiled arches and tall windows with Flamboyant Gothic tracery. The chancel has an ambulatory but no radiating chapels.

Collégiale and citadelle, Dinant

J. Evrard, Bruxelles

★**Citadelle** ⊙ – *Access by cable car, on foot (408 steps) or by car (the N 936 Sorinnes road).*
A castle was built here in 1051. The Bishop of Liège rebuilt it in 1523. The French destroyed it in 1703. Its present appearance dates from the Dutch occupation (1818-1821).
The citadel has been turned into a **museum.** The various rooms contain reconstructions, a few audio presentations, dioramas, a miscellany of exhibits and a small weaponry collection recalling the main events in the history of the citadel and the town.
There is a very pretty **view★★** from the top of the walls, 100m – 328ft above the Meuse. It encompasses the town in the shadow of the collegiate church, and the Meuse Valley with Bouvines.

★**Grotte la Merveilleuse** ⊙ – *West bank of the Meuse, Philippeville road.*
This cave is outstanding for the number of rock formations (drapes, waterfalls, colonettes) and the range of colours (white, brown, blue and pink). Visitors are taken along galleries on three levels.
A gallery-staircase with more than 120 steps brings visitors back out into the open air again.

★**Rocher Bayard** – This sharp jagged rock stands 1km – 0.75 miles south of the town *(on the N 95)*. It is said that Bayard the famous horse *(qv)* split the rock open with one blow of his hoof as he fled from Charlemagne. In days gone by there was only a narrow path along here but it was widened in 1661, then again in 1698, for Louis XIV's troops.

Parc de Mont-Fat ⊙ – The **Tour de Mont-Fat**, which can be reached by chairlift, stands in the centre of this amusement park. There is a panoramic view of Dinant and the Meuse Valley from the terrace.

Grotte de Mont-Fat ⊙ – The prehistoric caves lie halfway up the hillside. They can be reached by underground passageways and the aptly-named Trou du Diable (literally "Devil's Hole") or via the gardens.
The water which streams off the plateau and into the cracks in the cliff face has dug out a prehistoric dwelling which became a temple to Diana in Roman times, hence perhaps the name of the town.
The various chambers are adorned with rock formations.

EXCURSIONS

1 **Bouvignes** – *2km – 1.25 miles north on the N 96.*
Bouvignes and Dinant have merged to form a single conurbation. High above the town are the ruins of the Château de Crèvecoeur ("Heartbreak"), so named after being razed by the troops of King Henri II of France in 1554. **Herri met de Bles**, the marvellous landscape painter who continued to work in the style of Patinir *(qv)*, was born here. His paintings are unusual because they all include the little owl *(see Namur, Musée des Arts Anciens et du Namurois)* that he used as his signature.

Maison espagnole – The "Spanish House" with scrolled gables and Renaissance windows stands on Grand-Place. It was named after the period in which it was built (16C) and was once the Town Hall. It is now home to the **Musée de l'Éclairage** ⊙ appropriately containing a collection of old lamps.

Église St-Lambert ⊙ – The church dates from the 13C and 16C. It has been restored and contains some interesting works of art including the 16C *Christ Bound* and the 17C pulpit and lectern.
Near the church, a dig is revealing the remains of a castle thought to have been built in the 11C.

Château de Crèvecœur – *Access on the Sommière road (4km – 2.5 miles) or via a flight of stairs.* A reminder of the old fortifications, a gate, can be seen opposite the bottom of the steps. There is a beautiful **view★★** from the château of the town, the church, and the Spanish House, as well as of the Meuse Valley with Dinant in the distance.

★ 2 **Anseremme and Down the River Lesse** – *4.5km – 2.75 miles south on the N 95.*
★**Anseremme** – This little town, stretching along the right bank of the river to join Dinant, is a well-situated tourist centre at the confluence of the Lesse and the Meuse. Note in particular the 16C bridge, **pont St-Jean**, over the Lesse. To the south on the river bank in Old Anseremme is a 15C **priory** *(private property)* and its church surrounded by a graveyard.

Vallée de la Lesse – *4km – 2.5 miles.* A very narrow road runs through the steep-sided, verdant Lesse Valley, as far as the rocky spur topped by the Château de Walzin.

★**Down the River Lesse** ⊙ – It is possible to go down the Lesse River by canoe or a boat with a guide, from Houyet to Anseremme. Houyet can be reached by train from Anseremme, or by bus.
Cross the Lesse where it flows into the Meuse. The Freÿr Viewpoint *(qv)* in a bend near a café provides almost a **bird's eye view★** of the gardens around the Château de Freÿr *(qv)*. Further along the road, admire the **broad view★** of the valley from the next viewpoint, with the Freÿr crags and the château.

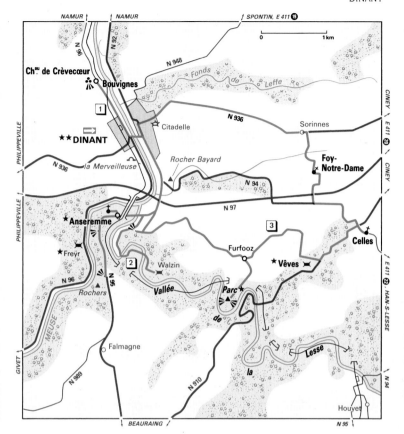

3 **Furfooz; Vêves; Celles; Foy-Notre-Dame** — *Round tour of 30km — 19 miles. Take the N 95 south and turn left on the Furfooz road.*

The road climbs and soon comes to a junction with a road on the right. A few yards from the fork there is a pretty **view★** down over Anseremme.

Furfooz — The **Parc de Furfooz ★** ⊘ lies in an area of chalk cliffs 500m — 0.3 miles south of the village, in a bend of the Lesse. The river has in fact dug out an underground course which has been explored since 1962. *Follow the signposted route.*
This site was a natural fortress and was occupied until the 10C, a fact recalled by the reconstructed Roman baths with hypocaust and the ruins at the top of the plateau (from which there is a beautiful view of the wooded Lesse Valley). The promontory is pitted with caves in which traces of prehistoric habitation have been found.

Vêves — An elegant **château ★** ⊘ stands out against the woods and overlooks the hamlet. Since the 12C it has belonged first to the Beaufort line, then to that of the Counts of Liedekerke Beaufort. The fortress was destroyed by the people of Dinant in revenge for its owner's involvement in the 1466 siege of the town. It was immediately rebuilt and was then altered during the Renaissance, and again in the early 18C. There is an arched gallery surmounted with half-timbering in the courtyard. 18C French furniture and family mementoes decorate the carefully restored interior.

Celles — A German tank at the north entrance to this village marks the furthest point of the 1944 German advance *(qv)*. The 11C **Romanesque church dedicated to St Hadelin** is an excellent example of the Mosan style: massive tower-façade flanked by two turrets, exterior decoration of lesenes, and half-domed vaulting in the apse. Inside there are 17C grisailles, 13C choir stalls, the oldest in Belgium, and superb 16C **tombstone★** made of black Dinant marble and depicting Louis de Beaufort and his wife on either side of the Cross. The church still has two 11C crypts.

Foy-Notre-Dame — A statue of the Virgin Mary was found in an old oak tree in Foy in 1609. Its miraculous gifts were acknowledged by the Prince-Bishop of Liège, and the village became a major place of pilgrimage. The church dates from 1623. There is Louis XIII panelling inside and a remarkable coffered timber **ceiling★** decorated with 145 paintings (17C) by the Stilmant brothers and Guillaume Goblet, all of them Dinant artists. The works were given to the church by pilgrims; they depict the Lives of the Virgin Mary and of Christ, the Evangelists, the Doctors of the Church and the Saints.
Return to Dinant via Sorinnes. This route skirts the citadel (qv).

Barrages de l'EAU D'HEURE ★

Hainaut-Namur

Michelin maps 409 G5 or 214 fold 3 – 32km – 20 miles south of Charleroi

This well-watered, undulating countryside was chosen for a series of reservoirs designed to supply the River Sambre and, consequently the Charleroi Canal in which the volume of water was insufficient once it was made accessible to international-sized vessels.

Two large dams have been created: Eau d'Heure, a huge rock-fill dam with a crest 250m – almost 0.25 miles long and La Plate-Taille, which has a hydro-electric plant. Plate-Taille is higher but the water supply is inadequate and it has to be filled by pumps during the night, using the Eau d'Heure turbo-pumps.

Three "fore-dams", Féronval, Ry-Jaune and Falemprise, were built to make the larger projects easier to carry out. They have also made it possible to create a new road network. An extensive tourist development programme is in progress on the shores of the lake, including various types of accommodation, sports amenities and amusements. The area is crisscrossed by more than 100km – 62 miles of footpaths.

★**Barrage de la Plate-Taille** – *Access by a wide road from Boussu-lez-Walcourt.*
The dam was built in 1977 and is the largest in Belgium. It is a gravity dam with a crest 790m – 0.5 miles long. The reservoir itself covers an area of 351 hectares – 867 acres and has a capacity of 68.4 million m^3 2 416 million cu ft of water. It is used for sailing, windsurfing and sub-aqua. A **viewing tower** 107m – 351ft high has been built on the crest.

Visitor Centre – There are audiovisual presentations about the dams and aquariums filled with regional fish.

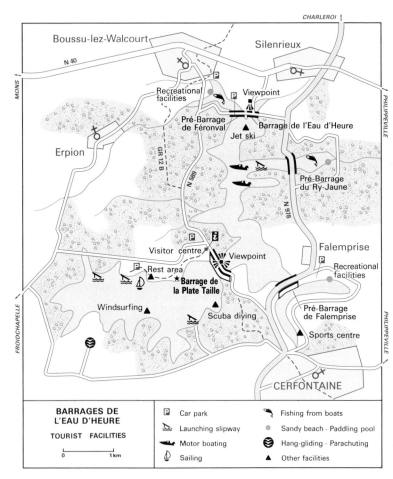

Constantly revised **Michelin Maps**, at a scale of 1:200 000, provide much useful motoring information

Keep current Michelin Maps in the car at all times

ENGHIEN

Hainaut – Population 10 101
Michelin maps 409 F3 or 213 fold 17

Enghien lies on the borders of the French- and Flemish-speaking areas of Belgium and was granted to the Arenberg family in 1606 by King Henri IV of France.

★**Park** ⊙ – The park was originally laid out in the 15C but it was not until the 17C, when Charles d'Arenberg was the owner of the estate, that it became one of the finest in Europe. The original stately home was demolished in the 19C and the tower from the chapel is all that remains of the building. The present house was built in 1913 on the site of the former orangery. The grounds include woodland, lawns, flowerbeds, and lakes, laid out around the 18C stables, the Chinese pavilion, and the Pavilion of the Seven Stars.

Église St-Nicolas – This vast Gothic church on Grand-Place has a carillon of 51 bells. Modern stained-glass windows (1964) by Max Ingrand can be seen inside. The main window represents the Apostolate. The Chapel of Our Lady of Messines, originally known as Chapelle St-Éloi, is the oldest part of the building. It contains a beautiful 16C altarpiece of uncertain origin, decorated with scenes depicting the Life of the Virgin Mary.

Maison de Jonathas – This 12C Romanesque keep only a few yards from the church was turned into a luxury residence in the 16C, unlike the Burbant Tower in Ath *(qv)* which has retained its military appearance. The small **musée de la Tapisserie** ⊙ serves as a reminder of the fact that Enghien had a number of major tapestry workshops from the 15C to the 18C. Note the fine series of five 16C Enghien *Verdures avec Jeux d'Enfants.*

Église des Capucins ⊙ – *Access via the Ninove road then via Rue des Capucins on the left.*
This 1616 church contains a beautiful Renaissance mausoleum in one of its chapels. It was designed by Emperor Charles V's sculptor, Jean Mone, for Guillaume de Cro, Cardinal-Bishop of Toldeo. The chapel on the opposite side is dedicated to Our Lady of Grace. Her statue, which is said to have miraculous powers, stands on the altar; it was a gift from Archduke Albert and Archduchess Isabella to Marie de' Medicis. On the high altar, there is an ebony and ivory altarpiece (17C) framing an *Adoration of the Magi* on which 51 of the figures are portraits of Arenburg family members.
The convent also includes a number of rooms which have been turned into the Musée de la Maison d'Arenberg. They contain sculptures, paintings, tapestries, family archives etc.

EUPEN

Liège – Population 15 503
Michelin maps 409 L4 or 213 fold 24
Town plan in the current Michelin Red Guide Benelux

Eupen lies on a slope of the Vesdre Valley, near the Hautes Fagnes. It is a large industrial town with factories scattered all along the river banks.
Eupen dates from the 18C, a period when its beautiful patrician houses were built by rich wool merchants from Ghent who were attracted by the waters of the Vesdre. The **Église St-Nicolas** with its amusing green onion-domed towers and exuberant Baroque altars also dates from this time.
A German dialect is spoken in Eupen, as it belonged to Germany for a century and only became part of Belgium in 1925, like Moresnet, Malmédy and St-Vith.

★★**Carnival** *(see the Calendar of Events)* – The carnival is a real Rhineland affair, and preparations begin in mid-November. On the Saturday His Madness the Prince appears, crowned with pheasant feathers. The children's parade takes place on the Sunday afternoon. The festivities reach their high point on the eve of Shrove Tuesday with the Rosenmontag (Rose Monday) Procession.

Musée de la ville d'Eupen ⊙ – *52, Gospertstrasse.*
The museum is in a picturesque 17C house and features watch- and clock-making, local history, the development of fashion, as well as a silver- and goldsmith's workshop and a collection of Raeren potteries *(see Introduction: Arts and Crafts).*

EXCURSIONS

★**Barrage de la Vesdre** – *(signposted: Talsperre) 5km 3.25 miles. Head southeast from Eupen on the N 67 and turn left.*
This dam lies upstream from the town, at the confluence of the Vesdre and the Getzbach. It was inaugurated in 1950 and is one of the largest projects of this type in Belgium, along with Gileppe dam and the Eau d'Heure dam complex.

It is a gravity dam, more than 63m – 207ft high and nearly 410m – 0.25 miles long, and is 55m – 180ft thick at the base. It has a capacity of 25 million m³ 883 million cu. ft.

Like the Gileppe dam, it was designed to supply water to the Eupen and Liège areas. It is equipped with a water-processing plant and a small electric power station. Sailing is permitted on the reservoir (Vesdre Yacht Club) but motorboats, fishing and swimming are prohibited.

Viewpoint ⊘ – The visitor can contemplate the lake and the surrounding Hertogenwald (spruces, birches).

Henri-Chapelle – *11km – 7 miles northwest on the N 67 then the N 3 on the left.* There is an **American cemetery** about 4.5km – 2.75 miles north of **Henri-Chapelle**, in Vogelsang-Hombourg. The remarkably well-maintained site blooms with roses and rhododendrons. It contains the graves of 7 989 American soldiers who died in the Ardennes or in Germany from 1944-1945. White marble crosses or stones carved with the Star of David for Jewish men are laid out in arcs of circles across the slightly sloping lawns. They all converge on the memorial which contains a small **museum** ⊘. The story and the maps of the end of the American campaign are carved into the marble.

From the terrace opposite the cemetery there is a **panoramic view★** of the Herve plateau, the fields edged with hedgerows, and the undulating countryside which is densely populated although the houses are well scattered across the entire area.

★Drielandenpunt – *18km – 11.25 miles north on the N 68.* After leaving the N 68 at Kettenis, the road crosses Walhorn and Astenet, where there is a small sanctuary in memory of St Catherine of Siena. Beyond Kelmis-La Calamine, it reaches Gemmenich via the Moresnet-Chapelle shrine to the Virgin Mary with its monumental calvary set amid the trees. From there a series of hairpin bends leads to the wooded plateau on which the borders of the Netherlands, Belgium and Germany meet. The border of the little neutral territory of Moresnet was also situated here until 1918; it is now part of Belgium. This is also the highest point in the Netherlands, with an altitude of 321m – 1 053ft. There is a beautiful **panoramic view ★** of the region from the top of the **Tour Baudouin** ⊘, a tall metal construction. The view encompasses the urban area of Aachen and the forests of the German Eifel, as well as Maastricht in the distance, amid wooded hillsides.

There is a beautiful **viewpoint★** 500m – 0.3 mile further on the Vaals (Netherlands) road. The German plain and Aachen can be seen on the right.

FOURNEAU-ST-MICHEL★★
Luxembourg
Michelin maps 409 J5 or 214 fold 6

Fourneau-St-Michel lies in the green fertile Masblette Valley, between wooded hills. The Benedictines once occupied this delightful valley. In the 18C the last abbot of St-Hubert, Nicolas Spirlet, set up a smelting works here. In 1966 this spot became the property of the province, and it was decided to set up a number of museums.

Le Musée de la Vie rurale en Wallonie, Fourneau St-Michel

★★Musée de la Vie rurale en Wallonie ⊙ – *There are two entrances. Allow 3 hours for this pleasant outing, with a stop for refreshment at the 18C Prévost inn or at the Tahons inn (playing field).*

This open-air museum, covering 40 hectares-99 acres, consists of old rural dwellings representing the various regions in Wallonia, rebuilt along a path about 2km 1.25 miles long. The buildings include a school, a chapel, a printshop, tobacco sheds, a washhouse, and a craft centre. A large traditional Ardennes building is home to the **musée du Cheval de trait ardennais** which illustrates aspects of the Ardennes draught horse and has an exhibition of the implements that this powerful working animal used to pull.

★Musée du Fer et de la Métallurgie ancienne ⊙ – *Time: allow 1 hour.*

This house was once the home of the owner of the ironworks. It is now a museum of iron and ancient metal-working and also includes exhibits relating to the various associated craft techniques. Objects made of iron (firebacks, irons, locks, religious objects, traps, etc.) are displayed next to the tools of the trade, once used by nail-makers, blacksmiths, coopers, and wheelwrights.

The tall furnace and the forge with its different types of bellows help to explain how iron was obtained in the 18C and 19C.

Musée P. J. Redouté ⊙ – This museum is contained in another part of the house, and is devoted to Pierre-Joseph Redouté, the "Raphael of flowers" who was born in 1759 in St-Hubert, and his brother Henri-Joseph, who provided the illustrations for *Description of Egypt*.

Les FOURONS
See VOERSTREEK

Château de FREŸR ★
Namur
Michelin maps 409 H5 or 214 fold 5 – Local map see La MEUSE NAMUROISE

The cliffs at Château de Frëyr

The estate is in a superb **setting**★★ beside the road running along the banks of the Meuse. The Classical buildings form a sharp contrast to the rough crags plunging down into the river on the opposite bank *(qv)*.

★Château ⊙ – The château was built from the 16C to the 18C, then restored in 1972. The style is Renaissance Mosan and Louis XV.

The tour takes visitors through a series of rooms with beautiful wood panelling and fireplaces, decorated with 17C and 18C furniture. Louis XIV was a guest here during the siege of Dinant in May 1675 and again in October for the signing of the Treaty of Freÿr. In 1785 the governor of the Low Countries, Archduchess Marie-Christine, also stayed here.

A large entrance hall is decorated with paintings representing hunting scenes (Snyders' studio). The beautiful wrought-iron balustrade on the balcony took its inspiration from Place Stanislas in Nancy, France.

Château de FREŸR

★Gardens ⊘ – The French-style gardens were designed in 1760 by the Counts of Beaufort-Spontin using the principles defined by Le Nôtre. They run parallel to the river, laid out in three terraces decorated with pools. The lowest terrace is shaded by lime trees and has a collection of 33 **orange trees** in tubs, some of which are three hundred years old. The other terraces include tall hedges that form a **maze**.
A pavilion at the highest point of the garden, near Frédéric Salle, overlooks the entire estate. It was decorated inside by the Moretti brothers, who also decorated Annevoie-Rouillon.

GEMBLOUX

Namur – Population 18 808
Michelin maps 409 H4 or 213 folds 19, 20

Gembloux, an agricultural and horticultural town, was famous for its Benedictine abbey. It was founded in the 10C and soon acquired great cultural influence. The monk **Sigebert**, who died in 1112, left a wide-ranging *Universal Chronicle* concerning the period of 381 to 1111. The abbey estate was abolished during the French Revolution, and since 1860 the building has been occupied by an agricultural college. The town still has several traces of its 12C ramparts.

Former Abbey – This group of buildings was constructed to designs by the architect Dewez from 1759 to 1779. Note the beautiful layout of the **main courtyard** with the old abbot's palace at the end. The sculptures on the pediment recall the abbot's powerful position as Count of Gembloux. The cloisters have been restored. They lead into a Romanesque room that is the only surviving part of the medieval abbey.
The 18C abbey **church**, now a parish church, is nearby.

Maison du Bailli ⊘ – This old 12C "fortified house" was extensively modified in the 16C. It is now the Town Hall.

EXCURSIONS

Corroy-le-Château – *5km – 3.25 miles southwest.*
This 13C **feudal castle★** ⊘ is surrounded by woods and reflected in the moat spanned by a stone bridge. The layout is an imitation of the royal castles built for Philip Augustus of France and it still has a military feel to it with its seven cylindrical towers and barbican.
The interior has been altered over the course of the centuries. The Gothic chapel on the mezzanine of the 7th tower in the outer wall, was restored in the 19C. The apartments are decorated with marble, paintings, some of which depict Flemish festivals, and 17C and 18C furniture. There is a beautiful collection of "jolités" (little painted boxes) from Spa *(qv)*.

Grand-Leez – *8km – 5 miles northeast on the Namur road, then turn left.*
The Defrenne **mill** dates from 1830 and is the only working mill left in the province of Namur. It still grinds corn. It is shaped like a truncated cone, with a rotating cap.

Corroy-le-Château

Gentinnes – *12km – 7.5 miles. Take the Charleroi road, then turn right.*
Gentinnes has had a seminary and study centre for prospective missionaries belonging to the congregation of the Fathers of the Holy Spirit since 1904.
The **Mémorial Kongolo** is a chapel built in 1967 in memory of the 21 Belgian missionaries from this order who were massacred in 1962 during a revolt in Kongolo in Zaïre. Their names are carved on the façade with the names of 196 other victims, religious or lay people, Catholic or Protestant.

GENK

Limburg – Population 45 906
Michelin maps 409 J3 or 213 fold 10
Town plan in the current Michelin Red Guide Benelux

Genk lies on the edge of the Kempen region, conveniently close to the Albert Canal and two motorways. It is Limburg's largest industrial centre, with two extensive industrial estates south of the town. Genk is also a prosperous town, with modern shopping centres and the **Limburghal** (1979), the convention and exhibition hall. The town also has the **Molenvijver**, superb public gardens covering an area of 15 hectares 37 acres including a vast lake and a watermill, as well as recreation parks such as the Kattevennen, or sports complexes such as Kattevenia.
On a small rise is a sombre-looking brick church (1954) with lofty vaulting.

EXCURSIONS

Natuurreservaat De Maten ⊘ – *2km – 1.25 miles. Hasselt road, then left after the railway bridge.*
The marshy area stretching between the heather-clad hills contains a string of lakes that are home to numerous water fowl *(footpaths)*.

Zwartberg – *6km – 3.75 miles north of the N 76.*
The 30 hectare-74 acre **Limburgse zoo** ⊘ has more than 4 000 animals, including bears, monkeys and birds.

Natuurreservaat De Mechelse Heide – *7km – 4.5 miles northeast on the N 75, then the N 763 toward Maasmechelen.*
This is an immense clearing (400 hectares – 988 acres) in the forest, with a magnificent landscape of heather-covered moors *(heide)*. Heather is one of the rare traces of early vegetation in the Kempen area. *Signposted footpaths.*

GENT★★★

GHENT – Oost-Vlaanderen **P**
Population 210 704
Michelin maps 409 E2 or 213 fold 4

Ghent is the spiritual citadel of Flanders, a university town, the second-largest Belgian port and a major industrial centre, in short, a city full of vitality. It is crisscrossed by canals and waterways, built as it is on numerous islets at the confluence of the Rivers Leie and Scheldt. **Emperor Charles V** (1500-1558) was born here, and Ghent is steeped in history and crammed with historic buildings. Furthermore, in its old districts and its quays between the cathedral and castle of the Counts of Flanders, there is a poetic, intimate atmosphere. Among the many famous citizens of Ghent is the great French-language writer, **Maurice Maeterlinck** (1862-1949).

Boat trips ⊘ – Trips (rondvaart) are available on the canals and the River Leie *(see Excursions below)*.

HISTORICAL NOTES

Ghent was one of the last havens of paganism in Gaul. St Amand, who came to evangelise the town in the 7C, was thrown into the Scheldt. Ghent later developed around two monasteries: St Peter's, founded by St Amand; and the future abbey of St Bavo, near the Leie.

A stone fortress was built in about 1000, on the site of the castle of the Counts of Flanders. It became the centre of a third urban settlement.

At the end of the 12C the clothmaking industry was flourishing. The city acquired borough status and gained important privileges. The wealthy merchant class built fortified stone homes called "stenen". In the middle of the 12C the église St-Jean was built. It is the cathedral church dedicated to St Bavo.

Count Philip of Alsace, wishing to make a show of his precedence over the powerful cloth merchants, had the castle rebuilt in 1180.

Incessant conflict – Before long Ghent succumbed to fierce internal conflicts. As in Bruges, the wool workers backed by Count Guy of Dampierre rebelled in 1280 against the patricians who were supported by the King of France *(see Bruges, Princely Receptions)*. In the 14C during the Hundred Years War, the situation developed into a battle against France. The Count of Flanders, Louis of Nevers, supported the King of France against England. As this blocked the importing of English wool into Flanders, the citizens of Ghent revolted again. They chose **Jacob van Artevelde** as their leader. He sided with the English and became the figurehead of the Flemish towns.

Van Artevelde was assassinated by the dean of the weavers' guild in 1345, but his son Philip managed to impose the supremacy of Ghent throughout Flanders. Finally, however, the Flemish were defeated by the French at the Battle of Westrozebeke in 1382 *(see Kortrijk, the Battle of the Golden Spurs)*.

In the 15C, when Ghent was ruled by the Dukes of Burgundy, the town rebelled against Philip the Good and his ideas of a new tax (1452). The citizens of Ghent were defeated at Gavere *(18km – 11 miles southwest)* and surrendered (1453). The town rebelled again against Charles the Bold in 1469, and in 1477 against Mary of Burgundy who had to grant new privileges to the Low Countries.

By the end of the century the clothmaking industry was in decline. Ghent, however, had become the main warehouse for Europe's grain, and this ensured renewed prosperity.

In the 16C the citizens rebelled again, this time against Emperor Charles V, who had himself been born in Ghent and who proudly proclaimed, "I could put the whole of Paris into a corner of my town of Ghent". The townspeople, meanwhile, refused to pay heavy taxes. Charles V responded with the **Caroline Concession** (1540) which stripped the borough of its privileges.

TIPS FOR GHENT

Tourist office – The Infokantoor Stad Gent, Stadhuis (crypt), Botermarkt, Gent, ☏ (09) 266 52 32 is open daily, April to 6 November, 9.30am to 6.30pm and the rest of the year 9.30am to 4.30pm.

City tours – To visit at a leisurely pace take one of the **carriages** which start from Sint-Baafsplein. Carriage rides are available between April and September from 10am to 7pm and the 30min-ride costs 700F.

During the summer season there is a choice of **boat trips** on the river Leie and one goes as far as Bruges. Departures from the Graslei, Kornelei and Recollettenlei.

Guided walks are organised by the tourist office between April and October; they leave from the Stadhuis in Botermarkt daily at 2.30pm.

Ghent by night – Many of Ghent's historic buildings and monuments are floodlit every evening until midnight between May and October and on Friday and Saturday evenings the rest of the year.

Religious strife disrupted the local way of life at the end of the century. The Duke of Alva put down a revolt by Calvinist iconoclasts in 1567, but the Protestants reacted strongly; four days after the "Spanish Fury" in Antwerp *(see Antwerpen)*, Philip II was forced to concede the famous **Pacification of Ghent** (1576) which freed the 17 provinces comprising the Low Countries of Spanish troops.

The town became a Republic in 1577, having revolted against the Spanish, but it was recaptured by Farnese in 1584. **Louis XVIII** took refuge in Ghent in 1815 in the old 18C Hane Steenhuyse mansion *(47 Veldstraat* **EZ A**). This was known as the "flight to Ghent".

From decline to renewal – Ghent's economic decline continued during the 17C. The 1648 closure of the Scheldt dealt a fatal blow to its commercial and industrial activities. However, Ghent was annexed to France in the early 19C and grew more prosperous through the cotton-weaving techniques developed by Ghent native **Lievin Bauwens**. He introduced the mule-jenny, an English method of spinning thread mechanically. Ghent spun and wove linen as well, since the waters of the Leie, as in Kortrijk, were suitable for the retting of flax. The textile industry has remained very important for Ghent's economy.

The 33km – 20.5 mile long canal from Ghent to Terneuzen has linked the **port** to the west stretch of the Scheldt since 1827. In 1968 it could handle 80 000-tonne vessels, and its international cargo traffic reached 25 million tons in 1990.

There are installations for the transhipment of cereal cargoes all along the canal. New industries have sprung up, including metal working, chemicals, petroleum products, and car assembly. The Sidmar steel works complex is in the north port area near the ore ship docking installations. It produces about 3.5 million tons of steel per year.

Ghent has also developed a prosperous regional horticultural industry which has earned it the nickname "city of flowers". A large proportion of its production is exported.

The town organises the world famous **Floralies gantoises** flower show every five years *(the next one will be in the year 2000).*

★★★**OLD TOWN** *time:-half a day*

> **Illuminations** ⊘ create a magical atmosphere for an evening stroll.

★★**St.-Baafskathedraal (FZ)** ⊘ – The cathedral stands on the site of the 12C église St-Jean of which a few traces have survived in the crypt. When Emperor Charles V had the Abbey of St Bavo *(qv)* demolished to make way for the Spanish palace, he ordered the renaming of the church after St Bavo and raised it to collegiate status. It became a cathedral in 1561. The cathedral was built in stages and shows various tendencies. There are elements of French Gothic (the chancel), Brabant Gothic (the tower) and Late Gothic (the nave). Yet despite this diversity, it gives an overall impression of harmony and solemn grace.

The remarkable **tower,** on the west side of the church, is also the entrance, as is the rule in Brabant Gothic architecture. There is an extensive **view** of Ghent and its surroundings from the top ⊘ of the tower.

The majestic effect of the **interior** is somewhat diminished by the neo-classical marble choir screen, decorated with 18C grisailles, which disrupts the beautiful arrangement of the nave. The lofty chancel built of Tournai stone, which is slightly higher than the nave, dates from the 14C. It was extended in the 15C by five radiating chapels and surmounted with a triforium. A certain rhythmic regularity is added to the ambulatory by marble columns and finely worked doors. The plain sandstone and brick nave dates from the 16C and harmonises well with the elegant Late Gothic balustrades and the densely-ribbed vaulting. This cathedral contains many valuable works of art.

★★★**Polyptych of the Adoration of the Mystic Lamb** *(Adoration de l'Agneau mystique)* ⊘ – In a chapel to the left near the entrance.

Polyptych of the Adoration of the Mystic Lamb (detail), Jan van Eyck

GIRAUDON

143

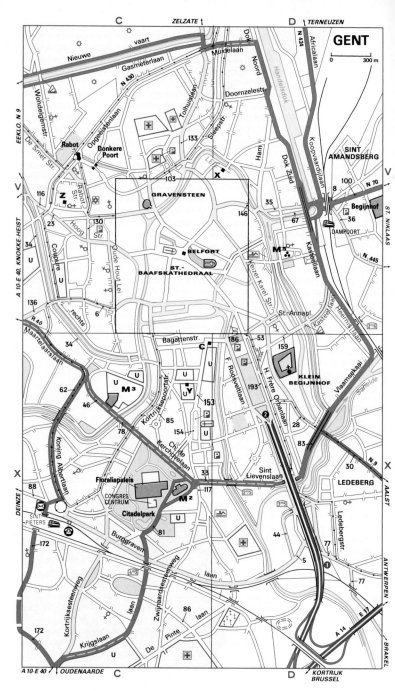

This superb polyptych has had many an adventure. It was donated to the church by Joos Vijd, and was solemnly placed in an ambulatory chapel in 1432. Philip II wanted to take possession of it, the Protestants wanted to burn it in 1566, Emperor Joseph II had the paintings of Adam and Ève removed as he found them shocking, and the French Directoire had it sent to Paris where it remained until 1815. It then lost several of its panels which were exhibited in the Museum of Berlin. It was put back together again in 1920, but the panel of the Righteous Judges was stolen in 1934. It has been replaced by a copy since 1941. The polyptych was first entrusted to the French during the Second World War, but the German authorities transferred it to Austria, where American troops found it in 1945 in a Styrian salt mine near Altaussee. The work was returned once more to the chapel chosen by the original donor, but was moved again in 1986 to a more secure location where viewing it would be easier. It is now exhibited in a chapel which has been converted into a strong room.

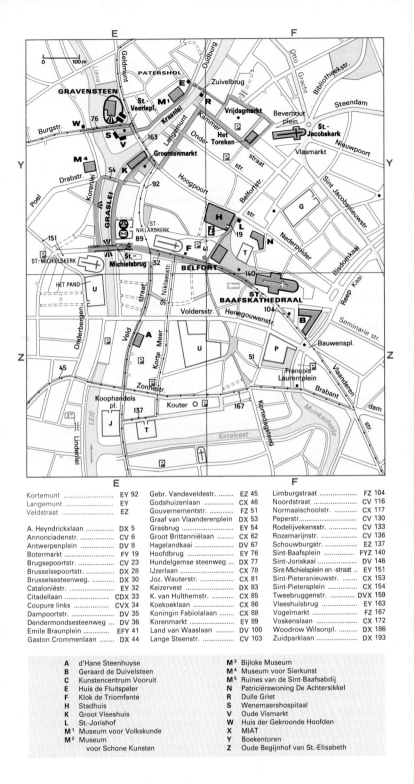

Kortemunt	EY	92
Langemunt	EY	
Veldstraat	EZ	

A. Heyndrickxlaan	DX	5
Annonciadenstr.	CV	6
Antwerpenplein	DV	8
Botermarkt	FY	19
Brugsepoortstr.	CV	23
Brusselsepoortstr.	DX	28
Brusselsesteenweg.	DX	30
Cataloniëstr.	EZ	32
Citadellaan	CDX	33
Coupure links	CVX	34
Dampoortstr.	DV	35
Dendermondsesteenweg	DV	36
Emile Braunplein	EFY	41
Gaston Crommenlaan	DX	44

Gebr. Vandeveldestr.	EZ	45
Godshuizenlaan	CX	46
Gouvernementstr.	FZ	51
Graaf van Vlaanderenplein	DX	53
Grasbrug	EY	54
Groot Brittaniëlaan	CX	62
Hagelandkaai	DV	67
Hoofdbrug	EY	76
Hundelgemse steenweg	DX	77
IJzerlaan	CX	78
Joz. Wauterstr.	CX	81
Keizervest	DX	83
K. van Hulthemstr.	CX	85
Koekoeklaan	CX	86
Koningin Fabiolalaan	CX	88
Korenmarkt	EY	89
Land van Waaslaan	DV	100
Lange Steenstr.	CV	103

Limburgstraat	FZ	104
Noordstraat	CV	116
Normaalschoolstr.	CX	117
Peperstr.	CV	130
Rodelijvekensstr.	CV	133
Rozemarijnstr.	CV	136
Schouwburgstr.	EZ	137
Sint-Baafsplein	FYZ	140
Sint-Joriskaai	DV	146
Sint-Michielsplein en -straat	EY	151
Sint-Pietersnieuwstr.	CX	153
Sint-Pietersplein	CX	154
Tweebruggenstr.	DVX	159
Vleeshuisbrug	EY	163
Vogelmarkt	FZ	167
Voskenslaan	CX	172
Woodrow Wilsonpl.	DX	186
Zuidparklaan	DX	193

A	d'Hane Steenhuyse
B	Geraard de Duivelsteen
C	Kunstencentrum Vooruit
E	Huis de Fluitspeler
F	Klok de Triomfante
H	Stadhuis
K	Groot Vleeshuis
L	St.-Jorishof
M¹	Museum voor Volkskunde
M²	Museum voor Schone Kunsten
M³	Bijloke Museum
M⁴	Museum voor Sierkunst
M⁵	Ruïnes van de Sint-Baafsabdij
N	Patriciërswoning De Achtersikkel
R	Dulle Griet
S	Wenemaershospitaal
V	Oude Vismarkt
W	Huis der Gekroonde Hoofden
X	MIAT
Y	Boekentoren
Z	Oude Begijnhof van St.-Elisabeth

The identity of its artist(s) has supplied endless material for discussion: is it the work of **Jan van Eyck** *(qv)* alone? Or are we to believe the Latin inscription on the frame, which says that it was begun by Van Eyck's older brother Hubert, although no other painting by this artist is known?

In any case, the colossal work depicts no fewer than 248 figures illuminated by a single light source on the right-hand side. The technique and the style are magnificent. The painting also bears witness to the Christian ideals of the Middle Ages.

The **paintings on the lower section** depict the Mystic Lamb on an altar surrounded by angels. Approaching the altar from either side of the Fountain of Life are the Knights *(photograph pp 44-45)* and the Righteous Judges, from the left, and the Hermits and Pilgrims, from the right. In the background the Virgins are gathered on the right, and the Martyrs and Confessors on the left.

The landscape is bright, the vegetation precisely detailed; botanists have identified 42 species of plants and flowers.

In the **upper section** we see Christ Triumphant, enthroned as the Great High Priest. To the left of Him are the Virgin Mary, a choir of angels, and Adam. To the right, St John the Baptist, a group of angel musicians, and Eve. The vivid realism of the figures and the decorative beauty of the fabrics are stunning.

When closed the panels represent the Annunciation in the centre, with the Prophets and the Sibyls above, and St John the Baptist, St John the Evangelist and the donors, Joos Vijd and his wife Elisabeth Borluut, below.

Cathedral furniture and works of art – The Baroque pulpit with its marble statues is by Laurent Delvaux. Hendrik Frans Verbruggen made the high altar in the chancel in the Baroque style. It depicts the *Apotheosis of St Bavo*. The mausoleum of Monsignor Triest (1654) by Jerome Duquesnoy the Younger is left of the chancel. The figure's weary expression is striking.

The altarpiece of **Jesus Among the Doctors** (1751), by Frans Pourbus the Elder is in the first ambulatory chapel to the south. Many famous figures feature on it, including Emperor Charles V in the lower left corner. Rubens' depiction of the **Vocation of St Bavo** (1624) can be seen in the tenth ambulatory chapel. The artist represented himself as a convert in a red cloak.

★**Crypt** – The crypt has the same layout as the chancel above it. The oldest part (1150) is marked out in black tiles on the floor. 15C and 16C naïve ex-votos are painted on the pillars and the Romanesque vaulting. There is also a valuable collection of church plate in the crypt including a silver reliquary of St Macaire by Hugo de la Vigne (1616), a 9C gospel-book and a necrological scroll describing monastic life in the Middle Ages. One of the chapels containing tombstones also includes the remarkable **Calvary triptych★** painted by Justus van Gent, a major work executed by the artist in 1466, before he left for Italy. The influence of Van Eyck and Van der Weyden is very clear (group of holy women in front of the Cross). This work is striking for the subtlety of the often acidic colours.

The 13C castle that belonged to Gerard the Devil, **Geraard de Duivelsteen (FZ B)**, is behind the east end of the cathedral. This austere medieval dwelling was restored in the 19C and belonged to a Ghent lord of this name.

★★★**Belfort** and **Lakenhalle (FY)** ☉ – The massive outline of the belfry (91m – 298ft), topped with a gilded copper dragon, symbolises the power of the guilds of Ghent during the Middle Ages. The belfry was built in the 13C and 14C and has frequently been altered and restored. It is adjacent to the 15C Cloth Hall, **Lakenhalle**. The carillon contains 52 chimes.

Inside the **belfry**, the room called "Secret" once contained the archives. There is a statue of a wild-looking man-at-arms, the only survivor of the four that once decorated the belfry's corners. Upstairs, a few historical mementoes and the carillon keyboard are worth a visit.

There is a beautiful view of the town from the upper platform. It was here that, while viewing the city, King Francis I of France said to Emperor Charles V: "How many Spanish skins would be needed to make a glove (*gant* in French, which sounds the same as the French name for Ghent, *Gand*) of this splendour?"!

Walk round the belfry to see the classical door (1741) of the **old prison** embellished with the "the man who suckles", the **mammelokker.** This Baroque low relief is a symbol of Christian charity. Cimon, an old Roman who was condemned to die of hunger, was suckled by his own daughter. A bell called the Triumphant, **Klok de Triomfante (EY F)** can be seen in the square at the foot of the belfry. This is the successor of the bell which once hung in the belfry and bore this legend: "This bell is called Roland; when it is set ringing, it sends a storm throughout the country."

Stadhuis (FY H) ☉ – Two distinct styles can be seen in the Town Hall. Building work began in 1518 to plans by Waghemakere *(qv)* and Keldermans. It was interrupted in 1535, however, and resumed 60 years later.

The **Huis van de schepenen van de Keure** (or Charter House) on the right is decorated with a corner turret and built in a florid 16C Gothic style. The chapel, a little balcony (for proclamations) and a flight of steps project beyond the north façade.

The left section, dating from the early 17C, took its inspiration from the Italian Renaissance. This is the **Huis van de schepenen van Gedele,** named after the aldermen responsible for settling disputes. Part of the Keure house is open to the public. The visit includes the hall of justice with its labyrinth pavement, which leads onto the balcony from which the Pacification of Ghent was proclaimed and a chapel with beautiful Gothic vaulting. The Throne Room upstairs has Renaissance vaulting.

The old crossbowmen's guild hall (1478), **St.-Jorishof (FY L)**, is opposite the Town Hall. It is now a hotel.

Graslei

Go past St.-Niklaaskerk to reach St.-Michielsbrug.

St.-Michielsbrug (**EY**) – There is a stunning **view★★★** of the old town's historic buildings and façades from this bridge. Turn round to admire the towers on the church dedicated to St Nicholas, the belfry and St Bavo's.

From the centre of the bridge, the view to the south reveals the apse of St.-Michielskerk and the old 15C Dominican convent next to it which is now a university building (Het Pand); and to the north the crenellations of the Counts of Flanders' castle and, in front of it, the houses on the quays known as Graslei and Korenlei.

★★★Graslei (**EY**) – *There is a good view of the house fronts from the Korenlei.* This used to be Ghent's harbour. The Graslei (literally "Herb Quay") is lined with 12C to 17C houses, in a very pure architectural style. From left to right, the most interesting houses are:

the 16C Gildehuis van de Metselaars, the masons' guildhall which has a tall stone façade crowned with graceful pinnacles;

the first Körenmetershuis (15C), the Grain Weighers' hall;

the large Romanesque Scaldian style Koornstapelhuis, which was a warehouse for grain taken as an in-kind customs duty payment;

the tiny Tolhuisje (1682), where the customs officer was lodged;

the second Gildehuis der Graanmeters (1698);

the Gildehuis der Vrije Schippers, the Free Boatmen's hall. The doorway is surmounted with the figure of a ship, and the wonderful façade is crowned with a gable with gently flowing lines, which dates from 1531.

Return to the Graslei.

Groentenmarkt (**EY**) – The vegetable market stands to the right of the meat market, **Groot Vleeshuis** (**K**), a building with a large number of crow-stepped dormer windows, dating from 1404.

Vrijdagmarkt (**FY**) – The enormous "Friday Market" was the scene of many historical episodes. The sovereigns of Flanders came here to address the people; weavers and wool workers fought bloody battles here in May 1345.

The house with the turret, on the far side of the marketplace, is **Het Toreken**. It dates from 1480 and belonged to the tanners' guild.

Further east are the three towers of **St.-Jacobskerk** (**FY**). The two towers on the west front are Romanesque, but one of them was given a sandstone roof with crockets in the 15C. The central statue is of Jacob van Artevelde.

Dulle Griet (**EFY R**) – The little 15C cannon, Mad Meg, was placed near a bridge over the Leie.

Kraanlei (**EY**) – Interesting houses line "Crane Quay", in particular the so-called Kite House, also known as the Flute Player's House, **Huis de Fluitspeler** (**E**). Next door to it is a house decorated with low reliefs representing works of mercy.

★Museum voor Volkskunde (**EY M¹**) ⊘ – The folk museum is housed in the cottages and Gothic chapel of the **almshouse, Alijsgodshuis,** which was founded in the 14C. The **inner courtyard★** makes a pretty picture with the delightful white houses and their tall dormer windows round about.

The museum describes Flemish popular arts and traditions. Among the forty or so rooms, there are remarkable reconstructions of shops (grocer's, bar, apothecary's), domestic interiors, craft workshops (cobbler's, wax-taper maker's, wood-turner's) recalling life in Ghent in *c*1900. The museum also has temporary exhibitions and a **theatre** ⊘ with traditional Ghent puppets.

St.-Veerleplein (**EY**) – This square, which was once used for executions, is surrounded by old houses. The **Wenemaershospitaal** (**S**), a hospice named after St Lawrence, has a façade dating from 1564. The old Baroque fish market, **Oude Vismarkt** (**V**), dating from 1690, has beautiful high reliefs representing Neptune and the rivers Leie and Scheldt.

Patershol (**EY**) – The Patershol, one of the city's oldest quarters, was saved from demolition in the 1980s. Today it is a lively corner with its many cafés and restaurants.

★★**Gravensteen** (**EY**) ⊘ – The castle of the Counts of Flanders was built in 1180 by the Count of Flanders, Philip of Alsace on the site of an older keep. It was extensively restored in the early 20C. At the time there was nothing left but a few ruins occupied by a spinning mill. Its architecture took its inspiration from the Crusaders' strongholds in Syria. The crown of curtain walls has oriels, watch turrets and merlons, all of which are reflected in the waters of the Lièvre.

Inside the curtain wall, it is possible to visit the watch-path (note the twin Romanesque windows in the east wall of the keep). Also open to the public are the beautiful rooms in the counts' palace, one of which was used by the seventh chapter of the Order of the Golden Fleece in 1445, presided over by Philip the Good. They now contain a collection of instruments of torture, recalling that the castle was also a prison for many years.

Gravensteen

From the top of the keep there is a superb **view**★ of Ghent and the surrounding area.

Go round the keep to enter the old stables. It has the layout of a double-naved crypt with ogive vaulting and contains a well.

On leaving the castle, note the **Huis der Gekroonde Hoofden (EY W)**, literally the "House of Royalty", at the beginning of Burgstraat. It is decorated with medallions containing busts of the counts of Flanders.

★★MAJOR MUSEUMS *time: allow half a day*

★★**Museum voor Schone Kunsten** (**CX M²**) ⊘ – This large art gallery stands on the edge of Citadelpark, which surrounds the **Floraliapaleis** *(qv)*. It houses extensive and interesting collections of ancient and modern art from the 15C to the 20C. Although some of the sculptures and the Brussels tapestries are outstanding, it is the paintings in particular that make this a gallery well worth a visit.

Ancient art *(left wing)* – The collection of old masters includes the delightful *Virgin with Carnation* by Van der Weyden and the two paintings by **Hieronymous Bosch** that deal with the same theme, that of good versus evil. The first of the two, **St Jerome**, is a work from his early years. The foreground represents evil, with the saint at prayer surrounded by terrifying objects and a menacing natural landscape; in the background, the peaceful landscape represents good. The **Bearing of the Cross**, one of the great painter's last works, reveals an extraordinary modernism in the way the mass of bloated, demonic faces is depicted, with the serene face of Christ in the centre. The figure of Christ is set between two diagonals: one symbolises evil with the beam of the Cross and the face of the bad thief on the lower right. The other links the face of the good thief with St Veronica withdrawing with the shroud.

Adriaan Isenbrant's *Virgin and Child* has a strikingly beautiful landscape. The work of 16C Ghent artist Gerard Horenbaut, who was best known as a miniaturist, is represented here by portraits.

The works of Pieter Brueghel the Younger and Roland Savery come next, then an admirable *Portrait of a Woman* by Pourbus the Elder, a number of works by Rubens, an unusually vigourous *Study of Heads* by Jordaens, Gaspar de Crayer's *Study of Young Moor's Head*, two works by Philippe de Champaigne *(Disciples on the Road to Emmaus)* and a *Portrait of Jean-Pierre Camus)*, a *Bittern* by Fyt and a portrait by Frans Hals.

The works by Antwerp painter Joachim Beuckelaer (1530-1574) in another part of the museum are realistic paintings of marketplaces and kitchens.

Modern painting *(right wing)* – The collection is extensive, displaying in particular paintings by the Belgian artists Ensor, Evenepoel *(Spaniard in Paris)*, Spilliaert, Emile Claus, and Van Rysselberghe *(Reading)*, as well as by the French artist Rouault and the Expressionists Kokoschka, Kirchner and Rholfs.

A few rooms have been given over to paintings by the first St.-Martens-Latem group *(qv)* including works by Minne, Van de Woestijne, De Saedeleer, and by the second St.-Martens-Latem group with paintings by Permeke, Gust De Smet, and Servaes.

The works from the 19C French school are all in one room. The collection includes Géricault's remarkable *Portrait of a Kleptomaniac*, and works by Corot, Courbet, Fantin-Latour, Daubigny, and Théodore Rousseau.

Museum van Hedendaagse Kunst – This museum, which was inaugurated in 1976, is in the same building. It deals exclusively with contemporary art movements presented through a series of temporary exhibitions. CoBrA, hyperrealism, minimalist art, conceptual art, Pop art and all the current movements are represented, and there are works by forerunners such as René Magritte, Paul Delvaux and Victor Servranckx.

★★**Bijloke Museum** (**CX M³**) ⊘ – The old Cistercian abbey was founded in the 13C. This remarkable group of brick buildings dates from the 14C to the 17C, and contains a museum of archaeology and history.

Inside the abbey buildings there are beautiful rooms in which old Ghent interiors have been reconstructed. Large **collections of decorative art** are exhibited in the galleries of the cloisters (ironwork, copperware, bronze, pottery and ceramics), along with the costume and arms collections.

The marvellous 14C **refectory** on the first floor has a large coffered vault and frescoes, one of which represents the Last Supper. There is a beautiful recumbant effigy made of Tournai stone in the centre of the room. It is the tomb of a Ghent nobleman who died in 1232.

The Guild Room, once the dorter, has magnificent 18C carved wooden *torchères* symbolising the different trades.

Two rooms on the ground floor contain collections relating to the various military brotherhoods in Ghent.

While crossing the little gallery looking out on a second courtyard, notice the refectory gable, delicately sculpted with moulded bricks.

In the 17C abbess' house, there are beautiful 17C fireplaces brought here from the Town Hall.

The wonderful silver insignia of the town musicians (15C and 16C) are displayed in the room dealing with the city of Ghent.

ADDITIONAL SIGHTS

★**Klein Begijnhof** (**DX**) – This calm enclosed Beguine convent was founded in 1234 by Joanna of Constantinople. It has not changed since the 17C and four Beguine nuns still live here. The charming brick houses, with small front gardens and whitewashed walls, surround the church and two meadows.

Museum voor Sierkunst (**EY M⁴**) ⊘ – The elegant rooms in the old 18C Coninck mansion contain beautiful furniture grouped by period, tapestries and objets d'art which recreate the atmosphere of a patrician home of days gone by. Certain rooms are decorated with painted canvas panels. The **dining room** (Room 7), with its painted ceiling, woodwork, furniture and Chinese porcelain, is a particularly elegant 18C interior. A new wing contains modern furniture.

St.-Baafsabdij (**DV M⁵**) ⊘ – The abbey was founded in the 7C and rebuilt in the 10C. It now lies in ruins.

In 1540, having proclaimed the Caroline Concession *(qv)*, Emperor Charles V turned the abbey into a citadel. It was demolished in the 19C.

Nothing remains of the abbey buildings but one gallery of the Gothic cloisters, the beautiful Romanesque lavabo, the twin Romanesque windows in the chapter-house and above all the vast 12C **refectory★**, with its magnificent timber ceiling shaped like a ship's hull. It contains Romanesque frescoes and a large collection of gravestones. There are also Romanesque and Gothic stones in the undercroft.

Museum voor Industriële Archeologie en Textiel (**MIAT**) (**DV X**) – *Minnemeers, 9.* This museum of industrial archeology and textiles is housed in an old cotton mill. It displays the city's industrial history.

Boekentoren (**CX Y**) – *Rozier 9.*
The central library of the University of Ghent (1933-1940) lies in a bustling district of the city. It was built to plans by the famous architect Henry van de Velde (1863-1957), the founder of the Kunstgewerbeschule in Weimar and forerunner of the Bauhaus movement. The 64m – 210ft tower has 26 storeys including a wonderful reception room (Belvedere) in which the architectural lines are particularly pure. This is a modernist construction with a very plain façade. It was built of concrete.

Kunstencentrum Vooruit (CX C) – *St.-Pietersnieuwstraat 23.*
This former Socialist "entertainment hall" was built by F Dierkens between 1911 and 1914. It now contains several different auditoriums used for drama productions, dance and concerts. The superb façade was designed in the Art Nouveau style.

Oude Begijnhof van St.-Elisabeth (CV Z) – The large Beguine convent was founded, like the small one, in 1234. When it became inadequate for their needs in the 19C the nuns left it and moved to St.-Amandsberg *(see below)*. All that now remains is a narrow picturesque street, **Proveniersterstraat**, near the church dedicated to St Elizabeth. There are also three pretty houses with crowstepped gables not far from the church entrance. They have been well-restored.

Begijnhoflaan leads northwards to the **Rabot** (CV). This gate (1489) with pepperpot roofs and crowstepped gables is in fact an old sluice into which the Lève disappears to flow underground. Not far from here is the **Donkere Poort**, all that remains of the palace (Prinsenhof) where Emperor Charles V was born.

Patriciërswoning De Achtersikkel (FY N) – This picturesque mansion, with its turrets and arcaded courtyard, was built in the 16C in a little street near the cathedral (Biezekapelstraat).
There is an entire row of old house fronts in Hoogpoortstraat nearby.

OTHER PLACES OF INTEREST

St.-Amandsberg – *Return to Land van Waaslaan* (DV **100**). *The entrance to the Beguine convent is at no 53.*

Begijnhof (DV) – In 1874 this succeeded the old Beguine convent of St Elizabeth *(see above)*, after which it was named. It is a huge enclosure with the traditional layout of Beguine convents. A neo-Gothic church stands in the middle. A few nuns still live here. The **museum** gives an insight into their way of life.

EXCURSIONS

Lochristi – *9km – 5.5 miles northeast on the N 70.*
The cultivation of summer-flowering begonias and azaleas predominates in this large agricultural centre.

Eeklo – *20km 12.5 miles northwest on the N 9.*
Eeklo has a pretty Renaissance **Town Hall,** with crowstepped gables and dormers and brightly-coloured shutters.

The 16C **Watervliet** church, 29km – 18 miles north on the N 456, near the border with the Netherlands, has a beautiful 15C triptych painted on wood, and interesting Baroque furniture.

★**Laarne** – *13km – 8 miles eastwards. Leave on the N 445 and turn left towards Heusden.* Magnificent estates can be seen along this road before reaching Heusden. *For a description of Laarne see Château de LAARNE.*

Leiestreek – *22km – 13.75 miles. Leave on the Koningin Fabiolalaan, near the station (St.-Pietersstation)* (CX).
The banks of the Leie have inspired many a painter. The name of the little town of **St.-Martens-Latem** has a permanent place in the history of art.
At the end of the 19C a group of artists formed around sculptor Georges Minne, who had lived in the village since 1897. Among the group's members were Gustave van de Woestijne (1881-1947), and the landscape painters Van den Abeele (1835-1918) and Valerius de Saedeleer (1867-1941).
Their research ended, after the war, in the very marked Expressionism of the second St.-Martens-Latem group, of which the forerunner was **Albert Servaes** (1873-1967). The main representatives were **Constant Permeke** (1886-1952), the leading figure **Gustave De Smet** (1877-1943) and **Frits van den Berghe** (1883-1939).
There is no road along the course of the Leie; a **boat trip** ⊙ is the best way to discover the countryside on its banks.

Afsnee – There are countless paintings of the charming Romanesque church, with its east end on the banks of the Leie.

St.-Martens-Latem – The area around this village near the Leie is very popular with people from Ghent. A 15C wooden windmill can be seen on the left from the road running through the village.

Deurle – *See DEURLE.*

Beyond Deurle the route initially follows the Leie (pretty view on the left), before crossing a bridge. There is then a beautiful **view** of the river running lazily between rich green meadows.

Kasteel van Ooidonk ⊙ – This 16C castle stands in a meander of the Leie, near the village of Bachte-Maria-Leerne. It replaced a medieval fortress that was inhabited by the lords of Nevele and destroyed during the Wars of Religion.

The present castle, surrounded by water and a wooded estate, is still inhabited. It is characteristic of the Hispano-Flemish style, with crowstepped gables and onion-domed towers. The interior was refurbished in the 19C and includes a beautiful suite of apartments. Among the 16C portraits are those of Philip of Montmorency, Count of Hornes and owner of the castle, and the Count of Egmont. Both were beheaded in Brussels in 1568.

Deinze – This small industrial town was built on the banks of the Leie. There is a beautiful **church** dedicated to Our Lady (Onze-Lieve-Vrouwekerk). It dates from the 13C and is an excellent example of Scaldian Gothic (triplets, tower above the transept crossing). A work by Gaspar de Crayer depicting the Adoration of the Shepherds can be seen inside.
A little further along, the white building of the **Museum van Deinze en Leiestreek** ⊙ can be seen through the trees. The St.-Martens-Latem group is well represented in the collections of paintings and sculptures by artists from the Ghent-Kortrijk area. The most outstanding works are *Beetroot Harvest* by Émile Claus, *Marshy Landscape* by Saedeleer and paintings by A Saverys, A Servaes, Van de Woestijne, G Minne, Van Rysselberghe, Van den Abeele and R Raveel. The museum also has an archeology and folklore section.

GERAARDSBERGEN ★

Oost-Vlaanderen – Population 30 193
Michelin maps 409 E3 or 213 fold 17

The name of this town is a reflection of its **location** ★ on a hillside overlooking the River Dender. It is famous in the world of cycle racing because of the irregularly cobbled path running up a terrible undulating hill. It is known as the "Geraardsbergen wall".
Geraardsbergen has a very large match factory. Mattentaart (fromage frais and curd tart) is a town speciality.

SIGHTS

Grote Markt – St.-Bartholomeuskerk stands on this square. The church was renovated in the neo-Gothic style in the 19C, as was the 19C Town Hall with its toothed gables and corner turrets. The little Manneken Pis against it is said to be the oldest in Belgium (1455). The statue has its own museum of costume on the ground floor of the building. In the centre of the square, the Gothic fountain called the Marbol dates from 1475.

St.-Adriaansabdij – *Follow Vredestraat to the left of the Town Hall, then turn right into Abdijstraat.*
A Benedictine monastery was founded here in 1081. The 18C abbey buildings have now been turned into a **museum** ⊙, with old paintings and furniture from St.-Bartholomeuskerk in Geraardsbergen and from the Hane Steenhuyse in Ghent *(qv)*. There are also some old paintings. The exhibits are displayed in various rooms and drawing rooms opening onto a wide vaulted corridor. On the second floor are various rooms with exhibits relating to the cultivation of tobacco, a flourishing business in Geraardsbergen from 1840 until the Second World War. There is a collection of pipes from all over the world. Another room has a display of black Chantilly lace which was made locally from 1870 onwards.
A park was laid out around a lake. The barns have been restored to provide exhibition space.

Oudenberg – *Access by car by Oude Steenweg then turn left into Driepikkel.*
A pilgrims' chapel containing a 17C statue of the Virgin Mary was built at the top of this hill, at an altitude of 110m – 364ft. There is a beautiful view of the surrounding countryside from the chapel. The **Krakelingenworp,** or "sugar bun throwing", festival takes place here *(see the Calendar of Events).*
A costumed procession of 800 people begins to climb the hill at 1500. When they reach the top 8 000 sugar buns called "Krakelingen" are thrown out over the crowd and the local celebrities must drink little live fish from a silver goblet. In the evening, a cask filled with tar and wrapped in straw is set on fire during the **Tonnekensbrand.** There are numerous stories and legends which claim to explain origin of this event, which is thought to be very old, yet despite them it remains a mystery.

GHENT ★★★

See GENT

Le GRAND-HORNU

Hainaut
Michelin maps 409 E4 or 214 fold 2

Hornu lies in the Borinage region near Mons. It has an industrial complex called Le Grand-Hornu, built between 1814 and 1832. This complex is a remarkable example of how workplace and home can be designed to make a unified whole, as had been done at the salt-works at Arc-et-Senans in France 25 years earlier.

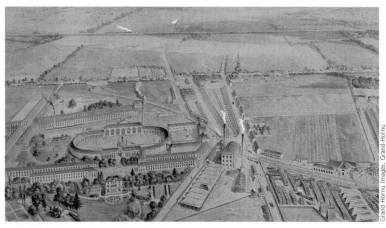

Panoramic view of the use of the Grand-Hornu area c1900

The founder of Le Grand-Hornu, the industrialist **Henri de Gorge** (1774-1832), assigned the design of the complex to architect Bruno Renard, who produced a layout for the site in the neo-classical style that was so much in vogue at the time. This can be seen from the use of arcades, pediments and half-moon windows. In addition to the industrial complex, 425 houses were built for the workers; they were exceptionally luxurious for the time.

Le Grand-Hornu ceased its activites in 1954, and was abandoned for several years. In 1969 a royal decree condemned it to demolition. Then in 1971 an architect from Le Grand-Hornu, Henri Guchez, bought the ruins of the site and undertook its restoration. Since 1989 Le Grand-Hornu has been the property of the Province of Hainaut.

TOUR ⊙

The tour takes visitors first into a closed courtyard bordered on the left by stables converted into an art gallery (doors sculpted by Félix Roulin); on the right is the hay loft. Then there is a vast oval courtyard surrounded by arcades and brick buildings, once the site of the workshops (they are now used as offices). The main workshop on the left made steam-powered machines. The pillars which used to support domes on pendentives can still be seen here. The administrative building opposite the machine shop is concealed behind a pedimented façade. The 425 workers' houses are arranged around the factory in rectilinear streets within a rectangle. The community consisted of 2 500 people in 1829.

HAKENDOVER

Vlaams-Brabant
Michelin maps 409 H3 or 213 fold 20 3km – 2 miles east of Tienen

This very old village is famous for its pilgrimages. The most spectacular one is the great procession of the Divine Redeemer (see the Calendar of Events), accompanied by riders on horseback. The procession wends its way through the meadows and fields already sown with seed which, despite being trampled down by the crowds, still apparently produce good harvests.

St.-Salvatorskerk ⊙ – The church was founded in 690. It has conserved a tower and part of the transept which are both Romanesque. The chancel was built in the 14C. The nave was enlarged in the 18C. A famous Brabant **altarpiece** ★ on the high altar is in wood and dates from 1400. It depicts in a lively yet elegant way the miraculous construction of the church, in thirteen scenes. Three virgins undertook the construction of the church in the 7C but angels demolished it during the night. On the thirteenth day after Epiphany a crow showed the virgins where they should build the church. They took on 12 workers, and a thirteenth one, who was none other than Christ, came to join them. This was how the church was completed.

HALLE★

Vlaams-Brabant – Population 32 310
Michelin maps 409 F3 or 213 fold 18
Town plan in the current Michelin Red Guide Benelux

Since the 13C town life has centred on worship of a Black Virgin, the object of a famous pilgrimage. The procession at Whitsun with its historical pageant *(see the Calendar of Events)* is the main procession. There are others on the first Sunday of September and the first Sunday of October.

The carnival *(on Refreshment Sunday, the third Sunday in Lent)* is famous.

★★ BASILIEK *time: allow 45 min*

The basilical church was built in the 14C. Its layout, without a projecting transept, is a good example of the early Brabant Gothic style. There is a powerful-looking square **tower** ☉ surmounted by bellcotes at the corners and, since 1775, also by a Baroque lantern. There is a little 15C baptistery on the south side, projecting from the main body of the basilica, with a bulbous roof. The carillon installed in 1973 consists of 54 chimes.

Note the **south doorway** and its carving of the Virgin and Child surrounded by angel musicians. A little further on, there is a little door decorated with a carving of the Coronation of the Virgin Mary. The harmoniously proportioned east end and the sides of the building are decorated with superb narrative corbels and two tiers of balustrades.

Interior – The elegant nave has a triforium with Flamboyant Gothic tracery. Above the porch, there is a double tier of windows, also in the Flamboyant Gothic style. There are many wonderful **objets d'art** in the church, as well as beautiful sculptures.

The font *(chapel south of the tower)* dates from 1466. It was made of brass and has a cover sumptuously decorated with apostles, horsemen (St Martin, St George, St Hubert) and a group representing the Baptism of Christ. In the chancel there are statues of the Apostles dating from 1410. They were inspired by Claus Sluter, the famous sculptor to the Dukes of Burgundy in Dijon. The famous Black Virgin is enthroned in the middle. The spandrils of the arches in the ambulatory are decorated with remarkable narrative carvings (15C).

An altarpiece in the Trazegnies chapel, which juts out from the basilica along the north aisle, represents the Seven Sacraments. It was made in the Italian Renaissance style by Jean Mone, sculptor to Emperor Charles V. Note also the tiny recumbent effigy of Joachim, the son of Louis XI, in a chapel on the north side of the chancel. The boy died in 1460, while his father, who was still Dauphin or heir apparent at that time, was in hiding in Genappe *(7km – 4.75 miles east)*.

Treasury ☉ – The most beautiful items of church plate are displayed in the crypt, bearing witness to the generosity of illustrious donors. Particularly outstanding examples include two Brussels monstrances, one dating from the 15C and donated by Louis XI, the other from the 16C, donated by Henry VIII of England.

ADDITIONAL SIGHTS

Grote Markt – The **Town Hall** next to the basilica was built in the early 17C in the Renaissance style. It was restored in the 19C, and now has a harmonious façade. A statue of the cellist **Adrien-François Servais** (1807-1866), who was born in Halle, stands in the middle of the square. Servais was an international success: Berlioz called him the Paganini of the cello and he was also the solo cellist of Leopold I.

Zuidwest Brabants Museum ☉ – The museum of southwest Brabant is housed in a 17C Jesuit school. It reflects the regional way of life in days gone by through objects found during archeological digs, old tools, baskets made in Halle in the 17C and 18C, Huizingen porcelain, etc.

EXCURSION

Rebecq – *10km – 6.25 miles southwest on the N 6, then a road to the right.*
A **tourist train** ☉ pulled by a little locomotive runs between the old Rebecq station and Rognon in the Senne Valley.
Exhibitions are organised in the **Arenberg Mill** on the Senne.

European industrial heritage sites

In the early days of the industrial age, industrialists had visions of utopian settlements where discipline and order reigned; only a few came to fruition: Wedgood's pottery works at Etruria, Owen's, New Lanark and Henri de Gorge's Le Grand-Hornu.

The village of New Lanark on the river Clyde is a good example of an 18C planned industrial village. Building started in 1785 and by 1799 the four mills were Scotland's largest cotton mill supporting a village population of over 2 000.

In Belgium an experimental mining village, Le Grand-Hornu, was built between 1814 and 1832 to work the coal seams of the Borinage coalfiled. In 1829 the township numbered 450 houses and accounted for a population of 2 500.

HAN-SUR-LESSE ★

Namur
Michelin 409 I5 or 213 fold 6

The **parc national de Lesse et Lomme** consists of vast limestone uplands crossed by two rivers. Han-sur-Lesse is famous for its magnificent cave and its animal reserve.

SIGHTS

★★★**Grotte de Han** ⊘ – *The entrance to the cave is at Le Trou de Salpêtre and can only be reached by tramway. The return trip is made on foot (400m – about 0.3 mile).* The tour takes visitors round one-fifth of the giant limestone cave gouged out by the Lesse over a distance of 15km – 9.50 miles. The cave served as a refuge from the end of the Neolithic period to the 18C. It is very damp, with a temperature of 13°C – 55°F, and gigantic concretions have formed at a rate of 4-5cm – 1.5-2in every one hundred years. They include the graceful **Minaret** stalagmite which is 5m – 16.25ft tall. Certain galleries have been open to the public since 1856 and have been blackened by the torches of the first visitors. The **Salle des Mystérieuses** has retained all the magic of a crystal palace, with its superb stalagmite in the shape of a tiara. The impressive **Salle d'Armes**, 50m – 164ft across, is crossed by the Lesse and features an outstanding sound and light show. Beyond it is the **Salle du Dôme** which is 129m – 423ft high. A torch-bearer can be seen here, rushing down the huge pile of boulders. Then comes the **Salle des Draperies** in which the ceiling bristles with marbled stalactites.

Large boats go down the subterranean stretch of the Lesse and emerge into daylight at the **Trou de Han** after a cannon is fired to demonstrate the echo in the gallery.

Spéléothèrme ⊘ – *At the exit to the cave, in an upper room of the Ferme de Dry Hamptay.* An audiovisual presentation reveals the other caves and galleries of the system which are only open to experienced potholers.

Musée du Monde souterrain ⊘ – This museum exhibits the results of regional archeological digs, mainly those conducted in the Han Cave, on the river bed or on the banks. The exhibits include Neolithic shaped flints, a remarkable collection of pottery, tools, weapons, jewellery, some of it gold jewellery from the Bronze Age (1100-700 BC), fibulae from the Iron Age, a fragment of an **official diploma ★** belonging to a Roman veteran, consisting of two bronze tablets, and various Gallo-Roman, Merovingian and medieval objects.

★**Réserve d'animaux sauvages** ⊘ – A small train takes visitors through the magnificent Massif du Boine estate covering an area of 250 hectares – 618 acres, where the Lesse flows underground. The reserves contain animals from the Ardennes forests (deer, stags, boars) and, in a vast clearing, the main wild animals that once lived in the region ie bison, brown bears, ibex, chamois, wolves, tarpans (small wild horses), wild oxen (this extinct animal was "recreated" by breeding) and Przewalski horses which originally came from the Russian steppe.

At the chasm known as the **gouffre de Belvaux**, the Lesse disappears beneath a rocky arch on Mont de Boine then re-emerges at Le Trou de Han *(see above)*.

EXCURSION

Lavaux-Ste-Anne – *10km – 6.2 miles west on the Dinant road.*
The **feudal castle**, surrounded by a moat fed by the Wimbe, looks like a fortress. It is still flanked at the corners by three massive 15C towers with onion domes and has a 15C keep. The original curtain walls between the towers were replaced by a U-shaped house in the 17C and 18C.

The castle houses the **musée de la Chasse et de la conservation de la Nature** ⊘, a museum concerned within hunting and nature conservancy. Stuffed animals, hunting trophies and documentation on European animals are on display.

HASSELT

Limburg ℙ – Population 64 722
Michelin maps 409 I3-J3 or 213 fold 9

Hasselt lies on the borders of the Kempen and Hesbaye regions. Since 1839 it has been the main city of Belgian Limburg, after a treaty signed in London divided the province, the remains of a former duchy, between Belgium and the Netherlands. It is a busy city, growing ever more so with the region's increasing industrialisation. An excellent gin-like spirit flavoured with juniper-berries (geneva) is made here *(see below)*. The Hasselt district includes no less than nine makers of this spirit, locally known as "witteke" (little white).

The town depended on the bishopric of Liège from the 14C to the 18C, although it rebelled from time to time, for instance in the 16C when Hasselt's Protestants took part in the religious disturbances fomented against the prince-bishops.

The Flemish peasants revolted in 1798 against the French occupiers who were pillaging the country and selling church estates as "national property". This revolt, called **Boerenkrijg**, ended in a bloodbath. The monument on Leopoldplein (**Z**) serves as a reminder that one thousand men died in Hasselt.

In 1959 Hasselt was endowed with a modern cultural centre(*via Kunstlaan*, **Z 32**). The diocese of Hasselt was founded in 1967 and covers the province of Limburg. The University of Limburg was founded in 1968 east of the town.

Hendrik van Veldeke – The first Dutch-language poet not to remain anonymous was born near Hasselt in the 12C. Hendrik van Veldeke died after 1210, and a statue in his memory stands in the little park at the corner of Dorpsstraat and Thonissenlaan.

Festivals – Every seven years in August *(see the Calendar of Events)* the Virgin Virga Jesse, patron saint of the town, is honoured by a large religious procession, presided over by Hasselt giant De Langeman or Don Christophe.

A folklore festival, the Meieavondviering, is held every year on 30 April on Grote-Markt. The May tree is brought there in a procession, then planted while witches dance and dummies representing winter are burned. The square then rings to the sound of local songs, especially the Meiliedeke.

SIGHTS

Grote Markt (**Z**) – A half-timbered house dating from 1659, now housing a chemist's, is named after its sign **Het Sweert** (**Z A**), the Sword.

St.-Quintinuskathedraal (**Z**) is nearby, its presence marked by a squat 13C tower topped by an 18C spire. The nave and side aisles of the cathedral were built in the 14C and gradually enlarged with the chancel, the side chapels, then the ambulatory.

O.-L. Vrouwkerk (**Z D**) – This 18C church dedicated to Our Lady contains marble sculptures brought here from the Cistercian Herkenrode Abbey *(5km – 3 miles northwest of Hasselt)*. The abbey was founded at the end of the 12C and abolished in 1797. Its church was destroyed in the 16C by a fire. The black and white marble **high altar** is a masterpiece by Liège sculptor Jean Delcour, who died in 1707 *(see Liège)*. The statues of St Bernard and the Immaculate Conception are also by Delcour. The two **mausoleums** in the transept for the abbesses of Herkenrode were created by two artists. The one on the right *(Christ in the Tomb)* was by Artus Quellin the Younger (1625-1700); the one on the left *(Resurrection of Christ)* by Laurent Delvaux (1696-1778). The 14C Virga Jesse, the origin of the septennial procession, is exhibited in the chancel.

HASSELT

Botermarkt .... Y 7
Demerstr. .... Y
Diesterstr. .... YZ 8
Grote Markt .... Z
Havermarkt .... Z 18
Hoogstr. .... Y 22
Koning Albertstr. .... Z 27
Ridder Portmanstr. .... Z 39

Badderijstr. .... Y 2
Dorpstraat .... Y 10
Kapelstr. .... Z 23
Kempischesteenweg ..... Y 24
Kolonel Dusartpl. .... Y 26
Koning Boudewijnlaan ... Y 28
Koningin Astridlaan .... Y 30
Kunstlaan .... Z 32
Lombaardstr. .... Y 34
Maastrichtersteenweg .. Y 35
Maastrichterstr. .... YZ 36
de Schiervellaan .... Z 43
St.-Jozefstr. .... Z 44
Windmolenstraat .... Z 50
Zuivelmarkt .... Y 51

A   Het Sweert
D   O.-L. Vrouwkerk
E   Refugiehuis van de abdij van Herkenrode

M¹ Nationaal Jenevermuseum
M² Museum Stellingwerff-Waerdenhof
M³ Stedelijk Modemuseum

★Nationaal Jenevermuseum Y M[1]) ⊘ – The geneva museum is in the farm-house of a former convent which was turned into a geneva factory in 1803. The factory remained operational until 1939. The museum has taken up geneva manufacture again, using 19C processes.

Ph. Gajic/MICHELIN

Geneva, a malt wine made with a base of barley and rye, has been made in Flanders since the 16C. Sprouted barley is put on the perforated floor of a kiln to dry. Then the malted barley and rye are ground to release the starch, and the mix (2/3 rye and 1/3 malted barley) is left to macerate at about 63°C – 145°F, so that the enzymes can turn the starch into sucrose. By adding yeast the sugars turn into alcohol, and the mix is distilled to separate the wort from the alcohol. A second distillation of this rough geneva produces the malt wine with a taste that varies depending on the flavourings (juniper berries, for example) added during the second distillation.

A numbered tour programme takes visitors through the old ox stables to the kiln. On the ground floor is the impressive steam machine that runs the millstones and the macerator. The 19C distillation machinery can still be operated. The exhibits on display in the old house concern the history, packaging and manufacturers' advertising of geneva. The tour ends with a tasting session.

Begijnhof (Y) – The garden of the old convent is still bordered by rows of 18C Beguine houses, with a little courtyard in front of them. They are in the Mosan style, with brick walls intersected with stone courses. A modern building is home to the **Provinciaal Museum** which organises exhibitions of international contemporary art. Ivy-clad ruins and a few carved stones are all that remain of the church which was destroyed by an air raid in 1944.

Museum Stellingwerff-Waerdenhof (YZ M[2]) ⊘ – The collections in this museum illustrate the history and artistic life of the town of Hasselt and the old Loon county. Besides the liturgical objects, including the world's oldest monstrance dating from 1286, there are some marvellous Art Nouveau ceramics from the Manufacture de céramiques décoratives founded in 1895, a collection of shop signs and some 19C and 20C paintings.

Refugiehuis van de abdij van Herkenrode (Y E) – This beautiful 16C Gothic-Renaissance building is now occupied by government offices. In times of trouble, this was a refuge for the Cistercians of Herkenrode.

Stedelijk Modemuseum (Y M[3]) ⊘ – *Gasthuisstraat 11.*
This new museum of fashion is housed in a 17C convent that has recently been refurbished. Its exhibits reflect changes in fashion from the 18C to the present day, through documents, accessories and clothes. The museum also organises temporary exhibitions.

Japanse tuin (Y) ⊘ – *East of the town via Koning Boudewijnlaan.*
This delightful Japanese garden lies outside the town centre. It was created with the assistance of the Hasselt's twin town, Itami in Japan. Its layout complies with the principles of Saku-tei-ki. The garden also includes a tea house and a ceremonial house that resembles something out of a fairytale.

EXCURSIONS

Round trip – *42km – 26 miles allow 3 hours. Leave by Kempischesteenweg (Y 24) and turn right after the bridge over the Albert Canal.*

★**Bokrijk Provincial Domain** – *See Provinciaal Domien van BOKRIJK.*
Go round the east side of the estate.

The road soon crosses magnificent heather-covered hills, that are characteristic of the Kempen, then passes the recreation park of **Hengelhoef**, before reaching the road from Houthalen to Zwartberg.

Kelchterhoef – This is a large wooded recreation area dotted with lakes *(fishing)*. An old half-timbered abbey farmhouse has been turned into an inn.
Head east to reach Zwartberg.

Zwartberg – *See GENK: Excursions.*

Genk – *See GENK.*

The return trip to Hasselt provides an opportunity to stop for a while at the **De Maten nature reserve** *(see Genk: Excursions).*

Heusden-Zolder; 't Fonteintje; Molenheide – *59km – 37 miles north. Leave via Koningin Astridlaan* (**Y 30**) *and turn right after going under the motorway.*

Heusden-Zolder – The **Zolder International Motor Racing Track** is south of the town near the pine-clad **Bolderberg** (alt 60m – 197ft). It is 4.19km – 2.6 miles long, and is an important centre of competitive motor sports. The Belgian Formula One Grand Prix is run here when it is not held at Spa Francorchamps.

't Fonteintje – This is a **recreation area** ⊙ east of Koersel-Beringen, surrounded by pines. There is a view of Kempenland from the top of the **tower** (uitkijktoren).

Molenheide – This 180 hectare – 445 acre park lies north of Helchteren-Houthalen. It is located in the woods and has various facilities. In the game park, **wild- en wandelpark** ⊙, animals such as deer, stags, etc. live in the wild. The park also provides many opportunities for sports (swimming, tennis, bicycles for hire).

HAUTES FAGNES★★
Liège
Michelin maps 409 L4 or 213 fold 24

The Hautes Fagnes region lies between Eupen and Malmédy, a wind-swept and desolate plateau steeped in nostalgia, with peat bogs and fields of flying bent (a smooth, herbaceous grass with a purplish blue panicle) stretching as far as the eye can see, broken up by the dark masses of spruce plantations and clumps of deciduous trees (beech, oaks and birches). This region is now practically deserted, but it was once densely populated. Traces have been found of a road, the Via Mansuerisca, which is thought to date back to the 7C.

Nature reserve ⊙ – *Photograph p 14.* The Réserve naturelle domaniale des Hautes Fagnes was created in 1957. It covers an area of over 4 200 hectares – 10 378 acres, providing complete protection for flora, fauna, soil and countryside within its boundaries. Most peat bogs lie within the nature reserve. The plateau is not very high, but its harsh climate makes it possible to breed several species of mountain animals and propagate a range of mountain plants, even from quite far north. There are two dangers threatening the peat bogs.

Firstly, being trampled on regularly stops their development and will ultimately lead to their destruction. This is why it is forbidden to leave the authorised signposted footpaths. Secondly, fire is absolutely fatal to this environment, and unfortunately occurs here all too often. Extreme caution is strongly recommended, especially in the dry season *(red flags = no admission).*

Nature park – Since 1971 the reserve has been part of the **Parc naturel Hautes Fagnes-Eifel**. This nature park includes the Robertville and Bütgenbach lakes in Gileppe and Eupen, and the Our Valley and the Eifel. It runs into the German Nordeifel nature park. The whole area is called the **Deutsch-Belgischer Naturpark**, and covers a territory of 2 400km^2 – 5 930 acres, of which 700km^2 1 730 acres are in Belgium. To the south, it joins the Germano-Luxembourg nature park *(qv).*

SELECTED SIGHTS

Centre Nature Botrange ⊙ – A vast, warm, well-lit building in pale wood greets visitors to the Hautes Fagnes. It houses an information centre, exhibitions, audiovisual presentations, and a bookshop.

Signal de Botrange – 694m – 2,277ft. This is the highest peak in Belgium. Together with the Baraque-Michel survey station it occupies the centre of this somewhat convex plateau of bleak marshy countryside sprinkled with shaggy tufts of white-plumed cotton grass.

There is a far-ranging panorama *(viewing tables)* from the top of the **tower** ⊙. On a clear day the **view★** is especially far-reaching to the northeast. Beyond the conifers, the moors dotted with trees stretch as far as Germany towards Roetgen and Aachen.

★Nature trail – *1 hour 15min on foot. Wellington boots are recommended. The beginning of the path is opposite the Signal de Botrange on the other side of the road.* This pleasant walk follows the boarding over the peat bogs, making it possible to appreciate the immensity of the landscape which disappears into the distance on all sides. It also provides an opportunity to see local birds and plants in close up. Among the plants are rowans, bilberry bushes, heather, birches, and conifers.

La Baraque-Michel – This is a land-surveying station (1886-1888) at an altitude of 675m – 2 214ft. The University of Liège has set up a scientific study station on nearby **Mont Rigi**.

Herentals was once a flourishing clothmaking town and it has kept a few mementos of its past, especially the south and east **gateways** (Zandpoort and Bovenpoort) from its 14C fortified enclosure.

SIGHTS

Stadhuis – The Town Hall is in the middle of the elongated Grand-Place and used to be the clothmakers' guild hall. Dating from the 16C, it was built in brick and sandstone and is surmounted with a tiny belfry with a carillon. The **Fraikinmuseum** ⊙ is on the top floor; it contains a collection of plaster works by sculptor Charles Fraikin, who was born in Herentals (1817-1893).

St.-Waldetrudiskerk ⊙ – This Brabant Gothic church dedicated to St Waudru still has its 14C square central tower. There are interesting furnishings inside. The **altarpiece★** represents the Martyrdom of St Crispin and St Crispinian, the patron saints of cobblers and tanners. It is a wood carving by Pasquier Borremans dating from the early 16C. Other interesting works include the 17C carved choirstalls, paintings by Ambrosius and **Frans Francken the Elder**, who was born in Herentals (16C and 17C), and other canvases by Pieter Jozef Verhaghen (18C). Note the Romanesque font.

Begijnhof ⊙ – *Access via Fraikinstraat and Begijnenstraat.*
The Beguine convent was founded in the 13C and was very prosperous. However the "iconoclasts" destroyed it in 1578, and it had to be rebuilt. The houses surround a garden in which there is a charming Gothic church (1614).

EXCURSION

Round trip – *65km – 40 miles to the northeast*

Geel – The town has earned a reputation for its colony of harmless mentally ill people, who are boarded out with local families. This special function of Geel is said to have followed the decapitation of the Irish princess St Dympna by her father, who had been driven mad by the devil.

St.-Dimpnakerk ⊙ lies on the outskirts of the town on the Mol road. The Late Gothic church has sumptuous furnishings. In the chancel, there is a beautiful black marble and alabaster **mausoleum★** dating from the 16C, by Antwerp artist Cornelis II Floris. An altarpiece (1513) illustrates the life of the saint. A late-15C Brabant altarpiece in the south transept represents scenes from the Passion of Christ and a 14C altarpiece in the first chapel of the ambulatory, showing the twelve Apostles.
A little building adjacent to the church tower, called the Chambre des Malades or Chamber of the Ill, has a pretty Renaissance façade.

Mol – Mol is reputed for its Nuclear Research Centre which was set up in 1952. **St.-Pieter-en-Pauluskerk** contains a thorn from Christ's crown. A procession is held in its honour (H. Doornprocessie) every year. Near the church is a **pillory.**

Jakob Smits (1855-1928), who lived in the village of **Achterbos**, is the greatest of Kempen painters. The old presbytery in the neighbouring village of **Sluis** has been turned into a museum, **Jakob Smits Museum** ⊙.

Ginderbuiten – The modern church, St.-Jozef Ambachtsman, built by Meekels, is most interesting.

Zilvermeer – This large provincial leisure area in the pine forests north of Sluis includes two lakes, one for swimming and boating, the other for sailing.

Abdij Postel – This is a Premonstratensian *(see Averbode)* abbey, founded in the 12C by the monks from Floreffe in the middle of a pine forest. The 18C buildings are flanked by a Renaissance tower with a carillon (concerts). The Romanesque **church** dates from the 12C and 13C but was altered in the 17C. Organ concerts are given here.
In summer the new room is used for chamber music concerts.

Kasterlee – This is the main tourist centre in the Antwerp Kempen region, located in the middle of a pine forest.
There is a pretty **windmill** to the south, opposite the little British Second World War cemetery abundantly decorated with flowers. Further south, on the River Nete, there is a watermill that has been turned into a restaurant *(signposted "De Watermolen")*.

Papekelders Viewpoint (Toeristentoren) ⊙ – *Shortly before the railway line just outside Herentals, turn right towards the Bosbergen Wood and continue on foot.*
A 24m – 74ft tower has been built at the wood's highest point (altitude 40m – 131ft). From it there is a panoramic view of the region.

HUY ★★

Liège – Population 17 336
Michelin maps 409 fold 14 or 213 fold 21

Huy (pronounced "oo-ee") is a charming little town huddled at the foot of its collegiate church and its fortress, at the confluence of the Meuse and the Houyoux. In days gone by Huy's inhabitants boasted that they possessed four wonders: "li pontia", the bridge (Gothic, rebuilt in 1956); "li rondia", the rose window in the collegiate church; "li bassinia", the fountain on Grand-Place; and "li tchestia", the fortress.

Huy was part of the Liège province from 985 to 1789. Its strategic location resulted in about thirty sieges and a long series of destructions.

The town produced famous Mosan goldsmiths in the 12C, among them **Renier de Huy**, creator of the font in St Bartholomew's church in Liège *(qv)*; and Godefroy de Claire, also known as **Godefroy de Huy**. Pewter has been a local speciality since the 7C.

In 1095 **Pieter the Hermit** preached the First Crusade here. He ended his days in the convent of Neufmoustier, where he was buried in 1115. His mausoleum (1857) is in the cloister ruins to the north of Rue de Neufmoustier *(access via Avenue Delchambre)*.

Boat trips on the Meuse ⊘ – Trips are organised on the lake.

SIGHTS

★**Collégiale Notre-Dame** (**Z**) – This is a vast 14C church. Flamboyant Gothic flourishes can be noted in the clerestory, which was finished at the end of the 15C. An impressive tower adorned with a beautiful rose window ("li rondia"), 9m – 30ft in diameter, precedes the main body of the church. The apse is flanked by two square towers, a very unusual feature in Belgium.

The nave and side aisles inside are lofty, harmonising with the lancet windows in the chancel rising to a height of 20m – 66ft. Their modern stained glass replaced the windows that were destroyed in 1944. The vaulting was rebuilt in the 16C and painted with Renaissance arabesques. A Romanesque crypt lies under the chancel.

Fabri medallion "The Tree of Life"
Treasury of the Collegiale Notre-Dame

Ph. Gajic/MICHELIN

★**Treasury** ⊘ – Apart from some interesting wooden statues of saints dating from the 14C and 16C, there is a rich collection of Mosan gold- and silverware. The most outstanding pieces are the four magnificent **reliquaries** from the 12C and 13C. The ones made for relics of the town's patron saints St Domitian and St Mengold have been attributed to Godefroy de Huy but are unfortunately severely damaged. The reliquary of St Mark (probably 13C) is remarkable for the lively little figures whose fluid lines are highlighted by the use of champlevé enamel. As to the reliquary of the Virgin Mary (c1265), it has repoussé copper figures set against a very ornate background.

Portail du Bethléem – *Go along the south side of the nave.* The 14C "Bethlehem Door" lies beside the chevet and once opened onto the cloisters. The carving on the tympanum represents the Nativity (shepherds to the left, the Magi to the right), with the Massacre of the Innocents above. The fluid folds of the drapery and the picturesque way in which certain details are rendered make this a very fine piece of work.

Ancien hospice d'Oultremont – The **tourist office** is located in this brick building, built in the 16C by Canon Gérard d'Oultremont, at the foot of the citadel. Note the beautiful staircase-tower. The **maison de Batta** (**Z A**) on the opposite bank is a house built in the Mosan Renaissance style.

★**Fort** (**Z**) ⊘ – *Access by foot or by cable car going to La Sarte.*
The fortress was built from 1818 to 1823 by the Dutch, on the site of the old prince-bishops' castle ("il tchestia") which had been demolished in 1717. It was used to imprison hostages and Resistance members from 1940 to 1944. More than 7 000 people were detained here.

A signposted route leads visitors through the dungeons, the interrogation room and the military museum. From the glacis there is a splendid **view** ★★ of the old town, the Meuse and the surrounding area. The Tihange nuclear power station (1975) can also be seen to the northeast.

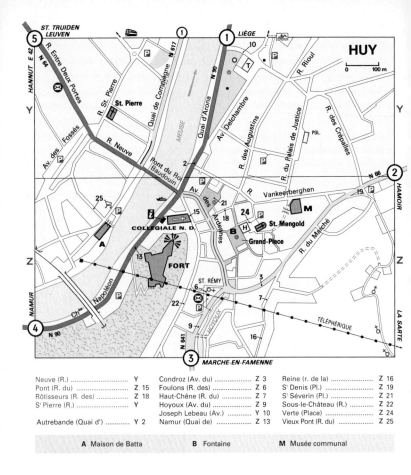

Neuve (R.)	Y	Condroz (Av. du)	Z 3	Reine (r. de la)	Z 16
Pont (R. du)	Z 15	Foulons (R. des)	Z 6	S¹ Denis (Pl.)	Z 19
Rôtisseurs (R. des)	Z 18	Haut-Chêne (R. du)	Z 7	S¹ Séverin (Pl.)	Z 21
S¹ Pierre (R.)	Y	Hoyoux (Av. du)	Z 9	Sous-le-Château (R.)	Z 22
		Joseph Lebeau (Av.)	Y 10	Verte (Place)	Z 24
Autrebande (Quai d')	Y 2	Namur (Quai de)	Z 13	Vieux Pont (R. du)	Z 25

A Maison de Batta	B Fontaine	M Musée communal

Grand-Place (**Z**) – The beautiful 18C **fountain** (**B**), "li bassinia", stands in front of the elegant Town Hall, which dates from 1766. The fountain is surmounted with bronze figures (Sts Mengold, Domitian, Catherine and the last count of Huy) dating from 1406 and 1597.

Charming little winding streets lead to the museum, via **Place Verte** overlooked by the pretty little Gothic church dedicated to its patron saint St Mengold.

★Musée communal (**Z M**) ⊘ – The museum is housed in the buildings and cloisters of the 17C Minim Brothers monastery. It has large local history and folklore collections including a regional interior decorated with a beautiful sandstone fireplace (1621), archeological finds, prints of the town, ceramics made in Huy in the 19C, pewter ware, and liturgical objects, including a 13C figure of Christ called the "handsome God of Huy".

Église St-Pierre (**Y**) – Romanesque font decorated with symbolic animals (lion, dragon).

La Sarte – The **playing fields** ⊘ beside the cable car terminus also have a children's playground.

EXCURSIONS

Amay – *8km – 5 miles east on the N 617 along the banks of the Meuse.*

Collégiale St-Georges – This was originally a Romanesque church but it was restored in the 18C. It is home to a beautiful piece of Mosan goldsmithing: the **reliquary★** in silver and gilded copper of St Oda and St George, created in about 1230 *(north transept).*

It also contains a **Merovingian sarcophagus★** *(beneath the chancel)* bearing the inscription Santa Chrodoara, but which could in fact be that of St Oda, a Merovingian noblewoman.

The little **musée communal d'Archéologie and d'Art religieux** ⊘ in the cloisters is a museum of archeology and religious art.

Flône Abbey, dating from the 17C and 18C, stands between the rock face and the Meuse about 2km – 1.25 miles from Amay. There is a beautiful 12C Romanesque font in the church.

★Château de Jehay  –
12km – 7.5 miles east. The château makes a very romantic picture with its walls in a white and brown stone checkerboard pattern reflected in the water of the moat. The building visitors see today dates from the 16C and is a beautiful example of a Mosan fortified manor-house, but the site was actually inhabited much further back in time. Archeological digs have unearthed traces of a lakeside town 10 000 years old. The present owner of the castle, a sculptor and archeologist, has redesigned the gardens.

There are marvellous **collections★** inside including furniture, tapestries, porcelain and gold- and silverware. In the smoking-room note the beautiful collection of silver- and goldware, a complete Koran on a single roll of paper, and a human head

Château de Jehay

shrunk by the Jivaros. The library contains a Brussels tapestry after Teniers and in the Queen Anne drawing room there is a rare 18C harpsichord.

The **Musée archéospéléologique** ⊘ is housed in the 13C cellars. It is an archeological and pot-holing museum displaying certain items found under the castle courtyard, including a fossilised bone patten.

IEPER ★

YPRES – West-Vlaanderen – Population 34 874
Michelin maps rpo B3 or zae folds 13, 14

Ypres, which was virtually flattened during the First World War, was rebuilt after the end of the conflict. It was one of the most powerful towns in Flanders in the 13C, together with Bruges and Ghent.

HISTORICAL NOTES

A great clothmaking town (12C-13C) – Founded in the 10C, Ypres is thought to have had a population of 40 000 by c1260. The markets and church dedicated to St Martin were built at this time. Ypres sided with England in the Hundred Years War in the 14C, which meant that it had the English wool it needed to continue clothmaking; as a result, it suffered reprisals from the King of France. This was the beginning of the town's economic decline, and Bruges replaced it on the international market. Ypres suffered from local problems too. The conflicts between the upper class and craftsmen eventually put power in the hands of the artisans, especially after the Battle of the Golden Spurs in 1302 *(see Kortrijk)*.

The decline of the town was accelerated first by an epidemic in 1316, then by the destruction of the workers' suburbs in 1383 during the siege by the people of Ghent and the English. By the 16C repression had given way to religious strife; many clothmakers left the country altogether. Ypres became an ecclesiastical town in 1559, when it was made the seat of a new bishropic (which was abolished in 1801). Several convents were built. One of the bishops was the famous Jansenius *(see Leuven)*.

A fortified site (17C-18C) – Its strategic location unfortunately made Ypres the victim of several sieges, and caused it to change hands on numerous occasions.

The French captured the town in 1678 and Vauban surrounded it with ramparts. During the reign of the Habsburgs, Ypres constituted the southern border of a vast empire and had its fortifications further reinforced.

The ramparts were demolished in 1852. They have since been turned into esplanades.

The Ypres Salient (1914-1918) – The town of Ypres was completely destroyed by the First World War, although it subsequently managed to rise from its ashes and revive its commercial activites (textiles and other industries). After the flooding at Nieuwpoort *(qv)* the Germans concentrated their attacks in October 1914 on the Ypres region. The town was the focus of bloody battles for four years, until October 1918, during the continuing struggle to capture the salient to the east of the town, held by mainly British troops. As was the case on the River Yser, the front hardly moved an inch, in spite of all the German efforts, in particular their use of a lethal new weapon, poison gas, in Steenstraat (north of Ypres) in April 1915.

In April 1918, a major German offensive was halted by Belgian troops at Merkem to the north of Ypres and in the Heuvelland (*see Ieper – Excursions*) by the British and French armies. From September onwards, the Allied counterattack led by Maréchal Foch was to succeed in liberating Belgium. More than 300 000 allied troops, including 250 000 British servicemen, were killed during the fighting. The countryside around Ypres is one vast graveyard; there are more than 170 military cemeteries. It was in **Poelkapelle** *(9km – 5.4 miles by ① on the town plan)* that the famous French airman Captain Guynemer was shot down in 1917 (memorial).

The tourist route marked with hexagonal signs, "Route 14-18" covers the places of interest and military cemeteries northeast of the town.

★LAKENHALLE (**ABX**) *time: allow 30 min*

The cloth halls were finished in 1304, but destroyed during the First World War. They were carefully rebuilt in sandstone in the original style.

They are in the form of a long rectangle surrounding two narrow courtyards. Seen from the Grote Markt Albert I they are 133m – 436ft in length, broken up by a very beautiful square **belfry** flanked with four turrets. Fluffy toy cats are thrown from the second floor of the belfry during the **Cat Festival**, which takes place every three years *(see the Calendar of Events)*. The festival dates back to the 10C when live cats were used to ward off the devil and witchcraft. Since 1955 the event has been introduced by a large procession of cats.

The halls stand to the right of the **Nieuwerk** (**BX H**), an elegant Renaissance building dating from 1619. It was built to house the Town Hall.

Ascent of the Belfry ⊙ – From the top there is a good view of the town and the cathedral *(264 steps)*.

Herinneringsmuseum ⊙ – There are many documents on the First World War and on the Battle of the Salient on the first floor of the cloth halls in this memorial museum. One of the display cases is devoted to Guynemer.

ADDITIONAL SIGHTS

Hotel-Museum Merghelynck (**BXY M¹**) ⊙ – This building dating from 1774 was destroyed in 1915 and rebuilt in 1932; luckily its collections were saved from the disaster. The beautiful furniture and objets d'art (paintings, porcelain) complement the refined 18C elegance of the reconstructed rooms.

Museum OCMW (**BX M²**) ⊙ – This museum is housed in the chapel of the **Hospice Belle**, which has beautiful Renaissance panels. The collection consists of antique furniture and works of art such as sculptures, silver- and goldwork, and paintings (including the *Virgin and Donors,* from 1420, a beautiful composition with a gold background).

Cat Festival, Witches' Parade

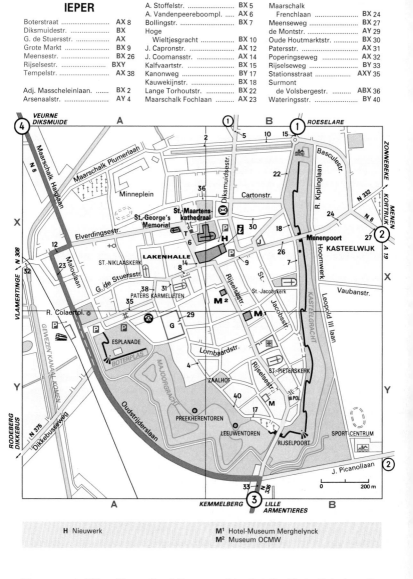

IEPER

Boterstraat	AX 8
Diksmuidestr.	BX
G. de Stuersstr.	AX
Grote Markt	BX 9
Meensestr.	BX 26
Rijselsestr.	BXY
Tempelstr.	AX 38
Adj. Masscheleinlaan.	BX 2
Arsenaalstr.	AY 4

A. Stoffelstr.	BX 5
A. Vandenpeereboompl.	AX 6
Bollingstr.	BX 7
Hoge Wieltjesgracht	BX 10
J. Capronstr.	AX 12
J. Coomansstr.	AX 14
Kalfvaartstr.	BX 15
Kanonweg	BY 17
Kauwekijnstr.	BX 18
Lange Torhoutstr.	BX 22
Maarschalk Fochlaan	AX 23

Maarschalk Frenchlaan	BX 24
Meenseweg	BX 27
de Montstr.	AY 29
Oude Houtmarktstr.	BX 30
Paterssstr.	AX 31
Poperingseweg	AX 32
Rijselseweg	BY 33
Stationsstraat	AXY 35
Surmont de Volsbergestr.	ABX 36
Wateringsstr.	BY 40

H Nieuwerk

M¹ Hotel-Museum Merghelynck
M² Museum OCMW

Menenpoort (BX) – The walls of the memorial called the Menin Gate bear the names of 54 896 Britons who died during the battles leading up to 16 August 1917.
The bugles of the fire brigade play the Last Post every evening at 8pm.

St.-Maartenskathedraal (ABX) – The cathedral was destroyed during the war, but rebuilt in its original style (13C-15C). Admire the 16C polyptych on the right near the entrance, and the 17C alabaster statues on the left on top of the parclose screen of the baptistery chapel.

St George's Memorial Church (AX) ⊘ – This Anglican church built in 1929 now commemorates the British servicemen who died during both World Wars. The furniture and the decoration were provided thanks to the generosity of donors from Great Britain and the Commonwealth.

EXCURSIONS

Bellewaerde Park – *5km – 3 miles east. Leave by ② on the town plan.*
The road goes past the Menin Gate and several military cemeteries, notably the **Hooghe Crater Cemetery** on the right, which contains over 6 800 British war graves.
In **Bellewaerde Park** ⊘ visitors can wander among antelopes, ostriches, stags, llamas and zebras. They can take a safari-tram through the tiger and lion enclosure, see a show given by an elephant, have a boat trip through an African landscape after passing beneath a magical waterfall and much more.

Tyne Cot Military Cemetery – *10km – 6.25 miles northeast on the N 332.* This British cemetery is the largest in the region. There are 11856 white tombstones standing out against the beautifully kept lawn and flower beds, arranged around the tall "Cross of Sacrifice". The curving semicircular wall enclosing the cemetery bears the names of almost 35000 soldiers who were lost after 16 August 1917. This site, from which there is a beautiful view, overlooks the surrounding country-side.

The village of **Westrozebeke** to the northeast *(13km – 8 miles)* recalls a 14C battle *(see Kortrijk: Battle of the Golden Spurs).*

Heuvelland (Flanders Uplands) – *17km – 10.5 south by ③ on the town plan. Take the N 331 on the right.*

Kemmelberg – This wooded hill (altitude 159m – 522ft) is a part of the Flanders Uplands which extend along each side of the border. Bitter battles were fought in the region in April 1918, at the beginning of the last major German offensive *(see Ieper, the Ypres Salient)*. The climb up the hill reveals some interesting views of the countryside. Near the top, there is a neo-Gothic **tower** ⊘ from which there is an interesting panoramic view. An obelisk on the south slope marks the site of the **French ossuary** where more than 5 000 unknown soldiers are buried.

Cross the N 375.

Rodeberg – This hill, also known as Mont Rouge, reaches an altitude of 143m – 469ft. Together with Zwarteberg (Mont Noir) in France it is a very popular tourist centre. There is a little windmill on the hill.

KNOKKE-HEIST ★★

West-Vlaanderen – Population 31 237
Michelin maps 409 C1 or 213 fold 3
Town plan in the current Michelin Red Guide Benelux

Heist, Duinbergen, Albert-Strand, Knokke and Het Zoute together constitute a single seaside resort, renowned for its elegance and what are considered the most beautiful villas on the coast, particularly in Het Zoute.

The resort offers a wide variety of entertainment. A traditional market takes place in the **Centre De Bolle** *(not far from Heist station)* on Thursday afternoons in July and August. Major exhibitions are organised every year in the **casino** and the **centre culturel Scharpoord** (Ontmoetingscentrum, *Meerlaan 32*), which is also used for conventions.

The resort is extremely well equipped for sports enthusiasts *(golf, swimming pools, archery, stadium and gymnasium)*. It also has a man-made lake (Zegemeer) and a thalassotherapy institute. A tramway provides a shuttle service between Knokke and De Panne *(qv)*.

Walks ⊘ – There are several pleasant walks starting from the resort. The signposted **promenade des Fleurs** (Bloemenwandeling) covers 8km – 5 miles and leads along willow-shaded avenues past Het Zoute's luxury villas half-hidden in beautiful gardens. Several of the walks in the surrounding area lead through green countryside scattered with pretty white farmhouses with red-tiled roofs.

SIGHTS

Kursaal – There is a beautiful Venetian crystal chandelier in the central foyer of the casino. A bronze statue (1965) by Zadkine, entitled *Le Poète*, stands in front of the building.

★**Het Zwin** – The Zwin, an arm of the sea which is now silted up, lies between the resort and the Belgian-Dutch border. It once served the ports in Sluis, Damme and Bruges.

This is a world of channels, tides and salt meadows, sur-rounded by dunes that isolate it from the sea and dikes that protect the countryside from flooding.

The Zwin was turned into a **nature reserve** ⊘ (150 hectares – 370 acres, of which 25 hec-tares – 62 acres are in the Netherlands) and is home to some very interesting flora and fauna. Part of the reserve (60 hectares – 148 acres) is open to the public.

Avocet

Antony/JACANA, Paris

The best times to visit are spring, for the birds, and summer, for the flowers. Indeed from mid-July to the end of August sea-lavender forms a marvellous mauve carpet.

Before beginning the walk, it is worth visiting the aviaries and the enclosure: storks nest and ducks splash about here, and it is possible to observe birds that come from the reserve itself. There is a view of the entire reserve from the top of the dike, on the other side of the woods.

The innumerable species living in the Zwin include terns, waders such as the avocet with its fine curved beak, ducks such as the red-beaked sheldrake and several migratory birds such as the grey plover and various species of sandpiper.

Avoid sightseeing in a church during a service.

KOKSIJDE

West-Vlaanderen – Population 18 354
Michelin maps 409 A2 or 213 fold 1

This locality which includes the seaside resort of **Koksijde-Bad**, also has the highest dune on the Belgian coast, the **Hoge Blekker** (**BX**) (33m – 108ft)

Among the many events in Koksijde, the large **flower market** ⊘ is interesting, as are the fishermen's folk festival and a procession "in homage to Flemish painting" *(see the Calendar of Events).*

Fishing on horseback for shrimps

A. Saucez/EXPLORER

SIGHTS

Duinenabdij (**BY**) ⊘ – The "abbey in the dunes" was founded in 1107 by the Benedictines and became Cistercian in 1138. The abbey reached its apogee in the 12C, then declined and was finally destroyed by the "iconoclasts" in 1566.

Archeological digs carried out since 1949 have uncovered certain **traces** of the original abbey, revealing the majestic lines of its church. The cloisters still have pretty corbels. The beautiful sandstone columns which belonged to the chapter-house and the lay-brothers' refectory still exist.

The finds uncovered during the digs are exhibited in the **museum** (**M²**). These collections concern archeology, history and regional flora and fauna (dioramas).

Near the abbey there is a wooden post **windmill** (Zuid Abdijmolen) (**BY**), dating from 1773.

O.L.V.-ter-Duinenkerk (**BX**) – This modern church, which was built in 1964, lies north of the abbey. It has great fluidity of line and is shaped like the arc of a circle. The undulating form of the roof and its navy-blue colour recall the waves of the ocean, and the beige colour of the brick walls reflects the tone of the nearby dunes. The stained-glass windows diffuse an iridescent light inside. The crypt *(access from outside)* contains a relic of St Idesbald, who was abbot of Dunes Abbey in the 12C.

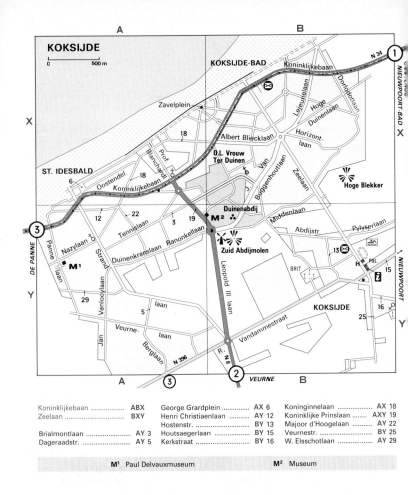

KOKSIJDE

0   500 m

Koninklijkebaan	ABX	George Grardplein	AX 6	Koninginnelaan	AX 18
Zeelaan	BXY	Henri Christiaenlaan	AY 12	Koninklijke Prinslaan	AXY 19
		Hostenstr.	BY 13	Majoor d'Hoogelaan	AY 22
Brialmontlaan	AY 3	Houtsaegerlaan	BY 15	Veurnestr.	BY 25
Dageraadstr.	AY 5	Kerkstraat	BY 16	W. Elsschotlaan	AY 29

M¹ Paul Delvauxmuseum   M² Museum

Paul Delvauxmuseum (**M¹**) ⊙ – *In St.-Idesbald*. It is possible to follow the artist's (1897-1994) development through the paintings, water-colours and drawings collected by the Paul Delvaux Foundation and exhibited here.

Paul Delvaux was born in 1897 in Antheit in the province of Liège. The museum has a collection of his post-Impressionist and Expressionist works, and includes the Surrealist paintings in which he developed a highly personal style.

Certain subjects were particularly interesting to the artist : stations (compare for example *Vue de la Gare du Quartier Léopold* (1922) and *Gare forestière* (1960) and above all women, whom he liked to represent more or less naked against a backdrop of Greek or Roman temples.

EXCURSIONS

Oostduinkerke – *4.5km – 2.75 miles east. Leave by* ① *on the town plan.*
A few people still fish on horseback for shrimps on the beach of **Oostduinkerke-Bad**. At low tide horses, now used in place of mules, pull heavy drag-nets and head into the water up to their breast. Each year the Shrimp Festival *(see the Calendar of Events)* takes place with a parade on Sunday.

Here, as well as in De Panne, the width of the beaches is ideal for sandyachting (SYCO club).

St.-Niklaaskerk ⊙ – This brown brick church, built in 1954, has great pointed roofs. Arcades join it to a massive square tower reminiscent of the one in Lissewege.

Yellow tones predominate inside, contrasting with the bluish colour of the flagstones. The originality of the building comes from the absence of any chancel and the series of closely spaced lancet arches which spring up from below ground level.

Nationaal Visserijmuseum ⊙ – *Pastoor Schmitzstraat 5.* The national fishing museum is in a modern building. There is a beautiful collection of model boats, nautical instruments and paintings by artists who worked in Oostduinkerke c1900, such as **Artan**, the Belgian painter born in The Hague (1837-1890). A typical fisherman's house was built beside the museum, with the north façade protected from the wind by a very low roof. There is also a 1920 tavern. A lifeboat and a shrimp boat are displayed in the courtyard.

Folklore Museum Florishof ⊘ – *Koksijdesteenweg 24.*
The museum includes a reconstruction of a regional interior, workshops (lace-maker's, clogmaker's, etc.), a chapel, a grocer's shop, a barn and a small school.

Abdijhoeve Ten Bogaerde – *4km – 2.5 miles south by* ③ .
This farm, a beautiful brick complex that once belonged to the Duinenabdij, is to the right of the road. The monumental barn, which bears similarities to the one in Ter Doest *(qv)*, now lies in ruins.

KORTRIJK ★

West-Vlaanderen – Population 74 044
Michelin maps 409 C3 or 213 fold 15
Plan of the conurbation in the current Michelin Red Guide Benelux

Kortrijk (Courtrai in French) is crossed by the River Leie. It is a dynamic business centre at the heart of a growing industrial area. Its pedestrian streets and luxurious boutiques are a major attraction throughout the region.
Roeland Savery (1576-1639) was born in Kortrijk. He was a remarkable painter of flowers and landscapes with animals. Savery worked in Prague for Emperor Rudolf II, travelled in the Alps to observe nature and spent the last years of his life in Utrecht. His art is very similar to that of Velvet Brueghel.

HISTORICAL NOTES

A prosperous town – Kortrijk has existed since the Roman period (a 1C Gallo-Roman cemetery was discovered in Molenstraat in 1959), but it reached the peak of its prosperity in the 15C when its cloth trade flourished. Wool-weaving soon gave way to linen-making, because of the Leie. The soft water of this river was ideal for retting flax. Kortrijk became famous for making linen, and damask linen became its speciality. Kortrijk has remained an internationally renowned textile centre (carpets, upholstery, ready-to-wear clothing).
There are several other expanding sectors : metallurgy, electronics, gold- and silver-work, oils, timber, chemical industries, construction.
The **Hallen** *(access by Doorniksewijk to the south)* is a modern architectural complex, dating from 1967. It is used for conventions, exhibitions and concerts. It bears witness to the town's industrial and cultural development. The town also plays an important role in education, notably because of the university (K.U.L.) campus *(see Leuven)*.

The Battle of the Golden Spurs

On 11 July 1302 a battle took place under the very walls of Kortrijk. It marked the Flemish struggle against the hegemony of the King of France. This battle had much to do with the creation of Belgium.
Philip the Fair's French cavalry was defeated by the craftsmen of Ypres and Bruges, under the command of Pieter de Coninck *(see Ghent, Princely Receptions)*. The golden spurs picked up on the battlefield by the victors carpeted the vaults of the Church of Our Lady until 1382, when they were recaptured by the victorious French army who had just defeated the Flemish in the Battle of Westrozebeke.
It was at this time that Philip the Bold, Duke of Burgundy, is said to have stolen the jack o' the clocks crowning the belfry. He gave them to Notre-Dame Church in Dijon, France. The symbolic return of the statues took place on 23 September 1961 and Manten and his wife Kalle again stand at the top of the belfry.

SIGHTS

Grote-Markt (**CDZ**) – This is the commercial hub of the town which has a large number of pedestrian streets.

Belfort (**CZ**) – The belfry dates from the 14C. The belfry stands in the middle of Grote Markt and is topped with five pointed turrets and the famous jack o' the clocks statue at the very top.
The imposing tower of the 15C **St.-Maartenskerk** (**DZ**) can be seen east of the square.

Stadhuis (**CZ H**) ⊘ – The Town Hall has a restored Late Gothic façade. The statues, which were replaced in the 19C, represent the Counts of Flanders.
The modernised interior still has magnificent rooms. The **Schepenzaal ★** or Aldermen's Chamber on the ground floor is decorated with a remarkable stone fireplace in the Late Gothic style (1527), with alcoves containing statues of the Virgin Mary and the

patron saints of towns in the region. The ends of the beams on the ceilings are decorated with picturesque coloured scenes featuring Justice, a crowned woman, as the principal character.

The **Oude Raadzaal**★, the former Council Chamber on the first floor; also has a fireplace dating from 1527. It is decorated with three rows of sculpture : at the top, the virtues; in the middle, on either side of Emperor Charles V, the vices; at the bottom, idolatry and the deadly sins.

The sculptures on the ceiling beams in this chamber represent very picturesque scenes depicting the evil influence of woman over man, for example in the illustration of the medieval poem, *Lay of Aristotle*, in which the philospher is being ridden by a woman.

★**Begijnhof** (DZ) – This is a charming little village between St.-Maartenskerk and O.-L.-Vrouwekerk. Its tranquillity comes as a surprise amid the hustle and bustle of the surrounding district.

The Beguine convent, founded in 1238, was richly endowed by the Countess of Flanders, Joanna of Constantinople, in 1242. There is a statue of the Countess in the convent. The present 41 cottages date from the 17C. The Mother Superior's House (no 27) stands out from the others because of its double gables. A small museum, **begijnhofmuseum** ⊘, restores the atmosphere of the past.

★**O.-L.-Vrouwekerk** (DY) ⊘ – The towers of the church dedicated to Our Lady look out over the picturesque little streets round about. Baldwin of Constantinople founded it in the 13C, and the poet Guido Gezelle *(see Brugge)* was vicar in the 19C.

The 14C chapel of the Counts of Flanders opens onto the south side of the ambulatory, and has arches with curious sculpted spandrils. It contains an alabaster **statue of St Catherine**★ (1380) attributed to Beauneveu. The drapery is extraordinary. A beautiful Van Dyck canvas, **The Raising of the Cross**★, is in the north transept; Rubens' influence is obvious.

Broeltorens (DY) – These towers were once part of the old fortifications destroyed by Louis XIV in 1684. They protected the bridge over the Leie (rebuilt after the First World War). The south tower dates from the 12C; the north one from the 13C.

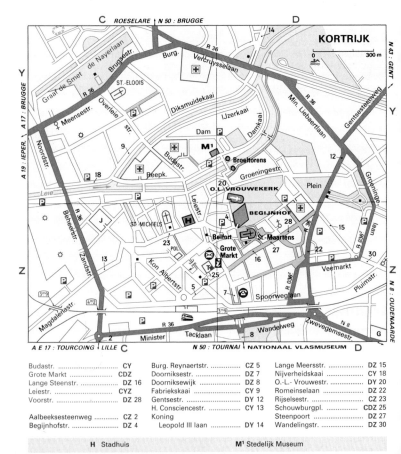

Budastr.	CY	Burg. Reynaertstr.	CZ 5	Lange Meersstr.	DZ 15
Grote Markt	CDZ	Doorniksestr.	DZ 7	Nijverheidskaai	CY 18
Lange Steenstr.	DZ 16	Doornieksewijk	DZ 8	O.-L.- Vrouwestr.	DY 20
Leiestr.	CYZ	Fabriekskaai	CY 9	Romeinselaan	DZ 22
Voorstr.	DZ 28	Gentsestr.	DY 12	Rijselsestr.	CZ 23
		H. Consciencestr.	CY 13	Schouwburgpl.	CDZ 25
Aalbeeksesteenweg	CZ 2	Koning		Steenpoort	DZ 27
Begijnhofstr.	DZ 4	Leopold III laan	DY 14	Wandelingstr.	DZ 30

H Stadhuis	**M¹** Stedelijk Museum

Begijnhof, Kortrijk

Stedelijk Museum (**CY M¹**) ⊙ – This well laid out museum has a beautiful collection of ceramics, silver, old items, sculptures and an interesting series of paintings from the 16C to the present day. Note Roland Savery's *Pillaging of a Village*.

★**Nationaal Vlasmuseum** ⊙ – *Etienne Sabbelaan 4. Via Doorniksewijk south of the map.*
The National Linen Museum is housed in a 19C farm originally intended for growing flax, one of Flander's most important activities, especially in the Leie region.
The successive steps in the growing of flax and the production of linen cloth as well as the development of the industry up to the use of the first machines (*c*1900) are evoked by paintings or life-size dummies dressed in traditional costume demonstrating each activity. One wing of the building illustrates the growing of flax and the production of linen, the other to crafts for domestic purposes.
Reconstructed interiors demonstrate the various steps: breaking, scutching, hackling, spinning and finally the weaving of linen.

EXCURSION

Rumbeke – *18km – 11 miles northwest towards Roeselare.*
A beautiful park (Sterrebos) surrounds the **château de Rumbeke** ⊙. The castle dates from the 15C and 16C. It bristles with turrets, including one with an onion dome, and crowstepped gables. Baldwin the Iron Arm, who had just kidnapped Judith, daughter of the King of France, Charles the Bald, sought refuge here in 862. It was after this incident that he obtained from the king the territory of Flanders of which he became the first count.

Château de LAARNE★

Oost-Vlaanderen

Michelin maps 409 E2 or 213 fold 5

The grey walls of **Château de Laarne** ⊙ are flanked with stone-roofed towers and a turreted keep. The castle is surrounded by a moat. It was built in the 12C to defend Ghent and was altered in the 17C. The main courtyard and present entrance, which is preceded by a stone bridge and surmounted by a loggia, date from this period.
The **interior** has been refurnished to recreate the atmosphere of a 17C stately home.
Large pieces of Antwerp and French furniture are arranged around the rooms, which have beautiful fireplaces. The walls are hung with marvellous tapestries. Two of the tapestries date from the 16C and come from Brussels. They were based on cartoons by B van Orley and belong to the hunting series known as *Hunts of Maximilian*. On the ground floor note the Renaissance vaulting in the gallery overlooking the inner courtyard. On the first floor there is an elegant 16C tapestry depicting the life of a nobleman. Finally, visitors should not miss the 15C-18C European **silver collection**★ donated by M Claude Dallemagne.

LESSINES

Hainaut – Population 15 780
Michelin maps 409 E3 or 213 fold 17

Lessines lies on the banks of the River Dender, in the middle of a region in which medicinal plants are grown (especially in Deux-Acren). The town has famous open-cast **porphyry quarries** ⊘ to the east.

The painter **René Magritte** was born here in 1898. He was one of the main figures in the Belgian Surrealism movement.

Lessines and its festivals – The **Penitents' Procession** takes place on Good Friday. It dates back to the 15C. During the procession, black penitents wearing hoods and rough homespun habits carry the instruments of Christ's Passion and the body of Christ part-way along the old town walls. They then lay the body in one of the chapels in église St-Martin. The **Saint Roch** Fair is held on the third Sunday in August. In the morning the "cayoteux" (the name given to quarry workers) work porphyry in the streets as they used to in days gone by, and in the afternoon there is a procession of giants, led by one embodying "El Cayoteu". The **cortège historique du Festin** takes place during the first weekend in September. It is a pageant commemorating the victory, in 1553, of Sebastian de Tramasure over the bands of pillaging English and Dutch who were trying to capture the town. More than 600 people in period costume take part in the procession and the dinner that rounds off the festival, when the captain symbolically places his sword at the foot of a statue of Our Lady.

★**Hôpital Notre-Dame-à-la-Rose** ⊘ – This hospital-cum-monastery was founded in 1242 by Alix de Rosoit, lady-in-waiting to Blanche of Castile and widow of Arnould IV d'Audenaarde, Grand Bailiff of Flanders and lord of Lessines. The buildings were reconstructed between the 16C and 18C in the Flemish Renaissance style around Gothic cloisters with a delightful garth. The hospital is now a museum that serves as a reminder of everyday life in the monastery and hospital down the ages. Its exhibits include furniture, paintings, gold and silver ware, and porcelain, all of them set out in the many rooms that have been reconstituted and turned into the museum. The 18C church was built at the end of the ward dating from the same period because of the principles on which care and treatment were based. They required that as much care be given to the soul as to the body, hence the close links between spiritual and temporal areas. The equipment used to make "helkiase" (from the Greek word for "wound") can be seen in the 19C infirmary. It was a cream used to treat skin diseases and ulcers and was invented by Sister Marie-Rose Carouy in the late 19C. It enjoyed enormous popularity.

EXCURSION

Ellezelles – *11km – 6.75 miles west.* 3km – 1.75 miles beyond the village on a hilltop with an altitude of 115m – 377ft is **De Kattenmolen** ⊘. It is a picturesque wooden post mill dating from 1751.

LEUVEN★★

Vlaams-Brabant – Population 80 439
Michelin maps 409 G-H3 or 213 fold 19

Leuven is the seat of a famous university. It stands on the banks of the River Dijle, and a number of beautiful historical religious buildings and an admirable Town Hall stand as reminders of its illustrious past.

HISTORICAL NOTES

Leuven's first castle was captured by the Vikings, who were defeated in turn soon afterwards by Arnulf of Carinthia (891). A new castle was built in the 11C by Lambert I the Bearded, Count of Leuven. This was to form the root of the town's development.

Leuven was the capital of the Duchy of Brabant. It lay in an enviable position at the end of the navigable section of the Dijle and on the route linking the Rhineland to the sea. It became a major clothmaking town. Town walls were built in the 12C, of which a few traces remain, especially in **St.-Donatus Park (Z)**. In the 13C a fortress was built to the north on **Cesarsberg (Y)**.

The **Joyous Entry**, a charter of Brabant's liberties to which all new sovereigns had to swear fealty, was signed in Leuven in 1356 and was effective until 1789.

Leuven then surrounded itself with a second set of walls about 7km – 4.25 miles long. However, violent conflicts pitted the clothmakers' guilds against the aristocracy, and a major riot broke out in 1378, culminating in the capture of the Town Hall. The aristocrats who had taken refuge there were thrown out of the windows. With its cloth trade ruined by civil war, Leuven was subjected to competition from

Brussels. Nevertheless, under Burgundian rule, the town acquired several large buildings (the Town Hall was built at the end of the 15C) and a university. Leuven
developed its commercial activities in the 18C, especially the brewing of beer, a
tradition dating back to the 14C. One of the large **breweries** ⊘ is open to visitors.
In 1914, when Leuven was sacked and set on fire, 1 800 houses and the university
library were destroyed. In 1940 the university was set on fire and the town heavily
bombed; in May 1944 Allied bombs also damaged the town. However, Leuven rapidly
rose from the ashes.

Katholieke Universiteit Leuven (Y) – The "Alma Mater" was founded in 1425 on the
initiative of Pope Martin V and at the request of John IV, Duke of Brabant. It soon
became one of the most prestigious universities in Europe. In 1517 Erasmus founded
the Three Languages College, where Hebrew, Latin and Greek were taught. It was to
serve as a model for the Collège de France in Paris. The University withstood the
religious strife of the 16C and remained a steadfast champion of orthodoxy for many
years. Several illustrious figures are associated with it : one of its rectors, the precep-
tor of Emperor Charles V, became Pope Adrian VI (1459-1523). In the 16C, Justus
Lipsius *(qv)* and Mercator *(qv)* both taught here. In the 17C, **Jansenius** (1585-1638)
was one of its lecturers. In 1640, after the death of Jansenius, the *Augustinus* was
published in Leuven, a work condemned by the Pope in 1642 but which was to give
rise to the Jansenist movement.
The University built up a magnificent library which was seriously damaged during the
two World Wars.
The Catholic University of Leuven has been split since 1968. The French-speaking
university, or Université Catholique de Louvain (U.C.L.) is in Louvain-la-Neuve *(qv)*. The
Flemish Katholieke Universiteit Leuven, called **K.U. Leuven,** has 25 000 students, including some 2 000 from abroad.

Dirk Bouts – Dirk Bouts ranks highly among 15C Primitive painters. Having studied
in Brussels in Van der Weyden's studio, this Haarlem-born (Dutch) artist settled in
Leuven in 1450, where he became the official painter in 1468. His masterpiece,
the *Last Supper*, can still be admired in St.-Pieterskerk. While the sparseness and austerity
of his composition reflect Van der Weyden's influence, his works nevertheless have a style
of their own. Facial expressions are impassive but tempered by the finesse of the brush
work, the colours are rich, and the background is meticulously painted. Dirk Bouts died in
Leuven in 1475. Both his sons, Dirk and especially **Albrecht,** inherited his talent.

Quentin Massys was born in Leuven in 1466. This remarkable portrait artist settled in
Antwerp and died there in 1530.

★★★STADHUIS (Z H) ⊘ – *time : allow 45min*

Mathieu de Layens built the Town Hall in the late Gothic style in the mid-15C, during
the reign of the Duke of Burgundy Philip the Good.
It needs to be studied at a distance to appreciate the vertical lines of this stone
reliquary, elegantly carved with gables, turrets and pinnacles, dormers, and almost
300 alcoves containing 19C statues. The alcove corbels are decorated with small
picturesque naïve scenes illustrating bible stories.

Stadhuis, engraving by Jacques Harrewyn

Inside several works by Constantin Meunier are exhibited in the lobby. Of the three reception rooms set one after the other, the last two are particularly richly decorated. Otto van Veen's *Resurrection of Christ* hangs in the Louis XVI room, which also has a painted ceiling. The large and small Gothic rooms on the first floor have oak ceilings. The archstones of the vaulting are decorated with scenes from the Old and New Testaments. Note also in the large room the 16C beams, on which the corbels are carved with biblical scenes.

A café and a small beer museum are to be found in the **cellars** (Raadskelder)

ADDITIONAL SIGHTS

★**St.-Pieterskerk** (Z) – The church dedicated to St Peter was built in the 15C, in the Brabant Gothic style, on the site of a Romanesque church.

The 16C façade was intended to have three tall towers, according to Joost Metsys's bold plans. The ground was unstable, however, and the west front remained unfinished.

The **interior** is outstanding because of the pure lines of the Gothic nave. Enormous pillars rise to the vaulting in a single sweep. There are two storeys, and a triforium extended by many tall lancet windows.

The 18C pulpit is exuberantly Baroque. St Norbert is seen struck down at the foot of a rock bristling with palm trees.

In front of the chancel are the three delicate arches of the **rood-screen**★ (1499). Above it is a wooden Crucifix. In the north transept is a *Sedes Sapientiae*, a statue of the Virgin and Child dating from 1441. The Virgin Mary is the patron saint of the University.

★★**Museum voor Religieuze Kunst** ⊙ – The ambulatory and chancel contain items from the treasury as well as magnificent paintings.

Dirk Bouts's **Last Supper**★★ (1468) is a calm, luminous masterpiece of marvellous simplicity. The depth of the perspective and the delicacy of the brush stroke are combined with the use of a wide range of colours. The painter, who represented himself standing to the right in a red hat, put the emphasis on the mystery of the Eucharist rather than on Judas' betrayal. Four richly-coloured biblical scenes on the leaves of the altarpiece prefigure the introduction of this sacrament.

The triptych known as the *Martyrdom of St Erasmus* shows the executioners winding out the saint's entrails with a winch. St Erasmus is totally impassive.

A small copy of the Van der Weyden triptych, *Descent from the Cross*, was painted by the great master in 1440. The original is in the Prado in Madrid.

A remarkable 13C wooden **Head of Christ**★, called "of the Tortured Cross", was damaged by fire in 1914. The face is especially moving.

A superb **tabernacle**★ stands in the chancel. The lace-like tracery of the tower was executed in Avesnes stone by Mathieu de Layens (1450). The 15C choir stalls are carved with satirical subjects.

The Romanesque crypt was a sepulchre for the Counts of Leuven. It now contains a display of 16C mantles and chasubles.

Naamsestraat (Z) – Several of the university colleges are to be found in this street.

Universiteitshalle (Z U¹) – In 1425 the University occupied this cloth hall built in the 14C. A new floor was added in the 17C. The entire building was reconstructed after its destruction in 1914.

It now houses the University offices.

Pauscollege (Z U²) – The Pope's College was founded by Pope Adrian VI *(qv)*. The vast 18C building has two wings and a severe-looking façade with a portico around the main courtyard.

St.-Michielskerk (Z B) – This church, dedicated to St Michael, was designed by Father Hesius in the 17C. The splendid Baroque **façade**★ is harmoniously proportioned, and has beautiful flowing lines producing an impression of verticality.

★★**Groot Begijnhof** (Z) – This Beguine convent, founded in about 1230, first consisted of the district near the church. In the 17C it was extended, covering an impressive area of 6 hectares – 15 acres. It is the largest Beguine convent in Belgium. The university bought it in 1962 and restored it as closely as possible to its original state. The houses have since provided accommodation for students. The last nun died in 1988.

This is a very beautiful group of buildings, crisscrossed by two arms of the Dijle and enclosed by an usual brick wall. The houses were built of brick and white stone. They have small arched doorways and some of them, like the houses in the Spanish district, have small alcoves decorated with statues. Some of the dwellings have gardens. While some of the richer nuns had their own homes (the Sint-Pauwel House (1634) at Middenstraat 65 is an example) others shared a convent.

The Gothic **church** is an austere building devoid of tower, transept and ambulatory. The chevet is lit by a beautiful double-lancet window. The decoration of the interior dates from the 18C.

LEUVEN

Bondgenotenlaan .... Z
Brusselsestraat .... Z 4
Fochplein .... Z 8
Naamsestraat .... Z
Tiensestraat .... Z

Aarschotsesteenweg .... Y 2
Blijde Inkomststraat .... Z
Bogaardenstraat .... Z
Brabançonnestraat .... Z
Broekstraat .... Z 3
Burchtstraat .... Y
Celestijnenlaan .... Z 5
Constantin Meunierstraat . Z 6
Deberiotstr. .... Z
Den Boschsingel .... Y
Diestsesteenweg .... Y 7
Diestsestraat .... Z
Diestsevest .... Y
Donkerstraat .... Y
Eén Meilaan .... Y
E. Ruelensvest .... Y
Frederik Lintsstraat .... Z
Geldenaaksebaan .... Y
Goudsbloemstraat .... Y 9
Grote Markt .... Z 10
Heilige Geeststraat .... Y 11
Herbert Hooverplein .... Z
Justus Lipsiusstraat .... Z 12
Kapucijnenvoer .... Y
Kardinaal Mercierlaan ..... Z
Karel van Lotharingenstraat . Z 13
Koning Albertlaan .... Z 14
Leeuwerikenstraat .... Y 16
Leopoldstraat .... Z
Leopold Vanderkelenstraat .. Z 17
Ludenscheidsingel .... Y
Margarethaplein .... Z 18
Maria-Theresiastraat .... Z 20
Martelarenplein .... Y 21
Mechelsevest .... Y
Minckelersstraat .... Z
Minderbroedersstraat ...... Z 22
Monseigneur Ladeuzeplein . Z 24
van Monsstraat .... Z
Naamsesteenweg .... Y
Naamsevest .... Y
Oude Markt .... Z 25
Pakenstraat .... Y
Parijsstraat .... Z
Parkstraat .... Z
Petermannenstraat .... Y 26
Redingenstraat .... Z 28
Riddersstraat .... Y
Rennessingel .... Y 27
Rijschoolstraat .... Z 29
Schapenstraat .... Z
Tervuursestraat .... Y 30
Tervuursevest .... Y
Tessenstraat .... Y 32
Tiensesteenweg .... Y 33
Tiensevest .... Y
Vaartstraat .... Z 35
Vesaliusstraat .... Z
Viadukt .... Y
Vismarkt .... Z 36
Vital Decosterstraat .... Z 37
Vlamingenstraat .... Z
Vuurkruizenlaan .... Y 38
Waversebaan .... Y 40
Weldadigheidsstraat .... Z 42

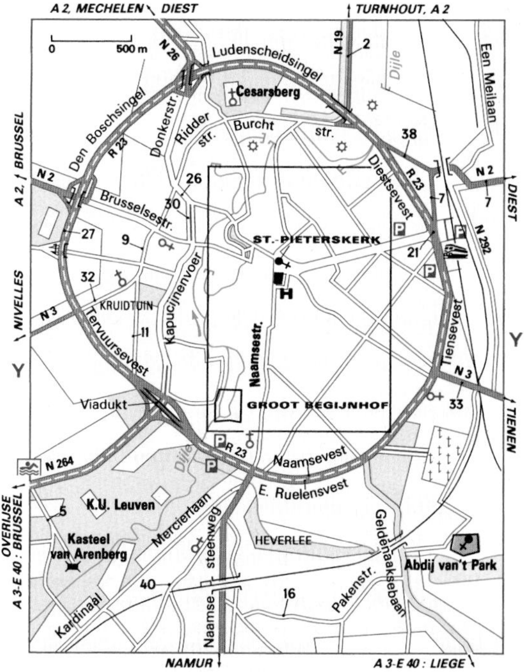

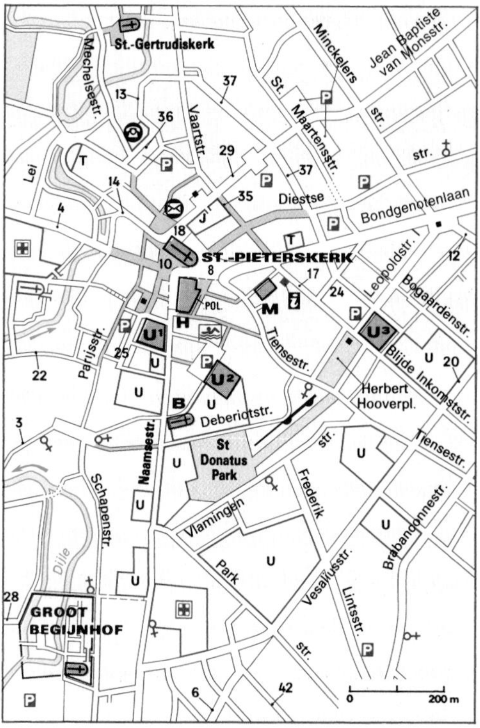

Map labels (upper)

A 2, MECHELEN \ DIEST — TURNHOUT, A 2
Ludenscheidsingel
Cesarsberg
A 2, BRUSSEL
NIVELLES N 3
Den Boschsingel — R 23
Donkerstr. — Ridder — str. — Burcht — str.
38
N 2
Brusselsestr.
30
26
27 9
ST.-PIETERSKERK
21
N 252 DIEST
32
KRUIDTUIN
11
Tervuursevest
Kapucijnenvoer
Naamsestr.
H
Diestsevest — Tiensevest
Y
N 3
Viadukt
GROOT BEGIJNHOF
33
N 264
Dijle
K.U. Leuven
5
Kasteel van Arenberg
40
Merciertaan
Naamsevest
E. Ruelensvest
HEVERLEE
16
Kardinaal
Naamse — steenweg
Pakenstr.
Geldenaaksebaan
Abdij van 't Park
NAMUR — A 3-E 40 : LIEGE

Map labels (lower)

St.-Gertrudiskerk
Mechelsestr.
Minckelers
Jean Baptiste van Monsstr.
13
37
St. Maartensstr.
36
Vaartstr.
29
37
str.
Lei
T
14
35
Diestse
Bondgenotenlaan
18
J
ST.-PIETERSKERK
8
17
Leopoldstr.
12
10
H
POL.
M
24
Bogaardenstr.
U¹
U³
25
U²
Tiensestr.
Blijde Inkomststr.
20
22
Palijsstr.
U
B
U
Deberiotstr.
Herbert Hooverpl.
3
St Donatus Park
Naamsestr.
Schapenstr.
Vlamingen
Frederik
Tiensestr.
Park
Vesaliusstr.
Lintsstr.
Brabançonnestr.
28
GROOT BEGIJNHOF
Dijle
6
42

B	St.-Michielskerk	U¹ Universiteitshalle
H	Stadhuis	U² Pauscollege
M	Stedelijk Museum Vander Kelen-Mertens	U³ Universiteitsbibliotheek

When driving in Belgian and Luxembourg towns use the plans in the **Michelin Red Guide Benelux** *which are updated each year to show:*

– *throughroutes, by-passes*
– *new roads, one-way systems*
– *car parks*

★**Museum Vander Kelen-Mertens (Z M)** ⊘ – The Vander Kelen-Mertens family mansion, which is now a museum with marvellous art collections, is entered through the Baroque doorway of the Savoy College.

Four rooms on the ground floor have been restored in the 19C neo-Gothic style. The ceramics section displays European faïence ware as well as Japanese and Chinese porcelain. There is also a collection of wonderful stained glass. The fine art section contains works by painters Van der Weyden and Massys (born in Leuven) and P J Verhaghen. The 11C *Sedes Sapientiae* stands out among the sculptures, as does an altarpiece dating from the second half of the 16C. The collection gives an idea of Brabant's great productivity in the 15C and 16C.

The University Library, **Universiteitsbibliotheek (Z U³)**, is nearby. Built in 1927 after the old library was destroyed (1914), this is an enormous neo-Gothic building crowned with a tower imitating the one on the Giralda in Seville. The building was damaged by fire in 1940 but has been restored.

St.-Gertrudiskerk (Z) ⊘ – The church dedicated to St Gertrude has a beautiful mid 15C tower designed by Jan van Ruysbroeck, the architect of the Town Hall in Brussels. The tower is surmounted by an openwork stone spire. Inside there are some interesting 16C wooden **choirstalls** carved with biblical scenes.

Abdij van 't Park (Y) ⊘ – *In Heverlee. Leave on Geldenaaksebaan and turn left after the railway bridge.*

The 16C-18C buildings of this Premonstratensian *(qv)* abbey stand on the edge of vast lakes fed by the Molenbeek. The abbey was founded in 1129 by Godfrey I the Bearded. Beyond several dilapidated porches, the water mill and the farmhouse is the prelate's courtyard, guarded by two stone lions.

The guided tour of the abbey buildings offers plenty of opportunity to admire the **ceilings**★ in the refectory (1679) and the library (1672). They are adorned with stucco high reliefs by Jean-Christian Hansche. The Romanesque church was altered in 1729. The Baroque interior is decorated with several canvases by P J Verhagen (in the chancel and gallery).

Kasteel van Arenberg (Y) ⊘ – *In Heverlee.*

This huge, early 16C castle has an impressive façade overlooking a wide lawn. It belongs to the university. The **science faculties** are in the grounds of the surrounding estate (120 hectares – 296 acres).

EXCURSION

IJse Valley – *25km – 15.5 miles southwest. Take the N 264 and turn left onto the N 253 towards Overijse.*

The road soon passes through pleasant countryside with rows of poplars.

Korbeek-Dijle St.-Bartholomeüskerk ⊘ has a superb sculpted wooden **altarpiece**★ (1522) with expressive figures and painted side panels. It illustrates the martyrdom and worship of St Stephen.

't Zoet Water – *3km – 1.75 miles from Korbeek-Dijle.* This pretty wooded beauty spot (the name means "Gentle Waters") has a succession of five lakes which are popular with tourists *(horse-riding, fishing, boating and recreation park)*. The Spanish house, a remnant of a 16C manor-house, has been turned into a restaurant. It is reflected in the waters of one of the lakes.

The road enters the valley of the IJse, a tributary of the Dyle, at Neerijse.

Huldenberg – The first **greenhouses for grapes** come into view at this point. The cultivation of vines in heated greenhouses began in the region in 1865 and is now commonplace throughout the IJse Valley and around Duisburg (Germany).

Overijse – **Justus Lipsius** (1547-1606) was born here. He was a 16C humanist who taught at Leuven and was a friend of Plantin *(qv)*.

Overijse, the heart of the wine-producing region, organises grape festivals every year *(see the Calendar of Events)*.

Hoeilaart – Hoeilaart was built on hillsides where the smallest plot of land is occupied by a greenhouse. Because of this, the town was nicknamed the "glass town". Major Grape Harvest Festivals take place here during the third weekend of September.

"The Steamship Novelist" – Georges Simenon 1903-1989

Simenon was one of the most popular and prolific writers and he came to be associated with his famous pipe-smoking police inspector Maigret. He was a native of Liège where he started his working life as a junior reporter but he soon moved to Paris where he wrote popular novels and stories under a variety of pseudonyms. The Maigret series of detective novels was launched in 1931.

LIÈGE★★

Liège P – Population 155 999
Michelin maps 409 J4 (enlarged inset map folds 17 and 18) or 213 fold 22
Plan of the conurbation in the current Michelin Red Guide Benelux

Liège lies at the confluence of the Meuse and Ourthe rivers, in a valley surrounded by hills. It is the third-largest city in Belgium and is a major economic and commercial centre. Liège is an important river port and benefits from its position at the intersection of major transport routes and its proximity to both the Netherlands and Germany. The glorious events in its history have brought the city a large number of churches and museums.

Perhaps the most striking features of Liège are its liveliness and the character of its people who are renowned for their friendliness, hospitality and light-hearted irreverence for authority. This reputation is enhanced by the many students from the Sart Tilman campus, who fill the cafés, bars and small restaurants in the "carré" (the area between Rue du Pot-d'Or, Rue St-Adalbert, Rue St-Gilles and Boulevard de la Sauvenière) after nightfall.

During the day the hustle and bustle is to be seen rather more in the shopping precincts around Place St-Lambert and between Feronstrée and the Meuse. On Sunday mornings the locals head for the **Marché de la Batte** (**FY**) on Quai de Maastricht and Quai de la Batte, where they can buy anything from antiques to poultry, household goods etc.

Viewpoints – To get an idea of the city's extended layout along the Meuse go to the **Citadel** (**DW**) *(by car, or on foot : 373 steps up montagne de Beuren)* where a viewing table gives an overall **view★★**. You can also go to **parc de Cointe** (**CX**). From a spot near the viewing table there is a scenic **view★**.

HISTORICAL NOTES

It is thought that Liège was founded in 705 after the assassination of St Lambert, Bishop of Tongeren and Maastricht. St Hubert built a chapel in honour of the saint and it rapidly became a major place of pilgrimage. In 721 it was decided to turn the town into a bishopric, but it was not until the 10C that the town really began to gain importance.

The ecclesiastical principality (10C-18C) – At the end of the 10C Bishop **Notger** turned his territories into a principality dependant on the Holy German Empire. It covered two-thirds of the present Wallonia. The history of this region was to be little more than a long series of battles. Some of the conflicts were instigated by princes anxious to retain their autonomy; others were rebellions by subjects against their prince.

Liège was granted certain privileges in 1316 and again in 1343. However, they were taken away in 1408 after the principality's communities revolted. Charles the Bold crushed another rebellion and had the town razed in 1468, sparing nothing but the churches. He later repented and presented Liège with the beautiful reliquary that is now part of the cathedral treasure.

In the 15C the savage William de la Marck, who was nicknamed "the Wild Boar of the Ardennes" because his followers wore boarskins, terrorised the principality and personally killed Prince-Bishop Louis de Bourbon (1482).

The town recovered its prosperity during the reign of Évrard de la Marck (1506-1538). On his death the struggle between the prince-bishop's followers and opponents broke out again.

In the 18C Liège threw itself into the Age of Enlightenment and welcomed the Revolution of 1789. The rule of the prince-bishops ended in 1794, and the town became French, then Dutch, territory until 1830.

In August 1914 the heroic resistance at the citadel and the line of forts (including **Fort de Loncin** ⊙, of which the ruins can be seen 8km – 5 miles north of Liège) made it possible for the Belgian and French troops to join forces and consolidate their position. More then 1,500 V1s and V2s fell on Liège between 1944 and 1945.

A major centre of Art – The Mosan school began to develop during the reign of Notger. It gained particular fame for its ivories in the 10C and 11C then, in the second half of the 11C, the 12C and the 13C, it began producing wonderful masterpieces in gold and silver, enamelwork and most outstandingly in cast iron, copper and brass *(see Introduction, Art)*.

Lambert Lombard (1505-1566) excelled in both painting and architecture during the Renaissance. **Jean Delcour** (1627-1707), who was trained by the Roman School

Reliquary
of Charles the Bold,
Cathédrale St-Paul

175

and sometimes called the Bernini of Liège, was the most productive sculptor of the 17C. His innumerable statues with their flowing drapery, including several graceful Madonnas, decorate the town's churches and fountains.

Architecture came into its own in the 16C and the 18C. The classical style triumphed but local particularities were retained, such as the use of brick lightened by white stone string courses and stone window mullions.

The great period of Liège cabinet-making was in the 18C when craftsmen sought inspiration in the Rococo style. Decorative carving was always done in the wood of the piece itself rather than being added afterwards.

Music flourished with composers such as **André-Modeste Grétry** (1741-1813), **César Franck** (1822-1890) and violinist **Eugène Ysaïe** (1858-1931).

Liège is also famous in literary circles with novels by **Georges Simenon** (1903-1989), who described his native city in several of his works. He was probably best known for his detective novels featuring Inspector Maigret.

Folklore is also an important part of Liège life. There are three puppet theatres. The best-known character is **Tchantchès**, a good-natured incarnation of a typical citizen of Liège.

Economic growth – Owing to the coal deposits discovered in the 12C, many blacksmiths plied their trade in Liège from the 14C onwards. The town soon earned a reputation for armour-making. Liège underwent massive industrial development in the 19C as a result of its location on a large navigable waterway and near a rich coal basin. Smelting works and heavy industries sprang up on the banks of the Meuse. Europe's first locomotive was built here, and the Bessemer steelmaking process was tested. The Fabrique nationale d'armes, a national armaments factory, was set up in Herstal in 1889.

Industrial growth was interrupted by the two World Wars, which hit Liège hard. Nevertheless, the building of the **Albert Canal** (1939) to link the Meuse and the Scheldt made Liège Europe's third-largest inland port. A tanker port was constructed between 1951 and 1964. Nowadays, metalworking remains one of the region's most important activities: iron and steel, heavy metalworking and processing, and the processing of non-ferrous metals, especially zinc (Seraing). There are also chemical and plastics plants, glass-making (Val-St-Lambert), cement works and rubber manufacturing.

★★OLD TOWN *time : allow half a day*

Leave from **Place St-Lambert** (**EY 138**), the centre of Liège's shopping district, where St Lambert's Cathedral once stood. The square is currently undergoing major refurbishment.

★**Palais des Princes-Évêques** – The palace of the Prince-Bishops was built *c*1000 by Bishop Notger, and was completely rebuilt after 1526 on the orders of Prince-Bishop Évrard de la Marck. The main façade was replaced after the fire in 1734, and the left wing dates from the last century. The building is now occupied by provincial government offices and the law courts.

The **main courtyard** ★★ is surrounded by arcades with raised arches and sixty massive yet elegant columns with entasis, surmounted by richly ornamented capitals. The variety of decoration on the columns is extraordinary. The **small courtyard**, which can be seen from the window of a corridor, seems more intimate.

★**Le Perron** (**EY A**) – The perron is a flight of steps perched on a monumental fountain by Delcour on the Place du Marché directly opposite the stately 18C Town Hall, which conceals a beautiful façade at the back. At the top of the perron, the Three Graces are holding a pine cone and a cross. This monument, which is the most

famous of its kind in Belgium, was erected in 1697 on the site of the old one that was destroyed in a storm. Initially the emblem of episcopal jurisdiction, the perron became a symbol of civil liberty. This explains why it was stolen in 1468 by Charles the Bold and taken to Bruges. It was not returned until 1478.

Hors-Château – This 11C street gots its name (literally "Outside the castle") from the fact that it was situated outside the town walls.

★★**Musée de la Vie wallonne** (**EY**) ⊙ – This museum, devoted to Walloon ethnography and folklore, is housed in an old Minorite monastery. It is a magnificent 17C Mosan Renaissance style residence elegantly combining brick and freestone. The museum illustrates life in the past through reconstructed interiors, workshops and traditional family scenes. It also has displays relating to regional arts and popular superstitions. Note the "nail oaks" in the room devoted to witchcraft. The sick would nail their clothing to these oaks to cure themselves of their illnesses.

An exceptional collection of sundials and a remarkable series of Liège puppets can be seen on the second floor. The museum also has a **puppet theatre** ⊙ and a room on dialects.

★**Musée d'Art religieux et d'Art mosan** (FY M⁵) ⊘ – The museum collections illustrate the changes in religious art in the Liège diocese since the early Middle Ages and include several masterpieces. Mosan Romanesque art is represented by numerous sculptures and pieces of gold and silver plate. The exhibits include the **Évegnée Madonna**, a very early (late 11C) statue, and the **Rausa Christ**, a 13C wooden sculpture showing the transition from the Romanesque (seated effigy) to the Gothic style (softness of the facial features and the folds of the garments). Among the Gothic paintings note the *Virgin with a Butterfly*, a rare 15C work by the Mosan school, and the marvellous **Virgin with Donor and St Mary Magdalene** (1475), attributed to the Master of St Gudula. The wooden **Berselius Madonna**, carved in 1530 by Swabian artist Daniel Mauch, shows a wriggling Infant Jesus and cherubs playing among the skirts of a beautiful Madonna.

Turn left from Rue Hors-Château towards the steps up the Montagne de Bueren, then turn left again into Impasse des Ursulines.

Impasse des Ursulines (FY 159) – This street is named after the community of nuns from the **old beguine convent of the Holy Spirit**. The beautiful half-timbered façades of the convent can be seen from the street. An old post stage has been rebuilt next door; it houses a reconstruction of violinist Eugène Ysaïe's studio.

Église St-Barthélemy (FY) ⊘ – This Romanesque church has a massive avant-corps surmounted with two towers, a feature that is very characteristic of the 12C Rhineland-Mosan style.
Inside the church there is a brass **font★★★** *(illustration p 24)* made by Renier de Huy between 1107 and 1118 for the Church of Notre-Dame-aux-Fonts *(qv)*. It was originally supported on 12 statues of oxen (only 10 of them have survived), symbolising the Apostles. The basin has five scenes depicted on it, the main one being the baptism of Jesus in the Jordan. The others represent the Preaching of St John the Baptist, the Baptism of the Catechumens, the Baptism of Cornelius the Centurion and the Baptism of the philosopher Crato. High-relief figures stand out against the smooth background. The fluidity of the stances and their highly stylised forms elevate them to a level of sculptural perfection reminiscent of the art of Antiquity.

★**Musée Curtius and Musée du Verre** (FY M¹) ⊘ – This tall aristocratic house dates from the early 17C. Jean Curtius, a rich commissary to the Spanish armies, had it built in the Mosan Renaissance style. It now houses valuable archeological and decorative arts collections. It contains in particular three remarkable Mosan works – the **Notger Gospels★★★**, an ivory dating from c1000 that is decorated with 12C champlevé enamel work and copper plaques added later on, the **Dom Rupert Virgin**, a 12C sandstone statue of the Virgin Mary which still has a Byzantine look about it, and the **Mystery of Apollo**, a carved stone tympanum dating from the 12C.
The Glass Museum at the end of the courtyard has a large **collection of glass objects★** dating from the origins of glass-making to the present day. On the ground floor, note the fine set of Art Nouveau and Art Deco vases by Gallé, Lalique, Daum, Val-St-Lambert etc. The furniture belonged to the decorator and cabinetmaker Serrurier-Bovy.

★**Musée d'Armes** (FY M³) ⊘ – The Arms Museum is housed in a fine 18C mansion. From 1800 to 1814 this was the *préfecture* of the *département* of Ourthe, the equivalent of county buildings today. Napoleon stayed here in 1803 and 1811. The museum displays to great advantage an exceptionally rich collection of portable arms, mainly firearms from the Middle Ages to the present, as well as a large collection of Napoleonic medals and decorations.

★**Musée d'Ansembourg** (FY M²) ⊘ – The contents of this beautiful 18C town house combine to give it the sophisticated atmosphere of the period. There are ceilings decorated with stuccowork, walls covered with Mechelen leather and Oudenaarde tapestries, furniture characteristic of Liège cabinet-making, and a kitchen adorned with Delft tiles.

En Féronstrée (FY) – This street is named after the *"férons"*, or ironworkers, who worked here in the Middle Ages.

Ilot St-Georges (FY M⁴) – The **Musée d'Art wallon** ⊘ exhibits its collections of works of art in a very unusual modern building. The museum is devoted to the works by painters and sculptors from Hainaut, the Namur region, Luxembourg, Liège and Walloon Brabant and Brussels. All the artists were part of the great European art movements from the 16C to the present. There are works by Lambert Lombard, Léonard Defrance, Antoine Wiertz, Félicien Rops, Henri Evenepoel, Constantin Meunier, and for the 20C, Anto Carte, Pierre Paulus, Léon Navez, Louis Buisseret (all four members of the Nervia group), Pol Bury, Jo Delahaut, René Magritte and Paul Delvaux. There is also a room for temporary exhibitions.

Vinâve d'Ile (EZ) – There is a *Virgin and Child* by Delcour above the fountain in this square, in the heart of the pedestrian shopping district.

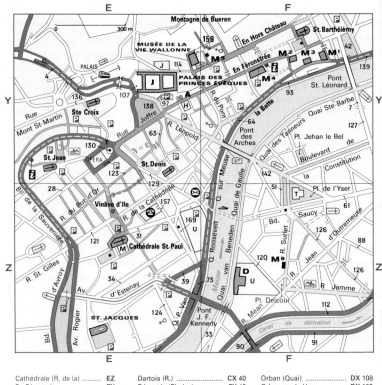

Cathédrale (R. de la)	**EZ**	Dartois (R.)	**CX** 40	Orban (Quai)	**DX** 108
En Férontrée	**FY**	Déportés (Pl. des)	**FY** 42	Orban ou de Huy	**DX** 109
Léopold (R.)	**EFY**	Dérivation (Quai de la)	**DW** 43	Ourthe (Quai de l')	**FZ** 112
Pont d'Ile	**EY** 123	Emile de Laveleye (Bd)	**DX** 49	Palais (R. du)	**EY** 114
Régence (R. de la)	**EYZ** 129	Est (Bd de l')	**FYZ** 51	Parc (R. du)	**DX** 115
Saint Gilles (R.)	**EZ**	Fer (R. du)	**DX** 54	Pitteurs (R. des)	**FZ** 120
Vinâve d'Ile (R.)	**EZ**	Fétinne (Pont de)	**DX** 57	Pont d'Avroy (R.)	**EZ** 121
		Georges Simenon (R.)	**FZ** 61	Prémontrés (R. des)	**EZ** 124
Académie (R. de l')	**EY** 4	Gérardrie (R.)	**EY** 63	Puits-en-Soc (R.)	**FZ** 126
Adolphe Maréchal (R.)	**FY** 7	Goffe (Quai de la)	**FY** 64	Ransonnet (R.)	**FY** 127
Amercœur (Pont d')	**DW** 9	Guillemins (R. des)	**CX** 66	Rép. Française (Pl. de la)	**EY** 130
Amercœur (R. d')	**DW** 10	Hauteurs (Bd des)	**CW** 69	Saint-Hubert (R.)	**EY** 136
Bois-l'Evêque (R.)	**CX** 15	van Hoegaerden (Quai)	**EFZ** 73	Saint-Lambert (Pl.)	**EY** 138
Bonaparte (Quai)	**DW** 16	Joie (R. de)	**CX** 78	Saint-Léonard (Quai)	**FY** 139
Bonnes-Villes (R. des)	**DX** 18	Lairesse (R.)	**DX** 84	Saint-Léonard (R.)	**DW** 141
Boverie (Quai de la)	**DX** 21	Léon Philippet (Bd)	**CW** 87	Saint-Pholien (R. et Pl.)	**FY** 142
Bressoux (Pont de)	**DW** 22	Liberté (R. de la)	**FZ** 88	Serbie (R. de)	**CX** 148
Bruxelles (R. de)	**EY** 24	Longdoz (Pont de)	**FZ** 90	Trappé (R.)	**CW** 156
Casquette (R. de la)	**EYZ** 28	Longdoz (Quai de)	**FZ** 91	Université (R. de l')	**EYZ** 157
Charles Magnette (R.)	**EZ** 31	Maastricht (Quai de)	**FY** 93	Ursulines (Imp. des)	**FY** 159
Churchill (Quai)	**FZ** 33	Maghin (R.)	**DW** 94	Vennes (Pont des)	**DX** 162
Clarisses (R. des)	**EZ** 34	Marché (Pl. du)	**EY** 97	Victor Hugo (Av.)	**CW** 163
Croisiers (R. des)	**EZ** 39	Notger (Square)	**EY** 107	20 Août (Pl. du)	**EZ** 169

A Le Perron	**M²** Musée d'Ansembourg	**M⁷** Musée d'Art moderne
B Tour Cybernétique	**M³** Musée d'Armes	**M⁸** Maison de la Métallurgie
D Aquarium	**M⁴** Ilot St-Georges	**M⁹** Musée Tchantchès
M¹ Musée Curtius et	**M⁵** Musée d'Art religieux	**M¹⁰** Musée des Transports
musée du Verre	et d'Art mosan	en commun

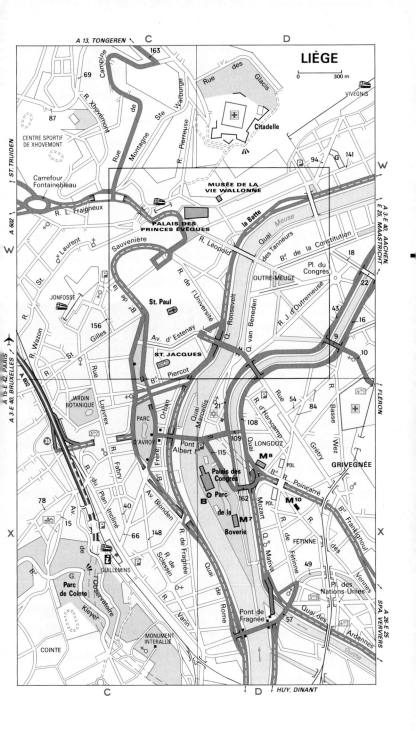

To plan a special itinerary:
– consult the **Map of Touring Programmes** which indicates the recommended routes, the tourist regions, the principal towns and main sights
– read the descriptions in the **Sights** section which include Excursions from the main tourist centres

Michelin Maps no 212, 213, 214 and 215 indicate scenic routes, interesting sights, viewpoints, rivers, forests etc

Cathédrale St-Paul (**EZ**) – This Gothic cathedral has three lofty naves and a triforium. It contains a few works by Delcour *(St Peter and st Paul, Christ in the Tomb)*, a pulpit carved by Willem Geefs in the 19C, and a remarkable collection of church plate.

★★Treasury ⊘ – The **reliquary of Charles the Bold★★** is in a room in the cloisters. The reliquary is made of gold embellished with enamelwork and was a gift from the Duke to the cathedral in 1471. The nobleman is depicted on it next to St George, whose face is identical to his. The majestic silver-gilt **bust reliquary of St Lambert** dates from 1512. It is 1.5m – 5ft tall and stands on an ornate base illustrated with scenes from the saint's life. Two 11C ivories, one Byzantine and the other Mosan, are also particularly worthy of note.

ADDITIONAL SIGHTS

West Bank

★★Église St-Jacques (**EZ**) ⊘ – Behind the west front of this Flamboyant Gothic church dedicated to St James is a Romanesque narthex that was once part of the Benedictine abbey church built here in the 11C. An interesting Renaissance façade (1558) by Lambert Lombard was added to the north porch. There is a 1380 low relief inside the porch, depicting the Coronation of the Virgin Mary.

Inside, the sumptuous architectural decoration is awe-inspiring. The **star vaulting in the nave★★** has a myriad of lierne and tierceron ribs framing painted portraits. There is a carved keystone at each intersection of the ribs. Great statues in painted limewood, most of them works by Delcour, back onto the line of columns. The chancel was decorated in an extraordinarily rich Flamboyant ogival style, with 16C stained-glass windows donated by the town's leading families.

An altarpiece with a 15C Pietà in its centre can be seen in the chapel on the north side of the chancel. There is also a 16C statue of the Immaculate Conception nearby in the transept. A superb 17C organ is supported on a loft at the end of the nave.

Star vaulting in the Église St-Jacques

Ph. Gajic/MICHELIN

Église St-Denis (**EY**) – This church was founded in the 10C by Bishop Notger and now stands at the heart of the shopping district. It has been altered several times, but still includes the base of a large 12C avant-corps.

The interior was altered in the 18C. An early 16C wooden Brabant style **altarpiece★** in the south transept illustrates the Passion of Christ with a crowd of figures. The predella, dating from somewhat later, depicts the life of St Denis.

Église St-Jean (**EY**) ⊘ – This church, dedicated to St John, was built in the shape of an octagon surmounted by a cupola. Its design was inspired by Aachen Cathedral. It was commissioned in the late 10C by Prince-Bishop Notger. The avant-corps was erected in c1200 and the nave rebuilt in the 18C. The rotunda and chancel inside were decorated in the neo-Classical style at the end of the 18C.

There is a 13C Calvary in the vestry, with beautiful wooden **statues★** of the Virgin Mary and St John. There is a magnificent Madonna and Child, or **Sedes Sapientiae★**, in a side chapel. The statue was carved in wood in about 1220. The clothing is draped in a remarkably fluid manner and the face is delicately feminine.

Openwork was added to the cloisters in the 16C, and more modifications were made in the 18C. The south gallery still has beautiful 16C vaulting in which the ribs and liernes form graceful rose patterns.

Église Ste-Croix (**EY**) – This is a hall church, with three equally high aisles, dating from the 13C and 14C. The avant-corps is Romanesque in style. The church is unusual in that it has two chancels opposite each other. The one at the west end is now used for christenings. The **treasury** ⊙ includes valuable liturgical ornaments and some gold and silver plate. One of the most valuable exhibits is a symbolic bronze key given by Pope Gregory II to St Hubert in 722. There is also a 12C triptych reliquary in gilded repoussé brass, attributed to Godefroy de Huy.

East Bank

Parc de la Boverie (**DX**) – This park is at the extreme south end of the island, between the Meuse on one side and the canal on the other.
The long façade of the **Palais des Congrès** is reflected in the water. It is a conference centre, situated near the **tour cybernetique** (**B**) 52m – 170ft high designed by Nicolas Schîffer. On the tower, a set of mobile blades indicates atmospheric changes. The building in the Louis XVI style set in the centre of the park was erected in 1905. It houses the **Musée d'Art moderne et d'Art contemporain** (**M⁷**) ⊙. The gallery has a fine collection of paintings and sculptures dating from the late 19C to the present day. There are works by French artists such as Gauguin *(Le Sorcier d'Hiva-Oa)*, Picasso (the famous *Famille Soler*, which is typical of his Blue Period), Monet, Signac, Derain etc. Belgian art is equally well represented with works by Van Rysselberghe, Claus, Ensor, Wouters, Khnopff, Evenepoel and the Flemish Expressionists. The gallery has an exhibition of works by contemporary artists including Mganelli, Arp and Ubac. In the basement, there is a collection of etchings. The basement is also used for temporary exhibitions.

Maison de la Métallurgie (**DX M⁸**) ⊙ – Here, in enormous 19C workshops, are a Walloon forge with a 17C coal-burning iron smelting kiln and two huge 18C "makas" (hydraulic hammers). The traditional work of Liège's "férons" or iron-workers is exhibited. They include firebacks and andirons.
The history of energy is illustrated in another room through an extensive collection of machinery, models and motors.

★**Aquarium** (**FZ D**) ⊙ – This beautiful aquarium belongs to the university's Institute of Zoology. Visitors can admire fish from all over the world in the 26 tanks in the basement of the building.
On the first floor there is an interesting collection of madrepores which were brought back from an expedition to the Great Barrier Reef in Australia.

Musée Tchantchès (**FZ M⁹**) ⊙ – This museum, which is located right in the centre of the Outre-Meuse district, belongs to an association called the République Libre d'Outre-Meuse. The association is devoted to Tchantchès (the Walloon equivalent of "Francis"), the popular hero of the Liège puppet theatre. The museum has the costumes which have been given to the puppet, and a collection of puppets from the Old Royal Imperial Theatre. **Puppet shows** ⊙ are performed here.
A Tchantchès monument stands on Place de l'Yser at the far end of Rue Surlet. There are several alcoves, known locally as "potales", containing statues of Christ or the Virgin Mary in the nearby streets. The Potales Festival takes place on August 15.

Musée des Transports en commun de la ville de Liège (**DX M¹⁰**) ⊙ – *9 rue Richard-Heintz.* The museum of transport boasts a collection of refurbished trams and buses, displayed in a large shed.

EXCURSIONS

Boat trips (**FZ**) ⊙ – A cruise is organised on the Meuse and the Albert Canal, from Liège to Maastricht.

★★**Blégny-Trembleur** – *20km – 12.5 miles northeast, in the Aachen direction. See Blégny-Trembleur.*

Sart Tilman – *10km – 6.25 miles south.* The **University of Liège** has an estate covering an area of 740 hectares – 1 828 acres on this wooded plateau and a centre for metallurgical research. The 17C Château de Colonster on the eastern edge of the estate has been turned into a conference centre and houses the Simenon Foundation (the writer's archives, manuscripts and library). The park also has an open-air museum.

Chaudfontaine – *10km – 6.25 miles on the Verviers road.* Chaudfontaine in the Vesdre Valley has been a popular spa since the late 17C. It has the only hot springs (38.6°C – 101.4°F) in Belgium. The water is used to treat rheumatism. Chaudfontaine also has an open-roofed hot-spring swimming pool and a **casino** with crazy golf.
The 17C restored **Maison Sauveur** ⊙ in the spa park is home to the tourist information centre.

Château d'Aigremont ⊙ – *16km – 10 miles west, on the E 40 motorway, leaving at junction 4.* The château d'Aigremont is located, like that of Chokier, on the top of a sheer cliff overlooking the Meuse. It is said that this castle was built by the four Aymon brothers. During the 15C it was one of the lairs of William de la Marck. The castle was rebuilt in the early 18C, in brick and stone. The interior is adorned with beautiful 18C furnishings. The most beautiful decorative feature is the stairwell with its *trompe l'œil* frescoes reproducing the architecture of an Italian palace. The walls of the kitchen are decorated with Delft tiles representing more than 1 000 different patterns.

There is a pretty French-style garden on the terraces.

Neuville-en-Condroz and St-Séverin – *27km – 16.75 miles southwest, in the Dinant direction.*

Neuville-en-Condroz – This is the site of the Ardennes American cemetery. A magnificent, well-tended park precedes the memorial and the lawn where 5 310 Americans are buried. The men died during the Second World War, most of them during the Battle of the Bulge. The white gravestones are arranged in the form of an immense Greek cross. Maps carved inside the memorial describe the famous battle.

St-Séverin – The **church★** in this small town is a harmonious 12C Romanesque building that was once a priory of Cluny Abbey (Burgundy, France). Indeed, the tower above the octagonal transept crossing is a copy of the "Blessed Water" (eau bénite) bell tower at Cluny. The volumes within the building vary attractively from one storey to the next and are best seen from the presbytery garden.

The ceiling in the nave is the same height as the vaulting in the transept and chancel whereas the ceilings in the apse and transept chapels are much lower. The décor in the great nave is discreet; it consists of alternating columns or groups of colonnettes and pillars with twisted twinned columns above.

The late-12C stone **font★** is original. The basin, supported by 12 colonnettes surrounding a central shaft, is sculpted with back-to-back lions. There is a head, of Syrian inspiration, at each of the four corners.

Visé – *17km – 10.5 miles north on the E 25.*

Visé is a very popular tourist resort on the banks of the Meuse. The town is well-known for its gastronomic speciality, goose prepared with a garlic sauce. Visé is also proud of its three guilds (crossbowmen, arquebusiers and free arquebusiers) who parade through the town during special events. The town has many tourist amenities including a cultural centre, a playing field, a nature reserve and Robinson Island.

Collégiale – The **reliquary of St Hadelin★** is in the south transept. This is a 12C Mosan work in repoussé silver. The end panels come from an older reliquary (1046). They show Christ crushing the asp and the basilisk (a mythological beast) on one side, and Christ crowning the two friends St Remaclus and St Hadelin on the other side. Some of the scenes on the side panels, illustrating the life of St Hadelin, are attributed to Renier de Huy. St Hadelin was the founder of Celles monastery near Dinant in the 7C. The community moved to Visé in the 14C.

LIER★★

Antwerpen – Population 30 246
Michelin maps 409 G2 or 213 fold 7

Many tourists, writers and artists have been attracted here by the atmosphere, the walks, the historical buildings and the old façades of a town that lies on the edge of both the Antwerp Kempen and Brabant regions. Lier still has its 16C walls, which have been turned into esplanades and edged with a canal.

Among the well-known people born here were the wrought ironsmith Van Boeckel (1857-1944), the portrait painter Opsomer (1878-1967), the writer **Felix Timmermans** (1886-1947) and the great clock and watch maker, Zimmer (1888-1970).

"Lierse Vlaaikens", or Lier tartlets, are a delicious local speciality.

★★ST.-GUMMARUSKERK (Z) *time : allow 45 min*

This Brabant Gothic church was built between the 14C and the 16C. The Keldermans and the de Waghemakeres *(qv)* were involved in the construction. The massive square tower, ending in a restored octagonal bell tower, has a 45-chime carillon.

There is a good view of the whole of the exterieur from near the north transept. Philip the Handsome married Joanna of Castile here in 1496.

The **interior** has some beautiful keystones, and the floor is paved with gravestones. The thick columns with great statues of the Apostles leaning against them, and the traceried triforium are characteristic of Brabant style. There are some interesting works of art.

The magnificent white stone **rood-screen★★**, which was made in the Flamboyant Gothic style despite its date of 1536, is the work of Mechelen sculptors. Statues of the Evangelists and the Fathers of the Church (re-executed in 1850) are displayed on columns; scenes from the Passion stand out against the rich decoration. The turret was added in 1850.

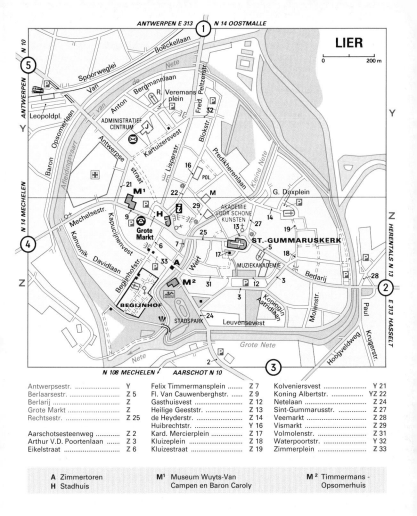

Antwerpsestr.	Y	Felix Timmermansplein	Z 7	Kolveniersvest	Y 21
Berlaarsestr.	Z 5	Fl. Van Cauwenberghstr.	Z 9	Koning Albertstr.	YZ 22
Berlarij	Z	Gasthuisvest	Z 12	Netelaan	Z 24
Grote Markt	Z	Heilige Geeststr.	Z 13	Sint-Gummarusstr.	Z 27
Rechtsestr.	Z 25	de Heyderstr.	Z 14	Veemarkt	Z 28
		Huibrechtstr.	Y 16	Vismarkt	Z 29
Aarschotsesteenweg	Z 2	Kard. Mercierplein	Z 17	Volmolenstr.	Z 31
Arthur V.D. Poortenlaan	Z 3	Kluizeplein	Z 18	Waterpoortstr.	Y 32
Eikelstraat	Z 6	Kluizestraat	Z 19	Zimmerplein	Z 33

A Zimmertoren	**M¹** Museum Wuyts-Van	**M²** Timmermans -
H Stadhuis	Campen en Baron Caroly	Opsomerhuis

The church has a beautiful collection of stained-glass windows. A 15C **window★** in the south aisle depicts the *Coronation of the Virgin* in a medallion. The fluidity of the drawing recalls the art of Van der Weyden. Maximilian of Austria presented the church with three of the stained-glass windows in the chancel during his visit in 1516. One of them shows him with his wife, Mary of Burgundy.

The choirstalls (1555) are carved with picturesque motifs. The copper lectern in the centre of the chancel dates from the 17C. The Baroque pulpit is the work of three artists, including Artus Quellin the Elder. A triptych is exhibited in the first ambulatory chapel on the north side. The leaves, representing St Clare and St Francis, are said to be by Rubens. The *Colibrant Triptych*, the *Marriage of the Virgin Mary* (1516), is attributed to Goswyn van der Weyden, grandson of Rogier. Note also in the south transept a triptych dating from 1612 by Otto Venius, Rubens's master (*Descent of the Holy Spirit*).

Once a year (*see the Calendar of Events*) the 17C repoussé silver reliquary containing the relics of St Gommarus is carried through Lier's streets in a procession.

ADDITIONAL SIGHTS

Zimmertoren (**Z A**) ⓦ – Two traces of the original 14C fortifications stand on the Zimmerplein: the Prisoners' Gate, **Gevangenenpoort**, and the Zimmer Tower, once known as the Cornelius Tower.

Astronomical Clock on the Zimmertornen

On the front of the tower is the astonishing **astronomical clock ★** made in 1930 by Zimmer of Lier. It has 11 different dials and two spheres, the earth and the moon. Every day at noon there is a procession of clockwork figures on the right side of the tower.

The **astronomical studio** inside the tower has 57 dials showing the lunar cycle, the tides, the zodiac and the main cosmic phenomena.

Another astronomical clock, the **Wonderklok,** can be visited in the pavilion next door to the tower. It has 93 dials and 14 automata. Zimmer's workshop is also open to visitors.

★Begijnhof (Z) – The Beguine convent was founded in the early 13C and altered in the 17C.

A monumental late 17C Renaissance portico marks the entrance. Above it is a statue of St Begga. There is a beautiful view from here of the Gevangenenpoort and the belfry.

Inside the enclosure the houses, some with gardens half-hidden behind low walls, line narrow paved streets along which there are the Stations of the Cross. The church has a 17C Renaissance façade topped with 18C scrolling and a lantern turret. The random arrangement of the roofs and dormer windows looks quite picturesque.

Grote Markt (Z) – The **Stadhuis (H)** in the centre is an elegant 18C structure. The windows containing more than 3 900 panes of glass. Beside the stadhuis is a slender Gothic **belfry** (1369) surmounted with four corner turrets. It includes a carillon which was once part of the old drapers' guild hall.

Several old guild halls surround the square, where a market is held every Saturday. Near the belfry the butchers' guild hall, with its crowstepped gables and perron guarded by two heraldic lions, is used for exhibitions (tentoonstelling).

Museum Wuyts-Van Campen en Baron Caroly (YZ M¹) ⊘ – This museum possesses a good art collection with works from the 16C to the present day.

Brueghel the Younger, Velvet Brueghel and Rubens feature among the Flemish painters; visitors should not miss **Frans Floris**'s truly remarkable group portrait of the *Van Berchem family.*

Also not to be missed are paintings from the Dutch (Van`de Velde, Jan Steen), Spanish (Murillo) and French (Poussin, Le Lorrain) schools, and 19C and 20C Belgian paintings (Ferdinand De Braekeleer, Tytgat, Opsomer). ·

Timmermans-Opsomerhuis (Z M²) ⊘ – This museum is devoted to contemporary Lier artists.

The **Van Boeckel** forge regroups, under a flowery chandelier, the works of art of the famous wrought ironsmith.

The reconstructed artist's studio belonging to **Baron Opsomer** contains landscapes *(Lier Beguine Convent)* and numerous portraits (Albert I, Félix Timmermans, Opsomer himself).

There are several rooms upstairs devoted to the Flemish writer **Félix Timmermans,** who was also a painter and creator of humourous drawings. Among his most famous works are *Tales of the Beguine Convent, Twilight of Death,* **Pallieter** (1916, a powerful, spirited book) and *Peasants' Psalms.*

Another room contains works and mementoes of the musician **Renaat Veremans** (1894-1969), author of *Vlaanderen* (Flanders), a well-known popular song.

LOMMEL

Limburg – Population 26 854
Michelin maps 409 I2 or 213 fold 9

Lommel's best-known feature is the large German military cemetery in the pine forests a few miles south of the town.

German military cemetery – German soldiers who fell in Belgium during the Second World War, and some who died in the former East Germany or during the First World War, lie in this 16 hectare – 40 acre enclosure.

There is a basalt calvary built above the crypt in front of the cemetery. It stands 6m – 20ft high. Almost 20 000 crosses (one cross for every two graves) are laid out in rows on a carpet of heather, dotted with pines and birches and separated by grassy paths.

Natuurreservaat Kattenbos – The nature reserve is part of the **Park der Lage Kempen,** the Lower Kempen Nature Park, together with the Pijnven Forest near Eksel to the south and the Holven Forest to the east near Overpelt. The park covers an area of 12 000 hectares – 29 652 acres spread throughout the province of Limburg.

A wooden post windmill (1809) stands near the road north of the nature reserve. This is the starting point for several signposted footpaths leading through the pine forest.

LOUVAIN-LA-NEUVE ★

Brabant-Wallon
Michelin maps 409 G3 or 213 fold 19 – 7km – 4.3 miles south of Wavre

Since Charleroi was founded in 1666, Louvain-la-Neuve has been the only new town to be founded in Belgium. Designed for 35 000 inhabitants, it extends over **Ottignies-Louvain-la-Neuve** (pop 21 665).

Université Catholique de Louvain (UCL) – Since the 1968 split in the Catholic University (founded in Leuven, in 1425), the French-language University has been in Louvain-la-Neuve. The medical students are the only exception. Their faculty is in **Woluwe-St-Lambert** (Brussels), in **Louvain-en-Woluwe**. The transfer took place from 1972 to 1979. The UCL has about 18 300 students, 14 000 of whom are in Louvain-la-Neuve.

Town and gown – Louvain-la-Neuve is an original idea, being not only an urban centre but also a university town. It is divided into four districts **(Hocaille, Biéreau, Bruyères** and **Lauzelle)** but the intermingling of shops, homes and faculties makes the division less apparent.

The **urban centre** in the heart of the town was designed as a meeting place and location for special events, reserved exclusively for pedestrians. The railway, motor traffic and car parks have been banished underground.

A science park was created for research companies and laboratories on the out-skirts of the town, along with the Cyclotron complex. The natural lie of the land was respected. The buildings are on four hills of the Lauzelle plateau which overlook the little Malaise valley.

The river has been covered over with a concrete slab to bear the weight of the town centre streets and buildings, including the University's central building, the **University Halls of Residence.**

Contemporary architecture serves town planning here, taking its inspiration from medieval towns and keeping everything on a human scale. Narrow streets, small squares, stairs, and buildings set back from the main line of frontages, all create an element of surprise and avoid monotony. Bricks and small white cobblestones predominate.

Several decorative elements have appeared since the town was created: a fountain (Place de l'Université) designed by a student and murals, including R Somville's great fresco ($400m^2$ – 478sq yds). The blue, white, grey and red of this fresco brighten up one of the walls of the University Halls on the Rue des Wallons side. There is a T Bosquet mural in the underground railway station depicting a 16C university town, with enlarged versions of Paul Delvaux's paintings of railway stations.

A motorway (Brussels-Namur) provides access to the town, as does the railway. A branch line off the Brussels-Namur route runs to the underground station. Maps and information are available in the information centre (follow the signs marked "REUL").

Musée de Louvain-la-Neuve (**Institut supérieur d'archéologie et d'histoire de l'art de l'U.C.L.)** ⊙ – *Place Blaise-Pascal.*

The collections include Egyptian, Greek and Roman antiquities, sculptures and masks representing African and South Sea primitive art, religious art (sculptures including a 16C *Christ and the Triumphal Entrance into Jerusalem*), porcelain, etc. The **Charles Delsemme legacy★** came to the museum in 1990. It represents the same universal quality. "By its diversity, its transcendence, this collection forms a desired whole", wrote the donor in his will. Note a Japanese theatrical mask, a Renaissance female figure, drawings by Picasso, and paintings by Delvaux and Magritte.

MAASEIK

Limburg – Population 20 214
Michelin maps 409 K2 or 213 fold 11

Maaseik is on the bank of the Meuse, at the extreme northeast of the Limburg Kempen region. The town is said to be the birthplace of the **Van Eyck** brothers, Jan *(qv)* and Hubert.

Maaseik's carnival procession (halfvastenstoet) halfway through Lent draws a consid-erable crowd *(see the Calendar of Events)*.

The town still has a few traces of the fortifications built in 1672 during the reign of Louis XIV. **Boat trips** ⊙ are organised on the Meuse.

SIGHTS

Grote Markt – This vast rectangular square, shaded by lime trees, is surrounded by 17C and 18C houses. Their narrow windows are often embellished with leaded lights.

The Town Hall (stadhuis) on the north side is housed in a beautiful 18C mansion. A statue of the brothers Jan and Hubert Van Eyck stands in the centre.

Museactron ⊙ – *Lekkerstraat 5.* The Museactron consists of three museums. The collections of the **musée d'Archéologie régionale** concern regional archeology and the history of the town. They include prehistoric objects, a few objects from the Roman period (a Roman doctor's instruments), and some from the Middle Ages. A footbridge links this museum to **Belgium's oldest apothecary's shop**, where the atmosphere of the past has been perfectly recreated. The **Bakery Museum** (Bakkerij-museum) is in the cellars.

Bosstraat – There are old houses all along this street.
The De Verkeerde Wereld (the World in Reverse) House, an old brick building, is at no 7. There is a half-timbered medieval house on the corner of the Halstraat.
The house at no 19 has a white façade (1620), projecting on arches, a feature common to this region. The Stenen Huis (Stone House), or the Drossaardshuis (Bailiff's House) at no 21 has a more austere Classical façade.

St.-Catharinakerk – This church dates from the 19C. The vestry is home to a remarkable **treasury** (kerkschat) ⊙. Most of the items in it come from the old Aldeneik Abbey *(see below)*. Note St Harlinde's gospel-book dating from the 8C, which is said to be the oldest book in Belgium, and a 10C silver-gilt reliquary.

Aldeneik – *2km – 1.25 miles east.* The **church** ⊙ in Aldeneik is the former minster of an 8C monastery founded by St Harlinde and St Relinde. It was enlarged in the 12C, and a Gothic chancel was added in the 13C. Restoration work was carried out in the 19C. The church still has its Romanesque central nave decorated with murals. There are 8C Merovingian sarcophagi.

*For historical background on the region
see the Historical Table and Notes in the Introduction*

MALMÉDY ★

Liège – Population 9 972
Michelin maps 409 L4 or 214 northwest of fold 9 – Local map see SPA: Excursions

Malmédy, on the River Warche, lies in a picturesque **setting** ★ in the middle of a hollow surrounded by steep wooded hills. The town itself is at an altitude of 340m – 1 115ft. **Ferme Libert** (north) is the place to go for downhill and cross-country skiing. **Ovifat** has the pistes for downhill skiing.
Malmédy's paper works and tanneries are well-known. "Baisers de Malmédy" ("Malmédy kisses") are a delicious local cake.
Together with Stavelot, the town formed an abbey principality until 1794. Malmédy, where the Walloon dialect is spoken, was Prussian from 1815 to 1925 *(see Eupen).* The town centre was destroyed in December 1944 by an air raid.
The French avant-garde poet Guillaume Apollinaire stayed in Malmédy in 1899. A monument was built in 1935 on the old Francorchamps road.

★ **Carnival** – *See the Calendar of Events.* Malmédy's very popular "Cwarmê" is one of the merriest carnivals in Belgium. The town is in a fervour for four days. On Saturday afternoon a humourous procession accompanies the "Trouv'lê", a sort of carnival king who is enthroned at the Town Hall. Sunday is the day of the great parade after which the "banes corantes" ("bands of running people") pursue the public. Steer clear of the **"haguètes"**, who have an Austrian eagle emblazoned on their backs and wear a bicorn hat embellished with feathers, and, most importantly, who are armed with long hinged pincers! On Monday short satirical sketches in the local dialect are performed in the streets.

Cathédrale Sts-Pierre-Paul-et-Quirin – This was once a Benedictine abbey church. It dates from 1782. The façade is framed by two tall towers. This was the Eupen-Malmédy diocesan cathedral from 1921 to 1925.
Inside, the furniture is particularly interesting (carved 18C pulpit, late 17C confessionals), as is the artwork : the 17C Delcour Virgin, the gilded wood St Quirin reliquary dating from 1698 and the silver bust-reliquaries of St Gereon and his companions, Roman soldiers (18C).

EXCURSIONS

Robertville – *10km – 6.25 miles northeast.* Robertville is part of the Hautes Fagnes-Eifel nature park *(qv).* The town is best known for its arch gravity **dam**, built in 1928, which overlooks the Warche from a height of 55m – 180ft. The reservoir forms a 62 hectare – 153 acre **lake** ★ which supplies Malmédy with drinking water and runs an electric power station in Bévercé. The lake is surrounded by a dense forest and offers many possibilities for sports enthusiasts. There is a beautiful view of the reservoir from just outside Robertville.

★**Château de Reinhardstein**
⊘ – *Access via a path start-ing from the dam, or on the first road on the left beyond the dam (sign-posted), then 800m – 0.5 mile on foot beyond the car park.*

The keep, surrounded by walls and standing on a rocky spur in the magnif-icent setting of a coniferous forest, gives the impression that the centuries have left it unchanged. It exudes the air of a fortress still ready to stand firm in the face of attack. However, in the early 1960s there was nothing on this site but

Château de Reinhardstein

ruins. Professor Overloop resurrected it by rebuilding it according to 17C engrav-ings depicting the fortress at the height of its splendour. At that time it was the property of the Metternich family.

The rooms with their stone walls and flagstone floors contain old furniture, tapestries, armour and works of art. The Knights' Hall and the chapel are partic-ularly eye-catching.

Bütgenbach – *15km – 9.3 miles east.* This dam (1928-1932) is also on the Warche. It has a vast 120 hectare – 296 acre reservoir, and is also a popular tourist attraction *(swimming, sailing, boating, pedal boats, fishing, tennis and wind-surfing).*

Round trip – *13km – 8 miles. Leave by the Stavelot road. Take a little road on the left before the viaduct, then a road on the right.*

★**Rocher de Falize** – This is a magnificent pinnacle of rock with sheer sides overlooking the Warche Valley. A spire on the opposite hilltop indicates Wavreumont Abbey, founded in 1950 by Benedictines from Leuven.

Bellevaux-Ligneuville – This village in the upper Amblève Valley still has a pretty half-timbered house, the Maison Maraite (1592), which is typical of the region.

Return to Malmédy via Hédomont.

Faymonville – *11km – 6.75 miles southeast.* A very old legend led to the villagers being known as "Turks". The name is reflected in the great carnival parade on Shrove Monday.

MECHELEN ★★

Antwerpen – Population 69 430
Michelin maps 409 G2 or 213 folds 6, 7
Plan of the conurbation in the current Michelin Red Guide Benelux

This is an ecclesiastical town, the residence of the Primate of Belgium. Mechelen is quiet and a bit old-fashioned with old houses lining the squares and the quaysides of the Dijle. High above the town is the magnificent tower on the cathedral with its famous carillon.

The traditional crafts such as lace or tapestry still exist here. It was a Mechelen workshop that produced the tapestry Belgium presented to the United Nations in 1954. It was originally intended for the United Nations Building in New York, but was given in 1964 to NATO in Paris. Mechelen is also a major centre of furniture-making. Brewing is also a fairly important industry in the town. Lastly, the region is famous for its market gardens (asparagus).

Mechelen carillons – In the Middle Ages Mechelen's bell-casters already had a reputation for excellence yet it was to a bellcaster from Amsterdam, Pieter Hemony, that Mechelen turned when, in 1674, it came to creating the carillon for the cathedral tower. In the late 19C the virtuoso carillon-player Jef Denyn made the chimes famous. He founded a school in 1922 and his students play throughout the world.

The first carillon in the cathedral (now restored) consisted of 49 chimes. A second set with the same number of chimes was added in 1981. Together the two sets of bells weigh 80 tons.

Carillon concerts ⊘ are given in the cathedral, at the church of Onze-Lieve-Vrouw-over-de-Dijle, or at the hôtel de Busleyden *(see below).*

HISTORICAL NOTES

Mechelen was a lakeside community in prehistoric times, and seems to have been converted to Christianity in the 8C by St Rumbald from Ireland. It belonged to the prince-bishops of Liège who surrounded it with a fortified enclosure.

Owing to its location on the Dijle, the town had a port, and trade prospered, especially with the advent of clothmaking. Mechelen gained a second set of ramparts in about 1300.

The golden age – Mechelen belonged to the Count of Flanders in the 14C, but legacies and bequests later brought it under the rule of the Dukes of Burgundy. This was the beginning of its most illustrious period. Charles the Bold established his Court of Accounts (combining those in Lille and Brussels) and the Parliament of Burgundian Estates here in 1473. The Parliament became the **Grand Council** in 1503, acting as a supreme court until the French Revolution.

The town enjoyed its greatest period of prosperity under **Margaret of Austria**, Emperor Charles V's aunt who governed until his majority, then under Emperor Charles V himself from 1519-1530. The highly cultivated princess loved the arts and surrounded herself with the greatest intellects of the day – philosophers Erasmus and Thomas More, historian Lemaire de Belges, musicians Pierre de la Rue and Josquin Des Prés, and painters Gossaert and Van Orley.

Margaret also commissioned the building of a large number of mansions. Mechelen architect Rombout Keldermans built a palace for her.

From the 16C to the present – The Court moved to Brussels in 1531. Although the Grand Council remained in Mechelen, the town's influence waned, except in the religious area. It was made an archbishopric in 1559 (a title shared with Brussels since 1961); Mechelen's prelate then became Archbishop of the Low Countries. The first man to sit on the episcopal throne was Cardinal de Granvelle, Philip II's minister.

The Spanish set fire to the town and massacred the inhabitants in 1572.

Nevertheless, by the 17C and the 18C Mechelen lace achieved fame far afield. Baroque furniture was produced in prolific quantities. The incomparable skills of Mechelen sculptors such as **Lucas Fayd'herbe** (1617-1697), Rubens' student, or **Theodoor Verhaegen** (1700-1759), Faydherbe's student, became famous.

Cardinal Mercier, Archbishop of Mechelen, amply illustrated the spirit of the city during the First World War by showing a quite extraordinary heroism and stoic resistance in the face of the invading forces.

THE HEART OF THE TOWN *time : 2 hours*

★**Grote Markt (ABY 26)** – The cathedral's impressive tower overlooks this square from the northwest. Beautiful 16C and 18C façades, with crowstepped or scrolled gables, line the other sides of the square. A statue of Margaret of Austria stands in the middle.

★**Stadhuis (BY H)** – The Town Hall stands on the east side of the square, occupying three adjacent buildings.

Building work began on the Late Gothic **Grand Council Building** on the left in the early 16C. It remained unfinished until the late 19C, when it was completed using Rombout Keldermans' original plans. A statue of Emperor Charles V stands in one of the alcoves. The building has been the Town Hall since 1913. The central façade is actually the front of the uncompleted 14C belfry. There are corbelled turrets at the top.

The former cloth hall, **Lakenhalle** (to the right) also dates from the 14C, although the gable was added in the 17C.

Schepenhuis (AY A) – The late 14C "old palace" is a rather isolated building set back from the main line of frontages to the southwest. It was the aldermen's house and now contains the town archives.

Postgebouw (AY) – This extensively restored mansion, now the GPO, used to be the Town Hall.

★★**St.-Romboutskathedraal (AY)** ⊘ – This Gothic building is remarkable for its grandiose tower which is as wide as the nave. Graceful pinnacles decorate the buttresses along the side aisles and elegant gables adorn the east end.

★★★**The tower** – This tower, considered the most beautiful in Belgium, forms the façade and porch; it measures 97m – 318ft in height. Begun in 1452, it was intended to reach the surprising height of 167m – 548ft, but the project was stopped in 1521. The Keldermans dynasty of architects directed the construction. The awesome proportions combine with powerful, yet subtle vertical lines to create an unforgettable impression. Vauban called this the eighth Wonder of the World. There are two carillons here *(concerts : see the Calendar of Events)*.

Interior – Enter by way of the south portal, which opens beneath a tall window with flamboyant tracery and a delicately arched pediment. The interior is surprisingly large (99m – 325ft long, 28m – 92ft high) but is nevertheless harmonious. The 13C central nave is 13m – 43ft wide, and has six bays. 17C statues of the apostles stand against stout cylindrical pillars to separate the bays. After the fire in 1342, the cathedral was embellished with an ambulatory and an apse with seven radiating chapels. The chapels in the north aisle were added between 1498 and 1502. Michel Vervoort's 18C pulpit displays a Rococo fig tree in which Adam and Ève are concealed, and a plethora of animals carved in full motion; a huge Crucifix dominates the scene of St Norbert's conversion.

Note among the **works of art** a moving Van Dyck *Crucifixion* in the south transept. The dull colours and the sorrowing faces of Mary and Mary Magadalene, as well as the attitude of the unrepentant thief, are particularly expressive. Lucas Faydherbe made the black-and-white marble altar. Artus Quellin the Younger is

St-Romboutskathedraal

said to have made the communion bench; this delicately executed work in white marble is in the Holy Sacrament chapel, at the end next to the tower. Cardinal Mercier's mausoleum is in the the north aisle in a chapel near the transept; he died in 1926.

Leave from the door in the north transept.

Notice the painting on the left; it depicts the inside of this city church in 1775.

Take the Wollemarkt leading to a small bridge. To the left there is a delightful **view★** (AY F) of the 16C **Sint-Truiden abbey refuge** (AY D). The crowstepped pediment and bellcote stand out against tall trees, while the pink brick walls seem to plunge into the canal covered in aquatic plants. At the end of Schoutetstraat the restored buildings (15C) of the former Tongerlo abbey refuge's house a tapestry factory.

★**Koninklijke Manufactuur van Wandtapijten** (AY M¹) ⊙ – The aim of the tapestry works is to preserve the Flemish tapestry-making tradition. Theodoor De Wit founded this factory in 1889, and it bears his son's name. Gaspard De Wit (1892-1971) was an artist and painter as well as an internationally famous weaver. He invented the "numbered cartoon", a black-and-white card with the design outlined only, and the colours indicated by number.

The guided tour takes in the workshops in which old tapestries are restored or new ones made. All the work is done by hand, as in the past. Several beautiful rooms serve as a decor for the tapestry collection. Developments in the art of tapestry from about 1500 to the present day are illustrated here, with an indication of the differences in style between various manufacturers *(qv)*.

Return to the little bridge and take the covered passageway opposite.

St.-Janskerk (BY) ⊙ – This 15C church dedicated to St John has Baroque furnishings and more particularly a 1619 Rubens triptych, the *Adoration of the Magi*. The central panel is a remarkable composition in two parts, one dark, the other light. The subtlety of the colours, the contrast between the gentle face of the Virgin Mary shown in profile and the softened ruggedness of the kings' faces as they gaze at the blond-haired Infant, make this an exceptional piece of work. Rubens' first wife, Isabella Brant, posed for the Virgin Mary's face.

To get to Frederik de Merodestraat go round the north side of the church.

Hof van Busleyden (BY M²) – This 16C turreted brick mansion was built for one of Emperor Charles V's councillors. It stands at the back of a courtyard adorned with lawns and lined with arcades. The bellringing school and municipal museum are housed in the mansion.

Reach the Veemarkt (cattle market) and Befferstraat.

St.-Pieter-en-Pauluskerk (BY) – This church, dedicated to St Peter and St Paul, has a beautiful restored Baroque façade.

Palais van Margaretha van Oostenrijk (BY J) – Rombout Keldermans built this palace in the early 16C; it became the seat of the law courts in 1796. The buildings, although Renaissance in style, are still influenced by Gothic ideas. They are laid out around a pretty arcaded courtyard.

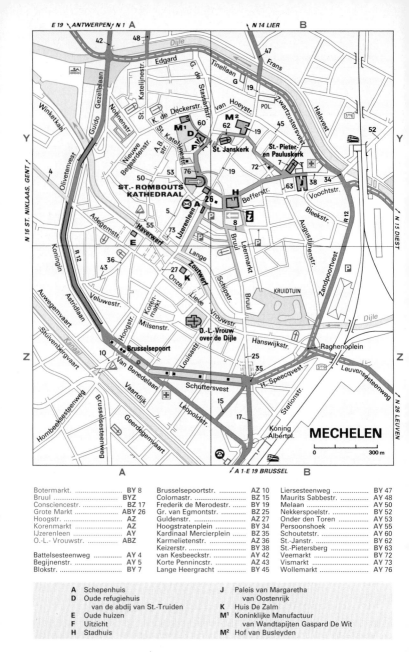

Botermarkt.	BY 8	Brusselsepoortstr.	AZ 10
Bruul	BYZ	Colomastr.	BZ 15
Consciencestr.	BZ 17	Frederik de Merodestr.	BY 19
Grote Markt	ABY 26	Gr. van Egmontstr.	BZ 25
Hoogstr.	AZ	Guldenstr.	AZ 27
Korenmarkt.	AZ	Hoogstratenplein	BY 34
IJzerenleen	AY	Kardinaal Mercierplein	BZ 35
O.-L.- Vrouwstr.	ABZ	Karmelietenstr.	AZ 36
		Keizerstr.	BY 38
Battelsesteenweg	AY 4	van Kesbeeckstr.	AY 42
Begijnenstr.	AY 5	Korte Penningcstr.	AZ 43
Blokstr.	BY 7	Lange Heergracht	BY 45

Liersesteenweg	BY 47
Maurits Sabbestr.	AY 48
Melaan	AY 50
Nekkerspoelstr.	BY 52
Onder den Toren	AY 53
Persoonshoek	AY 55
Schoutetstr.	AY 60
St.-Janstr.	BY 62
St.-Pietersberg	BY 63
Veemarkt	BY 72
Vismarkt	AY 73
Wollemarkt	AY 76

A	Schepenhuis	**J**	Paleis van Margaretha van Oostenrijk
D	Oude refugiehuis van de abdij van St.-Truiden	**K**	Huis De Zalm
E	Oude huizen	**M¹**	Koninklijke Manufactuur van Wandtapijten Gaspard De Wit
F	Uitzicht	**M²**	Hof van Busleyden
H	Stadhuis		

ADDITIONAL SIGHTS

IJzerenleen (AY) – This long square, which is a marketplace, is named after the wrought-iron balustrades along it which used to protect the 16C canal. There are some beautifully restored façades lining the square.

Zoutwerf (AZ) – This quayside is lined with several interesting façades, especially the one fronting the "Salmon House", **Huis De Zalm**, (AZ K), built in the 16C for the fishmongers' guild. The stone in the façade above the door bears a carving of a golden salmon.

Brusselsepoort (AZ) – This is the only remaining trace of the 14C fortifications. The gate is framed by two towers with pepperpot roofs dating from the 17C.

Kerk van O.-L.-Vrouw over de Dijle (AZ) ⊘ – This church contains a triptych by Rubens, *The Miraculous Draught of Fishes*.

Haverwerf (AY) – Three picturesque **old houses** (AY E) stand near a little bridge opposite the Fish Market, Vismarkt : St Joseph's House, with a scrolled gable ; Devil's House, a timbered house with caryatids ; and Paradise House, on which the tympana depict Adam and Ève.

EXCURSIONS

Fort Breendonk ⊙ – *12km – 7.5 miles west via Willebroek.*
This fort, a national memorial, was built between 1906 and 1914 to complete Antwerp's defences. Although bombarded in 1914, it was the last fort in Antwerp to surrender to the Germans. The Belgian Army chose it in May 1940 as its general headquarters (King Leopold III stayed here), but the German advance pushed the troops back to the coast, forcing them to abandon the fort. Between September 1940 and August 1944, the Nazis used it as a "reception camp" which was in reality a concentration camp; about 4 000 people were imprisoned here, some of whom were later deported.
A signposted tour, with recordings of survivors' accounts at certain places take visitors through the prisoners' rooms, the torture room, the huts used as living and sleeping quarters, the hostage execution enclosure and the gibbet used for prisoners sentenced to death. The documents in the small museum describe the two World Wars, and life in the Breendonk camp or in other similar Nazi installations.

From Mechelen to Elewijt – *12km – 7.5 miles, leave by Leuvensesteenweg* (**BZ**).

Muizen – The **parc zoologique de Planckendael** ⊙ is a vast zoological park covering an area of about a hundred acres to the south. It is planted with flowers and trees and is home to nearly 1 000 animals. There are rare or endangered species here, aviaries of tropical birds, and lakes with large colonies of water fowl.

Hofstade – This immense recreation park covers an area of almost 150 hectares – nearly 371 acres. It includes two lakes and an ornithological reserve.

Elewijt – **Het Steen** ⊙, to the west, is the castle where Rubens spent the last five years of his life (1635-1640). It still has a pretty north façade with crowstepped gables, as well as a 13C keep.

Keerbergen and Tremelo – *23km – 14.25 miles east, leaving by Nekkerspoelstraat* (**BY 52**).

Keerbergen – This is a pleasant holiday venue in the Brabant Kempen region. Luxurious villas are tucked amidst the pine forest.

Tremelo – The **Pater Damiaanmuseum** ⊙ is housed in the missionary's birthplace. **Father Damian** (1840-1889) died caring for Hawaii's lepers on Molokai Island. A collection of his personal belongings and an audio-visual presentation in several languages retrace his life.

La MEUSE NAMUROISE★★
Namur
Michelin maps 409 H5, H4, I4 or 213 folds 20, 21 and 214 fold 5

The Meuse rises in France at an altitude of 409m – 1 342ft. The river crosses Belgium and the south of the Netherlands, travelling 950km – 590 miles before flowing into the North Sea.

The Meuse in the Namur Region – The Meuse is at its most picturesque as it crosses the province of Namur. Its powerful rushing waters have gouged out a narrow valley at an altitude of 300m – 984ft before dropping down gradually as it heads north. The river, like most of the waterways in Belgium, flows initially from south to north. When it reaches Namur it suddenly bends to the east, flowing along a corridor. The variety of landscapes is a result of the types of soil. Shale-covered, wooded slopes alternate with hard rocks (limestone, sandstone). The bare stone forms a channel for the river, with magnificent escarpments, slender spurs or fine needles. In many places there are deep caves. All the rock faces are popular with climbers.
Numerous barges use the sections of the river that are navigable for 1 350-ton vessels (international standard) downstream of Givet, and along the stretch from Hermalle-s-Huy to Liège, handling 2 000-ton boats.

Boat trips, see Dinant, Huy, Namur.

The four Aymon sons
Ever since Renaud de Montauban's medieval verse-chronicle, the exploits of Renaud, Alart, Guichard and Richard have given rise to many different tales. The four young men were forced to flee the wrath of Charlemagne, whose beloved nephew had been killed by Renaud, on their magnificent **horse, Bayard**. The four sons of Duke Aymes of Dordogne took refuge only briefly in the Ardennes, on the banks of the Meuse, but their legend is still very much alive in many localities, especially along the Meuse in the Namur region.

★★ ① FROM HASTIÈRE-LAVAUX TO NAMUR

80km – 50 miles – allow 1 day – local map opposite

The impressive rocky cliffs and the ruins of a number of fortresses on top of them give this route a romantic atmosphere. The very presence of these fortresses underlines the valley's strategic importance. It lies on a traditional north-south route, and, because of this, was invaded on several occasions. One of the most disastrous of the invasions took place in 1554, when **King Henri II** of France was fighting Emperor Charles V.

The valley is more densely populated than the surrounding plateaux (Condroz to the east, Entre-Sambre-et-Meuse to the west). Straggling villages lie at the foot of the wild, rocky cliffs, while villas, inns and cafés crowd along the riverside.

Hastière-Lavaux – The **grottes du Pont d'Arcole** ⊙ *(Rue d'Anthée)* have five galleries adorned with rock formations. The caves also include a deep well with an underground river running at its bottom. The upper gallery has delicate stalactites, some of them an extraordinarily pure white in colour.

Hastière-par-delà – The **Église Notre-Dame** stands "on the other side" of the Meuse; it is actually the remains of a priory in the Mosan Romanesque style (1033-1035), except for the Gothic chancel. It has certain points in common with St Hadelin's in Celles *(qv)*, for example the large porch-tower, the pilaster strips, the nave with a wooden-ceiling, and the great arches supported on square pillars.

The 13C stalls were carved with a wide range of different motifs. The font dates from the 14C. The Romanesque **crypt** contains two Merovingian sarcophagi.

Return to the north bank.

Waulsort – This is a small tourist centre in a pleasant location. The huge Waulsort abbey was founded in the 11C. The former abbot's palace is all that now remains. The valley narrows beyond this point and beautiful rough grey rock faces plunge steeply into the Meuse on the opposite bank. These are the famous **rochers de Freÿr★**, cliffs that are the domain of the Belgian Alpine Club climbing school.

★ **Château de Freÿr** – *See Château de FREŸR.*

Before long, Viel Anseremme comes into view, a priory standing among beautiful trees in a bend in the river.

★ **Grotte la Merveilleuse** – *See DINANT.*

★★ **Dinant** – *See DINANT.*

Beyond Rocher Bayard, on the east bank, lies the southern end of Anseremme.

★ **Anseremme** – *See DINANT: Excursions.*

Return to Dinant and cross over to the west bank of the Meuse.

Bouvignes and Château de Crèvecœur – *See DINANT: Excursions.*

The ruins of the **Tour de Géronsart** and those of the **Château de Poilvache** ⊙ can be seen at a height of 125m – 410ft above the Meuse, overlooking the village of Houx. The people of Liège destroyed the castle in 1430 and it was then overrun by vegetation. Legend has it that the four Aymon sons built it. The 10C fortress was initially called Château d'Émeraude (literally "Emerald Castle") but was renamed Poilvache ("cowhide") in the 14C, as a result of a ruse. The besieged occupants slipped out of the castle in search of cattle and were captured by the people of Dinant, some of whom then disguised themselves in the prisoners' clothes while others covered themselves with animal skins and hid themselves amidst herds of cows. Their disguises enabled them to enter the castle. The **Molignée Valley★** *(qv)* lies beyond Anhée.

Cross the Meuse and head towards Yvoir.

Yvoir – Once a metal-working town, this is now a holiday resort which is popular for its island, now a **recreation centre** ⊙. It is possible to go caving and pot-holing nearby to the north. The **domaine de Champalle** ⊙ south of Yvoir includes botanical gardens, a castle and the Euro Butterfly Centre which has tropical greenhouses filled with hundreds of tropical butterflies, freshwater and sea fish, and brightly-coloured birds. The "breeding farm" gives visitors an insight into the development of butterflies, from egg to chrysalis; butterflies can be seen in their natural environment in a special garden (450m^2 – 92 sq yds).

The road out of Yvoir climbs a steep hill.

★ **Spontin** – *See SPONTIN.*

Crupet – This village lies between two valleys and has a beautiful **manor-house** (12C and 16C) surrounded by water. It is in fact a powerful square tower with a bartizan on one side. There is also a corner turret and half-timbered hoarding. The Carondelet family lived here until 1621, and the crest of this family from Franche-Comté can be seen on the pediment of the entrance porch. The noblemen's gravestones are in Crupet **church** left of the entrance. The lords themselves are depicted in stiff ceremonial clothing.

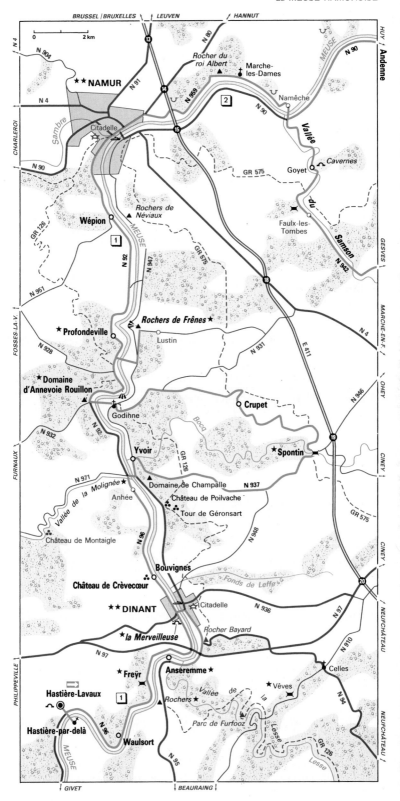

Cross the Meuse at the entrance to Godinne.

★**Annevoie-Rouillon** – *See Domaine d'ANNEVOIE-ROUILLON.*

There is a pretty **view**★ of Godinne priory a few miles beyond Annevoie. It is a charming 16C structure adjoining a 16C church with a Gothic chancel.

Cross the next bridge and take the Lustin road.

★**Rochers de Frênes** ⊘ – There is a beautiful **view**★ of the Meuse Valley and Profondeville from the viewpoint at the top of these rocks *(access through the café).*

Return to the west bank.

★**Profondeville** – This charming tourist centre is pleasantly located in a meander of the Meuse opposite the Rochers de Frênes.

Wépion – This town is renowned for its strawberry farms. The impressive **Rochers de Néviaux** cen be seen on the opposite bank.

Head for Namur (qv) via ⑤ on the town plan. The road arrives at the foot of the citadel.

★ ② FROM NAMUR TO ANDENNE

35km – 22 miles – local map on previous page

The Meuse broadens out along this stretch and the valley widens. Although stubbornly hard rock can still be seen here and there, the slopes are generally less steep. There are many working limestone and marble quarries along the riverbanks.

★★**Namur** – *See NAMUR.*

Leave Namur by ② on the town plan and drive along the north bank of the Meuse.

Rocher du roi Albert – Rocks rising 70m – 230ft above the Meuse can be seen on the left. It was here that **King Albert I** fell to his death on 17 February 1934 while rock-climbing. A cross halfway up the face marks the place where his body was found. The surrounding forest has become a **national park** and a little **museum** contains the gifts left by pilgrims to the spot.

Marche-les-Dames – The Cistercians founded the **abbaye Notre-Dame-du-Vivier** in the early 13C. It now accommodates the Little Sisters of Bethlehem. The abbey buildings date from the 13C and the 18C.

Cross the Meuse at Namêche and take the N 942 towards Gesves.

Vallée du Samson – This is a fertile, picturesque valley.

Goyet – The **cavernes** ⊘ give an idea of the way of life in prehistoric cave dwellings; other caves nearby contain beautiful concretions. A 19C **château** a short distance before Faulx-les-Tombes is a striking imitation of a medieval fortress.

Turn back and return to the Meuse Valley; follow it to Andenne.

Andenne – This little town grew up around the monastery founded in about 690 by St Begga, Charlemagne's great-great-great grandmother. The monastery became an aristocratic chapter of secular canonesses in the 11C.

The **War of the Cow** began in Andenne. A peasant had stolen a cow from a wealthy man in Ciney, and was recognised at the Andenne fair while he was trying to return the cow to its owner. He was arrested and hung by the men of Ciney. The Count of Namur came to revenge his serf's death, aided by the people of Luxembourg, and they laid siege to the town. Liège's prince-bishop, sovereign of Ciney, called on Dinant for help. The war lasted for two years and devastated the Condroz region.

Collégiale Ste-Begge – This collegiate church was built in the 18C to plans by Dewez; it was designed to replace the monastery's seven churches. The church contains St Begga's Gothic blue stone tomb *(chapel north of the chancel).* The church **museum** ⊘ contains the canonesses' treasury consisting of paintings, sculptures, manuscripts and the finely worked reliquary of St Begga (about 1570-1580).

Château de MODAVE★

Liège

Michelin maps 409 I4 or 214 fold 6

The first thing that strikes visitors on their arrival at the castle is the size of the buildings, but at this point there is no indication of the sheer drop down to the Hoyoux River on the other side. Certain parts of the castle (the keep) date back to the 13C; but for the most part the Count of Marchin, who restored it between 1652 and 1673, is responsible for the way it looks today. After him it belonged to Liège's prince-bishop, the Duke of Montmorency, and other families, before the Compagnie Intercommunale Bruxelloise des Eaux (Brussels Local Water Authority) bought it in 1941. The purchase was made necessary by the fact that the water used to supply Brussels was collected on the estate. Rennequin Sualem's hydraulic wheel, a model for the Marly machine, was constructed here in 1667.

TOUR ⊙

A great main courtyard precedes the classical façade. The rooms inside are elegantly furnished. Note **Jean-Christian Hansche's** extraordinary multicoloured stuccowork. The stucco in the guard room represents the family tree of the Counts of Marchin with their crests; the stucco work in the Hercules apartment depicts the hero's Labours. There is a beautiful **view**★ over the Hoyoux Valley from the terrace outside the Duke of Montmorency's bedchamber. The bedchamber of the Duchess of Montmorency, who owned the castle in the late 18C, is upstairs. A model of the hydraulic wheel can be seen in the cellars.

EXCURSION

Bois-et-Borsu – *7km – 4.3 miles southeast.*
The **Romanesque church** ⊙ **in Bois** (10C) still has its beautiful late 14C-early 15C **frescoes**★ illustrating the Coronation of the Virgin Mary, the Life of Christ and the legends of St Lambert and St Hubert on the vaulting and walls of the chancel and nave.
The village of **Ocquier** lies some 3.5km – 2 miles from Bois-et-Borsu. Its grey stone houses cluster around the Romanesque church of St Remaclus.

Vallée de la MOLIGNÉE★
Namur
Michelin maps 409 H5 or 214 folds 4, 5 – Local map see La MEUSE NAMUROISE

The Molignée is a small river that flows through a charming valley, wending its way between meadows and wooded slopes before it joins the Meuse. Villages of blue stone houses follow on from one another, and there are several abbeys on the hillsides.

FROM ANHÉE TO FURNAUX *24km – 15 miles allow 4 hours*

Château de Montaigle – This ruined fortress stands on an outcrop of rock. It was destroyed by Henri II in 1554.
Turn left at the old Falaën station.

Château-ferme de Falaën ⊙ – This 17C brick and limestone fortified farmhouse was once surrounded by a moat and defended by a drawbridge. It forms a square with a lofty tower at each corner. Inside there is a small museum on brotherhoods, with temporary exhibitions.

Abbaye de Maredsous – The Benedictines founded this abbey in 1872. It consists of a vast set of neo-Gothic buildings set on a wooded plateau overlooking a valley. The monks engage in a wide range of activities besides their usual hours of prayer, including teaching, computer technology, theological research, the hotel trade, cheesemaking, a bookshop etc.

Maredret – This village, which also has an abbey, specialises in crafts.

Ermeton-sur-Biert – The old castle overlooking this densely wooded area has become a convent.
Turn right beyond the station and go under the railway bridge.

Furnaux – The church has a magnificent **font**★ dating from about 1135-1150. Four lions support the Mosan Romanesque basin, decorated with scenes from the Old and New Testaments, in particular the Baptism of Christ.

MONS★
Hainaut **P** – Population 77 021
Michelin maps 409 E4 or 214 fold 2
Plan of the conurbation in the current Michelin Red Guide Benelux

Mons is both the capital of Hainaut province, a status which is emphasised by its belfry, and the commercial hub of the **Borinage** mining region near the French border. The steep old cobbled streets, with elegant 17C and 18C homes along them, are quite charming.
Sculptor and architect **Jacques Du Brœucq** (*c*1510-1584) was born here in the 16C, as was the musician **Roland de Lassus** (1532-1594).
The French poet **Paul Verlaine** was imprisoned in Mons for having shot his friend Rimbaud (*qv*). He wrote *Romances sans parole* and a few fragments of *Sagesse* during his term of imprisonment.
Since 1971 Mons has been the location of a five-faculty State University, including an international school of interpreting. The town also has a leading engineering college and a Catholic Faculty of Economic Sciences.
Lake Grand Large to the north in Péronne-lez-Antoing has a water sports centre.

A brief history – Mons, as the etymology of its name shows (mons/bergen: mountain), was built on a hillside. The town grew up around a convent founded by St Waudru, a lady of noble birth, in the 7C. Overlooking the convent were the ruins of a fortress.

The Counts of Hainaut later built a castle on the site.

The town reached the peak of its prosperity in the Middle Ages and during the reign of Emperor Charles V, due largely to its clothmaking activities. It was besieged several times, however, especially in the 17C and 18C, because of its strategic position on the border with France. Louis XIV captured the town in 1691 after a particularly devastating three-week siege, and in fact the architectural style of most of the houses dates from this period.

In 1792 in **Jemappes** *(5km – 3 miles west)* Dumouriez won a victory against the Austrians, temporarily making the country French.

For the British Empire, Mons became a symbol of the First World War. It was beneath its walls that General French held Von Kluck's German troops at bay for 48 hours. The Canadians finally liberated the city at dawn on 11 November 1918, after three days of fierce fighting.

SHAPE, the supreme command of European Allied forces, set up headquarters in Maisières and Casteau in the northeast in 1967.

Festivites of the Ducasse – Each year the Procession of the Chariot of Gold takes place on Holy Trinity Sunday (the weekend after Whitsun). Brotherhoods and trade guilds from the various parishes parade through the town with historical societies especially interested in the Renaissance, forming an escort for the reliquaries or statues of their patron saints. The procession ends with the appearance of St Waudru's processional chariot carrying her relics.

This procession is followed by the Lumeçon, a reminder of a "medieval game" opposing St George and a dragon. The combat, which involves several characters and some strange animals (the "*chinchins*"), is accompanied by traditional music and ends with the triumph of Good over Evil.

★★COLLÉGIALE STE-WAUDRU (Z) ⊘ *time : 1 hour*

This impressive Brabant Gothic church was commissioned by the aristocratic chapter of St Waudru canonesses between 1450 and 1686, and was built under the direction of **Mathieu de Layens** *(qv)*. It stands on the very site once occupied by the

modest monastery founded by St Waudru.

The exterior is impressive but somewhat squat, as the tower planned for the west front was never finished. It should have risen to a height of 190m – 618ft but instead its top is on a line with the roof of the nave. There are twenty-nine chapels around the church.

Interior – *Access by the south door.* The vast nave (108m – 354ft long) has fasciculated pillars rising in a single sweep up to the brick vaulting. The nave has three storeys. Jacques Du Broeucq's 16C Italianate Renaissance alabaster **rood-screen** was demolished in 1797 but the statues and bas-reliefs survived and are now distributed throughout the church (chapels, transept, high altar and sacristy).

Behind the west front, in front of the organ loft and its 18C instrument, is the **Car d'Or** (Chariot of Gold), built in 178. It used during the annual procession to carry St Waudru's 19C reliquary through the town.

The Chariot of Gold in the Collegiale Ste-Waudru

Seven splendid **allegorical statues★** carved in alabaster by Du Broecq are set out around the chancel. The four status representing the cardinal virtues and the three representing the theological virtues are particularly graceful. There is also a superb statue of St Bartholomew (1574).

The clerestory windows in the chancel contain beautiful 16C and 17C stained glass, and include the five "imperial windows" gifted by Maximilian of Austria. They were made by a master glass painter from Mons named Claix Eve.

In the first chapel on the south side of the ambulatory, there is a Gothic stone altarpiece called "Les Féries". The upper section dates from the 16C. The twelfth chapel contains a beautiful black marble and alabaster altarpiece by Du Broecq (1549), above which there is a lovely statue of Mary Magdalene surrounded by statuettes of the Evangelists. On the wall of the third chapel in the south aisle is a wonderful alabaster figure of Christ the Redeemer by the same artist.

Treasury ☉ – The church treasure is housed in the formed chapter house and includes a number of interesting religious artefacts dating from the 13C to 19C. Most of them bear the stamp of local craftsmen who were the official goldsmiths to the noble chapter of canonesses. Among the items on display are church plate, gold and silver objects including a 13C-14C finely worked silver-gilt reliquary of St Vincent, another reliquary (St Ely), and Parisian gold and silver plate dating from 1396. A superb piece of jewellery that belonged to St Waudru and is known as the "Benoîte affique" dates from the Merovingian period. It consists of an ancient gemstone decorated with the stylised figures of the Three Kings in *intaglio*. Since 1994, visitors have also been able to see the 10C shroud decorated with strips of tapestry in which the saint's body was wrapped.

A small room next to the treasure house contains Jacques Du Broecq's smaller sculptures.

ADDITIONAL SIGHTS

★**Beffroi** (Y) – *Illustration p 27*. The belfry was built at the highest point in the town on the charming square in front of the castle. From the square there are beautiful glimpses of the surrounding area, including the 11C-12C ruins of the outer walls of the **Counts of Hainaut's castle** (12C) and the Counts' private chapel, dedicated to St Calixte. Its crypt dates from the Romanesque period (11C).

The **belfry** (1662) is 87m – 285ft high, with graceful onion domes and a traceried lantern tower from which there is a superb panoramic view. This is the only Baroque belfry in Belgium. There are 47 smaller bells and one 5-tonne great bell in the carillon.

Hôtel de ville (Y H) ☉ – The Town Hall stands on Grand-Place. It was built in 1458. Construction was halted, for lack of money, when Charles the Bold died in 1477. It was taken up again in the 16C and was not completed until the 19C. The beautiful Gothic façade has a bell tower, framed by two 17C pavilions with scrolled pediments.

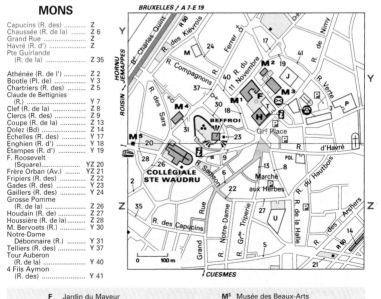

MONS

Capucins (R. des) .... Z
Chaussée (R. de la) .... Z 6
Grand Rue .... Z
Havré (R. d') .... Z
Pte Guirlande
  (R. de la) .... Z 35

Athénée (R. de l') .... Z 2
Bootle (Pl. de) .... Y 3
Chartriers (R. des) .... Z 5
Claude de Bettignies
  (R.) .... Y 7
Clef (R. de la) .... Z 8
Clercs (R. des) .... Z 9
Coupe (R. de la) .... Z 13
Dolez (Bd) .... Z 14
Échelles (R. des) .... Y 17
Enghien (R. d') .... Y 18
Étampes (R. d') .... Y 19
F. Roosevelt
  (Square).................... YZ 20
Frère Orban (Av.) .... YZ 21
Fripiers (R. des) .... Z 22
Gades (R. des) .... Y 23
Gaillers (R. des) .... Y 24
Grosse Pomme
  (R. de la) .... Z 26
Houdain (R. de) .... Z 27
Houssière (R. de la)........ Z 28
M. Bervoets (R.) .... Y 30
Notre-Dame
  Débonnaire (R.) .... Y 31
Telliers (R. des) .... Y 37
Tour Auberon
  (R. de la) .... Y 40
4 Fils Aymon
  (R. des) .... Y 41

F	Jardin du Mayeur	M³	Musée des Beaux-Arts
H	Hôtel de ville	M⁴	Le Vieux Logis
M¹	Musées du Centenaire	M⁵	Musée François Duesberg
M²	Musée de la Vie montoise		

Near the main door is the cast iron figure of a monkey, known as the "Singe du Grand-Garde". Its origins are a mystery. The monkey's head has been worn smooth by people stroking it for good luck. Note the 15C sculpted keystones in the porch. They are decorated with scenes symbolising the judicial functions of the town's aldermen.

There are many rooms **inside** from many different periods, decorated with beautiful furniture, paintings and tapestries. The beams in the Gothic room on the first floor are supported on beautiful carved corbels. The Gothic vaulting (17C) from the old St George's chapel is in the next room; temporary exhibitions are held here.

Jardin du Mayeur (Y F) – The Mayor's Garden was once the aldermen's orchard and farmyard. Nowadays, it forms a pretty complement to the old buildings behind the Town Hall; one of them, the old pawnshop, is now home to the musées du Centenaire. The "Joker's Fountain" sculpted by Gobert represents a little boy spraying passers-by with water.

Musées du Centenaire (Y M¹) $\odot$ – These museums include a War Museum, a Museum of Prehistoric and Gallo-Roman Archeology, a Numismatics Museum and most particularly a **Ceramics Museum** with works dating from between the 17C and the 20C. Note especially the ceramics from Delft, St-Amand-les-Eaux (France) and Brussels.

★**Musée du Folklore et de la Vie montoise (Y M²)** $\odot$ – The Maison Jean-Lescarts housing the folk museum stands alone at the end of a garden filled with archeological exhibits. A flight of steps leads to the museum entrance. It is a charming building dating from 1636, which used to be a convent infirmary.

The museum illustrates regional history and traditions through furniture, simple decoration, various collections and a range of different documents.

Musée des Beaux-Arts (Y M³) $\odot$ – Works of art from the 16C to the present day are exhibited on a rota basis in the art gallery. Major temporary exhibitions are held here every year.

Le Vieux Logis et la chapelle Sainte-Marguerite or **musées Chanoine-Puissant (Y M⁴)** $\odot$ – Before his death in 1934, Canon Puissant, a great art lover, installed extensive and wide-ranging collections of antique furniture, statues, gold and silverware, and sketches in this little 16C house and in the nearby chapel dedicated to St Margaret, a Romanesque building dating from the 13C. The chapel was once surrounded by the St Waudru parish graveyard (the "Attacat") and it was here that the canon was buried.

★**Musée François Duesberg (YZ M⁵)** $\odot$ – This museum is housed in the former premises of the national bank. Its interior layout is voluntarily austere in order to heighten the impact of the dazzling collection of clocks (1795-1815) made by the leading goldsmith-engravers in Paris. It was the popular enthusiasm for writers such as Daniel Defoe (*Robinson Crusoe*, 1719), Bernardin de Saint-Pierre (*Paul et Virginie*, 1787), or Chateaubriand (*Atala*, 1801) and the influence of the philosopher Jean-Jacques Rousseau that provided them with their creative inspiration. Ten different craftsmen were needed to produce a single clock on which the bronze was either given a black patina or gilded. Note the "Paul et Virginie" clock said to have been commissioned by the Parisian bronzesmith Pierre-Philippe Thomire in 1802 by Napoleon Bonaparte as a gift for the author whose work he so admired. The museum also has a teaching mission. Two display cases show the changes in clockmaking techniques and the clocks are accompanied by paintings, engravings and books focussing on the same themes.

EXCURSIONS

Cuesmes – *3.5km – 2 miles south. Leave from Grand-Rue.*

The **Maison de Van Gogh** $\odot$ stands in a pretty, rural setting. The artist lived here with a family of miners, the Descrucqs, in 1879 and 1880. He had come to the Borinage district in December 1878 to preach the gospel. He then began drawing the countryside and the miners' life in Cuesmes. Visitors can see a reconstruction of his room and a documents room containing an audio-visual presentation.

Le Grand-Hornu – *See Le GRAND-HORNU.*

Blaugies – *20km – 12.5 miles southwest of Mons.*

There is a little 15C polychrome wooden altarpiece in the **church**, representing an *Entombment* with a heightened sense of movement. There is also a 12C font, with images of dragons biting bunches of grapes on one side.

Roisin – *30km – 18.5 miles southwest of Mons.*

Verhaeren's house *(qv)* is north of the village, near **Le Caillou-qui-bique**. The writer lived here with his wife Marthe from 1900 to 1916, during the last years of his life. The little **musée Verhaeren** $\odot$ in the courtyard of the inn in Le Caillou includes a reconstruction of the poet's study.

NAMUR★★

Namur – Population 97 8450
Michelin maps 409 H4 or 214 fold 5 – Local map see La MEUSE NAMUROISE

This town has been a prime military site, owing to its location at the confluence of the Sambre and the Meuse spanned by the beautiful Jambes Bridge. The enormous citadel spread over Champeau Hill dominates the scene, while Namur itself is laid out around its many churches. It is now a prosperous city, where trade and tertiary sector offices are the main activities, in addition to tourism. Its university (Facultés universitaires Notre-Dame-de-la-Paix), founded in 1831, has a good reputation. Namur is currently the political capital of Wallonia, and the seat of the Walloon parliament.

A city often under siege – The history of the County of Namur is one of war. The city itself was often under siege because of its strategic position. Even in Roman times, Julius Caesar attacked the Aduatuci here when they sought refuge in the settlement. In 1577 Don Juan of Austria captured the castle, and from the 17C onwards assaults followed thick and fast. The 1692 siege led by Vauban in Louis XIV's presence had a great impact. The capture of Namur was celebrated in grandiloquent odes by Boileau and Racine, the Sun King's historiographers, and even in works by his official court painter, Van der Meulen. Vauban reinforced the fortifications, but Namur was recaptured again in 1695 by William III of Orange.

In 1746 the armies of Louis XV attacked the city, which was handed over to Austria 1748. Emperor Joseph II had the fortifications demolished.

The Revolutionaries took Namur in 1792, but they were forced out by the Austrians the following year. The last siege, in 1794, returned the town to the French.

After Waterloo in 1815 Grouchy's rear guard in Namur valiantly protected most of the field marshal's retreating forces heading for the Meuse Valley and Givet-Charlemont. The Dutch rebuilt the citadel in 1816.

Owing to the ring of fortresses built in the late 19C, Namur was able to put up heroic resistance against the enemy during the First World War. Nevertheless the town was eventually invaded, then pillaged and partly burned down on 23 August 1914. Namur was captured in May 1940 and suffered a number of air raids until 1944.

Festivals – Every year traditional folklore groups take part in the **Wallonia festivals** *(see the Calendar of Events)*. The **stilt-walkers,** whose existence has been traced back to the 15C, dress up in 17C costume and fight each other on stilts. The Canaris battalion distinguished itself during the Brabant Revolution.

Boat trips on the Meuse ⊘ – Boat trips are organised on the Meuse to Dinant and Wépion.

★CITADELLE (BZ) *time : 1 hour 30min*

Access via the Route Merveilleuse (1.5km – 1 mile) or by cablecar ⊘ leaving from the foot of the Citadel.

Route Merveilleuse – The **Tour Joyeuse (BZ)**, once part of the Counts' castle, is on the right as the road climbs.

A terrace in the northeast corner of a spur of rock at a bend in the road, affords a magnificent **panoramic view★★** of the valley of the Sambre and the Meuse. Not far from there, on the left, a narrow path leads down to Namur. From it, there is a view of the city's slate roofs and many bell towers.

The road then reaches the **donjon**, passing between two of the old castle's **towers** (**BZ A**) and crosses the moat separating the two main areas of the citadel.

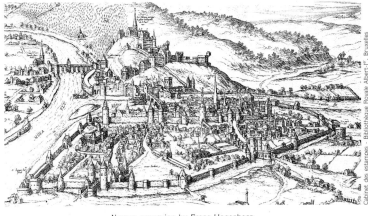

Namur, engraving by Frans Hogenberg

199

Fortifications ⊘ – The late 15C and 16C Mediane bastion was reinforced in 1640 by the addition of another bastion, the Terra Nova, built by the Spanish. A wide moat separates them.

A visit of the fortifications reveals the complex defensive architecture of each bastion, from both the outside *(recorded commentary)* and the inside with a guided tour of two underground passages.

Musée provincial de la forêt (AZ M¹) ⊘ – This forestry museum, surrounded by beautiful trees, provides an insight into the flora and fauna of Belgian forests.

The large diorama of the Ardennes Forest with sound effects is particularly interesting.

Tropical insect collections are on display upstairs. The butterflies are really remarkable.

Fort d'Orange – This fortress is near the **parc d'attractions Reine-Fabiola** (**AZ**), a local amusement park. The fortress was built in 1691 to protect the Terra Nova bastion. The Dutch partly rebuilt it in 1816.

Route des Panoramas (**AZ**) – This winding road heads down through the woods to the city centre.

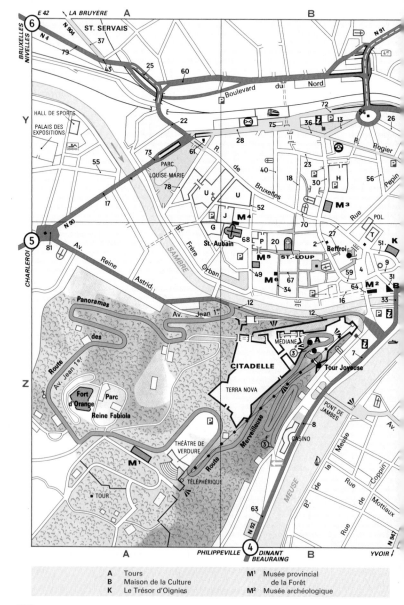

A	Tours	**M¹**	Musée provincial
B	Maison de la Culture		de la Forêt
K	Le Trésor d'Oignies	**M²**	Musée archéologique

★CITY CENTRE *time : half a day*

★**Musée archéologique** (**BZ M²**) ⊘ – The archeology museum is housed in the beautiful 16C building that was once the meat market. The exhibitions display the results of digs in the province. There are magnificent examples of 1C-7C jewellery and glassware.

The **Maison de la Culture** (**BZ B**) is an arts centre built in 1964. It lies behind the museum.

★★**Le Trésor d'Oignies aux Sœurs de Notre-Dame** (**BZ K**) ⊘ – The very rich Oignies priory **treasury**★★ is housed in one room; it was fortunately saved from the 1940 air raids. The display includes delicate early 13C Mosan gold and silverware by the monk **Hugo d'Oignies** including evangelistaries, reliquaries, etc. The delicacy of his workmanship is remarkable, especially the medallions on a black background, the filigree and the leaf decoration on which tiny hunting scenes can be seen.

Beyond the theatre, the **Tour St-Jacques** (**BZ**) comes into view on the left. The tower has an octagonal bellcote on top and has been used as a **belfry** since the 18C.

★**Musée des Arts anciens et du Namurois** (**BY M³**) ⊘ – This museum is housed in the **Hôtel de Gaiffier d'Hestroy**, an elegant 17C mansion, which contains beautiful collections of local works of art dating from the medieval to Renaissance periods.

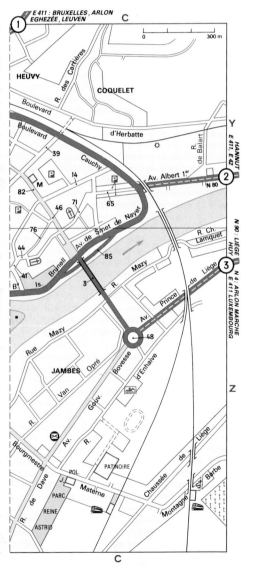

NAMUR

Ange (R. de l')	**BZ** 2
Fer (R. de)	**BY** 30
Marchovelette (R. de)	**BZ** 59
St- Jacques (R.)	**BYZ** 70
Ardennes (Pont des)	**CZ** 3
Armes (Pl. d')	**BZ** 4
Baron L. Huart (Bd.)	**BZ** 7
Baron-de-Moreau (Av.)	**BZ** 8
Bas-de-la-Place (R.)	**BZ** 9
Bord-de-l'Eau (R. du)	**ABZ** 12
Borgnet (Rue)	**BY** 13
Bourgeois (R. des)	**CY** 14
Brasseurs (R. des)	**BZ** 16
Cardinal-Mercier (Av.)	**AY** 17
Carmes (R. des)	**BY** 18
Collège (Rue du)	**BZ** 20
Combattants (Av. des)	**AY** 22
Croisiers (R. des)	**BY** 23
Croix-du-Feu (Av. des)	**AY** 25
Dewez (Rue)	**BCY** 26
Émile-Cuvelier (R.)	**BYZ** 27
Ernest-Mélot (Bd.)	**BY** 28
Fernand-Golenvaux (Av.)	**BCZ** 31
France (Pont de)	**BCZ** 33
Fumal (Rue)	**BZ** 34
Gare (Av. de la)	**BY** 36
Gembloux (Rue de)	**AY** 37
Général-Michel (Rue)	**CY** 39
Godefroid (Rue)	**BY** 40
Gravière (Rue de)	**CZ** 41
Hastedon (Pl. d')	**AY** 43
Ilon (Pl. d')	**CZ** 44
J.-B. Brabant (Rue)	**CY** 46
Joséphine-Charlotte (Pl.)	**CZ** 48
Joseph-Saintraint (R.)	**BZ** 49
Julie-Billiard (R.)	**BZ** 51
Lelièvre (Rue)	**BY** 52
Léopold (Pl.)	**BY** 54
Léopold II (Av.)	**AY** 55
Lucien-Namèche R.)	**BY** 56
Merckem (Bd de)	**AY** 60
Omalius (Pl. d')	**AY** 61
Plante (Av. de la)	**BZ** 63
Pont (Rue du)	**BZ** 64
Reine Élisabeth (Pl.)	**CY** 65
Rupplémont (Rue)	**BZ** 67
St-Aubain (Pl.)	**BZ** 68
St-Nicolas (R.)	**CY** 71
Square-Léopold (Av. du)	**BY** 72
Stassart (Av. de)	**AY** 73
Station (Pl. de la)	**BY** 75
Tanneries (Rue des)	**CYZ** 76
Vierge (Rempart de la)	**AY** 78
Waterloo (Chaussée de)	**AY** 79
Wiertz (Pl.)	**AYZ** 81
1er-Lanciers (R. du)	**BY** 82
4 Fils Aymon (Rue des)	**CZ** 85

M³ - Musée des Arts anciens et du Namurois
M⁴ - Musée diocésain et trésor de la Cathédrale

M⁵ Musée de Croix
M⁶ Musée Félicien Rops

The collection of gold- and silverware is particularly extensive. There are some beautiful Mosan reliquaries.

There are many sculptures in stone (fonts, tombs) as well as in wood (altarpieces, statues), and beaten copper, bearing witness to the interest in artistic production in the Namur region. Equally admirable are the four beautiful landscapes by Herri met de Bles *(qv)* from the early 16C.

★**Église St-Loup** (BZ) ⊙ – This used to be a Jesuit collegiate church and is now a school (Athénée Royal). It is a remarkable Baroque building, built from 1621 to 1645 to plans by Pierre Huyssens. Ringed columns, surmounted by a red and white marble entablature, support sandstone vaulting richly decorated in high-relief. Note also the lovely furniture.

Cathédrale St-Aubain (BYZ) – This Classical domed building was built in 1751 by the Italian architect Pizzoni. It is on the site of the old collegiate church of St Auban, founded in 1047. There are beautiful works of Baroque art inside, coming for the most part from the region's churches and abbeys. Note the Rubens school paintings above the choirstalls from Église St-Loup.

The old 18C bishop's palace is opposite the cathedral and is now used by the provincial government.

★**Musée diocésain et trésor de la cathédrale** (BYZ M⁴) ⊙ – Located to the right of the cathedral, the museum has a beautiful collection of religious objects: a priceless crown-reliquary in a case decorated with enamel discs (*c*1210), a portable altar decorated with ivory plaques (11C-12C), an arm-reliquary of St Adrian (*c*1235), a statue of St Blaise (*c*1280) in silver gilt, a Mosan statue of the Virgin Mary (*c*1220), a rare series of 16C-18C glassware, gold- and silverware, and sculptures.

★**Musée de Croix** (BZ M⁵) ⊙ – This museum is accommodated in an elegant 18C Louis XV style town house. Many of the rooms are open to the public. In them, the decoration integrates perfectly with the architecture. There are ceilings decorated with stuccoes, woodwork (panelling, doors, main staircase), and St-Rémy marble fireplaces.

Note the many high-corniced wardrobes decorated with inset Rococo panels; they are typical of Namur cabinet-making. There are also interesting pieces of regional art (paintings, sculptures, faïence, glass, gold- and silverware).

Musée Félicien Rops (BZ M⁶) ⊙ – This museum is devoted to the famous satirical cartoonist (1833-1898). It contains lithographs, etchings *(Sataniques)*, drawings and paintings.

EXCURSIONS

Franc-Waret – *12km – 7.5 miles northeast. Leave by ② on the town plan.*
The **château** ⊙, an impressive 18C building surrounded by a moat, is flanked by two wings set at right angles to it. A turret and a square tower, traces of the 16C construction, are hidden at the back. Inside, note the main double-spiral staircase, the rooms decorated with beautiful pieces of furniture, the Flemish and French paintings (Largillière portrait), 17C Brussels tapestries based on designs by P Coecke and F Boveman, and the porcelain collection. The visit ends in a beautiful vaulted room.

From Namur to Fosses-la-Ville – *18km – 11 miles west. Leave by ⑤ on the town plan.*
Floreffe – This **abbey** ⊙ overlooking the Sambre was founded in 1121 by the Premonstratensians *(qv)*, and was rebuilt in the 17C and 18C. It was enlarged by a long concrete construction in 1964. A small seminary now occupies this vast building.

The main courtyard opens onto a terrace bordered with 18C buildings. A tower and 17C porticoed building can be seen beyond the garden.

The **abbey church** (13C-18C), flanked by a tower, is 90m – 295ft long. In the 18C, Dewez altered the inside in the neo-Classical style. The immense chancel includes remarkable **choirstalls★** by Pieter Enderlin (1632 to 1648). He represented about forty figures, most of them the founders of religious orders, on the upper panels. The eight cherub musicians or singers decorating the end-pieces are particularly noteworthy.

The 13C mill-brewery down the hill below the abbey has been turned into an inn.

Fosses-la-Ville – This town in the Entre-Sambre-et-Meuse region *(qv)* grew up around a monastery in the 7C. It was besieged on countless occasions, especially in the 17C. **St Feuillen collegiate church,** which was rebuilt in the 18C, still has its late-10C Romanesque tower. The stalls were carved in 1524. The late-16C sculptures include an *Entombment*, and a late 16C bust-reliquary of St Feuillen. A "crypt" at the east end of the church was added on outside the main building in 1086. It is the only one of its kind still existing in Belgium.

The **"Petit Chapitre"**, a museum-gallery next to the church, was once the summer residence of the prince-bishops of Liège. It contains a **collection of costume dolls** ⊘. Lilette Arnould made the costumes of the 800 dolls by hand. The figures represent characters from Belgian folklore, such as Till Eulenspiegel *(qv)*, Tchantchès *(qv)*, the "Gilles" of Binche, the Chinels and the participants in St Feuillen's impressive military parade *(qv)* which takes place every seven years on the last Sunday in September *(next parade in 1998)*.

NIEUWPOORT

West-Vlaanderen – Population 97 470
Michelin maps 409 B2 or 213 fold 1

This is an old stronghold at the mouth of the River IJzer which was rebuilt after 1918 in the Flemish style. Nieuwpoort has an active fishing fleet and a large fish market.
As in Ostend, the harbour channel is protected by two long dikes extending far out into the sea and bearing two piers. Square fishing nets or dipping nets hang on the west pier *(for hire)*.
Nieuwpoort is also a seaside resort **(Nieuwpoort-Bad)** and a water sports centre. The marina has moorings for 3 000 boats.

The Battle of the Yser – The Nieuwpoort region was the scene of this terrible wartime episode. In August 1914 the Germans invaded Belgium then France. When Maréchal Joffre stopped them at the Marne, they immediately attacked Antwerp *(qv)*, leaving the Belgian troops just enough time to evacuate and dig in west of the River IJzer (Yser), under the command of King Albert. They were backed up by French and British troops.
The Germans launched an attack on the last bastion of Belgian territory on 16 October and succeeded in crossing the IJzer at Tervate, north of Diksmuide.
As the Allied reinforcements still had not arrived, the Belgians opened the sluice gates of the Veurne-Ambacht canal at Nieuwpoort on 28 October. The subsequent flooding of the surrounding polders immediately halted the German advance.
The front line then settled itself south of Diksmuide until the end of the war, and the Germans turned to the Ypres salient *(see Ieper)*.

SIGHTS

O.-L.-Vrouwekerk – The church tower was built in 1951. It contains a 67-chime **carillon** that can be heard twice a week and during **concerts** ⊘.

Koning Albertmonument ⊘ – This equestrian statue of the king, surrounded by a circular monument, is near the IJzer Bridge. There is an interesting **view** from the top over Nieuwpoort, Ostend, the IJzer, six locks in a fan-shape and the country-side beyond the polder region *(viewing table)*.

Musea – The Town Hall and market were rebuilt after the war. The **K.R. Ber-quinmuseum★** ⊘ is on the first floor of the market (stadshalle), in a large room in which the rafters are visible. The region's history and folklore is attractively presented. Note the diptych attributed to Lancelot Blondeel representing the port at the end of the 15C.
The little **Museum voor Vogels en Schaaldieren** ⊘ contains an ornithological collection on the ground floor of the **Town Hall** *(side entrance)*. There is a large diorama of birds and shellfish in their natural seashore environment.

De IJzermonding ⊘ – This nature reserve extends north of the resort, along the estuary of the River IJzer (Yser).

NINOVE

Oost-Vlaanderen – Population 33 534
Michelin maps 409 F3 or 213 fold 17

Ninove was renowned for its 12C Premonstratensian *(qv)* abbey, of which the beauti-ful **abbey church** (17C-18C) ⊘ remains. *Entrance through side door on the right.*
The church has the same layout as the one in Grimbergen and has some remarkable **wood panelling★**. There are two splendid confessionals at the end of the church, one of which is attributed to Theodoor Verhaegen (18C, north side) and is decorated with relief figures in a refined Baroque style. The same style is to be found in the side aisle panelling, executed by the same sculptor.
The 190 choirstalls, dating from 1635, are for their part more austere and elegant in style. Note the graceful 18C marble lectern decorated with cherubs in the chancel.

*Use the **Index** to find more information about a subject mentioned in the guide – towns, places, isolated sights, historical events or geographical features etc.*

NIVELLES ★

Brabant-Wallon – Population 21 883
Michelin maps 409 G4 or 213 fold 18

Nivelles, which was rebuilt after the war, is an elegant town with a famous collegiate church.

In the 12C, walls were built round the town and a few of the towers have survived, among them the Tour Simone in Rue Seutin. The abbey was turned into a chapter of canonesses and canons under the rule of an abbess. All the canonesses were high-born and they soon began leading a life of luxury. The abbey was very influential until its closure in 1798.

The collegiate church was badly damaged in 1940 when, along with 500 houses, it was set on fire. The town was later rebuilt. Its current wealth comes from the metal-working and paper-making industries.

Traditions – The **Tour de Sainte Gertrude** Procession *(see the Calendar of Events)* takes place in autumn. It was instituted at Michaelmas in the 13C, St Michael being the town's patron saint.

> ### Cradle of the Carolingian dynasty
>
> Nivelles was one of the cradles of the Carolingian dynasty. It grew up around an abbey dedicated to St Peter, founded in about 650 by Itta of Aquitaine, the wife of Pepin the Elder (Mayor of the Palace of the Austrasian kings and ancestor of Charlemagne). Their daughter, St Gertrude, later became the first abbess of a mixed religious order that became a noble chapter of canonesses and canons in the 9C.

The procession stretches over 14km – 8.5 miles up hill and down dale, following the route taken by St. Gertrude every day as she walked from her hermitage to the place where she had her meals. A 15C cart, drawn by six horses, carries the saint's reliquary.

As the procession wends its way back it is joined by giants (Argayon, Argayonne, their son Lolo and Godet the horse) as well as a group of canonesses in 17C dress. The local hero is the jack o' the clocks, Jean de Nivelles, the son of Jean de Montmorency, who is remembered in the popular French song "Cadet Rousselle".

The local speciality is a succulent cheese and vegetable quiche, served hot, known as "tarte al djote".

SIGHTS

★★**Collégiale Ste-Gertrude** ⊙ – This is an Ottonian Empire Romanesque abbey church, which was consecrated in 1046 by the Bishop of Liège in the presence of Emperor Henri III. The layout with two transepts and two opposing chancels is an architectural expression of the Holy Empire's double nature, representing the complementary elements of the emperor and the pope. The east chancel is raised, over a crypt with ribbed vaulting. The west chancel, representing imperial authority, is part of the 12C narthex.

This late-Romanesque **narthex** has an impressive solidity. It has five storeys accessible from two staircase towers and contains an apse, two chapel galleries, a vast upper chamber (19m – 63ft) called the "Imperial Hall", and an octagonal bell tower.

Collégiale Ste-Gertrude

J. Evrard, Bruxelles

The two doorways in the narthex are decorated with 12C Romanesque sculptures. On the south door is a carving of St Michael; on the north door is an illustration of the story of Samson.

The highest transept gable on the south side of the church, called St Peter's Gable, is decorated with Romanesque arches.

Interior – The size and the simplicity are striking. The long nave (102m – 331ft) was covered with ogive vaulting in the 17C and given a series of decorative features in the 18C. Restoration gave it back its original look while protecting it with a concrete ceiling made to look like wood. Note the graceful **Virgin of the Annunciation★**, a 15C painted wooden statue, the "Charles V" oak panel, the superb Renaissance choir stalls, a 16C marble and alabaster altarpiece said to have been made by Thonon, an artist from Dinant, and the 18C oak and marble pulpit representing the meeting between Jesus and the Woman of Samaria at Jacob's well by Laurent Delvaux. There are several other sculptures by this artist.

There is a 16C brass cupboard in the east chancel, above St Gertrude's mausoleum. A modern reliquary (1982) by F Roulin has replaced the magnificent 13C St Gertrude's reliquary destroyed in the fire caused by an air raid in May 1940. A copy of the original reliquary can be seen in the Imperial Hall.

Crypt and archeological basement – It was in the 11C crypt beneath the east chancel that pilgrims used to arrive to pray, just beneath St. Gertrude's reliquary. The archeological basement under the nave contains the ruins of the five churches, from the 7C to the 10C, which preceded the Romanesque one. The first Merovingian church (about 650) includes the tombs of St Gertrude and her parents. Another of the tombs contains the body of Charlemagne's first wife (8C) while the last church, dating from the Carolingian period (10C), has the tomb of Ermentrude, the granddaughter of Hugh Capet.

Cloisters – These 13C cloisters used to link the church to the monastery buildings which have now all disappeared. They serve as a reminder of the chapter of canons and canonesses who gradually replaced the monks and nuns of the early times. Only the north side of the cloisters is still entirely authentic.

Near the collegiate church are the 19C steps topped by a statue of St Michael, one of the town's patron saints.

The Law Courts were built in the neo-Gothic style. The **Porte de Saintes** is a gateway commemorating the twinning of Nivelles with the town of Saintes in Charente-Maritime, France.

Musée d'Archéologie, d'Histoire et du folklore ⊘ – *27 Rue de Bruxelles.*
This museum displays interesting collections of regional art in an 18C house and forms an ideal way to round off a visit to the collegiate church. Particularly noteworthy are the four stone limestone statues of the Apostle from the Gothic rood-screen in the church *(ground floor)*, the luxurious 16C Brussels tapestry, and a beautiful collection of Baroque terracottas by the sculptor Laurent Delvaux (1696-1778). The three allegorical figures were designed for the semicircular façade of Charles of Lorraine's apartments in Brussels *(qv)*.
Archeological collections covering the period between prehistoric and Gallo-Roman times are on the second floor.

Parc de la Dodaine – *South of the town.*
A flower-bedecked garden around a pond and a small lake is a beautiful setting for this park which is also well-equipped with a children's play area and sports facilities.

Following Avenue de la Tour-de-Guet west towards the motorway gives a view of the **Tourette**, a charming 17C square tower, on the right.

EXCURSIONS

Ronquières – *9km – 5.25 miles west.*
This charming village is well-known for its pretty view of the Charleroi Canal with its remarkable piece of technology.

The **Ronquières inclined plane★** ⊘, constructed in 1968, is 1 432m – 4 698ft long. It makes it possible for boats to transfer easily across a drop in the level of the canal of 68m – 223ft. Two containers 91m – 298ft long, filled with water, each with a 5 200-ton counterweight, can transport a 1 350-tonne boat, or four 300-tonne barges, from one canal reach to another, by running along a series of 236 rollers 70cm – 28in diameter. The whole installation is completed upstream by a canal bridge 300m – 984ft long and a **tower** 150m – 492ft high.

An exhibition inside the tower includes a film explaining the inclined plane and a view of the winch room. The upstream installations can be seen from the third floor. There is an audio-visual presentation on the Hainaut region on the second floor.

The visit can be completed by a **boat trip** ⊘ along the canal as far as Ittre. *Departure from the foot of the canal reach.*

Bois-Seigneur-Isaac; Braine-le-Château – *12km – 7.5 miles north.*

Bois-Seigneur-Isaac – The decoration in the 16C chapelle du St-Sang in the **abbey** is Baroque. On the high altar note Laurent Delvaux's sculptures and bas-relief *(Entombment)*. The Gothic vaulted vestry still has a reliquary containing a piece of sacred cloth stained with Christ's Blood. It resulted from a miracle which occurred during the Eucharist in 1405 when blood flowed from a sacred wafer onto the altar cloth and has since become an object of pilgrimage. The 18C **Château de Bois-Seigneur-Isaac** ⊙ opposite the abbey is an enormous building which houses some valuable collections.

Braine-le-Château – The castle, surrounded by water, is near a water mill (exhibitions). It belonged to the Counts of Hornes.

Maximilien de Hornes, Chamberlain to Emperor Charles V, had the **pillory** set up on the neighbouring market square in 1521. His alabaster mausoleum, by Jean Mone, is in the church.

Belgium and Luxembourg on a single sheet: Michelin map no 409 (1:350 000)

OOSTENDE ★

OSTEND – West-Vlaanderen – Population 67 257
Michelin maps 409 B2 or 213 fold 2
Plan of conurbation in the current Michelin Red Guide Benelux

There are two Ostends: one is the elegant seaside resort, the other is the fishing port, ferry terminal for crossings to England (Ramsgate) and hydrofoil terminal (Ramsgate). The **seaside resort** stretches between the **casino** (Kursaal) **(Y)**, opened in 1953 and the Thermae Palace Hotel, along the Albert I Promenade bordering the beach. One of the rooms in the casino was decorated by Paul Delvaux. The beach is popular with surfers. Nearby are the royal galleries built to plans by the French architect Charles Girault.

The old **fishermen's district** is near the harbour mouth and outer harbour. It consists of a network of narrow streets running down to the marina in the south. Further south again is a large park, the **Marie-Hendrikapark**, which has several small lakes for boating and fishing enthusiasts.

Ostend's famous oysters are matured in an 80 hectare – 198 acre basin, the Spuikom, southeast of the town.

The Siege of Ostend during the Eighty Years War is still famous. The story goes that Archduchess Isabella had vowed not to change her shift until the town was taken. The siege lasted for three years (1601-1604), hence the use of the word "isabelle" since that time to describe a certain unidentifiable colour.

The first Belgian sovereigns enjoyed staying in Ostend; Queen Louise-Marie died here in 1850.

Festivals – In 1896 James Ensor was one of the promoters of the **"Dead Rat Ball"**, a name chosen in memory of a Montmartre café called "The Dead Rat", frequented by Cœcilia Club members. This elegant annual philanthropic event *(see the Calendar of Events)* takes place on a Saturday in the casino and is attended by people in costume and masks on a chosen theme.

Among the other annual events, the Blessing of the Sea with a historical procession is interesting, as are Belgium Kites International and Ostend Jazz *(see the Calendar of Events)*.

Intrigue, by James Ensor

Musée des Beaux-Arts, Anvers/GIRAUDON, Paris

OOSTENDE

Adolf Buylstr.	CY 2	Ernest Feyspl.	CZ 6	Nieuwpoortsesteenweg	CZ 22
Alfons Pieterslaan	CZ	Filip Van Maestrichtpl.	CZ 8	Oesterbankstr.	CZ 24
Kapellestr.	CZ	Graaf de Smet de Naeyerlaan	CZ 9	Sir Winston Churchill Kaai	CZ 27
Vlaanderenstr.	CY 30	Groentemarkt	CY 10	Stockholmstr.	CZ 28
		Hendrik Serruyslaan	CZ 13	Wapenpl.	CZ 32
Edith Cavellstr.	CZ 4	Kanunnik Dr.		Warschaustr.	CZ 33
		Louis Colensstr.	CZ 14	Wellingtonstr.	CZ 35
		Koninginnelaan	CZ 18	Wittenonnenstr.	CY 36

A	Noordzeeaquarium
E	St.-Petrus-en-Pauluskerk
M¹	Stedelijk Feest-en Kultuurpaleis

M²	James Ensorhuis
M³	Provinciaal Museum
	voor Moderne Kunst

SIGHTS

Visserskaai (Y) – There is a virtually uninterrupted line of restaurants along this quay-side. The fishing harbour can be seen from here, as can the large fish market, the "**minque**", beyond the harbour mouth, where there are picturesque sales of fish and shellfish.

Weststaketsel (Y) – This is one of the two piers flanking the harbour mouth, or "havengeul". From here there is a view of the beach and the movement of the boats and ferries. At the far end, fishermen set up their dipping nets, square nets suspended on winches.

Noordzeeaquarium (Y A) ⊘ – The aquarium contains small tanks of North Sea fish and shellfish, and collections of shells.

Stedelijk Feest- en Kultuurpaleis (Y M¹) – The festival and arts centre overlooks the Wapenplein, the town's main square. It contains two museums.

Museum voor Schone Kunsten ⊘ – *Second floor*. Romantic to post-Impressionist Belgian paintings. Artists with works on show include Ensor, Spilliaert, Musin and Van Rysselberghe.

Heemkundig Museum De Plate ⊘ – *First floor*. This museum deals with regional history and traditions (banners, old Ostend society medals).
Ostend's maritime tradition is well illustrated in the reconstruction of a fishermen's café.

James Ensor (1860-1949)

Born in Ostend of an English father and a Flemish mother, this solitary genius rarely distanced himself from his native town and was recognised only much later by his contemporaries as one of the greatest painters of the late 19C.

Ensor painted initially in dark tones; later his palette brightened. Between 1883 and 1892 he used violent colours and a technique already tending towards Expressionism to illustrate macabre or satirical subjects which met with little public success. Ensor created an imaginary fantastic world, peopled with masked characters and skeletons, a squirming carnival atmosphere that paved the way for Surrealism.

His most representative work is *Entrance of Christ into Brussels* (1888), exhibited in the Malibu Museum, California.

James Ensorhuis (Y M²) ⊙ – The inside of Ensor's home has been reconstructed and turned into a museum. The entrance is through a seashell shop once run by his aunt and uncle. The artist's studio is on the second floor.

Opleidingszeilschip Mercator (CZ) ⊙ – This white three-master, once an officers' training ship for the Belgian merchant navy, has been tied up alongside in the marina since 1964. Although still in working order, the *Mercator*, which sailed the world's seas 41 times in its career from 1932 to 1960, is now a floating museum. There are several objects and photographs recalling its participation in scientific missions, including bringing back gigantic Easter Island statues or the mortal remains of Father Damien *(qv)*.

Provinciaal museum voor Moderne Kunst (Z M³) ⊙ – This museum exhibits Belgian paintings, sculptures, ceramics and graphic art, on the various floors of a former cooperative. The collections *(exhibited in rotation)* give an idea of trends in modern and contemporary art.

Expressionism is represented by the St.-Martens-Latem artists *(qv)*. Among the more recent movements on display are abstract art, pop art and conceptual art. The works of Panamarenko (1940-) and Jan Fabre are classed with contemporary art. The museum also organises temporary exhibitions with a national or international background.

St.-Petrus-en-Pauluskerk (Z E) – This church was built in 1905 in the neo-Gothic style and contains the mausoleum of Queen Marie-Louise.

The **Peperbus**, the bell tower of an 18C church destroyed by fire, stands nearby.

EXCURSIONS

Stene – *3km – 2 miles south by the N 33.*

The all white **St.-Annakerk** has a prettily proportioned exterior and a rustic interior. Only the north aisle existed in the 14C. The nave and the south aisle were added in the 17C. The presbytery to the south was added in 1764. It has now been restored.

Jabbeke – *17km – 10.5 miles east by the A 10 E 40. Leave the motorway at exit no 6.*

★**Provinciaal Museum Constant Permeke** ⊙ – Permeke (1886-1952) had this house, the Four Winds (Vier Winden), built in 1929 and lived here for more than 20 years. It now contains the artist's works from the beginning of his career onwards: his post-Impressionist period *(Landscape)*, as well as his Cubist *(About Permeke)* and Expressionist periods *(Sower, Dark Sea, Maternity, Daily Bread)* and, more recently, *Unfinished Landscape* (1951). The museum has almost all of Permeke's sculptures, some of which are exhibited in the garden *(Niobe, The Sower)*.

Gistel – *9km – 5.5 miles south on the N 33.*

The **St Godelive Procession** *(see the Calendar of Events)* takes place each year in this commercial centre. The **church** houses the tomb of the saint, whose name means "beloved of God". Godelive was married against her will to a lord called Bertulf, Lord of Gistel; she was later murdered and her body was thrown into a well in 1070.

Ten Putte Abbey *(3km – 2 miles west of Gistel)* was founded around the well standing in a charming garden enclosed by white walls. The cellar where the saint is said to have been imprisoned is under the stairs. She also is said to have accomplished a miracle in the corbelled chapel. The saint is represented on a little 16C triptych in the abbey church (1962). She can be recognised by her attribute, four crowns.

Michelin maps and town plans are oriented with north at the top of the page

Abbaye d'ORVAL ★★

Luxembourg
Michelin maps 409 J7 or 214 folds 16, 17

This abbey, tucked away in the Forest of Gaume *(qv)*, was founded in 1070 by Benedictines from Calabria in southern Italy. By the 12C it had become one of the most famous and richest Cistercian monasteries in Europe.

Legend and history – The name of the abbey ("Orval" means "valley of gold") and its coat of arms (in silver representing an azure rivulet from which a ring with three diamonds is emerging) recalls the legend of Countess Mathilda, Duchess of Lorraine. She was the abbey's protectress and she lost her wedding ring in a spring. It was miraculously returned to her by a trout.

The Church of Our Lady was built at the end of the 12C in the Gothic style, with a few remaining traces of Romanesque architecture. It was altered in the 16C and the early 17C. The abbey had to be rebuilt in 1637 after being burned and pillaged by Maréchal de Chatillon's troops. The monastery was so prosperous in the 18C, however, that new construction was undertaken by the architect Dewez. Hardly had this work been finished when General Loyson's soldiers laid waste to it (1793). The abbey was sold in 1797.

The new monastery – The restoration of the monastery was undertaken in 1926 by the Cistercian monks of the Abbey of Sept-Fons in the Bourbonnais region (Auvergne, France). It was completed in 1948 and the new building was erected on the site of the earlier 18C buildings. It is plain yet elegant, built of a warmly-coloured golden stone. The layout follows the true Cistercian tradition.

The façade of the new abbey church, including a huge representation of the Virgin and Child, faces onto the retreatants' courtyard. It has a great purity of line.

THE RUINS ⊙ *time: 1 hour follow the numbered tour.*

After a film on monastery life *(20min)*, the tour takes visitors round the ruins dating from the Middle Ages to the 18C. The Gothic ruins of the **Church of Our Lady** (église Notre-Dame) stand near the Mathilda Fountain, against a backcloth of trees and shrubs. The rose window in the north arm of the transept, the Romanesque capitals, and the Gothic and Renaissance pillars are remarkable. The tomb of Wenceslas, the first Duke of Luxembourg, is in the chancel. This chancel, with a flat Cistercian east end, was judged too small in the 17C, and an apse was added. The tour then visits the cloisters, which were rebuilt in the 14C, and the 18C undercroft. There is a garden of medicinal herbs in front of the museum of the monks' pharmacy.

OSTEND ★

See OOSTENDE

OUDENAARDE ★

Oost-Vlaanderen – Population 27 012
Michelin maps 409 D3 or 213 fold 16
Town plan in the current Michelin Red Guide Benelux

This Flemish town, rich in history and historic buildings, stands on the banks of the Scheldt, on the edge of Flanders and Brabant. **Adriaen Brouwer**, the painter of Flemish peasant life, was born here in 1605 (or 1606). His works sometimes bear a resemblance to Pieter Bruegel the Elder's paintings.

Oudenaarde is a centre for the textile industry. Its brown ale is also famous.

HISTORICAL NOTES

Baldwin IV, Count of Flanders, built a fortress here in the early 11C. Oudenaarde was repeatedly attacked by the people of Ghent in the 14C and 15C; indeed they lost their famous cannon known as "Mad Meg" (Dulle Griet) here. The cannon is now in Ghent near the Vrijdag Markt.

In 1521, Emperor Charles V besieged Oudenaarde during his conquest of the French enclave in the heart of his kingdom, the region around Tournai. While here, he fell in love with Johanna van den Geenst by whom he had a daughter, **Margaret of Parma.** She governed the Low Countries from 1559 to 1568.

Oudenaarde suffered many other sieges. The worst was that of 1684, led by Maréchal d'Humières, commanding Louis XIV's troops. The best known date in the town's' history, however, is 11 July 1708, when the Duke of Marlborough completely crushed the French army.

Oudenaarde tapestries

At the end of the 15C Brussels tapestry-makers produced marvellous works of art for the Dukes of Burgundy and the merchant class and the industry reached its peak in the early 16C. In Oudenaarde during the 15C high-warp tapestry began to replace the declining cloth industry and by the end of the century as many as 14 000 were involved in tapestry making. The town became a major centre of tapestry-making in the 16C and 17C, specialising in *verdures*, in which flowers and plants constitute the main part of the composition.

★★★ STADHUIS (YZ) ⊙

Hendrik van Pede built the Town Hall from 1526 to 1530, taking his inspiration from several of the region's town houses. Indeed, there are strong similarities between this building and others (Brussels and Leuven). The Town Hall overlooks the vast market square, **Grote Markt** (Z), and is adjacent to the old 13C cloth market.

The Town Hall is Late Gothic in style, already exhibiting hints of Baroque. Its lightness of line and its rich yet exquisitely tasteful ornamentation contribute in large part to its charm. Arcades support a projecting belfry, with a statue of an armed man on top, "Hanske de Krijger" (John the Warrior). Lovely slender bell-cotes decorate the corners.

In front of the façade the fountain adorned with dolphins was financed by Louis XIV.

Once inside, note the beautiful fireplace and carved wood of the door drum panelling (16C) in the **Council Room** by Van der Schelden. The "listener" responsible for noting the assembly's debates used to sit in the little lodge over the door. Note also some picturesque paintings by **Adriaen Brouwer**.

OUDENAARDE

Beverestraat .... Y 4
Broodstraat .... Z 9
Grote Markt .... Z
Hoogstraat .... YZ 17
Krekelput .... Z 23
Nederstraat .... YZ 35
Stationsstraat .... Y
Tussenbruggen .... Z 40

Aalststraat .... Z
Achterburg .... Z 2
Achter de Wacht .... Y 3
Baarstraat .... Z
Bekstraat .... Y
Bergstraat .... Z
Bourgondiëstraat .... Z 7
Burg .... Z 10
Burgschelde .... Z 14
Dijkstraat .... Y
Doornikstraat .... Z
Fortstraat .... Y
Gevaertsdreef .... Y
Jezuïetenplein .... Z 18
Kasteelstraat .... Z 21
Kattestraat .... Y
Louise-Mariekaai .... Z 26
Margaretha van Parmastr. . Z 32
Marlboroughlaan .... YZ
Matthijs Casteleinstr. ...... Z
Minderbroedersstr. .... Z 33
Parkstraat .... Y
Prins Leopoldstraat .... Y
Remparden .... Z
Tacambaroplein .... Y 38
Tussenmuren..................... Z
Voorburg .... Z 42
Wijngaardstraat .... Y 46
Woeker .... Y

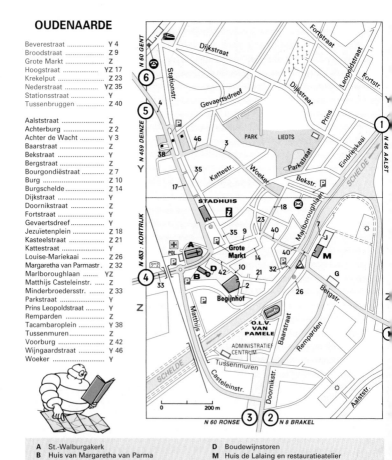

A   St.-Walburgakerk
B   Huis van Margaretha van Parma
D   Boudewijnstoren
M   Huis de Lalaing en restauratieatelier

ADDITIONAL SIGHTS

St.-Walburgakerk (Z A) – The east end of this large church stands west of the market square, Grote Markt. Its beautiful tower is 90m – 295ft high.

Huis van Margaretha van Parma (Z B) – Margaret of Parma's house is on the southwest side of Grote Markt. It features tall crowstepped dormers. To the left is the 11C tower, **Boudewijnstoren (Z D)**.

Begijnhof (Z) – The Beguine convent dates from the 13C. The simplicity of the chapel is very appealing.

★**O.L.-Vrouwekerk van Pamele (Z)** ⊙ – This beautiful 13C church was built by Arnould de Binche. It is typical of Scaldian Gothic architecture *(qv)*. Inside, there are three aisles and a transept with an ambulatory, which is fairly rare in Belgium. Two tombs, one from the early 16C and the other from the early 17C can be seen at the rear of the west front.

Huis de Lalaing en restauratieatelier (Z M) ⊙ – The Lalaing House has white walls decorated in Rococo style overlooking the Scheldt. It contains a workshop where old tapestries are restored and modern creations are woven.

EXCURSION

From Oudenaarde to Waregem – *15km – 9.3 miles northwest. Take the N 459 towards Deinze.*
In **Kruishoutem** the **Fondation Veranneman** (Stichting) ⊙ *(2 Vandevoordeweg, on the Waregem road then to the left)* is both an art gallery housing contemporary paintings by Mathieu, Permeke, Vasarely, Hartung, Wunderlich, Mara, Raveel, Botero, Arman, Bram Bogart and Vic Gentils, and a temporary exhibition centre. There are sculptures in the park by Dodeigne, Niki de St-Phalle, Vasarely, Gilioli, Schöffer, Antes, Rickey, Caro, Nigel Hall, Liberman, Niizuma and Vari.
The 17C **Château de Kruishoutem** ⊙ is surrounded by a moat. It has corners reinforced with four onion-domed towers. It stands in the middle of a large park.

Waregem – Flander's popular steeplechase which takes place on the Gaverbeek race course is a great crowd-puller *(see the Calendar of Events)*.

Vallée de l'OURTHE★

Liège-Luxembourg
Michelin maps 409 J4, J5, zae fold 22 or 213 fold 7

The Ourthe winds its way across the various northeast-southwest folds in the Ardennes plateau, cutting a deep course into it, before widening out in the plains, such as the Famenne, then flowing into the Meuse at Liège.
A long-distance waymarked footpath (GR 57) 170km – 106 miles long crosses the valley, running from Angleur near Liège to Houffalize in the province of Luxembourg.
The Ourthe Valley can be divided into two parts: the **Upper Ourthe★★** before La Roche-en-Ardenne *(qv)* and the **Lower Ourthe★** between La Roche-en-Ardenne and Liège.

★THE LOWER OURTHE

From La Roche-en-Ardenne to Liège
95km – 59 miles allow 1 day

★**La Roche-en-Ardenne** – *See La ROCHE-EN-ARDENNE. Time: 1 hour.*
Between La Roche-en-Ardenne and Liège the Ourthe flows through a delightful, tranquil valley, here and there bordered with rough escarpments, elsewhere with the limestone hollowed out into caves (Hotton, Comblain).
The road follows the Ourthe to Melreux. After Hampteau, a path to the left leads to the Hotton caves.

★★**Grottes de Hotton** ⊙ – Part of these caves, which were formed by a river gradually cutting a course underground, was discovered between 1958 and 1964. Only the Cave of the Thousand and One Nights (grotte des Mille et Une Nuits) at the end of the explored network is open to the public.
There is a great variety of concretions in the series of narrow chambers (temperature 12-16°C – 54-61°F). The delicacy of their shapes from transparent macaroni-shapes, to eccentrics, and undulating draperies is remarkable, but it is the splendour of their natural colours which is particularly striking. The calcite is pure white, dappled with red, brilliant orange, and delicate rose-pink from traces of iron. In the Friendship Gallery (Galerie de l'Amitié) this fairytale effect is accentuated by the clear reflections in the rock pools. The tour of the caves takes in a balcony 28m – 92ft over a chasm, in which the roar of a distant waterfall (at the far end of the Spéléo-Club passageway) can be heard.

Vallée de l'OURTHE

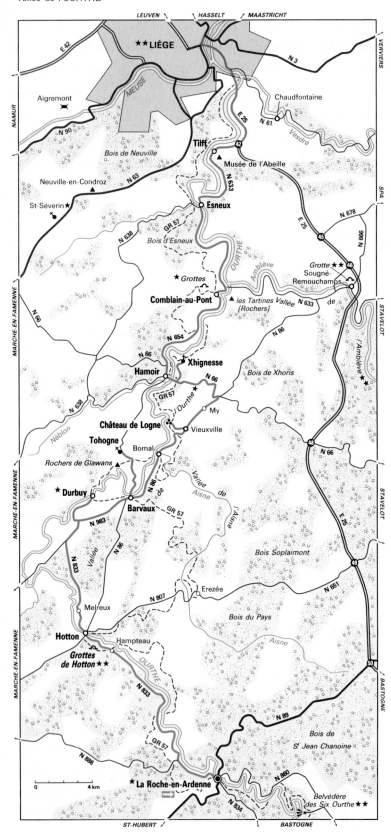

212

Hotton – The slate-roofed houses of this typical little town in the Famenne plain *(qv)* are strung out along the Ourthe, which has an island midstream at this point. There is an 18C watermill upstream on the Érezée road. Downstream from the bridge is a dam.

★**Durbuy** – The road rejoins the Ourthe again near Durbuy. The town is in a beautiful forested region and is one of the Ardennes' most pleasant holiday venues. This tiny settlement, promoted to the rank of town in 1331, was the world's smallest town with fewer than 400 inhabitants until it was merged with other communities in 1977. Durbuy has preserved its old character with its maze of medieval streets, the 17C castle, the old bridge and the half-timbered corn market. The charm of its streets and stone houses, where many craftsmen and artists live, combines well with the natural beauty of the site, at the foot of a spur of rock from which a spectacular geological fold, the Falize, can be seen.

Barvaux – This is another tourist centre in the Ourthe Valley. The river flows past the foot of the famous **Rochers de Glawans** downstream from here.

2km – 1.25 miles after Barvaux, take a road on the left for Tohogne.

Tohogne – This village has a well-restored **Romanesque church** in which there are works of art, including a 13C Mosan font and a 14C calvary.

Return to the N 86.

Beyond Bomal, where the River Aisne *(qv)* flows into the Ourthe, there is a pretty **view**★ of the valley, which is narrower here because of a rocky outcrop, beyond which the ruins of Château de Logne can be seen.

Château de Logne ⊘ – This was initially the property of the monks of Stavelot, then of the powerful La Marck family. This "eagle's nest" was one of the first fortresses adapted for firearms. It was destroyed in 1521 on the orders of Emperor Charles V. The objects found during digs inside the walls are exhibited at the **ferme de la Bouverie** ⊘ in Vieuxville. The village of Logne is a major tourist centre for sports enthusiasts.

Turn left after My.

Hamoir – This is a small community on the banks of the Ourthe. A statue of Jean Delcour *(qv)* stands in the central square; he was born here in 1627. The Town Hall is a charming 17C manor-house, hidden in a pretty park on the left bank.

Xhignesse – *Round tour of 4km – 2.5 miles from Hamoir.* The Mosan Romanesque church of St Peter has a remarkable apse decorated with blind arcading surmounted with niches.

Comblain-au-Pont – This small town lies at the confluence of the Ourthe and the Amblève, overlooked by an impressive cliff called the Tartines ("Sandwiches") because the rocks look as if they have been cut into slices *(qv)*.
Les **grottes de Comblain**★ ⊘ are caves 1km – 0.75 mile to the west on a little hill.

Esneux – This little town is built in tiers up a slope tucked in a coil of the Ourthe River.

Tilff – The **Musée de l'Abeille** ⊘ is a beekeeping museum housed in one of the castle farms. The museum contains interesting documents about beekeeping, collections of equipment, and hives (in some of them, the bees can be seen at work) as well as literature on the biology of bees.

★★**Liège** – *See LIEGE.*

Information in this guide is based on data provided at the time of going to press. Improved facilities and changes in the cost of living make subsequent alterations inevitable

De PANNE

West-Vlaanderen – Population 9 366
Michelin maps 409 A2 or 213 fold 1
Town plan in the current Michelin Red Guide Benelux

De Panne is a seaside resort on the border with France and is very popular with French tourists.
Its **beach**★ reaches 250m – 820ft in width in certain places at low tide and has no groynes. This makes it particularly suitable for sand-yachting *Illustration p 287*.
Near the beach is the **monument to King Leopold I**, marking the spot where Belgium's first sovereign landed in 1831, after travelling from England via Calais.
Queen Elizabeth stayed here during the First World War, while King Albert was at his HQ in Veurne.

EXCURSIONS

Westhoek – Part of the dunes lying around De Panne to the west form the Westhoek, a State nature reserve covering an area of 340 hectares – 840 acres up to the border. **Guided walks** ⊘ are organised.
Five signposted nature trails ranging in length from 1.6km – 1 mile to 2.4km – 1.5 miles cross the Westhoek.
Although sea reeds or shrubs (climbing willow, sea-buckthorn, common elder) cover most of the dunes, there is a bare open space in the middle, sometimes called the Sahara.

Oosthoek – This municipal nature reserve covers a 61 hectare – 150 acre area of dunes and woods southeast of De Panne.

Adinkerke – *3km – 1.75 miles south.*
Adinkerke is near the **Meli** ⊘, a 30 hectare – 74 acre recreation park. Its main theme is the bee (exhibition on bees, animals, attractions, fairytale village).

PHILIPPEVILLE
Namur – Population 7 206
Michelin maps 409 G5 or 214 fold 4

Founded in 1555 by Emperor Charles V to oppose Mariembourg, which had fallen to the French *(see Couvin)*, this citadel was called Philippeville in honour of the emperor's son, the future Philip II. In 1659 it fell into French hands. During the Revolution it was called the "Republican star".
Only a few underground passages and an old powder magazine survived the dismantling of the fortifications in 1860. An audio-visual presentation at the tourist office tells the story of Philippeville and its fortifications.

Underground passages ⊘ – The old powder magazine, now the **Chapelle Notre-Dame des Remparts**, still has its thick walls which used to house a ventilation system. Some of the 16C and 17C underground galleries extending for 10km – 6.5 miles under the town are open to visitors.

POPERINGE
West-Vlaanderen – Population 18 926
Michelin maps 409 B3 or 213 fold 13

Poperinge is an old clothmaking town, which became the centre of a hops-producing region *(see Introduction: Food and Drink Beer)* from the 15C onwards. It is proud of its three beautiful Gothic churches.
Every three years in September the **Hops Festival** *(see the Calendar of Events)* takes place with a picturesque procession. The hops fields stand out from the rest of the gently undulating landscape, because of the rows of tall stakes to support the plants.

SIGHTS

Hoofdkerk St.-Bertinus – *Vroonhof.* This 15C hall-church has a particularly beautiful 17C rood-screen, embellished with statues of Jesus and the Apostles. Note also the 18C pulpit and the richly decorated Baroque confessional.

Nationaal Hopmuseum ⊘ – *Gasthuisstraat 71.* The national hops museum is housed in an old public weighing station (stadsschaal) where, until 1968, the hops were weighed, selected, dried and pressed. Tools, machines, photographs and audio-visual presentations illustrate the cultivation and processing of hops.

O.-L.-Vrouwekerk – *Casselstraat.* This 14C hall-church, flanked by a tall tower with a stone spire, contains a wonderfully sculpted wooden communion bench.

St.-Janskerk – *St.-Janskruisstraat.* This church, dedicated to St John, has a massive tower similar to the bell tower of St Bertin's. Inside, there is beautiful 18C woodwork and a much venerated statue of the Virgin Mary which is carried in an annual procession on the first Sunday of July.

Weeuwhof – *St.-Annastraat, via Gasthuisstraat.* A little porch surmounted by a statue of the Virgin Mary leads into this 18C hospice, or "widows' courtyard", with picturesque cottages standing neatly around a flower garden.

EXCURSIONS

Lyssenthoek Military Cemetery – *3km – 1.75 miles south.*
More than 10 000 soldiers who died in the First World War, including many British men, lie in this impressive, flower-bedecked cemetery.

Haringe – *11km – 6.75 miles northwest.*
The inside of **St.-Martinuskerk** has a certain rustic charm. The organ was made by the Ghent craftsman Van Peteghem in 1778.

REDU-TRANSINNE

Luxembourg

Michelin maps 409 I5 or 214 fold 16

Lying in a magnificent undulating region of wooded countryside, the village of Redu is home to a European space station for telemetry and remote satellite control.

A book-worm's village – Redu is a paradise for lovers of old books. About thirty second-hand booksellers have opened shops here. The village comes alive with crowds of people during those ideal periods for reading books in the summer and at the weekends. A few antique dealers and restaurants have opened here as well.

⭐**Euro Space Center** ⊙ – *Situated near the E 411 motorway at exit 24.*
The latest audio-visual techniques have been used to present the great adventure of space: films of space missions in the auditorium, an explanation of the future Columbus space laboratory in the holorama, a description of the history of astronomy and black holes in the planetarium, tours of several spaceships and rockets including full-scale models of Ariane 4 and 5, and to finish, the thrills of the Space Show where mobile seats give the audience the impression of being right in the centre of a terrifying spaceship battle.
This is also a training centre for young people wishing to learn about space (courses lasting several days).

REULAND

Liège

Michelin maps 409 L5 or 214 fold 9 – 15km – 9.3 miles south of St-Vith

This is a picturesque village in the south of the Liège province in the Ulf Valley. It is overlooked by the ruins of its 11C fortress. From the keep there is a delightful **view**⭐ of the white houses with their heavy slate roofs, clustered around the onion-domed bell tower. Reuland is in the Hautes Fagnes-Eifel nature park *(qv)*.

La ROCHE-EN-ARDENNE ⭐

Luxembourg – Population 3 879

Michelin maps 409 J5 or 214 fold 7 – Local maps see Vallée de l'OURTHE and overleaf

Town plan in the current Michelin Red Guide Benelux

Long wooded spurs separated by deep valleys converge on this well-known tourist centre, famed for the beauty of its **setting**⭐⭐, in a loop of the Ourthe River. The river forms a wide stretch of water here *(canoeing and pedaloes)*. Numerous signposted footpaths (120km – 74.5 miles) have been set up in the area around La Roche.
The town was destroyed in 1944 and rebuilt after the war.
"Baisers de la Roche", or "Roche kisses", are cream-filled meringues, a speciality rivalled only by the delicious fruit or sugar tarts. The local blue sandstone ware is also famous.

J. Vernin/TRAVEL PICTURES, Bruxelles

La Roche-en-Ardenne

SIGHTS

Château ⊘ – *Access via a flight of stairs opposite the Town Hall.* The romantic-looking ruins of this impressive 11C castle stand right at the tip of the rocky **Deister** spur, bristling with ancient fir trees, overlooking the town.

The fortifications were strengthened after Louis XIV's siege in 1680. The castle was then demolished in the 18C on the orders of Joseph II.

Poterie de grès bleu ⊘ – *Rue Rompré, via Place du Bronze.* Blue sandstone ware, a speciality of La Roche, is made here. The engraved design is highlighted in blue.

The tour includes a visit to the old wood-burning kiln, the turning and decorating workshops as well as the factory museum.

Chapelle Ste-Marguerite – *Follow the Ourthe River towards Houffalize and take the road that climbs up to the left.*

The chapel is on the hill known as Deister, above the castle.

A viewpoint higher up can be reached by a little path that runs along the crest of the spur. There is a superb **panoramic view★★** of the town.

Parc "Nature et Santé" de Deister – *Follow the road beyond the Chapelle de Ste-Marguerite up to the top of the hill.*

The 15 hectare – 37 acre **Forest Park** is ideal for long walks. It lies on the Deister Plateau.

EXCURSIONS

★★**Upper Ourthe Valley** – *Round tour of 36km – 22 miles allow 4 hours local map above.*

The eastern Ourthe, which rises near the village of Ourthe on the border with Luxembourg, and the western Ourthe, which rises at Ourt, a village south of St-Hubert, converge to form the River Ourthe near Nisramont. Upstream from La Roche-en-Ardenne, the river is more like a torrent, gushing through wild and beautiful countryside.

Leave La Roche-en-Ardenne and head southeast towards Bastogne.

The road climbs the slopes up to the plateau, from which there is an open view of the rolling countryside.

Turn left towards Nisramont. Cross the bridge over the Ourthe and turn left towards Nadrin.

A **marble sculpture** to the left of the road represents a stylised portico in the form of a menhir. This is the work of Portuguese sculptor Joao Charters de Almeida, created in 1991 on the occasion of Europalia Portugal.

★★**Belvédère des Six Ourthe** – A **tower** ⊘ was built at the foot of the Hérou, a spur of schist 1 400m – 4 593ft in length. From the top of the tower *(120 steps),* there is a grandiose panoramic view of the wild beauty of this countryside so typical of the

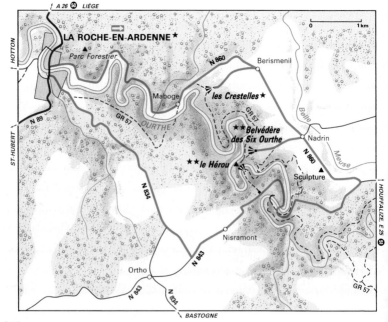

Ardennes. The winding River Ourthe has cut a serpentine valley around wooded spurs, often disappearing behind hillocks and then reappearing to sparkle again in the sun. The viewpoint is named after these "various" Ourthes.

★★**Le Hérou** – This awesome outcrop, hidden beneath luxuriant vegetation, is criss-crossed by pleasant signposted footpaths, including the GR 57. The rocky ground suddenly appears as the cliff drops sharply down to the river to the east *(allow 30min Rtn to be within sight of the cliff)*. At the foot of Le Hérou the river runs through a wild landscape. This spot is popular with rock-climbing schools.

Return to Nadrin, then turn left towards Berismenil. At the second left in Berismenil, head towards Crestelles.

★**Point de vue des Crestelles** – This is a remarkable viewpoint over a meander in the River Ourthe 200m – 656ft below. It is a departure point for hang-gliding and paragliding.

Return to the N 860. Go through Maboge (pretty view from the bridge), then return to La Roche-en-Ardenne.

★**Lower Ourthe** – *See Vallée de l'OURTHE.*

Houffalize – *25km – 15.5 miles east on the N 860.* This busy holiday location lies at the heart of the Ardennes, at an altitude of 370m – 1 214ft. Its **setting**★ in the green valley of the east River Ourthe is most attractive. The town was destroyed during the Battle of the Bulge *(qv)* in 1944, and has since been rebuilt. The roads arriving from the south and the west afford pretty views over the slate roofs.

The main car parks are shown on the town plans in this guide

ROCHEFORT ★

Namur – Population 11 208
Michelin maps 409 I5 or 214 fold 6

This little town on the edge of the Lesse and Lomme national park *(qv)* is a good base for holidays and excursions into the surrounding region.
The famous Trappist beer of Rochefort is made by the monks at the Abbey of St Rémy 2km – 1.25 miles from here. The famous marble quarries of St Rémy were also worked nearby (15C).
In August 1792 La Fayette, his life in danger for having defended Louis XVI, left the army and fled. With Chateaubriand he was given shelter at 8 Rue Jacquet before being arrested by the Austrians. Nearby is a monument in La Fayette's honour.

★**Grotte** ⊘ – This cave was originally gouged out by the Lomme and has a more rugged appearance than the one in Han. Its temperature (8°C – 46°F) is also lower. The first concretions come into view at the end of the man-made passage of non-porous marble. To the sound of background music, lights pick out the strange chaotic formations previously concealed in the shadows. The current course of the underground river and its successive riverbeds can be seen below. The little Hall of Arcades is hollowed out 80m – 262ft beneath the Château de Beauregard.
The **Hall of the Sabbath** is the most impressive one in terms of size: 65m – 213ft by 125m – 410f. A glowing air balloon allowed to float up to the roof gives an idea of the height (85m – 278ft). The tour returns via a man-made gallery opening onto a pretty view of the Lomme Valley.

EXCURSIONS

Grupont – *10km – 6.25 miles southeast.*
Grupont has a picturesque **Maison espagnole**, also called the Burgomaster's House. It is half-timbered and corbelled, and it dates from 1590.

Chevetogne – *15km – 9.3 miles northwest.*
Monastère de Chevetogne – An oecumenical community, celebrating the liturgy with Latin and Byzantine rites, settled here in 1939 in a 19C château. The **Eastern Orthodox Church** (1957) was built in the Novgorod Byzantine style. It is a square brick building, with a vast narthex surmounted by a little cupola on a drum base. The walls and vaulting inside are covered with frescoes. In the narthex are scenes from the Old Testament; in the nave, scenes from the life of Christ. An effigy of Christ Pantocrator dominates the cupola. The iconostasis, which isolates the sanctuary, is decorated with icons. The main ones, representing Christ and a Virgin and Child, are on either side of the Royal Doors. The shop can be accessed from the church. There are beautiful copies of old orthodox religious objets d'art on display.

★**Domaine provincial Valéry Cousin** ⊘ – This vast recreation park in a wooded setting with flowers surrounds a château and a string of lakes. It is very well-equipped for sports and other leisure activities and walks *(signposted paths)*.

Lessive – *6km – 3.75 miles southwest, via Eprave.*
The **Station terrienne belge de télécommunications spatiales** ⊙ is the Belgian telecom earth station set in the midst of woods south of the little village of Lessive. Equipped with three antennae and an impressively large radio relay tower, this has formed the link since 1972 between satellites and the national telecommunications network.

The guided tour of the station ends with an exhibition on current and future communications technology, a museum on past telephone and telegraph communications, and a film of a satellite launch.

From Rochefort to Marche-en-Famenne – *12km – 7.5 northeast on the N 86.*

Hargimont – The **Château de Jemeppe** was built in the 17C around a massive 13C keep.

Waha – This village has a charming sandstone **Romanesque church** dedicated to St Stephen. It was consecrated in the year 1050. There is a graceful 16C bell tower on top of the 12C tower. The square shapes are superposed in an imaginative way. The plain interior, with its massive pillars, houses some interesting works of art. Several gravestones can be seen in the porch. There is a beautiful Late Gothic (16C) calvary over the triumphal arch. The font in the south aisle (1590) is decorated with four carved heads. The consecration stone dating from 1050 can be seen mounted on one of the pillars near the entrance to the chancel. Reliquaries, old books and missals, chasubles, etc. are exhibited in a display case. The church also has some beautiful statues of popular art: St Nicholas (15C), St Barbara (16C), and St Roch, in polychrome wood (17C).

Marche-en-Famenne – This is the capital of the Famenne. In 1577 Don Juan of Austria, governor of the Low Countries, signed the Perpetual Edict here which confirmed the Pacification of Ghent *(qv)*, freeing the country of Spanish troops.

Château de Jannée ⊙ – *19km – 12 miles north on the N 949, N 929 and N 4.*
The Château de Jannée, surrounded by its park, dates back to the 12C. Reconstructions in the 17C and 19C have given it its current appearance. The 18 rooms open to the public serve as reminders of life in the past. There are old utensils and copper pans in the kitchen. The drawing rooms on the ground floor and the bedrooms are tastefully decorated. The furniture includes Louis XV wardrobes and a Mosan Louis XV desk. Note also the porcelain and the portraits of the owner's family.

RONSE

Oost-Vlaanderen – Population 22 672
Michelin maps 409 D3 or 213 fold 16

Ronse is set amidst the hills of the **Flemish Ardennes**, near the borders with French-speaking Wallonia.
The **Zotte Maandag** (Crazy Monday) festivities take place on the Saturday after Epiphany. The stars of this great popular festival are the masked characters called the "Bommels". The **Fiertel** takes place on Trinity Sunday, with a procession in honour of St Hermes. The reliquary is carried along a route 32.6km – 20.25 miles long.

St.-Hermes Collegiaal – The present church dates from the 15C and 16C. The south transept is devoted to the cult of St Hermes.
The church above a beautiful Romanesque **crypt★** ⊙ (1089) which is particularly vast, containing 32 pillars. Despite restoration in the 13C and a Gothic style extension (16C) to the east end, the church has an overall harmony. Two side doors, which have been walled up, recall the original purpose of the building. In the Middle Ages pilgrims came to process around the relics of St Hermes on display here. In Ronse, people prayed to the saint to ask him to cure mental illness.
The beautiful house (17C-18C) next to the church belonged to the canon of the St Hermes chapter (Museum of Folklore).

EXCURSION

From Ronse to Kluisberg – *15km – 9.3 miles west.*
There is a pretty view of the town from the gardens north of Ronse (Park de l'Arbre).
Take the N 60 towards Oudenaarde, then turn left towards Kluisberg at the top of the hill.
The mill, **Hotondmolen** ⊙, stands to the right of the road near an inn, at an altitude of 150m – 492ft. From the top of this squat building there is a vast panoramic view of the region and the Kluisberg *(viewing table)*.

Kluisberg – This hill, known as **Mont de l'Enclus** to French-speakers, has an altitude of 141m – 463ft. It lies exactly on the border between the French and Flemish-speaking regions and on the border between Oost-Vlaanderen and Hainaut. It is covered with pine woods and is much appreciated as a holiday venue.

ST-HUBERT ★

Luxembourg – Population 5 690
Michelin maps 409 J5 or 214 fold 16

The houses of St-Hubert nestle around the basilica, on a plateau in the heart of the Ardennes Forest, at an altitude of 435m – 1 427ft. The basilica was the site of major pilgrimages to St Hubert, patron saint of hunters and butchers. There is a beautiful **view** of the chevet of the basilica when approaching from the east.
St-Hubert was the birthplace of painter **Pierre Joseph Redouté** (1759-1840), the "Raphael of Roses". A museum is devoted to him at Le Fourneau-St-Michel *(qv)*.
Each summer the **Juillet Musical** organises concerts in the town and the surrounding area, as part of the Wallonia Festival.

The hunters' town – Each year during the first weekend in September, the **International Days of Hunting and Nature** take place. Hunting horns ring out from Saturday afternoon onwards. On Sunday, after a Solemn Mass and the blessing of the animals, a great historical procession takes place in the afternoon, recounting the story of St Hubert and the history of the abbey. More than 500 people in costume participate. On **3 November,** St Hubert's Day, the Solemn Eucharist is followed by the blessing of animals and various festivities.

The saint and his legend

One Good Friday in 683 AD, **Hubert,** son-in-law of the Count of Leuven, was hunting in the forest. The dogs raised a huge stag with ten points on its antlers. The animal was on the point of being captured when it turned and a blinding image of Christ on the Cross appeared between its antlers. A voice then reproached St Hubert for his immoderate love of hunting, and told him to seek out his friend Lambert, Bishop of Tongres-Maastricht, to be instructed in prayer and ministry.
In Rome Hubert learned of Lambert's martyrdom and was offered the vacant bishopric by the Pope. Hubert refused it, protesting his unworthiness. An angel then descended from the heavens to give him the white stole that was the symbol of the bishop's office, woven with gold by the Virgin Mary herself.
Once he had become Bishop of Maastricht, Hubert transferred the episcopal see to Liège *(qv)*.

★BASILIQUE ST-HUBERT ⊘ *time : 30min*

This old Benedictine abbey church was founded in the 7C. The relics of St Hubert were transferred here in the 9C, and have drawn crowds of pilgrims ever since. Several buildings have succeeded each other on this spot, and only the crypt remains of the original Romanesque church. The present Brabant Gothic church was rebuilt in 1526 after a fire (go round the south side of the church to see the Flamboyant Gothic section), but the façade was modified in the 18C. This explains why the two towers and the west front, on which the pediment depicts the miracle of St Hubert, are Baroque.

★★**Interior** – The interior is impressive, being 25m – 82ft high with five aisles. It has the layout of a pilgrims' church, with an ambulatory and radiating chapels. The first feature that strikes visitors is the colour in the brickwork, a combination of pink, grey and ochre stone beneath brick vaulting dating from 1683.
Willem Geefs' St Hubert mausoleum (1847) in the north transept depicts a slightly haughty, majestic figure. There are beautiful, delicately worked **stalls** (1733) in the chancel. Their panels depict the lives of St Hubert *(right)* and St Benedict *(left)*. The statue of the Virgin Mary on the high altar is from the school of Liège sculptor Delcour.
The Holy Stole woven with gold, dating from the 10C, is in the south transept on the St Hubert altar. An altarpiece with 24 Limoges enamels painted after Dürer's *Passion* is in the first chapel in the ambulatory. It was badly damaged by the Huguenots.
The Romanesque **crypt** under the chancel contains abbots' tombs. Their faces have been worn smooth by pilgrims' hands. The vaulting dates from the 16C.
Admire the Baroque organ before going out.

Abbey Palace – *On the left side of the square as you face the basilica.*
Built in 1728, this palace with an elegant façade and a pediment decorated with foliage now houses the province's Cultural Affairs offices. Exhibitions are organised here. There is some very beautiful wood panelling inside.

EXCURSIONS

★★Fourneau-St-Michel – *See FOURNEAU-ST-MICHEL.*

Parc à gibier ⊙ – *2km – 1.25 miles north.* Deer, boar, moufflons (wild sheep), wild boars etc. can be observed along three signposted routes in this game park. The road goes through beautiful forests of beech and conifers named after King Albert and St Michael.

Val de Poix – *9km – 5.5 miles to Smuid.* This peaceful rustic valley is crossed by a little river which is a tributary of the Lomme. There is a half-timbered house near a lake, to the left of the road, 3km – 1.75 miles from St-Hubert.

Vallée de la SEMOIS★★

Luxembourg-Namur
Michelin maps 409 J6, I6, H6 or 214 folds 15, 16

The River Semois (or Semoy in France) is a tributary of the Meuse; it rises near Arlon. It runs initially through a marshy depression called the "Belgian Lorraine", then meanders through the schist outcrops of the Ardennes range beyond Florenville.

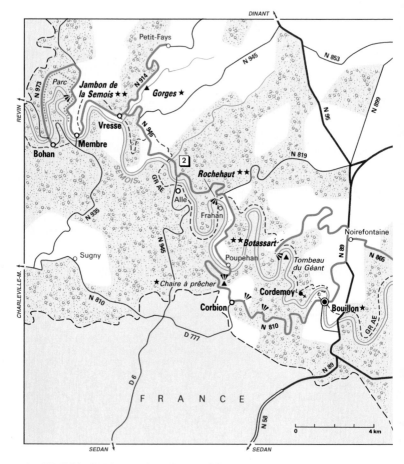

★⑪FROM CHINY TO BOUILLON

65km – 40 miles about half a day local map below

Chiny – The Semois, in cutting a course around Chiny, winds for a time through the Ardennes forests. Its valley becomes deeper and narrower, and the wild scenery can only be seen from a boat.

★Boat trip from Chiny to Lacuisine ⊙ – *8km – 5 miles. Landing-stage west of village, downstream from pont St-Nicolas (bridge).* The boat trip *(1 hour 15min)* follows the gorge known as Paradise, past the Côte de l'Ecureuil ("Squirrel Hill") and Rocher du Pinco ("Pinco Rock") to the right and the Rocher du Hât to the left. The return trip can be made on foot *(45min)* through the woods, following the signposted paths (route no 8).

Lacuisine – The turbulent waters calm down here. The river flows quietly through meadows past an old watermill.

★**Viewpoint over the Semois Gorge** – *2km – 1.25 miles north. Take the Neufchâteau road. Then 800m – half a mile north of the fork for Martué, pass a narrow road on the left and take the path on the right.*
Follow the white and orange signposts in the woods *(15min walk)* to reach a promontory with a bench. There is a **view** down onto the wild wooded river banks, often covered with white flowers.

Florenville – This holiday resort near the border is ideal as a touring centre. It is perched on a sandstone rise overlooking the Semois Valley.
From the terrace behind the east end of the church *(viewing table)* the valley can be seen cutting a great curve through the great sweep of arable countryside.
The church was destroyed in 1940 and has been rebuilt. The tower has a 48-chime carillon dating from 1955. From the **viewpoint** ⊙ at the top of the tower, there is a **view** of the slate roofs, the wide Semois Valley and the surrounding countryside *(220 steps)*.

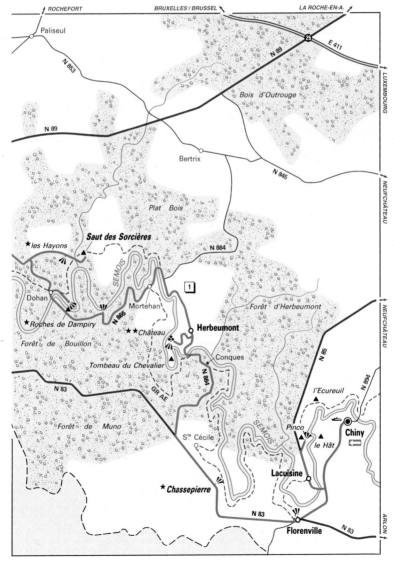

J. Évrard, Bruxelles

Tombeau du Chevalier, Herbeumont

★Chassepierre Viewpoint – This viewpoint (metal globe symbolising peace) is 5km – 3 miles from Florenville. It provides a beautiful view of the slate roofs in the village and the houses crowding on an outcrop of rock near an onion-domed church (1702). The River Semois meanders through the plain not far away.

Beyond Ste-Cécile, turn right towards Herbeumont.

Before crossing the river, notice the old priory of Conques (18C) on the right of the road. beyond Florenville In the Middle Ages this priory was a daughterhouse of Orval Abbey. It is now a hotel.

Herbeumont – The ruins of the 12C castle stand on the top of a hill. It was destroyed by Louis XIV's troops.

From the top, there is a magnificent **view★★** of the river's double meander encircling the **Tombeau du Chevalier,** a long wooded spur shaped like a medieval tomb, hence its name (literally "Knight's Tomb"). The Semois loops round the rock through magnificent landscape *(illustration above).*

Follow the river in Mortehan. Then, as the road climbs the hill, note the pretty views of the wild undulating countryside before the bend on the right. 2km – 1.25 miles on from a viewpoint near the **roches de Dampiry** (rocks), there is another **view★** of a beautiful loop in the Semois River.

2km – 1.25 miles beyond Dohan, take the road on the right to Les Hayons.

Just after Les Hayons, there is a pretty **glimpse★** of the River Semois and the valley in a great sweep of wooded countryside.

Saut des Sorcières – "Witches' Leap" is in fact a series of little waterfalls between lakes.

Return to the N 865. The road runs through Noirefontaine to Botassart.

Botassart – There is a remarkable **view★★** 2km – 1.25 miles beyond the hamlet, from the viewpoint with a telescope. This is one of the most typical and well-known views of the Semois. The river forms a magnificent meander around a long wooded hill called **Tombeau du Géant** ("Giant's Tomb") because here again, like the Knight's Tomb, the hillsides resemble the sides of a sarcophagus.

Turn back to take the road down to Bouillon.

★Bouillon – *See BOUILLON. Time : 1 hour.*

★★② FROM BOUILLON TO BOHAN

53km – 33 miles – about half a day – local map on previous page

★Bouillon – *See BOUILLON. Time: 1 hour.*

Leave Bouillon on the Corbion road, beyond the tunnel.

There is a viewpoint 5km – 3 miles along the road with a view of Cordemoy Abbey *(see Bouillon : Abbaye de Cordemoy).* Then 3km – 1.75 miles further, enjoy the panoramic view of the wooded crests, notably the Giant's Tomb.

Corbion – Reached by a path, the aptly-named **Chaire à prêcher** (pulpit) is a natural viewpoint in the form of a church pulpit. The **view★** encompasses a broad panorama of Poupehan, a village overlooking the Semois.

Rochehaut – There is a pretty **view**★★ from this hilltop village. The river encircles a promontory surrounded by meadows. The houses of the village of Frahan are built in terraces up the hillside.

Alle, on the opposite bank, is situated at the neck of an old meander which has now been truncated by the course of the river.

Take the road on the right to Le Petit-Fays.

★**Gorges du Petit-Fays** – The road climbs up along the edge of this rugged gorge thickly covered in vegetation.

Vresse-sur-Semois – The road rejoins the Semois here, at its confluence with the Petit-Fays. Vresse was once an important centre of tobacco-growing. It is now popular with holiday-makers and artists. The **Musée du Tabac et du Folklore** ⊙, situated in the tourist and cultural centre describes the traditional cultivation and use of tobacco.

Typical wooden **tobacco-drying sheds** can be seen here and there on the way to Bohan.

Membre – The start of the **Parc de Bohan-Membre** lies near this village. It covers 177 hectares – 437 acres and is crossed by the Semois. A scenic road runs round it.

In Membre, turn right.

3km – 1.75 miles further on there is a beautiful **view**★★ from the spot called **Jambon de la Semois**, a narrow wooded ridge.

Bohan – This little tourist centre is near the border.

SINT-NIKLAAS

Oost-Vlaanderen – Population 65 096
Michelin maps 409 F2 or 213 folds 5, 6
Town plan in the current Michelin Red Guide Benelux

The capital of the **Waas** region is a commercial and industrial centre, specialising in textiles (hosiery). A large market has been held here on Thursdays since the 16C.

SIGHTS

Grote Markt – This is one of the largest market squares in Belgium, covering 3.19 hectares – 7.8 acres. Some Flemish Renaissance houses stand at the east end of the square. From left to right they are the **Parochiehuis** (1663), which used to be the parish house and was then the Town Hall, **Cipierage** (1662), once a prison, and next to the post office, the **Landhuis** (1637), once used by the Waas regional government.

St.-Niklaaskerk ⊙ (13C-18C) is set back from the square. The church contains statues by Lucas Faydherbe and a Crucifix attributed to Duquesnoy.

The present Town Hall is neo-Gothic in style (1876).

Avenue Parklaan leads to the beautiful **municipal park,** in which the lake surrounds an extensively restored 16C castle.

Stedelijk Museum – The municipal museum is housed in several different buildings, each with its own collections.

Historisch Museum van het Land van Waas ⊙ – *Zamanstraat 49.* The regional history, folklore and crafts sections are in an old town house.

A modern building was added for the other sections. A large room is devoted to the geographer **Mercator** who was born in Rupelmonde *(12km – 7.5 miles southeast of St.-Niklaas)* in 1512. He was the inventor of a new technique of cartographic representation, called "Mercator's projection", in which the surface of the earth is projected onto a cylinder, thereby rendering the meridians completely parallel. The two globes, terrestrial and celestial, that he made for Emperor Charles V in 1541 and 1551, are on display as are the first edition of his Atlas (1585) and a second edition of the Atlas edited in Amsterdam by the Flemish geographer Hondius based on Mercator's maps. A second room deals with paleontology and archeology.

★**Afdeling Van Musiekdoos tot grammofoon** ⊙ – *Regentiestraat 61-63.* This section of the museum, entitled "From Music Box to Gramophone" houses a remarkable collection including a wide range of cylindrical phonographs, record players and mechanical music instruments. The guided tour explains the development of these instruments and gives visitors the chance to hear some of them.

Cultuurhistorische collecties ⊙ – *Regentiestraat 61-63.* The "**Barbierama**" includes four hair salons from the turn of the century (Art Nouveau and Classical styles) as well as many objects used in the past by barbers, surgeons and hairdressers.

Centre International de l'Ex-Libris ⊙ – *Regentiestraat 61.* Comparable to a library, this centre has a collection of nearly 120 000 ex-libris (16C-20C), drawn by 5 500 different artists of diverse origins.

Salons voor Schone Kunsten ⊙ – *Stationsstraat 73.* The drawing rooms of a private townhouse (1928), which once belonged to a textile manufacturer, contain paintings (Artans, Rops and Evenepoel), sculptures, furniture and objets d'art from the 16C to the 20C.

EXCURSION

Scheldt and Old Scheldt – *Round trip of 35km – 22 miles. Allow 2 hours (not including the tour of Kasteel van Bornem). Leave St.-Niklaas and head southeast on the N 16.*

Temse (Tamise) – This little town on the banks of the Scheldt specialises in ship-building. From the quay near the church the wide river can be seen, with a dike on the opposite bank.

A metal bridge, the longest in Belgium (365m – 0.25 mile long), spans the Scheldt.

Follow the N 16 and turn right after 5km – 3 miles towards Bornem. In the village follow the signs to Kasteel van Bornem.

Kasteel van Bornem ⊙ – This impressive neo-Gothic castle (1883-1895) was designed by architect H Beyaert, on the site of a fortress dating back to the 11C. The rooms open to the public contain family portraits, Chinese porcelain and antique furniture. The right wing is lived in by the Count of Bornem, John de Marnix de Sainte-Aldegonde. The most illustrious member of the Marnix family was **Philips Marnix van Sint-Aldegonde** (c1538-1598), a Calvinist writer and diplomat, and an ardent defender of William the Silent *(qv)*. He is said to be the author of the Dutch national anthem. A museum in the castle outbuildings houses a beautiful collection of European and American carriages.

Drive to St.-Amands via Zavelberg and Mariekerke.

St.-Amands – A terrace overlooks the Scheldt, which here forms a wide meander between lush green banks. The poet **Émile Verhaeren** (1855-1916) lies buried nearby, behind the church, next to his wife Marthe in a black marble tomb. The church tower "is mirrored in the churlish waters".

It was in Rouen, France, where he had just given a lecture, that Verhaeren died, crushed by a train. He was born in St.-Amands, and was the author of *All Flanders*. He always sang the praises of the Scheldt. A few verses, notably extracts from his *Hymn to the Scheldt*, are engraved on his tomb and a statue of the ferry-man who inspired his poem stands nearby. The old ferry-man's house (Het Veerhuis) has been reconstructed on the esplanade. The house where the writer was born is at 69, E Verhaerenstraat, the main street.

Take the road to Mariekerke again and follow the banks of the Scheldt towards Weert.

Before long the **road★** runs along the banks of the Old Scheldt (Oude Schelde), once an arm of the River Scheldt. The Kasteel van Bornem *(qv)* can be seen on the opposite bank. This is a picturesque marshy area, crisscrossed by canals surrounding orchards and fields covered with poplars, willows and reeds. Asparagus growing and basket-weaving are the main activities in these wetlands. **Weert** is the main town and it is very popular for Sunday outings.

The road ends at the N 16 leading back to St.-Niklaas.

SINT-TRUIDEN

Limburg – Population 36 724
Michelin maps 409 I3 or 213 fold 21

St.-Truiden, in the heart of the **Hesbaye** (Haspengouw) fruit-growing region well-known for its cherries, is a town that grew up around an abbey founded in the 7C by St Trudo. St.-Truiden is well-situated, on the main route from Cologne to Bruges, and was a prosperous merchant town in the 13C. Festivities take place in April when the fruit trees are in bloom.

SIGHTS

Grote-Markt (B) – This vast square is overlooked by the Town Hall and the Gothic collegiate church of Our Lady, surmounted by a 19C tower.

Oud Stadhuis (B H) – The former Town Hall is an impressive but gracious building, with a brick façade striped with bands of white stone. It is flanked by a 17C belfry containing a 41-chime carillon *(concerts)*. The steps at the foot of the belfry date from 1596.

The massive Romanesque bell tower of old St Trudo's Abbey is behind the Town Hall.

Abdij (A) – Benedictines occupied this former abbey until 1794. From 1839 to 1972 the buildings housed the seminary of the bishopric of Liège. The abbey is now essentially occupied by schools. An 18C porch (on the pediment: St Trudo healing a blind woman) leads into the main courtyard. On the left, a Louis XVI building houses the Imperial Hall (Keizerszaal), with ceiling frescoes dating from the 18C. The wall decoration and staircase are from later alterations.

Begijnhof (A) – The Beguine convent was founded in 1258. Its 16C, 17C and 18C Mosan houses stand round a rectangular square, in the middle of which is a church.

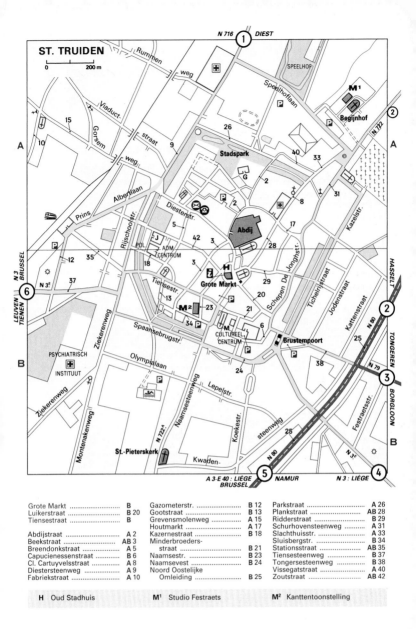

ST. TRUDEN

0 — 200 m

Grote Markt	B	Gazometerstr.	B 12	Parkstraat	A 26
Luikerstraat	B 20	Gootstraat	B 13	Plankstraat	AB 28
Tiensestraat	B	Grevensmolenweg	A 15	Ridderstraat	B 29
		Houtmarkt	A 17	Schurhovensteenweg	A 31
Abdijstraat	A 2	Kazernestraat	B 18	Slachthuisstr.	A 33
Beekstraat	AB 3	Minderbroeders-		Sluisbergstr.	B 34
Breendonkstraat	A 5	straat	B 21	Stationsstraat	AB 35
Capucienessenstraat	B 6	Naamsestr.	B 23	Tiensesteenweg	B 37
Cl. Cartuyvelsstraat	A 8	Naamsevest	B 24	Tongersesteenweg	B 38
Diestersteenweg	A 9	Noord Oostelijke		Vissegatstraat	A 40
Fabriekstraat	A 10	Omleiding	B 25	Zoutstraat	AB 42

H	Oud Stadhuis	M¹	Studio Festraets	M²	Kanttentoonstelling

Church – This has been turned into a museum of religious art. It dates from the 13C and 15C, and has 38 restored murals painted between the 13C and the 17C. Note the pulpit, the confessional, the sculptures and the liturgical ornaments.

Studio Festraets (A M¹) ⊘ – This contains most notably an **astronomical clock** built by one of the town's clock-makers. When the hour strikes, Death and a parade of medieval craftsmen appear.

Brustempoort (B) ⊘ – These are the underground remains of the 15C fortifications razed by Louis XIV's troops.

St.-Pieterskerk (B) – Like St Gingolph's Church, this church, dedicated to St Peter, is remarkable because of the contrasting colours in its walls (yellow ochre and brown).
This late 12C building is a fine example of the Mosan Romanesque style. It has a wide doorway with a bell turret and is closed off by three apses, the main one bearing a gallery with colonnettes. Inside, the three aisles have groined vaulting.

Kanttentoonstelling (B M²) ⊘ – The Lace Exhibition is housed in the Ursuline convent that was once the refuge for Averbode Abbey. The exhibition has examples of St.-Truiden bobbin lace made using the technique that was reintroduced in 1964 and developed with great originality.

Stadspark (A) – A pretty public park with a number of lakes.

SINT-TRUIDEN

EXCURSIONS

Borgloon and Klooster van Kolen – *12km – 7.5 miles east. Leave by ③ on the town plan.*

Borgloon – This was once the main town in the county of Loon after which it is named. It has a charming 17C Mosan Renaissance Town Hall with arcades, flanked by a tower. Note the statue of the Virgin Mary in a corner niche.

Take the Kerniel road northeast, and turn left before Kerniel.

Klooster van Kolen ⊙ – This former convent of the Croisiers order founded in Belgium in the 13C is now occupied by Cistercian nuns.

The vestry contains the **reliquary of St Odile** (1292). The painted wood panels, of the Mosan school, depict the legend of the saint, which is identical to that of St Ursula *(qv)*. The panels were unfortunately cut up in the 19C. The vestry's furnishings in the Louis XV style were made in Liège and are remarkably elegant. It is also possible to visit the church, which was decorated in the 18C.

Kortenbos – *6km – 3.75 miles northeast. Leave by ② on the town plan.*
The basilica church of Our Lady has a richly decorated Baroque interior. The nave has 17C oak panelling and confessionals decorated with heavy twisted columns.

Zepperen – *3km – 1.75 miles east by ② on the town plan.*

Sint-Genoveva, the church dedicated to St Genevieve, dates from the 15C and 16C and has a 12C tower at its entrance. Inside, in the south transept, there are several murals dating from 1509, representing the Last Judgement, St Christopher and the Life of St Genevieve.

Use the Index *to find more information about a subject mentioned in the guide – towns, places, isolated sights, historical events or geographical features etc.*

SOIGNIES ★

Hainaut – Population 22 087
Michelin maps 409 F4 or 213 fold 17

The town was built around an abbey founded in about 650 by St Vincent Madelgaire, husband of St Waudru of Mons. In honour of this saint, the Grand Tour takes place on Whit Monday *(see the Calendar of Events)*. It is a large procession covering a distance of 12km – 7.5 miles and ending in a historical parade depicting the life of the saint.

★★ COLLÉGIALE ST-VINCENT *time : 45min*

Building began in about 965 with the two opposite ends, narthex and chancel, in the Carolingian style. It was continued in the 11C in the Scaldian Romanesque style *(qv)*. The tower on the west front was completed in the 13C in the Gothic style. The collegiate church is a forbidding building of sandstone ashlar from nearby quarries, soberly decorated with pilaster-strips. Its layout in the shape of a Latin cross is arranged around the square transept crossing, which is decorated with pinnacles. Over the centuries, various sections have been added to the main building, including the 15C St Hubert's Chapel in the Gothic style and the remains of some early 13C cloisters, with visible timberwork. Both lie on the south side of the church.

Inside *(entrance via the north aisle)*, the nave (20m – 66ft high) is comparable to the one in Tournai. It is impressive for its alternating round and trefoiled pillars, its vast galleries opening onto rounded arches of the same size, and its Romanesque rafters which replaced the Gothic vaulting during restoration in 1898 designed to give the church back its original Romanesque appearance. Only the side aisles and the transept crossing have their original vaulting. The furnishings date mainly from the 17C and the Renaissance and Baroque styles predominate. This is evident in the ambo, a sort of rood-screen concealing the chancel and set between the huge pillars behind the transept crossing. Its architectural design, consisting of three surbased arches supporting a gallery, is Renaissance in style while its statues and decorative features are markedly Baroque. Note the superb statue of the Virgin Mary suckling the Infant Jesus in the niche on the south altar. It is made of painted white stone and dates from the 14C. Beyond the traceried door is the chancel and, behind the ambo gallery, is a huge white marble bas-relief representing the Resurrection of Christ. Behind the high altar is a cupboard containing the St Vincent reliquary and the 19C reliquary containing the saint's head. Both of them can be brought down onto the high altar using an ingenious pieces of 18C machinery.

In the ambulatory on the south side of the chancel is a niche containing an 15C stone **Entombment** with expressive faces. The statue stands out against the remains of a painted background illustrating a scene from Christ's Passion.

226

Treasury ⊙ – There are some 250 items in the church treasury including reliquaries, chalices, monstrances, church plate and vestments. They are displayed in the cloisters and the former chapter house, now a museum.

The **old cemetery** (vieux cimetière) near the church *(access via Rue Henry-Leroy)* has been turned into a public park. The Romanesque and Gothic chapel now houses an archaeological museum. This was once the last resting-place of local people and it is filled with gravestones and funerary monuments, the oldest of them dating from the 14C. Note 17C calvary and the Baroque gateway (at the end of the cemetery) which was part of the ornamentation of the church for two hundred years.

EXCURSIONS

Horrues – *4km – 2.5 miles northwest.* The **church** dedicated to St Martin is a pretty little 12C Romanesque building with a 13C chancel. It was built of local sandstone, like the collegiate church. An elegant 15C sculpted stone Gothic altar-piece depicting St Hubert's vision can be seen in the south aisle.

Ecaussinnes-Lalaing – *15km – 9 miles east.* An impressive **château** ⊙ perched on a crag overlooks the town and the River Sennette. It was built in the 12C but was later partially modified and enlarged with square and round towers.

The vast rooms, with carved mantelpieces adorned with heraldic coats-of-arms, constitute a museum. Exhibits include period furniture, works of art and collections of porcelain and glass.

The Virgin and Child in the chapel is attributed to the 14C Valenciennes artist Beauneveu. The kitchen still looks much as it did in the 15C.

Since 1903 a festival supper for the unmarried, called the matrimonial meal, has been held on Whit Monday on the market square of Ecaussinnes at the foot of the castle.

Le Rœulx – *8km – 5 miles south.* The **château** ⊙ of the Princes of Cro, a resplendent successor to the 15C fortress, has an elegant, 18C Classical façade in brick and stone, with numerous windows. Many famous guests have stayed here, including Philip the Good, Emperor Charles V, Philip II, and Maria de' Medici.

Inside there are rooms with groined vaulting (arms room, dining room) which remain from the 15C and 16C constructions. The collections are interesting: antique furniture, historical mementoes, objets d'art, porcelain, and paintings by old masters such as Van Dyck and Van Loo. The vast park has some magnificent trees and a beautiful rose garden.

SOUGNÉ-REMOUCHAMPS

Liège

Michelin maps 409 K4 or 213 south of fold 23 – Local map see Vallée de l'AMBLÈVE

Remouchamps is a pleasant holiday location on the banks of the Amblève, where a daisy festival is held on the last weekend in June.

★★**Grotte** ⊙ – This cave was discovered in 1828 and opened to the public in 1912. Visitors have an interesting tour, ending with a boat trip, through galleries gouged out of the rock by the Rubicon, a tributary of the Amblève. The last 80m – 260ft of the gallery were blasted using dynamite. The circular entrance was once a prehistoric rock shelter. A wide corridor leads to a precipice from which a flight of steps descends to the river.

Visitors pass a frozen waterfall and petrified rock pools *(gours)* in the Grand Gallery (20m – 66ft high), then descend to the Rubicon beneath the vault of sparkling stalactites. The tour takes them through the "Cathedral" measuring 100m – 328ft by 40m – 131ft with beautiful crystal concretions in three different colours, before reaching the Bridge of Titans. This is where the path goes down to the landing stage and the visit continues by boat for about 1km – 0.75 mile beneath strange, multicoloured rocks to the Precipice Chamber.

Grotte de Remouchamps

EXCURSION

From Sougné-Remouchamps to Tancrémont – *11km – 6.75 miles north.*

Deigné-Aywaille – The **parc safari du Monde Sauvage** ⊘ is in Deigné. Hippopotami, zebras, camels, giraffes, buffalo, rhinoceros and gazelles roam free; their area of the park can be visited by car or on the little train *(departures hourly next to the farm)*. The section consisting of the enclosures and islets is visited on foot. The park also has a sea lions' pool, a children's farm with a playground, an aviary of tropical birds and an auditorium in which visitors can watch 3D films.

Banneux-Notre-Dame – This has been the international place of pilgrimage to Our Lady of the Poor, since the eight apparitions to 11-year-old Mariette Beco during the winter of 1933. The Miraculous Spring, the Stations of the Cross and the chapels are dispersed throughout the neighbouring pine forest.

Tancrémont – A pilgrims' chapel contains a beautiful wooden **statue**★ of Christ which is the object of great veneration. This statue was discovered buried in the earth in about 1830. It depicts a crowned Christ in a robe that seems to be of Eastern influence, and is thought to date back to the 12C.

SPA★

Liège – Population 9 953

Michelin maps 409 K4 or 213 fold 23 Local map see Vallée de l'AMBLÈVE
Town plan in the current Michelin Red Guide Benelux

Spa lies in one of the most beautiful regions of the Ardennes, amidst wooded hills which take on marvellous hues in the autumn. It is a **spa town**★★ of some renown. Its clear waters are iron-bearing, bicarbonated and sparkling. They are used primarily for baths and for drinking as part of treatment for cardiac, rheumatoid and respiratory disorders. The town specialises in "jolités", little painted wooden ornaments.

A lengthy past – Spa's waters have been known about since Roman times. From the 16C onwards, it attracted huge crowds of "bobelins" (those taking the waters, from the Latin "bibulus": he who is a great drinker). Royalty such as Margaret of Valois (Queen Margot), Christina of Sweden, Peter the Great (whose name was given to the oldest source, or "pouhon"), and writers such as Marmontel and Victor Hugo all came here.

During the First World War the Kaiser Wilhelm II established himself here with his staff, and it was here that he abdicated in 1918. Two years later the Spa conference brought the Allies and the Germans together for an armistice committee.

The present spa town – Spa has a large number of springs. In addition to the Pouhon Pierre-le-Grand and the Pouhon Grand-Condé, there are also the Géronstère, Sauvenière, Groosbeek, Barisart, Tonnelet Springs and the only one to produce still water, Spa-Reine.

The **spa town architecture** of the late 19C and early 20C is particularly well represented. There are some lovely examples of neo-Classical and Rococo styles,

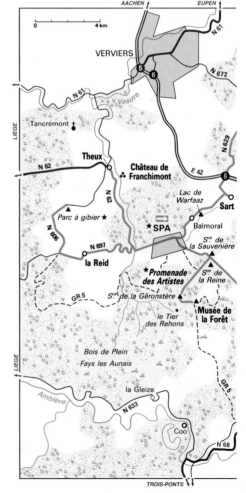

the use of metal frameworks and great painted frescoes. The finest examples are the **baths** built from 1862 to 1868, the **Pouhon Pierre-le-Grand** ⊘ inside a neo-Classical pavilion (1880), and the **Casino**. The current casino building replaced the 18C "Redoute" in 1919.

Spa the holiday resort – The many sports, artistic and cultural activities, the pleasant signposted walks, **guided tours** ⊘, and the interesting excursions into the surrounding area make Spa an excellent spot for a holiday.

The **Lac de Warfaaz** *(2.5km – 1.5 miles northeast)* is popular with water sports enthusiasts. Moreover, skiing and tobogganning are on offer at Le Thier des Raihons *(south)*. Among the many events, note the **autumn music season**, the **Spa Theatre Festival** *(see the Calendar of Events)* and major temporary exhibitions.

SIGHTS

Musée de la Ville d'eau ⊘ – *Avenue Reine Astrid 77 B.* This museum is in the central building of a royal villa which belonged to Queen Maria-Henrietta, a Habsburg princess and the second Belgian queen, who died in 1902. An extensive **collection of "jolités"**★ illustrates the history of the spa in the decoration on the painted wooden boxes, which actually depict different buildings in Spa from the 17C onwards.

Musée du Cheval ⊘ – *In the stables of the Maria-Henrietta villa.* The horse museum recalls Spa's prestigious "equestrian past" and the many outstanding horses and carriages which passed through the town, some of them among the finest in Europe. Spa also organised the first races.

★**Promenade des Artistes** – *Leave on the Sauvenière road (N 62).*

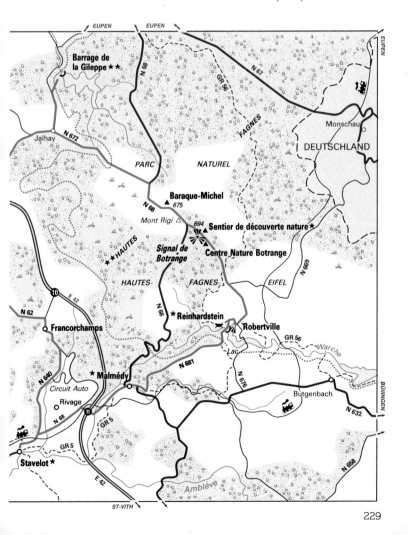

The suburb of Neubois, where Kaiser Wilhelm II established his headquarters in 1918, is on the left. Turn right onto the Fontaines road at the crossroads by the **Source de la Sauvenière.** The **Source de la Reine** is in the woods on the left. About 1.3km – 0.75 mile on from the crossroads a little stream called the Picherotte flows down to Spa. The path which follows this steeply sloping little valley, scattered with rocks and shaded by magnificent trees, is called the Promenade des Artistes.

Continue along the Fontaines road to reach the **Source de la Géronstère.**

EXCURSIONS

Musée de la Forêt ⊘ – *6km – 3.7 miles south in Berinzenne.*
The forestry museum is in a restored farmhouse in the depths of the Spa forest. It introduces visitors to various aspects of nature including vegetation, flora, local trees (in various woods), a geological exhibition, and forestry work. Fauna are also presented in large dioramas reproducing the animals' natural habitat in the Ardennes (deer, lynxes, wolves, foxes, etc.).

Sart – *5km – 3.25 miles northeast on the N 629.*
Place du Marché is embellished with a perron, a flight of steps that was a symbol of liberty in the Liège region. It is overlooked by a church with a 15C tower, as well as austere-looking stone houses.

Château de Franchimont et Theux – *8km – 5 miles northeast on the N 62.*
Château de Franchimont ⊘ – Set on a hill overlooking the Hoëgne Valley, the ruins of Franchimont (literally "mount of the Francs") hark back to the prince-bishops of Liège who used the castle as their summer residence from the 16C onwards. It also recalls the 600 proud men massacred in 1468 by Charles the Bold's troops, as they tried to defend the approach to Liège.

The haughty walls of the keep were protected by the pentagonal fortified enclosure with casemates at each corner.

Follow the numbered tour (explanatory plaques).

There is a pretty view of Theux from the chapel.

The building with the tea room and restaurant houses a historical museum.

Theux – A 17C and 18C Town Hall and old houses surround the square, in which there is an 18C perron, with a pine cone at the top.

The restored **église Sts-Hermès-et-Alexandre** ⊘ is nearby. There was originally a Merovingian chapel on the site, then a Carolingian church with a west tower, the vestiges of which have been found. In about the year 1000 a Romanesque nave was built here, followed by a fortified northern tower a short time later. It now has a hoarding. The chancel, dating from about 1500, is Gothic.

Note the sculpted Gothic stoops in the porch. The interior is unusual, with three arches separated by tall arches on pillars. This is the only hall-church with a flat Romanesque ceiling still in existence between the Loire and the Rhine. The ceiling in the nave was decorated in the 17C with 110 coffers painted with characters and scenes from the Life of Christ. The *Virgin Mary of Theux* (late 15C) is in a chapel on the north side of the chancel, and the Romanesque font is interesting, with dragons and four heads on the corners.

La Reid – *5km – 3.25 miles west on the N 62, then take the N 697.*
A **parc à gibier** ★ ⊘ (game park) has been set up west of the village. It is in a beautiful forest setting, in which the main species of Ardennes wildlife are on show, as well as a few rare specimens of various origins such as Dabowsky deer from Poland, yaks from Tibet, or racoons from America.

★**Round trip from Spa** – *75km – 47 miles allow 2 hours. Leave on the N 62 southeast in the direction of Malmédy.* Michelin map no 214 fold 8.

Francorchamps – This village is known for the Spa-Francorchamps motor racing circuit 7km – 4.3 miles long, to the south. Each year major races take place including the Belgian Grand Prix. A small modern church is also interesting.

Take the motor racing circuit to Stavelot.

This **route** ★ goes through magnificent countryside.

★**Stavelot** – *See STAVELOT below.*

From Stavelot to Malmédy take the Francorchamps motor racing circuit once more. It runs through very pretty scenery. The village of **Rivage** is located in the hills on the left, which are still dotted with traditional half-timbered farmhouses.

★**Malmédy** – *See MALMÉDY.*

Robertville and Château de Reinhardstein ★ – *See MALMÉDY: Excursions.*

After Robertville, the road crosses the Hautes-Fagnes plateau (qv). In Jalhay, turn right to reach Gileppe Dam (qv).

Return to Spa by taking the N 629 north and going through **Balmoral**, a suburb with luxurious villas half-concealed amidst the green hills.

SPONTIN ★

Namur

Michelin maps 409 I5 or 214 fold 5 – Local map see La MEUSE NAMUROISE

Spontin, in the Bocq Valley, is well-known for its castle and its mineral water springs. The water supplies a bottling plant which produces 30 million bottles of sparkling and still mineral water annually as well as sodas and fruit syrups.

★**Château** ⊙ – The castle is surrounded by the flowing waters of the Bocq and is a remarkable example of Belgian medieval architecture. It shows the development of aristocratic houses from the 12C to the 17C. Starting life as a simple keep in the 12C, it was enlarged into a fortress in the 14C, then restored at the end of the 16C in the Renaissance style and embellished with pink bricks and pepperpot roofs. The outbuildings were added in 1622, outside the moat, and now close off the main courtyard. The old keep can be seen in another courtyard

Château de Spontin

which also contains an elegant wrought-iron well canopy by Van Boeckel (19C). The austere rooms in the old main building, with their thick walls, sandstone floors, Gothic fireplaces and Louis XIII woodwork, form a sharp contrast to the apartments.

The south part was decorated in the neo-Gothic style in the 19C.

STAVELOT ★

Liège – Population 6 241

Michelin maps 409 K4 or 214 fold 8 – Local maps see Vallée de l'AMBLÈVE and SPA

Stavelot lies in the heart of a magnificent area of the Ardennes. It still has many old houses, some of them half-timbered.

The town grew up around an abbey, founded by **St Remaclus** in the 7C, at the same time as the abbey in Malmédy. It soon came under the Benedictine Rule and like its rival, Malmédy, became the seat of an ecclesiastic principality. Like the prince-bishops of Liège, the prince-abbots enjoyed absolute independence and bowed to no authority but that of the Empire. Nevertheless, Stavelot was incorporated into the Ourthe *département* in 1795.

The French poet Apollinaire spent the summer of 1899 in Stavelot. A memorial plaque can be seen on the side of the Hôtel du Mal Aimé, 12 Rue Neuve, where he stayed.

The town suffered extensive damage in December 1944 *(qv)*.

Two special events take place in the abbey during the summer months every year. They are Vacances-Théâtre and the Festival of Chamber Music *(see the Calendar of Events)*.

★★**Carnival** – Every year *(see the Calendar of Events)* more than 1 500 people parade through the streets during the extravagant Laetare procession. The parade has a great many floats and is enlivened by hundreds of **Blanc Moussis**, characters with long red noses and enormous white hooded costumes.

SIGHTS

Place St-Remacle – The **Fontaine du Perron** consists of a fountain and steps dating from 1769. Here, as in Liège, it symbolises the town's liberty.

Old Abbey – All that remains of the abbey church is its Romanesque tower with 16C porch. Around the main courtyard are the abbey buildings which were refurbished in the 18C and are now occupied by the Town Hall and museums. The old 18C monks' refectory is decorated with stuccowork, making an elegant setting for the festival's chamber music concerts. The undercroft is used for drama productions.

Museum – The museum is housed in the wing of the outbuildings. The **Musée religieux régional** ⊙ has some interesting works of art (14C to 19C) including a recumbant Christ attributed to Delcour, a 16C painted statue, gold and silver plate and liturgical vestments.

Regional history is illustrated by objects found during archeological digs on the site of the old abbey church as well as firebacks, models (abbey church, Château de Logne), seals, portraits, and the reconstruction of a printing works.

The **Tannery section★** on the top floor provides a pleasant insight *(recorded commentary)* into this local activity. The last tannery closed in 1947.

Three rooms have been arranged for temporary exhibitions. They display collections of modern and contemporary Belgian art (Degouve de Nuncques).

Musée Guillaume Apollinaire ⊘ – A little museum on the first floor of the Town Hall is devoted to the poet, with a reconstruction of his bedroom.

Musée du Circuit de Spa-Francorchamps ⊘ – An exhibition has been set up in the vaulted undercroft of the old abbey. It describes the history of the motor racing circuit *(qv)* from 1896 to the present day. Models of the winning cars and motorcycles, photos and posters recall the great moments of the famous track.

Ph. Calic/MICHELIN

Reliquary of St Remaclus (detail)

Église St-Sébastien – This church was built in the 18C and has an interesting **treasury** ⊘.

The monumental 13C **reliquary of St Remaclus★★**, of the Mosan school, is 2.07m – 6.72ft long. It is made of gilded metal highlighted with filigree and enamels, and is flanked by statuettes of St Remaclus, St Lambert, and the Apostles (fashioned in a more archaic style). On the ends are statuettes of Christ and the Virgin Mary. On the top are scenes from the New Testament.

Note the 17C bust-reliquary of St Poppo, former Abbot of Stavelot. Scenes from the life of the saint are on the base.

Rue Haute – *At the end of Place St-Remacle, up and to the right.*

This is one of the most picturesque streets in Stavelot. It leads to a charming little square with an old fountain and several old houses, half-timbered or with wooden façades.

THUIN

Hainaut – Population 13 994
Michelin maps 409 F4 or 214 fold 3

Thuin is the capital of the **Thudinie** region. It lies in a pretty **setting★** on a hillside separating the Sambre from the Biesmelle. It is overlooked by its tall square belfry (17C-18C), once the collegiate church tower.

Thuin was initially a possession of the Abbey of Lobbes *(qv)*, then was made part of the Liège principality in 888. Bishop Notger fortified the town in the 10C. The St Roch military march takes place in Thuin in May *(see the Calendar of Events)*, a parade which dates back to 1654. A speciality of Thuin is "spantôles", biscuits named after a cannon captured from the French in 1554.

SIGHTS

Place du Chapitre – There is an interesting **panorama** of the winding Sambre Valley, the Lower Town with its port and barges, and the picturesque town of Lobbes with the collegiate church on a hilltop.

The post office is not far from the square, in Grand-Rue, occupying what used to be the Lobbes Abbey refuge (16C, restored).

Remparts du Midi – Follow the sign marked "Panorama" in Grand-Rue, then take a picturesque little street running along the 15C ramparts and the east end of the church.

On the left is the **tour Notger**. This tower is all that remains of the ramparts built by the prince-bishop.

Hanging gardens – *Drive out of the town on the Biesme road.*

There is a pretty **view** of Thuin's terraced gardens from the public park (Parc du Chant des oiseaux) on the right. The view also includes the ramparts and the belfry, overlooking the Biesmelle Valley.

TIENEN

Vlaams-Brabant – Population 31 153
Michelin maps 409 H3 or 213 fold 20
Town plan in the current Michelin Red Guide Benelux

Tienen is in the agricultural region of **Hageland** ("hedge country"). It used to be a drapers' town and is now a centre of trade. It lies at the intersection of major road and rail links and is also an important centre for suger-beet growing and the local industry has a refinery capacity of 200 000 tonnes of sugar annually.

SIGHTS

★**O.L.-Vrouw-ten-Poelkerk** ☉ – This stone church built in the Brabant Gothic style stands on the huge market square. The 13C chancel is plain and harmonious, with a row of chapels, each with a decorated gable. The nave, however, was never built. The 14C transept has a square, onion-domed bell tower above it. There used to be a small lake nearby hence the church's name (Our Lady of the Lake). It has been drained, but a spring remains and is the site of a pilgrimage.
The beautiful deepset **doorways**★ by Jean d'Orsy date from 1360. Note the amusing little characters carved on the bases of the alcoves. The 14C statue of the Virgin Mary which used to decorate the central doorway was moved into the church and is now over the high altar.

Stedelijk Museum Het Toreke ☉ – The municipal museum is housed in an old 16C prison, in the courtyard of the Justice of the Peace. The collections (ceramics, gold and silver ware, archeology) illustrate the history of the town.

Wolmarkt – The restored Flemish Renaissance style **Van Ranst houses**, on the right at nos 19 and 21, are particularly outstanding.

St.-Germanuskerk – Built on the top of the hill, this church dedicated to St Germanus stands in the heart of the old town centre near the Veemarkt (cattle market).
In the 12C it was a four-towered Romanesque basilica.
The two towers of the forepart were built around 1225. They are typical of Mosan Romanesque architecture. Since the 16C they have framed a massive tower, which had a 54-chime carillon added to it in the 18C. The bells can be heard during **summer concerts** ☉. The interior is Gothic. Near the central altar there is a copy of the Romanesque font exhibited in the musée du Cinquantenaire in Brussels. The chancel houses a beautiful bronze lectern. Note the 15C *Miraculous Christ of the White Ladies* in the south transept chapel. In the north chapel, there is a Pietà, on which the breast is pierced by seven swords.

EXCURSION

From Tienen to Jodoigne – *13km – 8 miles southwest.*
Hoegaarden – This town is well-known for its pale ale.
There is a little folklore museum (Bier- en Streekmuseum) on the top floor of the 17C house known as **'t Nieuwhuys** ☉ *(2 Ernest Ourystraat).* The house was an inn during the Roman period. The museum contains objects concerning local history. The old beer cellar (kelder) is also open to visitors.

Jodoigne – Once a stronghold on a slope of the Gette Valley, Jodoigne is a major agricultural market town.
Église St-Médard was built in the late 12C, in a transitional style. The church is flanked to the west by a massive square tower. The **apse** is harmonious, with a double row of arches in which the arcades are supported by colonettes. The apse is framed by two apsidal chapels isolated from the chancel. The chancel itself has slender colonettes with capitals. Note the reliquary of St Médard in an alcove in the north transept, behind a grille.

MICHELIN GUIDES

The Red Guides (hotels and restaurants)

*Benelux – Deutschland – España Portugal – Europe – France –
Great Britain and Ireland – Italia – Switzerland*

The Green Guides (fine art, historical monuments, scenic routes)

*Austria – Belgium and Luxembourg – Berlin – Brussels – California – Canada –
Chicago – England: The West Country – Europe – Florida – France – Germany –
Great Britain – Greece – Ireland – Italy – London – Mexico – Netherlands –
New England – New York – Paris – Portugal – Quebec – Rome – Scandinavia
Finland – Scotland – Spain – Switzerland – Tuscany – Venice – Vienna – Wales –
Washington*

...and the collection of regional guides to France

TONGEREN ★

Limburg – Population 28 947
Michelin maps 409 J3 or 213 fold 22

Together with Tournai this is the oldest town in Belgium, and one of the richest in traces of the past. It is in the **Hesbaye** (Haspengouw), a gently undulating region of orchards.

A great Roman community – Tongeren was originally a camp established by Caesar's lieutenants, Sabinus and Cotta. Their legions were massacred nearby by **Ambiorix,**

the chief of the Eburones, who fomented a rebellion by part of Belgian Gaul against Caesar's armies in 54BC. During the Roman occupation the developing town was called **Atuatuca-Tungrorum,** and became a stopover on the Roman road from Bavay to Cologne. It actually covered a much greater area at the time, as shown by the remains of the late 1C town walls covering a distance of 4km – 2.5 miles. Traces also exist on the Legioenenlaan to the West. The barbaric invasions in the late 3C were so hard on the community that, in the early 4C, it withdrew into a much smaller area surrounded by walls, some traces of which have survived to the

Statue of Ambiorix

present day. St Servais was the first bishop of Tongeren in the 4C, but for security reasons the episcopal see was then moved to Maastricht. Gradually, under the protection of the principality of Liège, Tongeren began to prosper again. It organised an administrative system and built a third set of town walls in the 13C.

★★O.-L.-VROUWEBASILIEK (Y) ⓥ *time : 2 hours*

A statue (1866) of Ambiorix stands in the market square, in which the 18C Town Hall is also to be found. Pause to admire the impressive outline of the old collegiate church of Our Lady, a beautiful Gothic building (13C-16C) with a striking unfinished tower-façade (carillon).

Interior – *Go along the south side of the church and enter through the little doorway.*
There is a beautiful Romanesque (11C) painted wooden statue of Christ in the porch. The 13C nave is supported by cylindrical pillars, which have capitals with crockets. The elegant triforium is surmounted by a covered passageway. On the west side, beneath the rood-screen, there is a beautiful copper door dating from 1711. The 18C organ above it has been restored.
The most interesting works of art are in the chancel. The beautiful early 16C Antwerp wooden **altarpiece★** on the high altar represents the Life of the Virgin Mary.
Note also the great paschal candlestick and the lectern, both of them made in 1372 by a Dinant coppersmith.
A painted **statue★** of Our Lady of Tongeren, carved in walnut (1479), is in the north transept.
Concerts ⓥ are given in the basilica.

★★**Treasury** – Among the exhibited treasures, notice the 11C gospel-book covered with an ivory plaque (calvary scene), the 6C ivory diptych (St Paul), the 6C Merovingian gold clasp, the 14C monstrance-reliquary of St Ursula with an enameled base, the reliquary-triptych of the Holy Cross (12C) in silver-gilt highlighted with enamelwork, a Head of Christ in wood (11C), the reliquary of the Martyrs of Trier (13C) and the reliquary of St Remaclus (15C), decorated with paintings.
Every seven years *(see the Calendar of Events)* about a hundred priests wearing centuries-old liturgical vestments carry the reliquaries from the treasury in a procession.

★**Cloisters** – The charming cloisters have alternating single and double colonettes. There are interesting capitals on the row near the entrance. Gravestones have been set against the walls.

TONGEREN

Grote Markt .... Y
Hemelingenstraat .... Y 12
Maastrichterstraat .... Y
St.-Truidenstraat .... Y 42

Achttiende-
 Oogstlaan .... Y 2
Clarissenstraat .... Y 4
Corversstraat .... YZ 5
Eeuwfeestwal .... Y 6
Elisabethwal .... Z 9
Hasseltsesteenweg ..... Y 10
Hondsstraat .... Y 14
Luikerstraat .... Z 15
Looierstraat .... Z 17
Minderbroederstraat .. Y 19
Moerenstraat .... Y 20
Momberstraat .... Z 23
Muntstraat .... Z 24
Nevenstraat .... Y 25
Piepelpoel .... Y 27
Pleinstraat .... Y 28
Pliniuswal .... Y 30
Predikherenstraat .... Y 31
Regulierenplein .... Z 34
Riddersstraat .... Y 35
de Schiervelstraat .... Y 37
St.-Catharinastraat....... Y 38
St.-Jansstraat .... Z 39
St.-Maternuswal .... Y 41
Stationslaan .... Y 44
Vermeulenstraat .... Y 46
11 Novemberlaan .... Y 47

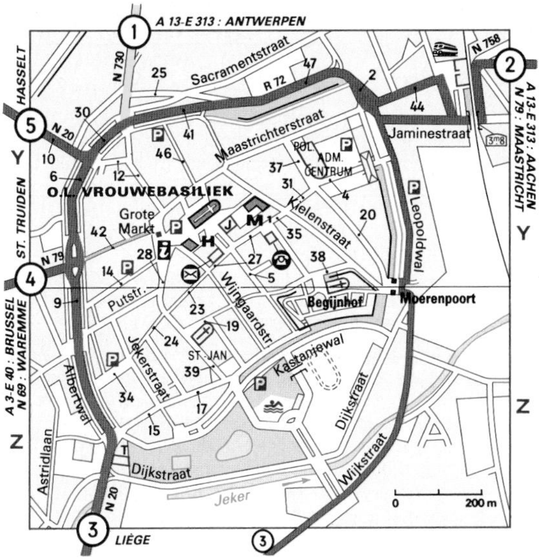

H   Stedelijk Museum   M¹   Gallo-Romeins Museum

ADDITIONAL SIGHTS

Gallo-Romeins Museum (Y M¹) ⊙ – This brand new Gallo-Roman museum on the site of a Roman villa is a museum unlike any other, and a visit here almost resembles an archeological expedition.
A reminder of the strange world of Piranesi has been laid out around a mysterious dodecahedron, a Gallo-Roman object whose exact purpose has never been discovered. The basement contains the prehistoric collections. The Gallo-Roman section is particularly descriptive of the town's past importance. Note the superb sculpture of Jupiter defeating two men with serpents' tails. The tour ends with the Merovingian collection.

Moerenpoort (YZ) – This 14C gate, once part of the medieval ramparts, is also the east entrance to the Beguine convent. The gate has been turned into a museum of local military history, the **musée de l'Histoire militaire de la ville** ⊙. One room is devoted to town militias. There is a view of the Beguine convent, the town and the collegiate church from here.

Begijnhof (Z) – Founded in the 13C, this convent was closed down during the French Revolution.
The Onder de Linde courtyard to the west still has a certain charm with the gardens preceded by a rounded gateway. A Gothic church with interesting furnishings stands in the centre of the enclosure.

Stedelijk Museum (Y H) ⊙ – The municipal museum contains paintings, engravings, sculptures and literature on the history of Tongeren.

EXCURSION

Alden Biesen – 10km – 6.25 miles; leave by ① on the town plan.
The Teutonic Order founded the **commanderie Alden Biesen** (Old Rushes Commandery) north of **Rijkhoven** in 1220. The present buildings were erected or modified between the 16C and the 18C. The castle is an impressive four-sided building, flanked by towers and surrounded by a moat. Louis XV attended a *Te Deum* in the church in 1747 to give thanks for victory at the Battle of Lawfeld (Lafelt) when the Austrians were defeated.
There is a small exhibition in the gallery beside the church.

BELGIUM and LUXEMBOURG: the Michelin map series at 1:200 000
When choosing a lunchtime or overnight stop
use the above maps as all towns listed in
the Red Guide Benelux are underlined in red
When driving into or through a town
use the map as it also indicates all places with
a town plan in the Red Guide Benelux. Common reference numbers make the
transfer from map to plan easier

TONGERLO

Antwerpen
Michelin maps 409 H2 or 213 fold 8

The famous Premonstratensian *(qv)* **abbey** stands to the west of the town, surrounded by a moat. It was founded in about 1130, then abandoned at the end of the 18C and partly destroyed. It was occupied once more in 1840 and has been rebuilt.

After going through the porch surmounted by three niches (14C), visitors enter the **courtyard,** with the farm (1640) and the tithe barn (1618) which is now used for an exhibition on the abbey and its monks. The **Prelacy** to the right has a beautiful Classical façade dating from 1725.

There is an ebony reliquary (1619) in the 19C **abbey church.** It contains the relics of St Siard, to whom farmers, young mothers and children come to pray. This is also a place of pilgrimage *(see the Calendar of Events)*.

★**Museum Leonardo da Vinci** ⊙ – *Access via the Prelacy.*

In a glass and concrete building there is an immense canvas, a copy of the **Last Supper** that Leonardo da Vinci painted on the wall of the convent of Santa Maria delle Grazie in Milan between 1495 and 1498. This faithful copy is surprisingly good, and was painted less than 20 years later. The Last Supper was bought in 1545 and hung in the abbey church for many years. It has been through numerous ups and downs and was ripped during a fire in 1929. It has been carefully restored in Belgium, and the emotional response it provokes in the viewer is as strong as ever. Early music and a well-chosen commentary heighten the dramatic intensity of the moment when Christ says, "One of you will betray me". Only Judas is outside the golden light reflected on each face.

From the garden in front of the museum, there is a beautiful view of the rear façade of the Prelacy and the graceful turret, once the lookout post, built in 1479.

TORHOUT

West-Vlaanderen – Population 18 346
Michelin maps 409 C2 or 213 fold 2

Torhout was a prosperous town in the 12C with a well-known fair.

St.-Pietersbandenkerk ⊙ – Rebuilt after having been bombed in 1940, this church has a pretty octagonal Romanesque bell tower with a carillon.
Models inside show changes in the church's development.

Stadhuis – This is a harmonious building dating from 1713. Widely spaced pilasters are topped by a high roof.

The **Château de Wijnendale** is 3km – 1.75 miles west of Torhout, a composite building (11C-19C) surrounded by a circular moat. The castle was built in the 11C by Robert the Frisian and became the favourite residence of the Counts of Flanders.
Mary of Burgundy had a fatal fall from a horse in the surrounding woods in 1482.

TOURNAI★★

Hainaut – Population 64 206
Michelin maps 409 D4 or 213 fold 15

Tournai grew up along the banks of the Scheldt which divides the city into two almost equal parts, overlooked by the five towers of its cathedral. It is at the heart of an essentially agricultural region and has had a prestigious past. Together with Tongeren, this is the oldest town in Belgium. One after the other the Romans, Franks, English, French and Austrians made this an important artistic centre. Unfortunately, the May 1940 bombings ravaged Tournai and destroyed most of its old houses. Boat trips are available on the Scheldt and provide a good view of the town. There are also day trips to various areas within the region.

HISTORICAL NOTES

The cradle of the French monarchy – Tournai was already an important city in Roman times. In the 3C St Piat converted the town to Christianity. It then came under Salian Frank domination in the 5C. This was followed by the Merovingian dynasty. Childeric died here in 481 and his son **Clovis,** who made Tournai a bishopric, was born here in 465.

The kings of France always considered Tournai as the cradle of their monarchy, and the town bears the royal fleur-de-lys in its coat of arms. Napoleon later adopted Childeric's symbol, the bee, for his own. It was during the 9C that a chapter of canons settled in the town and that its episcopal see was merged with the one in Noyon (they remained merged until 1146).

Philip Augustus visited the town in 1187 and won over the reigning bishop to his policies. The 12C and 13C were great periods of construction. A few Romanesque houses, religious buildings and some parts of the second set of town walls have survived to the present day.

Tournai remained faithful to France during the Hundred Years War. The town, called the "Chambre du Roy" (King's Chamber), was isolated in a Belgium which supported the English cause. The citizens of Tournai were invited by Joan of Arc to come to Charles VII's consecration in Rheims (1429) by calling them "gentilz loiaux Franchois" (kind loyal Frenchmen). When she was taken prisoner, Tournai sent her a pouch filled with gold to ease her captivity.

A centre of great artistic influence – Already well-known in the Merovingian period for its gold- and silversmiths, the town became a very important artistic centre in the late Middle Ages. With the 13C reliquary of St Eleutherius, the craftsmen of Tournai once more proved their excellence in the field of metalwork and in the 15C they were the respected rivals of Mosan art.

The use of local stone in buildings from the 12C onwards gave birth to a flourishing new school of sculpture. In the 15C, fonts and funerary monuments were carved in the very finely grained grey-blue stone, or sometimes in imported white stone.

In the 15C **Robert Campin** was born in Tournai (died in 1444). A contemporary of Van Eyck, he is thought by some scholars to be the **Master of Flémalle**, the anonymous artist responsible for a group of works discovered here in about 1900. The charm of his art lies in its colours, the precision with which he depicts interiors and their furnishings, and the sense of serenity.

In more serious subjects a more dramatic mode of expression is evident, which brought Robert Campin closer to his student **Rogier de La Pasture**, better known as **Van der Weyden.** This artist was born in Tournai (1399-1464) and became the official painter of the City of Brussels in 1436. His touching compositions are full of mysticism, while his neat precise drawing produced some remarkable portraits. His Virgins, with their soft oval faces and wide foreheads, have often been imitated.

The Belgian poet Georges Rodenbach was born in Tournai in 1855 but settled in Paris in 1887.

The high-warp **tapestry** of Tournai supplanted the production from its rival Arras as well as from other Flemish workshops. It was admired throughout Europe. The main features were the size of the tapestries, their lack of borders, the numerous figures depicted on them and the highly stylised manner *(see Introduction: Art)*.

A disputed stronghold – From 1513 to 1519, Tournai fell into the hands of King Henry VIII of England, who had a fortified district built there, with a keep now known as the **tour Henri VIII.**

The town then came under the rule of the Emperor Charles V and lost many of its privileges.

During a later period of religious strife, Tournai, under the heroic command of **Christine de Lalaing,** held out for two months in 1581 against Alexander Farnese.

The town again became part of France during the reign of Louis XIV, from 1667 to 1709. The fortifications were reinforced and bastions added to the 13C ramparts by Vauban. The many brick and stone houses date from this period. They are noticeable for their large windows and overhanging roofs.

A few of them are still standing despite the bombing of 1940, especially on Quai Notre-Dame. Tournai then became the seat of the Flemish Parliament, representing the sovereign's justice. It fell into the hands of the Austrians after the signing of the Treaty of Utrecht (1713), was returned to the French after the Battle of **Fontenoy** (1745) *(8km – 5 miles east)*, then was given back to the Austrians in 1748.

In the 18C, the coppersmithing industry and tapestry-making enjoyed a new lease of life in Tournai.

The porcelain works founded in 1751 by François-Joseph Peterinck were very much in vogue at this time. Soft porcelain was made here with rich colours and a great variety of decoration, although the Chinese style was very popular. The works finally closed in 1891.

Folklore and traditions – Tournai is one of the Belgian towns where traditions are still very important.

During the festival of the Nativity of Our Lady *(second Sunday in September at 3pm)*, which dates back to the Great Plague of 1090, the reliquary of St Eleutherius *(qv)* and certain items of the cathedral treasury are carried in a procession.

The days on which the four parades take place *(see the Calendar of Events)* combine publicity and folklore with giants representing figures who left their mark on the town's history such as Childeric and Louis XIV, a carnival parade, a procession of floral floats and a festival of military music.

★★★ CATHÉDRALE NOTRE-DAME (AZ) *time : 1 hour 30min*

The most striking and most unusual of Belgium's religious monuments stands in the centre of Tournai not far from the belfry. It influenced a great number of churches in the town itself and, since the diocese of Tournai once covered most of Flanders, its influence spread throughout the Scheldt Valley, giving birth to Scaldian art *(qv)*. The effect of the gigantic proportions of the building (134m – 440ft long, 66m – 216ft wide at the transept) and of the massive forms of its five famous towers is most impressive.

The five **towers,** each one different, stand at the transept crossing. The oldest one, in the centre, is supported on the pillars of the crossing itself. Its purpose was to bring more light into the transept crossing *(qv).*

The nave and the arms of the transept, which have semi-circular ends, date from the 12C. The slender Gothic chancel, which is taller than the nave and almost as long, replaced the Romanesque chancel in the 13C. This difference in style is evident both inside and outside the building.

Place P E Janson gives one of the best views of the cathedral as a whole.

Porte Mantile – This side door was so named to commemorate St Eleutherius' healing of blind Mantilius on this spot. The door still has some remarkable Romanesque carvings, especially on the string course flanking the top (struggle between the Merovingian monarchs and brothers, Sigebert and Chilperic) and the uprights (fight between Virtues and Vices).

Continue right round the east end of the church.

Porte du Capitole – This Romanesque doorway resembles the Porte Mantile, except that it is unfortunately in very bad condition. Indeed, it is difficult to pick out the carvings of the end of the world on the string course. The archivolt is supported by two knights with a shield.

Go through the Fausse Porte or "False Doorway", the arch topped by St Vincent's Chapel and linking the cathedral with the bishop's palace.

West front – The west front is flanked by the Old Priory (18C) on one side and the Bishop's Palace on the other. It was altered in the 14C and masked by a **porch** which underwent alterations in the 16C. In it there are three tiers of sculptures. On the bottom row are 14C high reliefs, including three scenes depicting the story of Adam and Eve, above that, 16C bas-reliefs, with the Tournai procession *(see above)* to the left, and the conflict between Sigebert and his brother Chilperic to the right and on the top row there is a line of Apostles and saints dating from the 17C. There is a beautiful 14C statue of the Virgin Mary on the central pillar. It is venerated under the name of Our Lady of the Sick (Notre-Dame des Malades).

Interior – This nave is a vast construction containing ten bays. It is four storeys high and has great triple-rolled arches supported on short pillars with beautifully carved capitals. Above that, the galleries are surmounted by a triforium of round arches with a blind bay in the centre. The uppermost level is lit by tall clerestory windows. The 18C vaulting replaced a wooden ceiling. A rood-screen made in 1572 cuts off the view along the nave.

The wall in the **south aisle** is covered with epitaphs.

Note the **capitals** on the pillars of the nave. They used to be painted. The carvings include plant decoration (**1**: bunches of grapes), animals (**2**: horses), human figures, often in a rather whimsical style (**3**: a falling man).

In Chapelle St-Louis, or the Chapel of the Holy Sacrament, there is a *Crucifixion* by Jordaens and finely carved 18C wooden panels from an abbey (scenes from the lives of St Benedict and St Ghislain). Especially outstanding is the second panel, depicting an abbey refectory in the 18C.

Crowned by a tall lantern (Anglo-Norman influence), the **transept** is magnificent in size and splendour, creating the effect of a "cathedral within a cathedral".

The layout is very unusual. Each transept ends in a semi-circle surrounded by an ambulatory. The four storey design echoes the design of the nave. The transept has traces of 12C frescoes and 16C stained-glass windows.

The frescoes (**4**) in the **south transept** above the altar dedicated to Our Lady of Tournai represent celestial Jerusalem. The windows depict the struggle between Sigebert and his brother Chilperic, the origin of the bishops' temporal power (further up, episcopal privileges such as the tax on beer).

Ph. Cajlo/MICHELIN

Detail of a stained glass window: beer tax

The **rood-screen** is the work of sculptor Cornelis Floris II de Vriendt *(qv)*. It is a magnificent piece of Antwerp Renaissance art, with different coloured marble finely chiselled into ornate decoration. The medallions and alabaster panels represent episodes from the Old and New Testament for example, Jonah being swallowed by the whale and the Entombment of Christ *(right)*.

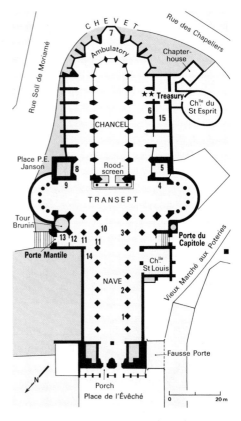

The **chancel** (1243) is very long and has seven bays. Its delicacy contrasts to the somewhat austere solidity of the nave. The French influence is manifest (Soissons).

The **ambulatory** called the "carolle" (from Old French *"caroler"*, meaning "to walk in a circle") ends in five radiating chapels. In the first chapel on the south side (**5**) note the *"Maidens'" Reliquary* (1572). In the next chapel (**6**) there is a *Raising of Lazarus* by Pourbus the Elder and a painting by Coebergher. In the axial chapel (**7**) there are *Scenes from the Life of the Virgin Mary* by Martin de Vos, a

work that is somewhat Italian in style. Behind the rood-screen in the first part of the chancel are the 18C canons' choirstalls and the sanctuary itself, with a high altar in the Classical style (1727). In the chapels in the north ambulatory, there are gravestones by the Tournai school (14C – 15C). Above the door leading into the room known as the "pilgrims' calefactory" is a painting of *Purgatory* (1635) (**8**) by Rubens. Opposite it are three *grisaille* works by Piat Sauvage (18C) hung one above the other.

Traces of frescoes (**9**) in the **north transept** depict the life and martyrdom of St Margaret. Here the stained-glass windows represent the separation of the Tournai diocese from the diocese of Noyon in France, to which it had been annexed in the 7C.

Among the capitals in the **north aisle**, note the swans (**10**), the imaginary animals (**11**), a woman being devoured by a monster (**12**) and on the other side (**13**), visible only in the porch, Fredegonde and Chilperic, and some birds drinking (**14**).

★★Treasury ⊙ – The most outstanding exhibits in this 15C vaulted chamber are two large reliquary chests dating from the 13C. They are the **Notre-Dame Reliquary** (1205) in silver and gilded copper, by Nicolas de Verdun, decorated with marvellously formed relief figures beneath sumptuous arcading and medallions depicting the Passion of Christ, and the **St Eleutherius Reliquary** (1247) which is decorated with a profusion of extraordinarily delicate statues of the Apostles set against a background of filigree, enamels and gems. Christ and St Eleutherius, who is holding the cathedral in his hand, are represented on the ends. Among the many valuable works note in particular the *Seven Joys of Mary* (c1546) by Pieter Pourbus, a reliquary of the True Cross called the *"Byzantine Cross"* of 5C or 6C oriental origin (gold, pearls, precious stones and a crystal glass panel through which the reliquary can be seen), an ivory reliquary chest called the *"Cologne"* reliquary (13C) which still has traces of painting, a clasp for a cape decorated with the figure of a young woman symbolising the fortified town of Tournai (15C) and the imperial cloak worn by Charles V in the cathedral in 1531.

In the Chapelle du St-Esprit or the Chapel dedicated to the Holy Spirit (17C) a long **tapestry** illustrates the life of St Piat, the apostle of Tournai, and that of St Eleutherius, the first bishop of Tournai. It was woven in Arras and donated in 1402 by a former chaplain to the Duke of Burgundy. The 18C French Regency woodpanelling in the chapter-house has been elegantly and finely carved to depict the Life of St Ghislain.

TOURNAI

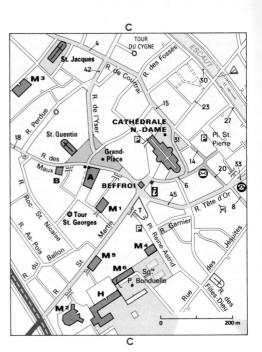

Chapeliers (R. des)	C 6
Cordonnerie (R. de la)	C 14
Gallait (R.)	C 20
Grand Place	C
Puits-d'Eau (R. des)	C 33
Royale (R.)	BY
Athénée (R. de l')	BY 2
Becquerelle (R. du)	AY 3
Bourdon St-Jacques	
(R. du)	C 4
Childeric (R.)	BY 7
Clairisses (R. des)	C 8
Clovis (Pl.)	BY 10
Curé-N.-Dame (R. du)	C 15
Delwart (Bd)	AY 17
Dorée (R.)	AZ 18
Hôpital-Notre-Dame	
(R. de l')	C 23
Lalaing (Bd)	AZ 25
Léopold (Bd)	AY 26
Marché-aux-Poissons	
(Quai du)	C 27
Montgomery (Av.)	AZ 29
Notre-Dame (Quai)	C 30
Paul-E. Janson (Pl.)	C 31
Poissonsceaux (Q. des)	BZ 32
Pont (R. de)	BYZ 34
Quesnoy (R. du)	BY 35
Saint-Piat (R.)	BZ 38
Sainte-Catherine (R.)	BZ 39
Tête-d'Argent (R.)	C 42
Volontaires (R. des)	BY 44
Wallonie (R. de la)	C 45

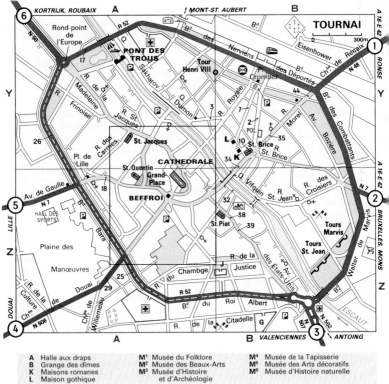

A	Halle aux draps	**M¹**	Musée du Folklore	**M⁴**	Musée de la Tapisserie
B	Grange des dîmes	**M²**	Musée des Beaux-Arts	**M⁵**	Musée des Arts décoratifs
K	Maisons romanes	**M³**	Musée d'Histoire	**M⁶**	Musée d'Histoire naturelle
L	Maison gothique		et d'Archéologie		

ADDITIONAL SIGHTS

* **Beffroi** (C) ⊘ – This is the oldest belfry in Belgium. The foundations date from the 12C. The base was then reinforced in 1294 by the addition of polygonal turrets and the upper sections were rebuilt in 1391 after a fire. Until 1817, several of the rooms were used as a prison.

  From the first floor there is an interesting **view** of the cathedral. There is also a good **view** of the city from the top of the tower (72m – 236ft high, 256 steps). The 44-chime carillon gives beautiful **concerts** ⊘ .

The best way of getting to the museum of fine art is to go back up Rue des Jésuites. The 12C **église St-Piat** (**BZ**) at the corner was built on the site of a Merovingian basilica (6C). It was dedicated to St Piat, the first Christian missionary to come to Tournai. He founded the town's first church. The town's first bishop was to be St Eleutherius *(qv)*.

Go up the street to the episcopal seminary (no 28) and take a look at the courtyard. Then walk through the town park to the art gallery.

★**Musée des Beaux-Arts** (**C M²**) ⊙ – This museum was designed by the famous Art Nouveau architect **Victor Horta** *(qv)* who gave it a star-shaped floor plan with all the rooms converging on the sculpture hall. This centralised layout and the huge glass roof is fronted by a curving façade surmounted by a bronze group by Guillaume Charlier called "Truth, Empress of the Arts". In front of the left side of the museum is a female sculpture by Georges Grard (20C). The museum houses works spanning the period between the 15C and the present day, in particular a collection of **Impressionist works** from the Brussels patron of the arts ⊙ Van Cutsem *(qv)*.

Among the series of **old masters** the most outstanding exhibits are Rogier Van der Weyden's *Virgin and Child*, Gossaert's *St Donatius*, and some delicate landscapes by Velvet Brueghel.

There is an educational display of all the works throughout the world by Rogier Van der Weyden, using photographs in the same format as the original canvases.

From the 17C the gallery has Jordaens canvases and a still life by Snyders. Two small pastoral scenes by Watteau represent the 18C. An entire room is devoted to the dark historical paintings of Tournai Romantic artist Louis Gallait (1810-1887).

19C and 20C Belgian painting is well represented through Henri De Braekeleer's intimist and realistic works, Charles De Groux, Meunier, Joseph Stevens (an animal painter), Hippolyte Boulenger (landscape artist), Ensor and Emile Claus. Sculpture is not forgotten (works by Charlier, Rousseau and Van der Stappen).

Two of **Manet's** famous compositions stand out among the Impressionist works. They are *Argenteuil* (1874) and *At Father Lathuille's* (1879). Works by Seurat, Monet and Fantin-Latour are on display in the same room.

The museum also has a large collection of drawings (Van Gogh, Toulouse-Lautrec, Khnopff).

Opposite the art gallery is the courtyard of the **Town Hall** (**C H**) which stands on the site of the old St Martin's Abbey (11C). The Romanesque crypt has survived. The **abbot's palace** (1763) was built to designs by Laurent Dewez *(qv)*. It has fine neo-Classical frontages.

Musée d'Histoire naturelle (**C M⁶**) ⊙ – The natural history museum overlooks the courtyard of the Town Hall. Its neo-Classical interior resembles the natural history laboratories of the 19C. The collections are set out in various glass display cabinets (some of them have an educational objective) around the main gallery. The square room at the end contains a series of dioramas and a chance to observe a number of living creatures in the reptile house is a pleasant way to round off the visit (lizards, snakes, fish, tortoises etc). Temporary exhibitions are often organised here.

Cross Square Bonduelle to Place Reine Astrid I.

Musée de la Tapisserie (**C M⁴**) ⊙ – The elegant façade of this museum overlooks Place de la Reine Astrid. The museum evokes an activity which flourished in Tournai from the 15C to the 18C. Tournai tapestry-making reached a peak between 1450 and 1550, and the small number of tapestries exhibited from this period show the main features including the variety in the subject matter (history, mythology, heraldry), bright colours and very elegant drawing. Numerous figures in 15C costume rival each other in magnificence in these lively, crowded compositions in which several scenes are superposed, as in the **Battle of Roncevalles** or **Famine in Jerusalem**.

A large part of the museum is given over to modern tapestry with the "Force murale" group from the 1940s (Louis Delfour, Edmond Dubrunfaut and Roger Somville) as well as contemporary tapestry where the play of textures is often a kind of sculpture. Temporary exhibitions complete this illustration of tapestry making.

The museum also has a workshop where tapestry-makers can be seen at work.

Grand-Place (**C**) – This square is in fact triangular and is overlooked by the cathedral towers. There is a statue of Christine de Lalaing in the middle. The belfry stands at one end, and **église St Quentin** at the other. This church has been completely restored. In the circular chapel on the north side is a 14C tomb decorated with weepers and topped by a silver statue of Notre-Dame-de-la-Treille which is carried in the procession held to celebrate the Feast of the Nativity.

The square was destroyed in 1940, but has had some beautiful houses rebuilt around it, such as the **clothmakers' hall** (1610) (**C A**), built in a transitional style from Gothic to Baroque. Further to the right, there is a beautiful brick house (**C B**) dating from the Baroque period. It used to be the tithe barn.

Carriage rides ⊙ and a small **tourist train** ⊙ all leave from Grand-Place.

Musée du Folklore (**C M**¹) ⊘ – *Take the Réduit des Sions from Grand-Place to reach the museum.*

The collections exhibited in the "Tournai House" (façades from 1673) bring to life the popular arts and traditions of Tournai and the surrounding area, as well as evoking everyday life. The house is typical of the Spanish style of architecture. There are interesting reconstructions on the ground floor including a public house, a "balotil" (hosier's) workshop with its knitting machine, and the craft room in which models serve as reminders of the many crafts of days gone by. On the first floor note the carnival room and the pharmacy. On the second floor, there is a model of 17C Tournai, which is a reproduction of one made for Louis XIV.

The **Tour St-Georges** is nearby (**C**). It used to be part of the initial 11C – 12C town fortifications.

Musée des Arts décoratifs (**C M**⁵) ⊘ – This museum has a large collection of porcelain from the royal and imperial works established in Tournai in the 18C. Note the service with the bird-motifs based on work by Buffon. It was ordered by the Duke d'Orléans. On the first floor is a collection of Tournai coinage and some remarkable pieces of silver plate including a soup tureen and its very rare silver-gilt interior dating from 1787.

Musée d'Histoire et d'Archéologie (**C M**³) ⊘ – This museum is in what used to be the pawnshop built by Coebergher in the 17C. On the ground floor there is a collection of Gallo-Roman exhibits uncovered during archeological digs. Note the extensive collection of ceramics and glassware including a 4C baby's feeding bottle and a 3C-4C **Gallo-Roman lead sarcophagus** ★ found in 1989 beneath a street near the museum. There is also a **Roman well** dug out of the trunk of a hollow oak tree. The Merovingian section on the first floor contains objects found around the royal tomb of Childeric, which was discovered in 1653. Among the exhibits is the skeleton of one of the horses sacrificed during the funeral. The second floor is given over to prehistory and protohistory.

★**Pont des Trous** (**AY**) – This bridge is a reminder of age-old military architecture. It was part of the second set of town walls erected in the 13C and was built to defend the entrance to the town from the River Scheldt that flows through it. There is a beautiful **view** ★ of the bridge from the neighbouring bridge (boulevard Delwart). This side of the bridge is rounded; the side facing the town is flat. Beyond it is the outline of the cathedral silhouetted in the distance. The bridge was raised 2.4m – 8ft in 1948 to ease access for river traffic.

Romanesque houses (**BY K**) – Near the church dedicated to St Brice, two houses have restored late-12C façades. They constitute a rare example of secular Scaldian Romanesque architecture *(qv)*, with windows divided by central colonettes and aligned between two stone string courses.

There is a Gothic house further along (13C-15C) (**BY L**), which develops the principles first seen in the Romanesque houses.

Tours Marvis (**BZ**) **and tours St-Jean** (**BZ**) – These four towers, which were once part of the 13C fortifications, overlook pretty gardens on Boulevard Walter de Marvis.

Tour Henri VIII (**ABY**) ⊘ – This powerful 16C tower built while Tournai was in the hands of Henry VIII of England now houses an **arms museum.**

Église St-Jacques (**C**) – The style of this church dedicated to St James is characteristic of the transition from Romanesque to Gothic architecture. The porch is surmounted by a thick square tower with turrets. An arcaded gallery runs along outside the nave; inside, this gallery forms an elegant traceried bridge over the transept crossing. It extends into the nave by a triforium.

EXCURSIONS

Château d'Antoing ⊘ – *6km – 3.75 miles southeast on the N 502.*
A few traces of the 12C walls, the 15C keep and the Renaissance façade recall the ancient origins of this castle, rebuilt in the 19C in the neo-Gothic style. Some of the outbuildings were lent to the Jesuits when they were forced to leave France. Charles de Gaulle was a pupil here from 1907-1908. The **chapel** still has a rich collection of carved gravestones, particularly those of the de Melun family (early 15C). From the top of the **keep,** there is a beautiful **view** of the region. The rooms in the keep (Gothic furniture) are open to visitors.

Mont-St-Aubert – *6km – 3.75 miles to the north.*
This hill rises to a height of 149m – 488ft and has become a holiday centre.
There is a beautiful **panoramic view** ★ of the Flanders plain from the cemetery near the church. Tournai and the cathedral can just be seen to the south, behind the trees. The conurbation of Roubaix-Tourcoing can be seen on the horizon to the west.

Pierre Brunehault – *10km – 6.25 miles by ③ on the town plan; at the Hollain exit, turn right.*

Near the ancient Roman road or "Brunehault road" from Tournai to Bavay stands the Brunehault Stone. It is a trapezoidal menhir 4.5m – 15ft high, similar to the Zeupire Stone *(see Charleroi, Gozée)*.

Leuze-en-Hainaut – *13km – 8 miles east by ② on the town plan.*
The vast **collegiate church** dedicated to St Peter was built in 1745 on the site of the old Gothic church destroyed by fire.
The plain exterior forms a stark contrast to the majesty of the interior. Note the beautiful 18C woodwork especially the Louis XV panelling, the confessionals carved with various motifs, the pulpit under which St Peter in chains is represented, and the organ case.

TROIS-PONTS
Liège – Population 2 183
Michelin maps 409 K4 or 214 fold 8

This is a picturesque village, well situated at the confluence of the Salm and the Amblève. It makes an excellent excursion centre.

EXCURSIONS

Salm Valley – *13km – 8 miles to Vielsam.*
This pleasant country valley was once a principality under the rule of the Princes of Salm. It was dependent upon the Duchy of Luxembourg. The River Salm flows rapidly along a winding course through a deep steep-sided valley. The road, edged with beautiful trees, runs alongside the river.

Grand-Halleux – The **domaine de Monti** ⊘ is nearby.
When leaving Grand-Halleux, take a road on the left and follow the signs. This estate has a vast forest in which the wild life of the Luxembourg Ardennes thrive (stags, roe deer, fallow deer, wild boars). There are also moufflons (wild sheep).

Vielsalm – The Macralles (witches') Sabbath takes place on the evening of 20 July in a wood near the town. The next day it is followed by the Bilberry Festival.

★**Circuit des Panoramas** – *44km – 27.3 miles.* This signposted tourist route consists of two circular tours wending their way up hill and down dale and offering extensive panoramic views of the Amblève or the Salm. The scenic route known as the "**boucle de Wanne**" to the southeast *(23km – 14.25 miles)* follows the lower course of the Salm *(see above)*. The road leaves the forest near Henumont before going down and then up again to Wanne, amid pretty landscapes. The road then reaches Aisomont. A dry ski slope (Val de Wanne) has been created to the right, just before this village. The next stop is Trois-Ponts.
Climb to the west by taking the "**boucle de Basse-Bodeux**" *(21km – 13 miles)* between the Salm and Baleur Valleys (towards Basse-Bodeux), then turn left towards Mont-de-Fosse. Beyond St-Jacques, Fosse and Reharmont, the scenic route crosses the N 651 and goes on to Haute-Bodeux. Just before Basse-Bodeux, turn left. The road crosses a beautiful forest near two of the upper basins of the power station, filled by pumping *(qv)*. Return to Trois-Ponts by going down through the hamlet of Brume.

TURNHOUT
Antwerpen – Population 36 547
Michelin maps 409 H2 or 214 fold 8 or 214 fold 16

Turnhout is the main town of the Antwerp Kempen region. It is also an industrial and commercial centre.
It was part of the Brabant province from the 12C to the 18C. Emperor Charles V made it a seigneury which he gave to his sister Mary of Hungary.
After the Treaty of Münster in 1648, Turnhout became a fiefdom held by the Orange-Nassau dynasty until 1753.
The Battle of Turnhout in October 1789 has remained famous. It resulted in the **Brabant Revolution** which rid the country of the Austrians for a short while. By the end of 1790, however, they had occupied the country again.
The town specialises in the production of playing cards.

SIGHTS

Grote Markt (**Z**) – **St.-Pieterskerk** is in the centre of the square. The church dates from the 15C and the 18C. It contains an interesting 19C pulpit, choirstalls dating from 1713 brought here from the old Corsendonk priory (in Oud-Turnhout, east of the town) and Baroque confessionals from 1740.
The neo-Classical Town Hall was inaugurated in 1961.

TURNHOUT

Baron Fr. Du Fourstr. ..... Y 2
Beekstr. .... Z 3
Deken Adamsstr. .... Z 5
Druivenstr. .... Z 6
Gasthuisstr. .... Z 7
Guldensporenlei .... Y 9
Hannuitstr. .... Y 12
Hofpoort .... Z 13
Kasteelstr. .... Y 14
Koningin
  Elisabethlei .... Y 16
Korte Gasthuisstr. .... Z 17
Kwakkelstr. .... Z 18
Mermansstr. .... Z 19
Otterstr. .... Z 21
Oude Vaartstr. .... Y 22
Renier
  Sniedersstr. .... Z 23
Sint Antoniusstr. .... Z 25
Spoorwegstr. .... Z 26
Veldstr. .... Z 28
Victoriestr. .... Z 29
Wezenstr. .... Y 31

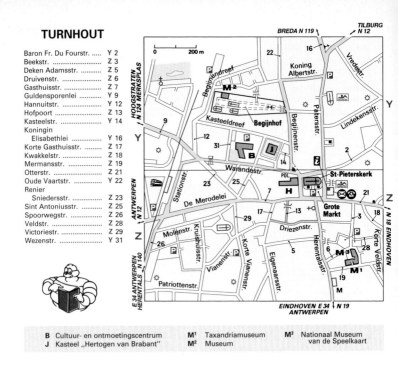

B Cultuur- en ontmoetingscentrum	M¹ Taxandriamuseum
J Kasteel „Hertogen van Brabant"	M² Museum
	M³ Nationaal Museum van de Speelkaart

Kasteel "Hertogen van Brabant" (Y J) – This solid, four-sided construction surrounded by water dates from the 13C to 17C. In the Middle Ages it was a hunting lodge for the Dukes of Brabant, who came to hunt the game in Kempen Forest. Mary of Hungary, who divided her time between Turnhout and Binche, made it into a luxurious residence. The castle now houses the Law Courts.
A modern **cultural centre** (Y B), De Warande, was built nearby in 1972.

Taxandriamuseum (Z M¹) ⏱ – This museum, in a 16C town house, deals with the archeology, local art and folklore of the Kempen region, which was called Taxandria in the days of the Ancient Romans.
There are extensive collections (note the Merovingian buckles) and an interesting reconstruction of a Kempen kitchen.

Begijnhof (Y) ⏱ – Founded in the 14C and rebuilt in the 16C and 17C after a fire, this is a charming enclosure in which the houses are arranged around a small triangular square overlooked by the Baroque church.
In the house at no 56, there is a small **museum** (Y M²) ⏱ devoted to life in the convent.

Nationaal Museum van de Speelkaart (Z M³) ⏱ – An old playing cards factory has been turned into a museum devoted to this industry which has existed in Turnhout since 1826. Besides the old machines used to make or print the cards, there is an extensive collection of packs of cards from all over the world, the oldest dating from about the year 1500.

Windmolen (*via Otterstraat*) (Z 21) – This pretty windmill was built in 1848 and has been restored. It is called "De Grote Bentel".

EXCURSIONS

Hoogstraten – *18km – 11 miles northwest*. Michelin map 212 fold 16.
A wide avenue planted with lime trees crosses this small town, overlooked by the magnificent tower-porch of its church, **St.-Catharinakerk** ⏱. The tower is built of brick with string courses of white stone. It was rebuilt after its destruction in 1944, and remains most impressive at a height of 105m – 344ft.
The church was designed by Rombout Keldermans (*qv*) in the 16C.
Beautiful 16C stalls can be seen inside in the chancel. The tomb of Antoine de Lalaing and his spouse Elisabeth de Culembourg, by Jean Mone, is equally admirable. Note too the wonderful 14-16C stained-glass windows and the series of tapestries.

Begijnhof – This Beguine convent was probably founded at the end of the 14C, and was rebuilt after having been burnt to the ground in 1506. It is a modest enclosure with modest cottages surrounding a shaded lawn. The 17C Baroque church has an elegant porch.

Baarle-Hertog – *14km – 8.5 miles north.* Michelin map 212 fold 16.

Baarle-Hertog is a Belgian enclave in Dutch territory. In the 12C the village of Baarle was divided into two. One part fell to the Duke of Brabant (Baarle-Hertog); the other was attached to the Breda seigneury and named **Baarle-Nassau** when Breda became the fiefdom of the Nassau family at the beginning of the 15C.

Each community now has its own Town Hall, church, police station, school and post office, and the border established in 1831 scrupulously respected community boundaries. However, except for the market square, which is definitely part of the Netherlands, the limits of the two territories get very confused.

The Belgian church can be recognised by its characteristic onion dome but it is less clear to which country the houses belong. Mind you, a close look at the plaques bearing the house numbers will help, since these are marked with the national colours.

VERVIERS

Liège – Population 46 997
Michelin maps 409 K4 or 213 fold 23
Plan of the conurbation in the current Michelin Red Guide Benelux

Verviers lies in the Vesdre Valley near the Hautes Fagnes. It is a large industrial town that once specialised in textiles.

It has few old historical monuments, as it was only recognised as a town in 1651. To the south the upper town consists of a well-to-do district, with expensive houses pleasantly situated amidst trees and shrubs.

Verviers is the birthplace of the violinist **Henri Vieuxtemps** (1820-1881). Henri Pirenne, author of a *History of Belgium* in seven volumes, was also born here (1862-1935).

Verviers' delicious gingerbread is famous.

Hôtel de ville (D H) – This elegant 18C building stands on a hill. It has many windows, highlighted with subtle ornamentation, and a **perron** *(see Liège)* in front of it.

★**Musée des Beaux-Arts et de la Céramique** (D M¹) ⊙ – Established in an old 17C hospice, this museum contains extensive collections of porcelain, Belgian and foreign glazed earthenware (faïence), old Raeren sandstone pottery and paintings and sculptures from the 14C to the 19C. They include Cornelis de Vos's *Portrait of a*

VERVIERS

Brou (R. du)	C 4	Carmes (R. des)	D 6	Paroisse (R. de la)	D 33
Crapaurue	D	Chêne (Pont du)	C 8	Raines (R. des)	D 34
Martyr (Pl. du)	C 28	Coronmeuse (R.)	D 10	Récollets (Pont des)	C 36
Saint-Laurent (Pont)	C 37	Harmonie (Av. de l')	C 22	Sommeville (Pl.)	D 39
Spintay (R.)	C	Lions (Pont aux)	D 25	Sommeville (Pont)	D 40
Verte (Pl.)	C	Maçons (Quai des)	D 27	Théâtre (R. du)	C 42
		Ortmans-Hauzeur (R.)	D 30	Thier-Mère-Dieu (R.)	D 43
		Palais de Justice (Pl. du)	D 31	Tribunal (R. du)	D 45

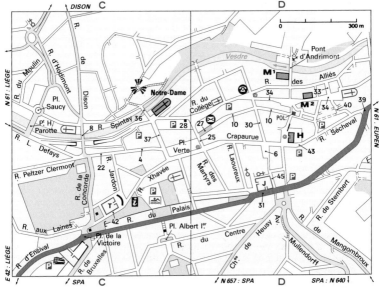

H Hôtel de ville	M¹ Musée des Beaux-Arts et de la Céramique	M² Musée d'Archéologie et de Folklore

Child highlighted against a froth of lace, and a panel by Pieter Pourbus depicting many characters. Engravings by artists from Liège dating from the period between the 16C and the present are kept in a chest of drawers. Upstairs, there is a collection of contemporary (Tytgat, Magritte) and non-figurative works.

Musée d'Archéologie et de Folklore (**D M²**) ⊘ – This museum occupies an 18C town house, containing furniture of various styles (Louis XIII and Charles X). It also has a collection of Dutch furniture (in the Main Drawing Room) and mementoes of the violinist Henri Vieuxtemps. On the first floor, there is a Louis XV drawing room with furniture made in Liège. On the second floor is the collection of objects unearthed during digs in the region. An interesting **lace**★ collection is displayed in drawers, with photographic enlargements making it possible to appreciate the delicacy of the work.

Musée de la Laine ⊘ – *8, route Séroule; take Chaussée de Heusy* (**D**).
Three rooms of the Institut supérieur national de l'État exhibit looms, tools, engravings and other documents on the subject of working with wool, thread and cloth before 1800.

Église Notre-Dame (**C**) – This church was rebuilt in the 18C. Since the 17C, pilgrims have come here to pray to the Black Madonna of the Recollects, a statue which was discovered in a strangely modified posture after an earthquake in 1692.

EXCURSIONS

★★**Barrage de la Gileppe** – *13km – 8 miles east on the N 61.*
This dam was built on a tributary of the Vesdre between 1869 and 1876, and raised between 1967 and 1971. It is 62m – 203ft high, 320m – 1 049ft long on a rock base of 235m – 771ft. Its capacity doubled and rose to 27 million m³ – 954 million cu.ft. It supplies the region with both drinking and industrial water.
There is a splendid **view**★★ of the wooded valley, the lion dominating the crest of the dam and the reservoir, which covers more than 120 hectares – 296 acres *(sports activities are prohibited on the reservoir and its shores).*

Limbourg – *7.5km – 4.5 miles east on the N 61.*
Perched on a rock above the town of Dolhain, which lies in the Vesdre Valley, Limbourg was the capital of a duchy until the 13C. After the Battle of **Worringen** in 1288, Limbourg was annexed to Brabant and shared its fortunes until the end of the 18C. It was a major stronghold and, as such, was besieged many times, notably by Louis XIV.
The town walls, the old Gothic church dedicated to St George, the quiet streets and the central paved square planted with lime trees, make a very picturesque scene.

From Verviers to Val-Dieu – *15km – 9.3 miles north. Leave on the E 42. At Battice, take the N 627, then turn right to Charneux. At Charneux, head for Thimister and turn left 1km – 0.5 mile after a small bridge.*

Croix de Charneux – This great concrete Cross was built on a hill 269m – 882ft high from which there is a beautiful view of the region. Nearby is the dome from an observation post (1932-1935) from the Battice fort that defended Liège.
Continue north to Val-Dieu.

Abbaye du Val-Dieu – This abbey lies in the charming Berwinne valley. The abbey was founded in about 1216, and has been occupied by the Cistercians since 1844. The vast courtyard of the abbey farm is in front of the guest quarters (1732), to the left of which are the abbey buildings and church. Rebuilt in 1934, the church still has a Gothic chancel. There are beautiful Renaissance stalls inside.

VEURNE★

West-Vlaanderen – Population 11 232
Michelin maps 409 B2 or 213 fold 1

Veurne's historical monuments are grouped around a magnificent market square, where the luxury of Flemish decoration is tempered by a slightly solemn dignity typical of the Spanish influence. Indeed, it was during the prosperous reign of the Archdukes Albert and Isabella that most of the historic buildings were erected. Veurne was a stronghold in the 9C. It expanded over the centuries and town walls were built in the 14C. Vauban laid out fortifications which were razed to the ground in 1783 on the orders of Emperor Joseph II. The town was the headquarters of the Belgian army in 1914 during the Battle of the Yser. It was bombed during both World Wars.
A large flower market is held annually on Whit Monday *(see the Calendar of Events)*. In August, the "Anno 1900" Festival takes place, with events featuring old costumes and demonstrations of crafts from the past.

Procession of the Penitents

★**Procession of the Penitents** – *See the Calendar of Events*. Every year the Sodality Brotherhood, founded in 1637, organises a procession through the town, consisting of floats where groups represent the life and death of Christ, followed by about two hundred penitents dressed in a sombre sackcloth robe with cowls over their heads. They walk barefoot and carry a heavy Cross. Georges Rodenbach describes them in *Le Carillonneur*. The Sodality Brotherhood also participates in a prayer meeting taking participants along the Stations of the Cross in the streets every Friday evening during Lent, every evening during Holy Week and on Maundy Thursday at midnight.

★★GROTE MARKT *time : 2 hours*

Veurne's vast market square is surrounded by beautiful monuments and old houses surmounted with imposing gables, pediments and cornices, most of them dating from the early 17C.

Stadhuis (**H**) ⊙ – The Town Hall was built in 1596 *(left)* and 1612 *(right)* in the Flemish Renaissance style, with a double pedimented façade and an elegant loggia. Towards the back of the building is a little onion-domed turret with a staircase in it. The walls inside are lined with magnificent **leather**★ from Cordoba (reception room) or from Mechelen (council chamber and registry office). The collegiate room is embellished with blue velvet from Utrecht. Note also the 18C furniture, and paintings including a still life attributed to Paul de Vos *(qv)*. The courtroom of the old law courts, which are accessed directly from the Town Hall, is also generally open to visitors.

Landhuis – Once a castellany (1618), the design for this building was inspired by the Stadhuis in Antwerp. Behind the old law courts stands the **belfry** (1628) (**A**), mainly Gothic in style but with a Baroque top section.

St.-Walburgakerk ⊙ – *Access via a narrow street to the right of the old law courts.*
The first church, which was destroyed by the Norsemen, was rebuilt in the 12C in the Romanesque style. A new building, on which work began in the 13C with ambitious plans, was never completed. Only the chancel was finished, and it is particularly impressive, being 27m – 88ft

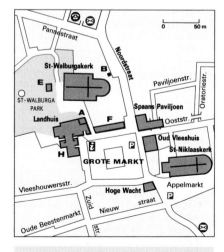

A Belfort	**F** Vijf huizen
B Klein monument	**H** Stadhuis
E Basis van een toren	

in height with numerous flying but tresses. In the 14C the base of a tower (**E**) was built in the neighbouring square. The Romanesque part of the church was renovated in the 20C.

Inside, the proportions are harmonious and impressive. Notice the Flemish Renaissance stalls (1596), a pulpit by H Pulinx (1727) representing the vision of St John in Patmos, 18C organ and rood-screen and 17C Flemish paintings.

The fortress built by Count Baldwin of the Iron Arm was built in the square west of the church.

North of the market square, note the group of **five houses**, with beautiful gables adorned with heavy windows with pilasters (**F**).

Noordstraat – In 1906 the Austrian writer Rainer Maria Rilke stayed in the old Inn of the Noble Rose, Die Nobele Rose (1572), which is now a bank. Opposite, a small monument (**B**) has been erected to commemorate the Nieuwpoort lock-keeper who caused flooding in 1914 *(qv)*.

Spaans Paviljoen – The 15C "Spanish Pavilion" on the corner of the market square and Ooststraat was the Town Hall until 1586. It was the Spanish officers' quarters in the 17C.

Oud Vleeshuis – This meat market was built in 1615 and has a pretty façade. It has been restored and now houses the town library.

Hoge Wacht – At the south end of the market square is an arcaded house built in 1636. It was once the guardroom. The side wall overlooks the apple market (Appelmarkt) and the church dedicated to St Nicholas.

St.-Niklaaskerk – This church has a beautiful massive brick **tower** ⊙ dating from the 13C and containing one of the oldest bells in Flanders, the Bomtje (1379). It is a hall-church, with three aisles of equal height inside. An interesting triptych (1534) on the high altar represents the Crucifixion. Some scholars attribute it to Van Aemstel, brother-in-law of Pieter Coecke, while others believe it to be by Van Orley.

EXCURSIONS

Lo – *15km – 9.3 miles southeast.* This little town still has a gateway flanked by turrets that was once part of the 14C ramparts. The beautiful 14C **hall-church**, surmounted with a crocketed spire, was partly reconstructed in 1924. There are interesting 17C and 18C furnishings inside.

From Veurne to Izenberge – *12km – 7.5 miles south.*

Wulveringem – Kasteel Beauvoorde ⊙ is a manor house built in the 16C and 17C on the site of a derelict castle. It is a charming building with crowstepped gables, surrounded by water and hidden behind the great trees of the park.

The interior was decorated by its last owner, Arthur Merghelynck *(qv)*. It includes 17C woodwork, extensive collections of antique furniture and objets d'art (paintings, ceramics).

Izenberge ⊙ – The **musée de plein air Bachten de Kupe** ⊙is an open-air museum also known as the "**Village of the Past**" (Antan Village). It consists of two sections – the Houtland Farm and the Village Square on which various rural buildings have been reconstructed. They contain old agricultural machinery from the province of West-Vlaanderen. A third section is being set up. There is an interesting Gothic church, with beautiful old woodwork inside. Note also the little 17C pilgrimage chapel nearby.

VILLERS-LA-VILLE ★★

Brabant Wallon – Population 8 192
Michelin maps 409 G4 or 213 fold 19

The wonderful **ruins** of Villers-la-Ville **Abbey**, north of the town, are the largest in Belgium.

★★**Abbey ruins** ⊙ – St Bernard laid the foundations of the abbey in 1147. The church and cloisters, however, were not built until 1198 and 1209. Both the Spanish and the Geuzen (Flemish and Dutch lesser nobility who initiated the revolt against Spanish rule) ransacked the convent in the 16C, and it was enclosed within fortifications in 1587. In 1789 the Austrians sacked the buildings which were then occupied by the French in 1795.

The old 13C **watermill** across from the ruins, on the Thyle, has been turned into a restaurant.

Follow the signposted tour.

Main courtyard – The courtyard is lined with 18C buildings now in ruins. The abbey palace is on the right.

Cloisters – The cloisters are vast. They were altered in the 14C and 16C. The arches surmounted by an oculus give them a certain elegant solidity.

The surrounding buildings are set out in typical Cistercian fashion. To the east is the **chapter-house**, which was refurbished in the 18C. Nearby is the 13C recumbent effigy of Gobert d'Aspremont. Above are the dorters which were also refurbished in the 18C. To the south are the calefactory, the refectory set at right angles to the cloisters and the kitchen. To the west is the undercroft with the lay-brothers' dorters above them. The abbey had up to 300 lay brothers in the 13C.

Church – The original church was built in the early 13C but collapsed in 1884. The church is sober in style, both impregnable-looking

Refectory, Villiers-la-Ville Abbey Ruins

and yet moving, as befitted a Cistercian building. The apse and transept were lit by oculi in the style of the Paris school, creating an unusual effect.

Leave the church by the west front and visit the 13C **brewery**, then go round the east end to go through the 17C and 18C **abbey quarters.**

Église de la Visitation ⊘ – This church has two beautiful Brabant **altarpieces** from the 15C and 16C illustrating the Life of the Virgin Mary and the Life of the Infant Jesus. Other noteworthy features include a 17C pulpit, a Christ Entombed from 1607, portraits of the abbots of Villers and the 17C funerary monuments of the Lords of Marbais. The eleven modern stained-glass windows were by F Crickx and G Massinon.

VIRTON

Luxembourg – Population 10 1090
Michelin maps 409 J 7 or 214 fold 11

Virton, a picturesque locality in the south of Belgium, is the capital of the **Gaume**, a region where the climate is more temperate than in neighbouring Ardennes.
In contrast to the regions situated in the east of the country, a Romance dialect is spoken in Gaume.

Musée gaumais ⊘ – *Rue d'Arlon.* This regional museum is in the old Recollects' convent, which has a jack o' the clocks. It specialises in local archeology and ethnography. There are reconstructed interiors (Gaume kitchen) and craft workshops.
Among the collections of industrial folk art, note the pieces of ornamental cast iron (firebacks and andirons) recalling that Gaume was once widely reputed for its iron smelting works.

EXCURSIONS

Montauban – *10km – 6.25 miles north. Take the Arlon road, then, in Ethe, a road to the left towards Buzenol.*
South of **Buzenol,** near the old ironworks on the edge of the stream stands a wooded promontory about 340m – 1 115ft high. It was occupied in prehistoric times, the Roman period and the Middle Ages. The remains of various fortifications can be seen here.

Musée des Sculptures romaines – This museum of Roman Sculpture includes a number of Gallo-Roman bas-reliefs discovered on the site. The most famous one represents the front part of the "vallus", the Celtic harvesting machine described by Pliny the Elder. A lifesize model was reconstructed based on a bas-relief in the Arlon Luxembourg Museum with a man working a "vallus".

From Virton to Torgny – *9km – 5.5 miles south on the Montmédy road. Turn right at Dampicourt.*

Montquintin – The village is perched on a crest with an altitude of more than 300m – 984ft. Near the church, a farm from 1765 contains the **Musée de la Vie paysanne** ⊙, a museum of rural life. The building itself is representative of traditional rural architecture and it serves as a reminder of life in Gaume in bygone days. Besides the living quarters, it is possible to visit the barn and the cowshed, with farm vehicles and agricultural machinery in the hayloft.

Return to the Malmédy road, then turn right towards Torgny.

Torgny – This is the southernmost locality in Belgium.
In this flower-bedecked village the houses are built of a slightly golden stone, sometimes covered with rough-cast. They have pantile roofs and stand in rows on the open slopes of a valley where the particularly temperate climate permits the cultivation of vines.

VOERSTREEK
Les FOURONS – Limburg – Population 3 593
Michelin map 409 K 3 or 213 fold 23

This is an enclave within the province of Liège, a lush green area in which small rivers such as the Voer, Gulp and Berwinne have carved out valleys that snake their way through delightful wooded hillsides, fertile pastures and orchards.

St.-Martens-Voeren – The most outstanding features are the church with its Romanesque tower and a small 18C chateau, Het Veltmanshuis, that is now used as an arts centre.

St.-Pieters-Voeren – Near a lake are the superb buildings that once formed a **Commandery** ⊙ of the Teutonic Order. It was first constructed in 1242 but was rebuilt in the 17C.

WALCOURT
Namur – Population 15 523
Michelin maps 409 G5 or 213 fold 3

This picturesque little old town stands on the site of a former stronghold.
Each year *(see the Calendar of Events)* there is a famous procession in honour of Our Lady of Walcourt. The participants parade right round the town's perimeter in what is called the "**Grand Tour**" accompanied by a "**military march**" *(see Charleroi,)* an escort dressed as Napoleonic soldiers or zouaves and playing fifes and drums.
In the middle of the day, the "Jeu scénique du Jardinet" is enacted around a birch tree, a short play commemorating the miracle of the statue of the Virgin Mary which is said to have fled the basilica when it burned down in the 13C and to have been later found in a tree.

★**Basilique St-Materne** – This basilica church stands at the top of a hill, on the site of a Mosan Romanesque building of which the lower section of the forepart and the Gothic church still remain. The church was built between the early 13C and the early 16C. It has an amusing 17C bell tower with an onion dome (rebuilt in 1926). The plain **interior**, consisting of five naves in grey stone and brick, is richly furnished. The remarkable white stone **rood-screen**★ (1531) is said to have been donated by Emperor Charles V. The structure is Gothic but the Renaissance decoration abounds with statues, medallions and ornamental foliage. A 16C calvary is at the top.
The very simple stalls dating from the 16C have misericords carved with satirical motifs. The statue of Our Lady of Walcourt is in the north transept. This 10C Virgin Mary in Majesty is one of the oldest Virgins in Belgium. The statue is made of wood covered with silver plates.

★**Treasury** ⊙ – The church plate is displayed in the presbytery. It includes valuable works of art such as a 15C monstrance, a 14C silver statue of the Virgin Mary, a little 13C turret-reliquary, and most outstanding of all a 13C reliquary-Cross with a delicate decoration typical of the style of the famous goldsmith Hugo d'Oignies *(qv)*.

If you intend combining a tour of Belgium and Luxembourg with a visit to one of the neighbouring countries, remember to take the appropriate Michelin Green Guide *to* Netherlands, Germany *or* France.

Brabant Wallon – Population 22 660
Michelin maps 409 G3 or 213 fold 18

Thou fatal Waterloo.
Millions of tongues record thee, and anew
Their children's lips shall echo them, and say -
"Here, where the sword united nations drew,
Our countrymen were warring on that day!"
And this is much, and all which will not pass away.
(Lord Byron)

It was at Waterloo on 18 June 1815 that the Allied Anglo-Dutch forces, under the command of the Duke of Wellington, and the Prussians, under von Blücher, put an end to the Napoleon's dreams of Empire-building, thereby turning over a new page in European history.

The Duchess of Richmond's Ball

On 15 June 1815, the Duchess of Richmond gave a ball in Brussels and it has remained famous because it was during the evening that a letter arrived informing the Commander-in-Chief of the Allied forces, the Duke of Wellington, that Napoleon was now only 14 miles from the capital. It is said that the ballroom emptied in a mere 20 minutes. Nobody knows exactly which of the private mansions in the town hosted the ball.

"...Everything was joyous as a church bell pealing merrily after a wedding ceremony. Then came silence! Listen! A sinister noise resounded, like the knell of the funeral bell! The fearsome sound can still be heard. It is as if the clouds were acting as echoes. It seems to be coming nearer and more distinct with each passing minute. It is more and more terrifying. It is the brazen voice of battle beginning its clamour!... (Lord George Byron)

The battle – After the Congress of Vienna signed on 25th March, France was threatened with encirclement and the danger was becoming increasingly evident, especially in the north where two Allied armies had already massed. Napoleon ordered forced marches and advanced to meet them with the cunning scheme of attempting to crush each army separately, before they had time to join forces. On 14 June Napoleon stopped at Beaumont *(qv)*. Two days later, he won his last victory against Blücher at **Ligny** *(northeast of Charleroi),* a victory which nonetheless cost him dearly in lives of men and failed to rout the Prussian army. Napoleon's Maréchal Ney had meanwhile failed to defeat the British in Quatre-Bras.

On 17 June Napoleon set off to do battle with Wellington. He arrived on the Mont St-Jean plain and, as darkness fell, established his headquarters at the farm known as **Le Caillou**. Wellington had set up his headquarters at **Waterloo**.

On 18 June bad weather delayed the arrival of some of the French troops, so the battle did not begin until almost noon, a delay which was to be vital to the final outcome of the battle.

While the French artillery and Napoleon's observation post were positioned near the staging-inn called **Cabaret de la Belle Alliance**, British and French troops engaged each other until nightfall in bloody combat by the **Hougoumont** farmhouse. This was one of three farmhouses which were key positions to be won by an army trying to gain possession of the Mont St-Jean. After hours of fierce skirmishing, the French troops gave up the assault and fell back.

The focus of the battlefield then shifted to **La Haie Sainte**, a farm which was eventually won by the French after a vicious struggle, and then on to the farm at **La Papelotte**. At about 4pm, beneath a leaden sky, French troops plunged into the famous **valley of the sunken road** ("chemin creux"), in which sweeping French calvary charges led by Ney and General Kellermann were savagely battered by British fire, but nonetheless managed to inflict heavy losses on Wellington's troops, who were now in urgent need of reinforcement from their Prussian allies.

Napoleon was waiting for reinforcements of 30 000 men led by Maréchal de Grouchy. They were expected to arrive from Wavre to the east. Blücher, however, having regrouped his troops and evaded Grouchy, circumvented the French army's right flank to join the British army. The Prussian front guard then took the village of **Plancenoit** and began to put pressure on Napoleon's southeast flank.

Surrounded, Napoleon finally sent his Imperial Guard to support Ney and engage with the British troops. The result was utter carnage on the sunken road, as Wellington had had time to reorganise his defence strategy to include the Prussian reinforcements, and the allied forces' fire shattered the closely packed ranks of Napoleon's Imperial Guard.

As night fell over the battlefield, littered with the bodies of 49 000 dead and wounded, the defeated French troops retreated, completely routed despite Ney's heroic efforts. Napoleon disappeared to Genappe under cover of darkness and Wellington joined Blücher at the **Belle Alliance inn**.

THE BATTLEFIELD

In 1861, Victor Hugo stayed in the Hôtel des Colonnes in Mont St-Jean (it no longer exists) to write the chapter in *Les Misérables* describing the battle. Stendhal had already done so in the opening pages of his novel *The Charterhouse of Parma* (1839).

The physionomy of the battlefield has changed greatly since 1815 (a motorway and a main road now cross it), but the plain is nevertheless dotted with historical buildings and commemorative monuments.

Every year a historical re-enactment is held here, with more than 2 000 participants.

Butte du Lion

Butte du Lion ⊘ – This 45m – 147ft high mound was constructed in 1826 by the kingdom of the Netherlands, on the spot where the Prince of Orange was wounded fighting the Imperial Guard. A cast-iron lion weighing 28 tonnes is at the top. Legend has it that the statue was made from the gunmetal of cannon captured on the battlefield but this is actually untrue.

There is a good general view of the site from the top. At the foot of the mound, to the south, the famous valley of sunken road *("chemin creux")* has been largely levelled out, as the surrounding earth was taken to build the mound.

Visitor Centre ⊘ – The centre stands at the foot of the Butte du Lion. An audiovisual presentation takes the audience into the very heart of events on 18 June 1815. A model 10m2 – 107ft2 situates the strategic points of the battle and depicts its main stages. The second part of the visit consists of a tourist film.

Panorama de la bataille ⊘ – This rotunda built in 1912 at the foot of the mound houses a grand panoramic painting 110m – 360ft in circumference and 12m – 39ft high created by the French painter Dumoulin and five other artists. It represents a few of the most striking episodes in the battle at the moment when Ney sent his calvary along the "sunken path".

On the ground floor, there is a permanent exhibition of costumes, weapons, and documents.

Musée de Cire ⊘ – This little waxworks museum stands opposite the Panorama. It contains a few waxwork figures representing Napoleon's last council-of-war with his staff at Le Caillou farm. Another display shows the three commanders of the Allied forces (the Prince of Orange, the Duke of Wellington and General Blücher).

Musée provincial du Caillou ⊘ – This museum is located south of the battlefield. Le Caillou was Napoleon's headquarters on the eve of the combat. The Emperor's bedroom still contains one of his campbeds and a few of his personal belongings. The other rooms contain the autographs of French generals involved in the 1815 campaign, maps, a bronze death mask of Napoleon on St Helena, and relics from the battlefield. In the garden, there is an ossuary dating from 1912 and the balcony from the Hôtel des Colonnes where Victor Hugo stayed in 1861. A memorial in the orchard recalls the final evening of the battalion of the Imperial Guard.

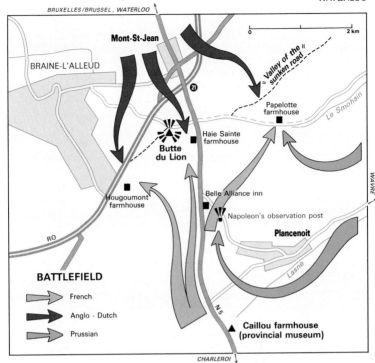

BATTLEFIELD

→ French

→ Anglo - Dutch

→ Prussian

THE TOWN

This hamlet was established from the 15C to the middle of the 17C, along the Genappe-Brussels road.

Musée Wellington ⊙ – The inn where Wellington set up his headquarters has been turned into a museum. There is the HQ itself, a museum illustrating the history of Waterloo and a library. The rooms, including Wellington's bedroom, contain engravings, arms, paintings, documents and mementoes describing Europe in 1815.

Beyond the garden is the vast, well-lit map room showing developments in the battle and containing exhibits of special historic interest such as "La Suffisante", a gun cast in Douai (1813) and captured at Waterloo.

Église St-Joseph – This church opposite the museum was originally no more than a forest chapel (1690) built to a central layout. It is still standing and now forms the entrance to the new church. Inside, numerous commemorative flagstones bear the names of officers and soldiers who fell at Waterloo.

Panorama Paintings

Grand panorama paintings were one of the most popular forms of mass entertainment in the 19C, before the advent of photography and the motion picture. They were usually exhibited in purpose-built rotundas and were often on huge cylindrical canvases which entirely surrounded the viewer, who stood on a central platform. The panorama painting technique is related to the exuberant mastery of Barque and the technique of trompe-l'œil and was originally the idea of Robert Baker, an Irishman. By portraying vast ponaramas in minute detail the painting enabled the public to glimpse foreign shores with an immediacy never before possible. Panorama paintings were usually created by teams of specialist artists. Their most common subject matter tended to be the glorification of warfare. Preliminary sketches were rescaled onto the enormous canvas using a grid, but this did not entirely eliminate distortions of perspective caused by the curve of the cylindrical canvas. It took about a year to complete a painting, which was then exhibited in its rotunda with the area between it and the viewing platform dotted with relevant objects to increase the effect of the illusion. Sadly, the popularity of the grand panorama diminished as that of the cinema grew, and many of the paintings were lost when the rotundas that housed them were demolished or put to other uses. There are now only nine left in western Europe (Austria: Salzburg and Innsbruck; Belgium: Waterloo and Brussels; Germany: Munich and Bad Frankenhausen; Switzerland: Einsiedeln, Thun and Lucerne).

WAVRE

Brabant Wallon **P** – Population 27 1620
Michelin maps 409 G3 or 213 fold 19

Wavre (pronounced "whaavre") lies amidst the hills in the Dijle Valley at the centre of a major communications network. The little statue of Maca, a laughing boy who symbolises the lighthearted spirit of the inhabitants, stands in an old church in front of the Town Hall.

Walibi ⊙ – *2km – 1.25 miles southwest on the N 238 towards Ottignies.*
This 50 hectare – 123 acre leisure park, opened in 1975, is the most popular in the country. It offers a multitude of attractions (the vertiginous Tornado, a 50m-164ft high Ferris wheel, Ali Baba's palace) and entertainments (trained dolphins, etc).
In 1987 the vast tropical-atmosphere swimming pool complex called **Aqualibi** ⊙ was inaugurated.

YPRES ★

See IEPER

*The **Michelin Green Guide France**
presents a selection of the most interesting and distinctive sights
on the main tourist routes*

ZEEBRUGGE

West-Vlaanderen
Michelin maps 409 C1 or 213 fold 3
Town plan in the current Michelin Red Guide Benelux

Zeebrugge (Bruges-sur-Mer to French-speakers) is the only Belgian deep-water coastal port. Inaugurated in 1907, it is linked to Bruges by the Baudouin Canal.
It is also a pleasant seaside resort with a small marina. Zeebrugge was a German submarine base during the First World War. It was made famous by the English operation here during the night of 22-23 April 1918 which blocked the canal and made the port unusable.

A multi-purpose port – The **outer harbour** is accessible to very large vessels. Like Ostend, it has regular passenger services to England (car-ferries to Dover, Felixstowe and Hull). It is also a container and ro-ro port, with links to England, Norway, Australia, North America, New Zealand and West and South Africa, and functions as a port of call for cruise liners and as a marina. Last but not least, it is Belgium's foremost-ranking fishing port, both in terms of the quantity of fish caught and the value of the catches.
A lock links the outer harbour to the **inner harbour** where there are three docks between the Baudouin Canal and the Leopold and Schipdonk penstocks.

Port extension – New installations intended to enlarge the outer harbour by extending it a further 3km – 1.75 miles out to sea are under construction. In particular to the east, a terminal is being built to offload and store natural gas from Algeria.
The construction of the new "West Breakwater" is being followed by the creation of two docks for container and roro ships.
The new inner harbour, a part of which has been finished since 1984, covers an area of 1 300 hectares – 3 212 acres.
The industrial estate within the harbour includes terminals to handle fruit, vegetables, cars, timber, coal, iron ore, etc.

SIGHT

Vissershaven – In front of the fishing harbour there is a marina. It is fun to watch the fishing boats, a picturesque and colourful sight.

EXCURSION

Lissewege – *4km – 2.5 miles by the N 31.*
The delightful village of Lissewege near the Baudouin Canal is overlooked by the impressive brick **tower** of its church. Built in the 13C and rebuilt in the 16C to the 17C, the church has retained its original charm (Tournai-style chancel, triforium).
All that remains of the **Ter Doest** *(1km – 0.5 miles south of Lissewege),* a daughter-house of the Abbaye des Dunes in Coxyde, are the chapel, a turreted farmhouse (part of which has been turned into a restaurant) and the vast and beautiful **abbey church** (13C), decorated with Gothic brick mouldings and surmounted by wonderful oak rafters.

ZOUTLEEUW ★

Vlaams-Brabant – Population 7 686
Michelin maps 409 I3 or 213 fold 21

This quiet and picturesque little Flemish town was once a stronghold protected by powerful walls (14C and 17C), in addition to being a clothmaking centre. It clusters around an interesting church.
Zoutleeuw was pillaged in 1678 by Louis XIV's troops. In the 18C its fortifications were demolished. Since then, the town has lived very much in the past.

★★ST.-LEONARDUSKERK ○ *time : 45min*

St Leonard's is a beautiful church that was constructed over several centuries. The east end was built in the 13C, encircled by an external passage with colonettes, and so was the north arm of the transept. The nave and the south arm of the transept were built in the 14C.
In the 15C, Mathieu de Layens built the charming Late Gothic sacristy opposite the Town Hall. The 16C bell tower, rebuilt in 1926, has a 39-chime carillon.

The interior escaped the 16C iconoclasts and is a veritable **museum**★★ of religious art.
A "marianum" (**1**) a double-sided statue of the Virgin Mary dating from 1530, hangs in the nave. The wooden altarpiece of St Anne (**2**) in the second chapel in the **south aisle** has painted panels (1565). Opposite it, there is a 16C gilded wooden triptych, also with painted panels, depicting the Glorification of the Holy Cross (**3**). In the third chapel, there is a triptych by Pieter Aertsen (1575). The medallions represent the Seven Pains of the Virgin Mary (**4**). An interesting 11C Romanesque Crucifix (**5**) surmounts the door into the sacristy.

The **south transept** has the most beautiful altarpiece (**6**) sculpted by Brussels artist Arnould de Maeler c1478, a work recounting the life of St Leonard. An older statue of the saint (1300)

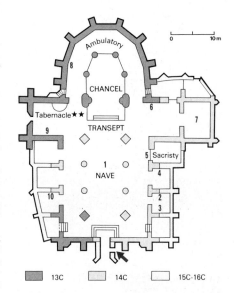

stands in the centre. The old St Leonard's Chapel (**7**) at the end of the transept contains a beautiful collection of 16C and 17C statues as well as an interesting **treasury** (gold and silver-work, copperware, and liturgical ornaments).
An exceptional series of 12C-16C statues runs along the **ambulatory.** There is also a superb six-armed brass paschal candle (**8**) made by Renier de Tirlemont in 1483. At the top there is a calvary with movingly plain figures.
The magnificent Avesne stone **tabernacle**★★ which is the pride of Zoutleeuw is in the **north transept.** This masterpiece was made in 1551 by the Antwerp artist Cornelis Floris II de Vriendt. Standing 18m – 59ft and 9 tiers high, it is decorated with groups consisting of 200 statues which are remarkably lifelike, both in their expressions and in the spontaneity of their poses. While the picturesque craftsmanship seems rather Gothic, the decoration and the composition show Italian influence.
Old Testament sacrifices decorate the base. Above them are scenes from the Garden of Eden then, above the tabernacle alcove, the Last Supper and episodes from the Old Testament. The upper tiers, superposed in a pyramid, are decorated with a multitude of characters (the Virtues, the Fathers of the Church) with the Virgin Mary right at the top. Frans Floris, brother of Cornelis, is thought to be the creator of the triptych (**9**) of the Baptism of Christ, opposite the tabernacle. Note the statues in the chapels in the **north aisle** and, in the second-last chapel (Lady Chapel), painted medallions representing the Seven Joys of the Virgin Mary (**10**) by Pieter Aertsen (1554).

ADDITIONAL SIGHT

Stadhuis – This charming Renaissance building was constructed during the reign of Emperor Charles V (1530) to plans attributed to Mechelen-born Rombout Keldermans. There is a traceried perron at the front. The façade is surmounted by a crowstepped gable and includes tall basket-handle windows. The Town Hall houses the tourist office.
The **drapers' hall** to the right, with a brick façade striped with bands of white stone, dates from the 14C.

Château de Vianden

Grand Duchy of
Luxembourg

BERDORF

Population 860

Michelin maps 409 M6 or 215 fold 3 – Local map see PETITE SUISSE LUXEMBOURGEOISE

This is a good departure point for excursions, situated at the heart of Luxembourg's so-called "Petite Suisse" (Mini-Switzerland) region, on a plateau with sides dropping steeply down to form crests or "escarpments" *(qv)* overlooking the Sûre Valley and the Mullerthal. A rock-climbing school comes here regularly to practise.

In the church, the high altar rests on a carved Roman block of stone depicting the four divinities Minerva, Juno, Apollo and Hercules.

RAMBLES

There are many footpaths which leave from Berdorf. They are marked on a noticeboard in the leisure centre next to the crazy golf course.

Promenade B – This path *(qv)* which runs along the edge of the "escarpment" to the northwest of Berdorf before dropping down to Grundhof, is particularly spectacular along this stretch. It links several viewpoints that can also be reached by road from Berdorf :

★★**Île du Diable** – *Leave the Mullerthal road on the left and carry on towards the cemetery. Once past this, take the footpath on the left with the campsite on the right.* Stroll through the pleasant pine forests to reach *(5min)* the end of the "escarpment". There are **magnificent views** of the Mullerthal and in the background the wild wooded countryside around Beaufort.

★**Sieweschluff** – *Take the Hammhof (Hamm farmhouse) road north, then turn left.* Follow the F 2 path then the footpath leading to the plateau *(10min)*. There is a marvellous **view** across the Sûre Valley and its wooded surroundings.

★**Kasselt** – This promontory 353m – 1 158ft in altitude lies to the north of the Sieweschluff and affords an extensive **view** of the Sûre Valley. The river forms a meander here at the point where it is joined by its tributary the Ernz Noire. The view also encompasses the village of Grundhof.

★**Werschrumschluff** – *2km – 1.25 miles south on the Mullerthal road.* The rock overhanging the road to the left is called the **pulpit** (Predigstuhl). From here it is possible to set off and explore the **Werschrumschluff**★, an immense gorge between two steep, rocky walls.

CLERVAUX★

Population 1 680

Michelin maps 409 L5 or 215 fold 10

Clervaux is a major tourist centre, built in a remarkable **setting**★★ in the heart of the thickly wooded Oesling region *(qv)*. The slate roofs cluster on a promontory formed by the River Clerve, around a feudal castle and the parish church which was built in 1910 in the Rhenish Romanesque style. The Abbaye St-Maurice et St-Maur, on the hill to the west, overlooks the valley, while its roofs disappear from view amidst the trees.

Clervaux is part of the Germano-Luxembourg nature reserve *(qv)*.

★★**Viewpoints** – On the road coming from Luxembourg, there are two viewpoints giving good overall views of the town's setting.

SIGHTS

★**Château** ⊙ – The château is a 12C fortress which was modified in the 17C and flanked by a number of towers. To the south are the Burgundy Tower surmounted by a small bellcote, and to the right the rather squat Brandenburg Tower.

In the restored Renaissance wing *(north)* there is an **exhibition of models**★ of the various manor-houses and fortresses in the Grand Duchy of Luxembourg.

On the second floor there is an exhibition of photographs by Edward Steichen, the American photographer of Luxembourg origin : **The Family of Man.**

Mementoes of the Battle of the Bulge *(qv)* are on display in the south wing.

Abbaye St Maurice et St Maur – This abbey was founded in 1909 by Benedictines from Solesmes, a French abbey in the Sarthe Valley. It is a vast set of buildings in brown schist, rebuilt in 1945.

The **abbey church,** which was rebuilt in a style rather different from the original Rhenish church, is fronted by a beautiful hexagonal tower in the Burgundy Romanesque style, reminiscent of the "Holy Water" (Eau Bénite) bell tower of the old Cluny Abbey.

The interior, which has all the austerity typical of Romanesque buildings, is lit by means of sparkling stained-glass windows. Near the entrance, on the left, there is a 15C Pièta altarpiece with canopies in a very delicate openwork dais. The high altar, by French sculptor Kaeppelin, is adorned with four winged subjects. There are two finely worked 16C Rhenish altarpieces, still essentially Gothic in style, in the arms of the transept, opposite one another.

An exhibition in the crypt explains 20C monastic life.

EXCURSIONS

Vallée de la Clerve – *11km – 6.75 miles south as far as Wilwerwiltz.*
The river which gave Clervaux its name flows through this pleasant valley of meadows at the foot of wooded slopes.

From Clervaux to Troisvierges via Hachiville – *23km – 14.25 miles northwest on the N 18, the N 12 and then a road on the left.*

Hachiville – Hachiville near the Belgian-Luxembourg border is a village typical of the Oesling region *(qv)*.
In the church there is an early 16C sculpted Brabant style **altarpiece.** It represents the joys and sorrows of the Virgin Mary in a series of attractive compositions.
Pilgrims have come to pray to the Virgin Mary in the **chapel-hermitage** built near a spring in the woods 2km – 1.25 miles northwest for 500 years.

From Hachiville return to the N 12 and take this road to Troisvierges.

Troisvierges – This village is located on a plateau at an altitude of over 400m – 1 312ft. The River Woltz (which becomes the Clerve at Clervaux) flows right through the town. Troisvierges has an onion-domed **church,** built by the Recollects in the 17C. The interior is decorated with beautiful Baroque furniture including the: pulpit and confessionals. The nave is separated from the chancel by two monumental altars. Niches in the left altarpiece contain statues of the three Virgins Faith, Hope and Charity which are venerated by pilgrims. *The Raising of the Cross* on the high altar is by the Rubens school.

Belgium and Luxembourg on a single sheet: Michelin map no 409 (1:350 000)

DIEKIRCH

Population 5 510
Michelin maps 409 L6 or 215 fold 3

Diekirch, a commercial and cultural centre, is spread along the lower Sûre Valley, on the borders of the Gutland and Oesling regions *(qv)*. The Herrenberg (at a height of 394m – 1 292ft) overlooking the town marks the first foothills of the Oesling.
Diekirch is well-known for its brewery, which produces the famous Diekirch beer.
This is also a pleasant tourist centre with a pedestrian precinct. The banks of the Sûre have been turned into a park. In the area around Diekirch, there are many signposted footpaths *(leaflet available from the tourist office)*.

SIGHTS

Musée ⊙ – *Place Guillaume, where the decanal church stands.*
This little museum is behind the bandstand. It houses in particular 3C **Roman mosaics.** The most remarkable of these pavements (3.5m – 11ft by 4.75m – 15ft) depicts at its centre the head of the Medusa with two faces.

Église St-Laurent ⊙ – *Access on foot from the decanal church via the Esplanade and the fourth street on the right.*
This little church dedicated to St Lawrence is hidden behind a circlet of houses in the old district of the town. It has been a religious site since the 5C.
The Romanesque nave on the right was built over a Roman building. The nave on the left is Gothic and contains frescoes dating from the 15C (above the altar) and the 16C (in the chancel).
About thirty sarcophagi were found beneath the church in 1961 during archeological digs. Most of them were Merovingian.

EXCURSIONS

Deiwelselter – *2km – 1.25 miles south on the Larochette road.*
After a hairpin bend and before the Gilsdorf road, take Footpath D on the right. It leads through the woods to this little monument called "Devil's Altar". The stones are said to have come from an ancient dolmen.
Outside the woods, there are beautiful views of the town.

Brandenbourg – *9km – 5.5 miles on the Reisdorf road to the east, and then the first left.*
This charming village is in the valley of the Blees, a tributary of the Sûre, and is overlooked by the ruins of a 12C castle on the top of a hill.
A small rural life museum has been set up in the **maison Al Branebuurg** ⊙. It contains literature on the region and a collection of everyday objects from times past.

ECHTERNACH ★

Located in the lower Sûre Valley, Echternach is a well-known tourist centre and the main town in the part of Luxembourg known as the "Petite Suisse" (Mini-Switzerland). Its overriding feature is the abbey founded in 698 by **St Willibrord.** This Anglo-Saxon, who was ordained Archbishop of the Frisons by the Pope, lived in Utrecht in the Low Countries before retiring to Echternach where he died in 739. To the south, the town has retained a few towers from the 13C town walls (Rue des Remparts, near the hospice).

Echternach is renowned for its dancing procession which dates back to the late Middle Ages. It honours St Willibrord, healer of St Vitus' Dance (chorea). The dancers cross the town in leaps and bounds, dancing to the tune of a polka march and linked to each other by white handkerchiefs.

At the beginning of the summer, during the Echternach International Festival, musical events take place in the basilica or in the Church of St Peter and St Paul.

Place du Marché

★**Place du Marché** – This is an attractive old market square ringed by traditional houses with flower-bedecked balconies. On one of the sides of the square stands the old Law Courts or **Denzelt,** a charming 15C building with arcades and corner turrets.

★**Abbey** – This Benedictine monastery, which was of great cultural influence during the Middle Ages owing to its famous scriptorium, was abandoned in 1797. The abbey buildings (1727-1731) are laid out in a quadrilateral and encircled by outbuildings. With the basilica next to them, they make a majestic and harmonious sight.

The **basilique St Willibrord** was built in the 11C on the site of a Carolingian church, of which the crypt still exists, and was then extended in the 13C. It was destroyed in December 1944, but its reconstruction gave it back its original charm. There is a neo-Gothic marble tomb in the crypt. The stone sarcophagus beneath it contains the relics of St Willibrord.

★**Musée de l'Abbaye** ⊘ – The abbey museum serves as a reminder of Echternach's eventful past since Roman days. In particular it illustrates the role of the abbey scriptorium, where the monks created the most beautiful illuminated manuscripts from the 9C to the 11C. An exhibition shows the different phases in the creation of these manuscripts and displays some reproductions. The most famous was the "Codex Aureus", a celebrated 11C gold gospel-book from Echternach that is now in the German National Museum in Nuremberg.

A pretty park north-east of the abbey extends as far as the Sûre, on the banks of which stands a graceful Louis XV style pavilion.

Villa romaine – *1km – 0.5 mile on the E 29, towards Luxembourg. Upon leaving Echternach, turn left into a large car park.*

The vestiges of a large Roman villa dating from 1C can be seen here on the edge of the town. The villa was originally symmetrical, but was then enlarged and modified over the course of the following three centuries.

EXCURSION

★★Wolfschlucht – *45min Rtn on foot. Take the car along Rue André Duscher from Place du Marché and turn right towards Troosknepchen after the cemetery. The footpath leaves from Rue Emersinde near the bus station.*
The route follows Footpath B up to the pavilion at the **Troosknepchen viewpoint** from which there are a number of beautiful **views★** of Echternach in the valley below. Continue on Footpath B, through a beech forest to Wolfschlucht (literally "Wolf Gorge"). A great pointed rock to the left of the entrance to the gorge is known as Cleopatra's Needle. A flight of steps crosses this dark, impressive cleft between two jagged, sheer walls of rock 50m – 164ft high. At the end of the gorge, a flight of steps to the right leads to the **Bildscheslay viewpoint** from which there is a pretty view of the Sûre flowing through rich green countryside.

Vallée de l'EISCH★

Michelin maps 409 K6-L6 or 215 folds 4 and 12

The River Eisch wends its way in meanders through meadows, forests and between high wooded walls of rock. The road runs along the river, past the six remaining **castles** in this valley, also known as the Valley of the Seven Castles. A footpath runs through the valley as well, from Koerich to Mersch.

FROM KOERICH TO MERSCH *26km – 16 miles allow 1 hour 30min*

Koerich – The **church** stands on a hill. It has beautiful Baroque furnishings, especially in the chancel. The ruins of a feudal **castle** stand near the river. It underwent alteration during the Renaissance period (note the fireplace).

Septfontaines – This is a picturesque village clinging to the slopes which drop steeply down towards the River Eisch. Above it are the ruins of the **castle** (13C-15C).
The **church** contains an interesting *Entombment*.
There are several elegantly carved Baroque stones forming Stations of the Cross in the **cemetery** around the church *(illustration right)*. At the foot of the castle are the seven springs (*"fontaines"* in French) which gave their name to the village.

Ansembourg – This little town has two **castles**. On the hillside there is a 12C castle that was altered in the 16C and 18C, and in the valley, a 17C castle that was the residence of the owner of the local iron smelting plant, with a turreted doorway and beautiful 18C gardens. **Hollenfels Castle** can be seen a little further on, on top of a ridge. It was enlarged in the 18C around a 13C keep. It now houses a Youth Hostel.

Hunnebour – *After the bridge over the Eisch, take the road on the right.*
At the foot of a high rocky ridge is the Hunnebour, a spring in a restful shady **setting★**.

Mersch – The feudal **castle** has been extensively re-stored. It is a tall square building in front of which there is a gateway with small turrets. Nearby is onion-domed **tour St-Michel**, the only trace of a church which has disappeared.

A Station of the Cross,
Septfontaines

ESCH-SUR-ALZETTE

Population 23 890
Michelin maps 409 K7 or 215 fold 14
Town plan in the current Michelin Red Guide Benelux

Esch-sur-Alzette, the Grand Duchy of Luxembourg's second largest town, is also the country's main iron and steel production centre. Its principal activity is steel manu-facture, owing to the large ARBED factory. This cosmopolitan town (more than 30% of the inhabitants are foreigners) also plays an important role in the world of commerce.

Parc de la ville – *Take the Dudelange road, then the first road on the right after the tunnel.*
This vast flower-bedecked park covers an area of 57 hectares – 140 acres. It is laid out in terraces on a hill overlooking the town to the east of the station. There is a small game reserve at the top (402m – 1 318ft in altitude) in the **Galgenberg** open-air centre.

Musée de la Résistance ⊙ – *Place du Brill.*
This little museum was built in 1956 in the town centre to commemorate the heroism of the Luxembourg people and their resistance to the occupying forces (1940-1944). The work in the mines and factories, the general strike of 1942, the struggle of the Underground movement and the deportations are described through bas-reliefs, frescoes, statues and documents.

EXCURSION

Rumelange – *6km – 3.75 miles. Take the Dudelange road, then turn right.*
This mining community near the French border has an interesting mining museum, the **musée national des mines** ⊙. Part of the iron mines worked until 1958 in the hill crossed by the border is open to the public. The tour of 900m – 0.5 mile of galleries (temperature: 12°C – 53°F), part of which is by a small train, gives an insight into the various extraction processes and the development of techniques and materials used since the mine was first opened.

LAROCHETTE ★
Population 1 420
Michelin maps 409 L6 or 215 fold 4

Larochette is a pleasant holiday location in the Ernz Blanche Valley, which is dominated by high rocky cliff walls of Luxembourg sandstone, on one of which there are two ruined castles.

Châteaux ⊙ – *Access via the Nommern road.*
The ruins of two buildings can be seen on the plateau. They are the 14C Gothic Palais des Créhange overlooking the town, and nearer at hand, the older Palais des Hombourg above the Mersch road.

EXCURSION

Round trip of 12km – 7.5 miles – *Allow 30min. Take the Nommern direction.*
On the outskirts of the pine forests note the nature reserve on the left. On the heathland amidst the broom there is the **Champignon** (Mushroom) rock, about 150m – 492ft from the road, a fine block of Luxembourg sandstone. There are good views of the locality from the road down to **Nommern.**
At Nommern, take the Larochette road.
The so-called motoring-pedestrian tour route *(circuit auto-pédestre)* no 2 begins at a left-hand bend. It takes visitors to the magnificent crags called the **Nommerlayen** ★ in the forest. They are walls of sandstone in a wide variety of shapes scattered among the trees.
Return to Larochette on the N 8.

LUXEMBOURG ★★
Population 74 400
Michelin maps 409 L7 or 215 fold 5

The first impressions of Luxembourg are unexpected, built as it is on a plateau crisscrossed by gullies, which are spanned by innumerable bridges. The city can come across as an urban, rural or military settlement, depending on the angle from which it is approached. Its squares, with their elegant façades painted in pastel colours, could be the backdrop for a theatre production. Its numerous viewpoints disclose vistas of lush green valleys. Yet for all its apparent tranquillity, there is behind the scenes all the liveliness and activity to be expected of a capital city, money market and the headquarters for various European institutions.
Luxembourg is also the headquarters for RTL, one of the largest broadcasting companies in Europe.

★★**A magnificent setting** – The city and fortifications are perched on top of a sandstone outcrop with steeply sloping sides, skirted by two rivers, the Alzette and the Pétrusse. The old town is separated from the modern one to the south by the deep gash known as the Pétrusse gorge, which is spanned by bridges such as the well-known **pont Adolphe** (1899-1903) (F), built in a bold, impressive style. To the north, it is linked to the Kirchberg plateau by the red-painted **pont Grande-Duchess Charlotte** (1964) (DY) spanning the Alzette. There are three districts in the valleys – Grund, Clausen and Pfaffenthal. Marvellous **views** of the city in all its varied guises can be enjoyed from every bend along the cliff roads.
In the high season the site is floodlit after dark, which shows it off to full advantage.

Festivals – The traditional folk festival of l'Emais'chen, when young lovers exchange terracotta ware sold especially for the occasion, takes place every year where the fishmarket used to be (Place du Musée). From the end of August onwards there is the big Luxembourg fair and market (Schueberfouer), which dates back to 1340.

View of the old town and the Église St-Jean du Grund

HISTORICAL NOTES

The history of the city is closely connected with that of the country itself.
In Roman times, Luxembourg was situated at the intersection of two Roman roads, one going from Trier to Rheims via Arlon (now Grand-Rue), and the other linking Metz to Aachen. The Bock rock had already been fortified. In the 10C, Count Sigefroi (from the Moselle), who styled himself Count of Luxembourg, built a castle near the upper town, on the Bock. A first defensive wall was erected around the upper town, then reinforced with a second the following century.
In the 12C the city, along with the Count of Luxembourg, came under the rule of Henry V the Blind, Count of Namur. His grandson **Henry VII** became **Holy Roman Emperor** in 1308. The House of Luxembourg held the imperial throne until 1437. In 1346 the son of Emperor Henry VII, **John the Blind,** King of Bohemia and Count of Luxembourg, was killed in the French ranks at the Battle of Crécy. In the 14C a third enclosure was built around the upper town, while the lower towns were also fortified.

Coveted territory – In the 15C, Luxembourg fell into the hands of the House of Burgundy. It next passed to Emperor Charles V (in 1555) who fortified the city, then to Philip II.
The city came under French rule in 1684, after being skilfully besieged by **Vauban,** who went on to strengthen its fortifications. Having fallen once more into the hands of the Spaniards in 1698, it was occupied by the French again in 1701, who were in turn replaced by the Austrians from 1714 to 1795. In spite of heavy reinforcement of its fortifications and the digging of casemates, the city surrendered to Carnot in 1795 and was administered as part of the Département des Forêts until 1814. After the defeat of Napoleon, the Duchy was raised to a **Grand Duchy** by the Congress of Vienna. It was administratively dependent on the German Confederation but belonged to the house of Orange-Nassau and was governed by William I, King of the Netherlands. As a result, the city was occupied by a Prussian garrison which did not leave Luxembourg until 1867. Once the country's neutrality had been declared in the Treaty of London, the three rings of fortifications were dismantled.
Despite its neutrality, Luxembourg was invaded by the German army in 1914 and again in 1940. It was liberated by the American army under General Patton on 10 September 1944.

European Institutions – In 1952 Luxembourg became the headquarters of the ECSC, the European Coal and Steel Community, the organisation which was to pave the way for a federal Europe. **Robert Schuman** (1886-1963), the French statesman born in Luxembourg, first mooted the idea, and **Jean Monnet** (1888-1979) put it into action. There were six member countries at that time – Belgium, France, Italy, Luxembourg, the Netherlands and West Germany.
Since the signing of the Treaty of Rome in 1957, Luxembourg has been home to **The General Secretariat of the European Parliament,** which holds sessions in Strasbourg and Luxembourg.

In 1966 the European Centre was inaugurated on Kirchberg. This building was intended to bring the various departments of the General Secretariat of the European Parliament together under one roof.

Since 1967, when the executive councils of three bodies ECSC, EURATOM and EEC merged to form a single commission with its headquarters in Brussels, many institutions have been set up on the Kirchberg plateau. They include the European Investment Bank, departments of the Commission of European Union (in particular the Statistics Department), the European School, the Court of Justice (founded in 1952) and the Court of Auditors of the European Union. As for the Official Publications Office for the European Union, it is established in Luxembourg-Gare.

Since 1965 the Council of Ministers, the main decision-making body within the European Union, has held its sessions in Luxembourg three times a year (in April, June and October). There are currently about 7 000 European civil servants in Luxembourg.

★★OLD TOWN *allow half a day*

Set off from Place d'Armes.

Place d'Armes (F) – This shady square is the lively centre of the city. In high season the cafés spill onto the pavements. Behind the bandstand is a column in honour of Michel Lentz, the author of the words for the Luxembourg national anthem, and Edmond de la Fontaine, an author and composer who was a native of Luxembourg. The main feature of the square is the **Palais Municipal** (F N), built in 1907, which houses the tourist information office. In a building on the corner of the square, on Rue du Curé, a **model** ⊙ of the Luxembourg fortress is on show.

From Rue du Curé, a delightful passageway leads to Place Guillaume.

Place d'Armes

Place Guillaume (F) – The equestrian statue of William II of the Netherlands (1792-1849), Grand Duke of Luxembourg, stands in the centre of the square. Building work began on the **Town Hall** (F H) in 1830, in the local architectural style.

Place de la Constitution (F) – This former bastion on the Beck, which includes a commemorative obelisk, affords marvellous **views**★★ across the Pétrusse gorge, laid out as gardens, and the pont Adolphe. The entrance to the Pétrusse casemates *(qv)* is to be found here.

Take Boulevard Roosevelt to Plateau St-Esprit.

Boulevard Roosevelt is lined with the buildings of the **old Jesuit college** (F V), including the new section of the cathedral.

Plateau St-Esprit (G) – This impressive citadel designed by Vauban contains the monument to National Solidarity. There are **views**★★ from the top of the citadel across the Pétrusse and Alzette Valleys, the Rham Plateau and the lower town of Grund with its church.

From Plateau St-Esprit, go down to the car park. From there take the steps, or, in a modern building nearby, the lift up to the cliff path and the Grund suburb.

★★**Chemin de la corniche** (G) – This has been called "the most beautiful balcony in Europe" because of its **views**★★. The path initially passes the old building in which the State Archives are kept, before joining the path that follows the old ramparts along the edge of the Alzette escarpment, and reaching the enormous gateway known as the **Porte de Grund** (1632) (**G E**). The elegant façades of houses belonging to the nobility line this path, overlooking the town of Grund and the spire of église St-Jean in the valley below.

Le Bock (**G**) – This spur of rock used to be linked to the town by a drawbridge (now the Pont du Château). It has been smoothed off somewhat by the construction of the road up from Clausen (Montée de Clausen).

The Bock forms the foundation of Luxembourg Castle (now ruined), which was built in the 10C, demolished in 1555 and converted into a small fort in the 17C. Destroyed in 1684 when the town was besieged by the French, it was rebuilt by Vauban.

In 1745 the Austrians took over the planning of the fortifications and dug the casemates. The Bock was razed in 1875. The only thing left standing is the tower called **Dent Creuse** (**G A**).

From the top of the ruins there are **views**★★ of the Rham plateau which was the site of a Gallo-Roman villa. To the left is the huge square gate called **Tour Jacob** (**G B**) or Dinselpuert. This was the Trier gateway and formed part of the 14C enclosure. The buildings on the right are the barracks built by Vauban (hospices). At the foot of the Bock, on the north side, is the old St-Esprit convent (17C).

★★**Casemates du Bock** ⊙ – In 1745, this defensive labyrinth was dug out of the sandstone outcrop which makes up the foundations of the city. There is a section open to the public a minute part of a network of 23km – 14 miles of passages which acted as a channel of communications between the various sections of the fortress and as a shelter during the Second World War. The archeology crypt contains remains of the fortress and an audio-visual presentation of the history of the site. Some of the openings have views of the gorge and Rham district.

On the right of the entrance to the upper town a **monument** has been built to commemorate visits to Luxembourg by famous people, most notably Goethe in 1792. Nearby is the porticoed building housing the **Council of State** (**G D**).

Place du Marché (**G 72**) – Once the intersection of Roman roads and formerly also the fish market, this square is surrounded by old houses. The one described as "Sous les piliers" (literally "under the pillars") has Flamboyant Gothic style windows and a niche in the same style containing a statue of St Anne and the Virgin Mary and Child, above a Renaissance portico. Further along on the left there is an attractive house with a corbelled turret.

★**Musée national d'histoire et d'art** (**G M¹**) ⊙

★**Gallo-Roman collection** – This collection is to be found mainly on the ground floor and is very extensive. Digs carried out in the south of the country (in Dalheim and Titelberg) revealed that the area was densely populated during Roman times. The exhibits are well-displayed and include bronzes, terracotta and fragile glassware.

A fireback (1586)

Musée national d'Histoire et d'Art, Luxembourg

The numerous funeral monuments should be compared with those in Trier and Arlon. The little house-shaped stones, which may have contained urns, and the stones carved with the four divinities were widespread in the south of Luxembourg. The Merovingian period has left a legacy of weapons and beautiful jewellery. The **salle des médailles,** or treasury, displays rare items from all historical periods, including the remarkable **bronze mask of Hellange** dating from 1C.

Fine Art collection – A range of religious sculptures (from the 11C to the 18C) is laid out in various rooms in this section, as well as in the Gallo-Roman section and in the rooms devoted to local lifestyles.

Ancient art *(third floor)* is represented principally by works from three collections – the Edmond Reiffers collection (Italian paintings from the 13C-16C), the Wilhelmy-Hoffmann collection (Northern European schools and Flemish works of the 16C and 17C; note a *Charity* by Cranach the Elder and a copy of the Hachiville altarpiece) and the Bentick-Thyssen collection (temporary exhibition).

Modern art *(first and second floors)* includes a few sculptures by Rodin, Maillol, Lobo, and Hadju, canvases and figurative or abstract tapestries by the Paris school (Bertholle, Bissière, Borès, Chastel, Estève, Fautrier, Gilioli, Lurçat, Pignon, Soulages, Tàpies, Veira da Silva) and works by the native Luxembourg Expressionist painter Joseph Kutter (1894-1941).

★★**Luxembourg Life section (decorative arts, folk art and tradition)** – *Access via the first floor of the Musée d'Histoire et d'Art.*
Some of the rooms may be closed for staffing reasons.
This outstanding section, set up in four old bourgeois houses, gives an insight into life in Luxembourg from the 17C to the 19C. The interiors are decorated with beautiful furniture, Boch faïence ware (Septfontaines), Nospelt pottery, pewterware, and a large collection of paintings under glass.
Firebacks *(qv)* are on display in the vaulted cellars. Part of the cellars is given over to the wines of the Moselle valley, an area famous for its white wine and sparkling wine.

Boulevard Victor Thorn (**G 121**) – This boulevard affords **views**★ of the Alzette Valley, spanned by the pont Vauban (**DY 118**), and the huddle of the Pfaffenthal suburbs. Above the valley, the pont Grande-Duchesse Charlotte connects the city with the Kirchberg plateau and the European Centre. The **Fort des Trois Glands** can be seen through a gap in the trees.

Porte des Trois Tours (**G**) – Built on the site of the second set of town walls, this is actually a gate flanked by two towers.

Now enter the city through the first **Porte de Pfaffenthal** (17C).

★**Palais Grand-Ducal** (**G**) ⊙ – The left wing, formerly the Town Hall, dates back to the 16C. Graceful turrets flank its façade, which is decorated with geometric patterns in bas relief.
The right wing, known as La Balance, was added in 1741, and the wing at the back, which has a view of the garden, in 1891. The building (1859) on the right of La Balance is the lower house of parliament.
Since 1895, most official functions have been held in this palace. A collection of well-preserved weapons is kept in the guardroom. The main staircase, with a charming balustrade decorated with the monogram of Adelaide-Marie, wife of the Grand Duke Adolf, leads off to the suites.
The former aristocrats' room, or **salon des Rois,** where portraits of all the past Grand Dukes are hung, is used for official audiences. In the dining room there are four tapestries which were a gift from Napoleon after his stay at the palace in 1804. They illustrate the story of Telemachus.

Place Clairefontaine (**FG 27**) – A monument to Grand Duchess Charlotte has been erected in this attractive square.

★**Cathédrale Notre-Dame** (**F**) – This old Jesuit church with delicate 20C spires actually dates from the 17C. On the north side there is an interesting **doorway** decorated with Renaissance and Baroque motifs.
It is a good example of a hall-church, all three of its aisles being of the same height. The style is on the whole Gothic, although the pillars are decorated with unusual arabesques in relief, and the gallery above the entrance is very delicately worked in a style that is half Renaissance and half Baroque. On the left of the nave there is a gallery reserved for the Grand Ducal family. The neo-Gothic style choir was added in the 20C. The miraculous statue of the Comforter of the Afflicted (national patron saint since 1678) is object of particular devotion. A pilgrimage is held here during the third week after Easter.
Leave the cathedral by the door on the south side of the chancel to get to the Treasury Chapel and the **crypt.** The treasury chapel contains the cenotaph of John the Blind (Jean l'Aveugle), who died at Crécy in 1346. The tomb was made in

1688 and depicts an Entombment. The crypt houses some interesting works by modern artists. It was in the cathedral that Josephine Charlotte of Belgium married Jean de Luxembourg in 1953. He went on to become Grand Duke in 1964 following the abdication of his mother, Grand Duchess Charlotte.

The Jesuit School, adjacent to the cathedral is now the National Library (Bibliothèque Nationale).

Return to Place d'Armes from the cathedral.

KIRCHBERG *allow 30min*

Several European institutions *(see below)* are on the Kirchberg plateau, which is crossed by a motorway. This has led to increased urbanisation (hotel, European school, etc.). The Parc des Expositions (exhibition centre) is beyond the plateau at the end of the motorway.

Before crossing the bridge leading to the Kirchberg, notice the **municipal theatre** (**CY T**) on the left. It was built in 1964 and has a long façade with windows arranged in a geometric pattern.

To the right of the road leading onto the bridge, there is a monument to Robert Schuman, designed by architect Robert Lentz (**CY S**).

★**Pont Grande-Duchesse Charlotte** (**DY**) – This bridge of steel boldly painted in red, is a symbol of the ECSC and was inaugurated in 1966. It crosses the Alzette, a distance of 300m – 984ft.

Take the second road on the right after the bridge, towards the European Centre.

Centre Européen du Kirchberg (**DEY**) – The 22-storey **tower block**, inaugurated in 1965, is occupied by the General Secretariat of the European Parliament. The Council of Ministers holds sessions here for three months every year. Additional space was created by a smaller building, the **Centre Robert Schuman**. A third construction, the **Hémicycle**, was finished in 1980 and is used as a conference centre.

Take the road which leads into the woods behind the European Centre to get to the Trois Glands.

Les Trois Glands (**DY**) – This is the old Thungen stronghold in the forest. On top of its towers are stones shaped like acorns ("glands" in French).

Turn left at the end of the lawn.

A small viewpoint overlooks Clausen and its church. To the left is a house with turrets, in which Robert Schuman was born (**DY Z**). To the right, there is a **view**★ of the city of Luxembourg, the Bock, and the Rham district with its tower blocks.

Return to the European Centre and go under the motorway to reach the Court of Justice.

Cour de Justice de l'Union Européenne (**DY**) – The dark-brown painted steel structure of the four-storey CJEC building, built in 1970, stands on a vast terrace on which there are also two sculptures by Henry Moore and Lucien Wercollier.

The nearby **bâtiment Jean Monnet**, with its walls of smoked glass houses the administration departments.

ADDITIONAL SIGHTS

Casemates de la Pétrusse ⊘ – *Entrance on Place de la Constitution* (**F**).
This is an extensive network of underground passages opening onto the Pétrusse Valley. It was created in 1746 by the Austrians to improve defences on the southern side of the plateau.

Musée J P Pescatore (**CY M²**) ⊘ – This museum in the sophisticated 19C interior of the Villa Vauban houses three collectors' legacies of Belgian, Dutch and French painting from the 17C to the modern day.

After a few paintings attributed to Canaletto (Room 3), note among the Flemish canvases works from the 17C by David Teniers the Younger *(Interior, The Smoker)*. The extensive 17C Dutch collection includes several genre paintings (Gérard Dou's *Empirical*, Jan Steen's *Festival of Kings*) and a Van de Capelle seascape.

19C French painting is represented notably by a Delacroix *(Young Turk Stroking his Horse)* and a Courbet *(Seascape)*.

The museum also organises temporary exhibitions.

Drive through the suburbs – A drive along the right bank of the Alzette through the suburbs of lower Grund, Pfaffenthal and Clausen reveals a completely different side of the city. These are working class districts, with maisonettes and breweries still producing local beers. There are also very different views of the old town and its fortifications from these districts at the bottom of the ravines.

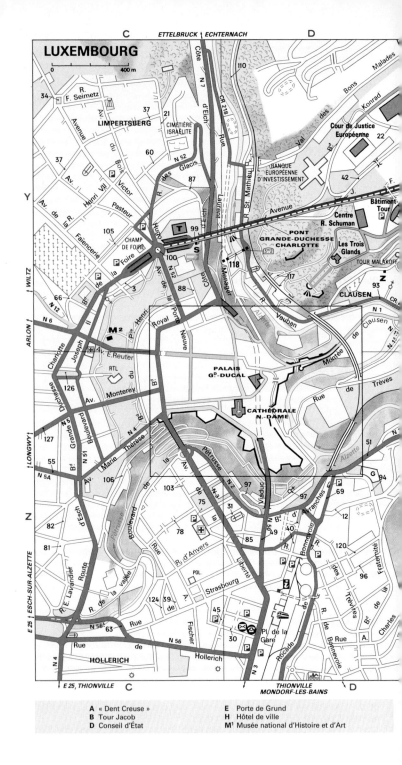

A	« Dent Creuse »	E	Porte de Grund
B	Tour Jacob	H	Hôtel de ville
D	Conseil d'État	M¹	Musée national d'Histoire et d'Art

Église St-Jean du Grund (**G**) – This church dedicated to St John belonged to the Benedictine abbey in Münster until the French Revolution.

The present building dates from 1705.

The interior is highlighted by three Flemish Baroque altarpieces in the chancel. Note also Stations of the Cross in 16C Limoges enamel made by Leonard Limosin, the 18C organ, the Gothic font and, in a chapel to the left of the nave, a graceful Black Virgin and Child by the Cologne school, carved in about 1360 and the object of great veneration.

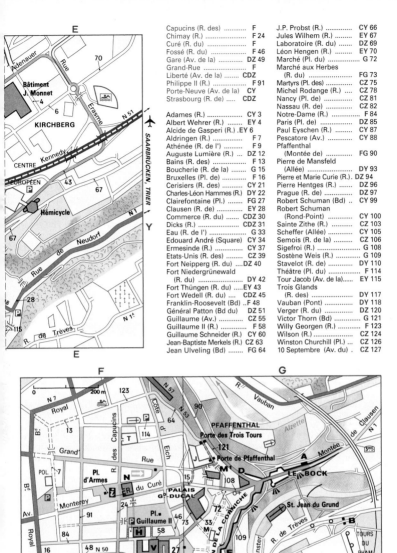

Capucins (R. des)	F	J.P. Probst (R.)	CY 66
Chimay (R.)	F 24	Jules Wilhem (R.)	EY 67
Curé (R. du)	F	Laboratoire (R. du)	DZ 69
Fossé (R. du)	F 46	Léon Hengen (R.)	EY 70
Gare (Av. de la)	DZ 49	Marché (Pl. du)	G 72
Grand-Rue	F	Marché aux Herbes	
Liberté (Av. de la)	CDZ	(R. du)	FG 73
Philippe II (R.)	F 91	Martyrs (Pl. des)	CZ 75
Porte-Neuve (Av. de la)	CY	Michel Rodange (R.)	CZ 78
Strasbourg (R. de)	CDZ	Nancy (Pl. de)	CZ 81
		Nassau (R. de)	CZ 82
Adames (R.)	CY 3	Notre-Dame (R.)	F 84
Albert Wehrer (R.)	EY 4	Paris (R. de)	DZ 85
Alcide de Gasperi (R.)	EY 6	Paul Eyschen (R.)	CY 88
Aldringen (R.)	F 7	Pescatore (Av.)	CY 88
Athénée (R. de l')	F 9	Pfaffenthal	
Auguste Lumière (R.)	DZ 12	(Montée de)	FG 90
Bains (R. des)	F 13	Pierre de Mansfeld	
Boucherie (R. de la)	G 15	(Allée)	DY 93
Bruxelles (Pl. de)	F 16	Pierre et Marie Curie (R.)	DZ 94
Cerisiers (R. des)	CY 21	Pierre Hentges (R.)	DZ 96
Charles-Léon Hammes (R.)	DY 22	Prague (R. de)	DZ 97
Clairefontaine (Pl.)	FG 27	Robert Schuman (Bd)	CY 99
Clausen (R.)	EY 28	Robert Schuman	
Commerce (R. du)	CDZ 30	(Rond-Point)	CY 100
Dicks (R.)	CDZ 31	Sainte Zithe (R.)	CZ 103
Eau (R. de l')	G 33	Scheffer (Allée)	CY 105
Edouard André (Square)	CY 34	Semois (R. de la)	CZ 106
Ermesinde (R.)	CY 37	Sigefroi (R.)	G 108
Etats-Unis (R. des)	CZ 39	Sostène Weis (R.)	G 109
Fort Neipperg (R. du)	DZ 40	Stavelot (R. de)	DY 110
Fort Niedergrünewald		Théâtre (Pl. du)	F 114
(R. du)	DY 42	Tour Jacob (Av. de la)	EY 115
Fort Thüngen (R. du)	EY 43	Trois Glands	
Fort Wedell (R. du)	CDZ 45	(R. des)	DY 117
Franklin-Roosevelt (Bd)	F 48	Vauban (Pont)	DY 118
Général Patton (Bd du)	DZ 51	Verger (R. du)	DZ 120
Guillaume (Av.)	CZ 55	Victor Thorn (Bd)	G 121
Guillaume II (R.)	F 58	Willy Georgen (R.)	F 123
Guillaume Schneider (R.)	CY 60	Wilson (R.)	CZ 124
Jean-Baptiste Merkels (R.)	CZ 63	Winston Churchill (Pl.)	CZ 126
Jean Ulveling (Bd)	FG 64	10 Septembre (Av. du)	CZ 127

M²	Musée J.-P. Pescatore	T	Théâtre municipal
N	Palais municipal	V	Ancien collège des Jésuites
S	Monument Robert Schuman	Z	Maison natale de R. Schuman

EXCURSIONS

Military cemeteries – *5km – 3 miles east. Leave via the Boulevard du Général Patton* (**DZ 51**). The Luxembourg American Cemetery at **Hamm**, just outside the capital, is one of thirteen American Second World War cemeteries overseas. It recalls the Grand Duchy of Luxembourg's gratitude to its liberators. This imposing 20 hectares – 50 acre cemetery is in woods, overlooked by a memorial chapel built in 1960, and contains 5 076 graves. Opposite the white crosses arranged in a curve stands the grave of General Patton who was killed in December 1945. His grave is identical to the others.

Further to the east *(access via the Contern road)* is the **Sandweiler German cemetery,** inaugurated in 1955. It comes into sight at a bend in the forest road. Broad lawns, on which trees have been planted and short crosses made of dark Black Forest granite arranged in groups of five, cover an area of 4 hectares – 9.8 acres. A monumental Cross stands over the common grave in which 4 829 soldiers out of the 10 885 buried in this cemetery have been laid to rest.

From Luxembourg to Bettembourg – *15km – 9.3 miles south, towards Thionville.*

Hespérange is a picturesque town on the banks of the Alzette. Above it are the ruins of a 13C-14C castle, among which small homes with tiny front gardens have been built.

Bettembourg has a large recreation park, the **Parc Merveilleux** ⊙. The 30 hectare – 74 acre grounds have animals and numerous attractions for children, in particular reconstructions of fairytale scenes.

From Luxembourg to Junglinster – *13km – 8 miles north, towards Echternach.* A beautiful road through the heart of a thick forest leads to Eisenborn, on the banks of the River Ernz Blanche. **Bourglinster,** a picturesque village at the foot of an old restored castle, is to the right.

Junglinster has a charming 18C stone-built church with beige rough cast, brightened by pastel-toned paintwork. It is surrounded by an old **cemetery** with 19C crosses that have a faintly archaic look.

MONDORF-LES-BAINS ★
Population 28 300
Michelin maps 409 L7 and 215 fold 5

This popular spa town near the border has two springs, the Kind and the Marie-Adélaïde bored respectively in 1846 and 1913. The water is used to treat liver and intestinal complaints as well as rheumatism. The spa establishment has modern facilities and is east of the old village.

★**Park** – Lying near the spa, this 36 hectare – 88 acre park, with beautiful trees and shrubs and colourful flowerbeds *(rose garden in June)*, extends over a hillside, offering several pretty views of the local countryside. The new pavilion for the Kind spring (1963) is in the centre of the park.

Église St-Michel ⊙ – This pink pebble-dashed church stands on a hill overlooking the old town. It was built in 1764 and is surrounded by a cemetery. Inside it has sumptuous Louis XV **furniture**★. The organ loft carved with musical emblems, the confessionals, the altars and the remarkable pulpit are all in perfect harmony with the stuccoes and *trompe-l'œil* frescoes painted by Weiser (1766), an artist who was born in Bohemia.

Vallée de la MOSELLE LUXEMBOURGEOISE ★
Michelin maps 409 M6-M7 and 215 folds 4, 5, 6

The Moselle (from the Latin name Mosella, or "little Meuse") separates the Grand Duchy of Luxembourg from Germany between the French frontier and Wasserbillig, at times reaching a width of about 100m – 109yds.
The navigability of the river has been substantially improved since the international agreement signed by France, Federal Germany and the Grand Duchy of Luxembourg. Canalisation work finished in 1964 has made it accessible to 3 200-tonne vessels between Thionville and Koblenz.
The Grevenmacher and Stadtbredimus dams, each equipped with a lock and a hydro-electric plant, interrupt the course of the river. So as not to disfigure the surrounding countryside, they were built at water level.
The main attractions of the route along this valley are the brilliance of the landscape and, on the west bank, hillsides carpeted with vines planted to grow up tall stakes (up to 2m – 6.5ft high).
Luxembourg Moselle wines can be tasted in the main wine cooperatives. There are white wines (Rivaner, Auxerrois, Pinot blanc, Pinot gris, Riesling, Traminer, Elbling) and sparkling wines.

Rambles – The Moselle footpath runs for about 40km – 25 miles along the river bank from Stromberg, a hill south of Schengen, and Wasserbillig.

Boat trips ⊙ – A boat trip down the Moselle between Wasserbillig and Schengen is a marvellous way to enjoy the peaceful countryside of this region dotted with wine-growing villages.

Luxembourg Moselle Valley

FROM SCHENGEN TO WASSERBILLIG
46km – 28 miles – allow half a day

Schengen – It is in this border village, the prime winegrowing area of the Luxembourg Moselle region (wine cellars), that government representatives from Luxembourg, Germany, France, Belgium and the Netherlands met on the "Marie-Astrid" pleasure craft on 14 June 1985. They signed the **Schengen Accord**, recognising the gradual abolition of international borders between these countries. In 1990 Italy also signed the accord.

Remerschen – Set back slightly from the river, this town is at the foot of the Kapberg, hills covered with vines supported by stakes. A calvary is at the top of the slope and can be reached via a steep flight of steps.

Schwebsange – In a garden to the right of the road are a 15C winepress and a fruit-crushing machine.
A few more winepresses can be seen opposite the church. In front of the church, the charming fountain known as the **Fontaine des Enfants aux raisins** is the site of the annual wine festival *(see the Calendar of Events)*.
Schwebsange also boasts the Grand Duchy's only marina.

Bech-Kleinmacher – The old winegrowers' houses, "A Possen" (1617) and "Muedelshaus", have been turned into the **Musée folklorique et viticole** ⊙.
Small rooms with rustic furniture (kitchen with an open fire) serve as reminders of life in the past. Traditional activities are presented in workshops and other attractions include a dairy, a wine museum and a wine cellar still with a grape-crushing vat.
Take the Wellenstein road which goes past the front of the museum.

Wellenstein – The **wine cooperatives** ⊙ are at the entrance to the village, which is surrounded by 70 hectares – 172 acres of vineyards. The impressive installations enable the storage of as many as 10 million litres (2.2 million gallons) of wine in enormous stainless steel vats, and a total of 1.5 million bottles.
The road climbs the **Scheuerberg** (views of the vineyards) then descends to Remich (views of the Moselle).
In Remich, return to the Moselle.

Remich – The town of Remich has several wine cellars. The **Caves St Martin** ⊙ to the north of the town, which have been hollowed out of the rock, specialise in the production of sparkling wines. The bank of the Moselle has been laid out at this point with a long footpath.

Stadtbredimus – Large wine cooperatives.
Shortly after Stadtbredimus, take the Greiveldange road on the left.
As the road climbs the hill there are beautiful **views★** of the Moselle's meandering course, the steep Luxembourg slopes covered with vines supported by stakes and, on the German side towards Palzem, a more gently undulating countryside which is also planted with vineyards.
Beyond **Greiveldange**, which has a large wine cooperative, return to the valley.

Ehnen – This winegrowing village is surrounded by vines on stakes and still has an old district with cobbled streets. In the heart of the old town stands a round church, built in 1826 and flanked with a Romanesque tower.

A winegrower's home has been turned into the **Musée du vin** ⏱. Tools used until the 1960s are on show here, and photographs give a pleasant illustration of the cultivation of vines and production of Moselle wine in days gone by. Related professions (coopering) are also mentioned, and the tour ends with some wine-tasting.

Wormeldange – This is the main town in the Luxembourg Riesling area. There are large **wine cooperatives** ⏱ near the exit of the town, on the left.

St Donat's Chapel is at the top of the plateau, on the spot known as **Koeppchen**, where an old castle once stood.

Machtum – This small village lies in a bend in the river. A winepress and a fruit-crusher are on display on a lawn.

The great **Grevenmacher dam-and-lock** is at the end of the meander. There is also an electric power station here.

Grevenmacher – Surrounded by vineyards and orchards, this little town is a major wine-growing centre with cooperative wine cellars and a private cellar. The **wine cooperatives** ⏱ are in the north of the town *(rue des Caves)*. South of the bridge are the **Caves Bernard-Massard** ⏱, founded in 1921. They produce a sparkling wine using the champagne method. The tour of the lower cellars ends with a documentary film on the Grand Duchy of Luxembourg, the Moselle, wine growing and the production of sparkling wine.

Mertert – This is an active river port linked to Wasserbillig by a footpath along the bank of the Moselle.

Wasserbillig – Situated at the confluence of the Moselle and the Sûre *(qv)*, the town also lies at the junction of several major international roads. It is a tourist centre and boat trips start from here.

PETITE SUISSE LUXEMBOURGEOISE ★★★

Michelin maps 409 L6-M6 and 215 folds 3, 4

The area known as Luxembourg's "Mini-Switzerland" because of its rich green, undu-lating landscape has a wealth of natural beauty spots. Its rock formations and vegetation are among its most attractive features.
Petite Suisse lies within the Germano-Luxembourg nature park *(qv)*.

Romantic scenery – Forests thick with beech trees, hornbeams, pines, birches and oaks, forest floors covered with ferns, heather, bilberry bushes and moss, foaming streams tumbling over rocky river beds and verdant pastures are all part of the characteristic scenery of Luxembourg's Petite Suisse.

Variety of rock formations – Strangely-shaped rocks lying hidden in the heart of the forest further add to the charm of the landscape.

Rock formations in Luxembourg's "Petite Suisse"

Luxembourg sandstone, a mixture of sand and limestone and part of one of the main Gutland "escarpments" *(qv)*, has been sculpted by Nature with amazing results. Erosion has worn grooves into the rocks, often making them look like tumble-down walls. Once water had eroded it, the sandstone plateau broke up, fissures appeared between the sedimentary layers, and huge blocks (diaclases) broke away and began to slide downhill towards the valley on their bed of argillaceous limestone.

The water table that collected in the lower section of the sandstone is the source of numerous springs. A kind of gully or crevice, known as a "**Schluff**", can appear between the rock faces. If the rockfaces are sloping, then an actual cave (schlucht) is formed. Some fifteen signposted footpaths offer opportunities to visit the Petite Suisse and discover its most beautiful nooks and crannies.

EXCURSION

Round tour of 34km – 21 miles from Echternach – allow 1 day.

★**Echternach** – *See ECHTERNACH. Allow 45min.*

From Echternach take the Diekirch road.

The road follows the course of the river Sûre and passes close by Wolfschlucht *(qv)*.

Take the next turning on the left towards Berdorf.

About 1km – 0.5 mile on from the fork the road is joined by **Footpath B** *(qv)* which goes down from Wolfschlucht into the Aesbach Valley.

Le Perekop – This is a rock about 40m – 131ft high, which overhangs the road on the right and looks like a set of ruins. A flight of steps in a crevice leads up to the top, where there is a view of the surrounding woods.

★★**Walk** – At Le Perekop **Footpath B** (Echternach to Grundhof) runs along at road level. The stretch towards the west along the banks of the River Aesbach until the point where the path diverges *(30min)* is among the most attractive in the area. Note the rocks worn down by erosion. They include the Tour Malakoff and, further on, the Chipkapass.

When the road leaves the woods, Berdorf comes into view ahead on the plateau.

Berdorf – *See BERDORF.*

From Berdorf take the Mullerthal road.

Not far along on the left is the **Predigstuhl**, a pulpit-shaped rock which partially conceals the **Werschrumschluff**★ (gully, *qv*) behind it.

The road slopes steeply down into the Mullerthal valley.

At Vugelsmullen (or Vogelsmuhle) in the Mullerthal (see below), take a right turn immediately followed by a left towards Beaufort.

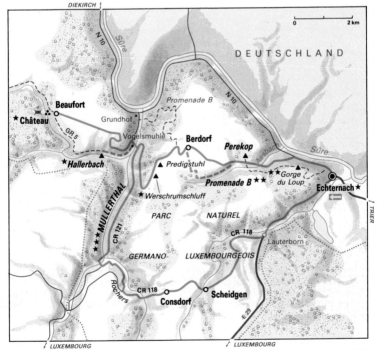

Beaufort – Set on a rise, this small town produces a blackcurrant liqueur called Cassero.

★**Château de Beaufort** ⊘ – The romantic-looking ruins of this fortress (12C-16C) stand in a wooded valley near a lake. In 1871, Victor Hugo wrote of the castle, "It comes into sight round a bend, at the foot of a gorge in a forest; it's like a vision. It's magnificent." The old castle consists of a huge, towering keep linked to a fortress. Restorations in 1930 cleared the approach roads and reinforced the entrances. The neighbouring castle was built by the lord of Beaufort in 1647.

The footpath from the west side of the lake leads towards the Hallerbach waterfall *(see below)*.

Return to Vogelsmuhle by car. Just before the hamlet, a small road branches off to the right along the Mullerthal.

About 300m – 328yds along this road, leave the car and take the Hallerbach footpath.

★**Hallerbach** – The rushing tumbling waters of the river can be seen through the woods gushing down through mossy boulders and farming charming little waterfalls *(allow 30min there and back)*.

Return to Vogelsmuhle and turn right.

★★★**Mullerthal** – This is the name given to the **Ernz Noire Valley.** Interrupted now and then by cascades, the river flows between two banks carpeted with meadows and backing onto wooded slopes. Spectacular outcrops of sandstone can be seen rising out of the trees.

About 200m – 218yds on from the Mullerthal, turn left towards Consdorf.

To get back to the top of the plateau the road goes along a little valley with attractive rock formations jutting out here and there along its sides.

Consdorf – This tourist village on the edge of the woods is very popular during the summer months.

Scheidgen – Holiday location.

Return to Echternach (qv) via Lauterborn.

RINDSCHLEIDEN★

Michelin maps 409 fold 18 and 215 fold 11 – Local map see Vallée de la SÛRE

This hamlet is tucked in the hollow of a valley around the parish church, which is much admired for the murals inside it.

★PARISH CHURCH

The church is Romanesque in origin. The chancel was modified in the Late Gothic period. The nave was enlarged in the 16C and given three equally high vaults.

Inside, all the vaulting and the walls of the chancel are covered with **frescoes.** Dating from the early 15C (chancel) and 16C (nave), they depict a multitude of figures, saints or royalty, and religious scenes in clear colours outlined in black.

Note also the 17C and 18C wooden statues as well as some sculptures in stone, the 15C eucharistic cabinet surmounted by an oculus, the keystones, the capitals and the 16C statues set on the springers.

The miraculous well of St Willibrord, the object of an annual pilgrimage, is in a little garden near the church. An old 15C font is nearby.

RODANGE

Michelin maps 409 K7 and 215 fold 13 – 3km – 1.75 miles west of Pétange

This is a small industrial town near the Belgian and French borders.

Tourist train ⊘ – *From 2km – 1.25 miles south of the church on the Lasauvage road, as far as "Bois de Rodange".*

This train, pulled by turn-of-the-century steam engines, travels about 6km – 3.75 miles through the **Fond de Gras** valley overlooked by the Titelberg *(see musée national d'Histoire et d'Art, qv)*. A shuttle service operates between the road and the old Fond de Gras station. Once an iron mineral mine, this has become the starting point for the train excursion.

EXCURSION

Bascharage – *6km – 3.75 miles northeast on the Luxembourg road.*

The **brasserie nationale** in this town makes lager-type beer distributed mostly in the Grand Duchy of Luxembourg.

In the **Taillerie luxembourgeoise de pierres précieuses** ⊘ *(Rue de la Continentale, east of the station)* precious stones from all the continents are cut and polished. The stone-cutters can be seen at work, and there is a large exhibition of minerals and jewels.

Vallée de la SÛRE★★

Michelin Maps 409 K6-L6-M6 and 215 folds 3, 4

The River Sûre, which rises in Belgium between Neufchâteau and Bastogne, crosses the Grand Duchy of Luxembourg as far as the River Moselle and the German border, which it marks from Wallendorf to Wasserbillig.
A large part of the valley can be explored by following signposted footpaths.

★★① THE UPPER VALLEY

From Hochfels to Erpeldange

68km – 42 miles – allow half a day – local map overleaf

This is the most spectacular stretch, where the river cuts deeply into the ancient Oesling rocks.
The valley through which the road runs is also followed by the Haute-Sûre footpath linking Martelange on the border to Ettelbruck 60km – 37 miles away.

★**Hochfels** – From near the chalet on this crest 460m – 1 509ft high, there is a **bird's-eye view** of the winding valley and its wooded slopes.

Travel via Boulaide and cross the Sûre at **Pont-Misère**, surrounded by pretty countryside, to reach Insenborn.
As the road goes back up to the plateau there are some lovely **views** of part of the Haute-Sûre lake downstream from the bridge, as well as of the river upstream at the foot of the Hochfels, with Boulaide on the horizon.

Insenborn – This town on the **lac de la Haute-Sûre★** is popular for water sports *(sailing, windsurfing, boating, swimming, fishing, diving)*. These activities are authorised upstream of Lultzhausen.

From Insenborn to Esch-sur-Sûre the road runs along the shore of the lake. There are remarkable **viewpoints★** over the green, winding river banks covered with broom and bristling with firs.

Barrage d'Esch-sur-Sûre – At the base of this 48m – 157ft high dam, which has a capacity of 62 million m^3 – 2 190 million ft^3, there is a hydro-electric plant. Two secondary dams have been built to absorb river flood tides – Bavigne *(northwest)* and Pont-Misère *(upstream)*.
There is a good **view★** of the lake from the Kaundorf road, in a bend 800m – 0.5 mile beyond the dam.

★**Esch-sur-Sûre** – This welcoming village, with its slate-roofed houses built in terraces up the hillside has a pretty setting. It is tucked inside a meander of the river, which has twisted in almost a full circle around a promontory topped by the ruins of a castle. A tunnel has been bored through the hill beneath it.
From the round watch-tower at the top of the hill, there is an interesting **view★** of the scenery with the castle keep and chapel in the foreground. The fortress dates back to the 10C and was demolished in 1795. The village still has some traces of its medieval walls.

Esch-sur-Sûre

Vallée de la SÛRE

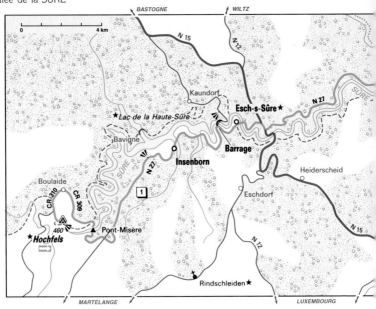

From Esch-sur-Sûre to Göbelsmuhle, the road rejoins the Sûre here and there, as it flows at the bottom of thickly wooded gorges.

Having entered the Germano-Luxembourg nature park *(qv)* and gone through Göbelsmuhle, the road comes within sight of the Château de Bourscheid, perched on a hilltop.

After Lipperscheid take the road on the left.

★★Point de vue de Grenglay – *15min Rtn on foot, on a footpath through fields, signposted "Point de Vue".*

From the top of this impressive escarpment there is a beautiful **view** of the Château de Bourscheid perched on a promontory in a meander of the River Sûre.

Return to the N 27 and turn right towards Château de Bourscheid.

★Château de Bourscheid ⊙ – The **ruins★** of this brown schist castle are 155m – 508ft above the Sûre. An 11C keep and a Gothic fireplace remain of the upper castle or fortress. The lower part of the castle, comprising the Stolzembourg mansion, was built in the 14C and altered many times up to the 18C. In the 19C it fell into ruins, but it has been restored since 1972 and is now a museum displaying objects uncovered during digs at the castle (pottery, architectural fragments). It is also used for temporary exhibitions. Note the two reproductions of drawings of the castle by Victor Hugo (1871) on the ground floor. The originals are in the Bibliothèque Nationale in Paris.

There are beautiful and varied **views★** of the valley and plateau from the towers of the fortress.

About 800m – 0.5 mile beyond the castle, on the right, there is the entrance to a campsite; a terrace here gives a pretty **glimpse★★** of the ruins and the valley.

Return to the valley.

From here the river descends southwards to Erpeldange. The **scenery★** of thickets and meadows is captivating.

★② THE LOWER VALLEY

From Erpeldange to Wasserbillig

57km – 35 miles – allow half a day

The lower Sûre is less austere and more pastoral. After emerging from the Ardennes massif, the river flows between gentler slopes and wider fields. The road follows the course of the river almost continually until the confluence with the Moselle.

Beyond Erpeldange, note the monument to General Patton on the other side of the bridge over the Sûre, towards Ettelbruck.

Ettelbruck – This is a road and railway junction at the confluence of the Sûre and the Alzette, as well as a commercial and agricultural centre.

Diekirch – *See DIEKIRCH.*

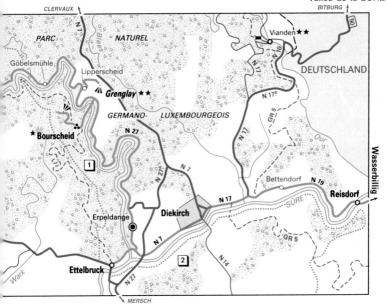

Reisdorf – This charming village was built at the end of the pretty Ernz Blanche Valley.

Shortly after the village, the river Our flows into the Sûre, near Wallendorf.

★**Echternach** – *See ECHTERNACH.*

Barrage de Rosport – Downstream from Rosport *(qv)*, the Sûre forms a gigantic loop. The river is contained by a large dam with a hydro-electric power station supplied by a pressure pipe installed at the mouth of the meander. The course of the river is therefore accelerated by an artificial variation in level.

At **Wasserbillig** *(qv)* the Sûre flows into the Moselle.

The diagram on the back cover shows the Michelin Maps covering the countries described in this Guide; the chapter headings specify the appropriate map for the local area

VIANDEN★★

Population 1 460
Michelin maps 409 L6 and 215 fold 3

The old houses in this charming little town cling to the slopes below Our Castle. It is a splendid **setting★**.

★★**Viewpoints** – The hills overlooking the town to the west offer beautiful views of Vianden and the surrounding countryside. The Mont St Nicolas *(qv)* road leads to a particularly interesting viewpoint. A **chairlift** ⊙ leads up to another viewpoint *(accessible also via a footpath from the castle)*. There is an extensive **panoramic view★★** over the town, the castle and the valley.

SIGHTS

★★**Château** ⊙ – *Illustration p 256.* The romantic outline of the castle dominates the town. It was built by the Counts of Vianden, and then belonged to the Orange-Nassau family from 1417 to 1977, except for a short period from 1820 to 1827, when it was bought by a speculator who left it in a severely damaged state.

In 1977 Grand Duke Jean gave it to the State of Luxembourg, and since then it has undergone a remarkable restoration which has given it back its late-18C appearance.

Archeological digs have revealed the presence of a small fortress constructed during the Dark Ages (5C) and a first Carolingian medieval enclosure dating from the 9C. The Counts of Vianden reached the height of their power from the 12C to the 13C, and it is from this period, a transition between Romanesque and Gothic, that most of the buildings date.

Tour – *1 hour 30min. A signposted route and numbered rooms lead the visitor through the maze of corridors, stairs and terraces.*

The castle consists of the 13C Petit Palais, a Romanesque building with Gothic pointed windows (Armoury and Byzantine Room) and the Grand Palais, with the gigantic **Knights' Hall** above the Counts' Hall.

The Romanesque **chapel** is at the east end. It has a ten-sided base from the Carolingian period which is extended by the chancel and surmounted by a hexagonal upper storey with colonnettes.

An archeological exhibition illustrates the various stages in the castle's construction.

From the watchpath and the garden, there are **views**★ of the Our Valley and the town.

Bridge over the Our – From this bridge, which is protected by a statue of St John of Nepomuk, patron saint of bridges, there is a pleasant **view** of the town and castle.

Maison de Victor Hugo ⊘ – After several trips through Vianden, Victor Hugo, in exile, stayed here in 1871 from 8 June to 22 August. The house has been turned into a museum and exhibits drawings and letters written by the great French author. There is a bust of Victor Hugo by Rodin opposite the house.

Musée d'Art rustique ⊘ – *98 Grand-Rue.*

This museum of rustic art is in an old patrician home. It consists of a delightful regional interior decorated with rustic furniture. There is a beautiful collection of firebacks and another of dolls.

Église des Trinitaires – *Grand-Rue.*

This old Gothic abbey church with two aisles dates from the 13C. It has pretty cloisters, also from the 13C, which have been restored.

THE DAM AND POWER STATION *tour : 2 hours*

Barrage de Lohmühle *1km – 0.75 miles north.*

This dam is the lower basin of a large hydro-electric plant. The reservoir, with a capacity of 10 million m^3 – 107 million ft^3, is 8km – 5 miles long. The **Église Neuve** (church), built in 1770 in the old plague victims' district, is on the west bank at the foot of the dam.

Hydro-electric pumping station – *5km – 3 miles north of the dam, beyond Bivels.*

Hollowed out of the rock, the machine room is the underground link between the upper basins in Mont St Nicolas and the lower Our reservoir. During hours of low consumption the reservoir water is pumped into the upper basins to be re-used in the periods of high consumption.

Annual energy production can reach 1 600 million kilowatts.

The **visitors' gallery** has models and illuminated explanatory displays.

Bassins supérieurs du mont Saint Nicolas – *5km – 3 miles west on the Diekirch road, then right.*

After the crossroads, there is a beautiful **view**★★ of the castle and the town roofs.

The **upper basins,** surrounded by 4.6km – 2.75 miles of dikes, form an artificial lake. This is between 14 and 35m – 45 and 114ft deep, and has a capacity of 6.6 million m3 – 71 million ft3. A flight of steps leads to one section of the dike. There is a **view** of the basin and the water tower, linked by a footbridge.

From the foot of the basins there is a **view**★ of the Our Valley gouged out of the cultivated Oesling plain and the hills in Germany.

EXCURSION

★★**Our Valley** – *20km – 12.5 miles as far as Dasburg in Germany.*

In the area around Ouren in Belgium and Wallendorf, the River Our marks the border between Germany and the Grand Duchy of Luxembourg. It cuts a deep and winding valley into the ancient rock, sometimes squeezing its way between sheer walls of stone.

Head north from Vianden.

The road runs initially along the crest of the **Lohmühle dam** *(qv).*

Bivels – This village is in a remarkable **setting**★ in the centre of an enormous meander of the Our.

Hydro-electric pumping station – *See above.*

Stolzembourg – The romantic ruins of a castle are perched on a hilltop above the village.

Dasburg – A charming town, in a pretty location on the German side of the river.

WILTZ

Population 3 880
Michelin maps 409 K6 and 215 folds 10, 11

Wiltz lies at an altitude of 315m – 1 033ft on the Oesling plateau *(qv)*. It is a commercial and industrial town (plastics, copper, brewing), a tourist centre and an international Scouting community. Twelve chalets and about fifteen campsites are dotted around the surrounding woods.

The lower town extends along the banks of the River Wiltz, while the upper town is a picturesque district squeezed onto a spur of rock between the church and the castle. Every year the castle gardens make a pretty setting for a European Festival of Open-air Theatre and Music *(see the Calendar of Events)*.

SIGHTS

Église décanale – This 16C church in the lower town was extended and restored in the 20C.

Its two Gothic aisles contain the tombstones of the Lords of Wiltz. A beautiful Louis XV grille closes off the counts' chapel.

On the climb up to the upper town, note a **monument** on the left, recalling that it was at Wiltz that the first general strike against the German occupation began in September 1942.

Château – The château of the Counts of Wiltz still has a square 13C tower, which was altered in 1722. The main wing dates from 1631. It has now been turned into an old people's home. An amphitheatre was created in 1954 at the foot of the main staircase. This is where the festival events take place.

Croix de Justice – Dating from the 16C, this "cross of justice" replaced a medieval cross symbolising the rights granted to the town (justice, freedom, trade).

Note also the statues of the Virgin Mary and St John of Nepomuk who is said to have saved the town from fire.

Monument Notre-Dame de Fatima – 1952. *Access via the Noertrange road, CR 329, to the west.*

The road passes a brewery where copper boilers can be seen. There is an interesting **view** from the monument of the white town with slate roofs arranged in tiers on the hillside.

The shrine is a pilgrimage site for Portuguese immigrants.

EXCURSION

Wiltz Valley – *11km – 6.75 miles east as far as Kautenbach.*
This pretty, winding valley runs between wooded hillsides.

Help us in our constant task of keeping up-to-date.
Send us your comments and suggestions to

Michelin Tyre PLC
Tourism Department
38 Clarendon Road – WATFORD Herts WD1 1SX
Tel: (01923) 415000

Practical
information

J. Évrard, Bruxelles

281

Travelling to Belgium and the Grand Duchy of Luxembourg

Formalities – Despite the new law which came into force on 1 January 1993 authorising the free flow of goods and people within the EU, it is nonetheless advisable that travellers should be equipped with some valid piece of identification such as a **passport.** Holders of British, Irish and US passports require no visa to enter Belgium and the Grand Duchy of Luxembourg, although visas may be necessary for visitors from some Commonwealth countries, and for those planning to stay for longer than 3 months. US citizens should obtain the booklet *Your Trip Abroad* (US $1.25) which provides useful information on visa requirements, customs regulations, medical care etc. for international travellers. Apply to the Superintendent of Documents, PO Box 371954, Pittsburgh, PA 15250-795, ☎ (202) 512-1800.

Customs Regulations – Since the implementation of the single European market in 1993, there are effectively no longer any restrictions on the quantities of goods which can be purchased within the EU by private travellers from its member states. A leaflet entitled *A Guide for Travellers* is avaliable from HM Customs, UK (or telephone) 0181 346 1144 or 0171 620 1313.
Non-residents of EU member states should enquire about customs regulations at their local customs service. US residents can obtain a free publication *Know Before You Go* from the US Customs Service, PO Box 7407, Washington, DC 20044, ☎ (202) 927-5580.

By air – Various international airline companies operate regular services to the international airports in Belgium (Brussels, Antwerp) and the Grand Duchy of Luxembourg (Luxembourg). Contact airlines and travel agents for information and timetables.

By sea – There are numerous cross-Channel services (passenger and car ferries, hovercraft, Sea Cat) from the United Kingdom and Eire. For details apply to travel agencies or to:

Hoverspeed, International Hoverport, Marine Parade, Dover, Kent CT17 9TG, ☎ (01304) 240 241.

P&O European Ferries, Channel House, Channel View Road, Dover, Kent CT17 9TJ, ☎ (0990) 980 980.

Sally Line, 81 Piccadilly, London W1V 9HF, ☎ (0171) 409 2240.
Argyle Centre, York St, Ramsgate, Kent CT11 9DS, ☎ (01843) 595 522.

Stena Line, Charter House, Park Street, Ashford, Kent TN24 8EX, ☎ (0990) 70 70 70.

Le Shuttle – Eurotunnel, ☎(0990) 35 35 35.

By rail – With **Eurostar,** it takes only three and a half hours to travel from London-Waterloo to Bruxelles-Midi. There are six trains a day from Monday to Saturday, and five on Sundays. Change at Bruxelles-Midi station to travel on to Luxembourg.

By road – When driving to the continent the ideal ports of entry for Belgium are **Zeebrugge** (from Hull and Felixstowe), **Ostend** (from Ramsgate) and **Calais** (from Dover). There is a wide choice of routes using motorways or national roads into Belgium and the Grand Duchy of Luxembourg.
Ostend to Bruges: 28km – 17 miles, to Ghent: 64km – 40 miles, to Brussels: 115km – 72 miles;
Zeebrugge to Bruges: 14km – 9 miles, to Brussels: 111km – 69 miles;
Calais to Brussels: 213km – 132 miles (via Ostend) 231km – 144 miles (via Lille);
Brussels to Luxembourg: 219km – 136 miles.

The Channel Tunnel

This undersea tunnel is the realisation of dreams of linking Britain to mainland Europe which date back over two hundred years. The Channel link consists of two single-track rail tunnels (7.60m – 24ft in diameter) for passenger and freight transport, and one service tunnel (4.80m – 15ft in diameter) for safety and ventilation. The tunnels are 50.5km – 31 miles long, 37km – 23 miles of which are under the Channel. Most of the tunnel is 40m – 131ft beneath the seabed, in a layer of blue chalk. The trains (800m – 2624ft long) have two levels for passenger cars (capacity 118 cars per shuttle) and one level for coaches and caravans. Special services operate for heavy goods vehicles. British, French and Belgian trains, including French TGVs, also use the tunnel. Journey time is ideally 35 minutes, 28 minutes of which are in the tunnel at a maximum speed of 130km – 80 miles per hour.

Touring in Belgium and Luxembourg

By car

Documents – A valid **driving licence** is essential. Third party insurance is the minimum cover required by insurance legislation in Belgium, but it is advisable to take out additional insurance for fully comprehensive cover (the Green Card).

Driving regulations – Traffic in Belgium and Luxembourg drives **on the right!** The minimum age for driving is 18 for cars and motor-cycles and 16 for mopeds. Children under 12 are not allowed to travel in the front seat as long as there is room for them in the back. Seatbelts are compulsory in the back as well as the front of the car. Amber headlights are not necessary. Dipped headlights (not sidelights) are compulsory at night.

Maximum **speed limits** for cars, caravans and small trailers are 50kph – 31mph in built-up areas, 90kph – 55mph on the open road, and 120kph – 75mph on motor-ways (minimum speed on motorways is 70kph – 45mph). Motorways are toll-free and all motorway junctions are numbered *(see the Michelin map series)*.

Priority must be given to cars coming from the right at junctions and on roundabouts, unless shown otherwise. Give way also to trams, pedestrians boarding or alighting from trams, and pedestrians crossing the road into which you are just turning.

The regulation **red warning triangle** must be carried, and displayed in the event of a breakdown. Dial 100 (in Belgium) for medical help for accidents involving injuries.

Accidents – In the event of an accident the emergency numbers are ambulance 100, police in Belgium 101 and police in Luxembourg 012. Emergency telephones are to be found alongside the main roads.

Breakdown service – The main organisations are:
– Touring Secours de Belgique, 44 rue de la Loi, 1040 Brussels, ☎ (02) 233 22 11 (for help anywhere in Belgium call ☎ (070) 344 777; this breakdown service operates round the clock; on motorways, use the emergency telephones)
– Royal Automobile Club de Belgique, rue d'Arlon 53, 1040 Brussels, ☎ (02) 287 09 00
– Vlaamse Automobilistenbond, Sint-Jacobsmarkt 45, 2000 Antwerp, ☎ (03) 253 63 63.
– Automobile Club du Grand Duché de Luxembourg, route de Longwy 54, 8007 Bertrange, ☎ 45 00 451.

Traffic and weather information – Useful numbers are:
Weather forecast – ☎ (0900) 27 003 (Institut Royal Météorologique).
Road and traffic conditions – ☎ 233 22 36 between 7am and 11pm (Touring Club) and ☎ 287 09 80 (Royal Automobile Club).

Petrol – Four-star ("super") petrol costs 37.50BF (29.40LF) per litre. Unleaded petrol, diesel and LPG are also available. Petrol is generally slightly more expensive in motorway service stations.

Access (Mastercard) and Barclaycard/Visa credit cards are not widely accepted at petrol stations; Eurocard, American Express and Diners Club are in wider use, but visitors are still strongly advised to have other means of payment with them.

Car Hire – Cars can be hired in most major towns and resorts. The minimum age limit is 21. A current driving licence is required.

Motorcyclists – Crash helmets are compulsory for drivers and passengers of motor-cycles of 50cc and over. Dipped headlights must be used at all times of the day or night.

Signposting – In Flanders, French towns are often signposted in Dutch, so Parijs for Paris, Rijsel for Lille etc.

By train

Tickets and fares – The Belgian railway system is run by the Société Nationale de Chemin de Fer de Belgique/Belgische Spoorwegen, whose symbol is a "B"in an oval. For further information and reservations apply to

London – Belgian Railways, Premier House, 10 Greycoat Place, London SW1, ☎ 0171 233 0360.

The Michelin Map-Guide "The Channel Guide" gives brief descriptions of the seaside resorts and historic cities at the other end of the tunnel. It includes a map showing the motorway networks at either end of the tunnel, site plans of the two terminals at Folkestone and Calais and includes a short history of the Channel Tunnel and details of the services offered by Eurostar and Le Shuttle.

General information

Currency – The unit of currency in Belgium is the Belgian franc, and in Luxembourg the Luxembourg franc. Belgian currency is used also in Luxembourg, but although the Luxembourg franc is theoretically valid currency in Belgium, it is generally only accepted in the province of Luxembourg.
Approximate exchange rate: £1 = 50BF.

To help with budgeting, here are some indications of **prices**:

	Belgian F	Luxembourg F
Four-star petrol (per litre)	37.50	29.40
Four-star unleaded petrol (per litre)	35.00	26.70
Diesel (per litre)	25.80	21.30
LPG (liquid petroleum gas)	10.80	10.47
Bus ride	50	
Underground ride (in Brussels)	50	
Taxi ride (town centre rates)	95 + 38F/km	
Local telephone call (2 min in town)	10	
Posting a letter/postcard within the EU	16	
Posting a letter/postcard outside the EU	30	
Cinema (average price)	250	
Theatre (average price)	600	

For indications of prices of hotels and restaurants, consult the current Michelin Red Guide Benelux.

Opening hours and public holidays

In Belgium:

Banks open from 9am to 12.30 noon and from 2pm to 3.30pm (until 4pm or even 6pm on Fridays in branches near major commercial centres); in town centres they open from 8.30am to 3.30pm (4pm on Fridays); closed at weekends.

Post offices open from 9am to 12 noon and from 2.30pm to4pm; in city centres from 9am to 5pm; closed at weekends. Some post offices house telephone facilities, but check the town map or a telephone book for those which do not. Central telephone agency (Belgacom) in Brussels at 19 boulevard l'Impératrice is open from 6pm to 8pm every day.

Shops open from 8am to about 6pm; closed on Sundays.

Public holidays are on 1 January, Easter Monday, 1 May, Ascension Day, Whit Monday, 21 July (national holiday), 15 August, 1 November, 11 November, 25 December. Local festivals *(see the Calendar of Events)* can also mean that various public facilities will be closed.

In Luxembourg:

Banks open from 8.30am to 12.30pm and from 1.30pm to 4.30pm; closed at weekends.

Post and telephone facilities are not always in the same place; consult a town map or the telephone book.

Public holidays in Luxembourg are the same as those in Belgium *(see above)* except for the national holiday, which is on 23 June, and 11 November, which is not a public holiday.

Telephone – The international dialling code for Belgium is 32, and for Luxembourg 352. To telephone the UK from Belgium or Luxembourg, dial 00 + 44 + STD code (minus preceding 0) + number.

Some useful telephone numbers:

	Belgium	Luxembourg
Operator	1307	017
Police	101	012
Fire Brigade/Ambulance	100	012
Weather forecast	1703	18

The Michelin Red Guide Benelux
which is revised annually
gives a selection of establishments offering

- *carefully prepared meals at reasonable prices*
- *simple meals at moderate prices*
- *prices including or excluding service*
- *car parking*

Accommodation

Hotels and restaurants – For choosing a stopover for a few hours or a few days, the current Michelin Red Guide Benelux is an indispensable complement to this guide. It is updated every year and offers a range of hotels and restaurants with an indication of their standard of service and comfort, their location, their degree of pleasantness and their prices.

Booking a room – Hotel accommodation can be booked through BTR (Belgian Tourist Reservation), 111 Boulevard Ampach, 1000 Brussels, ☎ (02) 513 7484, fax (02) 513 92 77. It is strongly advised to reserve hotel rooms in advance, especially for a weekend break, when visiting Bruges or any area where there is a local festival taking place.

Tips – It is customary to tip the waiter for particular service.
Tips are included in the prices of Belgian **taxis**.

Rented accommodation – Contact the local tourist office for details.

Farmhouse holidays – The following organisations provide information and make reservations:
– Fetourag, Fédération du Tourisme Agricole de l'Alliance Agricole Belge, rue de la Science 23-25, 1040 Brussels, ☎ (02) 230 72 95.
– UTRA, Fédération du Tourisme des Unions Professionnelles Agricoles de Belgique, rue A Dansaert 94-96, 1000 Brussels, ☎ (02) 511 07 37.
– For Flanders, contact:
– Vlaamse Federatie voor Plattelandstoerisme, Minderbroederstraat 8, 3000 Leuven, ☎ (016) 24 21 58 – this organisation brings out a brochure with addresses.
– For West Flanders, contact:
– VZW, Hoevevakantie Kraaiehof, Proostdijk 28, 8480 Veurne, ☎ (058) 31 16 42.
In Tielt, contact the VVV, Stadhuis, 8800 Tielt, ☎ (051) 40 10 11.
For the Ardennes, contact the tourist offices of the provinces of Liège, Luxembourg and Namur *(see addresses below)*.

Back-to-Nature holidays – There are many opportunities for returning to nature, in the Ardennes in particular, in places with a minimum of facilities: setting, accommodation, sport, recreation. These are indicated by a special sign and known locally as *Stations vertes de vacances*.

Camping and Caravanning – Belgium has more than 350 campsites, divided into four categories. They are extremely crowded in July and August. The Grand Duchy of Luxembourg has over 100 campsites. Independent camping is permitted in Belgium and Luxembourg, but do not forget to ask the permission of the landowner first!

Youth Hostels – Belgian Youth Hostel associations:
– Centrale Wallonne des Auberges de la Jeunesse, rue Van Oost 52, 1030 Brussels, ☎ (02) 215 31 00.
– Vlaamse Jeugdherbergcentrale, Van Stralenstraat 40, 2060 Antwerpen, ☎ (03) 232 72 18.
For information on accommodation for young people, contact Inforjeunes, 2 Impasse des Capucins, Namur *(on weekdays from 12 noon to 5.40pm; no information given by telephone)*, or JIAC, Place Ste-Catherine 16, Brussels, ☎ (02) 218 11 80 *(on weekdays from 10am to 7pm; Saturdays from 12 noon to 7pm)*.
Luxembourg Youth Hostel association:
– Centrale des Auberges de Jeunesse Luxembourgeoises, 18 place des Armes, – BP 374, 2013 Luxembourg, ☎ 22 55 88.

Tourist information

Belgian National Tourist Offices

London: 29 Princes Street, London W1R 7RG, ☎ (0891) 88 77 99.

New York: 780 Third Avenue, Suite 1501, New York, NY 10017, ☎ 1212 758 8130

Brussels: Rue Marché-aux-Herbes, 63, 1000 Bruxelles, ☎ (02) 504 03 90.

There are also **Regional Belgian tourist offices** for each province:
– Antwerpen: Karel Oomstraat 11, 2018 Antwerpen, ☎ (03) 216 28 10
– Brabant-Wallon: Chaussée de Bruxelles 218, 1410 Waterloo, ☎ (02) 351 12 00.
– Hainaut: Rue des Clercs 31, 7000 Mons, ☎ (065) 36 04 64
– Liège: Boulevard de la Sauvenière 77, 4000 Liège, ☎ (041) 22 42 10
– Limburg: Universiteitslaan 1, 3500 Hasselt, ☎ (011) 23 7980

- Luxembourg: Quai de l'Ourthe 9, 6980 La Roche-en-Ardenne, ☎ (084) 41 10 11
- Namur: Rue Notre-Dame 3, 5000 Namur, ☎ (081) 22 29 98
- Oost-Vlaanderen: PAC Het Zuid, Woodrow Wilsonplein 3, 9000 Gent, ☎ (09) 267 70 20
- Vlaams-Brabant: Diestsesteenweg 52-54, 3010 Leuven, ☎ (016) 26 76 20
- West-Vlaanderen: Kasteel Tillegem, 8200 Brugge, ☎ (050) 38 02 96

Luxembourg National Tourist Offices

London: 36-37 Piccadilly, London W1V 9PA, ☎ (0171) 434 2800.

Luxembourg: Air Terminus, place de la Gare, Luxembourg, ☎ 48 11 99; Luxembourg-Findel Aérogare, ☎ 40 08 08

Brussels: 104 avenue Louise, Brussels, ☎ (02) 646 03 70

In Belgium and Luxembourg tourist offices are indicated with 🅗 (information). The tourist office is called Office de Tourisme/Syndicat d'Initiative in French, and Dienst voor Toerisme/VVV (Vereniging voor Vreemdelingen Verkeer, or Foreigners' Travel Association) in Dutch. Addresses and telephone numbers are listed in the Times and Charges chapter of this guide.

Discovering Belgium and Luxembourg

Which is the best time of year to visit?

For those interested mainly in the cultural side of life, this can be enjoyed all year round. However, the countryside is at its best between April and October.

Spring – Burgeoning plant-life enhances avenues and squares, and delicate foliage along the borders of canals, in Bruges for example, makes a pretty scene. The forests of the Ardennes and Luxembourg are cloaked in myriad shades of green. In April, Watermael-Boitsfort, a suburb of Brussels, is a vision in pink amidst the blossom of its Japanese cherry trees.

Summer – The wide sandy beaches and sand dunes of the North Sea coast attract large crowds of holidaymakers. The rivers of the Ardennes cutting through their stunning backdrop of green hills are also extremely popular. In August the Lochristi region is resplendent with begonias in full bloom.

Autumn – This is the best time of year for visiting the Ardennes and Luxembourg, where richly stocked game forests take on magnificent seasonal hues. The city of Luxembourg is set jewel-like amidst the russet foliage of its trees.

Winter – Snow often covers the evergreen forests of the Ardennes, lending a magical quality to the beauty of the landscape. What better setting for a winter sports holiday?

Seaside resorts

The beautiful sandy Belgian coast boasts a series of lively seaside resorts each with a character all of its own. There are the well known resorts with all the traditional facilities and entertainment; Blankenberg provides fun for all the family while elegance and sophistication are the hallmarks of Knokke Heist and Ostend; then come a series of family resorts such as De Haan, Kokdijde and Middelkerke; and finally the tranquillity of more peaceful centres for the nature lover (Westende and De Panne).

There is free access to the dunes and beach almost everywhere and most beaches have hire facilities (deck chairs, sun loungers, parasols and wind screens). In the major resorts there are beach huts for rent per week or per month; the tourist office can provide the addresses of the local hire firms.

All the resorts have one thing in common: great stretches of golden sandy beach which are sometimes 500m wide at low tide. These are ideal for strolling barefoot at the water's edge, for taking the dog for a brisk and invigorating walk, for an early morning or late evening ride, or for sand-yachting, speed sailing (windsurfing on the beach) and skim-boarding.

Swimming – Large signs on the beach or promenade indicate the areas supervised by lifeguards and flags warn bathers of possible risks: green – safe bathing; yellow – be careful; red – bathing prohibited. When the yellow flag is up it is dangerous to take inflatable mattresses and dinghies into the sea; it is also dangerous to use them when the tide is going out. Lifeguards are normally on duty between 10am and 6pm.

Wind-surfing, surfing and skim-boarding – The Belgian coast is ideal for windsurfing, but for safety reasons on the popular beaches, windsurfers must set out from the specifically designated areas. The following resorts are popular with surfers Bredene, De Panne, Knokke-Heist, Nieuwpoort, Ostend, Wenduine, Westende and Zeebrugge. Surfing is possible at Ostend and skim boarders can be seen "skimming along" at the water's edge.

Office Belge de Tourisme, Paris

Sand-yachting

Sand-yachting and speed-sailing – The great expanses of hard sand at low tide are ideal for sand-yachting and one of the more popular stretches of coast for this sport is between De Panne and Oostduinkerke. Speed-sailing or windsurfing on wheels is growing in popularity.

Touring

Belgium has over 60 tourist trails indicated by hexagonal-shaped signposts carrying the name of the trail. The trails vary between 30km- and 130km-long and link the main tourist centres or follow the scenic routes. Many of the trails have a special theme: literature (Pallieter-route), history (Routes 14 to 18), geography (Scheideroute or River Scheldt) or present a particular feature of a region eg windmills (Molenlan-route or route des moulins) and vineyards (Druivenroute or route du raisin). Local book-shops and tourist information centres can provide brochures and leaflets on these trails.

Cycling

The flatter countryside of Flanders is good for cycling and has many cycling paths. A long-distance cycling path, the Grote Route 5, links Bokrijk in Belgium to Bergen op Zoom in the Netherlands. There are a large number of brochures in Dutch for special cycling tours. A bicycle can be hired from one railway station and returned to another one; it is best to book ahead. Reductions are offered to people with a railway ticket and to those who hire for more than three days.

Walking

An excellent network of clearly marked footpaths crisscrosses both Belgium, in partic-ular the Ardennes, and the Grand Duchy of Luxembourg. Grande Randonnée or GR (long-distance) footpaths are marked on Michelin maps 212, 213, 214 and 215.

Belgium – The network of marked footpaths covers 4 750km – 2 952 miles. The main footpaths are: GR 5 (Holland-Mediterranean), linking Rotterdam to Nice via the province of Liège (Spa, Liège) and the Grand Duchy of Luxembourg; GR AE (Ardennes-Eifel, part of European footpath 3) crossing the Ardennes from west to east through the Semois Valley; GR 12 (Brussels-Paris); GR 56 (Eastern Townships, Hautes-Fagnes, Helle Valley); GR 57 (Ourthe footpath linking Liège to the Grand Duchy); GR 129 (Scheldt-Meuse) linking Bruges with the Meuse Valley; GR 126 linking Brussels to the Semois Valley. There is also an interesting range of circular footpaths and footpaths in the Kempen region.

Two walking associations, "Sentiers de Grande Randonnée" (BP 10, 4000 Liège) and "Grote Routepaden" (Van Stralenstraat 40, 2060 Antwerpen, ☎ (03) 232 72 18), publish a quarterly periodical (GR Infos Sentiers and Wandelen GR) and have maps and literature on all the footpaths.

Elsewhere, public woods and recreation centres often have footpaths indicated by a special symbol depicting hikers. At the entrance to several nature reserves, routes for walks are suggested, with an indication of the length of the walk and posts painted in bright colours to act as markers.

Grand Duchy of Luxembourg – The national network of footpaths, marked in yellow, covers about 720km – 447 miles and is at its most dense around the main tourist centres: Diekirch, Echternach and Clervaux. The GR 5 crosses the country *(see above)*.

Leaflets and small maps are available from tourist offices. Topographical maps (1:20,000) are on sale in bookshops or at the central office of the Youth Hostel association *(see previous page)*.

Similarly there are 171 **drive-and-walk** routes and 25 **train-and-walk** routes. These vary in length from 5-15km – 3-9 miles and enable tourists to leave their car and go for a walk in areas of particular interest or natural beauty, using footpaths designed to return to the point of departure. There is a guide of such walks on sale in bookshops; the guide of the train-and-walk routes is available from the central office of the Youth Hostel Association or from bookshops.

Sport

Canoeing – Certain stretches of several rivers are suitable for canoeing. On the Ourthe, the Semois, the Sûre and the Amblève there are organisations which hire canoes. Going down the river Lesse by canoe or boat is an unforgettable experience *(qv)*. The Fédération royale belge de canoë can be contacted at Geerdegemvaart 79, 2800 Mechelen, ☎ (015) 41 54 59.

Waterskiing – One of the best places for this sport is on the Upper Meuse (at Wépion, Profondeville, Yvoir and Waulsort), in Liège, Mons, Manage and Ronquières, on the Eau d'Heure lake and on the Albert Canal. For further information contact Fédération francophone du ski nautique belge, rue de Tervaete 11, 1040 Brussels, ☎ (02) 734 93 73).

Yachting – There are several marinas along the coast, at Zeebrugge, Blankenberge, Ostend and Nieuwpoort. Useful addresses include: Ligue régionale du yachting belge, avenue du Parc d'Armée 90, 5100 Jambes, ☎ (081) 30 49 79, Landelijke Bond voor Watersportverenigingen in Belgiè, IJzerweglaan 72, 9050 Gent/Ledeberg, ☎ (09) 231 26 35, Vlaamse Vereniging voor Watersport, Beatrijslaan 25, 2050 Antwerpen, ☎ (03) 219 69 67.

Canoeing on the River Lesse

J. Evrard, Bruxelles

Shooting and wildfowling – Small game and wildfowl are to be found mainly to the north of the Sambre and Meuse valley, and large game (boar, stags, roe-deer) in the Ardennes. It is compulsory to have either a shooting permit or game licence. For further information contact the Royal St-Hubert Club, place Jean-Jacobs 1, 1000 Brussels, ☎ (02) 511 89 75.

Fishing – Belgium offers opportunities for all sorts of angling. It is compulsory to have a fishing permit valid for a year, which can be obtained from a post office. Further details from the national angling association, Fédération sportive des pêcheurs francophones de Belgique, rue de Wynants 33, 1000 Brussels, ☎ (02) 511 68 48.

Horse-riding – There are riding stables throughout Belgium and Luxembourg. Certain agencies organise horse-riding weekends. Horse racing takes place at Ostend, Groenendael, Watermael-Boitsfort, Kuurne and Sterrebeek (trotting), Waregem (steeplechase). Belgian horse-riding association: Fédération belge des sports équestres, Avenue Houba de Strooper 156, 1020 Brussels, ☎ (02) 478 50 56. Information on horse races can be obtained from the Jockey Club de Belgique, Avenue des Ombrages 16, 1200 Brussels, ☎ (02) 771 42 86.

Rock-climbing – A few of the rock faces overhanging the rivers of the Ardennes are sheer enough for rock-climbing *(qv)*. Belgian rock-climbing club: Club alpin belge, rue de l'Aurore 19, 1050 Brussels, ☎ (02) 648 86 11.

Winter sports – The Ardennes climate is harsh enough for there to be substantial snowfalls at quite low altitudes between December and March. In the provinces of Liège and Luxembourg, there are slopes for skiing and tobogganing. Equipment hire is available nearby. For further information contact the Liège or Luxembourg regional tourist offices *(qv)*.

Other sports – The reputation of Belgian cycling needs no further comment. Other popular sports in Belgium include swimming, tennis, bowling, clay-pigeon shooting and **balle-pelote**, a kind of bowls that is very popular in Wallonia.

A brochure published by the tourist office of the Grand Duchy of Luxembourg gives useful information about sports there.

Entertainment

Films are usually shown in their original language with subtitles in Flanders, or dubbed into French in Wallonia. In Brussels and Wallonia, **plays** are staged in French.
The Luxembourg tourist office publishes an Agenda Touristique six times a year which lists entertainments. See also the Calendar of Events at the end of the guide.
Belgians are great music-lovers and there are numerous **concerts** throughout the year, especially during festivals. From September to May, there is **opera** in Antwerp, Brussels, Ghent, Liège, Mons, Verviers and Charleroi, all of which have an opera house, as well as in Namur and Tournai.
In summer and autumn there are two major **festivals**, the Flanders Festival and the Wallonia Festival. These include various types of performances (opera, concerts, recitals, ballet) in various towns throughout the country, usually set against the magnificent backdrop of an ecclesiastical building (church or cathedral) or a castle.
For further information on the Flanders Festival contact the Secrétariat du Festival de Flandres, 60 rue Ravenstein, 1000 Brussels, ☎ (02) 548 95 95 or Kleine Gentstraat 46, 9051 St-Denijs-Westrem, ☎ (09) 243 94 94.
For further information on the Wallonia Festival contact ☎ (041) 22 32 48.
The **Europalia** Festival takes place every two years with a large number of events all over the country (theatre, music, literature, exhibitions, cinema, ballet). For information on the programme contact the Fondation Europalia International, ☎ (02) 507 85 94 or the Belgian Tourist Office, 29 Princes Street, London W1R 7RG, ☎ (0891) 88 77 99.
Last but not least, Belgium has no fewer than eight **casinos** open all year round in Blankenberge, Knokke, Ostend and Middelkerke on the coast, and Dinant, Chaudfontaine, Spa and Namur inland.
For entertainment in Luxembourg, consult the brochure available from the Luxembourg tourist office and the Calendar of Events in this guide.

Books and films

Access to the Channel Ports (Guide for the Disabled), available from Access Project, Pauline Hephaistos Survey Projects, 39 Bradley Gardens, London W13 8HE

A New Guide to the Battlefields of Northern France and the Low Countries, M Glover *(Michael Joseph)*

Passchendaele: The Untold Story, Robert Prior and Trevor Wilson *(Yale University Press)*

The Duke and the Emperor: Wellington and Napoleon, John Strawson *(Constable)*

Art Deco, A Duncan *(Thames and Hudson)*

The 19C in Belgium – Architecture and Interior Design, Jos Vandenbreeden and Françoise Dierkens-Aubry *(Lannoo)*

Art Nouveau in Belgium – Architecture and Interiors, Jos Vandenbreeden and Françoise Dierkens-Aubry *(Lannoo)*

Contemporary Architecture in Belgium, Geert Bekaert *(Lannoo)*

Blue Guide Belgium and Luxembourg, J Tomes *(A & C Black)*

Art in Belgium – From the Middle Ages to the Present Day, Colette Souillard, translated by Simon Honner *(Duculot)*

Civilisation (History/Flemish Primitives), K Clark *(Penguin)*

Dutch and Flemish Painting: Art in the Netherlands in the 17C, C Brown *(Phaidon)*

From Van Eyck to Brueghel, M Friedlander *(Phaidon)*

Rubens: A Double Life, Marie-Anne Lescourret *(A & C Black)*

Medieval Flanders, D Nicholas *(Longman)*

Pieter Paul Rubens: Man and Artist, C White *(Yale University Press)*

Niccolò Rising (fiction), D Dunnett *(Penguin)*

The Sorrow of Belgium (fiction), H Claus *(Penguin)*

Through the Dutch and Belgian Canals, P Bristow *(A & C Black)*

The Michelin Green Guide France
presents a selection of the most interesting and distinctive sights
on the main tourist routes

Phrasebook

Some tips for pronunciation of Flemish:

h: is sounded *(het = the)*
j: yeh *(kindje = small child)*
s: is soft *(except in "mus(z)eum")*
g: between "gentle" and "guest" *(Gent)*
ng: more "n" than "ng" *(Tongeren)*
ch: guttural, as in Scottish "loch" *(Mechelen)*
sch: s + ch as above *(Aarschot)*
sch (at end of word): sh *(toeristisch)*

aa, ae: ah *(Laarne, Verhaeren)*
ee: eh *(meer, zee)*
ie: ee *(Tienen, Ieper)*
oo: oh *(Oostende)*
ij: ay *(Kortrijk, Rijssel)*
oe: oo *(Doest)*

ou: ow *(Oudenaarde, Turnhout)*
ui: oi *(Diksmuide, St.-Truiden)*

Common words

NB For restaurant terminology, consult the current Michelin Red Guide Benelux.

Dutch	French	English	Dutch	French	English
U	vous	you	goedemorgen	bonjour	good morning
mijnheer	monsieur	Mr	goedemiddag	bonjour	good afternoon
mevrouw	madame	Mrs, Ms	goedenavond	bonsoir	good evening
juffrouw	mademoiselle	miss	tot ziens	au revoir	goodbye
toegang, ingang	entrée	entry	alstublieft	s'il vous plaît	please
			hoeveel?	combien?	how much?
uitgang	sortie	exit	dank u (wel)	merci (bien)	thank you (very much)
rechts; links	droite; gauche	right; left			
koffiehuis	café	café	postliggend	poste restante	poste restante
ja; nee	oui; non	yes; no	zegel	timbre	stamp

Tourist vocabulary

abdij	abbaye	abbey	lakenhalle	halle aux draps	cloth hall
beeld	statue	statue	meer; zee	lac; mer	lake; sea
beiaard	carillon	chimes	molen	moulin	(wind)mill
begijnhof	béguinage	beguine convent	museum	musée	museum
belfort	beffroi	belfry	natuur- reservaat	réserve naturelle	nature reserve
beurs	bourse	stock exchange	O.L.Vrouw	Notre-Dame	Our Lady
			oost; west	est; ouest	east; west
burcht	forteresse	fortress	oud, oude	vieux	old, former
eeuw	siècle	century	pastoor	curé	priest
gesloten	fermé	closed	paleis	palais	palace
gevel	façade	façade, front	plein	place	square
gids	guide	guide	poort	porte	gate
grote markt	grand-place	market square			
			schilderij	peinture	painting
haven	port	port	sleutel	clé	key
hof	cour	court(yard)	stadhuis	hôtel de ville	town hall
huis	maison	house	stedelijk	municipal	town
kaai	quai	quay	straat	rue	road, street
kapel	chapelle	chapel	toren	tour	tower
kasteel	château	castle	tuin	jardin	garden
kerk	église	church	uitzicht	vue, panorama	view
kerkschat	trésor	treasury	verdieping	étage	floor
koninklijk	royal	royal	vleeshuis	halle aux viandes	meat market
koster	sacristain	sacristan			
kunst	art	art	wandeling	promenade	walk
kursaal	casino	casino			

Road vocabulary

doorgaand verkeer	voie de traversée	through traffic
fiets; fietsen	bicyclette(s)	cycle(s)
ijzel	verglas	ice
let op	attention	Look out!
moelijke doorgang	passage difficile	poor road
schijf verplicht	disque obligatoire	(parking) disc compulsory
uitgezonderd plaatselijk verkeer	excepté circulation locale	local traffic only
uitrit	sortie	exit
weg	chemin	path
wegomlegging	déviation	detour
werken	travaux	roadworks

*Europe on a single sheet: **Michelin Map no** 970*

Bilingual list of place names

Official names are given in **bold** *typeface:* **blue** *for French and* **black** *for Flemish.*
There is a more comprehensive list on Michelin map 409

Aalst	Alost	**Lier**	Lierre
Aarlen	Arlon	Lombeek N.-D.	**O.-L.-V. Lombeek**
Aat	**Ath**	Louvain	**Leuven**
Alost	**Aalst**	Luik	Liège
Antwerpen	Anvers	Malines	**Mechelen**
Arlon	Aarlen	Mons	Bergen
Ath	Aat	Montaigu	**Scherpenheuvel**
Audenarde	**Oudenaarde**	Mont-St-Amand	**Sint-Amandsberg**
Auderghem	**Oudergem**	Namen	Namur
Baarle-Duc	**Baarle-Hertog**	Nieuport	**Nieuwpoort**
Bastenaken	Bastogne	Nijvel	Nivelles
Bergen	Mons	N.-D.-au-Bois	**Jezus-Eik**
Braine-le-Château	Kasteelbrakel	**O.-L.-V. Lombeek**	Lombeek N.-D.
Bruges	**Brugge**	**Oostende**	Ostende
Brussel	Bruxelles	**Oudenaarde**	Audenarde
Le Coq	De **Haan**	**Oudergem**	Auderghem
Courtrai	**Kortrijk**	De **Panne**	La Panne
Coxyde	**Koksijde**	Renaix	**Ronse**
Dendermonde	Termonde	Rhode St-Pierre	**Sint-Pieters-Rode**
Diksmuide	Dixmude	**Roeselare**	Roulers
Doornik	Tournai	**Ronse**	Renaix
Edingen	Enghien	Roulers	**Roeselare**
Ellezelles	Elzele	St-Nicolas	**Sint-Niklaas**
Elsene	Ixelles	St-Trond	**Sint-Truiden**
Elzele	**Ellezelles**	**Scherpenheuvel**	Montaigu
Enghien	Edingen	**Sint-Amandsberg**	Mont-St-Amand
Forest	**Vorst**	**Sint-Lambrechts-**	Woluwe-
Furnes	**Veurne**	**Woluwe**	St-Lambert
Gand	**Gent**	**Sint-Niklaas**	St-Nicolas
Geldenaken	Jodoigne	**Sint-Pieters-Rode**	Rhode St-Pierre
Gembloers	**Gembloux**	**Sint-Truiden**	St-Trond
Gent	Gand	Soignies	Zinnik
Geraardsbergen	Grammont	Tamise	**Temse**
De **Haan**	Le Coq	Terhulpen	La Hulpe
Hal	Halle	Termonde	**Dendermonde**
Hoei	Huy	**Tienen**	Tirlemont
La Hulpe	Terhulpen	**Tongeren**	Tongres
Huy	Hoei	Tournai	Doornik
Ieper	Ypres	Uccle	**Ukkel**
Ixelles	**Elsene**	**Veurne**	Furnes
Jezus-Eik	N.-D.-au-Bois	**Vilvoorde**	Vilvorde
Jodoigne	Geldenaken	**Vorst**	Forest
Kasteelbrakel	Braine-le-Château	**Watermaal-Bosvoorde**	Watermael-Boitsfort
Koksijde	Coxyde	Wavre	Waver
Kortrijk	Courtrai	Woluwe-	**Sint-Lambrechts-**
Léau	**Zoutleeuw**	St-Lambert	**Woluwe**
Lessen	Lessines	Ypres	**Ieper**
Leuven	Louvain	Zinnik	Soignies
Liège	Luik	**Zoutleeuw**	Léau

Provinces: **Oost-Vlaanderen**, East Flanders; **West-Vlaanderen**, West Flanders.
French cities: **Paris**, Parijs; **Lille**, Rijsel.

291

Calendar of events

The following list includes the principal events among the very many that take place. Other events are described in the main body of the text. Detailed lists are distributed by the Belgian and Luxembourg tourist offices.

Belgium

Saturday, Sunday and Monday after Epiphany

Ronse	Festival of Fools *(qv)*

Thursday, Saturday, Sunday, Monday and Shrove Tuesday

Eupen	**Carnival★★** *(qv)* and Rosenmontag

Saturday, Sunday, Monday and Shrove Tuesday

Blankenberge	Carnival *(qv)*
Malmédy	**Carnival★** *(qv)*

Sunday, Monday, Shrove Tuesday

Aalst	Carnival *(qv)*
Binche	**Carnival★★★** *(qv)*

Every Sunday in Lent

Ligny *(qv)*	Passion Play at 3.30pm (booking advisable, contact the Syndicat d'Initiative ☎ (071) 88 80 57

Refreshment Sunday (mid-Lent)

Halle	Carnival *(qv)*
Fosses-la-Ville	Carnival pageant with "Chinels" *(qv)*
Maaseik	Carnival pageant *(qv)*
Stavelot	**Carnival parade★★** with Blancs Moussis *(qv)*

Last Sunday in February

Geraardsbergen	Folklore pageant and Krakelingen-throwing *(qv)*

First Saturday in March

Ostend	Dead Rat Ball *(qv)*

Good Friday

Lessines	Procession of the Penitents at 8pm *(qv)*

Easter Monday

Hakendover	Procession of the Divine Redeemer at 11am *(qv)*

Second Sunday in May

Ypres	Cat Festival (every three years: 1997) *(qv)*

Sunday before Ascension Day

Mechelen	Procession of Our Lady of Hanswijk

Ascension Day

Bruges	**Holy Blood Procession★★★** *(qv)*

Ascension to weekend after Ascension

Blankenberge	Harbour festivals *(qv)*

Third Sunday in May

Thuin	St Roch military marches *(qv)*

Arlon...................... Maitrank festival *(qv)*

Halle .... Procession at 3pm *(qv)*

Écaussines-Lalaing .... Matrimonial meal *(qv)*
Gerpinnes.................. Folklore procession and procession of St Rolende *(qv)*
Soignies .... Grand Tour and Historical Pageant *(qv)*

Walcourt.................. Grand Tour and military march *(qv)*
Mons...................... The "Lumeçon" and Chariot of Gold Procession *(qv)*
Ronse .... The Fiertel *(qv)*

Koksijde .... Fishermen's Folklore Festival *(qv)*

Ligny *(qv)* .... Commemorative march celebrating Napoleon's last victory *(qv)*

Tournai.................... Day of Four Parades *(qv)*

Oostduinkerke.............. Shrimp Festival *(qv)*

St-Hubert.................. "Juillet musical" and Summer Academy *(courses)* *(qv)*
Blankenberge .... Blessing of the Sea *(qv)*
Tongeren .... Procession (every seven years: 2002) *(qv)*

Ostend .... Waltsing Mathille *(qv)*
Stavelot .... Vacances-Théâtre, then Festival of Chamber Music *(qv)*

Brussels .... Ommegang Procession at 9pm *(qv)*. Bookings at TIB (Town Hall), Grand-Place. ☎ (502) 513 89 40.

Gistel...................... St. Godelieve Procession *(qv)*

Schoten 213 fold 7 *(1)* .... World Folklore Festival

Jumet..................... Military march *(qv)*

Veurne .... **Procession of the Penitents**★★ at 3.30pm *(qv)*

Spa .... Spa Festival of Theatre *(qv)*
Hasselt .... Virga Jesse Madonna Procession (every seven years: 2003) *(qv)*

Koksijde .... Parade "In Homage to Flemish Painting" *(qv)*

14, 15, 16 August

Brussels . . . .   Carpet of Flowers on the Grand-Place (years ending in an even number)

15 August

Veurne . . . .   "Anno 1900" Festival *(qv)*

Sunday after 15 August

Ham-sur-Heure . . . .   Military march *(qv)*

Fourth Sunday in August

Ath . . . .   "Ducasse"★★ *(qv)*

Thursday after the fourth Sunday in August

Dendermonde . . . .   Parade of giants at 8pm *(qv)*

Last Sunday in August

Wingene 213 fold 3 *(1)* . . . .   **Brueghel Festival**★★: parade in costume, parts of which reproduce paintings by Pieter Brueghel, followed by a Brueghel-style dinner (every two years: 1997)

Blankenberge . . . .   Procession of floral floats *(qv)*

End of August

Overijse . . . .   Grape Festival *(qv)*) (02) 687 64 23

Tuesday following the last Sunday in August

Waregem . . . .   Flanders Steeplechase *(qv)*

First weekend in September

St-Hubert . . . .   International Days of Hunting and Nature *(qv)*

Third weekend in September

Namur . . . .   Wallonia Festival: battle of the stilt-walkers *(qv)*

Poperinge . . . .   Hops Festival (every three years: 1999)

29 September or the following Sunday

Nivelles . . . .   St Gertrude Procession *(qv)*

Sunday after 10 October

Lier . . . .   Procession *(qv)*

3 November

St-Hubert . . . .   St-Hubert's Festival *(qv)*

Sunday after 1 November

Scherpenheuvel . . . .   Candle Procession at 2.30pm *(qv)*

Sunday before 14 November

Tongerlo (Antwerp) . . . .   Pilgrimage *(qv)*

December

Bastogne . . . .   Walnut Fair *(qv)*

---

(1) Map references are given here for places not described in the main text of the guide.

Luxembourg

Easter Monday

Luxembourg .... "L'Emais'chen" Festival *(qv)*

Tuesday after Whitsun

Echternach................. Dancing procession at 9am *(qv)*

May-June

Echternach................. International Festival of Classical Music *(qv)*

July (every Friday, Saturday and Sunday)

Wiltz...................... Festival of Theatre and Music *(qv)*

September

Moselle Valley.............. Wine Festival at **Grevenmacher** and **Schwebsange** *(qv)*

Procession of Our Lady of Hanswijk at Mechelen

Admission times and charges

As admission times and charges are liable to alteration, the information printed below is for guidance only.

⏱: Every sight for which times and charges are listed below is indicated by the symbol ⏱ after the title in the Sights Section of the guide.

Order: The information is listed in the same order as in the Sights Section of the guide.

Dates: Dates given are inclusive.

Last admission: Tichet offices usually shut 30min before closing time. Some places issue timed tickets owing to limited space and facilities.

Charge: The charge given is for an individual adult. Concessionary rates may be available for families, children, old-age pensioners and the unemployed. Many places offer special rates for group bookings and some have special days for group visits. Large parties should apply in advance.

Churches: Churches cannot be visited during services and are usually closed between noon and 2pm. They are included in the following list if the interior is of particular interest.

Facilities for the disabled: As the range of possible facilities is great (for impaired mobility, sight and hearing) readers are advised to telephone in advance to check what is available.

Tourist offices: The addresses and telephone numbers are given for the local tourist offices, which provide information on local market days, early or late closing days as well as local events. Guided tours are organised on a regular basis during the tourist season in Antwerp, Bruges, Ghent, Liège, Mechelen, Namur, Tournai and Luxembourg. For information contact the tourist office.

Belgium

The prices are given in Belgian francs. The international dialling code for Belgium is 32.

A

AALST
🏛 Grote Markt – 9300 – ☎ (053) 73 22 62

Oud-Hospitaal– Open Tuesdays to Fridays, 10am to noon and 2pm to 5pm (7pm on Wednesdays). Saturdays and Sundays, 2pm to 5pm. Closed on Mondays, public holidays and between Christmas and New Year. No admission charge. ☎ (053) 70 26 60.

AARSCHOT
🏛 Grote Markt – 3200 – ☎ (016) 56 97 05

O.-L.-Vrouwkerk – Open daily from 9am to noon. ☎ (016) 56 97 05.

Vallée de l'AISNE

Tramway touristique de l'Aisne – Service runs daily (except Mondays) in July and August at 10.30am, 11.30am, 2pm, 3pm, and 4pm; at the same times on Sundays and public holidays from mid-April to June, and September to mid-October. 180F Rtn (children: 100F). ☎ (041) 84 42 97.

ANDERLECHT – See BRUSSELS

Domaine d'ANNEVOIE-ROUILLON

Gardens – Open daily, late March to early November, 9.30am to 6.30pm (there is a compulsory guided tour from the beginning of May to the end of August). 180F (combined ticket for the gardens and château: 210F). ☎ (082) 61 15 55.

Château – Guided tour only (20min) July and August, daily, 9.30am to 1pm and 1.30pm to 6pm; Easter to June and September, Sundays and holidays only, at the same times. 100F (children: 70F). Combined ticket for house and gardens: 210F (children: 145F). ☎ (082) 61 15 55.

ANTWERPEN
🏛 Grote Markt 15 – 2000 – ☎ (03) 232 01 03

Stadhuis – Open weekdays (except Wednesdays) 9am to 3pm, Saturdays 12 noon to 3.30pm. Closed Wednesdays, Sundays, and public holidays. 30F. ☎ (03) 232 01 03.

Kathedraal – Open Mondays to Fridays, 10am to 5pm, Saturdays 10am to 3pm, Sundays and public holidays 1pm to 4pm. The pamphlet available at the entrance contains a diagram indicating the location of the works of art. Closed during services. ☎ (03) 231 30 33.

Bellringing concerts – Concerts from 11.30am to 12.30pm on Fridays throughout the year, from 3pm to 4pm on Sunday afternoons from the beginning of May until the end of September, and from 9pm to 10pm on Monday evenings during July and August. ☎ (03) 232 01 03 (Tourist Office).

Oude Beurs – Open weekdays, 9am to 12 noon throughout the year. Closed on Saturdays and Sundays, as well as public holidays. ☎ (03) 232 01 03 (Tourist Office).

Vleeshuis – Open daily (except Mondays) from 10am to 4.45pm. Closed Mondays, and 1 and 2 January, 1 May, Ascension Day, 1, 2 and 11 November, 25 and 26 December. 75F (admission free for children). ☎ (03) 233 64 04.

Nationaal Scheepvaartmuseum – Open daily (except Mondays) from 10am to 4.45pm. Closed Mondays, and 1 and 2 January, 1 May, Ascension Day, 1 and 2 November, 25 and 26 December. 75F (children 30F). ☎ (03) 232 08 50.

Etnografisch museum – Open daily (except Mondays) from 10am to 4.45pm. Closed Mondays, and 1 and 2 January, 1 May, Ascension Day, 1 and 2 November, 25 and 26 December. 75F. ☎ (03) 232 08 82.

Volkskundemuseum – Open daily (except Mondays) from 10am to 4.45pm. Closed Mondays, and 1 and 2 January, 1 May, 1 and 2 November, 25 and 26 December. 75F (admission free for children). ☎ (03) 220 86 66.

Museum Plantin-Moretus – Open daily (except Mondays) from 10am to 4.45pm. Closed Mondays, and 1 and 2 January, 1 May, Ascension Day, 1 and 2 November, 25 and 26 December. 75F. ☎ (03) 233 02 94.

Museum Mayer van den Bergh – Same admission times and charges as the Museum Plantin-Moretus. ☎ (03) 232 42 37.

Maagdenhuis – Open daily (except Tuesdays), 1pm to 5pm. Closed Tuesdays, official and local public holidays. 75F. ☎ (03) 223 56 20.

Rubenshuis – Open daily (except Mondays) from 10am to 4.45pm. Closed on Mondays, 1 and 2 January, 1 May, Ascension Day, 1 and 2 November, 25 and 26 December. 75F. ☎ (03) 232 47 47.

St.-Jacobskerk – Open April to October, Mondays to Saturdays, 2pm to 5pm. Closed Sundays. 50F. ☎ (03) 232 90 45.

A flemish Proverb, by Bruegel the Elder, Museum Mayer van den Bergh, Antwerp

Ph. Cajic/MICHELIN

Handelsbeurs – Open Mondays to Saturdays, 8am to 6pm. Closed Sundays and public holidays. ☎ (03) 232 01 03.

St.-Carolus Borromeuskerk – ☎ (03) 233 02 29.

Rockoxhuis – Open daily (except Mondays), 10am to 5pm. Closed Mondays (except Easter and Whit Mondays), and 1 and 2 January, Ascension Day, 1 November, 25 and 26 December. No admission charge. ☎ (03) 231 47 10.

St.-Pauluskerk – Open May to September, daily, 2pm to 5pm. ☎ (03) 232 32 67.

Sint-Elisabethgasthuiskapel – Open Wednesdays to Fridays 1pm to 4pm. ☎ (03) 232 56 28.

Koninklijk Museum voor Schone Kunsten – Open daily (except Mondays) from 10am to 5pm. Closed Mondays, and 1 and 2 January, 1 May, Ascension Day and 25 December. 150F (free on Fridays and for children under 18). ☎ (03) 238 78 09.

Museum voor Fotografie – Open daily (except Mondays) from 10am to 5pm. Closed Mondays, and 1 and 2 January, 25 and 26 December. No admission charge. ☎ (03) 216 22 11.

Museum van Hedendaagse Kunst Antwerpen-MUHKA – Open daily (except Mondays) from 10am to 5pm. Closed Mondays, 1 January, Ascension Day, and 25 December. 150F. (free for children under 12). ☎ (03) 238 59 60.

Mini-Antwerpen – Open daily from 10am to 6pm. Closed 1 January and 25 December. 160F (children: 130F). ☎ (03) 237 03 29.

Dierentuin – Open daily, July and August, 9am to 6.30pm; mid-March to June and September 9am to 6pm; first fortnights in March and October 9am to 5.30pm; February and mid-October to November 9am to 5pm; January and december 9am to 4.45pm. 425F (children: 265F). ☎ (03) 202 45 40.

Openluchtmuseum voor Beeldhouwkunst Middelheim – Open daily (except Mondays) June and July, 10am to 9pm; May and August, 10am to 8pm; April and September, 10am to 7pm; October to March, 10am to 5pm. Closed Mondays, and 1 and 2 January, 1 May, Ascension Day, 1 and 2 November, 25 and 26 December. No admission charge. ☎ (03) 827 15 34.

Provinciaal Diamantmuseum – Open daily 10am to 5pm. Closed 1 and 2 January, 25 and 26 December. No admission charge, except during big summer exhibitions. ☎ (03) 202 48 90.

Begijnhof – Open daily 9am to 5pm. No admission charge. ☎ (03) 232 61 04.

Brouwershuis – Open by prior appointment only. 75F. ☎ (03) 232 65 11.

Museum Smidt van Gelder – Open by prior appointment only. 75F. ☎ (03) 239 06 52.

Provinciaal Museum Sterckshof – Open daily (except Mondays) 10am to 5.30pm. Closed Mondays and 25 December 2 January. No admission charge. ☎ (03) 360 52 50.

Scheldetocht: boat trip on the Scheldt – Apply to Flandria. ☎ (03) 231 31 00.

Havenrondvaart: boat trip round the harbour – Open continually from the end of April to the end of September, and also Easter weekend. Closed October to April. 375F (children: 250f). Departure from quai (kaai) no 13, Londenbrug. Further information: SA Flandria, Steenplein, Antwerpen. ☎ (03) 231 31 00.

Excursions

Oelegem: Textile Museum – Open March to November daily (except Mondays) 9am to 5pm (10am at weekends). Closed Mondays and 1 December to February. No admission charge. ☎ (03) 383 46 80.

Kalmthout: Arboretum – Open daily mid-March to mid-November 9am (10am weekends and public holidays) to 5pm. Closed mid-November to mid-March. 150F. ☎ (03) 666 67 41.

ARLON   🅱 Rue Faubourgs 2 – 6700 – ☎ (063) 21 63 60

Observation platform – Temporarily closed for work.

Musée luxembourgeois – Open Mondays to Saturdays 9am to noon and 2pm to 5pm throughout the year, Sundays mid-June to mid-September 9am to noon and 2pm to 5pm. 100F. ☎ (063) 22 61 92.

Roman tower – Visitors should apply to the Café d'Alby, Grand-Place 1. ☎ (063) 21 64 47. Closed Mondays. 10F.

Roman baths and Basilica – To visit call ☎ (063) 22 61 92 or (063) 22 12 36. No admission charge.

Excursion

Victory Memorial Museum – Open daily 10am to 5pm. Annual closure from 10 January until the Carnival holidays. 345F (children: 195F). ☎ (063) 21 99 88.

ATH   🅱 Rue Nazareth 2 – 7800 – ☎ (068) 28 01 41

Musée d'Histoire et de Folklore – Open on Sundays from April to September, 2pm to 6pm, and by appointment the rest of the year. 70F (children: 50F). ☎ (068) 28 01 41.

Excursions

Moulbaix: Moulin de la Marquise – Guided tours only (30 min) by appointment. For information apply to ☎ (068) 28 27 91. 30F.

Chièvres: Eglise St-Martin – Open daily April to September 9am to 7pm; the rest of the year 9am to 5pm. ☎ (068) 65 73 40.

Cambron-Casteau: Parc Paradiso – Open daily July and August 10am to 7pm; Easter to early November 10am to 6pm. Closed November to Easter. 385F (children: 250F). ☎ (068) 45 46 53.

ATTRE

Château – Guided tour only (1 hour) daily (except Wednesdays) during July and August, 10am to noon and 2pm to 6pm, weekends and public holidays only, April to June and September to October. 150F. ☎ (068) 45 44 60.

Abbaye d'AULNE

Abbey – Open April to September, Tuesdays to Fridays, throughout the year, 10.30am to noon and 1.30pm to 6pm, weekends and public holidays, 10.30am to noon and 1.30pm to 7pm. Closed Mondays. 40F. ☏ (071) 51 98 22.

AVERBODE

Abbey: Conventual buildings – Open daily 8am to 12.30pm and 1.30pm to 7.15pm. ☏ (013) 77 29 01.

B

BASTOGNE
🛈 Place Mac Auliffe 24 – 6600 – ☏ (061) 21 27 11

Bastogne Historical Center – Open July and August 8.30am to 7pm; May, June and September 9am to 6pm; April 9.30am to 6pm; October to March 10am to 5pm. Closed 10 January to Carnival holidays. 245F (children: 185F). ☏ (061) 21 14 13.

BEAUMONT
🛈 Grand-Place 10 – 6500 – ☏ (071) 58 81 91

Tour Salamandre – Guided tour (45min) daily July and August 10am to 7pm; in May, June and September on weekdays 9am to 5pm; October weekends 10am to 5pm. 50F. ☏ (071) 58 81 91.

Excursions

Solre-sur-Sambre: fortress – Closed to visitors. Restoration work in progress.

Rance: Musée national du Marbre – Open April to October Tuesdays to Saturdays 9.30pm to 6pm, Sundays 2pm to 6pm; the rest of the year, Tuesdays to Saturdays (closed Sundays and Mondays) 8.30am to 5pm. Closed Mondays, 1 and 11 November, and 15 December to 15 January, 1 and 11 January. 100F. ☏ (060) 41 20 48.

BEERSEL – See BRUXELLES

BELŒIL

Château and park – Open Easter to September, daily 10am to 6pm. Closed September to Easter. Entry to the estate (castle and gardens): 280F (children: 140F). ☏ (069) 68 96 55.

Excursion

Aubechies: Archéosite – Open Mondays to Fridays, throughout the year, 9am to 5pm, mid-April to October, weekends and public holidays, 2pm to 6pm. Closed for Christmas and the New Year. 150F (children: 50F). ☏ (069) 67 11 16.

BINCHE
🛈 Grand' place – 7130 – ☏ (064) 33 40 73

Chapelle St-André – Restoration work in progress, apply to Binche Tourist Office. ☏ (064) 33 40 73.

Collégiale St-Ursmer – Open July and August, guided tour only. Apply to Tourist Office, ☏ (064) 33 40 73.

Musée international du Carnaval et du Masque – Open April to October, Mondays to Thursdays 9am to noon and 2pm to 6pm, Saturdays 2pm to 6pm, Sundays and public holidays 10am to noon and 2pm to 6pm; the rest of the year Mondays to Thursdays 10am to noon and 1pm to 5pm, Saturdays, Sundays, and public holidays 2pm to 6pm. Closed on Fridays, and 22 December to 6 January, Shrove Tuesday, Ash Wednesday and 1 November. 150F (children: 75F). ☏ (064) 33 57 41.

Excursions

Domaine de Mariement: Park – Open daily April to September 9am to 6pm (7pm Sundays); February, March and October 9am to 5pm; January, November and December 9am to 4pm. ☏ (064) 21 21 93.

Domaine de Mariement: Museum – Open daily (except Monday) 10am to 6pm. Closed Mondays, as well as 1 January and 25 December. No admission charge. ☏ (064) 21 21 93. The library's special collection is open by prior arrangement, ☏ (064) 21 21 93.

Abbaye de Bonne-Espérance – Open daily 9am to 6 pm. ☏ (064) 33 96 75.

BLÉGNY-TREMBLEUR

Mine – Guided tour only (2 hours) daily from Easter to mid-September 10am to 4.30pm, March to November, weekends 10am to 4.30pm. 280F (children: 185F). ☏ (041) 87 43 33.

Tortillard: Tourist train – Departures daily in July and August at 2.30pm, 4.30pm and 5.30pm; March to June and September to November weekends and holidays only at 2.30pm, 3.30pm and 4.30pm. 120F (children: 80F). ☏ (041) 87 43 33.

Excursion

Mortroux: Musée de la Vie régionale – Open April to mid-September 11am to 7pm; mid-January to March and October to mid-December Sundays and public holidays only, 11am to 7pm. 60F. ☏ (041) 76 62 97.

Provinciaal Domein Van BOKRIJK

Openluchtmuseum – Open April to October daily 10am to 6pm. Closed the rest of the year. Admission charge varies according to the season. ☏ (011) 22 45 75.

Openluchtmuseum van Bokrijk

BOUILLON
🛈 Porte de France (Pavillon) – 6830 – ☏ (061) 46 62 57

Château – Open July and August daily 9.30am to 7pm; April, May, June and September daily 10am to 6pm; March, October, and November daily 10am to 5pm; February and December, weekdays, 1pm to 5pm (10am to 5pm at weekends); January weekends 10am to 5pm; daily 10am to 5pm during the Christmas and Carnival holidays. Closed on 1 January, and 25 December. 140F (children: 70F). Information ☏ (061) 46 62 57 or (061) 46 62 89 (during the season).

Musée Ducal – Open daily July and August, 9.30am to 7pm; April to June and September to November 10am to 6pm; November and December, weekends, 10am to 5pm; mid-January to March, weekends noon to 5pm. 120F (children: 60F). ☏ (061) 46 69 56.

BRUGGE
🛈 Burg 11 – 8000 – ☏ (050) 44 86 86

Reiefeest: Canal Festival – Next festival in 1998, on the 21, 22, 24, 26, 28, 29 August 9pm to midnight. The canals festival takes place every three years during August. ☏ (050) 44 86 86.

Belfort – Open April to September, daily 9.30am to 5pm; the rest of the year, 9.30am to 12.30pm and 1.30pm to 5pm. 100F . ☏ (050) 44 87 11.

Horse-drawn carriages – Daily 10am to 6pm. 900F. ☏ (050) 44 86 42.

Basiliek van het Heilig Bloed – Open April to September, daily 9.30am to noon and 2pm to 6pm; the rest of the year daily (except Wednesday afternoon) 10am to noon and 2pm to 4pm. ☏ (050) 44 86 86 (Tourist Office).

Museum – Closed Wednesday afternoons October to March, as well as 1 January, 1 November, and 25 December. 40F.

Stadhuis: Gothic Room – Open April to September, daily 9.30am to 5pm; otherwise daily 9.30am to 12.30pm and 2pm to 5pm. 60F. ☏ (050) 44 86 86 (Tourist Office).

Musée provincial du Franc de Bruges – Open daily (except Mondays) 10am to noon and 1.30pm to 5pm. Closed Mondays and in January. 20F. ☏ (050) 44 87 11.

Stedelijk Museum voor Schone Kunsten – Open April to September, daily 9.30am to 5pm, otherwise daily (except Tuesdays) 9.30am to 12.30pm and 2pm to 5pm. Closed 1 January, the afternoon of Ascension Day and 25 December. 200F. ☏ (050) 44 86 86 (Tourist Office) or (050) 44 87 11.

Memlingmuseum – Open April to September, daily 9.30am to 5pm; October to March daily (except Wednesdays) 9.30am to 12.30pm and 2pm to 5pm. Closed 1 January, afternoon on Ascension day and 25 December. 100F. ☎ (050) 44 87 11.

Begijnhuisje – Open April to September on weekdays 10am to noon and 1.45pm to 5.30pm, Sundays and public holidays 10am to noon and 1.45pm to 6pm; March, October and November 10.30am to noon and 1.45pm to 5pm; December to February, Wednesdays to Sundays, 2.45pm to 4.15pm (1.45pm to 6pm on Fridays). 60F. ☎ (050) 44 86 00 (Tourist Office).

Boottocht – March to November, daily 10am to 6pm; December to February weekends, public holidays and school holidays 10am to 6pm; 170F (children under 12: 85F). ☎ (050) 44 86 42.

Gruuthusemuseum – Open April to September, daily 9.30am to 5pm, otherwise daily (except Tuesdays) 9.30am to 12.30pm and 2pm to 5pm. 130F. ☎ (050) 44 87 11.

O.-L.-Vrouwekerk – Open Mondays to Saturdays 9am to 11.30am and 2.30pm to 5pm, Sundays 2.30pm to 5pm. ☎ (050) 34 53 14.

Brangwynmuseum – Open April to September daily 9.30am to 5pm; otherwise daily (except Tuesdays) 9.30am to 12.30pm and 2pm to 5pm. Closed 1 January, the afternoon of Ascension Day and 25 December. 80F (children: 40F). ☎ (050) 44 86 86 (Tourist office) or (050) 44 87 11.

Jeruzalemkerk – Open Mondays to Fridays 10am to noon and 2pm to 6pm, Saturdays 10am to noon and 2pm to 5pm. ☎ (050) 33 31 83.

Kantcentrum – Open daily (except Sundays) 10am to noon and 2pm to 6pm (5pm Saturdays). Closed Sundays, public holidays and Christmas to the New Year. 40F (children: 25F) ☎ (050) 33 00 72.

Museum voor Volkskunde – Open April to September, daily 9.30am to 5pm; otherwise daily (except Tuesdays) 9.30am to 12.30pm and 2pm to 5pm. 80F. ☎ (050) 44 87 11.

St.-Janshuismolen – Open May to September, daily, 9.30am to 12.15pm and 1.15pm to 5pm. 40F. ☎ (050) 44 87 11.

Guido Gezellemuseum – Open April to September daily 9.30am to 12.30pm and 1.15pm to 5pm; otherwise daily (except Tuesdays) 9.30am to 12.30pm and 2pm to 5pm. 1 January, afternoon of ascension Day, 25 December. 40F (children: 20F). ☎ (050) 44 87 11.

Schuttersgilde St.-Sebastiaan – Open daily (except Tuesdays and Thursdays) 10am to noon and 2pm to 5pm. 40F. ☎ (050) 33 16 26.

Engels Klooster – Open daily 2pm to 3.40pm, and 4.15pm to 5.15pm. Closed every first Sunday of the month. No admission charge. ☎ (050) 33 24 28.

St.-Salvatorskathedraal – Open daily (except on Sundays) 8.30am to 11.30am and 2pm to 6pm. ☎ (050) 33 68 41.

Schatzkamer – Open (except Wednesdays), April to September, weekdays 10am to 11.30am and 2pm to 5pm, Sundays 3pm to 5pm; the rest of the year daily (except Wednesdays, Sundays and public holidays) 2pm to 5pm. 60F.

Museum O.-L.-Vrouw ter Potterie – Open April to September, daily, 9.30am to 12.30pm and 1.15pm to 5pm April; the rest of the year daily (except Wednesdays) 9.30am to 12.30pm and 2pm to 5pm. Closed January, early February, afternoon of Ascension Day and 25 December. 60F. ☎ (050) 33 99 11.

Excursions

Access by boat (leaving Bruges) – Daily April to September. Closed October to March. 170F single (children under 12: 130F). ☎ (050) 35 33 19.

Sint-Michiels: Boudewijnpark – Open June to August 10am to 6pm; Easter to May and September 11am to 6pm. 510F. ☎ (050) 38 38 38.

Sint-Michiels: Dolphinarium – Shows 20 May to 30 June on weekdays at 10am; daily at 11am April to September; 18 May to 31 August daily at 2pm; March to October daily at 4pm and weekends November to February. Entrance ticket combines the dolphinarium and the Baudewijnpark: 510F (children: 410 to 460F). ☎ (050) 38 38 38.

Loppem: Kasteel – Open daily (except Mondays and Fridays) April to October 10am to noon and 2pm to 6pm. Closed Mondays and Fridays, and public holidays. 100F (children: 40F). ☎ (050) 82 22 45 or (050) 82 48 76.

Maze – Open 1.30pm to 6pm Easter to All Saints' during the holiday periods only. 40F. ☎ (050) 20 90 97

Male: Kasteel (abbey) – Open Mondays to Saturdays (except Thursday afternoons) 9am to 11.45am and 2pm to 5pm, Sundays and public holidays 10am to 11.45am and 2pm to 5pm. Closed the 1st fortnight of September, Easter and Christmas. ☎ (050) 35 02 11.

Grand-Place – Autoguide rental at the Tourist Office, Hôtel de Ville, Grand Place, daily (except Sunday mornings in winter), 9am to 5pm (no lunchbreak). ☎ (02) 513 89 40.

Musée de la Brasserie – Open daily (including weekends) 10am to 5pm. Closed Christmas and the New Year. 100F. ☎ (02) 511 49 87.

Hôtel de ville – Guided tour only (in French) without an appointment at 10.45am, and 2.30pm on Tuesdays, 2.30pm on Wednesdays, and 10.45am on Sundays and public holidays (Thursdays and Fridays by appointment only) April to September. Same times (no tours on Sundays and public holidays) October to March. Closed on 1 January, 1 and 11 November and 25 December. 80F (children: 50F). ☎ (02) 513 89 40.

Musée de la ville de Bruxelles – Open Mondays to Thursdays 10am to 12.30pm and 1.30pm to 5pm (4pm beginning October to end of March), on Saturdays, Sundays and public holidays 10am to 1pm. Closed Fridays, and 1 January, 1 May, 1 and 11 November and 25 December. 80F (children: 50F). ☎ (02) 279 43 55.

Église Notre-Dame-de-la-Chapelle – Open daily, June to September, 10am to 5pm. ☎ (02) 229 17 44.

Place du Grand-Sablon – *(Antique Dealers' District) Antiques and bric-à-brac market, Saturdays, 9am to 6pm, and Sundays, 9am to 2pm.* ☎ *(02) 513 39 72.*

Église Notre-Dame-du-Sablon – Open daily, 9am to 6pm. ☎ (02) 511 57 41.

Comic strip mural

Palais royal – Normally open 21 July to end of September, 9.30am to 3.30pm. Closed Mondays. No admission charge. ☎ (02) 513 89 40 (Tourist Office).

Hôtel Bellevue: Musée de la Dynastie – Open daily (except Mondays) Tuesdays to Sundays 10am to 4pm. Closed Mondays, 1 to 3 January, 1 May, 21 July, 1 and 11 November, 24 to 26 December. ☎ (02) 511 55 78.

Appartements de Charles de Lorraine – *A new museum was opened in 1996.* Apply to the Bibliothèque Royale Albert 1er, Bld de L'Empereur 4, 1000 Brussels, ☎ (02) 519 53 71.

Bibliothèque Royale Albert Ier – Guided tour (1 hour 30min to 2 hours) upon request to the Service éducatif, ☎ (02) 519 53 57 or (02) 519 53 71. Closed on Sundays, the last week in August, and 1 January, Easter, 1 May, Ascension, Whitsun, 21 July, 15 August, 2, and 15 November, 25 and 26 December.

Musée du Livre – Open Mondays, Wednesdays and Saturdays 2pm to 5pm. There is a guided tour (1 hour) available upon request. Closed on the same days as the library abnove. No admission charge. ☎ (02) 519 53 57.

Musée de l'Imprimerie – Open daily (except Sundays) 9am to 5.30pm (5pm on Saturdays). Guided tour (1 hour 15min) available upon request on (02) 519 53 56. Closed on the same days as the library above. No admission charge. ☎ (02) 519 53 56.

Toone Puppet Theatre – Performances throughout the year on Fridays and Saturdays at 8.30pm. For other days, call for details ☎ (02) 511 71 37 or (02) 513 54 86. Closed 1 January, Easter Monday and Whit Monday and 25 December.

Bruxella 1238 – Guided tours only, Wednesdays 10.15am, 11.15am, 1.45pm, 2.30pm and 3.15pm. Tours leave from the Hôtel de Ville. 80F. ☎ (02) 279 43 55.

Église St-Nicolas – Open daily 8am to 6pm. ☎ (02) 511 27 15.

Historium – Open daily 10am to 6pm. Closed 1 January, 21 July, and 25 December. 190F. ☎ (02) 217 60 23.

Centre belge de la Bande dessinée – Open daily (except Mondays) 10am to 6pm. Closed Mondays, 1 January, and 25 December. 180F (children under 12: 60F). ☎ (02) 219 19 80.

Cathédrale des Sts-Michel-et-Gudule – Open Apil to October weekdays 7am (7.30am Saturdays, 8am Sundays); November to March, 7am to 6pm. Accompanied tour by prior arrangement to the Animation Chrétienne en Tourisme, rue du Bois sauvage13, 1000 Brussels, ☎ (02) 219 75 30. Free entrance to the cathedral and 40F for the Crypt.

Musée d'Art ancien – Open daily (except Mondays) 10am to noon and 1pm to 5pm. Closed Mondays and 1 January, 1 May, 1 and 11 November and 25 December. No admission charge. ☎ (02) 508 32 11.

Musée d'Art moderne – Open daily (except Mondays) 10am to 1pm and 2pm to 5pm. Closed Mondays and 1 January, 1 May, 1 and 11 November and 25 December. No admission charge. ☎ (02) 508 32 11.

Musée Instrumental – Open Tuesdays to Fridays 9.30am to 4.45pm, Saturdays 10am to 4.45pm. Closed Mondays and Sundays as well as 1 January, 1 May, 1 and 11 November, and 25 December. No admission charge. ☎ (02) 511 35 95.

Musée Charlier – Open Mondays, Wednesdays and Thursdays 1.30pm to 5pm, Fridays 2pm to 4.30pm, Tuesdays 12.30pm to 5pm. ☎ (02) 218 53 82.

Palais de la Nation - Guided tour only (1 hour 30min) daily (except Sundays) at 10am, 11am, 2pm to 3pm, and 10am to 11am, and 2pm to 3pm by prior request for parties (two months in advance) to the Chambre des représentants, Service des Relations publiques et internationales, 1008 Brussels, ☎ (02) 519 81 36. Closed 1, 2, and 3 January, Easter weekend, Ascension, Whitsun weekend, 1 May, 21 July, 14 and 15 August, 1, 2, 11, and 15 November, and 24, 25, 26, and 31 December. No admission charge.

Église St-Jean-Baptiste-au-Béguinage – Open Tuesdays to Fridays 10am to 5pm; and the first, third and fifth Saturdays of the month, 9am to 5pm. The church is only open on Sundays during services (from 10am to 11am and at 8pm). ☎ (02) 217 87 42.

Maison de la Bellone – Open Tuesdays to Fridays 10am to 6pm. Closed Mondays, Sundays, public holidays and all July. ☎ (02) 513 33 33.

Musée du Costume et de la Dentelle – Open weekdays (except Wednesdays) 10am to 12.30pm and 1.30pm to 5pm (4pm October to March); Saturdays, Sundays, and public holidays 2pm to 5pm. Closed Wednesdays, 1 January, 1 May, 1 and 11 November and 25 December. 80F (children: 50F). ☎ (02) 512 77 09.

Palais de Justice – Open weekdays 9am to 4pm. Closed Saturdays, Sundays and public holidays. *No admission charge.* ☎ (02) 508 61 11.

Porte de Hal: Musée du Folklore – Open daily, except Mondays and public holidays, 10am to 5pm.

Place du Jeu de Balle: Flea Market – Every morning; especially 6am to noon on Sundays.

Le Botanique – Open daily 10am to 10pm. Daily during temporary exhibitions (except Mondays) 11am to 6pm. ☎ (02) 226 12 11.

Musées royaux d'Art et d'Histoire – Open Tuesdays to Fridays 9.30am to 5pm; weekends and public holidays 10am to 5pm. Closed Mondays, and 1 January, 1 May, 1 and 11 November and 25 December. 150F. ☎ (02) 741 72 11.

Musée royal de l'Armée et de l'Histoire militaire – Open daily (except Mondays) 9am to noon and 1pm to 4.30pm. Closed Mondays, 1 January, 1 May, 1 November and 25 December. *No admission charge.* ☎ (02) 734 52 52.

Autoworld – Open April to September, daily, 10am to 6pm; the resy of the year 10am to 5pm. Closed 1 January and 25December. 150F. (children: 80F). ☎ (02) 736 41 65.

Maison Cauchie – Open first weekend of every month 11am to 6pm. Closed at Christmas and New Year. 100F. ☎ (02) 673 15 06.

Musée des Sciences naturelles – Open Tuesdays to Saturdays 9.30am to 4.45pm, Sundays 9.30am to 6pm. Closed Mondays, 1 January and 25 December. 120F (children: 90F). ☎ (02) 627 42 38.

Musée Wiertz – Open Tuesdays to Fridays and every 2nd weekend 10am to noon and 1pm to 5pm. Closed Mondays, 1 and 11 November, 25 December and 1 January. ☎ (02) 648 17c18.

Bruxelles – Communes

Woluwe

Bibliotheca Wittockiana – Open Tuesdays to Saturdays 10am to 5pm. Closed Mondays, Sundays, Easter Monday, 1 and 25 May, 5 June, 21 July, 1 and 11 November, 24 December to 2 January. 100F. ☎ (02) 770 53 33.

Musée du Transport urbain bruxellois – Open April to beginning October weekends and public holidays 1.30pm to 7pm. ☎ (02) 648 17 18.

St-Gilles

Musée Horta – Open daily (except Mondays) 2pm to 5.30pm. Closed Mondays, 1 January, Easter, 1 May, Ascension Day, Whitsun, 21 July, 15 August, 1 and 11 November and 25 December. 120F (children: 80F), 200F the weekend (children: 160F). ☎ (02) 537 16 92.

Hôtel Hannon – Open daily (except Mondays) 1pm to 6pm. Closed Mondays, public holidays, 15 July and 15 August. 50F. ☎ (02) 538 42 20.

Hôtel Hannon

Ixelles

Musée communal – Open Tuesdays to Fridays 1pm to 7pm, Saturdays and Sundays 10am to 5pm. Closed Mondays and public holidays. Entrance to the permanent collections is free (admission charge for temporary exhibitions). ☎ (02) 511 90 84, extn. 1356.

Abbaye Notre-Dame-de-la-Cambre: Church – Open daily 9am to noon and 3pm to 6.30pm. Closed during services and public holidays. ☎ (02) 648 11 21.

Musée Constantin-Meunier – Open daily (except Mondays) 10am to noon and 1pm to 5pm. Closed Mondays, 1 January, 1 May, 1 and 11November and 25 December. No admission charge. ☎ (02) 508 32 11.

Uccle

Musée David-et-Alice-Van-Buuren – Guided tour only at 2pm and 4pm on Mondays (excluding public holidays). From Easter every Sunday 2pm to 6pm. Group visits by prior appointment Tuesdays to Saturdays. Closed between Christmas and the New Year. 300F (children: 200F). ☎ (02) 343 48 51.

Forest

Église St-Denis – Open Mondays and Wednesdays 10am to 11am, Tuesdays 9am to 10am, Thursdays and Fridays 3pm to 4pm. Apply to Abbé Wayembergh outside these times. ☎ (02) 344 87 19.

Anderlecht

Maison d'Érasme – Open daily (except Tuesdays and Fridays) 10am to noon and 2pm to 5pm. Closed 1 January and 25 December. 50F. ☎ (02) 521 13 83.

Collégiale des Sts-Pierre-et-Guidon – Open weekdays 9am to noon and 2.30pm to 6pm (5pm during winter). ☎ (02) 521 84 15.

Musée de la Gueuze – Open weekdays 8.30am to 4.30pm, Saturdays 10am to 5pm (10am to 1pm June to mid-October). Closed Sundays and public holidays. 70F (including wine tasting). ☎ (02) 521 49 28.

Erasmus' Study in Anderlecht

Koekelberg

Basilique nationale du Sacré-Cœur:

Gallery walkway – Open weekdays 8am to 6pm (5pm in winter). ☎ (02) 425 88 22.

Access to top of dome – Guided tour only, Easter to mid-October, weekdays at 11am and 15pm, Saturdays by appointment only, May to mid-October Sundays and public holidays 2pm to 5.45pm. Closed November to February, 21 July and 15 November. 70F. ☎ (02) 425 88 22.

Jette

Musée national de la Figurine historique – Open Tuesdays to Fridays 2pm to 5pm, also open the first Sunday of the month (at the same times). Closed Mondays and public holidays. No admission charge. ☎ (02) 479 00 52.

Laeken

Eglise Notre-Dame-de-Laeken – Open Sundays of the month only, 3pm to 5pm. ☎ (02) 478 20 95.

Crypte royale – Open the first Sunday of the month between March and October 3pm to 5pm; 17 February 2pm to 6pm; 31 July 10am to 5pm, 29 August, 25 September, 1 and 2 November 10am to noon and 3pm to 5pm, 15 November 3pm to 5pm, National Heritage Day 9.30am to 5pm. ☎ (02) 478 20 95.

Château royal de Laeken – Closed to the public.

Serres royales de Laeken – Open for a few days in the spring (April and May). Dates vary each year. For details telephone: ☎ (02) 513 89 40 (Tourist office). Free entrance during the day (Evenings: 200F).

Pavillon chinois – Open during the day (except Mondays) 10am to 4.45pm. Closed Mondays, 1 January, 1 May, 1 and 11 November and 25 December. 120F. ☎ (02) 268 16 08.

Tour japonaise – Open 10am to 4.45pm. Closed Mondays, 1 January, 1 and 11 November and 25 December. 50F. ☎ (02) 268 16 08.

Heysel

Atomium – Open daily April to August 9am to 8pm; September to March 10am to 6pm. 200F. ☎ (02) 477 09 77

Mini-Europe – Open daily July and August 9.30am to 8pm (midnight mid-July to mid-August); end of March to June, and September 9.30am to 6pm; October to early January 10am to 6pm. The brochure given with the admission ticket explains the identity of the models. Closed 8 January until 29 March. 380F (children 290F). ☎ (02) 478 05 50.

Excursions

Fôret de Soignes

Tervuren: Koninklijk Museum voor Midden-Afrika – Open mid-March to mid-October, daily (except Mondays) 9am to 5.30pm; the rest of the year daily (except Mondays) 10am to 4.30pm. Closed 1 January, and 25 December. 80F (children: 30F). ☎ (02) 769 52 11.

Tervuren: Arboretum – Open sunrise to sunset. Walks restricted to paths and lawns. No admission charge. ☎ (02) 769 20 81.

La Hulpe: Domaine Solvay: Park – Open daily April to September 8am to 9pm, the rest of the year daily 9am to 6pm. ☎ (02) 653 64 04.

Château de Rixensart – Guided tours only (35min) from the Sunday before Easter to the end of September, Sundays 2pm to 6pm. 150F (children: 100F). ☎ (02) 653 65 63.

Beersel and Huizingen

Beersel: Fortress – Open daily (except Mondays) March to mid-November, 10am to 6pm, and weekends from February to December, 10am to 6pm. A guided tour can be arranged, apply to Mr Cornelis. ☎ (02) 331 00 24. Closed Mondays and during January. 100F (children: 40F). ☎ (02) 735 09 65.

Huizingen: Domaine récréatif provincial – Admission to the estate: 100F (children: 50F) daily 9am to 8pm in summer; 9am to 5pm in winter. ☎ (02) 383 00 20.

Gaasbeek

Château et parc – Open April to October Wednesdays, Thursdays, weekends and public holidays 10am to 5pm. Closed Mondays and Fridays (Fridays only during July and August) and November to March. 120F (children 60F). ☎ (02) 532 43 72.

Meise

Plantentuin – Open daily Easter to October 9am to 5.30pm (6pm Sundays, and public holidays); the rest of the year daily 9am to 5pm. ☎ (02) 269 39 05 (extn 203).

Plantenpaleis (greenhouses) – Open Easter to October Mondays to Thursdays, Sundays 1pm to 4.30pm (Saturdays and Sunday morning are reserved for parties, by prior appointment). Otherwise 1pm to 4pm Mondays to Thursdays, Saturdays and Sunday mornings for parties (always by appointment). 120F (children: 50F). ☎ (02) 269 39 05 (extn 203).

Vilvoorde

O.-L.-Vrouwkerk – Open daily 10am to noon and 2pm to 4pm. ☎ (02) 251 06 79 or (02) 251 68 98.

C

Canal du CENTRE

Strepy-Thieu

Visitor Centre – Open daily 10am to 6pm. 40F. ☎ (065) 36 04 64 (Hainaut Tourisme).

Boat trips – Departures Saturdays in May, June, September and October 10am to 2pm, and Mondays to Saturdays during July and August (at the same times). For parties, all the year on prior request to the Compagnie du Canal du Centre a.s.b.l., ☎ (064) 66 25 61.

Exhibition – Open daily July and August 10am to 6pm; May, June and September, Saturdays, Sundays and public holidays, 10am to 4pm.

CHARLEROI   🛈 Avenue Mascaux 100 – 6000 – ☎ (071) 44 87 11

Gerpinnes: Musée des marches folkloriques de l'Entre-Sambre-et-Meuse – Open May to September Saturdays, Sundays, and public holidays 10am to 4pm. Closed during the week, and October to April. 50F (children: 25F). ☎ (071) 21 64 21.

Musée des Beaux-Arts – Open Tuesdays to Saturdays 9am to 5pm. Closed Mondays and Sundays, as well as 1 and 2 January, Shrove Tuesday, 1 May, Ascension Day, 27 September, 1, 2, and 11 November, 25 and 26 December. 50F. ☎ (071) 23 02 94 or (071) 23 03 01.

Musée du Verre – Same opening times and charges as for the Musée des Beaux-Arts. ☎ (071) 31 08 38.

Excursion

Mont-sur-Marchienne: Musée de la Photographie – Open daily (except Mondays) 10am to 6pm. Closed Mondays, and 1 January, Easter, 1 and 5 May, Whit Monday, Ascension, 21 July, 15 August, 1 and 11 November, and 25 December. 150F. ☎ (071) 43 58 10.

CHIMAY   🛈 Rue Noailles 4 – 6460 – ☎ (060) 21 18 46

Château – Guided tour only (45min) Easter to November daily 10.30am, 11.30am, 2.30pm, 3.30pm and 4.30pm; the rest of the year for parties only by prior arrangement. 200F (children: 100F). ☎ (060) 21 28 23.

Collégiale des Sts-Pierre-et-Paul – Open daily 8am to 6pm. ☎ (060) 21 12 38.

Excursion

Étang de Virelles – It has an area of 130 hectares, a picnic area, an adventure playground, and also pedalos and boating.

COUVIN

Cavernes de l'Abîme – Open July to mid-September, daily, 10am to noon and 1.30pm to 6pm; April and September, weekends only, 10am to noon and 1.30pm to 6pm; October Sundays and public holidays at the same times. Closed November to March. 140F. Combined ticket with the Grottes Neptune 320F. ☎ (060) 31 19 54 (in season) and (02) 731 59 67 (out of season).

Grottes de Neptune – Guided tour (45min) July and August, daily, 1am to 6.30pm; April to September daily 10am to noon and 1.30pm to 6pm; July and August, daily 10am to 6.30pm; October, weekends and public holidays, 10am to noon and 1.30pm to 6pm. Closed November to March. 230F (joint ticket with Cavernes de l'Abîme: 320F). ☎ (060) 31 19 54 (in season) and (02) 731 59 67 (out of season).

Mariembourg: Chemin de fer des Trois Vallées – Tourist train to Treignes and also towards Chimay (time 2 hours) daily July and August; April to October weekends and public holidays. Closed 1 November to 31 March. 250F Rtn (children: 150F). Information: ☎ (060) 31 24 40.

Excursions

Bruly-de-Pesche: Hitler's bunker – Open Easter to September, daily, 9.30am to noon, and 1pm to 6pm, as well as weekends in October. Closed November to Easter. 100F (children: 50F). ☎ (060) 34 74 63.

Cul-des-Sarts: Musée des Rièzes et des Sarts – Open Easter to September Tuesdays to Thursdays 9am to noon and 2pm to 4pm, Fridays 2pm to 4pm, weekends and public holidays 3pm to 6pm. Closed Mondays, Friday mornings, and October to Easter. 80F (children: 60F). ☎ (060) 34 60 35.

D

DAMME 🛈 Stadhuis/Markt – 8340 – ☎ (050) 35 33 19

Access by boat (leaving Bruges) – Daily April to September. Closed October to March. 170F single (children under 12: 130F). ☎ (050) 35 33 19.

Stadhuis – Open May to September weekdays 9am to noon and 2pm to 6pm; weekends and public holidays 10am to noon and 2pm to 6pm; the rest of the year, weekdays 9am to noon and 2pm to 5pm, weekends and public holidays 2pm to 5pm. Closed 1 January and 25 December. 30F. (children: 15F). ☎ (050) 35 33 19 (Tourist Office).

O.-L.-Vrouwekerk – Open daily April to September 10am to noon and 2.30pm to 5.30pm. ☎ (050) 35 33 19.

St.-Janshospitaal – Open April to October Tuesdays to Thursdays and Saturdays 10am to noon and 2pm to 6pm, Mondays and Fridays 2pm to 6pm; Sundays and public holidays 11am to noon and 2pm to 6pm. the rest of the year weekends only 2pm to 5.30pm. Closed 1 January, the 1st Sunday of September and 25 December. 40F (children: 20F). ☎ (050) 35 46 21.

Tijl Uilenspiegelmuseum – Closed for restoration work; scheduled to reopen 1997. Further information from the Tourist Office: ☎ (050) 35 33 19.

De Schellemolen – Open daily July and August, 10am to 12.30pm and 1.15pm to 5.45pm; June weekends 2pm to 5.30pm. Guided tours on request the rest of the year. ☎ (050) 35 33 19 (Tourist Office).

DENDERMONDE 🛈 Stadhuis/Grote Markt – 9200 – ☎ (052) 21 39 56

Stedelijk Oudeheidkundig Museum – Open April to October daily 9.30am to 12.30pm and 1.30pm to 6pm. Guided visits by appointment the rest of the year. Closed Mondays, 1 November to 31 March. ☎ (052) 21 30 18.

O.-L.-Vrouwekerk – Open July and August, daily, 2pm to 4.30pm; Easter to June and September, weekends 2pm to 4.30pm. Information from the Tourist Office. ☎ (052) 21 39 56.

Begijnhof: museums – Open daily (except Mondays) 9.30am to 12.30pm and 1.30pm to 6pm. Closed November to March. No admission charge. ☎ (052) 21 30 18.

DEURLE

Museum Gust De Smet – Open May to September, daily (except Mondays and Tuesdays) Mondays and Tuesdays 2pm to 6pm, Sundays 10am to noon and 2pm to 6pm; October to April, 2pm to 5pm. Closed Mondays, Tuesdays, and in January. 50F. ☎ (09) 282 77 42.

DEURLE

Museum Léon De Smet – Open February to December Wednesdays, Thursdays and weekends 2pm to 6pm (2pm to 5pm in winter). Closed Mondays, Tuesdays, and Fridays, and January. ☏ (09) 282 30 90.

Museum Mevrouw Jules Dhondt-Dhaenens – Open mid-February to mid-December Wednesdays to Fridays 2pm to 5pm (6pm April to October), Saturdays, Sundays and public holidays 10am to noon and 2pm to 5pm (6pm April to October). Closed Mondays and Tuesdays as well as mid-December to mid-February. 50F. ☏ (09) 282 51 23.

DIEST
🛈 Stadhuis/Grote Markt – 3290 – ☏ (013) 31 21 21

St.-Sulpitiuskerk – Open June to mid-September daily 2pm to 5pm. ☏ (013) 31 21 21 (Tourist Office) or (013) 32 34 24.

Stedelijk Museum – Open daily 10am to noon and 1pm to 5pm. Closed November to December. No admission charge. ☏ (013) 31 21 21.

Beguinhof: Church – Guided tour by prior appointment; contact the Tourist Office ☏ (013) 31 21 21.

St.-Barbarakerk – Open daily 7.30am to noon and 6.30pm to 7.30pm. ☏ (013) 31 10 41.

DIKSMUIDE
🛈 Grote Markt 28 – 8600 – ☏ (051) 51 00 88

Ijzertoren – Open July and August, daily, 9am to 6pm (weekends, 10am to 7pm); June daily 9am to 6pm (weekends 10am to 6pm); April to May and September to mid-November, daily, 9am to noon (weekends 10am to noon) and 1pm to 5pm. Closed mid-November to mid-March. 100F. ☏ (051) 51 91 46.

Dodengang – Open April to September daily 9am to 12.30pm and 1.30pm to 5.30pm; by appointment for parties the rest of the year. Closed October to mid-March. 60F. ☏ (051) 51 91 47 (Tourist Office).

DINANT
🛈 Rue Grande 37 – 5500 – ☏ (082) 22 28 70

Boat trips – Departures daily April to October. Information: C Marsigny, rue Daoust 64, 5500 Dinant, ☏ (082) 22 23 15.

Citadelle – Guided tour only (1 hour) daily July and August 10am to 7pm; April to June and September 10am to 6pm; the rest of the year daily (except Fridays) 10am to 4pm. Closed during the first fortnight in January, and Fridays October to March, 1 January and 25 December. 180F (children: 130F) ☏ (081) 22 36 70.

Grotte la Merveilleuse – Guided tour only (45min) July and August 10am to 6pm; May to June and September 10am to 5pm; April and October to mid-November 11am to 5pm; mid-November to March the cave is open during the holidays at the end of the year and during the carnival holidays. A guided tour upon request is available at other times, only for parties. Closed 1 January and 25 December. 180F (children: 120F). ☏ (082) 22 22 10.

Parc de Mont-Fat – Open daily April to August 10.30am to 7pm, March and September to October, weekends and public holidays noon to 5pm. Closed November to February, 1 January, 1 November, and 25 December. 150F: includes entrance to the tower, the cable car, the playing field and the Prehistoric Cave (children: 120F). ☏ (082) 22 27 83.

Grotte de Mont-Fat – Same admission times and charges as for Parc de Mont-Fat (above), but there is a guided tour only (25 min). ☏ (082) 22 27 83.

Excursions

Bouvignes: Musée de l'Éclairage – Open daily (except Mondays) April to the first weekend in October 1pm to 6pm. 70F. ☏ (082) 22 45 53.

Bouvignes: Église St-Lambert – Open by prior appointment, apply to Révérend Raty, rue des Potiers 1, 5500 Bouvignes. ☏ (082) 22 30 25 (Presbytery) or (082) 22 32 59.

Vallée de Lesse: Anseremme-Houyet – Access to Houyet by train and bus from Anseremme, several departures each morning. Bookings for trip down the Lesse: Lesse Kayaks, place de l'église 2, 5500 Dinant, ☏ (082) 22 43 97; at Meuse et Lesse, Libert Frères, rue Caussin 13, 5500 Dinant, ☏ (082) 22 61 86, or at Kayaks Ansiaux, rue du Vélodrome 15, 5500, ☏ (082) 22 23 25.

Furfooz: Parc de Furfooz – Open daily April to May 10am to 5pm, June to September 10am to 6pm; October to November 10am to 4.30pm. Closed late November to March. 100F (children: 40F). ☏ (082) 22 34 77.

Vêves: Château – Open daily (except Mondays) April to beginning of November 10am to 6pm. Closed Mondays (except in July and August) and November to March. 175F (children: 100F). ☏ (082) 66 63 95.

E

ENGHIEN

Park – Open Easter to September daily 1pm to 8pm; the rest of the year Saturdays, Sundays, and public holidays 1am to 6pm. 80F. ☎ (02) 395 84 48.

Musée de la Tapisserie – Open March to October, Tuesdays to Fridays 2pm to 5pm, Saturdays, Sundays and public holidays 2pm to 7pm; the rest of the year daily (except Mondays) 2pm to 5pm. Closed Mondays, except public holidays. ☎ (02) 395 83 60.

Église des Capucins – Guided tour only (1 hour) by written request to: J-P Tijtgat, Rue des Capucins 5, 7850 Enghien.

EUPEN   🛈 Marktplatz 7 – 4700 – ☎ (087) 55 34 50

Musée de la ville d'Eupen – Open Tuesdays to Fridays 9.30am to noon, and 1pm to 4pm, Saturdays 2pm to 5pm, and Sundays 10am to noon and 2pm to 5pm. Closed Fridays (except for parties, by prior appointment), and 23 December to 5 January, the weekend before the 24 June, and other public holidays. 30F (children: 15F). ☎ (087) 74 00 05.

Excursions

Barrage de la Vesdre: viewpoint – Access: 25F.

Henri-Chapelle: museum – Open daily 9am to 6pm (5pm November to March). No admission charge. ☎ (087) 68 71 73 (American cemetary).

Les Trois Bornes: Tour Baudouin – Open daily April to October 9am to 7pm; the rest of the year 9am to 5pm. 80F (children: 40F). ☎ (087) 78 76 10.

F

FOREST/VORST – See BRUXELLES

FOURNEAU-ST-MICHEL

Musée de la Vie rurale en Wallonie – Open daily July and August 9am to 6pm; daily March to June and September to November 9am to 5pm. Closed late November to February. 100F. ☎ (084) 21 06 13 or (084) 21 08 90.

An Ardennes draught horse in Fourneau-St-Michel

Musée du Fer et de la Métallurgie ancienne – Same admission times as for the Musée de la vie rurale en Wallonie. Closed 6 January to February. 100F. ☎ (084) 21 06 13.

Musée P. J. Redouté – Same admission times as for the Musée de la Vie rurale en Wallonie. Closed 6 January to February. 100F. ☎ (084) 21 06 13.

Château de FREŸR

Château and gardens – Open July and August, weekends and public holidays 2pm to 6pm. 200F. ☎ (082) 22 22 00.

G

GAASBEEK – See BRUXELLES

GEMBLOUX
🛈 Rue du 8 Mai 13 – 5030 – ☎ (081) 61 29 51

Maison du Bailli – Museum on local life and cutlery on the 2nd and 3rd floors. Open daily, except weekends, 9am to noon and 2pm to 4pm. ☎ (081) 61 51 71. Closed on public holidays.

Excursion

Corroy-le-Château: feudal castle – Guided tour only (1 hour) Saturdays, Sundays and public holidays May to September, 10am to noon and 2pm to 6pm. 150F (children: 80F). ☎ (081) 63 32 32.

GENK
🛈 Gemeentehuis, Dieplaan 2 – 3600 – ☎ (089) 30 91 11

Excursions

Natuurreservaat De Maten – Open sunrise to sunset July to February. Closed March to June. 100F. ☎ (089) 30 91 11.

Zwartberg: Limburgse Zoo – Open daily April to mid-November 9am to 6pm. 280F (children 2 to 12: 140F). ☎ (089) 38 18 44.

GENT
🛈 Botermarkt – 9000 – ☎ (09) 224 15 55

Boat trips – On the canals, daily 10am to 7pm. Departures Graslei (further information Benelux-Gent-Watertoerist, ☎ (09) 282 92 48) or Korenlei (information De Bootjes van Gent), ☎ (09) 223 88 53). Closed mid-November to March. 150F (children: 70F).

Old Town: illuminations – Every evening May to October; the rest of the year Fridays and Saturdays only.

St.-Baafskathedraal – Open April to October Mondays to Saturdays 9.30am to noon and 2pm to 6pm, Sundays and public holidays 1pm to 6pm; the rest of the year Mondays to Saturdays 10.30am to noon and 2.30pm to 4pm, Sundays and public holidays 2pm to 5pm. Closed 1 January and 25 December. To view the polyptych and visit the crypt: 60F. ☎ (09) 224 15 55.

Belfort – Open April to mid-November daily 10am to 12.30pm and 2pm to 6pm. 100F. ☎ (09) 233 07 72.

Stadhuis – Guided tour only (30min) April to October, Mondays to Thursdays at 2pm (in French) and 3pm (in English). Closed Fridays and weekends, late October to March, as well as public holidays (except 21 July). 100F. (No admission charge during the Gent holidays in the week of 21 July). ☎ (09) 233 07 72.

Museum voor Volkskunde – Open daily April to November 9am to 12.30pm and 1.30pm to 5.30pm; the rest of the year daily (except Mondays) 10am to noon and 1.30pm to 5pm. Closed 1 January and 25 December. 80F. ☎ (09) 223 13 36.

Puppet Theatre – Performances on Wednesdays at 2.30pm and Saturdays at 3pm throughout the year, and daily at 3pm during the Gent holidays (the week of 21 July). Closed 1 January and 25 December and during August. 80F (children 50F). ☎ (09) 223 13 36.

Museum voor Volkskunde, Gent

Gravensteen – Open daily April to September 9am to 5.15pm (4.15pm October to March). Closed 1 and 2 January, 25 and 26 December. 100F. ☎ (09) 225 93 06.

Museum voor Schone Kunsten – Open Tuesdays to Sundays 9.30am to 5pm. Closed Mondays, 1 and 2 January, 25 and 26 December. 100F. ☎ (09) 222 17 03.

Bijloke Museum – Open daily (except Mondays) 9.30am to 5.15pm. Closed 1 and 2 January, 25 and 26 December. 100F. ☎ (09) 225 11 06.

Museum voor Sierkunst – Open daily (except Mondays) 9.30am to 5pm. Closed Mondays, 1 and 2 January, 25 and 26 December. 100F (children: 40F). ☎ (09) 225 66 76.

St.-Baafsabdij – Open April to October daily (except Mondays) 9.30am to 5pm. Closed Mondays, 1 and 2 January, 25 and 26 December also 3 November to March. 80F (admission free for children). ☎ (09) 225 11 06.

Sint-Amandsberg: Begijnhof: museum – Open April to October, Wednesdays, Thursdays, Saturdays, Sundays, and public holidays 9am to 11am and 2pm to 5.30pm. Closed Mondays, Tuesdays and Fridays and November to March. 25F. ☎ (09) 228 19 13.

Lys: Boat trips – For information, apply to Rederij Benelux, Recollettenlei 10, 9000 Gent, ☎ (09) 224 32 33. 280F (children: 200F).

Excursions

Kasteel van Ooidonk – Guided tours only (1 hour) Easter to mid-September, Sundays and public holidays 2pm to 5.30pm, and Saturdays (at the same times) during July and August. Closed November to Easter. 150F. ☎ (09) 282 61 23.

Deinze: Museum van Deinze en Leiestreek – Open Mondays to Fridays 2pm to 5.30pm (except Tuesdays), Saturdays, Sundays and public holidays 10am to noon and 2pm to 5pm. Closed Tuesdays, 1 January, 25 and 26 december. 40F (children: 10F). ☎ (09) 381 96 70.

GERAARDSBERGEN

🚺 Stadhuis – 9500 – ☎ (054) 43 72 89

St.-Adriaansabdij: museum – Open April to September Mondays to Saturdays 9.30 am to 11.30am to 1pm to 4pm, Sundays 2pm to 6pm. Guided tour available, apply to Museum Abdij, Abdijstraat 10, 9500 Geraadsbergen, ☎ (054) 41 13 94.

Le GRAND-HORNU

Tour – Open March to September daily 10am to 6pm; October to February 10am to 4pm. Closed Mondays, 1 January, 25 December. 100F (children: 70F). ☎ (065) 77 07 12.

H

HAKENDOVER

St.-Salvatorskerk – To visit, contact Schoolpad 43, 3300 Hakendover, ☎ (016 78 80 98.

HALLE

🚺 Grote Markt 1, bus 1 – 1500 – ☎ (02) 356 42 59

Basiliek: treasury – Open daily (except during services) 8am to 5pm. Guided tour of the crypt upon request, ☎ (02) 356 42 59 (Tourist Office).

Zuidwest Brabants Museum – Open May to August weekends and public holidays 10am to noon and 2pm to 5pm; April, September and October, Sundays 2pm to 6pm. 40F (admission free for children) ☎ (02) 356 42 59 (Tourist Office).

Excursion

Rebecq: tourist train – Departures Sundays and public holidays May to September at 2.30pm, 4pm, and 5.30pm. Time: 1 hour. 100F (children: 60F). ☎ (067) 63 82 32 (Tourist Office).

HAN-SUR-LESSE

Grotte de Han – Guided tours only (1 hour 30min) daily May to August weekdays 9.30am to 11.30am and 1pm to 5pm, 5.30pm weekends and public holidays, 6pm July and August. Closed mid-November to mid-March. 315F (children: 220F). ☎ (084) 37 72 13.

Musée du Monde souterrain – Open daily mid-March to mid-November 11am to 5pm (7pm in July and August). Closed mid-November to mid-March. 120F (children: 80F). ☎ (084) 37 70 07.

Réserve d'animaux sauvages – Same opening times as for the Grotte de Han. 210F (children: 150F). ☎ (084) 37 72 13.

Excursion

Lavaux-Ste-Anne: Musée de la Chasse et de la conservation de la Nature – Open daily March to October 9am to 6pm, the rest of the year 9am to 5pm. 180F (children: 120F). ☎ (084) 38 83 62.

HASSELT

🚺 Lombaardstraat 3 – 3500 – ☎ (011) 23 95 40

Nationaal Jenevermuseum – Open Tuesdays to Fridays 10am to 5pm, Saturdays and Sundays and on public holidays 2pm to 6pm. Closed Mondays and in January, 1, 2 and 11 November, 24, 25, 31 December. 90F (admission free for children). ☎ (011) 24 11 44.

Museum Stellingwerff-Waerdenhof – Open Tuesdays to Fridays 10am to 5pm, weekends and public holidays 2pm to 6pm. Closed 24 December to end of January, and at Easter, 1, 2, 11 November. 90F. ☎ (011) 24 10 70.

Stedelijk Modemuseum – Open February to December Tuesdays to Fridays 10am to 5pm, weekends 2pm to 6pm. Closed Mondays, January, Easter, 1, 2 and 11 November, 25, 26 and 31 December. 90F. ☎ (011) 23 96 21.

Japanse tuin – Open April to October Tuesdays to Fridays 10am to 5pm, weekends and public holidays 2pm to 6pm. Closed Mondays, Easter and November to March. 100F. ☎ (011) 23 95 40.

Excursion

't-Fonteintje: recreation area – Open daily July and August, 10am to 7pm; May, June and September Wednesdays, Saturdays and Sundays 1pm to 5pm. 60F (children: 40F). ☎ (011) 42 20 61.

Molenheide: Wild- en wandelpark – Open daily 10am to 4pm (5.30pm in summer). 40F. ☎ (011) 52 10 40 or (011) 52 14 17.

HAUTES FAGNES

Nature reserve – Open daily 9am to 5pm. Guided tour available, mid-March to November at 11am on Sundays apply to Signal de Botrange, ☎ (080) 44 72 73. Zone C is closed mid-March to end of June to protect nesting birds (otherwise, guided tour only). 100F.

Centre Nature Botrange – Open Mondays 1pm to 6pm, and Tuesdays to Sundays 10am to 6pm. 150F (children: 70F). ☎ (080) 44 57 81.

Signal de Botrange: tower – Open daily except Tuesdays, 9am to 6pm (6.30pm on Sundays). Closed Tuesdays and at the end of June. 40F. ☎ (080) 44 56 00.

HERENTALS   🚹 Grote Markt 41 – 2200 – ☎ (014) 21 90 88

Fraikinmuseum – Temporarily closed during restoration work on the Town Hall.

St.-Waldetrudiskerk – Guided tour only (1 hour) on request; contact VVV Herentals (Tourist Office), ☎ (014) 21 90 88.

Excursions

Geel: St.-Dimpnakerk – Guided tour only Tuesdays to Sundays, by appointment, apply to St.-Dimpna-en Gasthuismuseum, Gasthuisstraat 1, 2440 Geel, ☎ (014) 59 14 43.

Sluis: Jakob Smits Museum – Open daily (except Mondays) 2pm to 6pm. Closed Mondays, and Tuesdays outside the holiday or exhibition periods, and also 1 January and 25 December. 50F. ☎ (014) 31 74 35.

Papekelders Viewpoint – Open daily May to September 10am to 6pm and during the Christmas and Easter holidays; the rest of the year weekends only. 25F. ☎ (014) 21 90 88. (Tourist Office).

HEYSEL – See BRUXELLES

LA HULPE – See BRUXELLES

HUY   🚹 Quai de Namur 1 – 4500 – ☎ (085) 21 29 15

Boat trips on the Meuse – Trips (1 hour) daily May to October at 2pm, 3pm, 4.30pm; extra trip at 5.30pm in July and August. Closed October to April. 120F (children: 100F). ☎ (085) 21 29 15.

Collégiale Notre-Dame: treasury – Guided tours daily 9am to noon, and 2pm to 5pm. 50F. ☎ (085) 21 29 15 (Tourist Office).

Fort – Open daily July and August 10am to 8pm; April to June and September to mid-October 10am to 5pm (6pm weekends). Closed mid-October to March. 120F (children: 80F). ☎ (085) 21 29 15.

Musée communal – Open April to October daily 2pm to 6pm. Closed November to March. 60F (children: 30F). ☎ (085) 23 24 35.

La Sarte – Open Easter to October daily 10am to 8pm. Closed November to Easter. 120F. ☎ (085) 23 29 96.

Excursions

Amay: Musée communal d'Archéologie et d'Art religieux – Open by prior arrangement only with Mr. J. Willems ☎ (085) 31 37 62 or Mr. E. Davin ☎ (085) 31 11 44. 25F.

Château de Jehay – Open July and August Saturdays, Sundays, and public holidays 2pm to 6pm. Closed September to June. 150F (joint ticket: castle and museum). ☎ (085) 31 17 16.

Jehay: Musée archéospéléologique – Same admission times and charges as for the château above. ☎ (085) 31 17 16.

I – J

IEPER
₿ Grote Markt – 8900 – ☎ (057) 20 07 24

Lakenhalle:

Ascent of the Belfry – Closed for an indefinite period.

Herinneringsmuseum – Open daily (except Mondays) March to mid-November 9.30am to noon, and 1.30pm to 5.30pm. Closed Mondays. 50F. ☎ (057) 20 07 24. The museum is to close for reorganisation between August 1997 and Easter 1998.

Hotel-Museum Merghelynck – Guided tour only (1 hour) daily 9am to noon and 1.30pm to 5.30pm only upon request to the Tourist Office, ☎ (057) 20 07 24. Closed during public holidays. 80F. ☎ (057) 22 85 55.

Museum OCMW – Open daily April to October 9.30am to noon and 1.30pm to 5.30pm. 50F. ☎ (057) 20 07 24 (Tourist Office).

St George's Memorial Church – Open daily 9am to 6pm. Closed during services. ☎ (057) 20 07 24 (Tourist Office).

Excursions

Bellewaerde Park – Open daily from the first weekend in July to the first weekend in September 9.30am to 7pm; first weekend in April to first weekend in July daily 10am to 6pm; first weekend in September to mid-October weekends only, 10am to 6pm. Closed the rest of the year. 650F (children: 590F). ☎ (057) 46 86 86.

Kemmelberg: tower – Open daily (except Tuesdays) 10am to 10pm. 20F. ☎ (057) 44 54 13.

IXELLES – See BRUXELLES

JETTE – See BRUXELLES

K

KNOKKE-HEIST
₿ Zeedijk Knokke 660 – 8300 – ☎ (050) 60 61 85

Walks – Contact the Tourist Office for suggested routes. ☎ (050) 63 03 80.

Het Zwin: nature reserve – Open daily April to September 9am to 7pm; the rest of the year daily (except Wednesdays) 9am to 5pm. Closed Wednesdays November to March. 150F (children: 90F). ☎ (050) 60 70 86. Only the accompanied tour gives access to the part of the reserve normally prohibited to the public (Thursdays in spring and summer and on Sundays throughout the year, boots essential, binoculars recommended).

KOKSIJDE
₿ Zeelaan (Gemeentehuis) 24 – 8670 – ☎ (058) 52 15 15

Flower market – Saturday 29 March in 1997. ☎ (058) 51 28 60.

Duinenabdij – Open mid-September to mid-June weekdays 9am to 12.30pm and 1.30pm to 5pm, weekends and public holidays 10am to 5pm; daily 10am to 6pm during the Easter holidays and mid-June to mid-September (Wednesdays in July and August 10am to 10pm); daily 10am to 5pm during the Christmas holidays. In January: open upon request. Closed 1 January and 25 December. 100F (children: 50 to 80F). ☎ (058) 51 19 33.

Sint-Idesbald: Paul Delvauxmuseum – Open July and August, daily 10.30am to 6.30pm; daily (except Mondays) in April, May, June and September 10.30am to 6.30pm; October, November and December on Fridays, Saturdays, Sundays and public holidays 10.30am to 5.30pm. Closed January, February and March. 150F. ☎ (058) 52 12 29.

Excursions

Oostduinkerke
₿ Oud-Gemeentehuis/Leopold II laan – 8670 – ☎ (058) 51 11 89

St.-Niklaaskerk – Visit on Sundays only by previous request. Apply to Pastorie, Witte Burg 90, 8670 Oostduinkerke, ☎ (058) 51 23 33.

Nationaal Visserijmuseum – Open daily (except Mondays) 10am to noon and 2pm to 6pm. Closed Mondays (except in July and August) 1 January, 1 and 11 November and 25 December. 80F (children: 50F). ☎ (058) 51 24 68.

Folklore Museum Florishof – Open daily (except Tuesdays) 10am to noon and 1pm to 5pm. Closed mid-September to mid-October. 60F (children: 50F). ☎ (058) 51 12 57.

KORTRIJK
🛈 Schouwburgplein 14a – 8500 – ☎ (056) 23 93 71

Stadhuis – Open weekdays 9am to noon and 2pm to 5pm. Closed weekends and public holidays. ☎ (056) 23 93 71.

Begijnhofmuseum – Open daily (except Wednesdays) 2pm to 6pm. ☎ (056) 24 48 02.

O.-L.-Vrouwekerk – Open weekdays 8.30am to noon and 2pm to 7pm, and 9.30am to 12.15pm on Sundays; the church is closed to visitors during services. ☎ (056) 21 38 09.

Stedelijk Museum – Open daily (except Mondays) 10am to noon and 2pm to 5pm. Closed Mondays, 1 January and 24, 25, 31 December. No admission charge. ☎ (056) 25 78 92.

Nationaal Vlasmuseum – Open March to November Tuesdays to Fridays 9.30am to 12.30pm and 1.30pm to 6pm (Mondays 1.30pm to 6pm), weekends 2pm to 6pm. Closed public holidays and December to February. 90F (children: 50F). ☎ (056) 21 01 38.

Excursion

Rumbeke: Château – Guided tours (1 hour 30min) upon request. ☎ (051) 20 63 45. 200F.

L

Château de LAARNE

Château – Open daily June to August 2pm to 5.30pm; Easter to May and September to October Sundays and public holidays 2pm to 5.30pm. Parties throughout the year by appointment only. ☎ (09) 230 91 55. Closed Mondays and Fridays, in January and 25 December. 150F (children: 50F).

LAEKEN – See BRUXELLES

LESSINES
🛈 Grand-Place 11 – 7860 – ☎ (068) 33 36 90

Porphyry Quarries – Closed to the public.

Hôpital Notre-Dame-à-la-Rose – Open daily (except Saturdays) July and August 2.30pm to 5pm. Guided tours (1 hour 30min) April to October at 3pm on Sundays and public holidays; conference tour (2 hours) April to October the first Sunday of every month at 2.30pm. ☎ (068) 33 36 90.

Excursion

Ellezelles: De Kattenmolen – Guided tour only (45min) May to September, Sundays and public holidays 2.30pm to 6.30pm, and by appointment only for parties the rest of the year. ☎ (068) 54 22 12 or (068) 64 51 55.

LEUVEN
🛈 Naamsestraat 1a – 3000 – ☎ (016) 21 15 39

Brewery – Group visits can be arranged in advance. Contact ☎ (016) 21 15 39 (Tourist Office).

Stadhuis – Guided tour only (30 min) weekdays at 11am and 3pm, weekends and public holidays at 3pm. Closed 1 January and 25 December. ☎ (016) 21 15 39.

St.-Pieterskerk: Museum voor Religieuze Kunst – Open Mondays to Saturdays (except Mondays between mid-October and mid-March) 10am to 5pm, Sundays and public holidays 2pm to 5pm. ☎ (016) 22 69 06.

Museum Vander Kelen-Mertens – Open Tuesdays to Saturdays 10am to 5pm, Sundays and public holidays 2pm to 5pm. Closed Mondays, 1 January and 25 December. 50F. ☎ (016) 22 69 06.

St.-Gertrudiskerk – Guided tours daily. Apply to the Tourist Office, ☎ (016) 21 15 40.

Abdij van 't Park – Guided tours only on Sundays at 4pm. 100F. ☎ (016) 40 36 40.

Kasteel van Arenberg – Closed to the public.

Excursion

Korbeek-Dijle: St.-Bartholmeüskerk – Open daily by prior arrangement to ☎ (016) 47 77 42.

LIÈGE
🛈 En Féronstrée 92 – 4000 – ☎ (041) 21 92 02

Fort de Loncin – Open (without access to buildings) April to September Wednesdays to Sundays 9am to 6pm, and October to March 10am to 4pm. Guided tour only of the buildings, pillboxes and turrets (2 hours 30min), April to October on the first and third Saturdays of every month at 2.30pm. Only by arrangement for parties the rest of the year. Closed Mondays and Tuesdays. 100F (children: 50F). ☎ (041) 63 42 35.

Musée de la Vie wallonne – Open Tuesdays to Saturdays 10am to 5pm, Sundays and public holidays 10am to 4pm. Closed Mondays, 1 January, 1 May, 1 November and 25 December. 80F. (children: 40F). ☎ (041) 223 60 94.

Puppet theatre – Performances (1 hour 30min) November to April on Wednesdays at 2.30pm and Sundays at 10.30am. 80F (free performance Christmas Day and Easter Saturday). ☎ (041) 223 60 94.

Musée d'Art religieux et d'Art mosan – Open Tuesdays to Saturdays 1pm to 6pm, Sundays and public holidays 11am to 4pm. Closed Mondays, 1 January, 1 and 8 May, 1, 2, 11 and 15 November, and 24, 25, 26 and 31 December. 50F (children: 20F). ☎ (041) 221 42 79 or (041) 221 42 25.

Église St-Barthélemy (font) – Open weekdays 10am to noon and 2pm to 5pm, Sundays 2pm to 5pm. 80F. ☎ (041) 223 49 98 or (041) 365 19 63.

Musée Curtius et Musée du Verre – Open Mondays, Thursdays and Saturdays 2pm to 5pm, Wednesdays and Fridays 10am to 1pm, second and fourth Sundays of the month 10am to 1pm. Closed Tuesdays, 1 January, 1 and 8 May, 1, 2, 11 and 15 November, 24, 25, 26 and 31 December. 50F (children: 20F). ☎ (041) 221 94 04.

Musée d'Armes – Open Mondays, Thursdays and Saturdays 10am to 1pm, Wednesdays and Fridays 2pm to 5pm, first and third Sundays of the month 10am to 1pm. Closed Tuesdays, 1 January, 1 and 8 May, 1, 2, 11 and 15 November, 24, 25, 26 and 31 December. 50F (children: 20F). ☎ (041) 221 94 16.

Musée d'Ansembourg – Open daily (except Mondays) 1pm to 6pm. Closed Mondays, 1 January, 1 and 8 May, 1, 2, 11 and 15 November, 24, 25, 26 and 31 December. 50F (children 20F). ☎ (041) 221 94 02.

Musée d'Art wallon – Open Tuesdays to Saturdays 1pm to 6pm, Sundays and public holidays 11am to 4.30pm. Closed Mondays, 1 January, 1 and 8 May, 1, 2, 11 and 15 November, 24, 25, 26 and 31 December. 50F. ☎ (041) 221 92 31.

Cathédrale St-Paul: Treasury – Open daily 10.30am to noon and 2pm to 4pm. No visits during services. To visit the treasury which is currently being restored, ☎ (041) 222 04 26.

West bank

Église St-Jacques – Open daily 8am to noon; mid-June to September and during Easter holidays 2pm to 6pm. ☎ (041) 222 14 41.

Église St-Jean – Open July to mid-September daily 10am to noon and 2pm to 5pm; the rest of the year Sundays only 11am to noon. ☎ (041) 223 70 42.

Église Ste-Croix: Treasury – Open daily 8am to 6pm; 9am to 5pm in winter. For the treasury, apply to the Sacristan, no 9 in the cloisters.

East bank

Musée d'Art moderne et d'Art contemporain – Open Tuesdays to Saturdays 1pm to 6pm; Sundays 11am to 4.30pm.

Maison de la métallurgie – Open weekdays 9am to 5pm, Saturdays 9am to noon. Closed Sundays and public holidays. 100F (children: 50F). ☎ (041) 342 65 63.

Aquarium – Open weekdays 10am to 12.30pm and 1.30pm to 5pm, weekends and public holidays 10.30am to 12.30pm and 2pm to 6pm. Closed 1January, 24, 25 and 31 December. 120F (children: 80F). ☎ (041) 366 50 21.

Musée Tchantchès – Open Tuesdays and Thursdays 2pm to 4pm. Closed in July. 40F. ☎ (041) 342 75 75.

Puppet shows – Shows (1 hour 30min) October to April Wednesdays at 2.30pm; mid-September to April Sundays at 10.30am . 80F. ☎ (041) 342 75 75.

Musée des Transports en commun de la ville de Liège – Open March to November weekdays, 10am to noon and 2pm to 5pm, weekends and public holidays 2pm to 6pm. 40F. ☎ (041) 361 91 11.

Excursions

Boat trips – Liège to Maastricht (3 hours 30min) July and August on Fridays: departures, Liège at 8.30am. 450F Rtn (children: 295F). ☎ (041) 222 42 10. In July and August a cruise is organised Liège to Visé, including a visit to the old Blégny coal mine, every Sunday, and only for parties by prior booking on Tuesdays, Thursdays, Fridays, Saturdays, and Sundays April to August. For further information, ☎ (041) 387 43 33.

Chaudfontaine: Maison Sauveur – Open Mondays to Fridays 9am to noon and 1.30pm to 5pm. Free entrance. ☎ (041) 65 18 34.

Aigremont: Château – Open daily (except Mondays), 10am to noon; also 2pm to 6pm June to August. Weekends only April to May and September and October. A guided tour can be arranged. Contact Madame Renard, ☎ (041) 36 16 87. Closed on Mondays during January, and on 25 December. 120F.

LIER
🛈 Stadhuis/Grote Markt – 2500 – ☎ (03) 489 11 11 (extn 212)

Zimmertoren – Open daily April to September 10am to noon and 1pm to 6pm; March and October 10am to noon and 2pm to 5pm; November to February 10am to noon and 2pm to 4pm. 50F (children: 30F). ☎ (03) 489 11 11.

Museum Wuyts-Van Campen en Baron Caroly – Open April to October daily 10am to noon and 1.30pm to 5.30pm. Closed Mondays and Fridays and 1 November to 31 March. 40F (children: 20F). ☎ (03) 489 11 11.

Timmermans-Opsomerhuis – Same admission times and charges as for the Museum Wuyts-Van Campen en Baron Caroly. ☎ (03) 489 11 11 (ext 275).

LOUVAIN-LA-NEUVE

Musée de Louvain-la-Neuve – Open weekdays 10am to 6pm, Sundays and public holidays (except in July and August) 2pm to 6pm. Closed Saturdays, public holidays and 24 to 31 December. 50F (admission free for children). Free entry on Sundays. ☎ (010) 47 48 41.

M

MAASEIK
🛈 Markt 45 – 3680 – ☎ (089) 56 63 72

Boat trips – Departures weekends in July and August, for information, apply to the Maaseik Tourist Office, Markt 45, 3680 Maaseik, ☎ (089) 56 63 72.

Museactron – Open July and August daily 10am to 6pm; otherwise daily 10am to noon and 2pm to 5pm. Closed Mondays (except in July and August), 1 and 2 January, 1, 2, 11, and 15 November, 25 and 26 December. 70F. ☎ (089) 56 68 90.

St.-Catherinakerk: Treasury – Open daily July and August 1pm to 5pm; April to June and September Tuesdays to Sundays 1pm to 5pm; the rest of the year weekends only 1pm to 5pm. ☎ (089) 56 68 90.

Aldeneik: Church – Open by arrangement with the Maaseik Tourist Office, (089) 56 63 72.

MALMEDY
🛈 Ancienne Abbaye, pl du Chatelet 10 – 4960 – ☎ (080) 33 02 50

Excursion

Reinhardstein: Château – Guided tour only (75 min) daily, July and August, Tuesdays, Thursdays and Saturdays at 3.30pm, Sundays and holidays 2.15pm, 3.15pm, 4.15pm and 5.15pm; 2nd fortnight in June, 1st fortnight in September, Ascension Day, Easter and Whit Sundays at 2.15pm, 3.15pm, 4.15pm and 5.15pm; the last Sunday in December2.15pm and 3.15pm. 150F. ☎ (080) 44 68 68 or 44 64 40.

MECHELEN
🛈 Stadhuis/Grote Markt – 2800 – ☎ (015) 29 76 55

Carillon concerts – Throughout the year: Saturdays 11.30am to 12.30pm and Sundays 3pm to 4pm. June to mid-September Mondays 8.30pm to 9.30pm. ☎ (015) 29 76 55.

St.-Romboutskathedraal – Open daily April to September 8.30am to 12.30pm and 2pm to 5.30pm; the rest of the year 8.30am to 12.30pm and 2pm to 4.30pm.

Koninklijke Manufactuur van Wandtapijten De Wit – Guided tour only (1 hour 30min) Saturdays at 10.30am. Any other time, for parties by previous appointment. Closed on public holidays, July, and during the period between Christmas and the New Year. 200F (children: 100F). ☎ (015) 20 29 05.

St.-Janskerk – Open July and August Sundays 2pm to 5pm. ☎ (015) 29 76 55 (Tourist Office).

Kerk van O.-L.-Vrouw over de Dijle – Open May to September on Wednesdays and Saturdays 2pm to 5pm. ☎ (015) 29 76 55 (Tourist Office).

Excursions

Breendonk: Fort – Open daily April to September, 9am to 6pm, the rest of the year, daily, 10am to 5pm. Closed on 1 January and 25 December. 75F. ☎ (03) 886 62 09.

Muizen: Parc zoologique de Plakendael – Open daily April to September 9am to 6.30pm; October to March, 9am to 4.45pm. 380F (children: 240F). ☎ (015) 41 49 21.

Elewijt: Het Steen – Can only be visited during Open Days; for further information contact the town hall (gemeentehuis) at Zemst (Elewijt).

Tremelo: Pater Damiaanmuseum – Guided tours during Easter holidays and July and August daily (except Mondays) 2pm to 6pm; April to July Saturdays 2pm to 5pm; throughout the year on Sundays and public holidays 2pm to 6pm. Closed Mondays, 1 November and 25 December. 60F (children: 30F). ☎ (016) 53 05 19.

MEISE – See BRUXELLES

La MEUSE NAMUROISE

Hastiere-Lavaux: Grottes du Pont d'Arcole – Guided tour only (50min) daily July and August 9am to 6pm; Easter to June and September 10am to 4pm; October to Easter Wednesdays and Thursdays 1pm to 4pm and Saturdays and Sundays 10am to 4pm. 170F (children: 150F). ☎ (082) 64 44 01 or (081) 56 88 07.

Poilvache: Château – Open daily July and August 10.30am to 6pm; April to June weekends 10.30am to 6.30pm; September (until 6pm). Closed October to March. 40F. ☎ (082) 61 35 14 or (082) 22 61 73.

Yvoir: recreation centre – Open daily May to September 9am to 9pm. 40F. ☎ (082) 61 21 77.

Yvoir: Domaine de Champalle – Open daily mid-June to mid-September 1pm to 6pm. 200F (children: 100F). ☎ (082) 61 10 84.

Rochers de Frênes – Open daily 10.30am to 7.30pm. Closed Wednesdays between September and June and the first fortnight in November. 60F. ☎ (081) 41 11 23.

Goyet: Cavernes – Guided tours only (1 hour 30min) March to November daily (except Wednesdays) 9am to 5pm. Closed December to February. 220F (children: 150F). ☎ (081) 58 85 45.

Andenne: Collégiale Ste-Begge: museum – Open by prior arrangement only on Sundays from mid-July to mid-August, 2pm to 6pm; otherwise on the first Sunday in May, June, September, and October at the same times. Apply to Mr R Frennet ☎ (085) 84 13 44.

Château de MODAVE

Château – Open April to mid-November daily 9am to 6pm. Closed mid-November to March. 150F (children: 90F). ☎ (085) 41 13 69.

Excursion

Bois-et Borsu: Church – Open on request to Monsieur le Curé, R. de l'Abattoir 11, 4560 Bois-et-Borsu, ☎ (086) 34 41 02.

Vallée de la MOLIGNÉE

Falaèn: Château-ferme – Open July and August, Mondays to Saturday, 1pm to 8pm, Sundays 11am to 8pm; April, May and September, Saturdays 1pm to 8pm, Sundays and public holidays 11am to 8pm; March and October to December Sundays and holidays 1pm to 8pm. Closed late December to February. 100F. ☎ (082) 69 96 26.

MONS   🄩 Grand'Place 22 – 7000 – ☎ (065) 33 55 80

Collégiale Ste-Waudru – Open daily 2pm to 5pm. Closed during services. ☎ (065) 33 55 80.

Treasury – Open daily 2pm to 5pm 23 April to 26 May and 11 June to 13 October. Closed Mondays. 30F (admission free for children). ☎ (065) 33 55 80.

Hôtel de ville – Guided tours only 9am to 5.30pm, upon written request (4 days before) sent to the Mons Tourist Office, Grand Place 22, 7000 Mons, ☎ (065) 33 55 80. Closed 1 and 2 January, Trinity weekend (from Saturday to Wednesday), 1 and 11 November, and 25 and 26 December.

Musées du Centenaire – Open daily noon to 6pm. Closed Mondays, 1 November and 25 December to 2 January. 60F (admission free for children). ☎ (065) 33 55 80.

Musée du Folklore et de la Vie montoise – Same admission times and charges as for the Musées du Centenaire above. ☎ (065) 33 55 80.

Musée des Beaux-Arts – Open daily noon to 6pm. Closed Mondays, 1 November, and 25 December to 2 January. 60F. ☎ (065) 33 55 80.

Le Vieux Logis: Musées Chanoine Puissant – Same admission times and charges as the Musées du Centenaire. ☎ (065) 33 55 80.

Musée François Duesberg – Open Tuesdays, Thursdays and weekends 2pm to 7pm. Closed Mondays, Wednesdays, Fridays and between Christmas and New Year. 100F. ☎ (065) 33 55 80.

Excursions

Cuesmes: Maison de Van Gogh – Open daily 10am to 6pm. Closed Mondays and Christmas to 2 January. 50F. ☎ (065) 33 55 80.

Roisin: musée Verhaeren – Open daily (except Fridays) by prior arrangement 10am to noon and 2pm to 5pm. 50F. ☎ (065) 75 93 52.

N

NAMUR ⚊ Rue de Fer 42 – 5000 – ☎ (081) 24 64 39

Boat trips on the Meuse – Rtn trip Namur-Dinant: in July and August daily 11.15am, 1.30pm, 3pm, 4pm and 5pm; in June at 11.15am, 3pm and 5pm. 180F. ☎ (082) 22 23 15.

Citadelle – Access by cablecar (time: 15min) April to May, weekends 11am to 5pm; June to September daily 11am to 5pm. Closed first weekend in August. 195F (children: 100F). ☎ (081) 22 68 29.

Fortifications – Open Easter to May weekends 11am to 5pm; June to September daily 11am to 5pm. Closed the first weekend in August. 195F. ☎ (081) 22 68 29.

Musée provincial de la forêt – Open mid-June to mid-September daily 9am to noon and 2pm to 5pm; April to mid-June and mid-September to October daily (except Fridays) 9am to noon and 2pm to 5pm. Closed November to March. 50F (children: 20F). ☎ (081) 74 38 94.

Musée archéologique – Open daily (except Mondays) 10am to 5pm (from 10.40am to 5pm on weekends and public holidays). Closed 1 January, Easter weekend, and 25 December. 80F. ☎ (081) 23 16 31.

Trésor d'Oignies aux Sœurs de Notre-Dame – Guided tours only (45min) on Mondays to Saturdays 10am to noon and 2pm to 5pm, Sundays 2pm to 5pm. Entrance located at no 17 Rue Julie Billiart. Closed Mondays, public holidays and 11 to 26 December. 50F (children: 20F). ☎ (081) 23 03 42.

Musée des Arts anciens et du Namurois – Open daily (except Mondays) Easter to 1 November 10am to 6pm; the rest of the year 10am to 5pm. Closed Mondays. 50F (children: 20F). ☎ (081) 22 00 65.

Église St-Loup – Currently being restored.

Musée diocésain et trésor de la cathédrale – Open Easter to October 10am to noon and 2.30pm to 6pm; the rest of the year 2.30pm to 4.30pm. Closed Mondays and Sunday mornings. 50F (children: 25F). ☎ (081) 23 13 59.

Musée de Croix – Guided tours only (1 hour) daily at 10am, 11am, 2pm, 3pm and 4pm. Closed Mondays and 23 December to 3 January. 80F (children: 50F). ☎ (081) 22 21 39.

Musée Félicien Rops – Open daily 10am to 6pm (5pm 1 November to Easter). Closed Mondays (except in July and August) and between Christmas and the New Year. 100F (children: 50F). ☎ (081) 22 01 10.

Excursions

Franc-Waret: Château – Guided tour only (1 hour) June to September Saturdays, Sundays and public holidays 2pm to 6pm. 120F. ☎ (081) 83 34 04.

Floreffe: Abbey – Guided tours only April to September, daily, at 1.30pm, 2.30pm, 4pm, and 5pm (additional tours in July and August at 10.30am, 11.30am and 6pm). ☎ (081) 44 53 03.

Fosses-la-Ville: Doll exhibition – Open weekends and public holidays 2pm to 6pm. 100F (children: 50F). ☎ (071) 71 12 02.

NIEUWPOORT ⚊ Stadhuis/Marktplein 7 – 8620 – ☎ (058) 23 55 94

O.-L.-Vrouwekerk: Carillon concerts – Mid-June to mid-September on Wednesdays and Saturdays at 8.30pm; mid-September to mid-June Sundays and Fridays at 11.15am. ☎ (058) 22 44 24.

Koning Albertmonument – Open daily May to September 9am to noon and 1.30pm to 7pm; October to April 9am to noon and 1.30pm to 5pm. 20F on foot, and 40F by lift. ☎ (058) 23 55 87.

K. R. Berquinmuseum – *Temporarily closed during restoration works.* ☎ *(058) 23 55 94.*

Museum voor Vogels en Schaaldieren – Closed temporarily for restoration work. ☎ (058) 23 55 94.

De IJzermonding – Guided tours during July and August at 10.30am. ☎ (058) 41 00 54.

NINOVE

Abbey church – Open daily 9am to 6pm. ☎ (054) 33 20 25.

NIVELLES

Collégiale Ste-Gertrude – Open weekdays 10am to 5pm, weekends 2pm to 5pm. ☎ (067) 21 93 58 or (067) 21 54 13.

Musée d'archéologie, d'Histoire et du Folklore – Open daily (except Tuesdays) 9.30am to noon and 2pm to 5pm. Closed Mondays, 1 January, Easter, 15 August and 25 December. 40F (children: 20F). ☎ (067) 88 22 80.

Excursions

Ronquières: Inclined plane – Open daily April to mid-November 10am to 7pm. 300F. ☎ (065) 36 04 64 (Hainaut Tourisme).

Ronquières: River boat trips – Departures daily (except Mondays and Wednesdays which are not holidays) April to mid-November, noon, 2pm, 3.30pm, and 5.30pm. 100F. ☎ (065) 36 04 64 (Hainaut Tourisme).

Bois-Seigneur-Issac: Château – Open 2pm to 6pm the two last Sundays in June, and the first Sunday in July, as well as the national heritage weekends (in September), and throughout the year, for parties only, by prior arrangement. ☎ (067) 21 38 80 or (067) 21 22 27. 150F.

OOSTENDE

Noordzeeaquarium – Open daily April to September 10am to noon and 2pm to 6pm, weekends 10am to 12.30pm and 2pm to 6pm. Closed 1 January and 25 December. 50F. ☎ (059) 32 16 69 or (059) 50 08 76.

Museum voor Schone Kunsten – Open daily 10am to noon and 2pm to 5pm. Closed Tuesdays, 1 January, 25 December. 50F (children under 14: free). ☎ (059) 80 53 35.

Heemkundig Museum De Plate – Open daily (except Tuesdays) mid-June to mid-September, Carnival, Easter, autumn and Christmas holidays 10am to noon and 3pm to 5pm. Closed on Tuesdays, 1 January and 25 December. 50F (children: 25F). ☎ (059) 70 82 15.

James Ensorhuis – Open daily (except Tuesdays) June to September 10am to noon and 2pm to 5pm; November to May weekends 2pm to 5pm. Closed Tuesdays during October, the 1st week of November, 1 January and 25 December. 50F (admission free for children). ☎ (059) 80 53 35.

Opleidungszeilschip Mercator – Open daily, Easter to September, 10am to 1pm and 2pm to 6pm (July and August 10am to 7pm); October to March weekends 11am to 1pm and 2pm to 5pm. Closed 1 January and 25 December. 100F ☎ (059) 70 56 54.

Provinciaal museum voor Moderne Kunst – Open daily (except Mondays) 10am to 6pm. Closed 1 January and 9 September to 4 October. 100F. ☎ (059) 50 81 18.

Excursion

Jabbeke: Provinciaal Museum Constant Permeke – Open daily (except Mondays) 10am to 12.30pm and 1.30pm to 6pm (5pm October to March). Closed Mondays, 1 January. 100F. ☎ (059) 50 81 18.

Abbaye d'ORVAL

Ruins – Open June to September 9.30am to 12.30am and 1.30pm to 6.30pm; November to February 10.30am to 12.30pm and 1.30pm to 5.30pm; the rest of the year 9.30am to 12.30pm and 1.30pm to 6pm. A guided tour is available on afternoons during July and August, and Saturday and Sunday afternoons Easter to September at 1.40pm, 2.30pm, 3.30pm, 4.30pm and 5.30pm (in French). 90F (children: 50F). ☎ (061) 31 10 60 or (061) 31 19 91.

OUDENAARDE

Stadhuis – Open April to October Saturdays 2pm to 4pm, Sundays and public holidays 2pm to 5pm. Closed November to March. 80F. To book guided tours, apply to the Oudenaarde Tourist Office. ☎ (055) 31 72 51.

O.-L.-Vrouwekerk van Pamele – Guided tours only daily 9am to noon and 1pm to 5pm by arrangement with the Oudenaarde Tourist Office. ☎ (055) 31 72 51.

Huis de Lalaing et restauratieatelier – Open weekdays 9am to 5pm. Closed public holidays and weekends. No admission charge. ☎ (055) 31 48 63.

OUDENAARDE

Excursions

Kruishoutem: Fondation Veranneman – Open daily (except Mondays and Sundays) 2pm to 6pm. Closed during August and public holidays. 50F (children: 25F). ☎ (09) 383 52 87.

Château de Kruishoutem – Not open to the public.

Vallée de l'OURTHE

Grottes de Hotton – Guided tour only (50min.) daily April to October 10am to 5pm (6pm in July and August). 200F (children: 100F). ☎ (084) 46 60 46.

Château de Logne – Open daily during the Easter holidays 1pm to 6pm, July and August 10.30am to 7pm, 26 to 31 December 1pm to 3.30pm, and only upon request (for parties) the rest of the year. 100F (children: 70F). ☎ (086) 21 20 33.

Logne: Ferme de la Bouverie – Open July and August weekends and public holidays 9am to 6pm and 1pm to 6pm. 50F (children: 30F). ☎ (086) 21 20 33.

Comblain-au-Pont: Grottes – Open daily April to mid-November 10am to 5pm. 230F (children: 180F). Combined ticket for entrance to the cave and the quarry: 330F (children: 250F). ☎ (041) 369 41 33.

Tilff: Musée de l'Abeille – Open daily July and August 10am to noon and 2pm to 6pm; April to June and September, weekends and public holidays 2pm to 6pm. 50F (children: 20F). ☎ (041) 88 22 63.

P

DE PANNE
🛈 Gemeentehuis/Zeelaan 21 – 8600 – ☎ (058) 42 18 18

Excursion

Westhoek Nature Reserve guided walks – Contact the Tourist Office: Dienst voor Toerisme, Gemeentehuis, Zeelaan 21, 8660 De Panne. ☎ (058) 42 18 18.

Adinkerke: Meli recreation area – Open April to mid-September, Mondays to Saturdays, 10am to 6pm, and Wednesdays, Saturdays, and Sundays from mid-September to the beginning of October. The park stays open until 7pm from the beginning of July until the beginning of September. 575F (children: 475F). ☎ (058) 42 02 02.

PHILIPPEVILLE
🛈 Rue Religieuses 2 – 5600 – ☎ (071) 66 64 96

Underground passages – Guided tours only (1 hour) daily July and August 2pm to 5.30pm. Closed 21 July and 15 August. 120F (children: 60F). ☎ (071) 66 64 96.

POPERINGE
🛈 Stadhuis/Grote Markt 1 – 8970 – ☎ (057) 33 40 81

Nationaal Hopmuseum – Open daily July and August and on Sundays in May, June and September 2pm to 5pm. 50F (children 25F). ☎ (057) 33 40 81.

R

REDU-TRANSINNE

Euro Space Center – Open daily April to September 10am to 5pm. Closed 1 January and 25 December. 395F (children: 300F). ☎ (061) 65 64 65.

LA ROCHE-EN-ARDENNE
🛈 Place du Marché – 6980 – ☎ (084) 41 13 42

Château – Open July and August daily 10am to 7pm; April, to June and September to October daily 10am to noon and 2pm to 5pm; otherwise weekdays 2pm to 4pm and weekends 10am to noon and 2pm to 4pm. 100F. ☎ (084) 41 13 42.

Poterie de grès bleu – Open weekdays 10am to 11.30am and 2pm to 5pm (5.30pm weekends and public holidays). Closed Mondays (except in July and August) and during the winter months. 95F. ☎ (084) 41 18 78.

Excursion

Belvédère des Six-Ourthe – Open all year round. 30F. ☎ (084) 44 41 93.

ROCHEFORT
🛈 Rue Behogne 2 – 5580 – ☎ (084) 21 25 37

Grotte – Guided tours (1 hour) daily (except Wednesdays in May and June) May to August every 45min 10am to 11.30am and 12.30pm to 5pm; April, September, October and November daily (except Wednesdays) 10am, 11.30am, 1.30pm, 3pm, and 4.30pm. Closed mid-November to March. 190F (children: 135F). ☎ (084) 21 20 80.

Excursions

Chevetogne: Domaine provincial Valéry Cousin – Open April to August 10am to 8pm. 200F per vehicle, valid throughout the year. ☏ (083) 68 88 21.

Lessive: Station terrienne belge de télécommunications spatiales – Open daily Easter to 1 November 9.30am to 5pm.

Jannée: Château – Guided tours only (35min) July and August daily 10am to 6pm; Easter weekend to June and September 10am to 6pm. Closed October to Easter, except for groups by appointment. 140F (children: 120F). ☏ (083) 68 86 31.

RONSE
🛈 Hoge Mote/Biezenstraat 2 – 9600 – ☏ (055) 21 25 01

St.-Hermes Collegiaal: crypt – Open Easter to mid-November Tuesdays to Saturdays 10am to noon and 2pm to 5pm, Sundays and public holidays 10am to noon and 3pm to 6pm; otherwise by appointment only, contact Stedelijke Musea Info, De Biesestraat 2, 9600 Ronse. 40F. ☏ (055) 21 17 30.

Excursion

Hotondmolen – Open all the year round. 5F. ☏ (055) 21 33 05.

S

ST-GILLES – See BRUXELLES

ST-HUBERT

Basilique St-Hubert – Open daily 9am to noon and 1pm to 6pm. Contact the warden at the basilica on (061) 61 23 88 or with Mr l'Abbé on ☏ (061) 61 10 85.

Excursion

Parc à gibier – Open daily 9am to 5pm (6pm April to October). 80F (children: 50F). ☏ (061) 61 17 15.

Vallée de la SEMOIS

Chiny
🛈 Petite Rue – 6822

Boat trip from Chiny to Lacuisine – Daily April to September 9am to noon and 1pm to 6pm by appointment. Apply to the Société des Passeurs Réunis, 6810 Chiny, ☏ (061) 31 19 03. Closed November to February. 200F.

Florenville: Viewpoint – Open July and August Mondays to Saturdays 10am to noon and 2pm to 6pm, Sundays 2pm to 6pm; June and December weekends and holidays 2pm to 5.30pm. Closed during religious services and October to May. 30F (children: 20F). ☏ (061) 31 12 29.

Vresse-sur-Semois: Musée du Tabac et du Folklore – Open daily in July and August 11am to 1pm, and 3pm to 7pm; the rest of the year, Mondays to Fridays 10am to noon and 1pm to 4pm, and Saturdays, Sundays and public holidays 10am to 1pm and 2pm to 5pm (except in January and February). Closed in January and February and on 25 December. 100F (children: 50F). ☏ (061) 50 08 27.

SINT-NIKLAAS
🛈 Grote Markt 45 – 9100 – ☏ (03) 777 26 81

St.-Niklaaskerk – Open daily 9am to 11.30am. ☏ (03) 777 01 92 ou (03) 776 08 22.

Historisch Museum van het Land van Waas – Open April to September by prior request. Closed Mondays and October to April. ☏ (03) 777 29 42.

Afdeling Van Muziekdoos tot grammofon – Same admission times and charges as Historisch Museum van het Land van Waas above.

Cultuurhistoriche collecties – Open April to October Tuesdays to Saturdays 2pm to 5pm, Sundays 10am to 5pm. Closed Mondays and October to March. 50F (children: 30F). ☏ (03) 777 29 42.

Centre international de l'Ex-Libris – Open April to October Tuesdays to Saturdays 2pm to 5pm, Sundays 10am to 5pm. Closed Mondays. 50F. ☏ (03) 777 29 42.

Salons voor Schone Kunsten – Open Tuesdays to Saturdays 2pm to 5pm and Sundays 10am to 5pm. Closed Mondays and 25 and 26 December. ☏ (03) 778 17 45.

Excursion

Kastel van Bornem – Guided tour only (2 hours Sundays in August and 15 August 1.30pm to 4.30pm; for parties from mid-April to October, by appointment only. 160F. Telephone before 9am or in the evening ☏ (03) 889 90 09 or (03) 889 22 01.

SINT-TRUIDEN

⊞ Stadhuis/Grote Markt – 3800 – ☎ (011) 68 62 55

Studio Festraets – Open April to September daily 3.30pm to 5.30pm. 60F (children: 30F). Closed Mondays and October to March. ☎ (011) 68 62 55.

Brustempoort – Guided tours (30min) April to September Sundays and public holidays at 2pm and 4pm upon request only, apply to the Tourist Office. ☎ (011) 68 62 55.

Kanttentoonstelling – Open 2pm to 5pm Sundays and public holidays. 30F (children: 20F) ☎ (011) 68 23 56.

Excursion

Borgloon: Klooster van Kolen – Open Mondays to Saturdays 2pm to 5pm, Sundays 3.30pm to 5.30pm. Closed on public holidays. *30F.* ☎ (012) 74 14 67.

SOIGNIES

Collégiale St-Vincent: Treasury – Open April to October Sundays and public holidays 2pm to 6pm. ☎ (067) 33 12 10.

Excursion

Ecaussinnes-Lalaing: Château – Open 10am to noon and 2pm to 6pm, on Saturdays, Sundays and public holidays in April, May, June, September and October, as well as 1 and 2 November. 150F. ☎ (067) 44 24 90.

Le Rœulx: Château – Closed for major restoration work. Date of reopening unknown.

SOUGNÉ-REMOUCHAMPS

Grotte – Guided tours daily February to November 9am to 6pm; December to January weekends and Christmas holidays 10am to 5.30pm. 290F (children up to 11: 190F). ☎ (04) 384 46 82.

Excursion

Deigne-Aywaille: Parc safari du Monde sauvage – Open daily, mid-March to mid-November 10am to 7pm; the rest of the year weekends and public holidays 10am to 5pm. 290F (children: 190F). ☎ (041) 360 90 70.

SPA

⊞ Place Royale 41 – 4900 – ☎ (087) 77 17 00

Pouhon Pierre-le-Grand – Open April to October daily 10am to noon and 2pm to 5.30pm; the rest of the year weekdays 2pm to 5pm, weekends and public holidays 10am to noon and 2pm to 5pm. Tasting: 7F per glass. ☎ (087) 77 17 00.

Guided tours – Accompanied walks are organised throughout the year. Contact Office du Tourisme, Place Royale 41, 4900 Spa. ☎ (087) 77 17 00.

Musée de la Ville d'eau – Open mid-June to mid-September and during school holidays daily 2.30pm to 5.30pm; the rest of the year weekends at the same times. Closed January to mid-March. 60F. ☎ (087) 77 44 86.

Musée du Cheval – Same admission times as Musée de la ville d'eau. 40F. ☎ (087) 77 44 86.

Excursions

Berinzenne: Musée de la Forêt – Open daily (except Mondays) in July and August 2pm to 5pm; March to June and September to mid-November, Wednesdays, weekends and public holidays. Closed on Mondays. 80F (children: 60F). ☎ (087) 77 33 20.

Franchimont: Château – Open daily April to September 10am to 7pm; the rest of the year, weekends, only, 10am to 7pm. 60F (children: 45F). ☎ (087) 54 10 27.

La Reid: Parc à gibier – Open daily April to September 9am to 6pm; the rest of the year 9am to 5pm. 120F (children: 70F). ☎ (087) 54 10 75.

SPONTIN

Château – Open daily July to October 10am to 5pm; April to June weekdays noon to 4pm, weekends and public holidays 10am to 5pm. 150F. ☎ (083) 69 90 55.

STAVELOT

⊞ Cour de l'Hôtel de Ville – 4970 – ☎ (080) 86 23 39

Musée religieux régional – Open daily April to beginning of November 10am to 12.30pm and 2pm to 17.30pm; the rest of the year 10.30am to 12.30pm and 2pm to 4.30pm. Closed 1 January, 3rd Sunday before Easter and 25 December. 125F (ticket also valid for the Musée du Circuit de Spa-Francorchamps). ☎ (080) 86 27 06.

Musée Guillaume Apollinaire – Open July and August daily 10am to 12.30pm and 2pm to 5.30pm; September to June Tuesdays 1pm to 4pm, Wednesdays 1pm to 5pm, Thursdays 9am to 11am and 2pm to 6pm, Fridays 4pm to 6pm, and Saturdays 9am to noon. 90F. ☎ (080) 86 41 13.

Musée du Circuit de Spa-Francorchamps – Open April to October daily 10am to 12.30pm and 2pm to 5.30pm; November to March daily, 10am to 12.30pm and 2pm to 4.30pm. Closed 1 January, Refreshment Sunday and 25 December. 125F (children: 50F). ☎ (080) 86 27 06.

Église St-Sébastien – Open daily 10am to noon and 2pm to 5pm. To visit the treasury apply to M Kint, Rue Neuve 109, 4970 Stavelot. ☎ (080) 86 44 37.

T

TERVUREN – See BRUXELLES

TIENEN   🛈 Grote Markt 4 – 3300 – ☎ (016) 81 97 8

O.-L.-Vrouw-ten-Poelkerk – Open during the week 9am to 7pm. ☎ (016) 81 97 85 (Tourist Office).

Stedelijk Museum Het Toreke – Open weekdays 9am to 12pm and 2pm to 4.30pm, weekends and public holidays 2pm to 6pm. Closed Christmas to New Year. No admission charge. ☎ (016) 81 97 85.

St.-Germanuskerk: summer carillon concerts – In July and August on Wednesdays at 8pm. ☎ (016) 81 97 85.

Excursion

Hoegaarden: 't Nieuwhuys – Guided tour only daily (except Wednesdays and Thursdays) 11am to 7pm. 65F. ☎ (016) 76 62 94 (Tienen Tourist Office).

TONGEREN   🛈 Stadhuisplein 9 – 3700 – ☎ (012) 39 02 55

O.-L.-Vrouwebasiliek – Open daily 10am to noon and 1.30pm to 5pm. ☎ (012) 23 42 94.

Concerts – For dates contact: Basilica Concerten, Vlasmarkt 4, 3700 Tongeren. ☎ (012) 23 57 19.

Gallo-Romeins Museum – Open Mondays noon to 6pm, Tuesdays and Fridays to Sundays 10am to 6pm, Wednesdays and Thursdays, 10am to 9pm. Closed Monday mornings, 1 January and 25 December. 200F (children: 75F). ☎ (012) 23 39 14.

Musée de l'Histoire militaire de la ville – Open May to September, weekends and public holidays 11am to 5pm. 30F (children: 20F). ☎ (012) 39 02 55.

Stedelijk Museum – Closed for restoration work.

TONGERLO

Museum Leonardo da Vinci – Open May to September weekdays (except Fridays) and Saturdays 2pm to 5pm; also Sundays 2pm to 5pm from March to October. Closed Fridays and at Easter, and October to February. 50F (children: 20F). ☎ (014) 54 10 01.

TORHOUT   🛈 Ravenhofstraat – 8820

St.-Pietersbandenkerk – Open daily throughout the year 8.30am to 6pm. ☎ (050) 22 07 70.

TOURNAI   🛈 Vieux Marché aux Poteries 14 – 7500 – ☎ (069) 22 20 45

A museum pass (which is valid for the seven Tournai museums) is available, price 320F. The Tourist Office also organises taxi tours (45min) with recorded commentary. For all information, contact the Centre de tourisme de la ville, Vieux Marché aux Poteries 14, 7500 Tournai, ☎ (069) 22 20 45.

Boat trips – Departures from Pont des Trous at 11am, 2.30pm, 4.15pm between May and August. Closed holidays which are not public holidays. 100F. ☎ (069) 22 20 45.

Cathédrale Notre-Dame: treasury – Open April to October daily 10am to 11.45am and 2pm to 5.30pm; November to March, 10am to 11.45am and 2pm to 3.30pm. ☎ (069) 22 20 45.

Beffroi – Closed for restoration work. ☎ (069) 22 20 45.

Carillon concerts – For further details of times telephone ☎ (069) 22 20 45.

Musée des Beaux-Arts – Open daily (except Tuesdays) 10am to noon and 2pm to 5.30pm. Closed Tuesdays, 1 and 2 January, the Monday of the annual jumble sale (in September), 11 November, 24, 25, 26 and 31 December. 80F. ☎ (069) 22 20 45.

Musée d'Histoire naturelle – Same admission times and charges as the Musée des Beaux-Arts. ☎ (069) 22 20 45.

Musée de la Tapisserie – Same admission charges and times as for the Musée des Beaux-Arts. ☎ (069) 23 42 85.

Carriage rides – July and August daily (on Mondays only when they are public holidays); April to September weekends 2pm to 6pm; time: 30min. 500F. ☎ (069) 22 20 45.

Tourist train – July and August daily (on Mondays only when thay are public holidays) at 3pm, 4pm and 5pm; April to June and September weekends and public holidays only; time: 1 hour. 100F. Apply to the tourist office, ☎ (069) 22 20 45.

Musée du Folklore – Same admission times and charges as the Musée des Beaux-Arts. ☎ (069) 22 40 69.

Musée des Arts décoratifs – Same admission times and charges as the Musée des Beaux-Arts. ☎ (069) 22 20 45.

Musée d'Histoire et d'Archéologie – Same admission times and charges as the Musée des Beaux-Arts. ☎ (069) 22 20 45.

Tour Henri VIII: Arms Museum – Same admission times and charges as for the Musée des Beaux-Arts. ☎ (069) 22 20 45.

Excursion

Antoing: Château – Guided tour only (1h 30min), mid-May to the end of September, on Sundays and public holidays, at 2.30pm, 3.30pm and 4pm. Closed October to mid-May. 120F (children: 100F). ☎ (069) 44 17 29.

TROIS-PONTS

Excursion

Grand-Halleux: Domaine de Monti – Open daily July and August 9am to 6pm; the rest of the year 9am to 5pm. 80F (children: 50F). ☎ (080) 21 76 02.

TURNHOUT   🖪 Grote Markt 44 – 2300 – ☎ (014) 42 21 96

Taxandriamuseum – Open Wednesdays, Fridays and Saturdays 2pm to 5pm; Sundays 10am to noon and 2pm to 5pm; Tuesdays and Thursdays in July and August only 2pm to 5pm. Closed Mondays 1 and 2 January and 25 December. 70F. ☎ (014) 44 33 55.

Begijnhof: museum – Open Wednesdays, Fridays and Saturdays 2pm to 5pm and Sundays 3pm to 5pm (July and August, Tuesdays and Thursdays 2pm to 5pm). Closed Mondays,1 and 2 January and Christmas. 70F (children: 50F). ☎ (014) 44 33 55.

Nationaal Museum van de Speelkaart – Open on Wednesdays, Fridays and Saturdays 2pm to 5pm and Sundays 10am to noon and 2pm to 5pm. In June, July and August open also on Tuesdays and Thursdays 2pm to 5pm. Closed Mondays, 1 and 2 January, 25 and 26 December. 90F (children: 50F). ☎ (014) 41 56 21.

Excursion

Hoogstraten: St.-Catharinakerk – Open daily April to October 9am to 7pm. ☎ (03) 340 19 55 (Tourist Office).

U – V

UCCLE – See BRUXELLES

VERVIERS   🖪 Rue Xhavée 61 – 4800 – ☎ (087) 33 02 13

Musée des Beaux-Arts et de la Céramique – Open Mondays, Wednesdays and Saturdays 2pm to 5pm and Sundays 3pm to 6pm. Closed Fridays and 1 January. 65F (combined ticket for the three museums), free admission weekends (admission free for children or 35F for the over 12). ☎ (087) 33 16 95.

Musée d'Archéologie et de Folklore – Open Tuesdays and Thursdays 2pm to 5pm, Saturdays 9am to noon and Sundays 10am to 1pm. Closed Fridays and 1 January. 65F (combined ticket for the three museums) free admission weekends. ☎ (087) 33 16 95.

Musée de la Laine – Open daily (except Sundays) 2pm to 5pm (6pm on Wednesdays). Closed Sundays and public holidays. 65F (combined ticket for the three museums). ☎ (087) 33 16 95.

VEURNE   🖪 Landhuis/Grote Markt 29 – 8630 – ☎ (058) 31 21 54

Stadhuis – Guided tours (45min) April to September daily 11am to 2pm and 3pm to 4.30pm; the rest of the year Mondays to Saturdays 11am to 3pm. Closed Sundays October to March. 50F (children: 30F). ☎ (058) 31 21 54.

St.-Walburgakerk – Open daily June to September. ☎ (058) 31 21 54.

St.-Niklaaskerk – Open daily 8am to 6pm (except Saturday afternoons). ☎ (058) 31 14 42.

Excursions

Wulveringem: Kasteel Beauvoorde – Guided tours only (1 hour) June to September at 2pm, 3pm, 4pm, and 5pm. The Gardens are open to walkers every day (except Mondays) 2pm to 6pm June to September. Closed Mondays and public holidays. 80F (children: 40F). ☎ (058) 29 92 29.

Izenberge: Musée de plein air Bachten de Kupe "Antan Village" – Open weekdays 1pm to 5pm, Saturdays, Sundays and public holidays 2pm to 6pm. Closed weekends mid-November to March, 1 January and 25 December. 120F (children: 60F). ☎ (058) 29 80 90.

VILLERS-LA-VILLE

Abbey ruins – Open April to October, Mondays and Tuesdays noon to 6pm, Wednesdays to Sundays, (and public holidays), 10am to 6pm (guided tour on Sundays at 3pm, without a booking); the rest of the year, Wednesdays to Fridays, 1pm to 5pm and weekends and public holidays 11am to 5pm (guided tour Sundays at 3pm without a booking). Closed Mondays and Tuesdays (from November to March), and also 1 January, 24, 25, and 31 December. 80F (children: 50F). ☎ (071) 87 95 55 or (071) 87 88 62.

Église de la Visitation – Guided tours only daily 3pm to 6pm. Apply to M Jean Roulin, Rue des Sart 20, 1495 Villers-La-Ville. ☎ (071) 87 73 27.

VILVOORDE – See BRUXELLES

VIRTON   🛈 Pavillon/Rue Grasses-Oies 2b – 6760 – ☎ (063) 57 89 04

Musée gaumois – Open April to November daily 9.30am to noon and 2pm to 6pm. Closed Tuesdays (except in June, July and August) as well as 1 December to 30 March. 100F (children: 30F). ☎ (063) 57 03 15.

Excursion

Montquintin: Musée de la Vie paysanne – Open daily in July and August 2pm to 6pm, and by appointment only the rest of the year. 50F (children: 30F). ☎ (063) 57 03 15.

VOERSTREEK

Sint-Pieters-Voeren: Commandery – Closed to the public.

#

WALCOURT

Basilique St-Materne: Treasury – Open daily 8.30am to 6pm. ☎ (071) 61 13 66 or the Office du tourisme, ☎ (071) 61 25 26.

WATERLOO   🛈 Chaussée de Bruxelles 149 – 1410 – ☎ (02) 354 99 10

At Waterloo, a "pass" gives access to all the museums on the 1815 site, at a special reduced price: 385F for individuals, and 300F for parties (on sale in each museum and in the Tourist Office). This ticket is valid for a year its date of issue.

Butte du Lion – Open April to September daily 9.30am to 6.30pm; October 9.30am to 5.30pm; March 10.30am to 5pm; November to February 10.30am to 4pm. Closed 1 January and 25 December. 40F (children: 20F). ☎ (02) 385 19 12.

Visitors centre – Open daily, April 10.30am to 5pm, May to September 9.30am to 6.30pm, October 9.30am to 5.30pm, November to March 10.30am to 4pm. Closed 1 January and 25 December. 300F (children: 190F). ☎ (02) 385 19 12.

Panorama de la bataille – Open May to September daily 9.30am to 6.30am; April 10.30am to 5pm; October 9.30am to 5pm; Novemnber to March 10.30am to 4pm. Closed 1 January and 25 December. 300F (children: 190F). ☎ (02) 385 19 12.

Musée de Cire – Open April to October daily 9.30am to 7pm; the rest of the year weekends and public holidays 10am to 6pm. 60F (children: 50F). ☎ (02) 384 67 40.

Musée provincial du Caillou – Open April to October daily (except Mondays) 10am to 6.30pm; November to March 1.30pm to 5pm. Closed Mondays and in January. 60F. ☎ (02) 384 24 24.

Musée Wellington – Open April to October daily 9.30am to 6.30pm; the rest of the year daily 10.30am to 5pm. Closed 1 January and 25 December. 80F (children 6 to 12: 40F). ☎ (02) 354 78 06.

Église Saint-Joseph – Open daily 7.30am to 7pm. ☎ (02) 354 00 11.

Walibi – Open daily May to June 10am to 6pm; July and August daily 10am to 7pm; September weekends and public holidays 10am to 6pm. 710F (children: 640F). ☎ (010) 41 44 66.

Aqualibi – Open daily (except Mondays) May to September 6pm to 10pm (11pm on Saturdays); October to April weekdays 2pm to 10pm, Saturdays 10am to 11pm, Sundays 10am to 10pm. 460F. ☎ (010) 41 44 66.

WOLUWE – See BRUXELLES

Y – Z

ZOUTLEEUW

St.-Leonarduskerk – Open April to October daily 2pm to 5pm. ☎ (011) 78 11 07 or (011) 78 18 49.

Maison Cauchie

Grand Duchy of Luxembourg

The prices are given in Luxembourg francs. The international dialing code for the Grand Duchy of Luxembourg is 352.

CLERVAUX
🏛 Château – 9748 – ☎ 92 93 95

Château – Exhibitions open daily, in June 1pm to 5pm, and July to mid-September 10am to 5pm. 40F (per exhibition). ☎ 91 142 (Tourist Office).

DIEKIRCH
🏛 Esplanade 1 – 9227 – ☎ 80 30 23

Musée – Open daily (except Thursdays) May to October 10am to noon and 2 pm to 6pm. Closed November to Easter. ☎ 80 30 23.

Église St-Laurent – Open daily (except Mondays) Easter to October, 10am to noon and 2pm to 6pm. Closed November to Easter. ☎ 80 30 23.

Excursion

Brandenbourg: Maison Al Branebuurg – Open in July and August, Sundays and public holidays, 2pm to 6pm; the first Sunday in the month for the rest of the year. 30F (children: 15F). ☎ 90 475.

ECHTERNACH
🏛 Porte St-Willibrord (Basilique) – 6401 – ☎ 7 22 30

Musée de l'Abbaye – Open Easter to 1 November daily 10am to noon and 2pm to 5pm. July and August 10am to 6pm. 50F. ☎ 72 74 72 or 478-6666.

ESCH-SUR-ALZETTE

Musée de la Résistance – Open Thursdays and weekends 3pm to 6pm. Closed 1 January, Easter Sunday and Whit Sunday, 1 May, 15 August and 25 December. No admission charge. ☎ 54 73 83.

Excursion

Rumelange: Musée national des mines – Guided tour only (1 h 30min) daily 2pm to 5pm Easter to October, and each 2nd weekend in the month the rest of the year. 120F (children: 60F). ☎ 56 31 21 1.

LAROCHETTE
🏛 Hôtel de Ville – 7619 – ☎ 8 76 76

Châteaux – Open Easter to October daily 10am to 6pm. Closed November to Easter. 50F. ☎ 8 74 97.

LUXEMBOURG
🏛 Place d'Armes – 2011 – ☎ 22 28 09

Model – Open daily during the school holidays 10am to 5.45pm. Closed at all other times. 60F (children: 40F). ☎ 22 28 09.

Casemates du Bock – Open daily March to October, 10am to 5pm. Closed November to February. 70F (children: 40F). ☎ 22 67 53 or 22 28 09.

House in the old town of Luxembourg displaying the national motto

Musée national d'histoire et d'Art – Open Tuesdays to Fridays 10am to 4.45pm, Saturdays 2pm to 5.45pm, Sundays 10am to 11.45am and 2pm to 5.45pm. Closed Mondays, 1 January, Easter, 1 May, 23 June, 15 August, 1 and 2 November, and 25 December. No admission charge. ☎ 47 93 30-1.

Palais Grand-Ducal – Guided tours mid-July to August, Mondays to Saturdays. Individual visitors must purchase their tickets at the tourist office. 200F. ☎ 22 28 09 (Luxembourg Tourist Office).

Casemates de la Pétrusse – Guided tour only (45 min) daily 11am to 4pm during the school holidays. 70F (children: 40F). ☎ 22 28 09 or 47 10 46.

Musée J-P Pescatore – Closed for restoration work.

Excursion

Bettembourg: Parc Merveilleux – Open daily April to October, 9.30am to 7pm. Closed November to mid-March. 130F (children: 100F). ☎ 51 10 48.

MONDORF-LES-BAINS

Église St-Michel – A guided tour on Wednesday 5.15pm to 6pm. ☎ 66 80 20 (presbytery).

Vallée de la MOSELLE LUXEMBOURGEOISE

Boat trips – Wasserbillig to Schengen Easter to September. Contact the Navigation Touristique de l'Entente de la Moselle Luxembourgeoise-Grevenmacher, ☎ 75 82 75. Selected railway stations sell joint tickets for trips by train and boat, or by bus and boat.

Bech-Kleinmacher: Musée folklorique et viticole – Open daily (except Mondays) March to December 2pm to 7pm. Closed January and February. 120F. ☎ 69 73 53.

Wellenstein: wine cooperatives – Guided tours only (1 hour) May to August weekdays 10am to noon and 1pm to 6pm, weekends and public holidays 11am to 6pm. 70F (children: 40F). ☎ 69 83 14.

Remich: Caves St-Martin – Guided tour only (40 min) April to October daily 10am to noon and 1.30pm to 6pm. Closed November to March. 90F (children: 70F). ☎ 69 90 91.

Ehnen: Musée du vin – Open daily (except Mondays) April to October 9.30am to 11.30am and 2pm to 5pm. Closed Mondays. 80F. ☎ 760 26.

Wormeldange: wine cooperatives – Guided tours only (1 hour) May to August weekdays 11am to 8pm, weekends and public holidays 11am to 6pm. 80F. ☎ 69 83 14.

Grevenmacher: wine cooperatives – Guided tour only (1 hour) May to August 9am to noon and 3m to 6pm (5pm Saturdays). 60F (children: 40F). ☎ 69 83 14.

Grevemacher: Caves Bernard-Massard – Guided tour only (1 hour) daily April to October 9.30am to 6pm. Closed November to March. 80F. ☎ 755 45 228.

PETITE SUISSE LUXEMBOURGEOISE

Château de Beaufort – Open daily April to September 9am to 6pm; October 9am to 5.30pm. 60F (children: 20F). ☎ 860 02.

RODANGE

Tourist train – Departures May to September Sundays and public holidays at 3pm and 4.40pm. Closed October to April and 23 June. 240F Rtn in 1st Class, 160F in 2nd Class. ☎ 31 90 69.

Excursion

Bascharage: Taillerie luxembourgeoise de pierres précieuses – Open daily (except Mondays and Sundays) 8am to noon, and 12.30pm to 5pm (4pm on Saturdays). ☎ 50 90 32.

Vallée de la SÛRE

Château de Bourscheid – Open July and August 10am to 7pm, May, June and September 10am to 6pm, April 11am to 5pm, October 11am to 4pm, November to March weekends only 11am to 4pm. 80F. ☎ 905 70.

VIANDEN   🄱 Maison Victor Hugo/Rue Gare 37 – 9420 – ☎ 8 42 57 – fax: 84 90 81

Chairlift – This runs daily April to September. Closed in the case of bad weather. 160F Rtn (children: 80F). ☎ 84 323.

Château – Open daily April to September 10am to 6pm, March 10am to 5pm, October to February 10am to 4pm. Closed 1 January, 2 November and 25 December. 120F (children: 40F). ☎ 84 92 91/84108.

Maison de Victor Hugo – Open mid-April to September, daily 9.30am to noon, and 2pm to 6pm, otherwise Mondays to Fridays (at the same times). Closed public holidays and possibly between October and March. 25F (children: 15F). ☎ 842 57.

Musée d'Art rustique – Open daily (except Mondays) Easter to October, 10am to noon and 2pm to 6pm. Closed Mondays. 100F. ☎ 845 91.

Index

Bruxelles *Brabant*. . . . . Towns, sights and tourist regions followed
by the name of the Province
Cloth Halls . . . . Sights in important towns
Egmont, Count of . . . . People, historical events, artistic styles and local terms

A bilingual list of place names is given on page 291

BELGIUM

A

Aachen, *Treaty of* 18
Aalst *Oost-Vlaanderen* 46
Aarschot
  Vlaams -Brabant 47
Abbaye: see under proper
  name
Achterbos *Antwerpen*
  158
Adinkerke
  West-Vlaanderen 214
Adolf of Nassau 19
Afsnee
  Oost-Vlaanderen 150
Aigremont (Château)
  Liège 181
Aisne (Vallée de)
  Luxembourg 48
Albert I 19
Albert II 19
Albert (Canal) 176
Albrecht 171
Alden-Biesen
  Limburg 235
Aldeneik *Limburg* 186
Alchinsky, Pierre 31, 105
Alle *Namur* 223
Almshouses 40
Alost: see Aalst
Alva, Duke of 18
Amay *Liège* 160
Ambiorix 234
Amblève (Vallée) *Liège* 48
Andenne *Namur* 194
Anderlecht *Brabant* 115
Annevoie-Rouillon
  (Domaine) *Namur* 49
Anseremme *Namur* 134
Antoing (Château)
  Hainaut 242
Antwerp: see Antwerpen
Antwerpen *Antwerpen*
  12, 50
  Begijnhof 62
  *Boat trips around the
    harbour* 63
  Boat trips on the Scheldt
    63
  Bourlaschouwburg 57
  Brabo Fountain 51
  Brouwershuis 62
  Cathedral 52
  Centraal Station 61
  Church: see under proper
    name
  Dierentuin 61
  Etnografisch museum 56

Fotografie
  (Museum voor) 61
Gildekamersstraat 56
Grote Markt 51
Guided tours 51
Handelsbeurs 58
Handschoenmarkt 52
Havenrondvaart 63
Hedendaagse Kunst
  Antwerpen-MUHKA
  (Museum van) 61
Hendrik Conscienceplein 59
Kapel: see under proper
  name
Kerk: see under proper
  name
Koninklijk Museum voor
  Schone Kunsten 59
Lange Wapper 56
Lillo-Fort 63
Maagdenhuis 57
Mayer van den Bergh
  (Museum) 57
The Meir 58
Mini-Antwerpen 61
Museum: see under proper
  name
Nationaal Scheepvaartmu-
  seum 56
Openluchtmuseum voor
  Beeldhouwkunst Mid-
  delheim 61
Oude Beurs 54
Plantin-Moretus (Museum)
  56
"Poesje" 55
The Port 63
The "Prince of Printers" 56
Provinciaal Diamantmu-
  seum 62
Provinciaal Museum
  Sterckshof 62
Public transport 51
Rockoxhuis 59
Rubenshuis 58
Scheldetocht 63
St.-Carolus Borromeuskerk
  59
St.-Elisabethgasthuiskapel
  59
St.-Jacobskerk 58
St.-Niklaaskapel 59
St.-Pauluskerk 59
Smidt van Gelder
  (Museum) 62
Stadhuis 51
Steenplein 56
Tourist office 51
Vlaaikensgang 52
Vleeshuis 54
Volkhuis "Help U zelve" 61
Volkskundemuseum 56
  Wijk Zurenborg 62

Woonhuizen "De Vijf
  Werelddelen" 51
Zilvercentrum 62
Appel, Karel 31, 105
Aqualibi *Brabant* 254
Ardennes 13
Ardennes, Battle of 68
Arenberg (Moulin) 153
Arlon *Luxembourg* 64
*Arras,
  Confederation of* 18
Art 23
Artan 166
Artevelde, Jacob van 142
Art Nouveau 28, 110
Ath *Hainaut* 65
Ath (Region) *Hainaut* 66
Attre *Hainaut* 67
Atuatuca-Tungrorum 234
Aubechies (Archéosite)
  Hainaut 71
Audenaarde: see Oude-
  naarde
Auderghem *Brabant* 115
Aulne (Abbaye)
  Hainaut 67
Austria, Margaret of 188
Austrian Netherlands 18
Averbode
  Vlaams-Brabant 68
*Aymon, Four brothers/
  sons* 191
Aywaille *Liège* 49

B

Baarle-Hertog
  Antwerpen 245
Baarle-Nassau
  Netherlands 245
Balmoral *Liège* 230
Banneux-Notre-Dame
  Liège 228
Baroque art 27
*Baroque civic
  architecture* 27
Baroque religious art 27
Baroque sculpture 27
Barrage: see under
  proper name
Barvaux *Luxembourg* 213
Bastin, Roger 28
Bastogne *Luxembourg* 68
Bastogne, Siege of 68
Baudouin I 19

Bauwens, Lievin 143
Beaumont *Hainaut* 69
Beauraing *Namur* 70
Beauvoorde (Kasteel)
    West-Vlaanderen 248
Beer 43
Beersel *Brabant* 120
Beguine convents 40
Belfries 25
Belgian Lorraine 14
Belgium, Central 13
Belgium, Lower 12
Bellewaerde (Park)
    West-Vlaanderen 163
Belœil *Hainaut* 70
Belvaux (Gouffre)
    Namur 154
Benoit, Peter 37
Benson, Ambrosius 82
Berchmans, St Jan 129
Berghe, Frits van den 150
Bettevaux-Ligneuville
    Luxembourg 187
Bilingual list 291
Binche *Hainaut* 71
Blancs-Mousais 38, 231
Blankenberge *West-*
    Vlaanderen 74
Blaton *Hainaut* 74
Blaugies *Hainaut* 198
Blégny-Trembleur *Liège*
    75, 181
Bles, Herri met de 134
Blue Sandstone
    Ware 216
Boeckel, Van 184
Boerenkrijg 155
Ten Bogaerde Farm
    West-Vlaanderen 167
Bohan *Namur* 223
Bohan-Membre (Parc)
    Namur 223
Bois-et-Borsu *Liège* 195
Bois-Seigneur-Isaac
    Brabant Wallon 206
Bokrij (Provinciaal
    Domein van)
    Limburg 76
Bolderberg *Limburg* 157
Bonfires 38
Bonne-Espérance
    (Abbaye) *Hainaut* 73
Bonnet, Anne 31
Bon-Secours *Hainaut* 75
Borgloon *Limburg* 226
Borinage (Region) *Hai-*
    naut 195
Bornem (Kasteel) *Oost-*
    Vlaanderen 224
Bosch, Hieronymous 104,
    148
Botassart *Luxembourg*
    222
Botrange (Signal) 14
Bouillon *Luxembourg* 77
Bouillon, Godefroy de 77
Bouts, Albrecht 171
Bouts, Dirk 29, 104, 171
Bouverie (Ferme)
    Luxembourg 213
Bouvignes *Namur* 134
Bouvines, Battle of 17
Brabant 13
Brabant Gothic 25

Brabant, Revolution 245
Braekeleer,
    Henri De 30, 60
Braine-le-Château
    Brabant Wallon 206
Brangwyn, Frank 86
Braschaat *Antwerpen* 63
Breendonk (Fort)
    Antwerpen 191
Brel, Jacques 35
Broeucq,
    Jacques du 27, 195
Bronne, Carlo 35
Brouwer,
    Adriaen 209, 210
Bruegel the Elder,
    Pieter 29, 60
Bruegel,
    Jan (Velvet) 30, 60
Bruegel the Younger,
    Pieter (Hell) 29, 60
Bruges: see Brugge
Bruges Matins 79
Brugge
    West-Vlaanderen 79
    Accommodation 82
    Basiliek van het Heilig
        Bloed 83
    Begijnhof 85
    Belfort-Hallen 83
    Bicycle 82
    Boat trips 82
    Bonne Chieremolen 87
    Boottocht 86
    Brangwynmuseum 86
    "Bruges Martins" 79
    Burg 83
    Church: see under proper
        name
    Collège d'Europe 82
    Covered market 83
    De Pelikaan 84
    Dijver 84
    Engels Klooster 87
    Ezelpoort 87
    Flemish primitives 80
    Franc de Bruges (Musée
        provincial du) 83
    Godshuizen 88
    Golden Tree Pageant 79
    Groene Rei 84
    Groeninge (Musée) 84
    Gruuthusemuseum 86
    Guido Gezellemuseum 87
    The Holy Blood Procession
        79
    Horse-drawn carriages 82,
        83
    Huidenvettershuis 84
    Huidenvettersplaats 84
    Jeruzalemkerk 87
    Kantcentrum 87
    Kerk: see under proper
        name
    Kruispoort 87
    Markt 83
    Memlingmuseum 85
    Minnewater 86
    Museum: see under proper
        name
    O.-L.-Vrouwekerk 86
    Onze-Lieve-Vrouw ter
        Potterie (Museum) 88
    Oude Griffie 83
    Paleis van het Brugse Vrije
        83
    Reiefeest (Festival) 79
    Rozenhoedkaai 84
    Sashuis 86
    Schatkamer 87

    Schuttersgilde St.-Sebas-
        tiaan 87
    St.-Annakerk 87
    St.-Donaaskerk 83
    St.-Janshuismolen 87
    St.-Nepomucenusbrug 84
    St.-Salvatorskathedraal 87
    Souvenirs 82
    Spiegelrei 86
    Stadhuis 83
    Stedelijk Museum voor
        Schone Kunsten 84
    Tourist office 82
    Transport 82
    Volkskunde (Museum voor
        Volkskunde) 87
    Windmills 87
Brûly-de-Pesche *Liège*
    127
Brunehault (Pierre)
    Hainaut 242
Brusselmans, Jean 30
Brussels: see Bruxelles
Bruxelles *Brabant* 90
    Appartements de Charles
        de Lorraine 97
    Armée et d'Histoire
        Militaire (Musée Royal
        de l') 108
    Art Ancien (Musée d') 101
    Art et d'Histoire (Musées
        Royaux d') 106
    Art Moderne (Musée d')
        104
    Autoworld 108
    Beaux-Arts de Belgique
        (Musées royaux des) 96
    Bibliothèque Royale
        Albert I 99
    Le Botanique 106
    Bourse 99
    Bruxella 1238 99
    Cabinets de donation 99
    Cathédrale Sts-Michel-et-
        Gudule 100
    Centre belge de la
        Bande dessinée 100
    Centre Berlaymont 110
    Charlier (Musée) 105
    Cinéma (Musée du) 96
    Coat of Arms 91
    Colonne du Congrès 105
    Costume et de la Dentelle
        (Musée du) 106
    Église du Finistère 105
    Église Ste-Catherine 105
    Église St-Jean-Baptiste-au-
        Béguinage 105
    Europalia Festival 90
    Galerie Bortier 99
    Galerie des Princes 99
    Galerie de la Reine 99
    Galerie du Roi 99
    Galeries St-Hubert 99
    Grand-Place 94
    Guided tours 92
    Guild Halls 94
    Historium 100
    Hôtel Bellevue 97
    Hôtel de ville 95
    Hôtel Ravenstein 97
    Imaginaire (Musée de l')
        100
    Imprimerie (Musée de l')
        99
    Institut Royal 109
    Instrumental (Musée) 96,
        105
    Lace making 106
    Livre (Musée du) 99
    Maison Cauchie 108
    Maison de la Bellone 106
    Maison du Roi 95

Manneken Pis 95
Markets 92
Le Mont des Arts 95
Museum: see under proper
  name
Notre-Dame-de-la-Chapelle
  96
Notre-Dame-du-Sablon
  96
Old England 97
Ommegang 93, 94
Palais d'Egmont 96
Palais de la Dynastie 99
Palais de la Nation 105
Palais des Académies 96
Palais des Beaux-Arts 96
Palais Royal 96
Parc de Bruxelles 97
Parc du Cinquantenaire
  106
Petite Rue des Bouchers
  99
Phone numbers 92
Place des Martyrs 100
Place des Palais 96
Place du Grand-Sablon 96
Place du Jeu-de-Balle 106
Place Poelaert 106
Place Royale 96
Porte de Hal 106
Public transport 92
*Queen Elisabeth Piano
  Competition* 90
Rue Neuve 100
Les Sablons 95
Sciences Naturelles
  (Muséum des) 109
September Days 91
Sgraffiti 109
Théâtre de la Monnaie 99
The Squares 109
Square du Petit-Sablon 96
TIB 92
Toone puppet theatre 99
Tourist office 92
Tourist Pass 92
Ville de Bruxelles (Musée
  de la) 95
Wiertz (Musée) 109
World Trade Center 90,
  93
Bulge, Battle of the 68
Burgundy, Dukes of 17
Bury, Pol 29
Burgundy, Mary of 17
Bütgenbach *Liège* 187
Butte du Lion
  Brabant 252
Buzenol
  Luxembourg 249

C

Le Caillou-qui-bique
  Hainaut 198
Calendar of events 292
Cambron-Casteau (Abbey)
  Hainaut 67
Campin, Robert 29, 101,
  237
Cantré, Joseph 28
Carillons 40, 187
Carlier, Maurice 29
Carnivals 37

*Caroline
  Concession* 142
Carolingian Empire 23
Caves 15
Celles *Namur* 135
Celts 16
Central Belgium 13
Centre (Canal)
  Hainaut 122
Ceramics 32
Chaire à prêcher
  Luxembourg 222
Charleroi *Hainaut* 124
Charles V 17, 142
Charles the Bold 17
*Charlotte of Luxembourg,
  Grand Duchess* 19
Charneux (Croix)
  Liège 246
Chassepierre viewpoint
  Luxembourg 221
Château: see under
  proper name
Chaudfontaine
  Liège 181
Chevalier (Tombeau)
  Luxembourg 229
Chevetogne
  Namur 217
Chièvres *Hainaut* 66
Chimay *Hainaut* 125
*Chimay,
  Princess of* 125
Chiny *Luxembourg* 220
Christus, Petrus 29, 80
Civic architecture 25
Claes, Ernest 36
Claus, Émile 30
Claus, Hugo 36
Clauwaerts 79
Clouet, Jean 60
Clovis 236
The Coast 12
CoBrA 31, 104
Coebergher 27, 65
Coecke, Pieter 32
Comblain-au-Pont
  Liège 213
Comic-strips 35
Concretions 15
Conscience, Hendrik 50
Coo *Liège* 126
Corbion
  Luxembourg 222
Cordemoy (Abbaye)
  Luxembourg 78
Corroy-le-Château
  Namur 140
Coster, Charles de 35
Courtrai: see Kortrijk
Couvin *Namur* 127
Cow, War of 194
Cranach, Lucas 60
Crestelles (Viewpoint)
  Luxembourg 217
Crèvecœur (Château)
  Namur 134
*Crommelynck,
  Fernand* 35
Crupet *Namur* 192
Cuesmes *Hainaut* 198
Cul-de-Sarts
  Liège 127
Cwarmê 38

D

Daisne, Johan 36
Damien, Father 191
Damme
  West-Vlaanderen 128
David, Gérard 29, 82, 84
Dead Rat Ball 206
Deigné-Aywaille
  Liège 228
Deinze
  Oost-Vlaanderen 151
Delcour, Jean 27, 175
Delvaux, Laurent 28
Delvaux, Paul 30
Dendermonde *Oost-
  Vlaanderen* 129
Deurle
  Oost-Vlaanderen 129
Deutsch-Belgischer
  (Naturpark) 157
Devolution, War of 18
Dewez, Laurent 28
Diamonds 51, 62
Diest *Vlaams-Brabant* 130
Diksmuide
  West-Vlaanderen 132
Dillens, Julien 28
Dinant *Namur* 133
Dodengang
  West-Vlaanderen 132
Doel *Antwerpen* 63
Ter Doest
  West-Vlaanderen 254
Drielandenpunt *Liège* 138
Ducasse 38, 65
Duivelsteen, Geraard de
  146
*Duquesnoy the Elder,
  Jerome* 27
*Duquesnoy the Younger,
  Jerome* 27
Duquesnoy, François 27
Durbuy *Luxembourg* 213
Dyck, Anthony van 29

E

Eau d'Heure (Barrages)
  Hainaut-Namur 136
Ecaussinnes-Lalaing
  Hainaut 227
Eekhoud, Georges 35
Eeklo
  Oost-Vlaanderen 150
Eggerickx, Jean-Jules 28
Egmont, Count of 91
Elewijt *Antwerpen* 191
Ellezelles *Hainaut* 170
Enclos (Mont) *Hainaut/
  Oost-Vlaanderen* 218
Enghien *Hainaut* 137
Ensor, James 30, 207
Entre-Sambre-et-Meuse
  Region *Hainaut* 124
Ermeton-sur-Biert
  Namur 195
Esneux *Liège* 213
Estaminets 40
Eulenspiegel, Till 128

Eupen *Liège* 137
Eyck,
    Hubert van 145, 185
Eyck, Jan van 29, 80,
    84, 145, 185

F

Fagne (Region) 14
Fagnes (Hautes)
    Liège 157
Faïence 32
Falaèn (Château-ferme)
    Namur 195
Falize (Rocher) *Liège* 187
Famenne (Region) 14
Fauna 15
Fayd'herbe, Lucas 27, 188
Faymonville *Liège* 187
Fétis, François Joseph 37
Fiertal 218
First World War 19
Flanders 16
Flemalle, Master of: see
    Campin, Robert
Flemish Ardennes 218
Flemish Expressionism:
    see Sint-Martens Latem
    Group
Flemish primitives 29, 80
Flône (Abbey) *Liège* 160
Flora 15
Floreffe *Namur* 202
Florenville
    Luxembourg 221
Floris II de Vriendt,
    Cornelis 26
Floris, Frans 184
Folklore and traditions 37
Folklore museums 39
Folon, Jean-Michel 35
Fondry des Chiens
    (Chasm) *Liège* 48
Fonds de Quareux
    Liège 48
't Fonteintje *Limburg* 157
Fontenoy, Battle of 237
Food and drink 41
Forest *Brabant* 115
Fosses-la-Ville
    Namur 202
Fouquet 60
Fourneau-St-Michel
    Luxembourg 138
Les Fourons: see Voer-
    streek
Foy-Notre-Dame
    Namur 135
Fraikin, Charles 28, 158
Franchimont (Château)
    Liège 230
Franck, César 176
Francken, Ambrosius 46
Francken the Elder,
    Frans 158
Francorchamps *Liège* 230
Franc-Waret *Namur* 202
Frênes (Rochers)
    Namur 194
Freÿr (Château)
    Namur 139
Froissart 125

Furfooz *Namur* 135
Furfooz
    nature reserve 15
Furnaux *Namur* 195
Furniture 32

G

Gaasbeek *Brabant* 120
Gastronomic glossary 42
Gaume (Region) 14
Geefs, Willem 28
Geel *Antwerpen* 158
Gembloux *Namur* 140
Geneva 156
Genk *Limburg* 141
Gent *Oost-Vlaanderen* 142
    Alijsgodshuis 147
    Alsmhouse 147
    Begijnhof 150
    Belfort 146
    Bijloke Museum 149
    Boat Trips 142
    Boekentoren 149
    Carriage tours 142
    City tours 142
    Donkere Poort 150
    Dulle Griet 147
    Gedele (Huis van de
        schepen van) 146
    Geraard de Duivelsteen 146
    Gekroonde Hoofden (Huis
        der) 148
    Graslei 147
    Gravensteen 148
    Groentenmarkt 147
    Groot Vleeshuis 147
    Guided walks 142
    Hedendaagse Kunst
        (Museum van) 149
    Huis de Fluitspeler 147
    Industriële Archeologie en
        Textiel (Museum voor)
        149
    Klein Begijnhof 149
    Kraanlei 147
    Kunstencentrum Vooruit 150
    Lakenhalle 146
    Keure (Huis van de
        schepenen van de) 146
    Mammelokker 146
    Museums: see under
        proper name
    Old prison 146
    Old Town 143
    Oude Begijnhof van
        St.-Elisabeth 150
    Oude Vismarkt 148
    Patershol 148
    Patriciërswoning De
        Achtersikkel 150
    Provenierssterstraat 150
    Schone Kunsten (Museum
        voor) 148
    Sierkunst (Museum voor)
        149
    St.-Amandsberg 150
    St.-Baafsabdij 149
    St.-Baafskathedraal 143
    St.-Jacobskerk 147
    St.-Jorishof 146
    St.-Michielsbrug 147
    St.-Veerleplein 148
    Stadhuis 146
    Het Toreken 147
    Theatre 148
    Tourist office 142
    Volkskunde (Museum voor)
        147
    Vrijdagmarkt 147

Gentinnes *Namur* 140
Genval (Lac) *Brabant* 120
Géant (Tombeau) *Luxem-*
    bourg 222
Geraadsbergen *Oost-*
    Vlaanderen 151
Géronsart (Tour) *Namur*
    192
Gerpinnes *Hainaut* 124
Geuzen 18, 82, 248
Gezelle, Guido 79
Ghelderode, Michel De 35
Ghent,
    Pacification of 18, 143
Ghent: see Gent
Giants 38, 65
Gijsen, Marnix 36
Gileppe (Barrage)
    Liège 246
The Gilles 72
Gilson, Paul 37
Ginderbuiten
    Antwerpen 158
Gistel
    West-Vlaanderen 208
Glassware 32
Glawans (Falaises)
    Luxembourg 213
Glossary of art 33
Glossary
    of gastronomy 42
Godelive, Saint 208
Goes, Hugo van der 29,
    81, 84
Golden Fleece,
    Order of the 17
Golden Spurs,
    Battle of 17, 167
Gorge, Henri de 152
Gossaert, Jan: see
    Mabuse
Gothic Art 25
Gothic decorative arts 26
Gothic sculpture 26
Goyet *Namur* 194
Gozée *Hainaut* 125
Grand-Halleux *Liège* 243
Le Grand-Hornu
    Hainaut 152
Grand-Leez *Namur* 140
Grand panorama
    paintings 253
Grard, Georges 28
's Gravenwezel *Ant-*
    werpen 63
Grétry,
    André-Modeste 176
Grimbergen *Brabant* 122
Groenendael *Brabant* 120
Groux, Charles de 30
Grupont *Luxembourg/*
    Namur 217
Gueuze 43, 115

H

De Haan
    West-Vlaanderen 74
Hadelin, Saint 182
Haen, Christina D' 36
Hageland
    (Region) 47, 233
Haguètes 186

Hainaut 13
Hakendover *Vlaams-Brabant* 152
Halle *Vlaams-Brabant* 153
Hamoir *Liège* 213
Ham-sur-Heure *Hainaut* 124
Han (Grotte) *Namur* 15
Hankar, Paul 28
Hanseatic League 79
Han-sur-Lesse *Namur* 154
Hargimont *Namur* 218
Haringe *West-Vlaanderen* 214
Haspengouw (Region): see Hesbaye
Hasselt *Limburg* 154
Hastière-Lavaux *Namur* 192
Hastière-par-delà *Namur* 192
Hautes Fagnes *Liège* 15, 157
Haute Fagnes-Eifel (national nature park) 15
Heizel: see Heysel
Hengelhoef (Recreation Park) *Limburg* 156
Henri II 192
Henri-Chapelle *Liège* 138
Henry VIII 237
Herbeumont *Luxembourg* 222
Herentals *Antwerpen* 158
Hergé 35
Le Hérou *Luxembourg* 217
Herve region 14
Hesbaye (Region) 13, 224, 234
Het: see under name
Heusden-Zolder *Limburg* 157
Heuvelland *West-Vlaanderen* 164
Heverlee *Brabant* 174
Heysel *Brabant* 117
Hoegaarden *Vlaams-Brabant* 233
Hoeilaart *Vlaams-Brabant* 174
Hofstade *Antwerpen* 191
Hoge Blekker *West-Vlaanderen* 165
Hooghe Crater (Cemetery) *West-Vlaanderen* 163
Hoogstraten *Antwerpen* 244
Hops festival 214
Horrues *Hainaut* 227
Horst (Château) *Brabant* 47
Horta, Victor 28, 111
Hoste, Huib 28
Hotond (Mill) *Oost-Vlaanderen* 218
Hotton *Luxembourg* 213
Hotton (Grottes) *Luxembourg* 211
Houffalize *Luxembourg* 217

Houtland (Region) 13
Hubert, Saint 219
Huizingen *Brabant* 120
Huldenberg *Vlaams-Brabant* 174
La Hulpe *Brabant* 120
Hundred Years War 17, 237
Huy *Liège* 159
Huy, Godefroy de 24
Huy, Renier de 24, 124, 141

I - J - K

Iconoclasts 17, 50, 82, 143
Ieper *West-Vlaanderen* 161
De Ijaermondrng *West-Vlaanderen* 203
Ijse (Valley) *Vlaams-Brabant* 174
Independence 18
Isenbrandt, Adriaen 82
Ixelles *Brabant* 111
Izenberge *West-Vlaanderen* 248
Jabbeke *West-Vlaanderen* 208
Jacmain, André 28
Jan-Berchmans, Saint 129
Jannée (Château) *Namur* 218
Jansenius 171
Jehay (Château) *Liège* 161
Jemappes *Hainaut* 196
Jemeppe (Château) *Luxembourg* 218
Jespers, Oscar 28
Jette *Brabant* 115
Jezus-Eik *Brabant* 120
Jodoigne *Vlaams-Brabant* 233
Jonckaere, Karel 36
Jordaens, *Jacob* 29, 60, 104
Joseph II 18
Joyous Entry (Charter) 170
Jumet *Hainaut* 124
Kalmthout Arboretum *Antwerpen* 64
De Kalmthoutse Heide *Antwerpen* 15, 64
Kasterlee *Antwerpen* 158
Keerbergen *Antwerpen* 191
Kelchterhoef *Limburg* 156
Keldermans, Rombout 188
Kemmelberg *West-Vlaanderen* 164
Kempen (Region) 13, 146, 198
Kermesse 38
Khnopff, Fernand 104
Klemskerke *West-Vlaanderen* 74
Kluisberg *Oost-Vlaanderen* 218

Knokke-Heist *West-Vlaanderen* 164
Koekelberg *Brabant* 115
Koksijde *West-Vlaanderen* 165
Koksijde-Bad *West-Vlaanderen* 165
Kolen (Klooster) *Limburg* 226
Kongolo (Mémorial) *Namur* 141
Korbeek-Dijle *Brabant* 174
Korstenbos *Limburg* 226
Kortrijk *West-Vlaanderen* 167
Kriek 43
Kruishoutem (Château) *Oost-Vlaanderen* 211

L

Laarne *Oost-Vlaanderen* 150
Laarne (Château) *Oost-Vlaanderen* 169
Lace 33, 106
Lacuisine *Luxembourg* 221
Laeken *Brabant* 116
Lalaing, Christine de 192
Lambeaux, Jef 24, 43
Lambert, Saint 138, 172
Lambic 43
Lampo, Hubert 30
Lancre (Mountain) *Liège* 92
Landscapes 12
Languages 22
Lassus, Roland de 195
Lavaux-Ste-Anne *Namur* 154
Layens, Mathieu de 171
Leie (Region) 117
Leiestreek *Oost-Vlaanderen* 150
Leisure parks 15
Leopold I 91, 213
Leopold II 18, 75
Leopold III 19, 91
Lesse (Vallée) *Namur* 134
Lesse et Lomme (National nature park) 141
Lessines *Hainaut* 170
Lessive *Namur* 218
Leuven *Vlaams-Brabant* 170
Leuze-en-Hainaut *Hainaut* 243
Liège *Liège* 13, 175
  Ansembourg (Musée d') 178
  Aquarium 181
  Armes (Musée d') 178
  Art moderne et d'Art contemporain (Musée d') 181
  Art religieux et d'Art mosan (Musée d') 177
  Art wallon (Musée d') 176
  Batte (Marché de la) 175
  Cathédrale St-Paul 180
  Citadel 175

Curtius (Musée) 178
East bank 181
Église St-Barthélemy 178
Église St-Denis 180
Église St-Jacques 180
Église St-Jean 180
Église Ste-Croix 181
En Féronstrée 178
Hors-Château 176
Ilot St-Georges 178
Impasse des Ursulines 178
Maison de la Métallurgie 181
Museum: see under proper name
Old Town 176
Palais des Congrès 181
Palais des Princes-Évêques 76
Parc de Cointe 175
Parc de la Boverie 181
Perron 176
Place St-Lambert 176
Puppet theatre 176
Tchantchès (Musée) 181
Transports en commun de la ville de Liège (Musée des) 181
Verre (Musée du) 178
Vie wallonne (Musée de la) 176
Vinâve d'Ile 178
West bank 180
Liège, principality 20
Lier *Antwerpen* 182
Ligny *Namur* 204
Lilar, Suzanne 30
Limbourg *Liège* 246
Limburg 12
Limburg, Jan and Herman van 24
Lipsius, *Justus* 46, 135, 138
Lissewege
  West-Vlaanderen 254
Literature 35
Lo
  West-Vlaanderen 248
Lobbes *Hainaut* 125
Lochristi
  Oost-Vlaanderen 150
Logne (Château)
  Luxembourg 213
Lombard, Lambert 175
Lommel *Limburg* 184
Loncin (Fort)
  Liège 139
Loon, Van 85, 102
Loppem
  West-Vlaanderen 88
Lorraine
  (Belgian region) 14
Lotharingia 16
Louis XVIII 143
Louvain-en-Woluwe
  Brabant 146
Louvain-la-Neuve *Brabant Wallon* 185
Lower Ardennes 14
Lower Belgium 12
Lumeçon 156
Luxembourg 13, 14
Lyssenthoek Military Cemetery
  West-Vlaanderen 214

M

Maaseik *Limburg* 185
Mabuse 50, 82
Mad Meg (Painting) 48
Maerlant, Jacob van 35, 128
Maeterlinck, Maurice 35, 142
Magritte, René 30
Maitrank 53
Male *West-Vlaanderen* 88
La Malibran 114
Mallet-Joris, Françoise 30
Malmédy *Liège* 186
Marche-en-Famenne
  Namur 218
Marches-les-Dames
  Namur 194
Maredret *Namur* 195
*Marck,
  Évrard de la* 64, 138
*Marck,
  William de la* 138, 144
Le Mardassou
  Luxembourg 57
Maredsous (Abbaye)
  Namur 195
Margaret of Austria 149
Margaret of Parma 168
Marie-Adélaïde 19
Mariembourg *Liège* 127
Mariemont (Domaine)
  Hainaut 73
Markets (Covered) 25
Martens, Dirk 46
Martini, Simone 60
Massys, Quentin 29
De Maten (Natuurreservaat) *Limburg* 141
McAuliffe, General 69
Mechelen *Antwerpen* 187
De Mechelse Heide (Natuurreservaat)
  Limburg 15, 141
Meise *Brabant* 121
Membre *Namur* 223
Memling, Hans 29, 81, 84, 85
Merovingians 16
Mertens, Pierre 35
Messina, Antomello de 30
Metsys, Quentin: see Massys
Meunier,Constantin 28
La Meuse namuroise
  Namur 191
Michaux, Henri 35
Middelheim
  Antwerpen 61
Minerva 108
Military parades 39
Miniaturists 29
Minne, Georges 28
Modave (Château)
  Liège 194
Moeschal, Jacques 29
Mol *Antwerpen* 158
Molenheide *Limburg* 157
Molignée (Vallée)
  Namur 195
Monde sauvage (Safari park) *Liège* 228
Mone, Jean 27

Mons *Hainaut* 195
Montaigle (Château)
  Namur 195
Montauban
  Luxembourg 249
Monti (Estate) *Liège* 243
Montquintin
  Luxembourg 250
Mont-sur-Marchienne
  Hainaut 125
Mortroux *Liège* 75
Mosan Romanesque Art 24, 177
Mosan School 175
Moulbaix *Hainaut* 66
Muizen *Antwerpen* 191
Münster, Treaty of 18
Music 37

N

Namur (Region) 13, 191
Namur *Namur* 199
Napoleon I 18
Nassau, Jean of 19
Nature reserves 15
Navez, Joseph 30
Neo-classicism 28
Neptune (Grotte)
  Liège 127
*Netherlands,
  War of the* 18
Neuville-en-Condroz
  Liège 182
Néviaux (Rochers)
  Namur 194
t'Nieuwhuys *Brabant* 233
Nieuwpoort
  West-Vlaanderen 203
Nieuwport-Bad
  West- Vlaanderen 203
Nijlen, Jean van 36
Nijmegen, Treaty of 18
Ninglonspo (Torrent)
  Liège 48
Ninove
  Oost-Vlaanderen 203
Nismes *Liège* 127
Nivelles *Brabant Wallon* 204
Nonceveux *Liège* 48
Norbert, Saint 68
Notger, Prince-bishop of Liège 16, 175
Notre-Dame-de-Scourmont (Abbaye)
  Hainaut 126

O - P

Oelegem *Antwerpen* 63
Oignies, Higo d' 24, 201
Ooidonk (Kasteel) *Oost-Vlaanderen* 150
Oostduinkerke *West-Vlaanderen* 166
Oostende
  West-Vlaanderen 206
Oosthoek
  West-Vlaanderen 214
Oost-Vlaanderen 12

Open-Air museums 39
Opsomer, Baron 184
Orange, House of 129
Orley,
    Bernard van 31, 104
Orval (Abbaye)
    Luxembourg 209
Ostend: see Oostend
Ottignies-Louvain-la-
    Neuve Brabant
    Wallon 185
Oudenaarde
    Oost-Vlaanderen 209
Oudenberg
    Oost-Vlaanderen 151
Oudergem: see
    Auderghem
Ourthe (Vallée) Liège-
    Luxembourg 211
Overijse
    Vlaams-Brabant 174
Ovifat Liège 186
Painting 29
Pageants 39
De Panne
    West-Vlaanderen 213
Pannemaker,
    Willem de 26
Papekelders
    Antwerpen 158
Park (Abdij)
    Brabant 174
Parma, Margaret of 209
Pasture, Rogier de la: see
    Weyden
Patinir, Joachim 133
Pax Romana 16
Peeters, Joseph 31
Penitents Procession 247
Permeke, Constant 30,
    50, 150
Petit-Fays (Gorges)
    Namur 223
Philip Augustus 17
Philip the Bold 17
Philip II of Spain 17
Philip the Good 17
Philip the Handsome 17
Philippeville Namur 214
Pierre Brunehault
    Hainaut 242
Pieter the Hermit 159
Plancenoit Brabant 251
Planckendael (Zoo)
    Antwerpen 191
Plantin,
    Christopher 50, 56
Plate-Taille (Barrage)
    Hainaut 136
Poelaert 28
Poelkapelle
    West-Vlaanderen 162
Poilvache (Château)
    Namur 192
Poix (Val)
    Luxembourg 220
Polders 13
Pont d'Arcole (Grottes)
    Namur 192
Poperinge
    West-Vlaanderen 214
Porcelain 32
Postel (Abdij)
    Antwerpen 158

Pourbus, Pieter 60, 82
Pousseur, Henry 37
"Pré-baroque" style 26
Prehistory 23
The Premonstratensians
    68
The Primitives 29
Processions 38
Profondeville Namur 194
Provost, Jan 82
Puissant, Adolphe 28
Puppets 39
Ten Putte (Abbaye)
    West-Vlaanderen 208
Pyrenees,
    Treaty of the 18

Q - R

Quellin the Elder,
    Artus 27
Quellin the Younger,
    Artus 27
Raeren Liège 32
Rance Hainaut 70
Ray, Jean 36
Rebecq
    Vlaams-Brabant 153
Redouté, Pierre-Joseph
    139, 219
Redu-Trasinne
    Luxembourg 215
Regions 12
La Reid Liège 230
Reinhardstein (Château)
    Liège 187
Religious Art 25
Remaclus, Saint 231
Rembrandt 60
The Renaissance 26
Renaissance
    architecture 26
Resurgences 15
Reuland Liège 215
Richmond,
    Duchess of 251
Rièzes et Sarts (Pays)
    Liège 14, 127
Rigi (Mont) Liège 157
Rijkhaven Limburg 235
Rivage Liège 230
Rixensart (Château)
    Brabant 120
Robertville Liège 186
Roche à Frêne
    Luxembourg 48
La Roche-en-Ardenne
    Luxembourg 215
Rochefort Namur 217
Rochefort (Grotte) 15
Rochehaut
    Luxembourg 223
Rockox, Nikolas 59
Rodeberg
    West-Vlaanderen 164
Rodenbach, Georges 35
Le Rœulx Hainaut 227
Roisin Hainaut 198
Romanesque Art 23
Romans 16
Ronquières Brabant
    Wallon 205

Ronse
    Oost-Vlaanderen 218
Rops, Félicien 30
Roulin, Félix 29
Royal Families 20
Rubens, Pieter Paul 29,
    50, 58
Rumbeke
    West-Vlaanderen 169
Rysselberghe,
    Théo van 30

S

Saedeleer, Valerius de 30
St: see also Sint
St-Aubert (Mont)
    Hainaut 242
St-Gilles Brabant 111
St-Hubert Luxembourg
    219
St-Séverin Liège 182
Salm (Vallée) Liège,
    Luxembourg 243
Sambre (Vallée)
    Hainaut 125
Samson (Vallée)
    Namur 194
Sart Liège 230
Sart Tilman Liège 181
Sarts (Pays) Liège 127
Saut des Sorcières
    Luxembourg 222
Savery, Roland 167
Sax, Adolphe 133
Scaldian Gothic 25
Scaldian Romanesque
    Art 23
Scheldt
    Oost-Vlaanderen 224
Scherpenheuvel
    Vlaams-Brabant 132
Schilde Antwerpen 63
Schoten Antwerpen 293
Second World War 19
Sedes Sapientiae 24
Segal, Georges 104
Semois (Vallée) Luxem-
    bourg-Namur 220
Semois
    (Gorge Viewpoint) 221
September Days 91, 99
Servaes, Albert 150
Servais,
    Adrien-François 153
Servranckx, Victor 31
Sgraffiti 109
Sigebert 140
Silent, William the 129
Simenon,
    Georges 35, 176
Sint-Aldegonde, Philip
    Marnis van 224
Sint-Amands Oost-
    Vlaanderen 224
St-Amandsberg Oost-
    Vlaanderen 150
Sint-Dimpnakerk Ant-
    werpen 158
Sint-Gilles: St.-Gilles
Sint-Idesbald West-
    Vlaanderen 166

Sint-Lambrechts-Woluwe
    Brabant 110
Sint-Martens-Latem
    Oost-Vlaanderen 150
Sint-Michiels West-
    Vlaanderen 88
Sint-Niklaas
    Oost-Vlaanderen 223
Sint-Pieters-Rode
    Vlaams-Brabant 47
Sint-Truiden Limburg 224
Sluis Antwerpen 158
Smet, De Gustave 150
Snyders, Frans 29
Sodality
    Brotherhood 247
Soignes (Forêt)
    Brabant 117
Soignies Hainaut 226
Solre-sur-Sambre
    Hainaut 70
Solvay (Domaine)
    Brabant 120
Sorcières (Saut)
    Luxembourg 222
Sougne-Remouchamps
    Liège 227
Spa Liège 228
Spanish Fury 18, 50
Spanish Succession, War
    of the 18
Spilliaert, Léon 105
Spontin Namur 231
Stalactites 15
Stalagmites 15
Stambruges Hainaut 75
Stavelot Liège 231
Het Steen Brabant 191
Stene
    West-Vlaanderen 208
Stevens, Alfred-Émile 30
Stoumont Liège 48
Strebelle, Claude 123
Strépy-Thieu Hainaut 94
Streuvels, Stijn 36
Symbolist movement 30

T

Tallien, Madame: see
    Chimay, Princess of
Tancrémont Liège 228
Tapestry 31
Taxandria: see Kempen
Tchantchès 176, 181
Temse
    Oost-Vlaanderen 224
Ten: see under name
Teniers the Younger,
    David 30
Ter: see under name
Tervuren Brabant 117
Tessenderlo Limburg 132
Theux Liège 230
Thiry, Marcel 35
Thudinie (Region) 232
Thuin Hainaut 232
Tienen
    Vlaams-Brabant 233
Tilff Liège 213
Timmermans, Felix 36,
    182, 184

Tohogne Luxembourg 213
Tongeren Limburg 234
Tongerlo Antwerpen 236
Tongre-Notre-Dame
    Hainaut 66
Tonnekensbrand 38, 151
Torgny Luxembourg 250
Torhout
    West-Vlaanderen 236
Tournai Hainaut 236
Town Halls 25
Townscapes 40
Traditions 37
Tremelo Antwerpen 191
Treviri (Region) 23
Trois-Ponts Liège 243
Truth pulpits 28
Turnhout Antwerpen 243
Tyne Cot Military
    Cemetery
    West-Vlaanderen 164

U -V - W

Uccle Brabant 114
Ukkel: see Uccle
Upper Ardennes 14
Utrecht, Union of 18
Val-Dieu (Abbaye)
    Liège 246
Valéry Cousin (Domaine
    Provinciaal)
    Namur 217
Valley: see under proper
    name
Val St-Lambert Liège 32
Van, Van den, Van der:
    see under name
Velde,
    Henry van de 28, 78
Veldeke, Hendrik van 155
Veranneman (Foundation)
    Oost-Vlaanderen 211
Verbruggen, Hendrik
    Frans 27
Verdun, Treaty of 16
Verdun, Nicolas de 24
Verdures 32, 137, 210
Veremans, Renaat 184
Verhaegen,
    Theodoor 28, 188
Verhaeren, Émile 35,
    198, 224
Verhaghen,
    Pieter Jozef 30
Verlaine, Paul 195
Verviers Liège 245
Vervoort the Elder,
    Michiel 28
Vesdre (Barrage)
    Liège 137
Veurne
    West-Vlaanderen 246
Vêves Namur 135
Victory Memorial
    Museum
    Luxembourg 65
Vielsalm Luxembourg 243
Vienna, Congress of 18
Vieuxtemps,
    Henri 37, 245

Villers-la-Ville Brabant
    Wallon 248
Vilvoorde Brabant 122
Vinçotte, Thomas 28
Virelles (Étang) Hainaut
    15, 126
Viroin (Vallée)
    Namur 127
Virton Luxembourg 249
Visé Liège 182
Voerstreek Limburg 250
Vonêche Namur 32
Vorst: see Forest
Vos, Cornelis De 30
Vos, Paul De 29
Vresse-sur-Semois
    Namur 223
Vrieselhof (Provinciaal
    Domein)
    Antwerpen 63
Waas (Region)
    Oost-Vlaanderen 223
Waha Namur 218
Walcourt Namur 250
Walibi Brabant 256
Wallonia Festivals 199
Walloon Art 177
Wanne Liège 243
Waregem
    Oost-Vlaanderen 211
Warfaaz (Lac) Liège 229
Waterloo Brabant
    Wallon 251
Waterloo,
    Battle of 18, 251
Watermael-Boitsfort
    Brabant 114
Watervliet
    Oost-Vlaanderen 150
Waulsort Namur 192
Wavre Brabant
    Wallon 254
Weert Antwerpen 224
Wellington, Duke of 251
Wenduine
    West-Vlaanderen 74
Wépion Namur 194
Wéris Luxembourg 48
Westrozebeke
    West-Vlaanderen 164
Westrozebeke, Battle of:
    Golden Spurs, Battle of
Westhoek
    West-Vlaanderen 214
West-Vlaanderen
    (Province) 12
Weyden,
    Rogier van der 29, 237
Wijnendale (Château)
    West-Vlaanderen 192
Wilderode, Anton van 36
Willebroek
    Antwerpen 191
Wiertz, Antoine 30
William IV 19
Woestijne,
    Gustave van de 30
Woluwe-St-Lambert
    Brabant 110
Woluwe-St-Pierre
    Brabant 110
Wouters, Rik 30
Wulveringem Beauvoorde
    West-Vlaanderen 248

X - Y - Z

Xhignesse *Liège* 213
Ypres: see Ieper
Ypres Salient 161
Ysaïe, Eugène 176
Yser, Battle of 132,
   203
Yvoir *Namur* 192
Zaventem *Brabant* 122
Zedelgem
   West-Vlaanderen 88

Zeebrugge
   West-Vlaanderen 254
Zepperen *Limburg* 226
Zeupire (Stone)
   Hainaut 125
Zeven-kerken
   West-Vlaanderen
   88
Zichem
   Vlaams-Brabant 132
Zilvermeer
   Antwerpen 158

't Zoet Water *Vlaams-
   Brabant* 174
Zotte mandag 218
Zoutleeuw *Vlaams-
   Brabant* 255
Zwaelmen, Van der
   28
Zwartberg
   Limburg 141
Het Zwin
   West-Vlaanderen 15,
   164

Grand Duchy of LUXEMBOURG

A - B - C

Ansembourg 261
Barrage: see under
   proper name
Bascharage 274
Beaufort 274
Beaufort
   (Château) 274
Bech-Kleinmacher
   271
Berdorf 258, 273
Bettembourg 270
Bivels 278
Blind,
   John the 263
Bourglinster 270
Bourscheid (Château)
   276
Brandenbourg 259
Charlotte,
   Grand Duchess 21
Château: see under
   proper name
Clervaux 258
Clerve
   (Vallée) 259
Consdorf 274

D - E

Dasburg 278
Deiwelselter 259
Diekirch 259
Echternach 260, 273
Ehnen 271
Eisch (Vallée) 261
Esch-sur-Alzette 261
Esch-sur-Sûre
   (Barrage) 275
Esch-sur-Sûre 275
Ettelbruck 276
*European
   Institutions*
   263

G - H - I

Galgenberg 261
Greiveldange 271
Grenglay (Point de vue)
   276
Grevenmacher 272
Grund 268
Gutland (Region) 14
Hachiville 259
Hallerbach 274
Hamm (American ceme-
   tery) 269
Haute-Sûre (Lac) 275
Henry VII 263
Hespérange 270
Hochfels 275
Hollenfels 261
Hunnebour 261
Independence 19, 21
Insenborn 275

K - L

Koerich 261
Larochette 262
Lohmühle (Barrage) 278
Luxembourg 262

M - N - O

Machtum 272
*Marie-Adélaïde, Grand
   Duchess* 21
Mersch 261
Mertert 272
Military cemeteries 269
Mondorf-les-Bains 270
Monnet, Jean 263
Moselle luxembourgeoise
   (Vallée) 270
Mullerthal 274
Nassau, Adolf 19
Nommern 262
Our Valley 278

P - R

Le Perekop (Rocher) 273
Petite Suisse luxem-
   bourgeoise 272
Pont-Misère 275
Reisdorf 277
Remerschen 271
Remich 271
Rindschleiden 274
Rodange 274
Rosport (Barrage) 277
Rumelange 262

S - T

Sandweiler (German
   cemetery) 270
St Nicolas 278
Scheidgen 274
Schengen 271
Schuman, Robert 263
Schwebsange 271
Septfontaines 261
Stadtbredimus 271
Stolzembourg 278
Sûre (Vallée) 275
Troisvierges 259

V - W

Vallée: see under proper
   name
Vauban 263
Vianden 277
Wasserbillig 272
Wellenstein 271
Werschrumschluff 258
Willibrord, Saint 260
Wiltz 279
Wiltz Valley 279
Wolfschlucht 261
Wormeldange 272

36 15 MICHELIN...

Minitel Service
to help you plan :

the best routes, mileages
tolls and journey times;

a suitable hotel, restaurant
or campsite;

suggestions for sightseeing ●●●

For route-planning in Europe

MANUFACTURE FRANÇAISE DES PNEUMATIQUES MICHELIN
Société en commandite par actions au capital de 2 000 000 000 de francs
Place des Carmes-Déchaux - 63 Clermont-Ferrand (France)
R.C.S. Clermont-Fd B 855 200 507

© Michelin et Cie, Propriétaires-Éditeurs 1997
Dépôt légal février 1997 – ISBN 2-06-151402-2 – ISSN 0763-1383

Printed in the EU 03-98/2
Photocomposition : A.P.S.-CHROMOSTYLE, Tours
Impression – Brochage : AUBIN Imprimeur, Ligugé

Illustration de la couverture par Claude MORÉNO/Y. AUSSET